KT-446-631

GUINNESS WORLD RECORDS 2004

British Library Cataloguing-in-Publication Data: a catalogue record for this book is available from the British Library.

ISBN 085112-180-2

MANAGING EDITOR
Claire Folkard

SENIOR EDITOR
Jackie Freshfield

EDITORS
Jennifer Banks
Simon Hall

PROJECT ART EDITOR
Johnny Pau

ASSISTANT DESIGNER
Violetta Wontor Pau

DESIGN CONCEPT
Bridgewater Book Company

COVER DESIGN
Ron Callow at Design 23

HEAD OF PICTURE/MEDIA DESK
Betty Halvagi

PICTURE RESEARCH
Maureen Kane
Mariana Sonnenberg
Caroline Thomas
Louise Thomas

VP CONTENT MANAGEMENT
Chris Sheedy

KEEPER OF THE RECORDS
Stewart Newport

RESEARCH TEAM
Stuart Claxton
Jerramy Fine
David Hawksett
Keely Hopkins
Della Torra Howes
Kim Lacey
Hein Le Roux
Chris Marais
Susan Morrison

PROOFREADING
Craig Glenday
Carla Masson

INDEX
Susan Bosanko

PRODUCTION DIRECTOR
Patricia Langton

PRODUCTION CO-ORDINATORS
Colette Concannon
David D'Arcy

PRINTING AND BINDING
Printer Industria Grafica, SA, Barcelona, Spain

COLOUR ORIGINATION
Colour Systems, London, UK

ILLUSTRATOR
Colin Brown

ACCREDITATION Guinness World Records Limited has a very thorough accreditation system for records verification. However, whilst every effort is made to ensure accuracy, Guinness World Records Limited cannot be held responsible for any errors contained in this work. Feedback from our readers on any point of accuracy is always welcomed.

ABBREVIATIONS AND MEASUREMENTS Guinness World Records Limited uses both metric and imperial measurements (US imperial in brackets). The only exception is for some scientific data, where metric measurements only are universally accepted, and for some sports data. Where a specific date is given the exchange rate is calculated according to the currency values that were in operation at the time. Where only a year date is given the exchange rate is calculated from December of that year. 'One billion' is taken to mean one thousand million. 'GDR' (the German Democratic Republic) refers to the East German state which unified with West Germany in 1990. The abbreviation is used for sports records broken before 1990. The Union of Soviet Socialist Republics split into a number of parts in 1991, the largest of these being Russia. The Commonwealth of Independent States replaced it and the abbreviation 'CIS' is used mainly for sporting records broken at the 1992 Olympic Games.

GENERAL WARNING Attempting to break records or set new records can be dangerous. Appropriate advice should be taken first and all record attempts are undertaken entirely at the participant's risk. In no circumstances will Guinness World Records Limited have any liability for death or injury suffered in any record attempts. Guinness World Records Limited has complete discretion over whether or not to include any particular records in the book.

Guinness World Records Limited is a Hit Entertainment Company

GUINNESS WORLD RECORDS 2004

CONTENTS

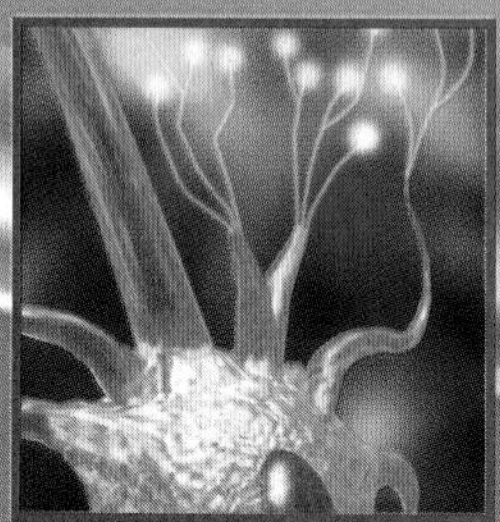

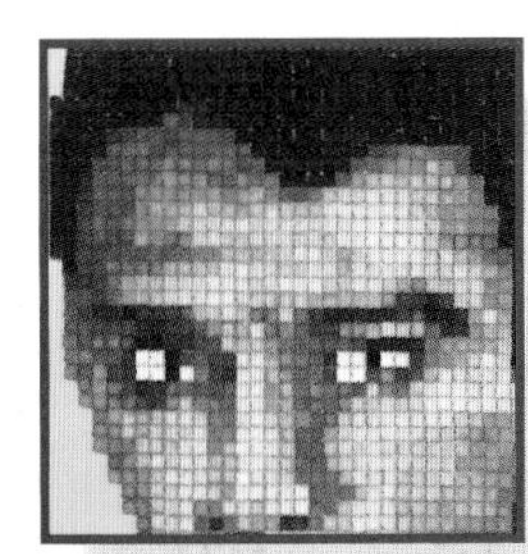

XXVII
OLYMPIAD
SYDNEY
2000

INTRODUCTION

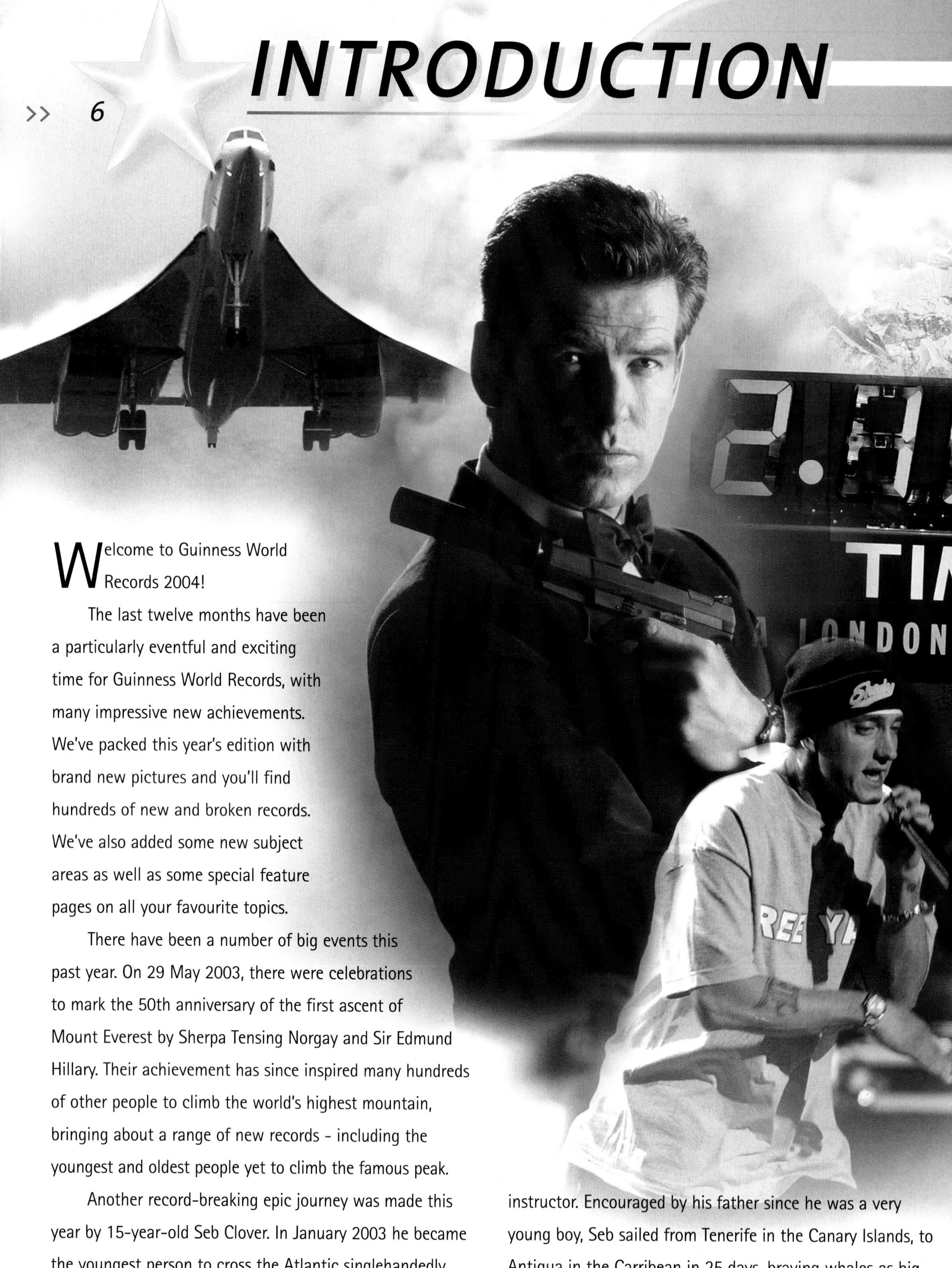

Welcome to Guinness World Records 2004!

The last twelve months have been a particularly eventful and exciting time for Guinness World Records, with many impressive new achievements. We've packed this year's edition with brand new pictures and you'll find hundreds of new and broken records. We've also added some new subject areas as well as some special feature pages on all your favourite topics.

There have been a number of big events this past year. On 29 May 2003, there were celebrations to mark the 50th anniversary of the first ascent of Mount Everest by Sherpa Tensing Norgay and Sir Edmund Hillary. Their achievement has since inspired many hundreds of other people to climb the world's highest mountain, bringing about a range of new records - including the youngest and oldest people yet to climb the famous peak.

Another record-breaking epic journey was made this year by 15-year-old Seb Clover. In January 2003 he became the youngest person to cross the Atlantic singlehandedly, in a race across the ocean against his father, a sailing instructor. Encouraged by his father since he was a very young boy, Seb sailed from Tenerife in the Canary Islands, to Antigua in the Carribean in 25 days, braving whales as big as his yacht and fierce Atlantic storms.

The athlete Paula Radcliffe also displayed great stamina and mental strength this year. Having set an incredible record time for the fastest marathon last year in London, she actually broke her own record this year, with an awe-inspiring time of 2 hours, 15 minutes and 25 seconds.

In the world of entertainment, the release of the 20th James Bond movie, *Die Another Day*, at the end of 2002 created yet more records for the movie series about the world's most famous secret agent. And in the music world, Eminem continues to be the most successful rap artist ever – his album *The Marshall Mathers LP* sold a record 1.76 million copies in its first week in June 2000 – and with the release of his debut movie *8 Mile* this year, the star continues to rule the world of rap.

Finally, 17 December 2003 marks the 100th anniversary of powered flight, since the Wright brothers made their first ground-breaking journey in the Wright Flyer. The end of 2003 also sees the last of commercial supersonic travel, with Concorde sadly being retired after 34 years of record-breaking transatlantic flights. But let's just imagine what another 100 years of air travel might bring!

So dive in and be inspired by the greatest the world has to offer. You don't have to be an athlete, a pop star or an explorer to hold a World Record - you could organise a group event or have a unique talent of your own. Next year we celebrate 50 years of Guinness World Records, so get thinking, and just maybe you too could be the proud owner of a Guinness World Record!

Editor, Guinness World Records

Clockwise from top left: Concorde, Pierce Brosnan as James Bond, Mount Everest; Paula Radcliffe, Seb Clover; Eminem

E.T.
THE EXTRA-TERRESTRIAL

HUMANS

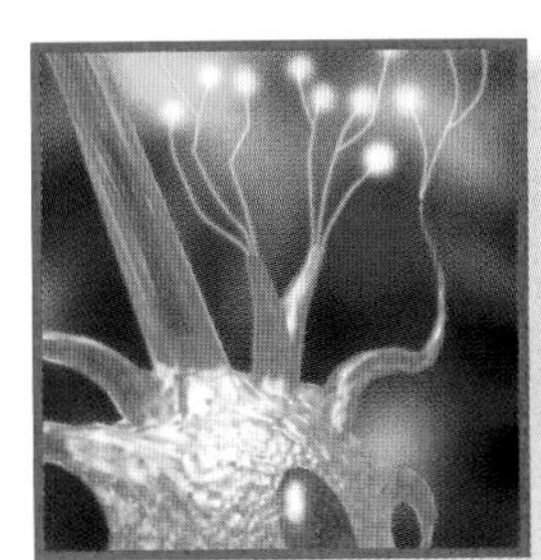

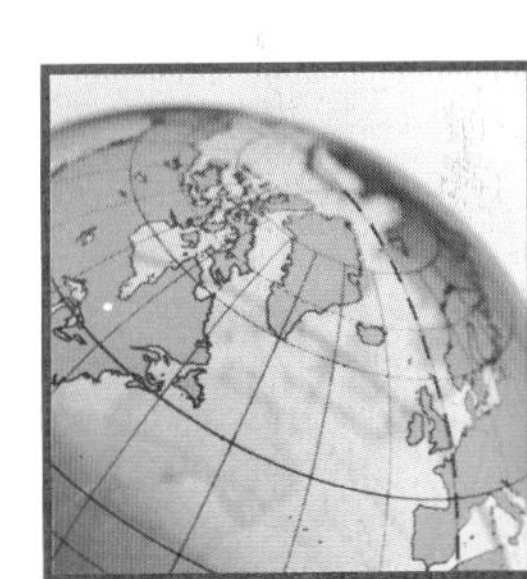

BODY EXTREMES

HEAVIEST MAN

The heaviest person in medical history was Jon Brower Minnoch (USA). He suffered from obesity as a child and, by 1963, when he was 22 years old and 1.85 m (6 ft 1 in) tall, he weighed 178 kg (28 stone). Four years later, he weighed 317 kg (50 stone), and by September 1976 he weighed 442 kg (69 stone 9 lb). He was rushed to hospital in 1978 with heart and respiratory failure, weighing an estimated 635 kg (100 stone). When he died in 1983 he was down to 362 kg (57 stone).

HEAVIEST WOMAN

Rosalie Bradford (USA) is claimed to have registered a peak weight of 540 kg (85 stone) in January 1987. In August of that year, she developed congestive heart failure and was rushed to hospital. She was consequently put on a carefully controlled diet and by February 1994 weighed 128 kg (20 stone 3 lb).

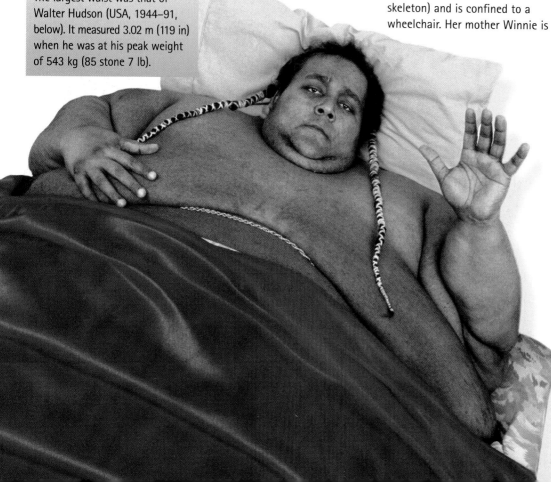

>> LARGEST WAIST

The largest waist was that of Walter Hudson (USA, 1944–91, below). It measured 3.02 m (119 in) when he was at his peak weight of 543 kg (85 stone 7 lb).

GREATEST WEIGHT DIFFERENTIAL BETWEEN A MARRIED COUPLE

Weighing 635 kg (100 stone), Jon Brower Minnoch (USA) married his 50-kg (7-stone 12-lb) wife Jeannette (USA) in March 1978. Their weight difference was 585 kg (92 stone 2 lb) – the greatest for a married couple.

MOST VARIABLE STATURE

At the age of 21 in 1920, Adam Rainer (Austria) measured 1.18 m (3 ft 10.5 in). He then had a rapid growth spurt and by 1931 had reached 2.18 m (7 ft 1.75 in). As a result, he became so weak that he was bedridden for the rest of his life. When he died in 1950, he measured 2.34 m (7 ft 8 in). He remains the only person to have been both a dwarf and a giant.

SHORTEST MAN EVER

The shortest mature human of whom there is independent evidence was Gul Mohammed (India). On 19 July 1990 he was examined at Ram Manohar Hospital, New Delhi, India, and found to be 57 cm (22.5 in) tall.

SHORTEST WOMAN

The shortest ever female was Pauline Musters (Netherlands). Born on 26 February 1876, she measured 30 cm (12 in) at birth. At nine years of age she was 55 cm (21.5 in) tall and weighed only 1.5 kg (3 lb 5 oz). She died of pneumonia with meningitis on 1 March 1895 in New York City, USA, at the age of 19. A post-mortem examination showed her to be exactly 61 cm (24 in) – there was some elongation after death.

The shortest living woman is Madge Bester (South Africa), who is only 65 cm (25.5 in) tall. She suffers from *osteogenesis imperfecta* (characterized by brittle bones and other deformities of the skeleton) and is confined to a wheelchair. Her mother Winnie is not much taller, measuring 70 cm (27.5 in), and is also confined to a wheelchair.

TALLEST WOMAN

Zeng Jinlian (China) of Yujiang village in the Bright Moon Commune, Hunan Province, measured 2.48 m (8 ft 1.75 in) when she died aged 17 years 232 days on 13 February 1982.

The tallest living woman is Sandy Allen (USA, b. 18 June 1955), who when last measured was 2.317 m (7 ft 7.25 in) tall. She stood 1.905 m (6 ft 3 in) by the age of 10 and was 2.16 m (7 ft 1 in) tall by 16.

TALLEST MAN

The tallest man in history for whom there is evidence is Robert Pershing Wadlow (USA, 1918–40) who, when last measured on 27 June 1940, was found to be 2.72 m (8 ft 11.1 in) tall. His amazing height was the result of an over-active pituitary gland which oversupplied his body with growth hormone.

LONGEST FINGERNAILS

The combined measurement of the five nails on the left hand of Shridhar Chillal (India) was 6.15m (20 ft 2.25 in) on July 8 1998, when they were measured on the set of *Guinness World Records: Primetime*, Los Angeles, California, USA. His thumbnail was the longest, measuring 1.42 m (56 in). The longest fingernails on a woman belong to Lee Redmond (USA). They measure a total length of 6 m 62.94 cm (29 ft 9 in). The longest nail is on her left thumb and measures 68.58 cm (2 ft 3 in).

LARGEST EVER FEET

Robert Wadlow (USA), the tallest ever man, wore US size 37AA shoes (UK size 36), equivalent to 47 cm (18.5 in) long. He died after attending a promotional march for Peter Shoes Company, the suppliers of his shoes. An infected blister on his left foot led to infection and he died in his sleep on 15 July 1940.

LONGEST MOUSTACHE

Kalyan Ramji Sain (India) has been growing his moustache since 1976, and by July 1993 it had reached a span of 3.39 m (11 ft 1 in). The right side measured 1.72 m (5 ft 7 in) and the left side 1.67 m (5 ft 6 in).

« TALLEST LIVING MAN

Radhouane Charbib (Tunisia, left) measured 2.359 m (7 ft 8.9 in) as a result of measurements taken on 22–23 April 1999 at Tunis, Tunisia.

LARGEST HANDS

Robert Wadlow (USA), famously the tallest man ever, had hands that measured 32.3 cm (12.75 in) from the wrist to the tip of his middle finger.

LARGEST NATURAL BREASTS

Annie Hawkins-Turner (USA) has an under-breast measurement of 109.22 cm (43 in) and an around-chest-over-nipple measurement of 177.8 cm (70 in). She currently wears a US size 52I bra, the largest available to buy, but by American bra estimation, her measurements would put her in a 48V bra, which is not a manufactured size.

LONGEST HAIR

The world's longest documented hair belonged to Hoo Sateow (Thailand), a tribal medicine man from the village of Muang Nga, Chang Mai, Thailand. On 21 November 1997 his hair was unravelled and officially measured at 5.15 m (16 ft 11 in) long. He stopped cutting his hair in 1929, believing that his long locks held the key to his healing powers.

LONGEST TONGUE

Stephen Taylor's (UK) tongue measures 9.4 cm (3.7 in) from the tip to the centre of his closed top lip. It was measured at Westwood Medical Centre, Coventry, Warwickshire, UK, on 29 May 2002.

GREATEST HEIGHT DIFFERENTIAL BETWEEN A MARRIED COUPLE

Fabien Pretou (France, above right), measuring 1.88 m (6 ft 2 in) tall, and Natalie Lucius (France, above left), who is 94 cm (3 ft 1 in) tall, were married at Seyssinet-Pariset, France, on 14 April 1990. The difference in height between the couple is 94 cm (3 ft 1 in).

AMAZING BODY

MOST ACTIVE MUSCLE
It has been estimated that the muscles of the eye (right) move more than 100,000 times a day. Many of these rapid eye movements take place during the dreaming phase of sleep.

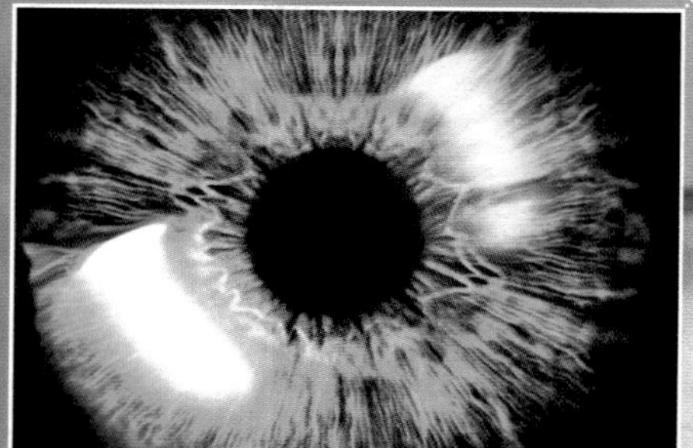

LARGEST MUSCLE
The bulkiest of the 639 named muscles in the human body is usually the *gluteus maximus* or buttock muscle (below), which extends the thigh. However, in pregnancy, the uterus can increase from about 30 g (1 oz) to over 1 kg (2 lb 3 oz) in weight.

LONGEST CELL
Motor neurons (left) are some 1.3 m (4 ft 3 in) long; they have cell bodies (grey matter) in the lower spinal cord with axons (white matter) that carry nerve impulses from the spinal cord down to the big toe. The cell systems that carry certain sensations (vibration and positional sense) back from the big toe to the brain are even longer – about equal to the height of the body.

LARGEST ARTERY
The aorta is 3 cm (1.18 in) in diameter where it leaves the heart (outlined above). By the time this artery divides at the level of the fourth lumbar vertebra, it is about 1.75 cm (0.68 in) in diameter.

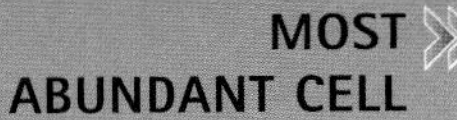

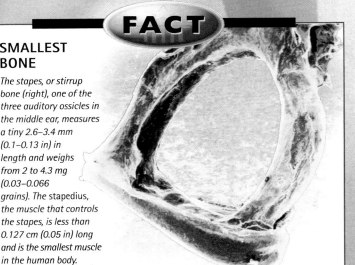

MOST ABUNDANT CELL

The body contains around 30 billion red blood cells (erythrocytes, right), with approximately 5 x 10^{12} in every litre of blood (8.75 x 10^{12} in every pint). Red blood cells are produced in bone marrow, and their function is to carry oxygen and carbon dioxide around the body.

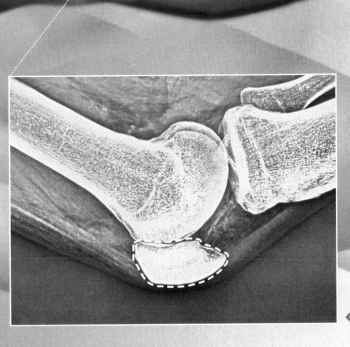

LARGEST SESAMOID BONE

The largest sesamoid bone in the body is the patella or knee cap (outlined above). Most other sesamoids are only a few millimetres in diameter and are shaped like a sesame seed, hence the name. They are usually formed in tendons close to joints or where the tendons angle sharply around bone. Their function is to take compression when a tendon is going around a joint, as when kneeling.

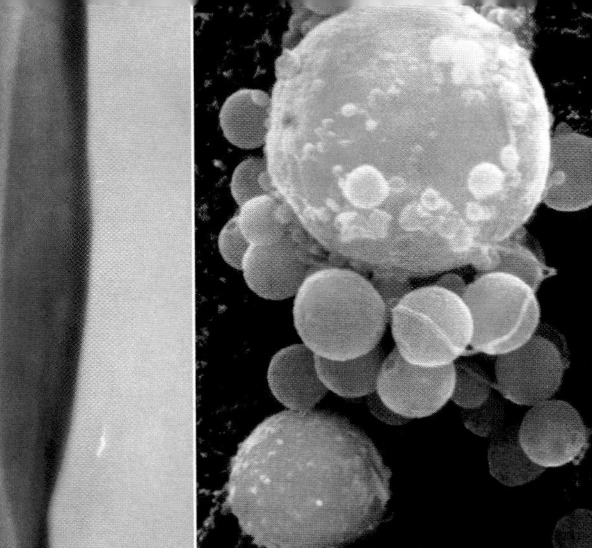

LONGEST MEMORY OF A CELL

Lymphocytes (above) are a type of white blood cell produced by the immune system. The largest of the lymphatic tissues is the spleen. Each successive generation of lymphocytes produced contains the 'memory' of previous illnesses that the body has fought throughout its lifetime.

SMALLEST BONE

The stapes, or stirrup bone (right), one of the three auditory ossicles in the middle ear, measures a tiny 2.6–3.4 mm (0.1–0.13 in) in length and weighs from 2 to 4.3 mg (0.03–0.066 grains). The stapedius, the muscle that controls the stapes, is less than 0.127 cm (0.05 in) long and is the smallest muscle in the human body.

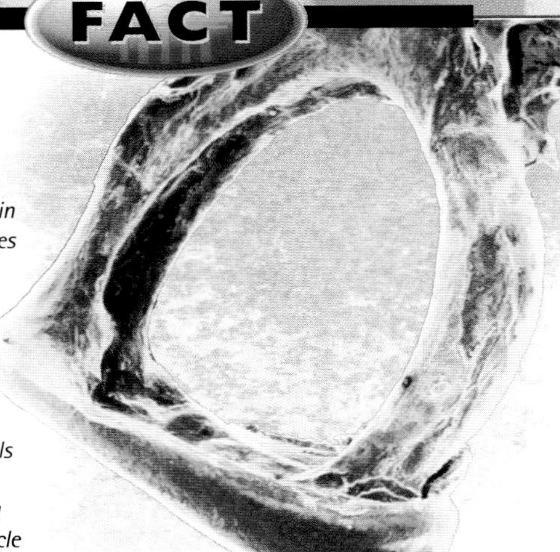

MEDICAL PHENOMENA

MOST COMMON CAUSE OF SUDDEN DEATH

Coronary heart disease is the most common cause of sudden death. The main factors that put an individual at risk of the disease are cigarette smoking, high blood pressure and high levels of cholesterol.

MOST COMMON INFECTIOUS DISEASE

The common cold, caused by a group of rhinoviruses, of which there are at least 180 types, affects almost everyone on Earth, except for those living in small isolated communities or in the frozen wastes of Antarctica. There are at least 40 different viruses, either airborne or transmitted by direct contact, which cause symptoms such as sneezing, coughing, sore throat, running eyes and nose, headache and mild fever.

MOST TEETH AT BIRTH

The first deciduous or milk teeth – the upper and lower jaw first incisors – normally appear in infants at 5–8 months. There are many recorded examples of children born with teeth. Sean Keaney (UK) was born on 10 April 1990 with 12 teeth. They were extracted to prevent possible feeding problems, and he grew his second full set of teeth at 18 months. Molars usually appear at 24 months, but in a case recorded in Denmark in 1970, a six-week premature baby was documented with eight teeth at birth, with four in the molar region.

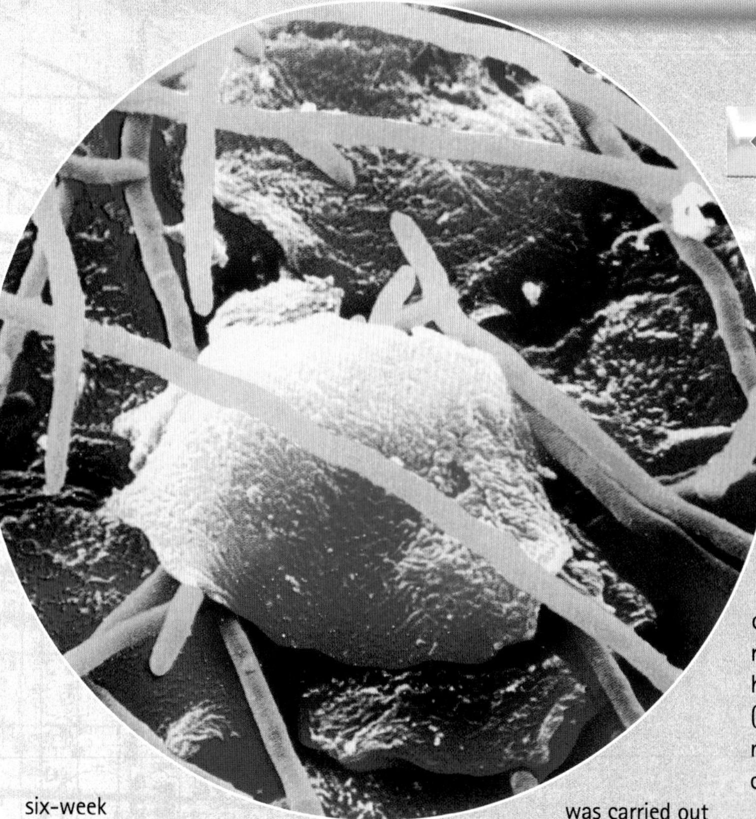

LARGEST TUMOUR AT BIRTH

The largest tumour ever recorded at birth weighed 311 g (11 oz) and was pressing against the windpipe of Ryan James Shannon (USA). He was born seven weeks early by Caesarean section on 2 January 1996 and weighed 2.8 kg (6 lb 2 oz). The tumour weighed 10% of his body weight. An operation to remove the growth was carried out nine days after the birth. The procedure lasted four hours and was a complete success.

LARGEST TUMOUR EVER OPERATED

An ovarian cyst estimated to weigh 148.7 kg (328 lb) was drained during the week prior to surgical removal of the cyst shell, in Texas, USA, in 1905 by Dr Arthur Spohn (USA). The patient recovered fully.

MOST SARCOMAS EXCISED FROM A PATIENT

From 1977 to 2001 a total of 1,674 sarcomas were excised under local anaesthetic from the skin of a British male patient by Dr Cecil Weintraub (South Africa). Sarcomas are malign tumours of the supporting tissues of the body. They can occur in blood vessels, muscle, fat, or in any of the other tissues that support, surround and protect the organs of the body.

LONGEST CARDIAC ARREST

The longest cardiac arrest lasted four hours in the case of fisherman Jan Egil Refsdahl (Norway), who fell overboard off Bergen, Norway, on 7 December 1987. He was rushed to Haukeland Hospital after his body temperature fell to 24°C (75°F) and his heart stopped. He made a full recovery after being connected to a heart-lung machine.

MOST COMMON SKIN INFECTION

Tinea pedis, commonly known as 'Athlete's foot' (seen left, under a microscope), is the most common skin infection in humans. The fungus afflicts up to 70% of the worldwide population and almost everyone will get it at least once in a lifetime. It affects the skin between the toes, which becomes dry, itchy and sore.

LONGEST HEART STOPPAGE

The longest recorded heart stoppage is a minimum of 3 hr 40 min in the case of Jean Jawbone (Canada) who, at the age of 20, was revived by a team of 26 medical staff using peritoneal dialysis in the Health Sciences Centre, Winnipeg, Manitoba, Canada, on 8 January 1977.

LONGEST SURVIVAL WITH THE HEART OUTSIDE THE BODY

Christopher Wall (USA, b. 19 August 1975) is the longest known survivor of the condition *ectopia cordis*, where the heart lies outside the body. The mortality rate is high, with most patients not living beyond 48 hours. He currently works for a construction tubing company in Philadelphia, USA.

LONGEST COMA

Elaine Esposito (USA) never regained consciousness after undergoing an appendectomy on 6 August 1941, aged six. She died on 25 November 1978, aged 43 years 357 days. She had been in a coma for 37 years 111 days.

OLDEST DISEASE

Leprosy is the oldest disease, with cases described in ancient Egypt as early as 1350 BC. (The disfigured hands of a leprosy victim are pictured on the right.) *Tuberculosis schistosomiasi*, an infectious disease of the lungs, has also been seen in Egyptian mummies dating from the 20th dynasty (1250 to 1000 BC).

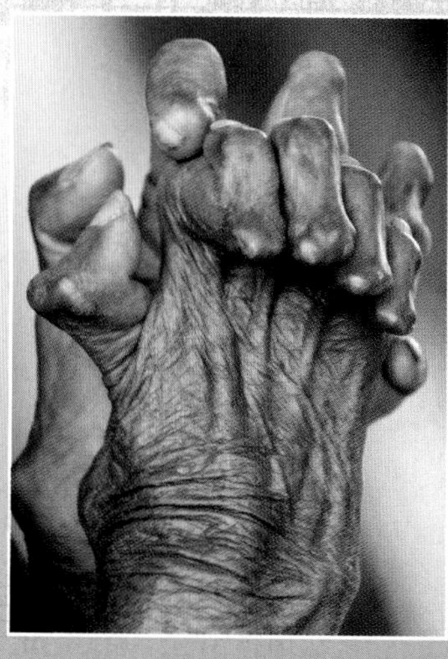

LONGEST TIME SURVIVED WITHOUT A PULSE

The longest time a human has survived without a pulse in their vascular system is three days. Julie Mills (UK) was at the point of death due to severe heart failure and viral myocarditus when, on 14 August 1998, cardiac surgeons at The John Radcliffe Hospital, Oxford, UK, used a non-pulsatile blood pump (AB180) to support her for one week, during which time her heart recovered and the pump was removed.

LOWEST HEART RATE

The lowest resting heart beat on record is 28 bpm (beats per minute), and belongs to the cyclist Miguel Induráin (Spain) who was tested at the University of Navarra, Pamplona, Spain, in 1995. The average resting heart rate is 66–72 bpm, with most athletes having 40 bpm. Induráin also has a lung capacity of 8 litres (14 pints) and a heart capable of pumping 50 litres (88 pints) of blood per minute – double that of a normal healthy man.

LOWEST BODY TEMPERATURE

The lowest authenticated body temperature is 14.2°C (57.5°F) (rectal temperature) for Karlee Kosolofski (Canada) then aged two, on 23 February 1994. She had accidentally been locked outside her home for six hours in a temperature of -22°C (-8°F). Despite severe frostbite, which meant the amputation of her left leg above the knee, she made a full recovery.

HIGHEST BODY TEMPERATURE

Willie Jones (USA) was admitted to Grady Memorial Hospital, Atlanta, Georgia, USA, with heatstroke on 10 July 1980, a day when the temperature reached 32.2°C (90°F) with 44% humidity. Jones's temperature was found to be 46.5°C (115.7°F) and he was discharged after 24 days.

HIGHEST BLOOD ALCOHOL LEVEL

The University of California Medical School, Los Angeles, USA, reported in December 1982 the case of a confused but conscious 24-year-old female who was shown to have a blood alcohol level of 1,510 mg per 100 ml – nearly 19 times the UK driving limit (80 mg of alcohol per 100 ml of blood) and triple the normally lethal limit.

HIGHEST BLOOD SUGAR LEVEL

Twelve-year-old Michael Dougherty (USA) had a blood sugar level 19 times above average at 2,350 while still conscious on 21 November 1995. The normal blood sugar range is between 80 and 120.

MOST ARTIFICIAL JOINTS

Anne Davison (UK) had 12 major joints (both shoulders, elbows, wrists, hips, knees and ankles) and three knuckles replaced by the age of 47. Diagnosed with arthritis at the age of 13, the first joint that Anne had replaced was her right knee, at the age of 27. The record is shared with Charles N Wedde (USA), who has rheumatoid arthritis, and also had 12 major joints replaced, between 1979 and 1995.

LONGEST ATTACK OF HICCUPS

Charles Osborne (USA) began hiccuping in 1922 while attempting to weigh a hog before slaughtering it. He was unable to find a cure but led a normal life in which he had two wives and fathered eight children. He continued hiccuping until one morning in February 1990, 68 years later.

LONGEST SNEEZING FIT

The longest recorded sneezing fit is that of Donna Griffiths (UK). She began sneezing on 13 January 1981 and sneezed an estimated one million times in the first 365 days. Her first sneeze-free day came 978 days later on 16 September 1983.

FASTEST SNEEZE

The highest speed at which expelled particles from a sneeze have been measured to travel is 167 km/h (103.6 mph).

LOUDEST SNORING

Kåre Walkert (Sweden), who suffers from the breathing disorder apnea, recorded peak snoring levels of 93 decibels on 24 May 1993.

LARGEST TUMOUR REMOVED INTACT

The largest tumour ever removed intact was a multicystic mass of the right ovary (below) weighing 137.6 kg (303 lb). The operation, which took over six hours, was performed by Professor Katherine O'Hanlan of Stanford University Medical Center, California, USA. The growth had a diameter of 1 m (3 ft) and was removed in its entirety in October 1991 from the abdomen of an unnamed 34-year-old woman. The patient made a full recovery. She left the operating theatre on one stretcher, with the tumour on another.

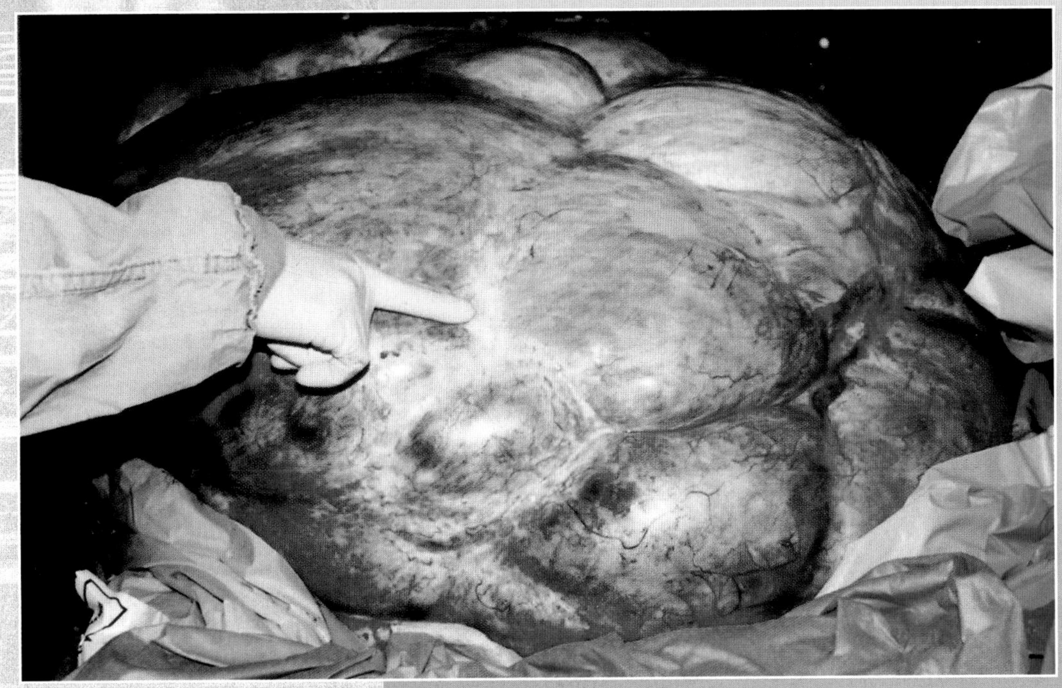

BIRTH & LIFE

OLDEST LIVING TRIPLETS

Douglas Haig Wilkins, Winnie Elsa Le Notre and Elsa Winnie Luxon (all UK, left and below) were verified on 4 March 2002 to be the oldest living triplets, aged 84 years 349 days. They were born in Guernsey, UK, on 21 March 1917 to Mary and Frederick Wilkins.

MOST PROLIFIC MOTHER EVER

The greatest recorded number of children born to one mother is 69, to the first wife of Feodor Vassilyev (Russia). In 27 pregnancies between 1725 and 1765 she gave birth to 16 pairs of twins, 7 sets of triplets and 4 sets of quadruplets. Only two of the children failed to survive their infancy. The mother also holds the records for giving birth to the most sets of twins and the most sets of quadruplets.

LONGEST FAMILY TREE

The lineage of K'ung Ch'iu or Confucius (China, 551–479 BC) can be traced back further than that of any other family. His great-great-great-great-grandfather Kung Chia is known from the 8th century BC. Kung Chia has 86 lineal descendants.

GREATEST NUMBER OF DESCENDANTS

In polygamous countries, the number of a person's descendants can be incalculable. Moulay Ismail, the last Sharifian Emperor of Morocco, was reputed to have fathered a total of 525 sons and 342 daughters by 1703, and achieved a 700th son by 1721. The most recorded living descendants of a monogamous person, however, is 824, by Samuel S Mast (USA). At the time of his death on 15 October 1992 aged 96, he had 11 children, 97 grandchildren, 634 great-grandchildren and 82 great-great-grandchildren.

MOST CHILDREN DELIVERED AT A SINGLE BIRTH

The highest medically recorded number of children born at a single birth is nine to Geraldine Brodrick (Australia) at the Royal Hospital for Women, Sydney, NSW, Australia, on 13 June 1971. None of the children (five boys [two stillborn] and four girls) lived for more than six days.

LONGEST INTERVAL BETWEEN BIRTHS

The longest interval between the birth of two children to the same mother is 41 years for Elizabeth Ann Buttle (UK), who had a daughter, Belinda, in 1956 and a son, Joseph, on 20 November 1997.

MOST PREMATURE BABY TO SURVIVE

James Elgin Gill was born to Brenda and James Gill (both Canada) on 20 May 1987 in Ottawa, Ontario, Canada, 128 days premature and weighing 624 g (1 lb 6 oz). The normal human gestation period is 280 days (40 weeks). Much of James's body was still developing, including his skin, hands, ears and feet, with his eyes still fused shut. James survived and is now a healthy teenager.

OLDEST MOTHER

It was reported that Rosanna Dalla Corte (Italy, b. February 1931) gave birth to a baby boy on 18 July 1994 when aged 63 years. This record is also attributed to Arceli Keh (USA, b. February 1933) who was thought to be aged 63 when, after IVF treatment, she gave birth to a daughter at Loma Linda University Medical Center, California, USA, on 7 November 1996.

OLDEST LIVING MAN

Yukichi Chuganji (b. 23 March 1889) of Ogori, Fukuoka Prefecture, Japan, became the oldest man in the world on 4 January 2002 at the age of 112 years 288 days.

OLDEST MAN EVER

The greatest age to which any man has ever lived is 120 years 237 days in the case of Shigechiyo Izumi of Isen, Tokunoshima – an island 1,320 km (820 miles) south-west of Tokyo, Japan. He was born on 29 June 1865 and was recorded as a six-year-old in Japan's first census of 1871. He died at 12:15 GMT on 21 February 1986 after developing pneumonia.

OLDEST LIVING WOMAN

The oldest living woman in the world whose date of birth can be fully authenticated is Kamato Hongo (Japan, b. 16 September 1887). She took the title aged 114 years 183 days on the death of Maude Farris-Luse (USA, b. 21 January 1887), who died on 18 March 2002.

OLDEST WOMAN EVER

The greatest fully authenticated age to which any human has ever lived is 122 years 164 days by Jeanne Louise Calment (France). Born on 21 February 1875, she died at a nursing home in Arles, southern France, on 4 August 1997.

MOST CHILDREN DELIVERED AT A SINGLE BIRTH TO SURVIVE

A set of septuplets (four boys and three girls, left) was born to Bobbie McCaughey (USA) on 19 November 1997 at the University Hospital, Iowa, USA. Conceived by in vitro fertilization, the babies were all delivered after 31 weeks by caesarean in the space of 16 minutes. They weighed between 1.048 kg and 1.474 kg (2 lb 5 oz and 3 lb 4 oz).

Another set of surviving septuplets was born eight weeks prematurely on 14 January 1998 to 40-year-old Hasna Mohammed Humair (Saudi Arabia). The four boys and three girls, the smallest of which weighed just under 907 g (2 lb), were born at the Abha Obstetric Hospital, Aseer, Saudi Arabia. The unplanned pregnancy was the result of a fertility drug prescribed to regulate the mother's menstrual cycle.

OLDEST LIVING MALE TWINS

William and Fred Barrett (UK, b. 5 May 1904) have lived in the southwest of the UK all of their lives, and became the oldest male twins living in the world on 16 April 2001, aged 96 years 346 days.

OLDEST LIVING MALE CONJOINED TWINS

Ronnie and Donnie Galyon (USA, b. 25 October 1951) are the oldest living conjoined male twins. For 36 years, they travelled in side shows, carnivals and circuses, but they retired in 1991, and now live in Ohio, USA.

OLDEST FEMALE CONJOINED TWINS

Masha and Dasha Krivoshlyapova (Russia, b. 3 January 1950) were rare conjoined twins with the condition known as *dicephales tetrabrachius dipus*. Between them they had two heads, four arms and two legs. They died aged 53 in April 2003, within 17 hours of each other.

OLDEST LIVING MIXED TWINS

Louisa Dunn (*née* Adams) and Fred Adams were born on 9 March 1907 in Wood Green, London, UK. They became the oldest living mixed twins on 3 November 1999, aged 92 years 199 days.

OLDEST EVER QUADRUPLETS

The quadruplet siblings Adolf, Anne-Marie, Emma and Elisabeth Ottman (Germany) were born on 5 May 1912. All four quads lived to the age of 79.

HEAVIEST QUADRUPLETS AT BIRTH

The heaviest quadruplets weighed a total of 10.426 kg (22 lb 15.75 oz) at birth. The two girls and two boys were born to Tina Saunders (UK) at St Peters Hospital, Chertsey, Surrey, UK, on 7 February 1989.

MOST SINGLE SIBLINGS SHARING THE SAME BIRTHDAY

There is one verified example of a family producing five single children with coincident birthdays. Carolyn and Ralph Cummins' (USA) children Catherine (1952), Carol (1953), Charles (1956), Claudia (1961) and Cecilia (1966), amazingly, were all born on 20 February. The odds against five single siblings sharing a birthdate are one in 17,797,577,730 – almost four times the world's population.

LONGEST SEPARATED TWINS

On 27 April 1989, through the New Zealand television programme *Missing*, twins Iris Johns and Aro Campbell (New Zealand, b. 13 January 1914) were reunited after 75 years of separation.

OLDEST FEMALE TWINS EVER

Kin Narita and Gin Kanie (Japan, b. 1 August 1892, right), whose names mean gold and silver, were the oldest authenticated female twins. Kin died of heart failure on 23 January 2000 at the age of 107 years 175 days. They lived in Nagoya, Japan, the town of their birth.

ASTONISHING OLDIES

OLDEST BADMINTON PLAYER

As of February 2003, 96-year-old Henry Paynter (Canada, b. UK, 27 February 1907, above) was still a regular player at the Kelowna Badminton Club, Kelowna, British Columbia, Canada.

OLDEST OLYMPIC GOLD MEDALLIST

Oscar Swahn (Sweden) was in the winning Running Deer shooting team at the 1912 Olympic Games in Sweden, aged 64 years 258 days. In the same event at the 1920 Olympics in Belgium he won silver, becoming the oldest winner of any Olympic medal at 72 years 280 days.

OLDEST COMPETITOR AT A WINTER OLYMPIC GAMES

The oldest ever competitor at the Winter Olympic Games is James Coates (GB) who competed in the skeleton at St Moritz, Switzerland, in 1948 aged 53 years 328 days.

The oldest female competitor at a Winter Olympic Games is Anne Abernathy (US Virgin Islands) who took part in the luge at Salt Lake City, USA, on 13 February 2002 aged 48 years 307 days.

OLDEST SNOWBOARDER

George Blair (aka Banana George, USA, b. 22 January 1915) of Winter Haven, Florida, USA, is the world's oldest active snowboarder, snowboarding for between 45 and 60 days a year.

OLDEST MAN TO REACH THE SUMMIT OF MT EVEREST

Yuichiro Miura (Japan, b. 12 October 1932) reached the summit of Everest aged 70 years 222 days on 22 May 2003, becoming the oldest person ever to have accomplished this feat.

OLDEST WOMAN TO REACH THE SUMMIT OF MT EVEREST

Tamae Watanabe (Japan, b. 21 November 1938) was aged 63 years 177 days when she reached the summit of Mt Everest at 9:55 am on 16 May 2002, becoming the oldest woman ever to do so.

Watanabe reached the summit on its busiest day ever, when 54 other climbers reached the top of the 8,848-m (29,028-ft) peak.

OLDEST PERSON TO FLY SOLO ROUND THE WORLD

Fred Lasby (USA, b. 28 May 1912) completed a solo round-the-world flight at the age of 82 years 84 days in his single-engined Piper Comanche. Leaving Fort Myers, Florida, USA, on 30 June 1994, he flew west for 37,366 km (23,218 miles), making 21 stops and arriving back at Fort Myers on 20 August 1994.

OLDEST AERONAUTICAL RECORD BREAKER

The oldest pilot to have set a world record as recognized by the world governing body, the Fédération Aéronautique Internationale (FAI), is retired Wing Commander Kenneth Wallis (UK). Wallis was 85 years 213 days old when, on 16 November 2002, he set a speed record of 207.7 km/h (129 mph) over a distance of 3 km (1.8 miles) in a piston-engine-powered autogyro over Norfolk, UK.

OLDEST BASE JUMPER

BASE jumpers parachute from high manmade structures and natural formations. On 2 August 2002 James Talbot Guyer (USA, b. 16 June 1928) parachuted from the 148-m-high (486-ft) Perrine Bridge near Twin Falls, Idaho, USA, aged 74 years 47 days.

OLDEST WOMAN TO MAKE A SOLO PARACHUTE JUMP

Sylvia Brett (UK) was 80 years 166 days old when she parachuted over Cranfield, Bedfordshire, UK, on 23 August 1986.

OLDEST FOOTBALL PLAYER

Enrique Alcocer (Mexico, b. 28 August 1924) is currently the world's oldest regular football player. He plays for the Reforma Athletic Club in Mexico City, Mexico. Alcocer began playing regularly in 1936 for Grosso junior and high school in Mexico City. He then played professionally for the Marte Football Club in Mexico's first division in 1944 before joining his current club in 1952.

OLDEST BALL BOY IN A MAJOR TENNIS CHAMPIONSHIP

The oldest ball boy to participate in a major tennis championships is Manny Hershkowitz (USA) who worked on court at the US Open at Flushing Meadow, New York, USA, in September 1999 aged 82.

OLDEST ENGLISH CHANNEL SWIMMER

The oldest person to swim the English Channel was Bertram Batt (Australia, b. 22 December 1919), who was aged 67 years 241 days when he swam from Cap Gris-Nez, France, to Dover, UK, in 18 hr 37 min from 19–20 August 1987. The oldest woman to achieve the feat was Susan Fraenkel (South Africa, b. 22 April 1948), who was 46 years 103 days old when she did the swim in 12 hr 5 min on 24 July 1994.

OLDEST WINDSURFER

Otto Comanos (Australia, b. Greece, 16 November 1913) took up the sport of windsurfing shortly after his retirement in 1986 and regularly windsurfs two to three times a week in the lakes in and around Sydney, New South Wales, Australia.

OLDEST DRAG BOAT RACE CHAMPION

Paul Showman (USA) is recognized by the International Hot Boat Association (IHBA) as being the oldest person to compete in an officially sanctioned drag boat race and the oldest ever IHBA Champion in the 12-second class, when he won in 1998 at the age of 83 in his boat *The Legend.*

OLDEST BOXING CHAMPION

Archie Moore (USA) was recognized as a light heavyweight champion up until 10 February 1962 when his title was removed. His date of birth is uncertain, but he was believed to be between 45 and 48 years old. During his career (1936–63) he won a record 145 fights by knockout.

OLDEST COMPETING FEMALE BAREBACK BRONC RIDER

Jan Youren (USA, b. 2 October 1943) has ridden bulls and broncs for over 35 years and is a former world champion in the sport.

OLDEST TIGHTROPE WALKER

The oldest known tightrope walker is 'Professor' William Ivy Baldwin (USA, 1866–1953), who crossed a portion of the Eldorado Canyon, Colorado, USA, on his 82nd birthday. He walked a 97.5-m (320-ft) long wire spanning a 38.1-m (125-ft) drop.

OLDEST CLOWN

The record for world's oldest professional clown is held jointly by Josep Andreu I Lasserre (aka Charlie Rivel, Spain) and Arnold Schmidt (aka Guggele, Denmark). Both clowns were entertaining circus crowds up until the age of 87.

OLDEST FORMULA ONE GRAND PRIX WINNER

The oldest Grand Prix winner (in pre-World Championship days) was Tazio Giorgio Nuvolari (Italy, 1892–1953), who won the Albi Grand Prix at Albi, France, in his Maserati 4CL on 14 July 1946 aged 53 years 240 days.

OLDEST DRIVERS

There are three drivers who were issued with new driving licences at age 104: Maude Tull (USA) of Inglewood, California – who took to driving aged 91 after her husband died – was issued a renewal to her licence on 5 February 1976 when aged 104; Layne Hall (USA), whose date of birth is uncertain (b. 1884 or 1880), was issued with a New York State licence on 15 June 1989 when he was either 104 or 109; and most recently, Fred Hale Sr (USA, b. 1 December 1890) was issued with a driving licence on 29 February 1995 at age 104. The licence was valid until his 108th birthday in 1998.

OLDEST BELL RINGER

As of 10 March 2003 Reginald Bray (UK, b. 28 October 1902) was still an active member of the bell ringing team of St Cyr and St Julitta, Newton St Cyres, Devon, UK, ringing bells regularly aged 100 years 133 days.

OLDEST FEMALE CHORISTER

Clarissa Lee (UK, b. 20 October 1892) was a chorister at St Mary and St Andrew Church, Pitminster, Somerset, UK, from 1914 to the end of 1996, when she was 104. She sang with the choir every week.

OLDEST MALE STRIPPER

Bernie Barker (USA, b. 31 July 1940), a regular performer at Club LeBare, Miami Beach, Florida, USA, began his career in 2000 at the age of 60 as a way to get in shape after recovering from prostate cancer. Since leaving his previous job of selling real estate, he has won over 30 male stripping contests.

OLDEST FEMALE SINGER TO REACH NO.1 IN THE UK CHART

Deborah Harry (USA, left, b. 1 July 1945), the lead singer of Blondie, became the oldest female vocalist to top the UK charts when she went to No.1 with 'Maria' on 13 February 1999 at the age of 53 years 227 days.

OLDEST LIFEGUARD

The oldest lifeguard in the world is Haywood Leroy Stewart (USA, b. 22 May 1916, below) of Wheat Ridge, Colorado, USA, who has been a lifeguard since 1938.

FOOD FEATS

FASTEST TIME TO DRINK A PINT OF BEER UPSIDE-DOWN

Peter G Dowdeswell (UK) of Earls Barton, Northamptonshire, UK, drank a pint of beer in 3 seconds while standing on his head at BBC Radio Leicester studios, UK, on 16 February 1988. He also holds the record for drinking the fastest yard of ale (1.42 litres or 2.5 pints), which he achieved in 5 seconds at RAF Upper Heyford, Oxfordshire, UK, on 5 May 1975.

FASTEST TOMATO KETCHUP DRINKER

Dustin Phillips (USA) consumed 91% of a standard 397-g (14-oz) bottle of Heinz tomato ketchup though a 0.63-cm-diameter (0.25-in) drinking straw in just 33 seconds at the studios of *Guinness World Records: Primetime*, Los Angeles, California, USA, on 23 September 1999.

MOST CREAM CRACKERS EATEN

Ambrose Mendy (UK) ate three cream crackers in a record time of 49.15 seconds at the offices of Guinness World Records, London, UK, on 29 October 2002.

MOST MEATBALLS EATEN IN ONE MINUTE

Nick Marshall (UK) consumed 27 meatballs in one minute using a toothpick, during a national meatball eating competition held at IKEA, Leeds, West Yorkshire, UK, on 18 November 2002.

MOST HOT DOGS EATEN IN THREE MINUTES

Peter Dowdeswell (UK, right) ate four hot dogs (sausages and buns) in three minutes as part of the Wimpy National Hotdog Championships at the Trocadero Centre, London, UK, on 27 July 2001.

FASTEST SAUSAGE SWALLOWER

Jimmy Sköld (Sweden) swallowed whole seven cooked sausages – each measuring a minimum of 16 cm (6.29 in) long and 1.75 cm (0.68 in) in diameter – in one minute on the set of *Guinness World Records: Primetime*, Los Angeles, USA, on 11 March 2001.

MOST BAKED BEANS EATEN WITH A COCKTAIL STICK IN FIVE MINUTES

The greatest number of baked beans eaten with a cocktail stick in five minutes is 226 by Andy Szerbini (UK) at London Zoo, London, UK, on 18 November 1996.

MOST WORMS EATEN IN 30 SECONDS

Mark Hogg (USA) swallowed a total of 94 night crawler worms in 30 seconds on the set of the *Regis Philbin Show* in October 2000. Although Hogg can swallow handfuls of live worms – which have been thoroughly washed – without hesitation, he doesn't care for eating sushi.

MOST BIG MACS CONSUMED

Donald Gorske (USA) has eaten Big Macs daily since 1972. He consumed his 18,250th on 7 March 2002.

MOST JAM DOUGHNUTS EATEN IN THREE MINUTES

The record for most jam doughnuts eaten in three minutes without licking the lips is six and is held by Steve McHugh (UK) who achieved this at the offices of Guinness World Records, London, on 28 June 2002.

MOST ICE-CREAM EATEN IN 30 SECONDS

The world record for the most ice-cream eaten in 30 seconds with a teaspoon is 167 g (5.8 oz) and belongs to Jaime André Sargento da Silva (Portugal) who achieved his feat in Lisbon, Portugal, on 11 November 2002.

MOST SMARTIES EATEN WITH CHOPSTICKS IN THREE MINUTES

The record for the most Smarties eaten with chopsticks in three minutes is 108 by Kathryn Ratcliffe (UK) at WH Smith's store in Gateshead, Tyne & Wear, UK, on 28 September 2002.

LARGEST BUBBLEGUM BUBBLE BLOWN WITH THE MOUTH

Susan Montgomery Williams (USA) blew the world's largest bubblegum bubble in New York, USA, on 19 July 1994. Measured under the strict rules of this competitive activity, it had a 58.4 cm (23 in) diameter.

MOST HAMBURGERS STUFFED IN THE MOUTH

The record for stuffing the most regulation size hamburgers (including buns and condiments) in the mouth at one time is three. Johnny Reitz (USA, right) performed this feat on the set of *Guinness World Records: Primetime* on 17 June 1998. The rules of the event require the participant not to swallow any of the hamburgers.

FURTHEST MARSHMALLOW NOSE-BLOW

The furthest a marshmallow has been blown out of one person's nostril and caught in the mouth of another person is 4.96 m (16 ft 3.5 in), by blower Scott Jeckel (USA) and catcher Ray Perisin (USA) on the set of *Guinness World Records: Primetime* in Los Angeles, California, USA, on 13 August 1999.

FURTHEST SPAGHETTI NASAL EJECTION

Kevin Cole (USA) holds the record for the longest spaghetti strand blown out of a nostril in a single blow. On 16 December 1998 Cole successfully achieved a record distance of 19 cm (7.5 in) on the set of *Guinness World Records: Primetime* in Los Angeles, California, USA.

MOST M&MS FLIPPED AND CAUGHT IN ONE MINUTE

The record for flipping peanut M&Ms from the back of one person's ear into another person's mouth is 16 in one minute by Mark Needle (USA) who flipped the sweets to his brother, Ben, on the set of *Guinness World Records: Primetime*, Los Angeles, USA, on 18 August 1998.

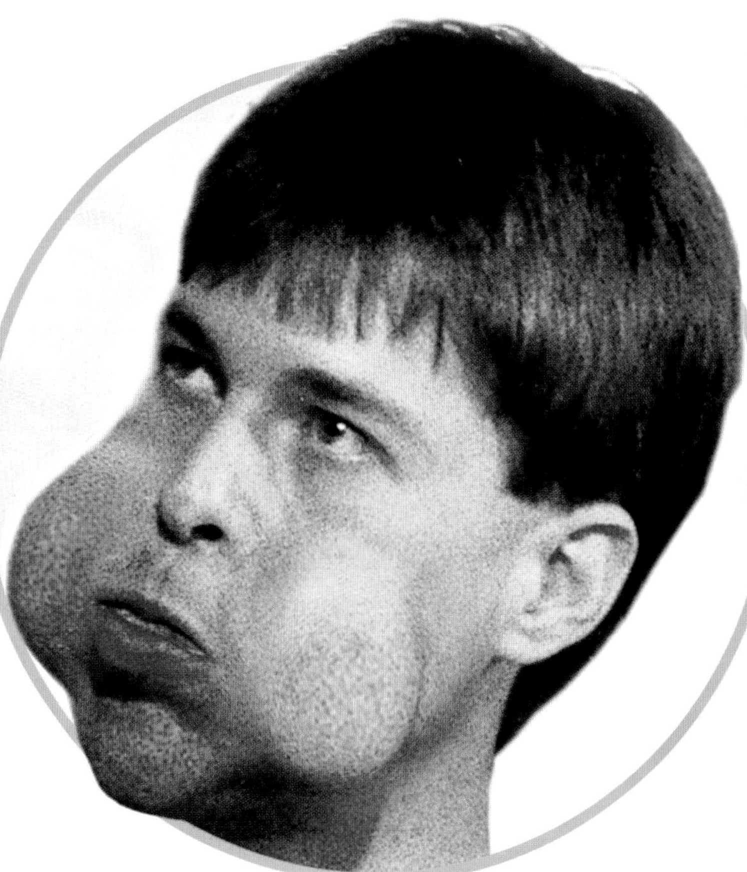

Treading Championships, Villa Franca del Bierzo, Castilla-León, Spain, on 30 August 1998.

FASTEST SANDWICH MADE USING FEET

Using just his feet, Rob Williams (USA) made a Bologna smoked sausage, cheese, lettuce, sliced tomato, mustard, mayonnaise and sliced pickle sandwich – complete with olives on cocktail sticks – in 1 min 57 sec on the set of *Guinness World Records: Primetime* on 10 November 2000.

MOST PANCAKES MADE IN EIGHT HOURS BY A TEAM

The most pancakes made in eight hours is 30,724 by members of the Lubbock Lions Club, Lubbock, Texas, USA, at the 50th Annual Pancake Festival, Lubbock Memorial Civic Center, on 23 February 2002.

FASTEST CHICKEN PLUCK

On 19 January 1939 Ernest Hausen of Fort Atkinson, Wisconsin, USA, was timed at 4.4 seconds for completely plucking a chicken.

HIGHEST FORMAL MEAL EATEN

The highest altitude at which a formal meal has been eaten is 6,768 m (22,205 ft), at the top of Mt Huascarán, Peru. On 28 June 1989 nine members of the Ansett Social Climbers from Sydney, Australia, scaled the mountain with a Louis XIV dining table, chairs, silverware, a candelabra, wine and a three-course meal.

LARGEST PIZZA ORDER

On 19 August 1998 Little Caesar's took an order from the VF Corporation of Greensboro, North Carolina, USA, for 13,386 pizzas for 40,160 employees at 180 locations across the United States. The average cost of each pizza was $7.99 (then £4.94), which resulted in a total cost of $106,959.41 (then £66,077.40).

LONGEST PIZZA DELIVERY

On 22 March 2001 Bernard Jordaan of Butlers Pizza, Cape Town, South Africa, hand delivered a pizza to Corne Krige, the captain of the Fedsure Stormers rugby team, in Sydney, Australia – a distance of 11,042 km (6,861 miles) as the crow flies.

LONGEST CURRY DELIVERY

MadAboutCurry.co.uk arranged for a vegetable biryani curry and a peshwari naan to be delivered from the Rupali restaurant, Newcastle-Upon-Tyne, Tyne and Wear, UK, to Rachael Kerr (UK) in Sydney, Australia, a distance of 17,398 km (10,811 miles) as the crow flies. The delivery arrived at its destination on 26 February 2001.

MOST GRAPES TRODDEN IN TWO MINUTES

Angel Amigo and Juan Manuel Fuertes (both Spain) trod 50 kg (110.2 lb) of grapes in two minutes, resulting in 15 litres (26.4 pints) of juice, at the International Grape

LARGEST GINGERBREAD HOUSE

Roger A Pelcher (USA) built a gingerbread house with an internal volume of 940 m³ (33,196 ft³) at Wolfchase Galleria, Memphis, Tennessee, USA, in December 2001. The house (right) was 17.5 m (57.5 ft) tall at its highest point, and approximately 9 m² (29.5 ft²) at the base.

ODD TALENTS

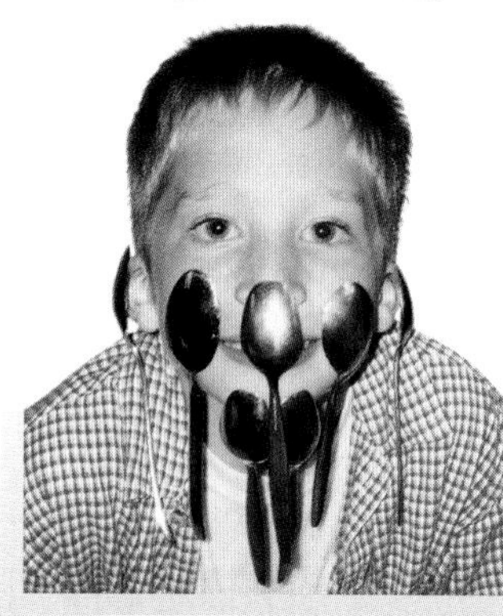

MOST SPOONS BALANCED ON THE FACE

Jonathan Friedman (USA, above) balanced seven stainless steel spoons on his face for five seconds at Lake Oswego, Oregon, USA, on 24 February 2002. The spoons weighed 19.8–42.5g (0.69–1.4 oz). He placed one on each ear and cheek, one on his nose and two on his chin.

MOST CLOTHES PEGS CLIPPED ON A FACE

Garry Turner (UK), known for his unusually stretchy skin, managed to clip 133 ordinary wooden clothes pegs on his face, at the offices of Guinness World Records, London, UK, on 3 August 2001.

GREATEST VERTICAL HEIGHT WALKED ON STILTS

On 9 June 2002, Colin Tschida and Ryan Hamilton (both USA) hiked 4.82 km (3 miles) on wooden stilts to reach the top of Harney Peak, which has an elevation of 2,207 m (7,242 ft), in the Black Hills of South Dakota, USA. The climb took 2 hr 25 min 21 sec. Walking on stilts with footholds 60 cm (2 ft) above the ground, they rested on four occasions, remaining on their stilts by leaning against trees. They fell off their stilts a total of nine times between them.

FASTEST HUMAN CRAB OVER 20 M

Agnès Brun (France) travelled a distance of 20 m (65 ft) in a crab position in 33.3 seconds at the studios of *L'Émission des Records* in Paris, France, on 30 November 2001.

MOST CARTWHEELS IN ONE MINUTE WITHOUT HANDS

Mohammed Elachi (France) completed 32 cartwheels in one minute without using his hands and without straying out of a 60-cm diameter (2-ft) circle in Paris, France, on 28 May 2002.

FASTEST FROG JUMP

Bastien Lecomte (France) covered a distance of 10 m (32 ft 6 in) frog jumping (holding on to his toes) in a time of 11.58 seconds at the studios of *L'Émission des Records* in Paris, France, on 23 May 2002.

MOST SOAP BUBBLE DOMES

Soap bubble artist Fan Yang (Canada) set the world record for the most soap bubble domes created inside one another at the studios of *Guinness World Records* in Helsinki, Finland, on 20 October 2001. He blew a total of 12 soap bubble domes within each other in the manner of a Russian matriska doll.

LONGEST CARD THROWING DISTANCE

The record for the longest throw of a single playing card is 65.96 m (216 ft 4 in) by Rick Smith Jr (USA). The record was set at the Cleveland State Convocation Center, Ohio, USA, on 21 March 2002.

MOST PACKS OF CARDS MEMORIZED

Dominic O'Brien (UK) memorized, on a single sighting, a random sequence of 54 separate packs of cards all shuffled together (2,808 cards in total) at Simpson's-In-The-Strand, London, UK, on 1 May 2002. He memorized the cards in 11 hr 42 min then recited them in the exact sequence in a time of 3 hr 30 min. With only a 0.5% margin of error allowed (no more than 14 errors), he broke the record with just eight errors.

MOST BASKETBALLS SPUN SIMULTANEOUSLY

The most basketballs spun simultaneously is 28 by Michael Kettman (USA, pictured right, spinning 20 basketballs) on 25 May 1999 in London, UK.

FURTHEST EYEBALL POPPER

Kim Goodman (USA), can pop her eyeballs to a protrusion of 11 mm (0.43 in) beyond her eye sockets. Her eyes were measured achieving this feat on the set of the US television show *Guinness World Records: Primetime* on 13 June 1998.

LARGEST SIMULTANEOUS ONE-HANDED HAT SPIN

Francois 'Jester Coco' Chotard (France) spun with one hand a total of 23 hats simultaneously, balanced on the tops of individual poles measuring between 170 cm and 220 cm long (67–87 in) at Bolton, Greater Manchester, UK, on 14 September 2001.

MOST BOWLING BALLS STACKED IN THREE MINUTES BY A TEAM

Jäni Yli-Länttä and Niko Korkeakangas (both Finland) managed to stack nine standard bowling balls vertically without the use of adhesives in three minutes on the set of *Guinness World Records* in Helsinki, Finland, on 23 October 2001.

MOST LAYERED BED OF NAILS SANDWICH

The most layered bed of nails sandwich was made up of four people lying between three double-sided beds of nails in Deal, Kent, UK, on 27 August 2001.

HEAVIEST BED OF NAILS CONCRETE BLOCK BREAK

Ciro Gallo (UK) had 37 concrete blocks weighing a total of 235.8 kg (519.8 lb) placed on his chest and broken with a 6.35-kg (14-lb) sledgehammer while he lay on a bed of nails at Hemel Hempstead, Hertfordshire, UK, on 24 August 2002.

MOST BALLOON SCULPTURES IN ONE HOUR

John Cassidy (USA) made 494 balloon shapes in one hour in New York, USA, on 29 August 2002. He broke his own record of 468 balloons.

MOST TIGHTROPE SKIPPING JUMPS

Juan Pedro Carrillo (USA) achieved 780 consecutive turns skipping with a rope on a high-wire in San Antonio, Texas, USA, on 30 June 2000. The tightrope was 7.9 m (26 ft) high.

LONGEST FULL-BODY ICE CONTACT ENDURANCE

Wearing only his swimming trunks, Wim Hof (Netherlands) endured standing in a tube filled with ice cubes for 1 hr 6 min 4 sec in London, UK, on 13 March 2002.

HIGHEST FLAME BY A FIRE BREATHER

Henrik Segelström (Sweden) blew a flame to a height of 3 m (9.8 ft) in Stockholm, Sweden, on 28 November 2001.

MOST BRAS UNHOOKED IN ONE MINUTE WITH ONE HAND

Jason Dahmer (Canada) unhooked one-handed 16 bras worn under t-shirts at Columbus, Ohio, USA, on 17 August 2001.

LONGEST TIME SPINNING A FRYING PAN ON A FINGER

Anders Björklund (Sweden) was able to spin a frying pan on his finger for 14 minutes on the set of *Guinness Rekord TV*, Stockholm, Sweden, on 29 November 2001.

MOST CHAINSAW JUGGLING THROWS

Tom Comet (Canada, above) juggled three petrol-driven chainsaws for 44 throws (14 complete rotations and two catches) on 5 August 2002 at Princess Street Gardens, Edinburgh, UK.

MASS PARTICIPATION

LARGEST DOG WALK

On 20 April 2002, 3,117 dogs took part in the world's largest dog walk. The dogs were taken on the 5.5-km (3.4-mile) Mighty Texas Dog Walk, starting from Austin High School, Austin, Texas, USA. The event was organized by Texas Hearing & Service Dogs.

LARGEST GROUP HUG

A total of 4,703 people hugged each other for at least 10 seconds at the Scout 2001 event at Rinkaby skjutfält, Kristianstad, Sweden, on 3 August 2001. The record-breaking hug was televised for the *Guinness Rekord TV* show.

LARGEST HUMAN CENTIPEDE

A total of 2,026 people - Nagoya Otani High School students, their parents and teachers - succeeded in creating the world's largest human centipede at Tsuruma Track and Field Stadium, Nagoya, Japan, on 13 June 2001. The ankles of all participants were firmly tied to the ankles of the next person. The human centipede successfully moved a distance of 30 m (98 ft 6 in) without any mishaps.

MOST PEOPLE MAKING SNOW ANGELS SIMULTANEOUSLY

A record 1,791 people made snow angels on the grounds of the Capitol Mall at Bismark, North Dakota, USA, on 23 March 2002. The event (below) was organized by the State Historical Society of North Dakota.

LARGEST MASCOT GATHERING

On 29 September 2002, a record total of 90 costumed mascots gathered to compete in the British Mascot Grand National (right) at Huntingdon Racecourse, Huntingdon, UK.

LARGEST MEXICAN WAVE

The world's longest Mexican wave consisted of 5,805 participants and occurred on Aberavon beach, Neath Port Talbot, UK, on 14 April 2002, in support of the British Heart Foundation.

LARGEST GATHERING OF SANTAS

The world's largest gathering of Santas took place on 7 December 2002, when 2,685 costumed Santas paraded down the streets of Bralanda, Sweden. All participants wore red Santa costumes with matching hats and fake white beards.

MOST PEOPLE ON A SINGLE PAIR OF SKIS

A total of 80 people skied a distance of 120 m (394 ft) on a 76-m long (250-ft) pair of skis at the Norway/Keskinada Giant Ski Event at Ottawa, Ontario, Canada, on 2 February 2002. The participants were led by the Governor General of Canada, Adrienne Clarkson, and the Norwegian Ambassador to Canada, Ingvard Havnen. The event was organized by the Norwegian Embassy and the executive committee of the Keskinada Loppet cross-country ski race. It took place at Rideau Hall, the Canadian Governor General's residence.

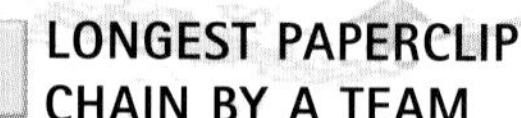

LONGEST PAPERCLIP CHAIN BY A TEAM

A 32.2-km-long (20-mile) paperclip chain was made in 24 hours by 60 people as part of an art exhibition at the SKOL Contemporary Art Centre, Montreal, Canada, on 1 April 2001.

LARGEST HUMAN IMAGE

On 24 July 1999 a total of 34,309 people, organized by Realizar Eventos Especiais of Portugal, gathered at the National Stadium of Jamor, Lisbon, Portugal, to create the Portuguese logo for Euro 2004. The event was part of the successful Portuguese bid to UEFA to hold the European football championship in 2004. The kicking leg of the player in the logo was composed of 651 gymnasts wearing black and white capes, which, when turned over, created the illusion of the player kicking the ball. Once the ball was kicked, it released 10,000 red and green helium balloons - the colours of the Portuguese flag.

LARGEST GROUP DRUM ROLL

A total of 1,434 drummers, led by Micky Dolenz (USA), Davy Jones (UK) and Peter Tork (USA) - former members of The Monkees - played a drum roll for 3 min 22 sec to mark the opening of the Hard Rock Hotel at Universal Orlando, Florida, USA, on 27 February 2001.

LARGEST SIMULTANEOUS YODEL

The world's largest simultaneous yodel involved 937 people, yodeling the popular Swiss song 'Von Luzern uf Wäggis zue' for more than one minute at the Ravensburger Spielland, Meckenbeuren, Germany, on 5 October 2002.

LARGEST BELL RINGING ENSEMBLE

At an event held in the city of Gdańsk, Poland, 10,000 people gathered in Dlugi Targ Street and rang their bells simultaneously on 31 December 2000 to celebrate the turn of the century.

LARGEST SIMULTANEOUS YO-YO

On 13 June 2002 the world's largest yo-yo took place at the Royal Dublin Society, Dublin, Republic of Ireland, with 426 people yo-yoing for two minutes.

MOST PEOPLE JUGGLING AT THE SAME TIME

At the European Juggling Convention held in Edinburgh, UK, on 7 August 1998, a total of 1,508 people juggled a minimum of three balls each for ten seconds.

MOST PEOPLE FIRE BREATHING

A total of 50 people, organized by Frankenberg Entertainment (Sweden), gathered in Stockholm, Sweden, to blow fire from torches on 3 October 2001.

LARGEST SIMULTANEOUS WHOOPEE CUSHION SIT

The record for the most people to sit on whoopee cushions at the same time was broken by 982 people, all employees of Walkers Ltd (UK), at the International Convention Centre in Birmingham, UK, on 15 January 2002.

MOST TREES PLANTED IN A DAY

The most trees planted in 24 hours is 80,244 by a team comprising 300 citizens of Nagapattinam District, Tamil Nadu, India, on 4 December 2002.

MOST COUPLES ON SIMULTANEOUS BLIND DATES

A total of 123 couples (246 people) participated in blind dates as part of the 'Desperate and Dateless Ball' organized in aid of The British Red Cross on 16 February 2002. Couples met at a bar before attending the party at Planit Arches, London, UK. Before the event, singles completed a questionnaire stating their likes and dislikes and were computer matched by internet dating agency loveandfriends.com.

LARGEST AEROBICS DEMONSTRATION

The largest number of participants in an aerobics display is 38,633. They took part in the University of Guadalajara's Capital Aeróbica event held in Guadalajara, Mexico, on 6 June 1998.

LARGEST TYRE-ROLLING GROUP

On 13 October 2001, 81 people rolled a tyre down a 100-m (328-ft) course in the 'Running of the Tires,' (below) in Toronto, Ontario, Canada. The event was sponsored by Dunlop Tires and Big Brothers of Toronto.

LARGEST TAP DANCE

The greatest ever number of tap dancers in a single routine was 6,951, gathered at the City Square, Stuttgart, Germany, on 24 May 1998. The routine, choreographed by Ray Lynch (USA), lasted 2 min 15 sec and was danced to the tune 'Klicke-di-Klack' that Lynch composed for the event.

LARGEST MOTORCYCLE PYRAMID

The Dare Devil's Team of the Indian Army Signal Corps (India) achieved a motorcycle pyramid consisting of 210 men balanced on a total of 10 motorcycles on 5 July 2001, at Gowri Shankar Parade Ground, Jabalpur, India. The pyramid travelled a distance of 129 m (424 ft).

LONGEST SCARF KNITTED BY A TEAM

The longest scarf ever knitted measured 32.2 km (20 miles). It was created by the able hands of the residents of Abbeyfield Houses for the Abbeyfield Society of Potters Bar, Hertfordshire, UK, and was completed on 29 May 1988.

MASS PARTICIPATION

LARGEST SIMULTANEOUS PERCUSSION PERFORMANCE

The world's largest percussion performance (left) was held at the Hong Kong Coliseum, Hong Kong, China, on 2 July 2002. A record 10,102 people played a percussive rhythm for over six minutes as part of 'The Music of the Dragons' concert.

LARGEST MULTIPLE-VENUE SIMULTANEOUS DANCE

A total of 196,569 people from 681 schools across Canada danced simultaneously for eight minutes from 11:15 am CST (10:15 am PDT/ 2:15 pm ADT) during 'activ8 the Nation's Schools Hokey Pokey Challenge' on 9 April 2002.

MOST PEOPLE TO PARACHUTE FROM A BALLOON SIMULTANEOUSLY

A total of 16 members of the Velvet Toilet Tissue Team simultaneously jumped from a hot-air balloon at an altitude of 3,200 m (10,500 ft) over Peterborough, Cambridgeshire, UK, on 31 May 2002. They all jumped from a single large basket suspended beneath the balloon. The balloon was captained by David Fish (UK) and the skydiving team was led by Ian Ashpole (UK).

LARGEST MULTIPLE-VENUE SIMULTANEOUS TAP DANCE

Organized by the North London Performing Arts Centre, London, UK, a total of 7,596 children from 40 schools across north London tap danced simultaneously to the tune 'To the Show' for five minutes from 10:00 am on 22 March 2002.

LARGEST SIMULTANEOUS BALLOON POP

A total of 368 people popped balloons simultaneously at the Mid States Camping Conference in the Pheasant Run Resort and Conference Center, Charles, Illinois, USA, on 4 April 2002.

LARGEST SIMULTANEOUS JUMP

The largest ever simultaneous jump occurred on 7 September 2001 to celebrate the launch of Science Year in the UK. At precisely 11:00 am, 559,493 people began jumping up and down for one minute. The total number of participants was 569,069. The extra numbers represent disabled pupils who contributed to the seismic activity by dropping objects on the ground or hitting the ground with their fists.

MOST PEOPLE HULA-HOOPING SIMULTANEOUSLY

The record for the most people hula-hooping simultaneously is 2,290 and was set during an event organized by the China Food GMP Development Association and the Bureau of Health, Kaohsiung City Government, at Chung Cheng Stadium, Kaohsiung City, Taiwan, on 28 October 2000.

MOST PEOPLE BRUSHING TEETH SIMULTANEOUSLY

A total of 2,883 individuals simultaneously brushed their teeth for one minute on 3 February 2001 at Yuba City High School, California, USA.

LARGEST LINE DANCE

A record total of 11,967 people took part in a line dance organized by NTUC Income Insurance Cooperative Ltd, Singapore, at the Singapore Expo Centre, Singapore, on 1 May 2002, dancing to 'Rasa Sayang' for 7 min 9 sec.

LARGEST SIMULTANEOUS CHEERLEADING

The largest simultaneous cheerleading event (right) occurred when 328 past and present cheerleaders between the ages of 4 and 60 performed a cheer in full uniform on the field of Cardinal Stadium, Louisville, Kentucky, USA, on 20 October 2001. The event was organized by the Power Cheer Training Center.

LARGEST SIMULTANEOUS BASE JUMP

The largest simultaneous BASE jump involved 15 participants from five countries who skydived from the Petronas Towers, Kuala Lumpur, Malaysia, seconds before midnight on 31 December 1999 as part of the new millennium celebrations.

MOST TREES PLANTED SIMULTANEOUSLY

On 15 October 2000, 10,000 people at 152 locations throughout Malaysia planted 110,461 trees simultaneously. The event was organized by the Government of Malaysia through the National Landscape Department of the Ministry of Housing and Local Government, Kuala Lumpur City Hall, The Tree Planting Group of the Malaysia Nature Society and all state governments.

LARGEST SIMULTANEOUS MULTIPLE-VENUE SING-ALONG

The largest simultaneous sing-along was staged by Young Voices, Sargent Cancer Care for Children and EMI (all UK). There were 83,121 participants from hundreds of schools across the UK who simultaneously sang a specially written song, 'Tell Me Why', at different venues on 9 December 2002.

LARGEST 'YMCA' DANCE

A total of 13,588 people danced to the song 'YMCA' for five minutes prior to the baseball game between the Spikes and the Salt Lake Stingers at Johnny Rosenblatt Stadium, Omaha, Nebraska, USA, on 4 July 2001.

MOST PEOPLE SKIPPING WITH THE SAME ROPE

The record for the most people skipping with the same rope is 220. The record was set by a team of skippers at the International Rope Skipping Competition, Greeley, Colorado, USA, on 28 June 1990.

LARGEST SALSA DANCE

A total of 3,868 people danced to Pérez Prado's 'Mambo No. 5' for five minutes to create the largest salsa dance on 19 October 2000, at Palau Sant Jordi, Barcelona, Spain.

The record for most salsa-dancing couples was set by a total of 173 couples, who danced a rueda at Bayfront Park, Florida, USA, on 24 June 2001.

MOST PEOPLE DOING THE TWIST

To raise money for Breakthrough Breast Cancer (UK), a total of 1,150 people 'twisted away' on the beach at Burnham-on-Sea, Somerset, UK, for five minutes on 11 August 2002.

LONGEST CONGA LINE

The Miami Super Conga consisted of 119,986 people who gathered to conga in Miami, Florida, USA, on 13 March 1988.

LARGEST CHRISTMAS CRACKER PULL

On 2 December 2001, 971 people participated in a simultaneous Christmas cracker pull at a party to celebrate the 25th birthday of the Museum of London, London, UK.

LARGEST MULTIPLE-VENUE SIMULTANEOUS QUADRILLE

A total of 7,518 dancers danced a quadrille in nine towns across Slovenia on 24 May 2002 (above). A quadrille is a French square dance originating from the 18th century and is executed by four couples.

STRENGTH

HEAVIEST COMBINED WEIGHT BALANCED ON THE HEAD IN ONE HOUR

The heaviest combined weight balanced on the head in one hour is 5,180 kg (11,420 lb) by John Evans (UK) at the Lowestoft Motorcycle Show, Lowestoft, Suffolk, UK, on 23 July 2000. This record load was the combined weight of 92 people Evans balanced individually on his head for at least ten seconds.

MOST TELEPHONE DIRECTORIES TORN IN THREE MINUTES

Rick Belden (USA, below) ripped 19 telephone directories, each with 1,494 pages, in a record time of 3 minutes in Charlotte, North Carolina, USA, on 2 November 2002.

MOST WEIGHT ON THE BODY

Eduardo Armallo Lasaga (Spain) lay on a wooden board beneath 1,399.8 kg (3,086 lb) of concrete blocks, in Madrid, Spain, on 18 October 2001.

HEAVIEST BOAT PULLED

On 19 November 1988 in Rostock, Germany, David Huxley (Australia) pulled the *Delphin*, weighing 1,006 tonnes (2,217,847 lb) with a cargo of 175 cars plus passengers, over a distance of 7 m (23 ft).

HEAVIEST WEIGHT LIFTED WITH THE EAR

The heaviest weight lifted using only the ear is 50 kg (110 lb) by Li Jian Hua (China), who lifted a column of bricks hanging from a clamp attached to one of his ears and held the weight for 9.3 seconds on 17 December 1998 at the studios of *Guinness World Records: Primetime* in Los Angeles, USA. The column of bricks was stacked in a metal casing and suspended from the ear clamp by a chain.

HEAVIEST TRAIN PULLED

Juraj Barbaric (Slovakia) single-handedly pulled a 20-car freight train weighing 1,000 tonnes (2.2 million lb) a distance of 4.5 m (14 ft 9 in) along a railway track in Kosice, Slovakia, on 1 June 1999. He trained for eight months prior to the record attempt, with weekly train-pulling practice sessions.

HEAVIEST TRUCK PULLED OVER 100 FEET

The heaviest truck pulled over 100 ft (30.5 m) weighed 24.64 tonnes (54,320 lb) and was pulled by Kevin Fast (Canada) at Cobourg, Ontario, Canada, on 30 June 2001.

HIGHEST BEER KEG TOSS

Juha Rasanen (Finland) threw a 12.3-kg (27-lb) beer keg over a bar at a height of 6.93 m (22 ft 9 in) on the set of *El Show de los Récords* in Madrid, Spain, on 21 September 2001.

MOST MILK CRATES BALANCED ON THE HEAD

John Evans (UK, left) balanced 96 milk crates on his head in Hyde Park, London, UK, on 6 April 2001. John has several other outstanding strength records, including balancing the heaviest car on his head, when he sustained a gutted Mini car weighing a total of 159.6 kg (352 lb) on his head for 33 seconds at The London Studios, London, UK, on 24 May 1999.

MOST CONSECUTIVE ONE ARM CHIN-UPS

On 3 December 1982 Robert Chisholm (Canada) completed 22 consecutive one-arm chin-ups using a ring at Queen's University, Kingston, Ontario, Canada.

HEAVIEST HOD CARRIED ON THE FLAT AND UP A LADDER

Russell Bradley (UK) carried bricks weighing 264 kg (582 lb) in a hod weighing 48 kg (105 lb 13 oz) a distance of 5 m (16 ft 5 in) on the flat, before ascending a ladder to a height of 2.49 m (8 ft 2 in) at Worcester, Worcestershire, UK, on 20 November 1993.

FASTEST PIANO SMASHING

The record time for demolishing an upright piano with a sledge hammer and passing the entire wreckage through a circle 22.8 cm (9 in) in diameter is 1 min 37 sec by six members of the Tinwald Rugby Football Club, Ashburton, New Zealand, on 6 November 1977.

FASTEST CONCRETE BLOCK BREAK ON BODY

On 28 September 2002 Frederick Burton (UK) piled 16 concrete building blocks on his chest and had them systematically broken with a sledgehammer by Peter Johnson (UK) in 12.7 seconds, in Cheadle, Staffordshire, UK.

MOST TRUCKS PULLED SIMULTANEOUSLY

The most trucks pulled simultaneously at several locations is 21 for the Motability and National Freight Consortium (now Exel plc) Truck Pull held in the UK on 11 September 1999. A total of ten trucks were pulled a distance of at least 30 m (100 ft) by teams of differing sizes.

MOST DECKS OF CARDS TORN IN HALF IN 30 SECONDS

Scott Fraze (USA) ripped 13 decks of cards (with 52 cards and two jokers in each) in a time of 30 seconds on the set of *Guinness World Records: Primetime* in Los Angeles, California, USA, on 21 December 2000.

HEAVIEST WEIGHT PULLED WITH THE TEETH

Walter Arfeuille (Belgium) used his teeth to pull eight railway carriages, with a total weight of 223.8 tonnes (493,570 lb), a distance of 3.2 m (10 ft 5 in) along rails at Diksmuide, Belgium, on 9 June 1996.

MOST WEIGHT LIFTED WITH THE EARS, TONGUE AND NIPPLES

The most weight simultaneously lifted using the ears, tongue and nipples is 13.19 kg (29 lb 1.6 oz) by Joe Hermann (USA), a member of the Jim Rose Circus (USA). He successfully lifted two standard 1.04-kg (2-lb 4.8-oz) steam irons with his earlobes, picked up a 2.26-kg (5-lb) car battery with his tongue and supported the weight of a 7.12-kg (15-lb oz) cinderblock from his nipples on the set of *Guinness World Records: Primetime* in Los Angeles, California, USA, on 25 September 1998.

HEAVIEST SINGLE PLANE PULLED

David Huxley (Australia) pulled a Boeing 747-400 aeroplane weighing 187 tonnes (412,264 lb) a distance of 91 m (298 ft 6 in) in 1 min 27.7 sec on 15 October 1997 at Sydney, Australia.

HEAVIEST WEIGHT LIFTED WITH A BEARD

The heaviest weight lifted with a human beard is 61.3 kg (135 lb) when Antanas Kontrimas (Lithuania, below) lifted Ruta Cekyte (Lithuania) off the ground for 15 seconds on 18 August 2001 at the VIII International Country Festival 2001 in Visaginas, Lithuania.

MARATHON FEATS

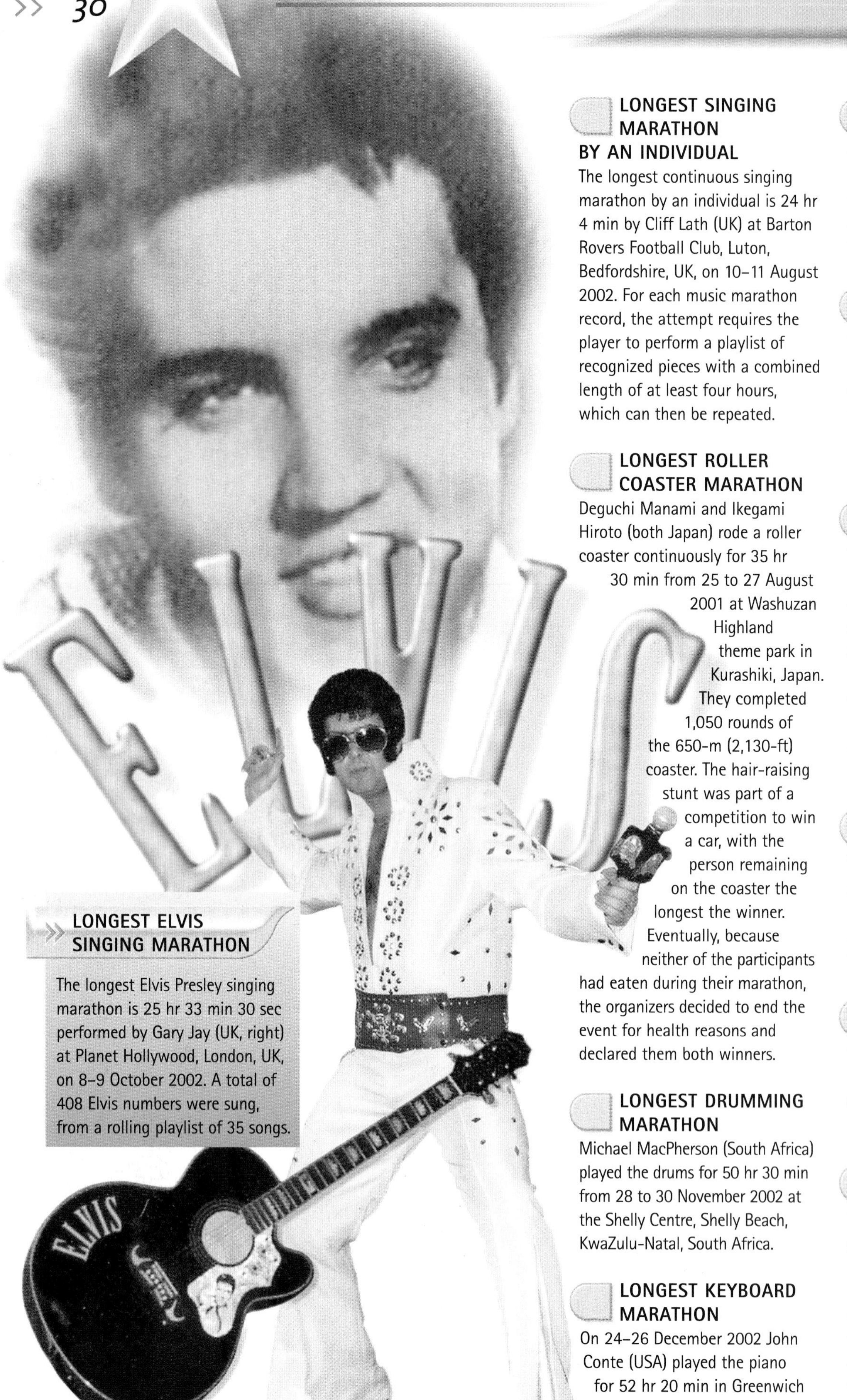

LONGEST ELVIS SINGING MARATHON

The longest Elvis Presley singing marathon is 25 hr 33 min 30 sec performed by Gary Jay (UK, right) at Planet Hollywood, London, UK, on 8–9 October 2002. A total of 408 Elvis numbers were sung, from a rolling playlist of 35 songs.

LONGEST SINGING MARATHON BY AN INDIVIDUAL

The longest continuous singing marathon by an individual is 24 hr 4 min by Cliff Lath (UK) at Barton Rovers Football Club, Luton, Bedfordshire, UK, on 10–11 August 2002. For each music marathon record, the attempt requires the player to perform a playlist of recognized pieces with a combined length of at least four hours, which can then be repeated.

LONGEST ROLLER COASTER MARATHON

Deguchi Manami and Ikegami Hiroto (both Japan) rode a roller coaster continuously for 35 hr 30 min from 25 to 27 August 2001 at Washuzan Highland theme park in Kurashiki, Japan. They completed 1,050 rounds of the 650-m (2,130-ft) coaster. The hair-raising stunt was part of a competition to win a car, with the person remaining on the coaster the longest the winner. Eventually, because neither of the participants had eaten during their marathon, the organizers decided to end the event for health reasons and declared them both winners.

LONGEST DRUMMING MARATHON

Michael MacPherson (South Africa) played the drums for 50 hr 30 min from 28 to 30 November 2002 at the Shelly Centre, Shelly Beach, KwaZulu-Natal, South Africa.

LONGEST KEYBOARD MARATHON

On 24–26 December 2002 John Conte (USA) played the piano for 52 hr 20 min in Greenwich Village, New York, USA.

LONGEST ORGAN PLAYING MARATHON

On 13-14 June 2002 Matthew Penn (UK) played a church organ for 24 hr 17 min at the Holy Trinity Church, Stratford-upon-Avon, Warwickshire, UK.

LONGEST TUBA PLAYING MARATHON

The longest tuba marathon by an individual lasted for 24 hr 8 min and was achieved by Rodney Kenny (UK) on 16–17 August 2002 at The Salvation Army, Gosport, Hampshire, UK.

LONGEST SKIING MARATHON

The longest time spent skiing non-stop is 150 hr 12 min 44 sec by Franz Frank (Austria) at Wagrain, Austria, between 27 January and 2 February 2002. During that time, Frank skied a combined distance of a staggering 1,659.7 km (1,031.2 miles) and a combined altitude of 401,737 m (1,318,034 ft).

FASTEST MARATHON SKIPPING

The fastest marathon run whilst skipping is 5 hr 19 min 14 sec by Carlos Argüeta López (Guatemala) at the Los Angeles Marathon, California, USA, on 5 March 1995.

LONGEST CLUB DJ MIXING SESSION

The longest club DJ mixing session is 74 hours by Martin Boss (USA) at Vinyl Frontier in Orlando, Florida, USA, on 1–4 February 2002.

LONGEST TV WATCHING MARATHON

The record for the longest time spent watching television is 47 hr 16 sec and belongs to Steven Hayes, Adam King, Nick Tungatt and Sam Beatson (all UK), who continually watched TV on 4–6 December 2002 at Covent Garden, London, UK, and at The Printworks, Manchester, UK.

FASTEST ORANGE NOSE PUSH

Myles Anderson (UK, right) pushed an orange with his nose for 1.6 km (1 mile) in 1 hr 14 min from London Bridge to Bishopsgate, London, UK, on 22 March 2002.

LONGEST LECTURE

Dustin Buehler's (USA) lecture on 'The History and Evolution of the American Presidency' at Willamette University, Salem, Oregon, USA, on 25–27 April 2003 lasted for a record 51 hrs 44 min 17 sec.

FASTEST COAL BAG CARRYING MARATHON

Brian Newton (UK) covered a distance of 42.195 km (26 miles 385 yd) whilst carrying 50.8 kg (112 lb) of household coal in an open bag in a time of 8 hr 26 min on 27 May 1983.

LONGEST NETBALL MARATHON

The longest endurance marathon for a game of netball is 54 hr 15 min by members of Castle View School, Canvey Island, Essex, UK, from 22–24 March 2002.

LONGEST POOL MARATHON

The longest pool marathon lasted 103 hr 5 min and was set by a team at the Prince of Wales pub, Bracknell, Berkshire, UK, from 27 to 31 January 2002. Team members were Dean Howell, Gary Lynn, Jon Moss and Anthony McDonagh (all UK).

LONGEST HULA-HOOPING MARATHON

The longest recorded marathon for a single hoop is 72 hours by Kym Coberly (USA) in Denton, Texas, USA, on 17–20 October 1984.

LONGEST READING ALOUD MARATHON

The longest reading aloud marathon is 53 hr 2 min and was set by a team of six people – Carlo Marzani, Ivana Albergo, Lorenzo Cantori, Graziano Ferrari, Giovanni Garau and Paola Giovanazzi (all Italy) at the cultural centre of Rovereto, Tento, Italy, from 29 November to 2 December 2002.

LONGEST TATTOO SESSION

The longest tattoo session lasted for 33 hours and was completed by Chris Goodwill (UK), who tattooed Kevin Budden (UK) at the Electric Pencil Tattoo Studio, Plumstead, Greater London, UK, on 12–13 April 2003. Eight designs were tattooed onto Budden's body during the attempt.

LONGEST SOFTBALL MARATHON

The longest game of softball lasted 30 hr 5 min at Shelbyville softball complex, Indiana, USA, on 14–15 September 2002. The first pitch was thrown at 8:08 am on 14 September 2002 and the game ended at 2:13 pm the next day. Played between Bat-a-Ball-a-Harda and United Players, Bat-a-Ball-a-Harda won, with a score of 322 runs to 292.

LONGEST TIME SPENT LIVING WITH SCORPIONS

Kanchana Ketkaew (Thailand) lived in a glass room measuring 12 m^2 (130 ft^2) which contained 3,000 scorpions for 32 days, from 21 September to 23 October 2002 at Royal Garden Plaza, Pattaya, Thailand. Over the course of the 32 days over 400 scorpions were born and 200 died, replaced by a further 400 on the 19th day. Ketkaew was stung a total of nine times.

LONGEST KISS

Louisa Almedovar and Rich Langley (both USA) kissed for a record 30 hr 59 min 27 sec on 5 December 2001 at the television studios of *Ricki Lake*, New York City, USA.

LONGEST WATER-SKIING MARATHON

Ralph Hildebrand and Dave Phillips (both Canada) water-skied for 56 hr 35 min 3 sec around Indian Arm at Rocky Point, BC, Canada, from 9 to 12 June 1994. They covered a distance of 2,152.3 km (1,337.46 miles) at an average speed of 48 km/h (30 mph).

LONGEST MOVIE WATCHING MARATHON

An audience of 23 people (all South Africa) watched 32 films for 59 hr 27 min at an event (below) at Northgate SterKinekor cinema, Johannesburg, South Africa, from 26 to 28 August 2002.

INSPIRING PEOPLE

MOST PROLIFIC PAINTER

In a career that lasted 75 years, Pablo Diego José Francisco de Paula Juan Nepomuceno de los Remedios Crispín Cipriano de la Santísima Trinidad Ruíz y Picasso (Spain, above) was the most prolific of all professional painters. It has been estimated that he produced about 13,500 paintings and designs, 100,000 prints and engravings, 34,000 book illustrations, and 300 sculptures and ceramics. His oeuvre has been valued at £500 million ($788 million) and by May 1997, his works had been sold at auction 3,579 times.

LONGEST PERIOD OF INCARCERATION FOR A COUNTRY'S FUTURE HEAD OF STATE

The former President of the Republic of South Africa, Nelson Rolihlahla Mandela, spent almost 27 years in prison in South Africa from 1964 until his release on 11 February 1990. He had been found guilty of sabotage and treason during the years of the government's apartheid system. Four years later, on 10 May 1994, he was elected State President of the Republic of South Africa – the first democratically elected President in South Africa's history.

LONGEST SERVING 20TH CENTURY BRITISH PRIME MINISTER

Margaret Thatcher, now Baroness Thatcher (UK), was the longest-serving British Prime Minister of the 20th century. She was in office for 11 years 208 days from 4 May 1979 to 28 November 1990.

LONGEST BIOGRAPHY

The longest biography in publishing history is the ongoing biography of Winston Churchill (UK), begun by his son Randolph and continued by biographer Martin Gilbert (both UK). The book currently comprises eight volumes plus a total of 16 companion volumes, all containing around 10 million words.

MOST FIRE PERSONNEL LOST IN ONE INCIDENT

According to the International Association of Fire Fighters, the unprecedented tragedy of 11 September 2001 claimed the lives of 344 New York City fire personnel in just one incident. Their rescue efforts saved thousands of civilian lives. This was the largest single-event loss of life sustained by modern-day fire service personnel in war or peace times. In contrast, a total of 102 US fire fighters died nationwide in 2000. The most US fire fighters lost at once prior to 11 September was 24, during an incident that occurred over 100 years ago.

MOST MONEY RAISED BY AN INDIVIDUAL MARATHON RUNNER

Retired advertising executive John Spurling (UK) raised a record £1.13 million ($1.87 million) for charity by running the London Marathon in London, UK, on 18 April 1999.

LARGEST FUNDRAISING CHARITY

For 10 consecutive years the Salvation Army, USA, has raised more funds annually than any other charity. In 2001 alone, the charity raised $1.39 billion (£889 million), down from $1.44 billion (£921 million) the previous year.

MOST ARTISTS SAVED

Varian Fry (USA), known as 'The Artists' Schindler', journeyed from the USA to France in 1940 with a list of 200 prominent artists and intellectuals known to be in parts of Nazi-occupied Europe. He subsequently helped to save around 4,000 people from the Gestapo, among them some of the most famous cultural figures of our age, including Max Ernst (Germany), Marc Chagall (France), André Breton (France) and Nobel Prize-winning chemist Otto Meyerhof (Germany).

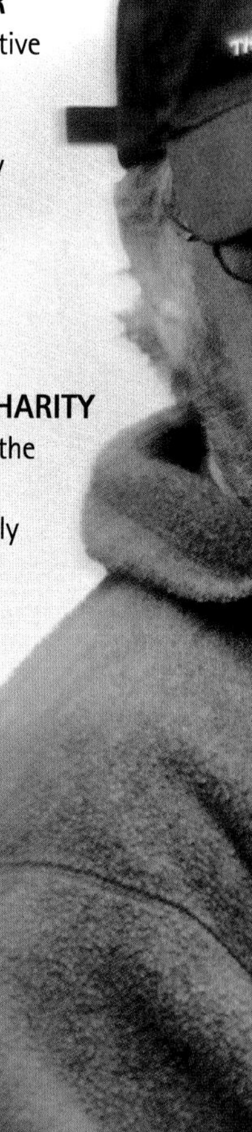

LARGEST RACIAL EQUALITY RALLY

On 28 August 1963 civil rights leader Martin Luther King Jr (USA) led more than 250,000 demonstrators in a march down the Mall in Washington DC, USA. They gathered in front of the Lincoln Memorial to call for equal civil rights for all Americans, irrespective of race or colour.

LARGEST VOLUNTEER AMBULANCE ORGANIZATION

Abdul Sattar Edhi (Pakistan) began his ambulance service in 1948, ferrying injured people to hospital in Karachi. Today, his radio-linked ambulance fleet is 500 vehicles strong and operates all over Pakistan, through $5 million (£3,050,000) funding raised annually. Edhi has also established 300 relief centres, three air ambulances, 24 hospitals, three drug rehabilitation centres, women's centres, free dispensaries, adoption programmes and soup kitchens that feed 100,000 people a month. He has paid for and supervised the training of 17,000 nurses. The ambulance service even picks up corpses, and the organization arranges Muslim burials. Edhi has not taken a holiday in 45 years.

MOST CASH RAISED FOR CHARITY BY A SPORTING EVENT

The London Marathon, run annually since 1981 through the streets of London, UK, raises more money for charity than any other single sporting event in the world. A record total of £31 million ($48.7 million) was raised in April 2002, the last year for which figures were calculated.

ROYAL PATRON TO THE MOST CHARITIES

As of December 2000 Princess Anne, the Princess Royal (UK) was patron of a record 233 charity organizations. She is best known for her charity work with Save the Children UK, of which she has been president since 1970. She also heads her own Princess Royal Trust for Carers, which raises awareness of the UK's estimated six million carers.

FIRST POWER-DRIVEN FLIGHT

The first controlled and sustained power-driven flight occurred near the Kill Devil Hill, Kitty Hawk, North Carolina, USA, at 10:35 am on 17 December 1903. Orville Wright (USA) flew the 9-kW 12-hp chain-driven *Flyer I* for a distance of 36.5 m (120 ft) at an airspeed of 48 km/h (30 mph), a ground speed of 10.9 km/h (6.8 mph) and an altitude of 2.5–3.5 m (8–12 ft) for about 12 seconds. He was watched by his brother Wilbur and four other men. The *Flyer I* is now exhibited in the National Air and Space Museum at the Smithsonian Institution, Washington DC, USA.

» EARLIEST PERFUME LAUNCHED BY A COUTURIER

Fashion designer Gabrielle (Coco) Chanel (France, right), whose name became synonymous with elegance and chic, launched her Chanel No.5 perfume in 1921. A designer ahead of her time, Chanel was always sharp and elegant. The clothes she designed transformed the way women looked and how they looked at themselves.

MOST HEAVYWEIGHT WORLD TITLE RECAPTURES

Three boxers have regained the heavyweight championship twice: Muhammad Ali (USA), Evander Holyfield (USA) and Lennox Lewis (UK). Ali first won the title on 25 February 1964, defeating Sonny Liston (USA). He defeated George Foreman (USA) on 30 October 1974, having been stripped of the title by the world boxing authorities on 28 April 1967, and won the WBA title from Leon Spinks (USA) on 15 September 1978, having previously lost to him on 15 February 1978.

MOST OSCARS WON IN A LIFETIME

Walt Disney (USA) won more Oscars than any other person, with a record 26 awards from 64 nominations between 1932 and 1969. He won his first Oscar for a short cartoon entitled *Flowers and Trees* (USA, 1932).

MOST CHARTS TOPPED AROUND THE WORLD WITH THE SAME ALBUM

Since its release on 13 November 2000, the album entitled *1*, by the Beatles – a compilation of every No.1 hit they ever had in the UK and the US – has topped the charts in 35 countries from Australia to Venezuela.

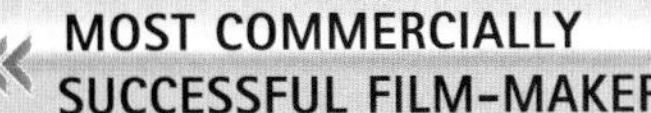

« MOST COMMERCIALLY SUCCESSFUL FILM-MAKER

Three of Steven Spielberg's (USA, left) films are in the top 10 grossing movies of all time and have grossed $2.23 billion (£1.39 billion) in total. The films are: No. 3, *Jurassic Park* (USA, 1993) $920.1 million (£570 million; No. 7, *ET the Extra Terrestrial* (USA, 1982) $700.8 million (£434.1 million); No. 10, *Jurassic Park: The Lost World* (USA, 1997) $614.1 million (£380.4 million).

MOST GRAMMY AWARDS WON BY A FEMALE ARTIST

Aretha Franklin (USA) is the female recording artist to have won the most Grammys. She has won a total of 15 since receiving her first in 1967 for Best Female R&B Vocal Performance with 'Respect'. She won her 15th Grammy in 1988, for Best Female Soul Gospel Performance, with 'One Lord, One Faith, One Baptism'.

COURAGE & ENDURANCE

DEEPEST SEAWATER DIVE

The deepest scuba dive was one of 307.8 m (1,010 ft) made by John Bennett (UK) on 6 November 2001 off Escarcia Point, Puerto Galera, The Philippines. The descent, aided by a weighted sled, took just over 12 minutes. The ascent, however, took 9 hr 36 min to allow for decompression, and Bennett needed 60 oxygen tanks. At the bottom of the dive he lost his vision and experienced muscle spasms. The highest pressure on his body was 3,309 kPa (480 lb/in^2).

LONGEST UNDERWATER SCUBA SUBMERGENCE IN A CONTROLLED ENVIRONMENT

The continuous duration record – with no rest breaks – for remaining underwater using breathing apparatus is 212 hr 30 min by Michael Stevens (UK) in a Royal Navy tank at the National Exhibition Centre, Birmingham, UK, on 14–23 February 1986.

LONGEST OPEN FRESHWATER SCUBA DIVE

Jerry Hall (USA) spent 71 hr 39 min 40 sec underwater on 6–9 August 2002 in South Holston Lake, Bristol, Tennessee, USA. Using scuba gear for his dive, Hall spent most of the time reclining on a wooden platform suspended by cables underwater.

DEEPEST FRESHWATER CAVE DIVE

On 23 August 1996, Nuno Gomes (South Africa) scuba-dived to a depth of 282.6 m (927 ft 2 in) at the Boesmansgat Cave, Northern Cape, South Africa.

LONGEST DISTANCE BY KITE SURFER

Neil Hutchinson, Kent Marincovik and Fabrice Collard (all USA) travelled a distance of 88 nautical miles (163 km or 101.3 miles) between Key West, Florida, USA, and Varadero, Cuba, on boards pulled by kites, on 21 December 2001. Their journey, during which they were not permitted to touch any other vessel, lasted 8 hr 38 min, and was completed at an average speed of 12 knots (22 km/h or 14 mph).

FASTEST SOLO ROW ACROSS THE ATLANTIC

The fastest solo trans-Atlantic row, as recognized by the Ocean Rowing Society, is 46 days 4 hr by Fyodor Konyukhov (Russia), who rowed from San Sebastian, Gomera, Canary Islands, Spain, to Port St Charles, Barbados, from 16 October to 1 December 2002. The journey was made in the 6.9-m (22-ft 7.2-in) fibreglass *Uralaz*, which weighed 350 kg (771 lb) empty and 650 kg (1,433 lb) fully loaded. It had solar panels, a gas cooker and navigation equipment.

FASTEST TRANS-ATLANTIC ROW

In 1997, Phil Stubbs and Rob Hamill (both New Zealand) rowed across the Atlantic, from the Canary Islands to Barbados, in 41 days. Despite having to anchor for two days to ride out a 96-km/h (60-mph) storm, they beat the previous record, set in 1971 by Don and Geoff Allum (UK), by 32 days.

GREATEST DISTANCE BY PEDAL BOAT

Kenichi Horie (Japan) crossed the Pacific Ocean by pedal boat, from Honolulu, Hawaii, USA, to Naha, Okinawa, Japan, from 30 October 1992 to 17 February 1993. He covered a record distance of 7,500 km (4,660 miles).

LONGEST TIME ADRIFT AT SEA

The longest known time that anyone has survived adrift at sea is approximately 484 days, by Japanese captain Oguri Jukichi and one of his sailors Otokichi. They were shipwrecked in a storm off the Japanese coast in October 1813 and drifted in the Pacific Ocean before being rescued by a US ship off California on 24 March 1815.

GREATEST DISTANCE COVERED IN 24 HOURS BY WHEELCHAIR

Rafael Emilio de León Lebrón (Dominican Republic) wheeled himself a distance of 181.147 km (112.5 miles) in 24 hours on 13–14 December 2001 at the Juan Pablo Duarte Centro Olímpico, Santo Domingo de Guzmán, Dominican Republic.

LONGEST WHEELIE IN A WHEELCHAIR

Robert Hensel (USA) travelled 9.943 km (6.178 miles) non-stop on the rear wheels of his wheelchair at Scriba, New York, USA, on 3 October 2002.

LONGEST JOURNEY BY WHEELCHAIR

Rick Hansen (Canada), who was paralysed from the waist down in 1973 as a result of a motor accident, wheeled his wheelchair 40,075.16 km (24,901.55 miles) through four continents and 34 countries. He started his journey from Vancouver, British Columbia, Canada, on 21 March 1985 and arrived back there on 22 May 1987.

FASTEST SEVEN SUMMIT ASCENT

Andrew Salter (UK) climbed the highest peak on each continent in a record 288 days between 16 May 2000, when he reached the summit of Mt Everest in Nepal (Asia), and 27 February 2001, when he climbed Aconcagua in Argentina (South America). He also scaled the Vinson Massif in Antarctica, Mt McKinley in Alaska (North America), Mt Kilimanjaro in Tanzania (Africa), Puncak Jaya in Indonesia (Australasia) and Elbrus in Russia (Europe).

EARLIEST ASCENT OF MT EVEREST

The summit of the world's highest mountain Mt Everest (8,848 m or 29,029 ft) was first reached at 11:30 am on 29 May 1953 by Edmund Hillary (New Zealand), and Sherpa Tenzing Norgay (Nepal). The successful expedition was led by Col (later Hon Brigadier) Henry Cecil John Hunt (UK).

FASTEST ATLANTIC CROSSING BY AQUABIKE

Alvaro de Marichalar (Spain, left) crossed the Atlantic on an aquabike in 17 days 1 hr 11 min, departing from Hierro, Canary Islands, Spain, on 4 May and reaching English Harbour Town, Antigua, on 21 May 2002.

MOST CONQUESTS OF MT EVEREST

Apa Sherpa (Nepal) completed his 13th successful climb of Mt Everest on 26 May 2002.

FIRST SOLO ASCENT OF MT EVEREST

Reinhold Messner (Italy) was the first person to successfully climb Mt Everest solo, reaching the summit on 20 August 1980. It took him three days to make the ascent from his base camp at 6,500 m (21,325 ft), and the climb was made all the more difficult by the fact that he did not use bottled oxygen.

LONGEST DRIVEN JOURNEY

Emil and Liliana Schmid (both Switzerland, below) have covered over 567,000 km (352,000 miles) in their Toyota Land Cruiser since 16 October 1984, crossing 135 countries in the process.

FASTEST ASCENT OF MT EVEREST

Lakpa Gelu Sherpa (Nepal) made a successful ascent of Mt Everest in 10 hr 56 min 46 sec on 26 May 2003, the fastest ever climb from base camp to the summit of the world's tallest mountain.

YOUNGEST PERSON TO CLIMB MT EVEREST

Temba Tsheri Sherpa (Nepal) reached the summit of Mt Everest on 23 May 2001, aged 16 years 7 days. He had attempted to climb Mt Everest in 2000 at the age of 14, but had to turn back just 22 m (72 ft) from the summit. He lost parts of several fingers to frostbite.

LONGEST JOURNEY BY SKATEBOARD

Jack Smith (USA) travelled just under 4,830 km (3,000 miles) on a skateboard from Lebanon, Oregon, to Williamsburg, Virginia, USA, in July 1976 and July 1984. The same journeys also broke the record for the fastest trans-America skateboard trip. The first trip took him 32 days, with two companions, and the second trip, made with three team members, took 26 days.

FASTEST TRANS-USA JOURNEY ON INLINE SKATES

Russell 'Rusty' Moncrief (USA) crossed the USA on inline skates in 69 days 8 hr 45 min from 5 January to 15 March 2002. He skated from Crescent Beach, near Jacksonville, Florida, to Soltana Beach, near San Diego, California, covering 4,175 km (2,595 miles).

MOST CRASH TESTS

By February 2003 WR 'Rusty' Haight (USA) had endured 718 collisions in cars as a 'human crash test dummy', thanks to his work as a traffic collision reconstructionist.

FASTEST CIRCUMNAVIGATION BY CAR

The fastest circumnavigation of the world by car, under the rules applicable in 1989 and 1991, embracing more than an equator's length of driving (40,075 km or 24,901 road miles), is held by Mohammed Salahuddin Choudhury and his wife Neena (both India). The journey took 69 days 19 hrs 5 min from 9 September to 17 November 1989, starting and finishing in Delhi, India. Guinness World Records no longer endorses car circumnavigation attempts.

LONGEST TAXI RIDE

The longest taxi ride is a 34,908-km (21,691-mile) journey costing £40,210 ($63,500), when Jeremy Levine, Mark Aylett (both UK) and Carlos Arrese (Spain) went from London, UK, to Cape Town, South Africa, and back, from 3 June to 17 October 1994.

LONGEST BICYCLE WHEELIE JOURNEY

Kurt Osburn (USA) travelled 4,569 km (2,839.6 miles) on his bicycle, doing a wheelie the whole way, from the Guinness World of Records Museum in Hollywood, California, to the Guinness World of Records Museum in Orlando, Florida, USA, between 13 April and 25 June 1999.

FASTEST TRANS-USA UNICYCLE RIDE

Akira Matsushima (Japan) crossed America, from Newport, Oregon, to Washington, DC, by unicycle in a record 23 days, from 10 July to 22 August 1992.

FASTEST MOTORCYCLE CIRCUMNAVIGATION

Kevin Sanders, with his wife Julia (both UK, above) as a passenger, circumnavigated the world on a motorcycle in 19 days 8 hr and 25 min between 11 May and 22 June 2002. Guinness World Records no longer endorses such attempts.

HIGHEST ALTITUDE CYCLING

Siegfried Verheijke, Luc Belet (both Belgium) and Martin Adserballe (Denmark) rode mountain bikes at an altitude of 7,008 m (22,992 ft) on the slopes of the Muztagata peak in China on 11 August 2000.

LONGEST WIND-POWERED LAND JOURNEY

Robert Torline (USA) travelled from Brownsville, Texas (on the Mexican border), to Maida, North Dakota (on the Canadian border), USA, covering 3,410 km (2,119 miles) on his wind-powered street sailor from 29 April to 16 June 2001.

EPIC JOURNEYS

FASTEST SOLO CROSSING OF ANTARCTICA

The fastest and first ever unaided solo crossing of the Antarctic continent was achieved by Borge Ousland (Norway, left), who completed the 2,690-km (1,671-mile) trek on 18 January 1997, 64 days after setting out on 15 November 1996. He dragged his 185-kg (408-lb) supply sled from Berkner Island in the Weddell Sea to Scott Base in McMurdo Sound.

LONGEST SOLO TREK ACROSS ANTARCTICA

Japanese adventurer Mitsuro Ohba (above, centre) walked, skied and parasailed a total of 3,824 km (2.376 miles) across the Antarctic continent in 99 days from 9 November 1998. Ohba began his trek on the South African side of continent and was aiming to reach Walgreen Coast, facing Chile, but he was picked up by plane when bad weather forced him to abandon his attempt 200 km (124 miles) short of his intended target.

FASTEST SOLO TRANS-PACIFIC ROW

Jim Shekhdar (UK, right) rowed unaided across the Pacific Ocean in 273 days 13 hr 12 min, beginning from Ilo in Peru on 29 June 2000, and ending near Brisbane, Australia, on 30 March 2001.

FASTEST SOLO SAILING CIRCUMNAVIGATION BY A WOMAN

Ellen MacArthur (UK, left) circumnavigated the globe in 94 days 4 hr 25 min 40 sec, starting and finishing at Les Sables d'Olonne, France, from 5 November 2000 to 11 February 2001.

LONGEST SUCCESSFUL SOLO BALLOON FLIGHT

On 4 July 2002, on completion of his 33,195-km (20,627-mile) solo circumnavigation of the Earth by balloon, Steve Fossett (USA, left) set the record for the longest successful solo balloon flight.

FIRST SUCCESSFUL MT EVEREST ASCENT

At 11:30 am on 29 May 1953 Edmund Hillary (New Zealand, above left) and Sherpa Tenzing Norgay (Nepal, above right) became the first people to reach the summit of Mt Everest.

YOUNGEST SOLO TRANS-ATLANTIC SAILOR

Sebastian Clover (UK, right) sailed across the Atlantic Ocean singlehandedly from Santa Cruz de Tenerife, Canary Islands, Spain, to English Harbour, Antigua & Barbuda, aged 15 years 362 days, from 19 December 2002 to 12 January 2003.

YOUNGEST PERSON TO CYCLE THE PAN-AM HIGHWAY

Emmanuel Gentinetta (USA, above), was 18 years 266 days old when he completed his solo cycle journey of the Pan-American Highway from Prudhoe Bay, Alaska, to Bahia Lapataia, Tierra del Fuego, Argentina, from 23 June 1999 to 9 March 2000. The trip took 261 days and covered some 24,516 km (15,234 miles).

FACT

DID YOU KNOW...?

That the Earth is not perfectly round? It is actually slightly flatter at the poles and bulges at the Equator, the result of the planet spinning on its own axis. So if it were possible to walk around the Earth in a straight line, circumnavigators would be better off walking pole-to-pole rather than following the Equator, because the Earth's equatorial circumference is 133 km (82.6 miles) greater than its polar circumference.

NATURAL WORLD

THE EARTH

OLDEST VOLCANIC ROCKS ON EARTH

Volcanic rocks dated at 3.825 billion years have been discovered in the Inukjuak area in the northern reaches of Quebec, Canada. The precise dating of the rocks was performed by the University of Quebec, Montreal, Canada, and the Simon Fraser University in British Columbia, Canada, in 2002.

EARLIEST EVIDENCE FOR PLATE TECTONICS

On 8 July 2002 a team of Chinese and US scientists announced their discovery of rocks indicating that plate tectonics were active on Earth some 2.5 billion years ago. This is 500 million years earlier than previously thought. The evidence comes from a belt of rock not far from the Great Wall of China at Dongwanzi, Hebei. The 2.5-billion-year-old rock contains chromite (iron chromium oxide), which is only normally found in rocks deep on the ocean floor.

LARGEST CONTINENT EVER

Over 250 million years ago all of today's continents were joined together as one 'supercontinent', named Pangea (meaning 'all lands' in Greek). However, around 180 million years ago, plate tectonics caused Pangea to slowly break apart, eventually resulting in the continents we know today. Evidence of Pangea can be seen by observing the way existing coastlines from different continents, such as Africa and South America, seem to fit together.

OLDEST CONFIRMED IMPACT ON EARTH

On 23 August 2002 a team of US scientists led by Gary Byerly and Donald Lowe announced their discovery of a 3.47-billion-year-old asteroid impact on Earth. They had studied ancient rock samples from Australia and South Africa and analysed the spherules contained within. These tiny particles are a common by-product of meteoritic impact and were used to date the impact, along with local zircon crystals. The 20–30-cm-thick (8–12-in) spherule beds in the rock indicate that the impacting body had a rough diameter of 20 km (12 miles). However, no crater has been found, as Earth's geological processes have had time to erase it.

FASTEST MELTING GLACIER

A volcanic eruption under Vatnajokul glacier in Iceland (Europe's largest) in October 1996 topped Lake Grimsvotn with meltwater. The meltwater flowed from the lake at an estimated 45,000 m^3/sec (1.6 million ft^3/sec), making it the greatest melting of a glacier in recorded history.

LARGEST SINGLE CRYSTAL ON EARTH

The Earth's mostly iron spherical inner core is around 2,400 km (1,500 miles) across. At 5,000–6,000°C (9,000–11,000°F) it is solid rather than liquid, due to the immense pressures in the Earth's interior. Many geologists now believe that this gigantic ball of iron is actually a single crystal. The core is about three-quarters the size of the Moon, and has a mass of around one hundred million million million tonnes.

HIGHEST MOUNTAIN

Mount Everest in the eastern Himalayas on the Tibet-Nepal border has a height of 8,848 m (29,028 ft). It was officially recognized as the world's highest mountain in 1856, following surveys carried out by the Indian government. The mountain was named after Col Sir George Everest (UK), Surveyor-General of India from 1830 to 1843.

LARGEST DOLINE

A doline is typically a funnel-shaped basin formed when limestone caves subside. Xio Zhai Tien (The Great Doline) is the largest doline in the world. Situated in the Sichuan region of central southern China, this huge depression measures 500 m (1,600 ft) across and 660 m (2,100 ft) deep.

LARGEST ACTIVE VOLCANO

Mauna Loa, Hawaii, USA, which last erupted in 1984, rises 4,170 m (13,680 ft) above sea level, has the shape of a broad, gentle dome and is 120 km (75 miles) long and 50 km (31 miles) wide. It has a volume of 42,500 km^3 (10,200 $miles^3$) of which 84.2% is below sea level. Its caldera (crater), Mokuaweoweo, measures 10.5 km^2 (4 $miles^2$) and is 150–180 m (500–600 ft) deep.

LARGEST STEAM RINGS

The active volcano Mount Etna, in Sicily, Italy, is the tallest and most active in Europe. A complex physical process, thought to involve the unusual geometry of the shape of one of the volcano's vents, is causing the volcano to produce huge steam rings (above). The steam rings are around 200 m (650 ft) across and can last for up to 10 minutes as they slowly drift upwards to a height of 1,000 m (3,300 ft) above the volcano.

MOST ACTIVE VOLCANO

The world's most active volcano is Kilauea, in Hawaii, USA, which has erupted on a continuous basis since 1983 and is discharging lava at a rate of 5 m^3 (176 ft^3) per second.

LARGEST GEOLOGICAL FEATURE DISCOVERED FROM SPACE

The Richat Structure in the Sahara Desert of Mauritania (right and above) is a multi-ringed sedimentary basin around 50 km (30 miles) in diameter. Originally thought to be an impact crater, it is now believed to be the eroded remains of an uplifted sedimentary dome. This 'bullseye' was discovered from orbit by US astronauts Jim McDivitt and Ed White during the *Gemini IV* mission in June 1965.

GREATEST ERUPTION VOLUME

The total volume of matter discharged in the eruption of Tambora, a volcano on the Indonesian island of Sumbawa, between 5 and 10 April 1815, was estimated to be 150–180 km^3 (36–43 $miles^3$). This is the greatest known eruption volume from any volcano, comparing with a probable 60–65 km^3 (14–16 $miles^3$) ejected by Santoriní (Greece) in 1628 BC and 20 km^3 (5 $miles^3$) ejected by Krakatoa (Indonesia) in 1883.

DEEPEST LAVA CAVE

The deepest lava cave – an open tube down the inside of a solidified lava flow – is Kazumura Cave, on Hawaii, USA. It is 59.3 km (36.9 miles) long and descends 1,099 m (3,605 ft) down the eastern flank of Kilauea volcano.

HIGHEST TEMPERATURE IN A FUMEROLE

The highest temperature in a fumerole or smoke vent was 941°C (1,726°F) and was recorded in the hot dome (central section) of the Kudryavy volcano, Iturup, Kurile Islands, Russia, in 1996–97.

TALLEST GRANITE MONOLITH

El Capitan, in Yosemite National Park, California, USA, is 1,095 m (3,593 ft) tall.

DEEPEST VALLEY

The Yarlung Zangbo valley in Tibet is 5,000 m (16,400 ft) deep on average. Its deepest point has been measured at 5,382 m (17,657 ft).

LONGEST RIFT SYSTEM

The East African Rift System (left) is approximately 6,400 km (4,000 miles) long with an average width of 50–65 km (30–40 miles). The escarpments around the edge of the valley have an average height of 600–900 m (2,000–3,000 ft). The rift system begins in Jordan and extends southwards to Mozambique in southern Africa. This extensive rift system has been gradually forming for around 30 million years, as the Arabian peninsula has separated from Africa.

WATER WORLD

LARGEST OCEAN

The Pacific Ocean is the largest ocean in the world. (Bora Bora Island, located in the Pacific, is pictured below). Excluding adjacent seas, the Pacific represents 45.9% of the world's oceans and covers an area of 166,241,700 km² (64,186,000 miles²). The average depth is 3,940 m (12,925 ft).

DEEPEST POINT IN THE OCEAN

The Marianas Trench in the Pacific Ocean was first pinpointed as the deepest part of the ocean in 1951 by HM Survey Ship *Challenger*. On 23 January 1960 the US Navy bathyscaphe *Trieste* descended to the bottom, and on 24 March 1995 the unmanned Japanese probe *Kaiko* also reached the bottom and recorded a depth of 10,911 m (35,797 ft). This is the most accurate measurement to date.

FASTEST OCEAN CURRENT

During the monsoon season, the Somali current in the northern Indian Ocean flows at 12.8 km/h (9 mph).

LARGEST CONTINUOUS OCEAN CURRENT SYSTEM

The thermohaline conveyor belt is a vast global system of ocean circulation, driven by differences in sea water density and salinity. It transports cold and salty deep water from the north Atlantic down to the Southern Ocean, where it travels east and north to the Indian and Pacific Oceans. Here it rises and becomes warm, travelling back westwards where it sinks again in the north Atlantic. The entire cycle can last for a thousand years.

MOST SOUTHERLY OCEAN

The most southerly part of the oceans is located at 87°S, 151°W, at the snout of the Scott Glacier, 320 km (200 miles) from the South Pole.

HIGHEST WAVE

The highest officially recorded sea wave was calculated at 34 m (112 ft) from trough to crest. It was measured by Lt Frederic Margraff (USA) from the USS *Ramapo*, proceeding from Manila, Philippines, to San Diego, California, USA, on the night of 6–7 February 1933 during a hurricane that reached a speed of 68 knots (126 km/h or 78 mph).

LARGEST BAY

The world's largest bay by shoreline length is Hudson Bay in Canada, with 12,268 km (7,623 miles) of shoreline and an area of 1,233,000 km² (476,000 miles²). Measured by area, the Bay of Bengal, in the Indian Ocean, is larger, at 2,172,000 km² (839,000 miles²).

HIGHEST OCEAN TEMPERATURE

The highest temperature ever recorded in an ocean is 404°C (759°F), measured above a hydrothermal vent some 480 km (300 miles) off the American west coast in 1985 (an example of a hydrothermal vent is pictured right). The record temperature was measured by an American research submarine examining these largely unexplored ocean features.

TALLEST HYDROTHERMAL VENT

The tallest known hydrothermal vents on the ocean floor measure around 55 m (180 ft) high. They were discovered by researchers from the Woods Hole Oceanographic Institution (USA) in December 2000. These vents, dubbed 'The Lost City', are part of a system of hydrothermal vents on the mid-Atlantic Ridge, itself the largest system of vents discovered.

LARGEST AQUIFER

The Great Artesian Basin underlies around one fifth of Australia. This huge underground water resource extends over 1,711,000 km^2 (660,000 miles^2) and has an estimated water storage volume of 64,900 million million litres (14,200 million million gal). The basin, consisting of alternating layers of water-bearing sandstone and non-water-bearing siltstones and mudstones, was formed between 100 and 250 million years ago.

DEEPEST BRINE POOL

The Orca Basin in the Gulf of Mexico lies 2,200 m (7,200 ft) below sea level. This 7-x-21-km (4-x-13-mile) depression is filled with water that has a salt content of 300 g per litre – around eight times saltier than the Gulf itself. Effectively a hypersaline lake at the bottom of the sea, its salinity is caused by salt leaching out of the salt deposits under the sediment on the sea floor.

GREATEST SUBMARINE MOUNTAIN RANGE

The greatest of all mountain ranges is the submarine Mid-Ocean Ridge, which extends 65,000 km (40,000 miles) from the Arctic Ocean to the Atlantic Ocean, around Africa, Asia and Australia, and under the Pacific Ocean to the west coast of North America. It has a maximum height of 4,200 m (13,800 ft) above the base ocean depth.

LARGEST SEA CAVE

The Sea Lion Caves close to Florence on the Oregon coast, USA, have a chamber 95 m (310 ft) long, 50 m (165 ft) wide and around 15 m (50 ft) high, in a wave-cut passage 400 m (1,315 ft) long.

LARGEST LAGOON

Lagoa dos Patos, located near the seashore in Rio Grande do Sul, southernmost Brazil, is 280 km (174 miles) long and extends over 9,850 km^2 (3,803 miles^2), separated from the Atlantic Ocean by long sand strips. It has a maximum width of 70 km (44 miles).

LARGEST ICEBERG

The largest known tabular iceberg was over 31,000 km^2 (12,000 miles^2) in area. It was 335 km (208 miles) long and 97 km (60 miles) wide (larger than Belgium), and was sighted 240 km (150 miles) west of Scott Island, in the Southern Ocean, Antarctica, by the USS *Glacier* in November 1956.

LARGEST SUBGLACIAL LAKE

Lake Vostok in Antarctica was discovered in 1994 by analysing radar imagery of the icy continent. Buried under 4 km (2.5 miles) of the East Antarctic Ice Sheet, it is the most pristine lake on Earth, having been completely isolated from the rest of the world for at least 500,000 years and perhaps much longer. With an area of some 14,000 km^2 (5,400 miles^2), it is the world's 18th-largest lake and has a depth of at least 100 m (330 ft).

LARGEST FRESHWATER LAKE BY VOLUME

The freshwater lake with the greatest volume is Lake Baikal in Siberia, Russia, with an estimated volume of 23,000 km^3 (5,500 miles^3). With a maximum depth of 1,637 m (5,371 ft), Lake Baikal is also the world's deepest lake. It contains one-fifth of all the world's fresh surface water.

LARGEST LAKE

The largest inland sea or lake is the Caspian Sea in Azerbaijan, Russia, Kazakhstan, Turkmenistan and Iran. It is 1,225 km (760 miles) long and has a total area of 371,800 km^2 (143,550 miles^2). Of its total area, 38.5% (143,200 km^2 or 55,280 miles^2) is in Iran. Its maximum depth is 1,025 m (3,360 ft), and the surface is 28.5 m (93 ft) below sea level.

LARGEST UNDERGROUND LAKE

The largest underground lake is that in the Drachenhauchloch (Dragon's Breath) cave near Grootfontein, Namibia, discovered in 1986. When surveyed in April 1991 the surface area was found to be 2.61 ha (6.45 acres). The surface is some 66 m (217 ft) underground, and the lake has a depth of 84 m (276 ft).

SALTIEST LAKE

Don Juan Pond in Wright Valley, Antarctica, is so salty that it remains liquid even at temperatures as low as -53°C (-63.4°F). The percentage of salt by weight is 40.2%, compared to 23.1% and 3.38% for the Dead Sea and the world's oceans respectively.

LARGEST LAKE IN A LAKE

The largest lake in a lake is Manitou Lake, with an area of 106 km^2 (41 miles^2). It is found on the world's largest lake island, Manitoulin Island (with an area of 2,766 km^2 or 1,068 miles^2), in the Canadian part of Lake Huron.

GREATEST RIVER FLOW

The Amazon in South America discharges an average of 200,000 m^3/sec (7,100,000 ft^3/sec) into the Atlantic Ocean, increasing to more than 340,000 m^3/sec (12,000,000 ft^3/sec) in full flood. The lower 1,450 km (900 miles) averages 17 m (55 ft) in depth, but the river has a maximum depth of 124 m (407 ft). Although it is shorter than the Nile, its flow is 60 times greater.

LARGEST ATOLL

The atoll with the largest land area is Christmas Atoll (above), in the Line Islands in the central Pacific Ocean. It has an area of 649 km^2 (251 miles^2), of which 321 km^2 (124 miles^2) is land.

The world's largest atoll is Kwajalein in the Marshall Islands, in the central Pacific Ocean. Its slender 283-km (176-mile) long coral reef encloses a lagoon of 2,850 km^2 (1,100 miles^2).

LONGEST RIVER

The Nile is credited as the world's longest river. Its main source is Lake Victoria in East Africa. From its farthest stream in Burundi, it extends 6,695 km (4,160 miles) in length.

WEIRD PLANTS

LARGEST SEED

The largest seed in the world is that of the giant fan palm, (*Lodoicea maldivica*) – commonly known as the double coconut or coco de mer – found wild only on the Seychelle islands in the Indian Ocean. The single-seeded fruit (above) weighs up to 20 kg (44 lb), can be larger than a basketball and take 10 years to develop. The seeds grow on the palm until they are too heavy, when they fall to the ground.

TALLEST LIVING TREE

The world's tallest living tree is the 'Stratosphere Giant', which measured 112.6 m (369 ft 4.8 in) in 2002. This coast redwood (*Sequoia sempervirens*) was discovered by Chris Atkins (USA) in August 2000 in the Rockefeller Forest of the Humboldt Redwoods State Park, California, USA.

LARGEST LIVING TREE

The world's largest living tree is 'General Sherman', a giant sequoia (*Sequoiadendron giganteum*) growing in the Sequoia National Park, California, USA. It stands 82.6 m (271 ft) tall, has a diameter of 8.2 m (27 ft 2 in) and a circumference of 25.9 m (85 ft). The trunk had a volume of 1,487 m^3 (52,508 ft^3) in 1980 when it was last measured accurately, but it is now thought to be almost 1,500 m^3 (53,000 ft^3). The tree is estimated to contain the equivalent of 630,096 board feet of timber – enough to make over five billion matches – and its red-brown bark is up to 61 cm (24 in) thick in parts. The tree's weight, including its vast root system, is estimated to be 2,000 tonnes (4,000,000 lb). 'General Sherman' is thought to be 2,100 years old.

LARGEST TREE EVER

The world's largest ever tree was the 'Lindsey Creek Tree', a coast redwood (*Sequoia sempervirens*) that grew in California, USA, until it was blown over in a storm in 1905. The tree had a total mass of 2,720 tonnes (6,000,000 lb).

LIVING TREE WITH THE GREATEST GIRTH

The living tree with the greatest circumference (girth) is 'El Arbol del Tule', in Oaxaca state, Mexico. This Montezuma cypress (*Taxodium mucronatum*) was last measured in 1998, and was 42 m (137 ft) tall, had a diameter of 11.5 m (38 ft) and a girth of 36 m (119 ft), taken at 1.5 m (5 ft) above the ground.

MOST MASSIVE PLANT

The world's most massive plant was reported in December 1992 to be a network of quaking aspen trees (*Populus tremuloides*) growing in the Wasatch Mountains, Utah, USA, from a single root system covering 43 ha (106 acres) and weighing an estimated 6,000 tonnes (13,227,720 lb). This network of trees (belonging to the willow family) is a genetically uniform clonal system and acts as a single organism, with all the component trees changing colour or shedding leaves in unison.

HEAVIEST PINE CONE

The heaviest pine cones belong to the Coulter pine (*Pinus coulteri*) of North America. The average weight of the cones, when green, is 0.4–2.2 kg (1–5 lb). However, the heaviest recorded weighed 4 kg (9 lb).

LARGEST LEAF

The largest leaves of any plant are those of the raffia palm (*Raphia farinifera*) of the Mascarene Islands in the Indian Ocean, and the Amazonian bamboo palm (*Raphia taedigera*) of South America and Africa. The leaf blades on each of these plants can measure 20 m (65 ft 7 in) long, with petioles (the stalk by which a leaf is attached to a plant) measuring up to 4 m (13 ft).

FASTEST GROWING PLANT

The world record for the fastest growing plant belongs to certain species of the 45 genera of bamboo, which have been found to grow at up to 91 cm (35 in) per day.

FASTEST GROWING FLOWERING PLANT

The world's fastest growing flowering plant is a *Hesperoyucca whipplei* of the Liliaceae family which had grown 3.65 m (11 ft 11 in) in 14 days, a rate of about 25.4 cm (10 in) per day. This was reported by people from Tresco Abbey, Isles of Scilly, Cornwall, UK, in July 1978.

SLOWEST FLOWERING PLANT

The slowest flowering plant is the rare *Puya raimondii*, the largest of all herbs, discovered at a height of 3,960 m (12,992 ft) in Bolivia in 1870. The flowering parts of the plant emerge after about 80–150 years of the plant's life, which then dies. One specimen planted near sea level at the University of California's Botanical Garden, Berkeley, USA, in 1958 grew to 7.6 m (24 ft 11 in) and bloomed in 1986, after only 28 years.

LONGEST DISTANCE TRAVELLED BY A DRIFT SEED

The record for the longest distance travelled by a drift seed belongs to Mary's bean (*Merremia discoidesperma*). It has the widest documented drift range for any seed or tropical fruit, travelling over 24,140 km (15,000 miles) from the Marshall Islands in the north Pacific Ocean to the beaches of Norway on the northern Atlantic Ocean. The bean can be traced along this distance as it only comes from a few locations in the Pacific.

>> LARGEST PREY CONSUMED BY A CARNIVOROUS PLANT

Of all the carnivorous plants, the ones that consume the largest prey are the pitcher plants of the Nepenthaceae family (genus *Nepenthes*, below). Both the *Nepenthes rajah* and *Nepenthes rafflesiana* have been known to digest frogs, birds and even rats. These species are commonly found in the rainforests of Asia, particularly in Borneo, Indonesia and Malaysia.

DEEPEST LIVING PLANT

The greatest depth at which plant life has been found is 269 m (882 ft) for algae found by Mark and Diane Littler (both USA) off San Salvador Island, Bahamas, in October 1984. The maroon-coloured plants survived although 99.9995% of sunlight was filtered out.

OLDEST PLANT CLONE

Clonal plants flower but do not produce any seeds. They spread by dropping parts of their branches, which take root and form new plants that are genetically identical to the parent plant. The oldest known colony of genetically identical plants is one of King's holly (*Lomatia tasmanica*) which was found in Tasmania's (Australia) south western wilderness region and is believed to be over 43,000 years old.

OLDEST TREE CLONE

The world's oldest colony of genetically identical trees is the stand of Huon pines (*Lagarostrobus franklinii*) on the west coast of Tasmania, Australia. The stand is believed to have developed from an original tree 10,500 years old, but no individual tree is that age.

OLDEST LIVING INDIVIDUAL TREE

The oldest living individual tree is the ancient bristlecone pine (*Pinus longaeva*) 'Methuselah', which is 4,767 years old. It was found by Edmund Schulman (USA) in the White Mountains, California, USA, and dated in 1957.

HIGHEST TREE RING COUNT

The highest actual ring count made on any tree is held by 'Eon Tree', a redwood that fell in a storm in the USA in late 1977. Ron Hildebrant (USA) counted 7,223 annual rings at 42.6 m (140 ft) above the base. The age of the tree is estimated to be over 9,000 years.

EARLIEST SURVIVING TREE SPECIES

The oldest surviving species of tree is the maidenhair (*Ginkgo biloba*) of Zhejiang, China, which first appeared about 160 million years ago. It was rediscovered by Engelbert Kaempfer (Germany) in 1690, but has been grown in Japan since c. 1100, where it is known as *ichou*.

MOST POISONOUS COMMON PLANT

Based on the amount it takes to kill a human, the most poisonous common plant in the world is the castor bean (*Ricinus communis*). According to the *Merck Index: An Encyclopedia of Chemicals, Drugs, and Biologicals* (1997) a dose of 70 micrograms (2 millionths of an ounce) is enough to kill a person weighing 72 kg (160 lb or 11 st 4 lb). The plant's poison is called ricin and is a protein found in the seeds of the castor bean.

MOST POISONOUS FUNGI

The world's most poisonous fungi is the death cap (*Amanita phalloides*), which can be found worldwide, including in North America and the UK. It is responsible for 90% of all fatal poisonings caused by fungi. Cooking does nothing to neutralize the poisonous chemicals in this fungus. If eaten, it destroys the liver and kidneys. Symptoms begin to occur between six and 15 hours after eating. The effects are vomiting, delirium, collapse and death.

>> SMELLIEST FLOWER

Commonly known as the corpse flower, *Amorphophallus titanum* (right) is the smelliest flower on Earth. When it blooms it releases a foul odour similar to that of rotten flesh that can be smelled half a mile away.

GARDEN WONDERS

LONGEST BEETROOT
The world's longest beetroot measured 5.504 m (18 ft 0.6 in). Peter Glazebrook (UK) presented his winning beetroot at the UK National Giant Vegetables Championship 2002, Shepton Mallet, Somerset, UK, on 6 September 2002.

LARGEST BUNCH OF BANANAS
The largest bunch of bananas, containing 473 individual bananas, was grown by Kabana SA and Tecorone SL (Spain) on the island of El Hierro, Canary Islands, Spain, and weighed 130 kg (287 lb) on 11 July 2001.

LARGEST PUMPKIN
The largest pumpkin weighed 606.7 kg (1,337 lb 9 oz) at the pumpkin weigh-off at Topsfield Fair, Massachusetts, USA, on 5 October 2002. It was grown by Charles Houghton (USA, right) and later carved into this Halloween image by Scott Cully (USA).

LARGEST CANTALOUPE MELON
A cantaloupe weighing 28.8 kg (63 lb 8 oz) with a circumference of 114 cm (45 in) and a length of 53 cm (21 in) was grown by Bill Rogerson (USA) of Robersonville, North Carolina, USA, in 1997.

TALLEST UMBRELLA PLANT
The world's tallest umbrella plant (*Schefflera arboricola*) measured 8.22 m (27 ft) on 4 January 2002. It is currently growing inside Konsta's Restaurant, Richmond, Virginia, USA, which is owned and managed by Konstantinos Xytakis and Sara Guterbock (both USA).

MOST HEADS ON ONE SUNFLOWER PLANT
The world record for most heads on one sunflower plant (*Helianthus*) is 837. The sunflower plant was grown by Melvin Hemker (USA) on his farm in St Charles, Michigan, USA, and the heads were counted on 18 September 2001.

LARGEST SUNFLOWER HEAD
A sunflower (*Helianthus*) with a diameter of 82 cm (32 in) was grown by Emily Martin of Maple Ridge, British Columbia, Canada, in 1983.

TALLEST SUNFLOWER
In 1986 M Heijms (Netherlands) grew a sunflower (*Helianthus*) that reached a record height of 7.76 m (25 ft 5.4 in).

LARGEST ROSE BUSH
A specimen of the rose bush Lady Banks (*Rosa banksiae*), at Tombstone, Arizona, USA, has a trunk circumference of 4.09 m (13 ft 6 in), stands around 2.75 m (9 ft) high and covers an area of 743 m² (8,000 ft²) .

LONGEST CARROT
Bernard Lavery (UK) grew a 335-cm (132-in) carrot in 1987. Internationally famous, Dr Lavery has held 26 world records for his out-sized plants and vegetables.

HEAVIEST LEEK
The world's heaviest leek (right) weighed 8.1 kg (17 lb 13 oz). Grown by Fred Charlton (UK), it was entered in the UK National Giant Vegetable Championship 2002, in Shepton Mallet, Somerset, UK, on 6 September 2002.

LONGEST CORN COB
A corn cob grown by Bernard Lavery of Llanharry, Rhondda Cynon Taff, UK, in 1994 measured 92 cm (36.25 in) in length.

TALLEST RUNNER BEAN PLANT
In 1992 Bernard Lavery (UK) grew a 10.7-m (35-ft) bean plant (*Phaseolus vulgaris*).

LARGEST KOHLRABI

The largest kohlrabi was grown by Scott Robb (USA) and weighed 19.8 kg (43 lb 11 oz) at the Alaska State Fair, Palmer, Alaska, USA, on 29 August 2001. The kohlrabi was a giant winter kohlrabi (*Brassica oleracea*). Robb has also broken the world record for the heaviest rutabaga (swede).

LONGEST CUCUMBER

The world's longest cucumber measured 1.1 m (43.5 in) and was grown by AC Rayment of Chelmsford, Essex, UK, in 1986.

LONGEST PARSNIP

A 5-m-long (16-ft 4.5-in) parsnip was grown by Peter Glazebrook (UK). He presented the parsnip at the UK National Amateur Gardening Show Giant Vegetable Championship, held on 1 September 2000.

LARGEST GOURD

Robert Weber (Australia) grew a gourd 177 cm (70 in) in circumference and presented it at the Australasian Giant Pumpkin and Vegetable Competition in Victoria, Australia, on 7 April 2001.

TREE BEARING THE MOST DIFFERENT FRUIT

The greatest number of different fruits produced from the same tree is five: apricot, cherry, nectarine, plum and peach. The fruit species were grafted onto a prune tree in 2000 by Luis H Carrasco E of Lo Barnechea, Santiago, Chile.

TALLEST FUSCHIA

A fuchsia (*Begonia fuchsioides*) grown by Bernard Lavery (UK) in 1995 grew to a height of 4.2 m (13 ft 9 in).

ROSE WITH THE MOST BLOOMS

A 'Cecile Brunner' rose (family *Rosaceae*) with 5,470 blooms was grown by Clifton Martin of Merrylands, New South Wales, Australia, in 1982.

TALLEST HOLLYHOCK

A hollyhock (*Alcea rosea*) 5.97 m (19 ft 7 in) in height was grown by George Palmer (UK) in 1978.

TALLEST DAFFODIL

A daffodil (*Narcissus*) grown by M Lowe of Chessell (UK) in 1979 reached a height of 1.55 m (5 ft 1 in).

TALLEST HOME-GROWN CACTUS

The tallest home-grown cactus (*Cereus uruguayanus*) measured 18.2 m (60 ft) on 10 December 2002 and was grown by Pandit Munji in Dharwad, Karnataka, India.

TALLEST ORCHID

A height of 15 m (49 ft) has been recorded for the orchid *Galeola foliata*, a saprophyte of the vanilla family that grows in the decaying rain forests of Queensland, Australia. It is not free-standing but is supported by other trees in the rain forest.

TALLEST GERANIUM

A geranium (*Pelargonium x hortorum*) grown by B Tournebize (France) of Puy-de-Dôme, France, grew to a height of 6.1 m (20 ft).

TALLEST ROSE BUSH

The world's tallest rose bush (family *Rosaceae*) measured 3.38 m (11 ft 1 in) on 29 January 2003 and grows in the garden of Kathleen Mielke-Villalobos (USA), who lives in San Diego, California, USA.

MOST LEAVES ON A CLOVER

A red clover (*Trifolium pratense*) with a record 14 leaves was reported by Paul Haizlip (USA) at Bellevue, Washington, USA, on 22 June 1987. Another record-breaking 14-leafed clover, this time a white one (*Trifolium repens*), was found by Randy Farland (USA) near Sioux Falls, South Dakota, USA, on 16 June 1975.

LARGEST VINE

As of December 2002 the 'Great Vine' at Hampton Court Palace, Greater London, UK, had a record circumference of 3 m (9 ft 10 in) and branches up to 33 m (108 ft 3 in) long. Planted in 1768, the 'Great Vine' produces an average yield of 318.8 kg (703 lb) of grapes every year.

LONGEST COURGETTE

The world's longest courgette measured 1.34 m (53 in) on 1 October 2002. It was grown by Sher Singh Kanwal (USA, below) at his home in Niagara Falls, New York, USA.

★ HEAVIEST FRUITS & VEGETABLES ★

FRUIT/VEGETABLE	WEIGHT	NAME AND VENUE	DATE
Apple	1.67 kg (3 lb 8 oz)	Alan Smith, Loddington Farm, Linton, Kent, UK	1997
Beetroot	23.4 kg (51 lb 9.4 oz)	Ian Neale, National Giant Vegetable Championship, Shepton Mallet, Somerset, UK	2001
Broccoli	15.87 kg (35 lb)	John and Mary Evans, Palmer, Alaska, USA	1993
Brussels sprout	8.3 kg (18 lb 3 oz)	Bernard Lavery, Llanharry, UK	1992
Cabbage	56.24 kg (124 lb)	Bernard Lavery, Llanharry, UK	1989
Celery	23.8 kg (52 lb 7.5 oz)	Ian Neale, Abertysswg, Mid Glamorgan, UK	2001
Garlic	1.19 kg (2 lb 10 oz)	Robert Kirkpatrick, Eureka, California, USA	1985
Grapefruit	3.065 kg (6 lb 12 oz)	Debbie Hazelton, Queensland, Australia	1995
Lemon	3.88 kg (8 lb 8 oz)	Donald and Charlotte Knutzen, California, USA	1983
Mango	1.94 kg (4 lb 4 oz)	John Painter, Bokeelia, Florida, USA	1999
Marrow	61.23 kg (135 lb)	John Handbury, Temple Normanton, Chesterfield, UK	1998
Onion	7.03 kg (15 lb 7.9 oz)	M Ednie, Anstruther, Fife, UK	1997
Parsnip	2.56 kg (5 lb 13.5 oz)	Barry Micklethwaite, Barnsley, South Yorkshire, UK	2000
Peach	725 g (25.6 oz)	Paul Friday, Michigan, USA	2002
Pineapple	8.06 kg (17 lb 12 oz)	E Kamuk, Ais Village, Papua New Guinea	1994
Potato	3.5 kg (7 lb 13 oz)	K Sloane, Patrick, Isle of Man, UK	1994
Quince	2.34 kg (5 lb 2 oz)	Edward Harold McKinney, Alabama, USA	2002
Radish	31.1 kg (68 lb 9 oz)	Manabu Oono, Kagoshima, Japan	2003
Rhubarb	2.67 kg (5 lb 14 oz)	E Stone, East Woodyates, Wiltshire, UK	1985
Squash	436 kg (962 lb)	Steve Hoult, Ontario, Canada	1997
Strawberry	231 g (8.17 oz)	G Andersen, Folkestone, Kent, UK	1983
Swede	34.35 kg (75 lb 12 oz)	Scott Robb, Palmer, Alaska, USA	1999
Sweet potato	22.5 kg (49 lb 9 oz)	Belinda Love, Gingin, Western Australia	1998
Tomato	3.51 kg (7 lb 12 oz)	G Graham, Edmond, Oklahoma, USA	1986
Watermelon	118.84 kg (262 lb)	B Carson Arrington, Tennessee, USA	1990

MAMMALS

ONLY TRANSIENT MASCULINIZATION

The only female mammal that temporarily changes sex is the juvenile female fossa (*Cryptoprocta ferox*, above) of Madagascar. Research from Aberdeen University (UK) discovered that young female fossas have a protrusion resembling male genitalia but outgrow this state as adults, when ready to mate and raise young.

LARGEST CARNIVORE ON LAND

The largest of all the carnivores is the polar bear (*Ursus maritimus*, above). Adult males typically weigh 400–600 kg (880–1,320 lb), and have a nose-to-tail length of 2.4–2.6 m (7 ft 10 in–8 ft 6 in).

LARGEST HERD

The largest herds on record are those of the springbok (*Antidorcas marsupialis*, left) during migration across the plains of the western parts of southern Africa in the 19th century. A mass migration of the springbok was observed in 1849. It was said to have taken three days for the animals to pass through the settlement of Beaufort West, Western Cape, South Africa.

LONGEST TONGUE

South America's giant anteater (*Myrmecophaga tridactyla*, above) has the longest tongue on a mammal relative to its body size. With an average body length of 1–2 m (3–6 ft), its tongue typically measures 60 cm (23 in) long.

MOST EFFICIENT SCAVENGER

The spotted hyena (*Crocuta crocuta*, above) utilizes the carcasses of its prey more efficiently than any other carnivore. It is the only animal with a digestive system that can break down bones, hooves, horns and hides.

LARGEST MAMMAL TO BUILD A NEST

The 175-kg (385-lb) European wild boar (*Sus scrofa*, above) has such small piglets that the mother builds a nest to protect them from predators.

HIGHEST FREQUENCY HEARING

Bats (family Vespertilionidae, above) have the most acute hearing of any land animal, using frequencies in the 20-80 kHz range, compared with 20 kHz for humans.

MOST NAMES

Because of its wide distribution across North and South America, the mammal with the highest number of different names is the puma (*Puma concolor*, right). In the English language alone, it has over 40, including cougar, mountain lion, red tiger, catamount and Florida panther.

FASTEST HEARTBEAT

The shrew (family Soricidae, above) has the fastest heartbeat of any mammal, with a rate of 1,200 beats per minute, which is similar to that of a hummingbird when hovering.

LONGEST GESTATION

The Asiatic or Indian elephant (*Elephas maximus*, above) has an average gestation period of one year nine months and a maximum of two years one month – over twice that of a human pregnancy.

LARGEST COLONY OF MAMMALS

A colony of black-tailed prairie dogs (*Cynomys ludovicianus*, above) discovered in 1901 contained around 400 million individuals and was estimated to cover 61,400 km^2 (23,700 miles^2).

PETS & DOMESTIC ANIMALS

TALLEST DOG

Harvey, a Great Dane born in 1993 and owned by Charles Dodman of Marford, Clwyd, UK, stands at 105.4 cm (41.5 in) tall, as measured from the the ground to the top of the shoulder. The Great Dane is one of the tallest of the working dog breeds, yet the average Great Dane stands around 75 cm (29.5 in) tall. Harvey is also the longest dog alive, measuring 231.14 cm (7 ft 5 in) from nose to tail tip. He weighs 88.45 kg (14 st 1 lb) and eats 3.6 kg (7 lb 14 oz) of food daily.

Harvey shares the tallest dog record with Shamgret Danzas, a Great Dane owned by Wendy and Keith Comley of Milton Keynes, Buckinghamshire, UK. Their dog also stood 105.4 cm (41.5 in) tall. Shamgret Danzas died on 16 October 1984.

OLDEST DOG

The world's oldest living dog is Butch, a 27-year-old beagle. Butch was bought in 1975 as a puppy and is owned by Gregory Duncan of Keswick, Virginia, USA.

Most dogs live for 8–15 years but the greatest reliable age recorded for a dog is 29 years 5 months for an Australian cattle dog named Bluey, owned by Les Hall of Rochester, Victoria, Australia. Bluey was bought as a puppy in 1910 and worked among cattle and sheep for nearly 20 years before retiring. He finally passed away on 14 November 1939.

LONGEST GOAT HORNS

The world's longest goat horns were measured tip-to-tip at 1.09 m (3 ft 6 in) on 9 April 2002. They belong to a goat (right) owned by Amilcar Reis Mendes (Portugal), who lives in Casal Branco, Ourém, Portugal.

DOG WITH THE LONGEST EARS

The dog with the longest ears is Mr Jeffries (above), a bassett hound whose ears measured 29.2 cm (11.5 in) on 3 November 2002. Mr Jeffries lives with his owner, Phil Jeffries (UK), in Southwick, West Sussex, UK.

SMALLEST DOG

The world's smallest living dog is Whitney, a Yorkshire terrier who measured 7.6 cm (3 in) to the shoulder and 24.1 cm (9.5 in) from nose to tail-tip on 26 November 2002. Whitney is owned by Christopher and Patricia Sheridan of Shoeburyness, Essex, UK. The smallest dog ever on record is a fist-sized, dwarf Yorkshire terrier owned by Arthur Marples of Blackburn, Lancashire, UK. When fully grown, this tiny dog stood 7.11 cm (2.8 in) at the shoulder and measured 9.5 cm (3.75 in) from the tip of its nose to the tip of its tail. The dog died in 1945, just before its second birthday.

OLDEST DOG BREED

The world's oldest known breed of domesticated dog is the saluki, believed to have emerged in 329 BC. Saluki dogs were revered in ancient Egypt and they were kept as royal pets.

LONGEST EYELASHES ON A DOG

The longest eyelashes ever measured on a dog were 9 cm (3.5 in) long on 27 April 2002 and belong to Borders, a Lhasa apso owned by Angela Barrett of Belleville, Ontario, Canada.

LONGEST DOG SWIM

On 2 September 1995 two black Labradors named Kai and Gypsy swam the 'Maui Channel Swim' from Lanai to Maui Island, in Hawaii, USA – a distance of 15.2 km (9.5 miles). The swim took 6 hr 3 min 42 sec and owner Steve Fisher (USA) swam along aside them all the way.

DEEPEST SCUBA DIVE BY A DOG

Dwane Folsom (USA) regularly takes his dog, Shadow, a black mongrel (half retriever, half Labrador) scuba diving off the coast of Gran Cayman Island. The deepest the pair usually go is approximately 4 m (13 ft). When diving, Shadow wears a specially adapted diving suit made up of a helmet, weighted dog jacket and breathing tube which is connected to his owner's air tank.

HIGHEST JUMP BY A GUINEA PIG

The world record for the guinea pig high-jump belongs to Puckel Martin, who jumped 20 cm (7.8 in) on 16 March 2003. Puckel Martin is owned by Madde Herrman (Sweden) of Vargön, Sweden.

HIGHEST JUMP BY A RABBIT

The world record for the highest rabbit jump is 46 cm (18 in) and was achieved by Golden Flame on 29 August 2002. Golden Flame is a three-year-old castor satin rabbit belonging to Sam Lawrie of Havant, West Sussex, UK.

RABBIT WITH THE LONGEST EARS

The longest ears on a rabbit belong to Toby III, a black male English lop rabbit whose ears measured 76.8 cm (30.25 in) long and 19.7 cm (7.75 in) wide on 3 June 2002 when he was two years old. Toby III is owned by Phil Wheeler of Barnsley, South Yorkshire, UK.

LONGEST GOLDFISH

The longest goldfish (*Carassius auratus*) in the world measures 37.2 cm (14.6 in) from its snout to the end of its tail fin. Bruce, as the goldfish is called, is two years old and owned by Chan Chun Ping Louis and Jackie Chan (both China), who run the Tung Hoi Aquarium Company Ltd in China.

OLDEST PET PARROT

The longest lived pet parrot was one called Prudle, who was reared by Iris Frost, of East Sussex, UK, as a pet after being found in Jinja, Uganda, in 1958. Prudle learned over 800 different words and could even conduct polite conversation, before its death in 1994, aged 35.

CAT WITH THE LONGEST TAIL

The longest tail of a domestic cat belongs to Furball, who lives with her owner, Jan Acker (USA), in Battle Creek, Michigan, USA. Furball's tail measured 40.6 cm (16 in) on 21 March 2001.

CAT WITH THE MOST TOES

The cat-toe record holder is Jake, a five-year-old male ginger tabby who has 28 toes, with 7 on each paw. Jake lives in Bonfield, Ontario, Canada, with his owners, Michelle and Paul Contant (both Canada). The toes were officially counted on 24 Sept 2002, with each toe having its own claw, pad and bone structure.

LONGEST CAT

The world's longest cat is Verismo's Leonetti Reserve Red (aka Leo), who measured 121.9 cm (48 in) from his nose to the tip of his tail on 10 March 2002, aged five. Leo is a male Maine Coon cat who lives with his owners, Frieda Ireland and Carroll Damron, in Chicago, Illinois, USA. Leo has a normal diet, but prefers to eat blue cheese.

MOST FLIGHTS MADE BY A CAT

The world record for the most flights made by a cat is held by Smarty, who made his 64th flight on 6 May 2002. All of Smarty's flights have been trips between Cairo, Egypt, and Larnaca, Cyprus, with his owners Peter and Carole Godfrey (UK) who live in Cairo. Smarty also holds the record for most quarantined domestic animal, with 32 stays in quarantine.

LONGEST CAT'S WHISKERS

The longest whisker on a cat measured 13.9 cm (5.5 in) on 18 February 2003 and belongs to Sylvester, a black and white long-haired cat owned by Amy Heckethorn of Burlington, Iowa, USA.

TALLEST LIVING HORSE

The world's tallest living horse is Lyrical Bend (above), a dark bay Percheron/Thoroughbred cross gelding (male) born on 6 May 1994. He measures 19.37 hands (193.99 cm or 76.375 in). Lyrical Bend is owned by Lucinda W Fayrer-Hosken (USA) and lives on her farm in Monroe, Georgia, USA. The tallest horse ever was the shire gelding Sampson (UK). Foaled in 1846, he measured 21.2½ hands (2.19 m or 7 ft 2.5 in).

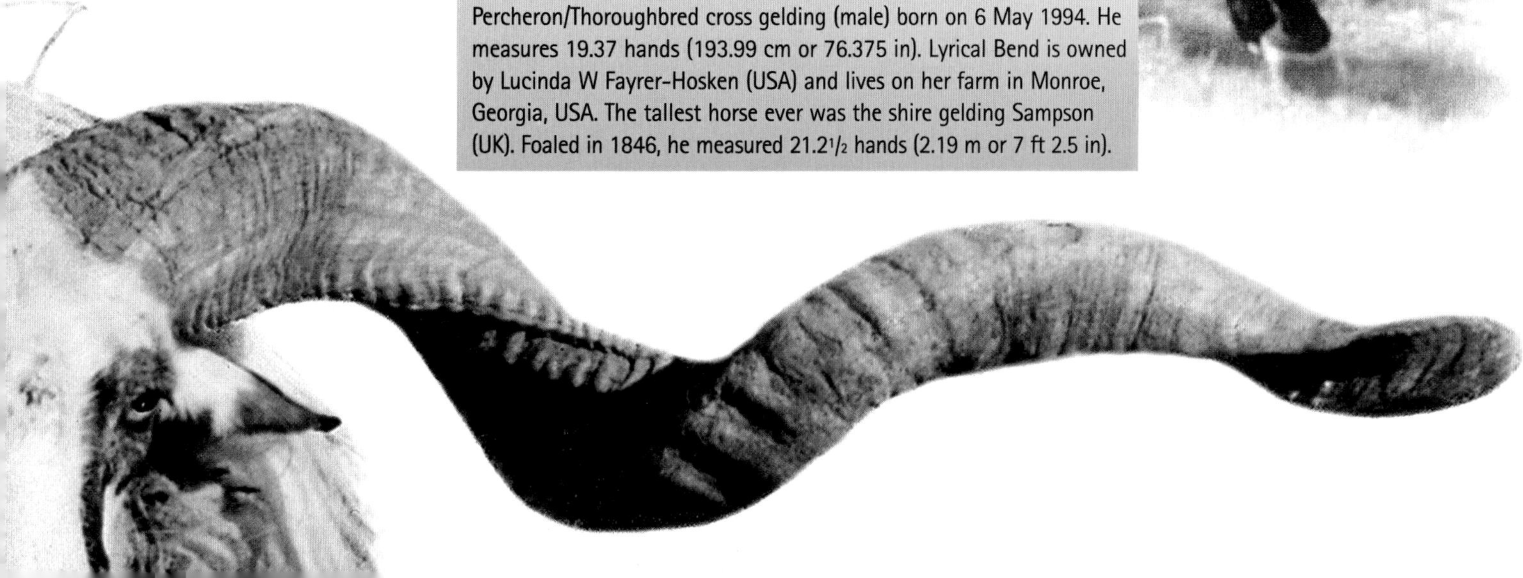

SPEED

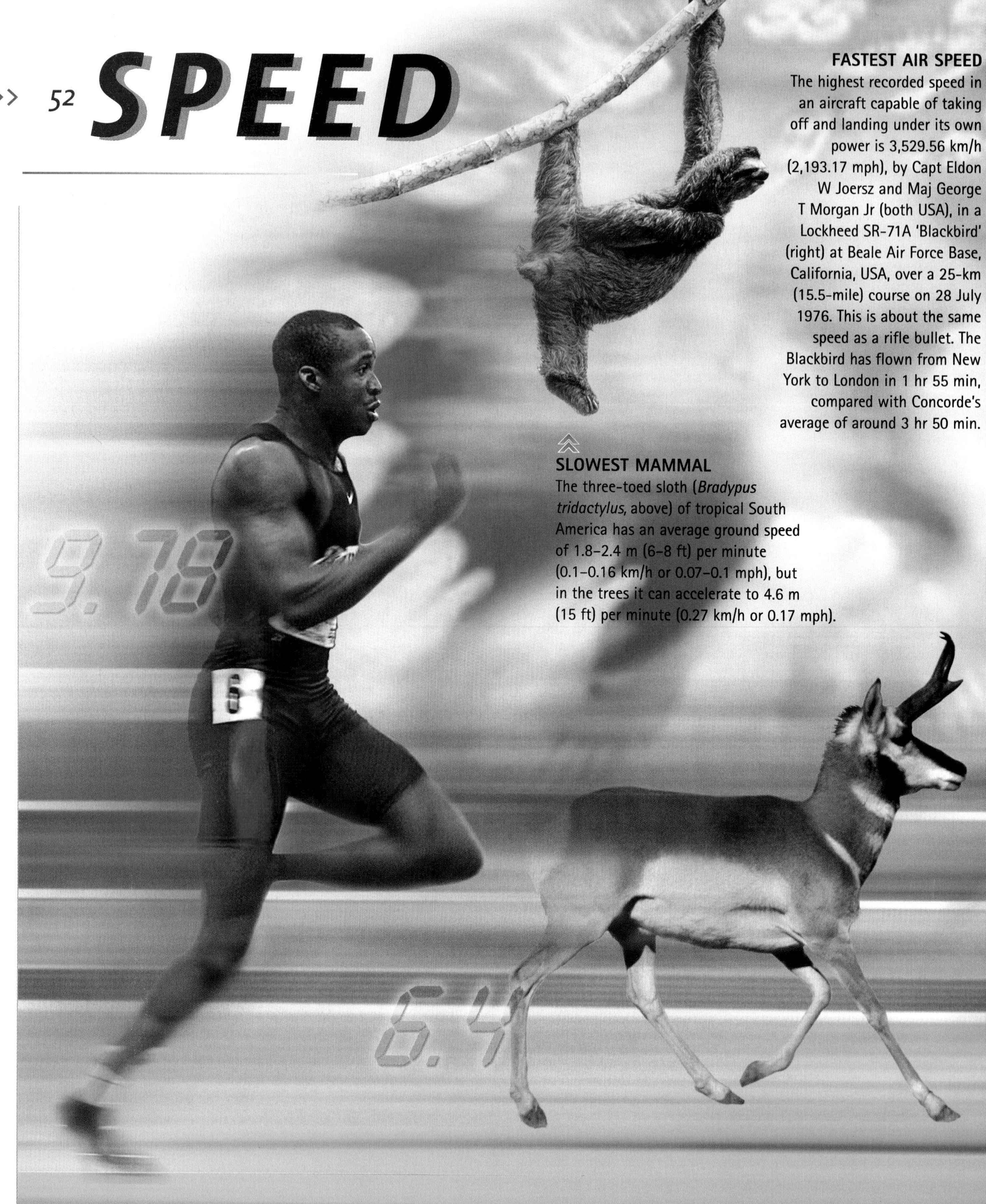

FASTEST AIR SPEED

The highest recorded speed in an aircraft capable of taking off and landing under its own power is 3,529.56 km/h (2,193.17 mph), by Capt Eldon W Joersz and Maj George T Morgan Jr (both USA), in a Lockheed SR-71A 'Blackbird' (right) at Beale Air Force Base, California, USA, over a 25-km (15.5-mile) course on 28 July 1976. This is about the same speed as a rifle bullet. The Blackbird has flown from New York to London in 1 hr 55 min, compared with Concorde's average of around 3 hr 50 min.

SLOWEST MAMMAL

The three-toed sloth (*Bradypus tridactylus*, above) of tropical South America has an average ground speed of 1.8–2.4 m (6–8 ft) per minute (0.1–0.16 km/h or 0.07–0.1 mph), but in the trees it can accelerate to 4.6 m (15 ft) per minute (0.27 km/h or 0.17 mph).

FASTEST MAN

The men's 100-m record is 9.78 sec and is held by Tim Montgomery (USA, above). The record was set in Paris, France, on 14 September 2002. This equates to 36.8 km/h (22.9 mph).

FASTEST LAND MAMMAL OVER DISTANCE

The American antelope (*Antilocapra americana*, above) is the fastest land animal when measured steadily over a long distance. It has been observed to travel continuously at 56 km/h (35 mph) for as far as 6 km (4 miles). It is found in western USA, southwestern Canada and parts of northern Mexico.

FASTEST LAND SPEED

The official one-mile land-speed record is 1,227.985 km/h (763.035 mph or Mach 1.020), set by Andy Green (UK) on 15 October 1997 in the Black Rock Desert, Nevada, USA, in Thrust SSC (right). The supersonic car is powered by two Rolls-Royce Spey 202 jet engines which generate 222 kN (50,000 lb) of thrust.

FASTEST KANGAROO

A speed of 64 km/h (40 mph) was recorded for a female eastern grey kangaroo (*Macropus giganteus*, below). The highest sustained speed is 56 km/h (35 mph) recorded for a large male red kangaroo which died from its exertions after being paced for 1.6 km (1 mile).

FASTEST BIRD IN LEVEL FLIGHT

Ducks and geese (*Anatidae*, below) are the fastest fliers in level flight. The red-breasted merganser (*Mergus serrator*), the eider (*Somateria mollissima*), the canvasback (*Aythya valisineria*) and the spur-winged goose (*Plectropterus gambensis*) can reach up to 90–100 km/h (56–62 mph).

FASTEST LAND MAMMAL OVERALL

When measured over a short distance, the cheetah (*Acinonyx jubatus*, above right) can maintain a steady maximum speed of approximately 100 km/h (62 mph) on level ground. That's nearly the UK national speed limit!

FACT

Compare the speed....

36.8 km/h 56 km/h 56 km/h 62 km/h 1,227.985 km/h

BIRDS

HEAVIEST FLYING BIRD

The heaviest flying bird is the mute swan (*Cygnus olor*), which can grow to a weight of 18 kg (40 lb). There is a record from Poland of a cob (male) weighing 22.5 kg (49 lb 10 oz) that had temporarily lost the power of flight.

LARGEST BIRD EVER

The largest bird that ever lived is the elephant bird or vouron patra (*Aepyornis maximus*) which became extinct about 1,000 years ago (although sightings were reported as late as 1658). This flightless bird from the island of Madagascar grew to around 3–3.3 m (10–11 ft) tall and weighed about 500 kg (1,100 lb).

BIRD WITH THE LARGEST VOCABULARY

A budgerigar called Puck, owned by Camille Jordan (USA), knew an estimated 1,728 words before its death in 1994.

MOST AIRBORNE BIRD

The most airborne of all birds is the sooty tern (*Sterna fuscata*, above). After leaving the nesting grounds as a youngster, it remains aloft for 3–10 years whilst maturing, settling on water from time to time, before returning to land to breed as an adult.

MOST ABUNDANT BIRD

The most abundant bird is the red-billed quelea (*Quelea quelea*), a seed-eating weaver of the drier parts of sub-Saharan Africa, which has an estimated adult breeding population of 1.5 billion. At least 200 million of these 'feathered locusts' are slaughtered annually without having any impact on this number.

LONGEST FEATHERS

The longest feathers on a bird found in the wild and not bred for ornamental purposes are those of the male crested argus pheasant (*Rheinhartia ocellata*). The feathers reach a length of 1.73 m (5 ft 8 in).

OLDEST BIRD

The greatest irrefutable age reported for any bird is over 80 years for a male sulphur-crested cockatoo (*Cacatua galerita*) named Cocky, who died at London Zoo, UK, in 1982. An unconfirmed age of 82 years was reported for Wolf, a male Siberian white crane (*Grus leucogeranus*) at the International Crane Foundation, Baraboo, Wisconsin, USA. Wolf died in 1988 after breaking his bill while repelling a visitor near his pen.

Excluding the ostrich, which has been known to live up to 68 years, the longest lived domesticated bird is the goose (*Anser domesticus*), which has a normal lifespan of about 25 years. On 16 December 1976 a gander named George, owned by Florence Hull (UK), died aged 49 years 8 months.

LONGEST BILL

The longest bill is that of the Australian pelican (*Pelecanus conspicillatus*). It is between 34 and 47 cm (13 and 18 in) long.

The longest beak in relation to overall body length is that of the sword-billed hummingbird (*Ensifera ensifera*) found in the Andes from Venezuela to Bolivia. The beak measures 10.2 cm (4 in), making it longer than the bird's actual body if the tail is excluded.

LARGEST BIRD

The largest living bird is the north African ostrich (*Struthio camelus camelus*). Male examples of this flightless (ratite) sub-species have been recorded up to 2.75 m (9 ft) tall and weighing 156.5 kg (345 lb).

>> RAREST BIRD OF PREY

Only 49 Californian condors (*Gymnogyps californianus*, right), most of which were bred in captivity, exist in the wild, with about 99 in captivity following a recent study, making it one of the rarest birds of prey.

MOST DANGEROUS BIRD

The most dangerous of all birds are all three species of cassowary (family Casuariidae, above) which live in New Guinea and north-eastern Queensland, Australia. They are large birds (up to 2 m or 6 ft 6 in tall) and on each foot they have three forward-pointing toes with strong claws to provide grip while running, the inner toe having a 12-cm-long (5-in) spike for defensive purposes which it kicks out when cornered. A cornered or wounded bird can be extremely dangerous and will leap into the air and kick, damaging vital organs or causing massive bleeding to its victim. Its kick is powerful enough to rip open a person's stomach or even kill.

SMALLEST FLIGHTLESS BIRD

The Inaccessible Island rail (*Atlantisia rogersi*) of Inaccessible Island, South Atlantic, weighs a mere 40 g (1.4 oz). First discovered in 1870, and described as being the size of a three-day-old black chicken, the adult birds are a dark chestnut brown above and grey-brown below. The males are darker than the females, but both adult birds have fiery-red eyes.

LARGEST WINGSPAN

The largest wingspan of any living species of bird was that of a male wandering albatross (*Diomedea exulans*) of the southern oceans, with a wingspan of 3.63 m (11 ft 11 in). It was caught by members of the Antarctic research ship USNS *Eltanin* in the Tasman Sea on 18 September 1965.

SMALLEST BIRD

The smallest bird is the bee hummingbird (*Mellisuga helenae*) of Cuba and the Isle of Pines (New Caledonia). Males measure 57 mm (2.25 in) in length, half of which is taken up by the bill and tail, and weigh 1.6 g (0.056 oz). Females are slightly larger. This is believed to be the lowest weight limit for any warm-blooded animal.

LARGEST BIRD EGG

The largest bird egg on record was an ostrich egg weighing 2.35 kg (5 lb 2 oz). It was laid in June 1997 at Datong Xinda ostrich farm, Datong, Shanxi, China.

HIGHEST FLYING BIRD

The highest altitude recorded for a bird is 11,300 m (37,000 ft) for a Ruppell's vulture (*Gyps rueppellii*), which collided with a commercial aircraft over Abidjan, Ivory Coast, on 29 November 1973. The impact damaged one of the plane's engines, but it landed safely.

HEAVIEST BIRD OF PREY

The heaviest bird of prey is the Andean condor (*Vultur gryphus*), males of which average 9–12 kg (20–27 lb) and have a wingspan of 3 m (10 ft).

A weight of 14.1 kg (31 lb) has been claimed for a male Californian condor (*Gymnogyps californianus*), now preserved in the California Academy of Sciences at Los Angeles, California, USA. This species is generally much smaller than the Andean condor and rarely exceeds 10.4 kg (23 lb).

MOST POISONOUS BIRD

The hooded pitohui (*Pitohui dichrous*) from Papua New Guinea is one of a small number of poisonous birds in the world. It was discovered in 1990 and has puzzled scientists ever since. Its feathers and skin contain the powerful poison homobatrachotoxin, the same one secreted by the dart frogs of South America. Like many other poisonous animals, this bird also emits a foul smell and advertises its toxicity with bright colours. The venom affects the nerves of the victim but it is not known how the species acquired it.

STRONGEST BIRD OF PREY

The bird of prey capable of killing and carrying away the largest animal is the female Harpy eagle (*Harpia harpyja*) which, in spite of its weight (9 kg or 20 lb), manages to hunt animals of equal or superior size. A Harpy eagle swooping down at 32 km/h (20 mph) generates around 8,300 Newton-meters (13,500 foot-pounds) of energy. That is more than twice the muzzle energy of a bullet shot from a rifle.

TALLEST FLYING BIRD

The tallest of the flying birds are cranes (below), which are waders belonging to the family Gruidae. The largest can stand to a height of almost 2 m (6 ft 6 in) high.

AQUATIC LIFE

SHORTEST LIVED FISH

The shortest-lived fish are probably certain species of Killifish (family Aplocheilidae) which are found distributed broadly throughout a variety of fresh and brackish water habitats in Africa. They normally live for about eight months in the wild.

STRONGEST BITE

Experiments carried out with a 'Snodgrass gnathodynamometer' (shark-bite meter) at the Lerner Marine Laboratory in Bimini, Bahamas, revealed that a 2-m-long (6-ft 6.75-in) dusky shark (*Carcharhinus obscurus*) could exert a force of 60 kg (132 lb) between its jaws. This is the same as a pressure of 3 tonnes/cm^2 (42,500 lb/in^2) at the tip of its teeth. The bite of a larger shark such as a great white (*Carcharodon carchrias*) must be considerably more spectacular, but it has never been measured.

LARGEST FISH

The world's largest fish is the rare plankton-feeding whale shark (*Rhincodon typus*, below), which is found in the warmer areas of the Atlantic, Pacific and Indian Oceans. The largest scientifically recorded example was 12.65 m (41 ft 6 in) long, measured 7 m (23 ft) around the thickest part of the body and weighed between 15 and 21 tonnes (33,000-46,300 lb). It was captured off Baba Island, near Karachi, Pakistan, on 11 November 1949.

LONGEST SURVIVAL OUT OF WATER

The six species of lung fish (Lepidosirenidae, Protopteridae and Ceratodidae) live in freshwater swamps that frequently dry out for months or even years at a time. Two of the four species found in Africa are considered to be the real experts. As the water recedes, they burrow deep into the ground and secrete a mucus to form a moisture-saving cocoon around their bodies. They then build a porous mud plug at the entrance of the burrow – and wait. Abandoning gill breathing in favour of their air-breathing lungs, they can live for up to four years in this dormant position.

LARGEST OYSTER

In 1999 a common oyster (*Ostrea edulis*) from Chesapeake Bay, Virginia, USA, weighed in at 3.7 kg (8 lb 2.5 oz). It was 30 cm (12 in) long and 14 cm (5.5 in) wide.

HEAVIEST SPONGE

In 1909 a wool sponge (*Hippospongia canaliculatta*) measuring 1.83 m (6 ft) in circumference was collected off the Bahamas. It initially weighed between 36 and 41 kg (80–90 lb) but this fell to 5.5 kg (12 lb) after it had been dried and drained of all excrescences. It is now preserved in the National Museum of Natural History in Washington DC, USA.

LARGEST INVERTEBRATE

The largest invertebrate is the Atlantic giant squid (*Architeuthis dux*). The heaviest ever recorded was stranded aground in Thimble Tickle Bay, Newfoundland, Canada, on 2 November 1878. Its body was 6.1 m (20 ft) long and one tentacle measured 10.7 m (35 ft).

DEEPEST FISH

The 20-cm-long (8-in) *Abyssobrotula galatheae*, a species of the cuskeel (family Ophidiidae), has been collected from the Puerto Rico Trench at a depth of 8,370 m (27,455 ft).

OLDEST MOLLUSC

The longest lived mollusc is the ocean quahog (*Arctica islandica*), a thick-shelled clam found on both sides of the Atlantic and in the North Sea. A specimen with 220 annual growth rings was collected in 1982. Although this implies an age of 220 years, not all biologists accept these growth rings as an accurate measure of age.

HIGHEST DENSITY OF CRABS

An estimated 120 million red crabs (*Gecarcoidea natalis*) live on the 135-km² (52-mile²) Christmas Island, Pacific Ocean, a density of approximately one crab per square metre for the whole island. They occur nowhere else in the world.

MOST ABUNDANT ANIMAL

Copepods are crustaceans and are found almost everywhere where water is available. They have colonized almost every habitat – from 10,000 m (32,800 ft) down in the deep sea to lakes 5,000 m (16,400 ft) up in the Himalayas – and from subzero polar waters to hot springs. They include over 12,000 species and, with krill, form the most important members of zooplankton. They form groups that can reach a trillion individuals. Most are very small, less than 1 mm (0.04 in) long, but some rare oceanic species are over 1 cm (0.4 in).

SMALLEST SPONGE

The widely distributed *Leucosolenia blanca* is just 3 mm (0.11 in) tall when fully grown.

SMALLEST MARINE FISH

The shortest recorded marine fish – and the shortest known vertebrate – is the dwarf goby (*Trimmatom nanus*) of the Indo-Pacific. Average lengths recorded for a series of specimens collected by the 1978/79 Joint Services Chagos Research Expedition of the British Armed Forces were 8.6 mm (0.34 in) for males and 8.9 mm (0.35 in) for females.

LARGEST MARINE CRUSTACEAN

The largest of all crustaceans is the Japanese spider crab (*Macrocheira kaempferi*, below) which is found off the southeastern coast of Japan and has an average body size of 25.4 x 30 cm (10 x 12 in) and an average leg span of 2.43–2.74 m (8–9 ft).

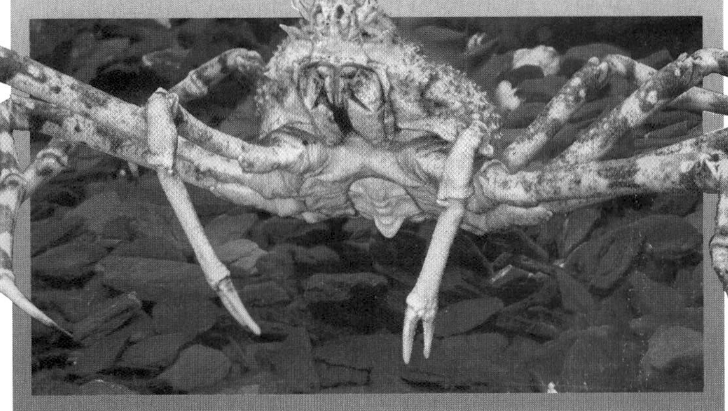

LARGEST CLAM

The largest of all existing bivalve shells is that of the marine giant clam (*Tridacna gigas*, below), found on the Indo-Pacific coral reefs. One 115-cm-long (3-ft 9.25-in) specimen weighing 333 kg (734 lb) was collected off Ishigaki Island, Okinawa, Japan, in 1956.

SMALLEST FRESHWATER FISH

The shortest and lightest freshwater fish is the dwarf pygmy goby (*Pandaka pygmaea*), a colourless and nearly transparent species found in the streams and lakes of Luzon in the Philippines. Males are only up to 9.9 mm (0.38 in) long and weigh 4-5 mg (0.00014–0.00018 oz).

LONGEST LIVING MARINE INVERTEBRATE

The tubeworm *Lamellibrachia*, which survives by digesting seeps of oil leaking from the sea floor, can live for 170–250 years.

LARGEST STARFISH

Out of the 1,600 known species, the largest starfish in the world is the very fragile brisingid (*Midgardia xandaros*). In 1968, a specimen was collected in the Gulf of Mexico by a Texas AM University research vessel *The Alaminos*. The starfish measured an astonishing 1.38 m (4 ft 6 in) from tip to tip.

SMALLEST STARFISH

The smallest known starfish is the asterinid sea star (*Patiriella parvivipara*) discovered on the west coast of the Eyre peninsula, South Australia, in 1975. It has a maximum radius of only 4.7 mm (0.18 in) and a diameter of less than 9 mm (0.35 in).

DEEPEST DIVE BY A MAMMAL

The deepest authenticated dive by a mammal was made by a bull sperm whale (*Physeter macrocephalus*) off the coast of Dominica in the Caribbean Sea in 1991. Scientists recorded the dive to be 2,000 m (6,500 ft) deep, lasting a total of 1 hr 13 min.

FASTEST MARINE MAMMAL

On 12 October 1958 a bull killer whale (*Orcinus orca*) estimated to be 6.1–7.6 m (20–25 ft) long was timed at 55.5 km/h (34.5 mph) in the Pacific. Similar speeds have been reported for Dall's porpoises (*Phocoenoides dalli*) in short bursts.

LARGEST JELLYFISH

An Arctic giant jellyfish (*Cyanea capillata arctica*) of the northwestern Atlantic that washed up in Massachusetts Bay, USA, in 1870 had a bell diameter of 2.28 m (7 ft 6 in) and tentacles stretching 36.5 m (120 ft). Their sting can be fatal to humans, but they live very deep in the ocean.

CREEPY CRAWLIES

STRANGEST INSECT DEFENCE MECHANISM

The bombardier beetle (genus *Brachinus*, right) stores two benign chemicals in a chamber in its abdomen. When threatened, they are released into a second chamber and mix with an enzyme causing a violent reaction and the release of considerable heat (up to 100°C or 212°F) from its anus.

DANGEROUS BEE

The Africanized honey bee (*Apis mellifera scutellata*, right) will generally only attack when provoked but is persistent in pursuit. Its venom is no more potent than that of other bees, but the number of stings it inflicts, which can result in death, is greater than any other.

LARGEST MOTH

The atlas moth (*Attacus atlas*, above) of southeast Asia has a wingspan of 30 cm (12 in) and is often mistaken for a bird. They have no mouth, and therefore live for only about four days.

FASTEST CATERPILLAR

The larvae of the mother-of-pearl moth (*Pleuroptya ruralis*, above) can travel 38.1 cm/sec (15 in/sec) – the equivalent of 241 km/h (150 mph). It reaches this speed by forming into a 'wheel' and rolling away.

MOST VENOMOUS SCORPION

The Tunisian fat-tailed scorpion (*Androctonus australis*, above) is responsible for 80% of stings and 90% of deaths from scorpion stings in north Africa.

STRONGEST SPIDER »

The Californian trap-door spider (*Bothriocyrtum californicum*, right) has been proved to be able to resist a force 38 times its own weight attempting to open its trap-door – a silken structure covering the entrance to its underground burrow. This is the same as an 82-kg (180-lb) man trying to keep a door closed which was being pulled on the other side by the weight of a small jet.

« MOST DESTRUCTIVE INSECT

The single most destructive insect is the desert locust (*Schistocerca gregaria*, left), native to the dry and semi-arid regions of Africa, the Middle East and western Asia. Individuals are only 4.5–6 cm (1.8–2.4 in) long but can eat their own weight in food every day. In a single day, a 'small' swarm of about 50 million locusts can eat food that would sustain 500 people for a year.

LARGEST SPIDER »

The world's largest known spider is a male goliath bird-eating spider (*Theraphosa blondi*, right) collected by members of the Pablo San Martin Expedition at Rio Cavro, Venezuela, in April 1965. It had a record leg span of 28 cm (11 in) – sufficient to cover a dinner plate.

STRONGEST INSECT

In proportion to their size, the strongest animals are the larger beetles of the Scarabaeidae family (above). In tests they were found to support 850 times their own weight upon their back. A human can support up to 17 times his own body weight.

FACT

KILLER ANT!

The most dangerous ant is the bulldog ant (Myrmecia pyriformis, right) found in Australia. It is so named because of its ferocity and determination during an attack. The ant stings its prey a number of times – injecting more venom each time. In an attack, the ant will hold on to its victim with long toothed mandibles, curl its body underneath and thrust its long barbless sting into the skin. This sting has been known to kill adult humans within 15 minutes.

REPTILES

LARGEST TORTOISE

Goliath, a Galapagos tortoise (*Chelonoidis nigra*), resided at the Life Fellowship Bird Sanctuary in Seffner, Florida, USA, from 1960 until his death in November 2002. He was 1.358 m (4 ft 5.5 in) long, 1.02 m (3 ft 3.6 in) wide, 68.5 cm (2 ft 3 in) tall, and weighed 417 kg (920 lb).

FASTEST CHELONIAN

The highest speed claimed for any reptile in water is 35 km/h (22 mph) by a frightened Pacific leatherback turtle (*Dermochelys coriacea*).

LARGEST LIZARD

The largest lizard is the Komodo dragon (*Varanus komodoensis*, below), also known as the Komodo monitor or ora, which is found on the Indonesian islands of Komodo, Rintja, Padar and Flores. Males average 2.25 m (7 ft 5 in) in length and weigh about 59 kg (130 lb). The largest accurately measured specimen was a male presented to a US zoologist in 1928 by the Sultan of Bima. In 1937 it measured 3.1 m (10 ft 2 in) in length and weighed 166 kg (365 lb).

OLDEST LIZARD

The greatest age recorded for a lizard is over 54 years for a male slow worm (*Anguis fragilis*) kept in the Zoological Museum in Copenhagen, Denmark, from 1892 until 1946.

HEAVIEST VENOMOUS SNAKE

The heaviest venomous snake is the eastern diamondback rattlesnake (*Crotalus adamanteus*) of the southeastern USA, which weighs 5.5–6.8 kg (12–15 lb) and is 1.52–1.83 m (5–6 ft) in length. The heaviest on record weighed 15 kg (34 lb) and was 2.36 m (7 ft 9 in) long.

LONGEST SNAKE

The reticulated python (*Python reticulatus*) of southeast Asia, Indonesia and the Philippines often exceeds 6.25 m (20 ft 6 in), and the record length is 10 m (32 ft 9.5 in) for a specimen shot in 1912 in Celebes, Indonesia.

MOST DANGEROUS LIZARD

The Gila monster (*Heloderma suspectum*, below) is a large – up to 60 cm (24 in) long – heavily built, brightly coloured lizard that lives in the arid parts of Mexico and southwestern USA. It has eight well-developed venom glands in its lower jaws and carries enough venom to kill two adult humans. The venom is not injected but seeps into the wound caused when the Gila monster bites its victim with its sharp fragile teeth. Because of this, the lizard may continue to hang on after it has bitten and chew for several minutes. In one study of 34 people bitten by the Gila, there were eight fatalities.

SHORTEST VENOMOUS SNAKE

The namaqua or spotted dwarf adder (*Bitis schneideri*) of Namibia has an average length of 20 cm (8 in).

SMALLEST LIZARD

The title of smallest lizard is held by both the *Sphaerodactylus parthenopion* and *Sphaerodactylus ariasae* which have both been recorded as having an average snout-to-vent length of only 16 mm (0.6 in). They both share the distinction of being the smallest of the approximately 23,000 species of amniote vertebrates.

LONGEST FANGS

The longest fangs of any snake are those of the highly venomous Gaboon viper (*Bitis gabonica*) of tropical Africa. In a specimen 1.83 m (6 ft) long, the fangs measured 50 mm (2 in). The Gaboon viper is considered to produce more venom than any other venomous snake. A single adult male may have enough venom to inject lethal doses into 30 individual men. Not only do they produce more venom than any other snake but they also inject more deeply.

HEAVIEST SNAKE

The heaviest snake is the green anaconda (*Eunectes murinus*) of tropical South America and Trinidad. The normal length is 5.5–6.1 m (18–20 ft). A female shot in Brazil c. 1960 was 8.45 m (27 ft 9 in) long with a girth of 1.11 m (44 in), and was estimated to have weighed 227 kg (500 lb).

SMALLEST CHELONIAN

The smallest chelonian is the speckled cape tortoise or speckled padloper (*Homopus signatus*), which has a shell length of between 6 and 9.6 cm (2.3 and 3.7 in). The smallest marine turtle in the world is the Atlantic ridley (*Lepidochelys kempii*), which has a shell length of 50–70 cm (20–28 in) and a maximum weight of 80 kg (176 lb).

LONGEST VENOMOUS SNAKE

The longest venomous snake is the king cobra (*Ophiophagus hannah*), also called the hamadryad, which measures 3.65–4.5 m (12–15 ft) in length and is found in southeast Asia and India. The head of the king cobra is as big as a man's hand and it can stand tall enough to look an adult human being in the eye. Its venom can stun the nervous system and cause asphyxiation while other toxins start digesting the paralysed victim. The venom in a single bite from a king cobra is enough to kill an elephant or 20 people.

MOST VENOMOUS LAND SNAKE

The most venomous land snake in the world is the inland taipan or small-scaled (or fierce) snake (*Oxyuranus microlepidotus*), which measures up to 1.7 m (5 ft 7 in) and is found mainly in the Diamantina River and Cooper Creek drainage basins in Queensland and western New South Wales, Australia. In a single strike, a taipan can inject 60 mg (0.002 oz) of venom, sufficient to quickly paralyse a small marsupial but also more than enough to kill several human adults. The average venom yield after milking is 44 mg (0.00155 oz) but one male specimen yielded 110 mg (0.00385 oz), enough to kill 250,000 mice. Fortunately this species only lives in the arid deserts of central eastern Australia and no human death has been reported from its bite.

LARGEST CROCODILIAN

The largest reptile in the world is the estuarine or saltwater crocodile (*Crocodylus porosus*), which ranges throughout the tropical regions of Asia and the Pacific. The Bhitarkanika Wildlife Sanctuary in Orissa State, India, houses four protected estuarine crocodiles measuring more than 6 m (19 ft 8 in) in length, the largest being over 7 m (23 ft) long. There are several unauthenticated reports of specimens up to 10 m (33 ft) in length. Adult males typically measure 4.2–4.8 m (14–16 ft) in length and scale about 408–520 kg (900–1,150 lb).

LONGEST LIZARD

The Salvadori or Papuan monitor (*Varanus salvadorii*, left) of Papua New Guinea has been measured at up to 4.75 m (15 ft 7 in) in length, but nearly 70% of its total length is taken up by the tail.

SMALLEST CROCODILIAN

The Cuiver's dwarf caiman (*Paleosuchus palpebrosus*) of northern South America is the smallest crocodilian in the world today. Females rarely exceed 1.2 m (4 ft) in length and males rarely grow to more than 1.5 m (4 ft 11 in).

SHORTEST SNAKE

The world's shortest snake is the very rare thread snake (*Leptotyphlops bilineata*), known only in Martinique, Barbados and St Lucia. The longest known specimen was 10.8 cm (4.25 in) long, and had such a matchstick-thin body that it could have entered the hole left in a standard pencil after the lead has been removed. The Brahminy blindsnake (*Ramphotyphlops braminus*) is also under 10.8 cm (4.25 in) long.

SLOWEST CHELONIAN

In a speed test carried out in the Seychelles, a male giant tortoise (*Geochelone gigantea*, below) could only cover 4.57 m (14 ft 11 in) in 43.5 sec (0.37 km/h or 0.23 mph), despite the enticement of a female tortoise.

OLDEST CHELONIAN

The greatest authentic age recorded for a chelonian is at least 188 years and was set by a Madagascar radiated tortoise (*Astrochelys radiata*) that was presented to the Tonga royal family by Captain Cook in either 1773 or 1777. The animal was called Tui Malila and remained in their care until its death in 1965.

MOST WIDELY DISTRIBUTED VENOMOUS SNAKE

The saw-scaled or carpet viper (*Echis carinatus*), which is found from West Africa to India, bites and kills more people in the world than any other species.

OLDEST SNAKE

The greatest reliable age recorded for a snake is 40 years 3 months 14 days for Popeye, a male common boa (*Boa constrictor*) who died at Philadelphia Zoo, Pennsylvania, USA, on 15 April 1977.

CONSERVATION

ENDANGERED SPECIES

Many animals are only known from a single or type specimen and the population size of others is unknown. This makes it very difficult to establish the identity of the world's rarest species and, consequently, this selection simply highlights some of the better known examples from the 2002 International Union for the Conservation of Nature's Red List of Threatened Species.

RAREST BIRD

The blue macaw (*Cyanopsitta spixii*) is considered to be one of the rarest birds in the world. The only hope for the survival of this species lies with the 66 individuals kept in captivity. In 2000, this species was judged to be critically endangered and extremely close to extinction. The single known wild bird almost certainly died towards the end of 2000 and thus the species may now be extinct in the wild.

MOST ENDANGERED FISH

The Devil's Hole pupfish (*Cyprinodon diabolis)*, which number between 200 and 500, are restricted entirely to an unusual system of water holes in Nevada, USA. Their main threat comes from the pumping of groundwater for irrigation, and the introduction of exotic fish species in the area.

RAREST LAND MAMMAL

The Javan rhinoceros (*Rhinoceros sondaicus*), a solitary, single-horned species, is considered to be the world's rarest large mammal. Once widely distributed in southeast Asia, its population has declined to an estimated 60 animals (about 50 on the remote western tip of Java, Indonesia, and the rest in Vietnam).

RAREST MARINE MAMMAL

The baiji, or Yangtze River dolphin (*Lipotes vexillifer*), has an estimated population of only a few dozen. The population is still falling owing to competition with fisheries, accidental capture in nets, pollution, disturbance and habitat destruction. The baiji is also killed for its meat and oil. The few survivors live mainly in the middle reaches of the Yangtze River, China. Despite being a national treasure in China, the baiji is expected to become extinct soon.

RAREST AMPHIBIAN

The golden toad (*Bufo periglenes*, above) is found in a small area (less than 10 km² or 4 miles²) contained in the Monteverde Cloud Forest Preserve in the Cordillera de Tilaran, near Monteverde, Provincia de Puntarenas, Costa Rica. Its numbers mysteriously plummeted in little over a decade, with the last recorded sighting of one specimen dating back to between 1988 and 1989.

MOST ENDANGERED PRIMATES

Because of the difficulty in establishing definite numbers for individual primates, there are several species which are considered critically endangered.

Although the species was only discovered in 1985, there are believed to be only approximately 1,000 golden bamboo lemurs (*Hapalemur aureus*) living wild in Madagascar's eastern rainforest. The main threat to its existence is the rampant slash-and-burn agriculture around its habitat.

The total number of remaining Cross River gorillas (*Gorilla gorilla diehli*) on the Nigeria-Cameroon border in 2000 is somewhere between 150 and 200 individuals. Bushmeat trade is popular in this part of the world and this has greatly reduced numbers.

There are only about 400 black-faced lion tamarins (*Leontopithecus caissara*) in the states of Paraná and São Paulo, Brazil. Their discovery in 1990 was considered one of the most significant primatological events of the 20th century because they had been undetected for so long in what is a very densely populated area of Brazil.

The Cat Ba Island golden-headed langur (*Trachypithecus poliocephalus*) is only found on the island of Cat Ba, the largest of more than 3,000 islands located in northeastern Vietnam's Halong Bay. There are estimated to be only approximately 100 left in the wild as they have suffered over the years from human encroachment and hunting.

RAREST INSECT

Scientists believe there may be as few as ten specimens of the Lord Howe Island stick insect (*Dryococelus australis)* in existence. The giant stick insect evolved before the dinosaurs and was presumed extinct for 80 years until scientists rediscovered it on a remote island off Australia in February 2001. Several eggs were also found. This species can grow up to 15 cm (6 in) long and their bodies are 1.3 cm (0.5 in) thick.

MOST ENDANGERED WILDCAT

The Iberian lynx (*Lynx pardinus*, left) is restricted to Spain and Portugal and in 2000 it was estimated that there were only 600 survivors in an extremely fragmented population. The Iberian lynx was once widespread all over Spain but through agriculture and development has lost a lot of its habitat. A major cause of the decline in numbers was the introduction of the disease myxomatosis in an attempt to reduce the rabbit population. As rabbits are the Iberian lynx's main food source, this had a direct impact on the population. This wildcat is now legally protected.

LARGEST TROPICAL FOREST RESERVE

The Tumucumaque National Park in the northern Amazonian state of Amapa, Brazil, measures some 38,875 km² (15,010 miles²) in area, and contains many endangered species of plant and animal. The creation of the park was announced on 22 August 2002.

LARGEST AFFORESTATION PROJECT

The world's largest afforestation project is the 'Green Great Wall'. This 4,480-km-long (2,783-mile) forest belt is being created in northwest China in order to combat the threat of desertification and over-farming, which has ruined vast areas of cultivated land. The project was initiated in 1978, and is set to last until 2050 when a total of 35.6 million hectares (87.9 million acres) of land will be afforested. It is currently being coordinated by the State Forestry Administration of China.

LARGEST LANDSCAPE RESTORATION PROJECT

The largest ecological restoration project in history is the current $8 billion (£5 billion) project that will restore the Everglades wetlands of Florida, USA.

RAREST TREE

The Wollemi pine (*Wollemia nobilis*), a member of the Araucaria family, was discovered in Wollemi National Park, 150 km (93 miles) northwest of Sydney, Australia, in 1994. Only 43 adult trees have been found, all growing in a 0.5-ha (1.5-acre) grove in the park in three small stands. The pine is unusual in being covered with brown, knobbly, spongy bark. The trees grow on wet ledges in a deep, sheltered gorge. The tallest measures 40 m (131 ft) and has a girth of some 3 m (9 ft).

EARLIEST ZOO

The earliest known collection of animals was established at modern day Puzurish, Iraq, by Shulgi, a 3rd-dynasty ruler of Ur from 2097–2094 BC.

LARGEST ENVIRONMENTAL PETITION

Greenpeace collected 8.5 million signatures worldwide in 1995 to call upon France's President Jacques Chirac to end French nuclear testing in Mururoa in the South Pacific. Despite worldwide condemnation, France completed six nuclear tests. However, as France had initially intended to perform eight tests, Greenpeace took it as a success that they only performed six.

HIGHEST DIVERSITY OF PLANTS PER UNIT AREA

The area of the world regarded as having the greatest diversity and endemism of plants per unit area is the small island of Juan Fernández in the Pacific Ocean off the coast of Chile, which has a total surface area of 100 km² (39 miles²). In this small area scientists have so far identified 209 species of vascular plants (126 of which are endemic), an endemic plant family (Lactoridaceae), a primitive dicotyledon and 12 fully endemic plant genera.

MOST ENVIRONMENTALLY FRIENDLY COUNTRY

The country regarded as the most environmentally sustainable is Finland, which heads the Environmental Sustainability Index (ESI) compiled in 2002 by the World Economic Forum. Based on 20 core indicators covering five broad areas – environmental systems (eg air and water quality), reducing environmental stress (eg pollution levels), reducing human vulnerability to environmental degradation, social and institutional capacity to respond to environmental threats, and contribution to global stewardship – Finland scored 73.9 out of 100. The lowest was Kuwait with 23.9. The USA was 45th with 53.2. The UK was 91st with a score of 46.1. In total, 142 countries are listed.

GREATEST ENVIRONMENTAL MANAGEMENT

In terms of receiving ISO 14001 certification for environmental management, Japan leads the world with 8,123 certifications as of December 2001. ISO 14000 provides guidelines for organizations that need to systematize and improve their environmental management efforts. The ISO 14000 standards came as a result of the 1992 Rio Summit on the Environment.

GREATEST BIODIVERSITY

The area considered to have the greatest biodiversity is the tropical Andes region (left) covering 1,258,000 km² (485,716 miles²). This area runs through Venezuela, Colombia, Ecuador, Peru, Bolivia and northern Argentina. So far, 45,000 species of vascular plant have been described (15–17% of the world's species) as well as 1,666 bird species, 414 mammal species and 1,309 reptile and amphibian species.

PREHISTORIC LIFE

LONGEST PREHISTORIC SNAKE

The longest prehistoric snake was the python-like *Gigantophis garstini*, which inhabited what is now Egypt about 38 million years ago. Parts of a spinal column and a small piece of jaw discovered at Fayum in the Western Desert indicate a length of about 11 m (36 ft). This is 1 m (3 ft 3 in) longer than the reticulated python, the present-day longest snake.

OLDEST VOMIT

On 12 February 2002, a team of palaeontologists, led by Peter Doyle (Greenwich University, UK) announced their discovery of the fossilized vomit of a marine reptile. Discovered in a quarry in Peterborough, Cambridgeshire, UK, the 160-million-year-old vomit could provide an insight to the feeding habits of ichthyosaurs.

EARLIEST ANIMAL TO WALK ON LAND

The earliest animal to walk on land was *Pederpes finneyae*, which lived around 350 million years ago. This tetrapod was discovered in 1971 north of Dumbarton, UK. The identification of the legs and one complete foot was announced on 4 July 2002. The identification was made by Jenny Clack (UK), from the University Museum of Zoology, University of Cambridge, UK.

LONGEST PREHISTORIC TUSKS

The longest tusks of any prehistoric animal were those of the straight-tusked elephant (*Hesperoloxodon antiques germanicus*), which lived in what is now northern Germany about two million years ago. The average length in adult bulls was 5 m (16 ft).

OLDEST FLOWERING PLANT

On 3 May 2002, scientists announced the discovery of the fossilized remains of the earliest flowering plant discovered to date. At least 125 million years old, and named *Archaefructus sinensis* ('ancient fruit from China'), it was found in stone in northeast China and is possibly the ancestor of all the flowering plants in the world today. Its closest living relative may be the water lily, as the ancient plant lived in clear shallow water, with its flowers and seeds extending above the surface.

LARGEST EVER CARNIVORE

In 1995, a skeleton of the largest predatory dinosaur was discovered in Neuquen, Patagonia, Argentina. This new dinosaur, *Giganotosaurus carolinii* (above), was 12.5 m (40 ft) long, and weighed 8 tonnes (17,000 lb). The bones suggest that it was both taller and more heavily built than *Tyrannosaurus rex*. It lived about 110 million years ago so is 30 million years older than *T. rex*.

LARGEST PREHISTORIC FLYING BIRD

The largest known flying bird was the giant teratorn *Argentavis magnificens*, which lived in Argentina about 6–8 million years ago. Fossil remains discovered at a site 160 km (100 miles) west of Buenos Aires, Argentina, in 1979 indicate that this gigantic vulture-like bird had a wing span of possibly up to 7.6 m (25 ft) and weighed about 80 kg (176 lb).

EARLIEST BIRD

The earliest fossil bird is known from two partial skeletons found in Texas, USA, in rocks dating back 220 million years. Named *Protoavis texensis* in 1991, this pheasant-sized creature has caused much controversy by pushing the age of birds back many millions of years from the previous record, that of the more familiar *Archaeopteryx lithographica* found in Jurassic sediments in Germany. It is unclear whether *Protoavis* will be widely accepted as a true bird, making *Archaeopteryx*, the 153 million-year-old crow-sized flier, the earliest unambiguous fossil bird.

EARLIEST DINOSAUR

Fossils of the oldest known dinosaur were found in 1996 in Madagascar by international scientists led by John Flynn (USA). Believed to date from 230 million years ago during the Triassic period, they may belong to prosauropods – plant-eating dinosaurs the size of a kangaroo, with a small head and a long neck.

LARGEST DINOSAUR EGGS

The largest known dinosaur eggs are those of *Hypselosaurus priscus* ('high ridge lizard', right), a 12-m-long (40-ft) titanosaurid which lived about 80 million years ago. Examples found in the Durance valley in France in October 1961 would have been, uncrushed, 30 cm (12 in) long – about the height of this page – and a diameter of 255 mm (10 in).

OLDEST FOSSIL SPIDER TRAPPED IN AMBER

The oldest fossil spider trapped in amber (below) has been dated to 125–135 million years old. It is from the family Linyphiidae, and was discovered in Lebanon and analysed by David Penney and Paul Selden (both University of Manchester, UK) who announced their discovery on 26 December 2002.

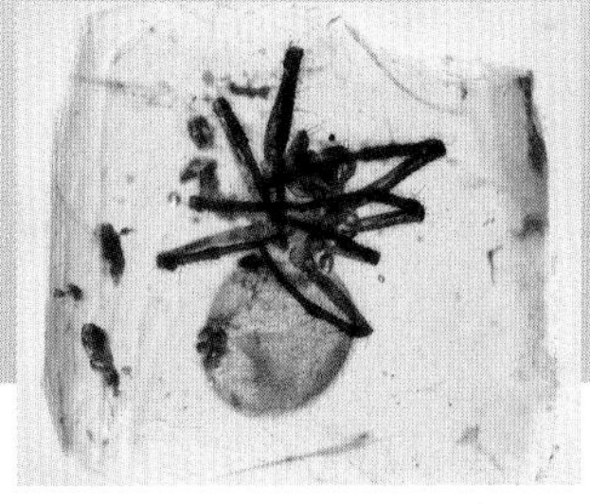

OLDEST CERATOPSIAN DINOSAUR

The oldest ceratopsian dinosaur discovered to date is *Liaoceratops*. It was discovered in the Yixian Formation, a fossil-rich rock bed in northeast China. The rocks date the creature at having lived 120–145 million years ago. This dog-sized herbivore was a precursor to the more famous *Triceratops*. The discovery was announced on 21 March 2002.

LARGEST FLYING CREATURE

The largest ever flying creature was the pterosaur *Quetzalcoatlus northropi* ('feathered serpent'). About 70 million years ago it soared over what is now Texas, Wyoming and New Jersey in the USA, Alberta in Canada, Senegal and Jordan. Partial remains found in Big Bend National Park, Texas, USA, in 1971 indicate that it must have had a wing span of 11–12 m (36–39 ft) and weighed about 86–113 kg (190-250 lb).

LARGEST PREHISTORIC CARNIVOROUS BIRD

The largest ever carnivorous bird was the *Titanis walleri*, known to have lived until the late Pleistocene (Ice Age) in Florida. It had a total body height of 2.5 m (8 ft) and its weight probably reached 200 kg (440 lb).

LARGEST TRILOBITE

The largest fossil trilobite was discovered in northern Manitoba, Canada, and measures over 70 cm (27.5 in) in length – more than 30 cm (12 in) longer than the previous largest trilobite. The discovery of the 445-million-year-old specimen was announced on 9 October 2000.

LARGEST PREHISTORIC INSECT

The largest prehistoric insect was the dragonfly *Meganeura monyi* which lived about 280 million years ago. Fossil remains found at Commentry, France, indicate a wing expanse possibly up to 70 cm (27.5 in).

LARGEST PLESIOSAUR

The largest plesiosaur ever to swim in the oceans was *Liopleurodon*, which was up to 25 m (82 ft) long. *Liopleurodon* was carnivorous and had a long (3 m or 10 ft) head, a short neck and four powerful flippers. These cousins of the dinosaurs lived in the late Jurassic period, between 165 and 150 million years ago.

BEST PRESERVED DINOSAUR REMAINS

'Leonardo', the fossilized remains of a 77-million-year-old duck-billed dinosaur, was discovered in northern Montana, USA, in the summer of 2000. The 7-m-long (23-ft) *Brachylophosaurus* is the fourth dinosaur ever discovered to be classified as a mummy. Around 90% of its body is covered in fossilized soft tissue, including skin, muscles, scales, footpads, and even its last meal has been preserved in its stomach. The creature was between three and four years old when it died.

LONGEST DINOSAUR

The longest vertebrate on record was a diplodocid excavated in 1980 from New Mexico, USA. Named *Seismosaurus halli*, it was estimated to be 39–52 m (128–170 ft) long based on comparisons of individual bones. In 1999, the bones were reconstructed at the Wyoming Dinosaur Center, to measure a total length of 41 m (134 ft). It was disassembled in August 1999 to tour the USA.

LARGEST DINOSAUR FOOTPRINT

In 1932 the gigantic footprints of a large bipedal hadrosaurid ('duckbill') measuring 1.36 m (4 ft 5.5 in) in length and 81 cm (32 in) wide were discovered in Salt Lake City, Utah, USA.

TALLEST DINOSAUR

Dinosaur remains found in 1994 in Oklahoma, USA, belong to what is believed to be the largest creature to have ever walked the earth. The *Sauroposeidon* stood at 18 m (60 ft) tall and weighed 60 tonnes (132,000 lb). Its neck is about a third longer than that of the *Brachiosaurus*, its nearest competitor. It lived about 110 million years ago, during the mid-Cretaceous period.

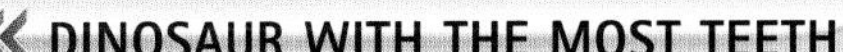

DINOSAUR WITH THE MOST TEETH

The dinosaur with the most teeth was the duck-billed hadrosaur (left), which, despite being a herbivore with a toothless beak, had up to 960 self-sharpening cheek teeth in the side of its strong jaws for chewing tough plants.

THE UNIVERSE

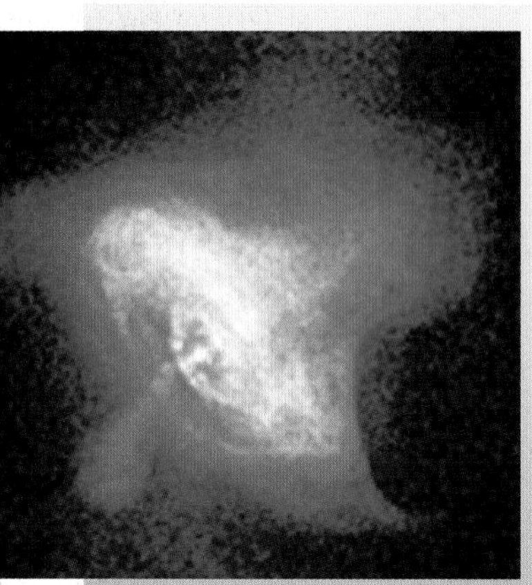

BRIGHTEST REMNANT OF A SUPERNOVA

The Crab Nebula (M1, above) in the constellation of Taurus is the brightest supernova remnant in the sky. It has a magnitude of 8.4. The picture above, captured by the Chandra X-ray space telescope in August 1999, shows the rapidly spinning pulsar at its centre.

LONGEST CHANNEL IN THE SOLAR SYSTEM

The longest channel in the Solar System is Baltis Vallis on Venus. It is around 7,000 km (4,300 miles) in length and has an average width of around 1.6 km (1 mile). It was discovered by the Magellan radar mapper, which orbited Venus from May 1989 to October 1994, and is believed to have been formed by molten lava.

LARGEST KUIPER BELT OBJECT

The Kuiper Belt is a vast belt of icy bodies beyond the orbit of Neptune. The largest object found there is 2002 LM60, which measures around 1,300 km (800 miles) across. It was first discovered by Chad Trujillo and Mike Brown (both USA) at Caltech, Pasadena, California, USA, on 4 June 2002. It is the largest object discovered in the Solar System since Pluto was found in 1930. The discoverers have proposed the name 'Quaoar' for this new world, after a creation god of the Tongva tribe – the original inhabitants of the Los Angeles area. It orbits the Sun at a distance of around 6 billion km (4 billion miles) and has an orbital period of 288 years.

FAINTEST PLANET IN THE SOLAR SYSTEM

The faintest of the nine planets as seen from Earth is Pluto (magnitude 15.0), which can only be viewed through a telescope.

PLANET WITH THE GREATEST AXIAL TILT

Uranus has the greatest axial tilt of all the planets in the Solar System. Its axis of spin is tilted 97.86 degrees from the plane of its orbit. The Earth's axis of tilt is 23.45 degrees.

LARGEST STRUCTURE IN THE UNIVERSE

The largest structure found to date in the universe is the Great Wall. This giant sheet or filament of galaxies was discovered in 1989 by Margaret Geller and John Huchra (both USA) while analysing data from the Harvard-Smithsonian Center for Astrophysics (CfA) Redshift survey. It has been estimated at being around 270 x 700 million light years in extent, and around 15 million light years thick. One light year is the distance light travels in a year, about 9.5 trillion km (6 trillion miles). Although invisible to the naked eye, the Great Wall stretches across the whole of the northern sky.

NEAREST BROWN DWARF

Brown dwarfs are often called 'failed stars'. Like other stars, they form from clouds of galactic gas and dust that collapse under their own gravity. The nearest brown dwarf to the Earth is Epsilon Indi B, a companion to the star Epsilon Indi which is 11.8 light years away. First seen in archive photographs, its nature was confirmed by astronomers using the 3.5-m (11-ft 6-in) New Technology Telescope at La Silla Observatory, Chile. Its discovery was announced on 15 January 2003.

MOST LUMINOUS OBJECT

Believed to be the most luminous object in the universe, quasar APM08279+5255 was discovered in March 1998 by a team of astronomers using the 2.5-m (8-ft) Isaac Newton Telescope (INT) at La Palma, Canary Islands, Spain. This quasar is between four and five million billion times brighter than the Sun and is estimated to be more than 10 times brighter than any other known quasar.

FASTEST METEOR SHOWER

The fastest annual meteor shower is the Leonids, which occurs between 15 and 20 November. Entering the Earth's atmosphere at around 71 km (44 miles) per second, the Leonids begin to glow at an altitude of around 155 km (96 miles). The high speed of the Leonids is because the motion of the parent meteoroid stream from comet P/55 Tempel-Tuttle is almost directly opposite to the orbital motion of Earth around the Sun. This causes an almost head-on collision between the tiny particles and the Earth.

MOST DISTANT OBJECT IN THE UNIVERSE

It was announced on 15 March 2002 that astronomers using the Keck II observatory in Hawaii, USA, have discovered a galaxy (HCM 6A) with a redshift of 6.56, corresponding to a distance of around 13 billion light years. Light from the galaxy provides a snapshot of the universe when it was just 780 million years old.

LARGEST VISIBLE LUNAR CRATER

The largest wholly visible crater is the walled plain Bailly, towards the Moon's South Pole, which is 295 km (183 miles) across, with walls rising to 4,250 m (14,000 ft).

FASTEST WINDS IN THE SOLAR SYSTEM

The planet Neptune (below) has the fastest winds of any world in the Solar System. Measured by NASA's Voyager 2 probe in 1989, they blow at around 2,400 km/h (1,500 mph).

PLANET WITH THE MOST SATELLITES

In March 2003 astronomers announced the discovery of four new tiny moons orbiting the giant planet Jupiter, bringing its total number of natural satellites to 52. A team led by Scott Sheppard and David Jewitt (both USA) of the University of Hawaii, USA, made the discovery using the 3.6-m (11-ft 9.6-in) Canada France Hawaii Telescope, Hawaii, USA.

YOUNGEST LUNAR CRATER

In December 2002 US scientists announced their discovery of a fresh crater on the Moon. The 2-km (1.2-mile) wide crater is in the same location as a bright flash photographed in 1953 by amateur astronomer Leon Stuart (USA). This is the only lunar crater known to have been formed in modern times. The asteroid that caused this crater would have been around 300 m (980 ft) across and would have detonated on impact with a force around 35 times more powerful than the Hiroshima bomb.

MOST MASSIVE STAR VISIBLE TO THE NAKED EYE

Eta Carinae (seen above in an image by the Hubble Space Telescope) is a rare supergiant, some 9,000 light years from Earth. With a mass estimated at between 100 and 200 times that of the Sun, it is one of the most massive stars in the galaxy. Today, along with its surrounding gas, it is just visible to the naked eye, with a magnitude of 6.21. Around 150 years ago it became one of the brightest stars in the sky, as it underwent massive explosive outbursts. It is one of the most unstable stars known to astronomers, and will almost certainly destroy itself in a supernova at some time in the future.

MOST DISTANT PLANET

The most distant extrasolar planet detected to date is around 5,000 light years away. Roughly the same size as our own giant planet Jupiter, this world, known as Ogle-TR-56b, orbits its parent star once every 29 hours. It was discovered by astronomers at the Harvard-Smithsonian Center for Astrophysics, Massachusetts, USA, and announced on 6 January 2003.

OLDEST STAR IN THE MILKY WAY

In 2002 a team led by Norbert Christlieb (Germany) announced that they had identified the oldest star in our own Milky Way galaxy. Called HE0107-5240, it is a giant star around 36,000 light years from Earth. Its age is measured by its composition. When the universe was formed, it consisted of hydrogen with some helium. As it evolved, the rest of the chemical elements appeared, formed by nuclear synthesis in stars. HE0107-5240 has almost no metal content in it – it has only 1/200,000th of the metal content of our own Sun, meaning it must have formed from clouds of gas consisting of almost pure hydrogen and helium when the universe was young. It could date back to over 13 billion years ago.

NEAREST SUPER-MASSIVE BLACK HOLE

Unlike normal black holes, which weigh several times the mass of the Sun, supermassive black holes reside in the hearts of galaxies and can be as massive as several hundred million times that of the Sun. Many astronomers now believe that such a terrifying force exists at the centre of our own galaxy, the Milky Way, only 30,000 light years away.

NEAREST PLANETARY NEBULA

At a distance of around 400 light years, the Helix Nebula (also known as NGC 7293) is the closest planetary nebula to the Earth. It formed when a dying star threw off its outer layers, which are gradually expanding into space. Planetary nebulae are so called because astronomers originally believed they were new planets. The Helix Nebula is around 100 times more distant than the nearest stars (excluding the Sun). If the Helix Nebula was bright enough to be visible to the naked eye, it would cover an area around half the size of the full Moon.

CLIMATE & WEATHER

WARMEST YEAR ON RECORD
The warmest year since records began (around 1880) was 1998. It was 0.57°C (1.026°F) warmer than the average global temperature, measured between 1961 and 1990. The 1990s was the warmest decade on record: the six warmest years on record were all in the 1990s.

GREATEST DISPLAY OF SOLAR HALOS
On 11 January 1999 at least 24 types of solar halo (below) were witnessed by scientists at the geographic South Pole. They are formed by sunlight being reflected and refracted by ice crystals in the atmosphere, causing rings around the Sun and bright coloured patches in the sky. Atmospheric conditions at the South Pole are conducive to this type of phenomenon.

MOST POWERFUL SHORT-TERM NATURAL CLIMATE CHANGE
The El Niño Southern Oscillation occurs as a result of cyclic warming of the eastern and central Pacific Ocean. Apart from the seasonal effects of the Earth moving around the Sun, it is the most powerful short-term natural climate change on Earth. The entire cycle of El Niño and La Niña (its cooler counterpart and opposite) lasts between three and seven years. It causes unusual weather conditions all around the world, particularly notable in the 1982/83 and 1997/98 events.

EARLIEST IMAGE OF A SPRITE
Sprites are atmospheric electrical phenomena associated with lightning. These unusual flashes shoot upwards from the tops of thunderstorms to altitudes up to 100 km (62 miles) above the surface of the Earth. Historical reports of these phenomena were not taken seriously until the first image was taken, accidently, in 1989 when a low-level-light TV camera was pointed above a thunderstorm. Sprites have since been caught on video from the US space shuttle. Scientists have yet to fully understand them.

GREATEST TEMPERATURE RANGE
The greatest recorded temperature ranges in the world are around the Siberian 'cold pole' in the east of Russia. Temperatures in Verkhoyansk (67°33'N, 133°23'E) have ranged 105°C (188°F), from -68°C (-90°F) to 37°C (98°F).

The greatest temperature variation recorded in a single day is 56°C (100°F). The temperature fell from 7°C (44°F) to -49°C (-56°F) at Browning, Montana, USA, between 23 and 24 January 1916.

CLOUDS WITH THE GREATEST VERTICAL RANGE
In the tropics, cumulonimbus has been observed to reach a height of nearly 20,000 m (65,600 ft), nearly 2.5 times the height of Mt Everest.

HIGHEST ATMOSPHERIC PHENOMENA
Of all the phenomena visible in our skies, the very highest are the aurorae, also known as the northern and southern lights. Often visible at night from low and high latitudes, these coloured, shimmering lights are the result of charged particles from the Sun interacting with the upper atmosphere. The lowest aurorae occur at altitudes of around 100 km (62 miles), with highest extending up to around 400 km (248 miles).

MOST STROKES IN A LIGHTNING FLASH
Most lightning flashes consist of several 'strokes' - major pulses of current. It is these pulses which cause some flashes to appear to flicker. The most pulses detected in a single flash is 26, in a cloud-to-ground flash in New Mexico, USA, noted by Marx Brook (USA) in 1962.

WETTEST PLACE
By average annual rainfall, the wettest place in the world is Mawsynram, in Meghalaya State, India, with 11,873 mm (467 in) per annum.

DRIEST PLACE
Between 1964 and 2001 the average annual rainfall for the meteorological station in Quillagua, in the Atacama Desert, Chile, was just 0.5 mm (0.02 in). This discovery was made during the making of the documentary series *Going to Extremes*, by Keo Films in 2001. The weather station has an 802-m (2,631-ft) elevation and is located at 21°38'S, 69°33'W.

LARGEST SNOWFLAKE
It is reported that on 28 January 1887 at Fort Keogh, Montana, USA, ranch owner Matt Coleman (USA) measured a snowflake that was 38 cm (15 in) wide and 20 cm (8 in) thick, which he later described as being 'larger than milk pans' in *Monthly Weather Review* magazine.

HEAVIEST HAILSTONES
The heaviest hailstones on record weighed up to 1 kg (2 lb) and are reported to have killed 92 people in the Gopalganj area of Bangladesh on 14 April 1986.

GREATEST MONTHLY RAINFALL
For a calendar month, the rainfall record is 9,300 mm (366 in) at Cherrapunji, Meghalaya, India, in July 1861, and the 12-month record was also set at Cherrapunji, with 26,461 mm (1,041.75 in) between 1 August 1860 and 31 July 1861.

>> LARGEST MIRAGE
The largest mirage on record was that sighted in 1913 in the Arctic at 83°N, 103°W by Donald B MacMillan (USA). It appeared as the same 'hills, valleys and snow-capped peaks' that Robert Peary (USA) had misidentified as Crocker Land six years earlier.

On 17 July 1939 a mirage of Snaefellsjkull (alt 1,446 m or 4,744 ft) on Iceland was seen from the sea from 540–560 km (335–350 miles) away.

HIGHEST SHADE TEMPERATURE

The highest shade temperature ever recorded is 58°C (136°F) at Al'Aziziyah in the Sahara Desert, Libya, on 13 September 1922.

GREATEST RAINFALL IN 24 HOURS

A record 1,870 mm (73 in) of rain fell in 24 hours in Cilaos (alt 1,200 m or 3,940 ft), Réunion, Indian Ocean, on 15 and 16 March 1952. This is equal to an astonishing 7,554 tonnes (16,653,700 lb) of rain per acre.

FASTEST WIND SPEED

Scientists using the 'Doppler on Wheels' mobile weather observatory (University of Oklahoma, USA) recorded a 486 +/-32 km/h (302 +/-20 mph) wind speed associated with a large tornado near Bridge Creek, Oklahoma, USA, on 3 May 1999. The previous record was measured using a 3-mm Doppler radar, which registered a 460-km/h (286-mph) wind speed associated with a tornado near Red Rock, Oklahoma, USA, on 26 April 1991. For both speeds, the measurement was taken 30–60 m (100–200 ft) above the ground. The ground speed is not known.

MOST INTENSE RAINFALL

Difficulties attend rainfall readings for very short periods, but the figure of 38.1 mm (1.8 in) in one minute at Basse-Terre, Guadeloupe, in the Caribbean, on 26 November 1970 is seen as the most intense recorded by modern methods.

MOST TORNADOES BY AREA

The highest frequency of tornadoes by area is reported in the UK where in an average year one tornado is reported per 7,397 km^2 (2,856 mile^2). The equivalent figure for the USA is one tornado per 8,663 km^2 (3,345 mile^2).

LARGEST PIECE OF FALLEN ICE

On 13 August 1849 a 6-m-long (20-ft) piece of ice was reported to have fallen from the sky in Scotland, UK, after a clap of thunder. The ice was clear but looked like it was made up of smaller pieces. One possible explanation is that hailstones were fused together by lightning.

COLDEST PERMANENTLY INHABITED PLACE

The coldest permanently inhabited place is the Siberian village of Oymyakon (pop 4,000), 63°16'N, 143°15'E (alt 700 m or 2,300 ft), in Russia, where the temperature reached -68°C (-90°F) in 1933, and an unofficial -72°C (-98°F) has been published more recently.

MOST TORNADOES IN 24 HOURS

The record number of tornadoes over a 24-hour period is 148. They swept through 'Tornado Alley' – the southern and mid-western USA – between 3 and 4 April 1974.

LARGEST MEASURED TORNADO

The largest measured tornado occurred on 3 May 1999 near Mulhall, Oklahoma, USA. Its diameter, around 1,600 m (5,250 ft), was measured using the University of Oklahoma's 'Doppler on Wheels' mobile weather observatory operated by Joshua Wurman (USA).

LONGEST ICE AGE

Geological evidence suggests that Earth endured many severe ice ages in its early history. The longest and most severe was between 2.3 and 2.4 billion years ago, and lasted around 70 million years.

NATURAL DISASTERS

WORST DROUGHT FAMINE

The worst famine caused by drought was in northern China in 1876–79, when between 9 and 13 million people are estimated to have died after the rains failed for three consecutive years. At around the same time (1876–78), approximately five million Indians died when the monsoon failed in successive years.

GREATEST RECORDED CLIMATIC IMPACT OF A VOLCANIC ERUPTION

The cataclysmic 1815 eruption of the Tambora volcano in Indonesia caused global average temperatures to drop by as much as 3°C (5.4°F). It led to 1816 being known as 'the year without summer', with massive crop failures and other weather-related disruptions throughout Europe and North America. The eruption killed around 92,000 people – the highest death toll from a volcanic eruption.

GREATEST FLOOD

Roughly 18,000 years ago an ancient 120-km (75-mile) long lake in Siberia ruptured, causing the greatest freshwater flood in history. The discovery of this event in 1993 suggests a catastrophic flood 490 m (1,600 ft) deep and travelling at 160 km/h (100 mph).

HIGHEST DEATH TOLL FROM A FLOOD

When the Huang He (Yellow River), Huayan Kou, China, flooded its banks in October 1887, 900,000 people are believed to have been killed.

WORST HOMELESS TOLL FROM A FLOOD DISASTER

Monsoon rains caused extensive river flooding in India's Bengal state during September 1978 with 15 million out of a population of 44 million made homeless. London's population is just over seven million: this disaster would have made twice London's population homeless.

FURTHEST DISTANCE FROM WHERE A VOLCANIC ERUPTION HAS BEEN HEARD

On 27 August 1883, when the Krakatau volcano on the island of Rakata, Indonesia, erupted, it was heard by people on Rodriguez Island 4,653 km (2,908 miles) away. According to witnesses, it sounded like the distant roar of heavy guns and continued at intervals of three to four hours during the night. Krakatau erupted with a force nearly 10,000 times that of the atom bomb dropped on Hiroshima, Japan. It caused a tsunami wave 40 m (131 ft) high, throwing a steamship 2.5 km (1.6 miles) off course.

COSTLIEST NATURAL DISASTER

The devastating Kobe earthquake of January 1995 in Japan resulted in overall losses of $100 billion (£63.04 billion), making it the costliest natural disaster to befall any one country. The quake measured 7.2 on the Richter scale, killed more than 6,400 people and injured around 27,000.

HIGHEST DEATH TOLL FROM A TSUNAMI

Up to 27,000 people drowned when a giant tsunami inundated the Japanese coastline on the Sea of Japan in 1896. Japan has about 1,500 seismic occurrences every year, the most recent major one being in Kobe in January 1995.

GREATEST MASS EXTINCTION

Approximately 248 million years ago, at the end of the Permian geological period, a mass extinction wiped out around 90% of all marine species and 70% of all higher land animals. Its cause is not known.

MOST PEOPLE TRAPPED IN AN AVALANCHE DISASTER

A total of 240 people died and over 45,000 were trapped on 20 January 1951 when a series of avalanches, caused by a combination of hurricane-force winds and wet snow (due to heavy rain) overlaying powder snow, thundered through the Swiss, Austrian and Italian Alps.

>> FASTEST AVALANCHE

The volcanic explosion of Mt St Helens, Washington, USA (right), on 18 May 1980 triggered the fastest recorded avalanche in history down its north slope. The velocity reached a staggering 402.3 km/h (250 mph).

WORST DAMAGE TOLL FROM A CYCLONE DISASTER

Hurricane Andrew (above), which hit Homestead, Florida, USA, between 23 and 26 August 1992, caused an estimated $15.5 billion (£7.8 billion) worth of damage in terms of insured losses.

WORST DEATH TOLL FROM AN AVALANCHE DISASTER

An estimated 40,000–80,000 men died during the First World War in the Tyrolean Alps, owing to avalanches triggered by gunfire.

HIGHEST TSUNAMI WASH

The highest tsunami ever reported was 524 m (1,719 ft) high and occurred along the fjord-like Lituya Bay, Alaska, USA, on 9 July 1958. It was caused by a giant landslip and moved at a terrifying 160 km/h (100 mph). This wave was so high it would easily have swamped the Petronas Towers in Kuala Lumpur, Malaysia, which at 452 m (1,483 ft) are the world's tallest office buildings.

WORST HOMELESS TOLL FROM A CYCLONE DISASTER

Hurricane Mitch, which struck Central America (Honduras and Nicaragua) between 26 October and 4 November 1998, destroyed 93,690 dwellings and left around 2.5 million people dependent on international aid.

WORST DAMAGE TOLL FROM A LANDSLIDE DISASTER

A total of $138 million (£57 million) worth of damage was caused in southern California, USA, by a series of mudslides brought about by nine days of torrential rain and a subtropical storm that raged between 18 and 26 January 1969.

DEADLIEST LAKE

The lake responsible for the most deaths without drowning is Lake Nyos in Cameroon, west Africa, where toxic gases have claimed nearly 2,000 lives in recent decades. On one night in August 1986, between 1,600 and 1,800 people and countless animals were killed by a large natural release of carbon dioxide gas. Scientists disagree on the source of Lake Nyos' deadly gas. Some believe that the decomposition of organic material near the bottom of the lake causes the gas to build up, and seasonal changes in surface temperature triggers mixing of deep and shallow water, allowing the gas to be released. Because Nyos lies in the crater of an old volcano, others believe that the gas is volcanic in origin.

HIGHEST TSUNAMI LANDSLIDE

The highest tsunami triggered by a submarine landslide was one which struck the island of Lanai in Hawaii, USA, c.105,000 years ago. It deposited sediment up to an altitude of approximately 375 m (1,230 ft).

WORST DEATH TOLL FROM A LIGHTNING STRIKE

A total of 81 people aboard a Boeing 707 jet airliner died when the plane was struck by lightning near Elkton, Maryland, USA, on 8 December 1963.

HIGHEST EARTHQUAKE TSUNAMI

The highest tsunami or giant wave caused by an offshore earthquake appeared off Ishigaki Island, Ryukyu island chain, Japan, on 24 April 1771. It was possibly as high as 85 m (279 ft), and tossed a 750-tonne (1,653,000-lb) block of coral more than 2.5 km (1.5 miles) inland.

MOST TREES DESTROYED BY STORMS

Around 270 million trees were felled or split by storms that hit France on 26 and 27 December 1999. The storm lasted 30 hours and caused 87 deaths. The damage was estimated at FF 52.3 billion (£5 billion or $8 billion). In Paris, the Bois de Boulogne and Bois de Vincennes lost 140,000 trees. It will take an estimated 100 to 200 years to replace some of the forests.

MOST WATERLOGGED CITY

Venice (below) is the most frequently flooded city on Earth. Early in the 20th century Venice flooded four or five times a year; by 1989 this number had increased to 40. By 1998 the squares and streets were flooded one day in three. In the next 50 years it is estimated that the water level in Venice will rise by 20.3 cm (8 in).

HIGHEST WASTE GENERATION

The USA produces the most municipal waste per capita in the world, according to figures issued by the Organization for Economic Cooperation and Development in 1999. The estimated figure stands at 720 kg (1,585 lb) per capita.

WORST COASTAL DAMAGE FROM AN ENVIRONMENTAL DISASTER

On 25 March 1989 the *Exxon Valdez* oil tanker ran aground in Prince William Sound, Alaska, USA, spilling over 41 million litres (9 million gal) of oil. In total 2,400 km (1,500 miles) of coastline was polluted.

WORST OIL TANKER SPILL

The collision of the *Atlantic Empress* with the *Aegean Captain* off Tobago in the Caribbean Sea on 19 July 1979 resulted in the loss of 161.6 million litres (35.5 million gal) of oil.

WORST OIL SPILL DISASTER

The world's worst oil spill occurred as a result of a marine blow-out beneath the drilling rig *Ixtoc I* in the Gulf of Campeche, Gulf of Mexico, on 3 June 1979. The oil slick reached an incredible length of 640 km (400 miles) by 5 August 1979. It was eventually capped on 24 March 1980 after an estimated loss of up to 635 million litres (140 million gal).

MOST ACIDIC ACID RAIN

A pH reading of 1.87 was recorded at Inverpolly Forest in the Scottish Highlands, UK, in 1983, and 2.83 was recorded over the Great Lakes, USA/Canada, in 1982. These are the lowest pH levels ever recorded in acid precipitation, making it the most acidic acid rain. pH values range from 0 to 14, with 7 being neutral. The lower the number, the higher the acid level of any given substance.

MOST POLLUTED MAJOR CITY

Mexico City (above) is the world's most polluted major city and the most polluted capital city. It is classified as having serious problems with sulphur dioxide, suspended particulate matter, carbon monoxide and ozone – in all of which World Health Organization (WHO) guidelines are exceeded by more than a factor of two – plus moderate to heavy pollution for lead and nitrogen dioxide. The city's altitude, its climate and its location contribute to the problem, since emissions are trapped by the surrounding mountains.

WORST ACID RAIN DAMAGE TO FORESTS

The Czech Republic has the greatest damage to forests caused by acid rain, with 71% of the country's forests being affected. Temperate forests are the most seriously affected by acid rain.

WORST MARINE POLLUTION

A fertilizer factory on Minamata Bay, Kyushu, Japan, deposited mercury waste into the sea between 1953 and 1967. Up to 20,000 people were affected, 4,500 seriously, and 43 people died from the poisoning.

GREATEST SULPHUR DIOXIDE POLLUTION

The Bulgarian Maritsa power complex releases 350,000 tonnes (770 million lb) of sulphur dioxide into the Maritsa River every year. Sulphur dioxide is an acidic gas which, when released into the atmosphere, combines with water vapour in the clouds to form sulphuric acid. This is one of the major causes of acid rain.

WORST NUCLEAR WASTE ACCIDENT

The overheating of a nuclear waste container caused the December 1957 explosion at a complex at Kyshtym in Russia, which released radioactive compounds that dispersed over a vast area. More than 30 small communities within a 1,200-km² (460-mile²) area were eliminated from maps of the USSR in the three years following the accident, and about 17,000 people were evacuated.

MOST DEVASTATING AIR POLLUTION

More than 6,300 people have died from the effects of a poisonous cloud of methyl isocyanate that escaped on 3 December 1984 from a Union Carbide pesticide plant near Bhopal, Madhya Pradesh, India. The gas was released into the air when a valve in the underground storage tank failed. Survivors still suffer from damage to their brains, lungs, livers and kidneys, as well as being blinded.

LARGEST DEFORESTATION

Between 1990 and 2000 Brazil cleared an average area of forest of 22,264 km² (8,596 miles²) every year (an area almost equivalent to El Salvador). Between 1994 and 1995, deforestation rates in Brazil nearly doubled to about 29,000 km² (11,200 miles²) annually. This is the greatest increase in the rate of deforestation ever recorded. Since then, rates have returned to the levels of the early 1990s – about 13,000 km² (5,000 miles²) per year.

WORST NUCLEAR REACTOR DISASTER

A nuclear reactor disaster at Chernobyl No. 4 (right) in the former USSR (now Ukraine) on 26 April 1986 at 1:23 am local time resulted in an official Soviet death toll of 31 people. No proper records were kept of subsequent deaths, but over 1.7 million people were exposed to radiation.

MOST DEVASTATING ANIMAL INTRODUCTION

In 1859 a farmer introduced 24 wild rabbits to Australia. With few natural predators, the rabbit population exploded. They eat crops, chew the bark of young trees and their burrows damage the soil. There are now over 300 million rabbits in Australia.

WORST DESTRUCTION OF THE NATURAL ENVIRONMENT BY FIRE

Deliberately-lit forest fires made 1997 the worst year in recorded history for the destruction of the natural environment. The largest and most numerous were in Brazil, where they ranged along a 1,600 km (1,000 mile) front.

WORST RIVER POLLUTION

On 1 November 1986 firemen fighting a blaze at the Sandoz chemical works in Basel, Switzerland, flushed 30 tonnes (66,150 lb) of agricultural chemicals into the river Rhine. Half a million fish died as a result.

LOWEST RECORDED OZONE LAYER LEVELS

Ozone levels reached a record low on 28 September 1994 over the South Pole in Antarctica, when a figure of 88 Dobson units (DU) was recorded. A figure of 300 DU is considered adequate to shield the Earth from solar ultraviolet radiation and sustain our biological systems.

LARGEST HOLE IN THE OZONE LAYER

In September 2000, scientists at NASA's Goddard Space Flight Center, Maryland, USA, detected the largest hole so far in the ozone layer. With an area of around 28.3 million km^2 (11 million miles^2), the hole above Antarctica is three times the area of the USA.

LOWEST CARBON DIOXIDE EMISSIONS

Of the major industrialized nations, France has the lowest emissions of carbon dioxide (CO_2). France's commitment to nuclear power has helped cut her fossil fuel-related CO_2 emissions. In 1999 France released around 400 million tonnes (880 billion lb) of CO_2 into the atmosphere.

HIGHEST CARBON DIOXIDE EMISSIONS PER CAPITA

The United Arab Emirates (UAE) has the highest carbon dioxide (CO_2) emissions per capita. In 1995 the emissions level reached 30.9 tonnes (68,100 lb) of CO_2 per capita. The total amount of CO_2 emissions for the UAE in 1995 was 68.3 million tonnes (150.5 billion lb).

WORST MARINE OIL POLLUTION

In the 1991 Gulf War, Saddam Hussein (Iraq) ordered oil refineries in Kuwait to release a total of 908 million litres (200 million gal) of oil into the Persian Gulf. This was over 20 times larger than the oil spill from the *Exxon Valdez*. Iraqi forces set fire to 600 oil wells, which created clouds of black smoke that deposited soot as far away as the Himalayas in India.

HIGHEST CARBON DIOXIDE EMISSIONS

The USA has the highest emissions of CO_2, one of the key gases responsible for the 'greenhouse effect'. In 2000 the USA emitted around 5,800 million tonnes (11,600 billion lb) of CO_2, a 3.1% increase on 1999. The burning of fossil fuels is a primary cause.

MOST LETHAL SMOG

Between 3,500 and 4,000 people, mainly the elderly and children, died in London, UK, from acute bronchitis caused by thick smog between 4 and 9 December 1952. It was caused by the burning of fossil fuels combined with a weather inversion that trapped smoke particles near the ground. Visibility in the streets was only 30 cm (12 in) and cinemas had to close because it was impossible to see the screens.

LONGEST RUNNING ENVIRONMENTAL CAMPAIGN

Greenpeace has been campaigning against nuclear testing since it was founded in 1971, with the first campaign directed against nuclear testing off the Alaskan coast. The environmental organization is still campaigning on the nuclear issue worldwide.

LARGEST PRODUCER OF COMMERCIAL ENERGY

In 1995 the USA produced 75,387 petajoules (joules x 10^{15}) of commercial energy. USA resources include solid (eg coal), liquid (oil), and gaseous fuels as well as primary electricity.

DEEPEST UNDERGROUND NUCLEAR EXPLOSION

A 2.5-kiloton nuclear device was detonated at the bottom of a shaft 2,850 m (9,350 ft) deep at a location 60 km (37 miles) south of Nefte-yugamsk, Siberia, Russia, on 18 June 1985. The detonation was carried out in an attempt to stimulate oil production. For a comparison, the Hiroshima bomb had a yield of 20 kilotons.

LARGEST DIAMOND

A 3,106-carat diamond was found on 26 January 1905 at the Premier Diamond Mine, near Pretoria, South Africa, and presented to the reigning British monarch, Edward VII. Named 'The Cullinan', it was cut into 106 polished diamonds.

LARGEST MANMADE EXCAVATION

The Bingham Canyon copper mine near Salt Lake City, Utah, USA, is the world's largest manmade excavation. Since it began operations in 1906, more than 5.4 billion tonnes of rock have been excavated from it. It measures 4 km (2.5 miles) across and 0.8 km (0.5 miles) deep and is visible from space.

GREATEST OIL GUSHER

The greatest 'wildcat' ever recorded blew at Alborz No. 5 well, near Qum, Iran, on 26 August 1956. An incredible 62,100 kPa (9,000 lb/in²) of pressure blasted the uncontrolled oil to a height of 52 m (170 ft), producing 120,000 barrels per day. It was closed after 90 days' work by B Mostofi and Myron Kinley of Texas, USA.

OLDEST MINE

The oldest mine in the world is the chert (silica) mine at Nazlet Sabaha, Garb, Egypt. It is thought to have first been in use around 100,000 years ago.

LARGEST PRODUCER OF NATURAL DIAMONDS

The world's largest producer of natural diamonds is Australia, which provides around 34% of the world's annual production of 110 million carats. Owing to their relatively low quality, they only account for 5% of the annual value. Botswana diamonds are much higher quality and account for 21% of the world's annual production in terms of value.

LARGEST CRATER FROM AN UNDERGROUND NUCLEAR EXPLOSION

On 15 January 1965, a 104-kiloton nuclear device was detonated at the Semipalatinsk Test Site, Kazakhstan, 178 m (583 ft) beneath the dry bed of the Chagan river, leaving a crater 408 m (1,338 ft) wide with a maximum depth of 100 m (328 ft). A major lake later formed behind the 20–35 m (65–114 ft) upraised lip of the crater, which was then cut through with earthmoving equipment to allow it to be used as a reservoir.

HIGHEST OIL CONSUMPTION

The largest oil consumer in the world is the USA with 19.6 million barrels per day in 2001, 25% of the world's total.

LARGEST OIL FIELD

The Ghawar field in Saudi Arabia, developed by Saudi company Aramco, stretches over 240 x 35 km (150 x 22 miles), and has an EUR (estimated ultimate recovery) of 82 billion barrels of oil.

LARGEST OIL PRODUCING COMPANY

The world's largest oil producing company is the Saudi Arabian Oil Co. (Saudi Aramco) supplying 11% of the world's oil demand and controlling oil reserves of approximately 259 billion barrels (roughly 25% of the world's total and 12 times the US reserves).

FASTEST TIME TO SINK A MINE SHAFT

The one-month (31-day) world record for sinking a standard shaft, 7.9 m (26 ft) in diameter, is 381.3 m (1,251 ft) at Buffelsfontein Mine, Northern Province, South Africa, in March 1962.

LARGEST SOURCE OF WORLD ENERGY BY FUEL TYPE

In 1996 the largest source of world energy by fuel was oil, which generated 41% of the world's total energy. Coal was second, with 24% of the total.

LARGEST HYDROGEN BOMB CRATER

On 1 March 1954, the US government performed its largest ever nuclear weapons test on Bikini Atoll, Marshall Islands (Pacific Ocean). The 13.6-megaton hydrogen bomb explosion, code-named 'Bravo', vaporized two and a half islands and millions of tonnes of sand, coral, and sea and plant life. It left behind a crater (right) with a diameter of around 1,800 m (6,000 ft) and a depth of around 70 m (240 ft).

HEAVIEST OIL PLATFORM

The world's heaviest oil platform is the *Pampo* platform in the Campos Basin off Rio de Janeiro, Brazil, built and operated by the Petrobros company. Opened in the 1970s, the platform weighs 24,000 tonnes (52.9 million lb), covers 3,900 m² (42,000 ft²) and produces 33,000 barrels per day.

LARGEST PIECE OF AMBER

The largest piece of amber was unearthed in Sarawak, Malaysia, in 1991. The original size of the piece was several square metres, but it was impossible to excavate in one piece. It was broken up into smaller fragments, the largest of which weighs 23 kg (50 lb) and is now in the Staatliches Museum für Naturkunde in Stuttgart, Germany. This largest fragment of the original piece still breaks the previous record.

LONGEST ICE CORE

The longest ice core in the world measures 3,623 m (11,886 ft) in length and was drilled from the ice above Lake Vostok, Antarctica, in 1998. The drilling stopped at around 150 m (492 ft) above the surface of the lake in order to avoid possible contamination of the lake's pristine environment.

LARGEST NATURAL GAS PRODUCTION

The world's largest producer of natural gas in 2001 was the USA, with 697 billion m³ (24,641 billion ft³).

LARGEST NATURAL GAS FIELD

The Urengoy gas condensate field in Siberia, Russia, is the world's largest, with estimated reserves of 8 trillion m³ (282 trillion ft³). Discovered in 1966, it provides one third of the total annual Russian gas production.

DEEPEST PENETRATION INTO THE EARTH'S CRUST

A geological exploratory borehole near Zapolyarny on the Kola peninsula of Arctic Russia was begun on 24 May 1970. It reached a depth of 12,261 m (40,236 ft) by 1983, when work stopped due to lack of funds. The temperature of the rocks at the bottom of the hole is about 210°C (410°F). The object of the Kola hole was not oil or gas extraction but first-hand knowledge of the nature of the Earth's interior, particularly the 'zone of discontinuity'.

LONGEST OIL PIPELINE

The world's longest crude oil pipeline is the Interprovincial Pipe Line Inc. installation. It spans the North American continent from Edmonton, Alberta, Canada, through Chicago to Montreal – a distance of 3,787.2 km (2,353 miles). Along the pipe, 82 pumping stations maintain a flow of 254,000 m³ (1.6 million barrels) a day.

DEEPEST WATER BORE

The world's deepest water bore is the 2,231-m (7,320-ft) Stensvad Water Well 11-W1 drilled by the Great Northern Drilling Co. Inc. in Rosebud County, Montana, USA, from October/November 1961. The Thermal Power Co. geothermal steam well, begun in Sonoma County, California, USA, in 1955 is down to 2,752 m (9,029 ft).

GREATEST GEOTHERMAL POWER CAPACITY

The USA has the capacity to generate 2,700 megawatts of electricity directly from the Earth. The Geysers Power Plant, California, USA, is the largest geothermal plant in the world, and can generate 1,700 megawatts of electricity.

DEEPEST MINE

The Western Deep Levels gold mine in Carletonville, Gauteng, South Africa (below), is the world's deepest mine. A depth of 3,581 m (11,749 ft) was attained on 12 July 1977. The shaft is 2,072 m (6,800 ft) deep with a lift that winds at a maximum speed of 1,095 m (3,595 ft) per minute.

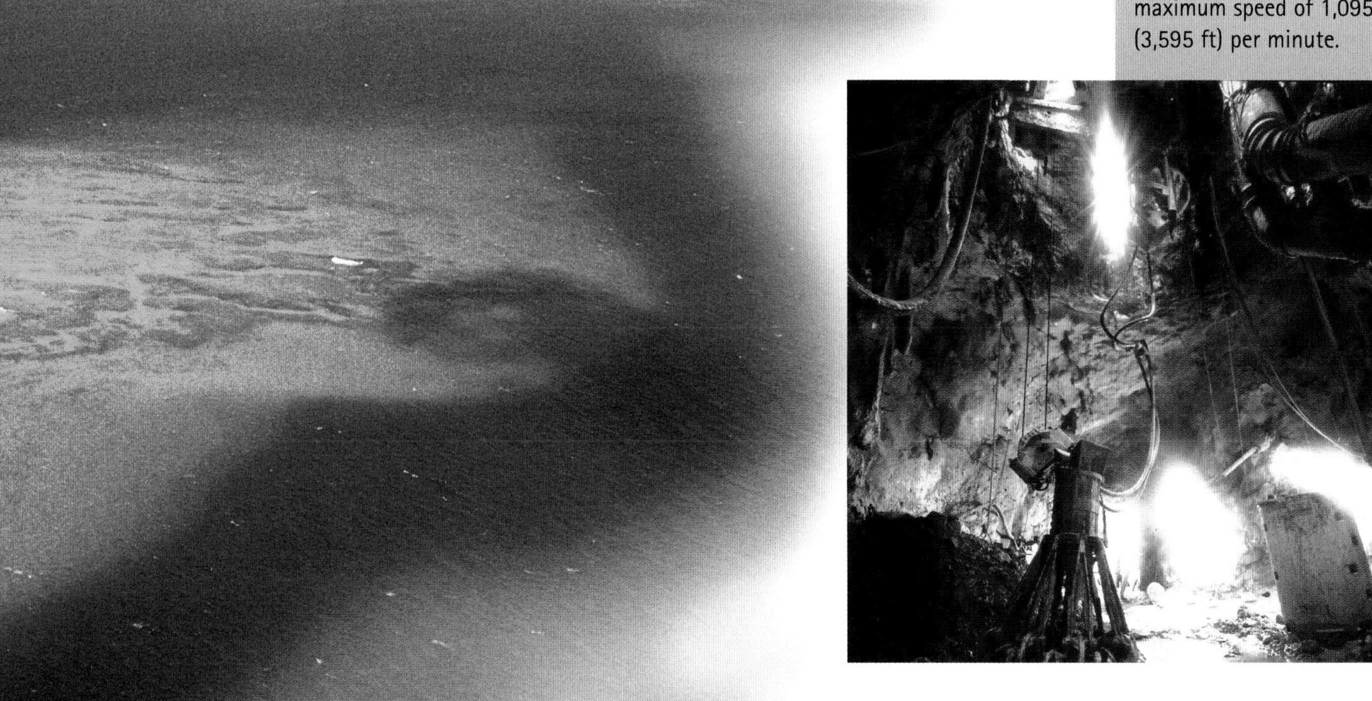

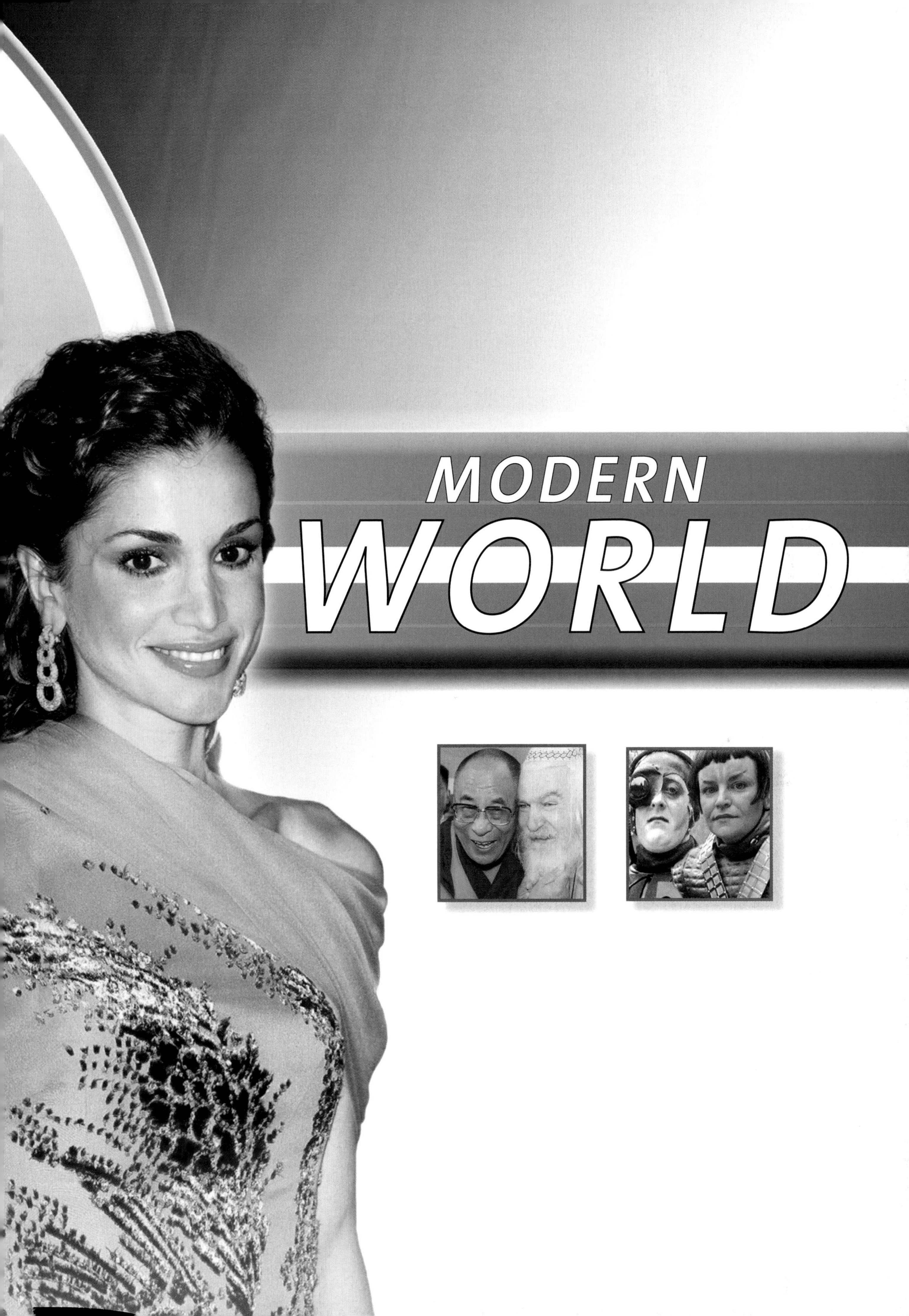

MODERN WORLD

NATIONS

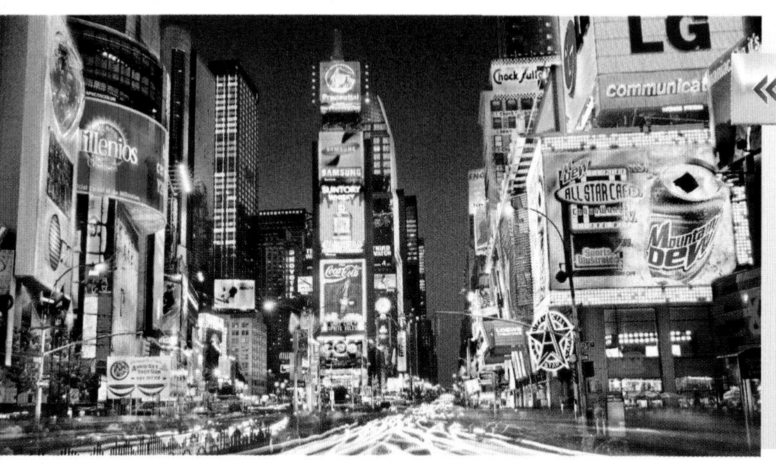

LARGEST ADVERTISING EXPENDITURE

The USA (Times Square, New York, USA, shown left) has the largest advertising expenditure, with $236.3 billion (£155.9 billion) spent in 2000. The estimated expenditure for 2001 was $233.7 billion (£161.2 billion) and the forecast for 2006 is $285 billion (£177 billion).

MOST COMMON SURNAME

The most common surname in the world is Li. China alone has 87 million people with this surname – accounting for 7.9% of the total population.

LARGEST SHORTAGE OF MEN

The country with the largest recorded shortage of males is Latvia, where 54% of the population is female.

MOST REMOTE CITY FROM THE SEA

The city most remote from the sea is Urumqi, the capital of China's Xinjiang Uygur autonomous region, which lies at a distance of about 2,500 km (1,500 miles) from the nearest coastline.

MOST CROSSED FRONTIER

The border crossed most often is that between the USA and Mexico. In 2000, over 290 million people crossed from Mexico into the USA, and a similar number passed in the opposite direction. This is equivalent to the entire population of the USA crossing the border twice in one year. Of the travellers crossing into the USA, 47 million were on foot, while the rest were carried in approximately 91 million personal vehicles and 270,000 buses. The border extends for 3,110 km (1,933 miles), with numerous border-crossing points.

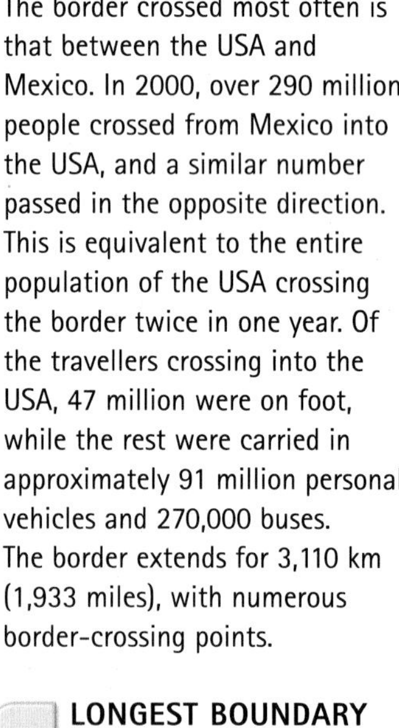

LONGEST BOUNDARY

The world's longest boundary lies between Canada and the USA. Including the Great Lakes boundaries but excluding the 2,547-km (1,582-mile) frontier with Alaska, the border extends for 6,416 km (3,986 miles). If the Alaskan boundary is added, the US-Canada boundary is 8,963 km (5,569 miles) long.

LONGEST COASTLINE

Canada has the longest coastline of any country in the world, with 243,798 km (151,489 miles) including islands.

MOST MARITIME BOUNDARIES

The country with the largest number of maritime boundaries is Indonesia, with 19 (including boundaries with disputed territorial claims).

HIGHEST GNI PER CAPITA

According to the World Bank Atlas, the country with the highest gross national income (GNI) for 2001 was Luxembourg, with a GNI of $41,777 (£28,826). GNI is the total value of goods and services produced by a country in one year, divided by its population. GNI per capita shows what part of a country's GNI each person would have if GNI were divided equally. The 2001 World Bank figures (of 205 countries) reveal that the USA ranks seventh with $34,870 (£24,060), and the UK is 16th with $24,230 (£16,718).

LOWEST GNI PER CAPITA

According to the World Bank Atlas, Ethiopia (members of Ethiopia's Karo tribe shown right) had the lowest GNI per capita in 2001, with a GNI of only $100 (£69).

LOWEST ROAD FATALITY RATE

Malta has the lowest fatality rate in road accidents with 1.6 per 100,000 population.

LOWEST AND HIGHEST LIFE EXPECTANCY

The country with the lowest life expectancy at birth, as of 2000, is Zambia with 38 years. Japan is the country with the highest life expectancy at birth, in 2000. The average for the total population is 80.7 years.

LARGEST SHORTAGE OF WOMEN

The country with the largest recorded shortage of women is the United Arab Emirates, where the male population numbers 66.6%.

OLDEST CAPITAL CITY

The oldest capital city in the world is Damascus (Dimashq), Syria. It has been continuously inhabited since c. 2500 BC. In 1998 it had an estimated population of 1,431,821.

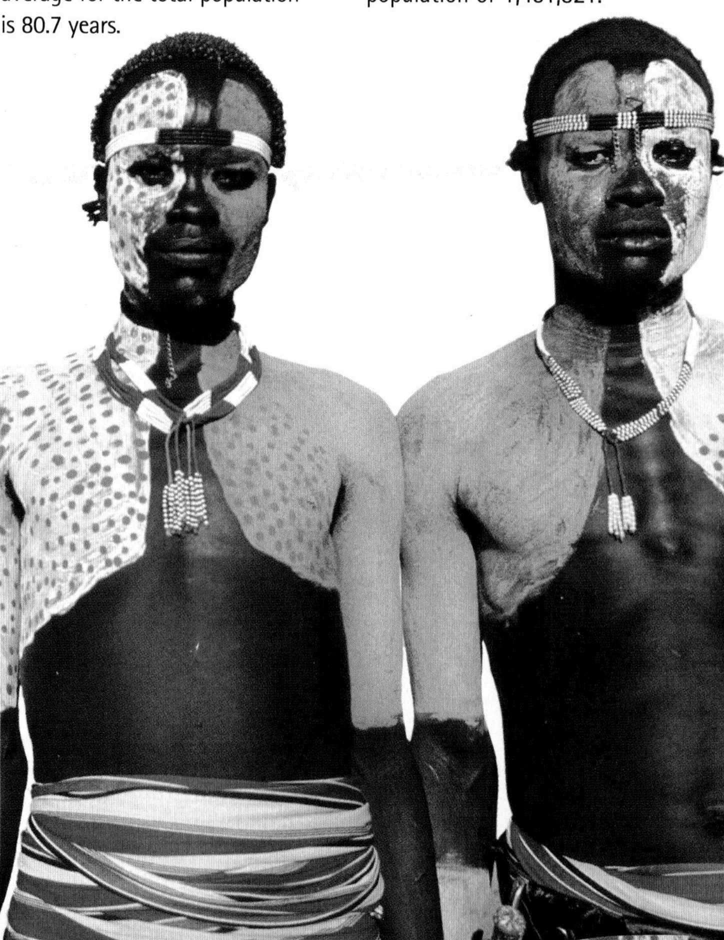

MOST BOUNDARIES BY CONTINENT

There are 306 national land boundaries in the world. The continent with the greatest number is Africa, with 112. Part of the border between Zambia and Zimbabwe is formed by the mighty Victoria Falls (left).

MOST POPULOUS CITY

The largest conurbation in Asia, and the most populous urban agglomeration in the world, is Tokyo, Japan, with an estimated population of 26.4 million in March 2000 according to the United Nations.

MOST POPULOUS COUNTRY

China is the world's most populated country. It had an estimated population of 1,274,915,000 in 2001.

LEAST POPULOUS COUNTRY

The Vatican City or the Holy See has the world's smallest population with just 890 inhabitants in 2001. With an area of only 44 ha (108.7 acres) the Vatican is also the world's smallest country.

MOST SPARSELY POPULATED COUNTRY

The most sparsely populated sovereign country is Mongolia, with a population of 2,435,000 (2001) in an area of 1,564,160 km^2 (603,930 miles^2), giving a density of 1.6 people to every 1 km^2 (4 people to every 1 mile^2).

MOST POPULOUS ISLAND

The world's most populous island is Java, Indonesia, which, in 1999, had an estimated population, of 121,193,000, all living in an area of 127,499 km^2 (49,227 miles^2).

MOST DENSELY POPULATED ISLAND

The world's most densely populated island is Ap Lei Chau, off the southwest coast of Hong Kong Island. Ap Lei Chau has a population of 80,000 living in an area measuring 1.3 km^2 (0.5 miles^2). The actual population density, therefore, is 60,000 per 1 km^2 (160,000 per 1 mile^2).

MOST DENSELY POPULATED COUNTRY

Monaco is the most densely populated country. It had a population density of 16,307 per km^2 (42,400 per mile^2) in 2001.

COUNTRY WITH MOST OFFICIAL LANGUAGES

The Republic of South Africa has 11 official languages. These are: English, Afrikaans, isiZulu, isiXhosa, Sesotho, Setswana, Sepedi, Xitsonga, siSwati, isiNdebele and Tshivenda. The population of South Africa was 43,792,000 in 2001.

MOST PRIVATE HOUSING

The greatest percentage of private housing is in Mongolia where, in 1997, 100% of homes were owner-occupied.

LEAST PRIVATE HOUSING

The smallest percentage of private housing is in Estonia where, in 1995, only 18.3% of property was owner-occupied.

LOWEST SUICIDE RATE

Antigua and Barbuda (1995), the Dominican Republic (1994), Saint Kitts and Nevis (1995) and St Vincent and The Grenadines (1986) all recorded the lowest suicide rates with no cases reported in the years shown.

HIGHEST SUICIDE RATE

The country with the highest suicide rate is Lithuania with 87 per 100,000 people in 1998.

YOUNGEST ELECTED AS US PRESIDENT

John F Kennedy (USA, above), the Democratic victor in the 1960 US presidential election, was, at the age of 43, the youngest man ever to win the American presidency. Winning by a narrow margin in the popular vote, Kennedy became the first Roman Catholic president. He was also the youngest to die in office.

LARGEST GATHERING OF WORLD LEADERS

The United Nation's 55th session of the General Assembly began with the Millennium Summit held in New York, USA, between 6 and 8 September 2000. It brought together 144 kings, presidents, prime ministers and heads of state.

MOST DESCENDANTS TO BECOME PRIME MINISTER

Since 1947 a total of three descendants of the Nehru-Gandhi family have become Prime Minister of India. Jawaharlal Nehru became India's Prime Minister when the country attained independence in August 1947, and remained in power until his death in 1964. His daughter Indira Gandhi served as Prime Minister from 1966 to 1977 and from 1980 until she was assassinated on 31 October 1984. Rajiv Gandhi, Indira's eldest son, became Prime Minister following his mother's death and won the 1984 elections by a landslide. He served until 1989 and was assassinated while campaigning for the premiership on 21 May 1991.

LONGEST REIGNING LIVING QUEEN

Currently, the longest-reigning, living queen is Her Majesty Queen Elizabeth II (b. 1926), who succeeded to the throne on 6 February 1952 on the death of her father. Elizabeth II is Queen of the UK and Head of the Commonwealth. The year 2002 saw the Queen's Golden Jubilee, marking the 50th anniversary of her accession.

The longest reigning queen ever was Victoria, Queen of Great Britain (1837–1901) and, from 1876, Empress of India, who reigned for 63 years 216 days.

MOST HANDSHAKES BY A HEAD OF STATE

President Theodore Roosevelt (USA) set a record for a head of state by shaking hands with 8,513 people at an official White House function in Washington DC, USA, on 1 January 1907.

YOUNGEST MAYOR

Shane Mack (USA, b. 15 November 1969) was elected mayor of Castlewood, South Dakota, USA, at the age of 18 years 169 days on 3 May 1988. He held office for eight years.

MOST SPENT PER VOTE IN AN ELECTION

Michael R Bloomberg (USA), the Republican candidate for the 6 November 2001 New York City mayoral election, spent $92.60 (£56.65) for each of the 744,757 votes he won against Democrat Mark Green (USA), a total campaign spend of $68,968,185 (£44,446,855). His opponent spent roughly $16.5 million (£11.2 million) on his campaign.

HEAVIEST MONARCH

The world's heaviest monarch is King Taufa'ahau Tupou IV of Tonga, who, in September 1976, was weighed on the only adequate scales in the country – at the airport – recording a weight of 209.5 kg (33 st or 462 lb). By 1985 he was reported to have slimmed down to 139.7 kg (22 st), in early 1993 he was 127 kg (20 st), and by 1998 he had lost more weight as a result of a fitness programme.

MOST PRESIDENTS IN THREE WEEKS

In December 2001, amidst intense rioting due to an economic crisis, Argentina had five presidents within a three-week period.

EARLIEST COUNTRY TO PASS WOMEN'S SUFFRAGE

The 1893 Women's Suffrage Petition led to New Zealand becoming the earliest self-governing nation to grant women the right to vote. Governor Glasgow signed the Electoral Bill on 19 September 1893.

MOST CANDIDATES ON A BALLOT PAPER

For the November 1994 municipal elections in Prague, Czech Republic, there were 1,187 candidates on the ballot for the single city constituency.

MOST VOTES FOR A CHIMPANZEE IN A POLITICAL CAMPAIGN

In the 1988 mayoral election campaign in Rio de Janeiro, Brazil, the anti-establishment 'Brazilian Banana Party' presented a chimpanzee called Tião as their candidate. The chimp came third out of 12 candidates, taking just over 400,000 votes. Known for his moody temper, Tião's campaign slogan was 'Vote monkey – get monkey'. Tião passed away in December 1996 aged 33.

COUNTRY OF ORIGIN FOR MOST REFUGEES

The country with the most people seeking asylum elsewhere is Afghanistan. According to the 2001 figures from the United Nations High Commission for Refugees, Afghans (above) account for approximately 3.8 million, or one-third, of the 12-million global refugee population.

OLDEST EVER ROYAL

Prussian Princess Leonilla Bariatinskaya of Sayn-Wittgenstein-Sayn (1816–1918) is the oldest known royal in history, with a lifespan of 101 years 268 days. Princess Leonilla lived 30 days longer than HM Queen Elizabeth, the Queen Mother (UK), who died in March 2002, and held the record for the oldest king's consort.

MOST FAILED ASSASSINATIONS

The target for the most failed assassination attempts on an individual head of state in modern times was Charles de Gaulle (France), President of France from 1958 to 1969. He was reputed to have survived no fewer than 31 plots against his life between 1944 and 1966.

COUNTRY RECEIVING MOST APPLICATIONS FOR POLITICAL ASYLUM

According to the United Nations High Commission for Refugees (UNHCR) 2001 statistical report, a total of 915,000 asylum applications were submitted to 144 countries during 2001. The country that receives the highest number of applications for political asylum is the UK. According to figures from the UNHCR, the UK received 92,000 applications in the year 2001. Germany was the second most popular with 88,300 applications, followed by the USA with 83,200. Afghanistan was the main country of origin for political asylum seekers in 2001 (66,800 people), followed by Iraq (60,800) and Turkey (41,300).

OLDEST PRESIDENT

Joaquin Balaguer (1907-2002) was president of the Dominican Republic 1960–62, 1966–78 and 1986–96. He ultimately left office at the age of 89. He held the presidency for no fewer than 22 years.

MOST IMMIGRANTS

The USA regularly receives the most legal immigrants. The Immigration and Naturalization Service (USA) website shows that between 1820 and 1996 the USA received 63,140,227 official immigrants. In 1996 the illegal alien population was 5 million, of which 2.7 million were Mexican.

MOST PRESIDENTIAL PALACES

As of February 2003, Saddam Hussein (Iraq), President of Iraq since 1979, had eight principal palaces plus other minor residences throughout Iraq, which contain a total of 1,058 buildings. In Babylon, Saddam has a palace built alongside the remains of the palace of Nebuchadnezzar II (620– 562 BC); every brick is stamped with the legend 'The Leader, Saddam Hussein, Victor of Allah'.

LARGEST PARLIAMENT

The largest legislative assembly in the world is the National People's Congress of the People's Republic of China. The Eighth National People's Congress, the first session of which was convened in March 1993, is composed of 2,978 deputies indirectly elected from 22 provinces, five autonomous regions and four municipalities directly under the Central sGovernment, and from the Chinese People's Liberation Army; it represents the Communist Party of China, eight allied 'democratic' parties and 'people without any political affiliations'. The Congress is elected for a term of five years.

LONGEST EMBASSY SIEGE

In September 1979 a crowd of about 500 people seized the US embassy in Tehran, Iran. Of the approximately 90 people inside the embassy, 52 remained in captivity until the end of the crisis 444 days later, on 20 January 1981.

LONGEST SERVING US SENATOR

The longest serving senator in US history is Republican Strom J Thurmond (b. 1902) who served the state of South Carolina, USA, a total of 48 years in the Senate between 1954 and 2002, seeing the terms of 18 US presidents.

MOST WOMEN MINISTERS

Worldwide, the greatest representation of women in a government cabinet is in Sweden where, following a general election in March 1996, a new cabinet containing 11 women out of 22 ministers was formed.

YOUNGEST CURRENT QUEEN

HM Queen Rania Al-Abdullah of Jordan (b. 31 August 1970, below), wife of King Abdullah Bin Al-Hussein, is currently the youngest queen in the world. Married on 10 June 1993, her husband was crowned on 7 February 1999 when she was just 28 years 160 days.

WAR & PEACE

LARGEST MILITARY EVACUATION

The greatest military evacuation was that carried out by 1,200 Allied naval and civil craft from the beachhead at Dunkerque (Dunkirk), France, between 26 May and 4 June 1940 (evacuees shown right). A total of 338,226 British and French troops were taken off the beaches in the face of advancing German troops. The expression 'Dunkirk spirit' is still used to describe a refusal to concede in a crisis.

YOUNGEST GUERRILLA LEADERS

On 24 January 2000, a renegade ethnic group from Myanmar (Burma) led by two 12-year-old twins Luther and Johnny Htoo said to possess 'mystical powers', took 700 people hostage for 24 hours at a hospital in Ratchaburi, Thailand. The hostage-takers, known as 'God's Army', demanded that doctors treat wounded colleagues at their mountain base. All hostages were later freed during a military operation carried out by Thai commandos on the morning of 25 January 2000.

YOUNGEST NOBEL PEACE PRIZE WINNER

In 1992 Rigoberta Menchú Tum (Guatemala, b. 1959), was awarded the Nobel Peace Prize 'in recognition of her work for social justice and ethnocultural reconciliation based on respect for the rights of indigenous people.' At age 33, she was the youngest person ever to receive this honour.

LARGEST ARMED FORCES

The strength of China's People's Liberation Army in 1997 was estimated to be 2.84 million (comprising land, sea and air forces). The reserves that can be mobilized number around 1.2 million, plus many more for local militia duty.

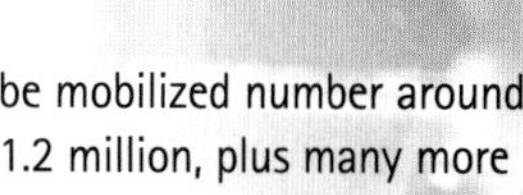

LARGEST CONTRIBUTORS TO PEACEKEEPING

Canada and the island nation of Fiji have taken part in virtually every one of the 55 United Nations (UN) peacekeeping operations to date.

PEACEKEEPING MISSION WITH MOST CONTRIBUTING NATIONS

The United Nations Mission in Bosnia and Herzegovina (UNMIBH) drew troops from 44 nations. UNMIBH was an umbrella organization overseeing the activities of the International Police Task Force (IPTF) set up in Bosnia and Herzegovina after the United Nations Protection Force (UNPROFOR) mission came to an end in 1995.

LONGEST RUNNING PEACEKEEPING OPERATION

The United Nations Truce Supervision Organization (UNTSO) has been in place since June 1948. UNTSO's headquarters are in Jerusalem, but it maintains military observation posts throughout the Middle East. This was also the first UN peacekeeping operation.

LARGEST PEACEKEEPING DEPLOYMENT

The UN peacekeeping mission with the largest deployment was UNPROFOR, which took place in the former Yugoslavia from February 1992 to March 1995. The mission reached a strength of 39,922 personnel in September 1994, including a 'Rapid Reaction Force'.

MOST EXPENSIVE PEACEKEEPING OPERATION

The most expensive UN peacekeeping mission to date is UNPROFOR, which cost a massive $4.6 billion (£2.96 billion). This included all the missions deployed in the former Yugoslavia during this period.

BLOODIEST UN PEACEKEEPING OPERATION

The conflict in the Balkans during the 1990s led to more fatalities than any other UN peacekeeping mission. The total number of fatalities for all missions in the region is 268, including 210 fatalities in UNPROFOR alone.

OLDEST ARMY

The oldest established military unit is the 80–90-strong Pontifical Swiss Guard in the Vatican City, with a regular foundation dating back to 1506. Its origins, however, predate 1400.

MOST NATIONALITIES IN A SINGLE MILITARY FORCE

As of February 2003 the French Foreig Legion (in training, right) had 7,700 me serving in its ranks with a diverse rang of nationalities from 136 countries. Most new recruits hail from former Eastern Bloc nations.

BLOODIEST WARS

By far the most costly war in terms of human life was World War II (1939–45), in which the total number of fatalities, including battle deaths and civilians of all countries, is estimated to have been 56.4 million, assuming 26.6 million Soviet and 7.8 million Chinese fatalities. The country that suffered most in proportion to its population was Poland, with 6.028 million or 17.2% of its population of 35.1 million killed.

BLOODIEST SIEGE

The worst siege in history was the 880-day siege of Leningrad, USSR (now St Petersburg, Russia), by the German Army from 30 August 1941 until 27 January 1944. The best estimate is that between 1.3 and 1.5 million defenders and citizens died. This included 641,000 people who died of hunger in the city and 17,000 civilians killed by shelling. More than 150,000 shells and 100,000 bombs were dropped on the city. The longest recorded siege was that of Azotus (now Ashdod), Israel, which according to Herodotus was besieged by Psamtik I of Egypt for 29 years in the period 664–610 BC.

BLOODIEST MODERN BATTLE

The greatest death toll in a battle has been estimated at 1.109 million in the Battle of Stalingrad, USSR (now Volgograd, Russia), which started in the summer of 1942 and ended with the German surrender on 31 January 1943. Approximately 650,800 Soviet soldiers were wounded but survived.

LARGEST CIVILIAN EVACUATION

An estimated two million Germans were evacuated from East Prussia in 1945 when the region was ceded to the Soviet Union under the Potsdam Agreement. The German population of East Prussia was replaced by Russians, Belorussians, Ukrainians and other Soviet citizens.

MOST NOBEL PEACE PRIZES BY NATIONALITY

The majority of Nobel Peace Prize winners have been from the USA. Between 1907 and 2002, 270 Americans received the award including former US president Jimmy Carter (above), who was awarded the Peace Prize in 2002 for his decades of untiring efforts to find peaceful solutions to international conflicts.

LARGEST ANTI-WAR RALLY

On 15 February 2003, anti-war rallies took place across the globe, the largest occurring in Rome, Italy, where a crowd of three million gathered to protest against the USA's threat to invade Iraq. On the same day, 1.3 million people attended a peace rally in Barcelona, Spain, and one million people participated in a peace march through the streets of London, UK. Police figures from around the world reported that millions more demonstrated in nearly 600 cities worldwide.

GREATEST AIR AND SEA BATTLE

The greatest battle involving both ships and aircraft was the World War II Battle of Leyte Gulf, in the Philippines, in which 218 Allied warships battled 64 of their Japanese counterparts over six days from 22 to 27 October 1944. In the skies above, 1,280 US and 716 Japanese aircraft were engaged in combat. In the end, 26 Japanese and six US vessels were sunk.

GREATEST ANCIENT NAVAL BATTLE

The greatest of ancient naval battles was the Battle of Salamis, Greece, in September 480 BC. There were an estimated 800 vessels in the defeated Persian fleet and 380 in the victorious fleet of the Athenians and their allies, with a possible involvement of 200,000 men.

GREATEST MODERN NAVAL BATTLE

The greatest purely naval battle of modern times was the World War I Battle of Jutland on 31 May 1916, in which 151 British Royal Navy warships squared up against 101 German warships. The Royal Navy lost 14 ships and 6,097 men, and the German fleet 11 ships and 2,545 men.

CRIME & PUNISHMENT

LARGEST JEWEL ROBBERY

At the Antwerp Diamond Centre, Belgium, over the weekend of 15/16 February 2003, 123 of the 160 vaults were emptied, with an estimated loss of at least $100-million (£62-million) worth of jewels. There was no sign of a break-in, alarms did not go off, and the bomb-proof vault doors were not tampered with.

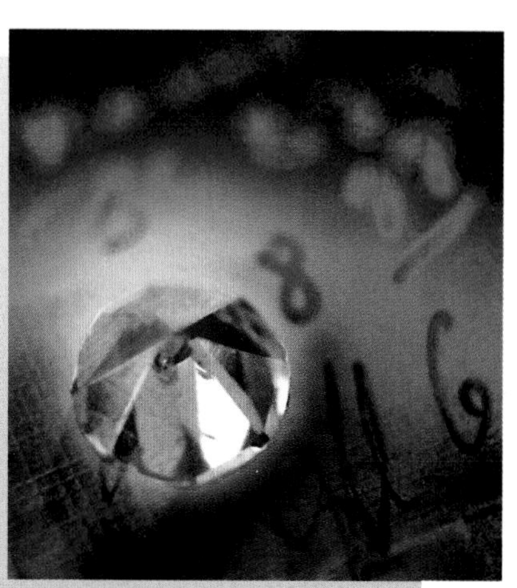

LARGEST COMPENSATION FOR WRONGFUL IMPRISONMENT

Robert McLaughlin (USA) was awarded $1,935,000 (£1,225,000) in October 1989 for wrongful imprisonment after a murder in New York City, USA, in 1979, which he did not commit. The 29-year-old had been sentenced to 15 years in prison and actually served six years, from 1980 to 1986, before his foster father proved to the authorities that he had nothing to do with the crime, resulting in Robert's release.

LARGEST PRISON CAPACITY

The largest prison recorded in modern times (from countries in which figures are kept) was the State Prison of Southern Michigan, USA, which had a maximum capacity of 6,500 inmates. It no longer houses such a large number.

The largest prison currently in existence, in terms of inmates, is San Quentin State Prison, California, USA, with 5,967 prisoners as of January 2003.

MOST PROLIFIC MURDER PARTNERSHIP

Sisters Delfina and María de Jesús Gonzáles (Mexico) abducted girls to work in bordellos, and are known to have murdered at least 90 of them and their clients. The sisters were sentenced to 40 years imprisonment in 1964.

LARGEST SEX DISCRIMINATION PAYOUT FOR AN INDIVIDUAL

The largest payout ever awarded to an individual in a sex discrimination case was £1,412,823 ($2.2 million) to Julie Bower (UK) in April 2001. She was awarded compensation after a British tribunal ruled that she had been forced out of her job as a result of sex discrimination by her former employer, Schroder Securities. The Equal Opportunities Commission supported her case.

MOST PEOPLE KILLED IN A TERRORIST ACT

The most individuals killed in a terrorist act, according to the official count from the authorities, is 2,823, as a result of the attack on the World Trade Center, New York City, USA, on 11 September 2001. The total number of people killed aboard the two aircraft that crashed into the twin towers was 157. On the same day, a hijacked aircraft was crashed into the Pentagon, Washington DC, USA, with the loss of 189 lives, and a fourth plane crashed in a field in Pennsylvania, killing 44 people.

MOST HANGINGS SURVIVED

The survivor of the most legal hanging attempts is Joseph Samuel, a 22-year-old who was sentenced to death for murder in Sydney, Australia. On 26 September 1803 the first attempt at execution failed when the rope broke. The second attempt failed when the rope stretched so much that the victim's feet touched the ground. At the third attempt, the second replacement rope broke. Samuel was then reprieved.

John Lee (UK) also survived three attempted hangings in Exeter, Devon, UK, in 1885, when each time the trap door failed to open.

MOST VIEWED TRIAL

A daily average of 5.5 million Americans watched live coverage of the OJ Simpson (USA) trial on three major cable television networks between 24 January and 3 October 1995. Simpson, an American football player and actor, was on trial for the murder of his ex-wife, Nicole, and a waiter, Ronald Goldman (both USA) on 12 June 1994. He was acquitted of the charges when the jury reached a verdict of not guilty on 3 October 1995.

MOST COMMON METHOD OF EXECUTION

The most common method of execution in the world is by firing squad, which is practised in 73 countries. Hanging is the second most common method, practised in 58 countries worldwide. Beheading is still practised in three countries, while electrocution is practised only in the USA.

LARGEST ROBBERY BY A MUGGER

Treasury bills and certificates of deposit worth £292 million ($435 million) were stolen when a mugger attacked a money-broker's messenger in the City of London, UK, on 2 May 1990. As details of the documents stolen were quickly flashed on the City's market dealing screens and given to central banks worldwide, the chances of the thief benefiting from the theft were considered to be very remote.

SHORTEST JURY DELIBERATION

On 2 June 1998, in the case of *Eastwood* v. *Capriotti* in the 234th Judicial District Court of Harris County, Texas, USA, the jury of 12 people ruled in favour of the defendant after only two minutes of deliberation. Shannon Eastwood (USA) had brought the suit against Robert Capriotti (USA) and the Capriotti Cosmetic and Laser Surgery for negligence and carelessness.

LARGEST SEIZURE OF NARCOTICS ASSETS

In December 1998 illicit drugs profits of nearly $280 million (£120.7 million) were seized by the US government, making it the largest narcotics bust in history.

LAST LEGAL EXECUTION FOR WITCHCRAFT

The last legal execution of a witch was that of Anna Göldi at Glarus, Switzerland, on 18 June 1782. It is estimated that at least 200,000 witches were executed during the European witch hunts of the 16th and 17th centuries. At the village of Quedlingburg, near Leipzig, Germany, 133 witches were burnt in one day in 1589.

LONGEST SERVING EXECUTIONER

The longest period of office for a public executioner is 45 years (1829–74), served by William Calcraft (UK) who officiated at Newgate Prison, London, UK.

MOST PROLIFIC SERIAL KILLER

The Shipman Inquiry concluded that family doctor Harold Shipman (UK, above) murdered 215 of his patients between 1975 and 1998. He killed his elderly (mainly female) victims with the administration of drugs. Found guilty in January 2000, he will spend the rest of his life in prison.

MOST PROLIFIC 'HANGING' JUDGE

In 1685 George Jeffreys (UK), the Chief Justice who presided over the trials known as the 'Bloody Assizes', sentenced approximately 320 alleged rebels to death in Somerset, Dorset and Devon, UK. Most were hung, drawn and quartered.

LARGEST RACE DISCRIMINATION SETTLEMENT

The Coca-Cola company (USA) agreed to pay out $192.5 million (£121.3 million) in November 2000 after four African-Americans, representing 2,000 other employees, accused the company of race discrimination. Every employee involved in the case was ordered to receive in the region of $40,000 (£27,900) in compensation and back pay, while the four who took the case to court could receive up to $300,000 (£209,000) each.

LARGEST DRUG SEIZURES

On 29 September 1989 in Sylmar, California, USA, officers from the Drug Enforcement Administration based in Alexandria, Virginia, USA, seized 21,570 kg (47,554 lb) of cocaine. The largest heroin seizure took place in Bangkok, Thailand, on 11 February 1988 when officers seized 1,277 kg (2,816 lb) of heroin.

MOST CRIMINALS POSITIVELY IDENTIFIED FROM THE COMPOSITES OF ONE ARTIST

Since 1982 more than 135 criminals have been positively identified and brought to justice in Texas, USA, thanks to the detailed composites drawn by forensic artist Lois Gibson (USA). Police officials claim these criminal cases dealing with murder, rape and robbery would have gone unsolved without Lois's drawings.

HIGHEST MODERN KIDNAP RANSOM

Two Hong Kong businessmen, Walter Kwok and Victor Li, paid off gangster Cheung Tze-keung (aka 'Big Spender') a record total of $206 million (£127.3 million) in return for their freedom after they were kidnapped in 1996 and 1997, respectively. Cheung Tze-keung, who orginally planned to kidnap the top 10 tycoons in Hong Kong, was executed in China on 5 December 1998.

LARGEST PAYOUT IN COMPENSATION BY A TOBACCO COMPANY

The most compensation paid to and received by an individual is $1.1 million (£668,000), awarded to a 70-year-old ex-smoker in 1995 by Brown & Williamson Tobacco (USA).

MOST CIVIL DAMAGES AWARDED TO A COMPANY

The most damages awarded in legal history were the $11.12 billion (£7.69 billion) damages due to Pennzoil Co. against Texaco Inc. concerning the latter's allegedly unethical tactics to break up a merger between Pennzoil and Getty Oil Co. in January 1984. An out-of-court settlement of $5.5 billion (£3 billion) was reached on 19 December 1987 after a 48-hour negotiation period.

LONGEST SERVING PRISONER ON ALCATRAZ

Killer, thief and kidnapper Alvin Karpis, known as 'Public Enemy No. 1', spent 26 years as an inmate of Alcatraz prison (left), San Francisco, California, USA, from August 1936 to April 1962 when he was transferred to USP McNeil Island.

LARGEST CURRENCY INTRODUCTION

The largest currency introduction took place on 1 January 2002 when 15 billion euro banknotes and 50 billion euro coins – with a value of over €664 billion ($592 billion or £407 billion) – were put into circulation in Austria, Italy, Belgium, Finland, France, Germany, Greece, Ireland, Luxembourg, The Netherlands, Portugal and Spain.

LARGEST AIRLINE CORPORATION

The largest airline corporation is AMR, based in Fort Worth, Texas, USA, which had a total revenue of $17,299 million (£11,709 million) and profits of around $3,511 million (£2,376 million) in 2002 with a workforce of over 125,000 employees. As well as a fleet of over 800 jetliners and hubs in Chicago, Dallas/Fort Worth, Miami, and San Juan, Puerto Rico, it also heads Oneworld, a global marketing alliance with British Airways and others.

LARGEST SINGLE TRADING FLOOR

The largest single trading floor (below) belongs to the financial service firm UBS (formerly known as UBS Warburg) in Stamford, Connecticut, USA, and covers an area of 8,625 m^2 (93,070 ft^2). There are 1,400 traders occupying the space sitting alongside 5,000 computers. The trading floor is the size of 20.5 basketball courts or 44 singles tennis courts.

GREATEST RISE OF THE DOW JONES INDUSTRIAL AVERAGE

On 16 March 2000 the Dow Jones Industrial Average gained 499.19 points (4.93%), the greatest rise in history, closing at 10,630.6 points.

GREATEST FALL OF THE DOW JONES INDUSTRIAL AVERAGE

On 17 September 2001 the Dow Jones Industrial Average fell by 684.81 points (7.13%) to 8,920.70, the biggest points loss in history. This occurred when the New York Stock Exchange re-opened after the attack on the World Trade Center on 11 September 2001.

GREATEST ANNUAL PROFIT EVER

In the year 2000 the integrated oil company Exxon Mobil based in Irving, Texas, USA, had profits of $17 billion (£12 billion), equivalent to a net increase in growth in one year of 124%.

GREATEST PERCENTAGE FALL OF THE FTSE 100

The greatest percentage fall in a day's trading of the FTSE 100 share index was 12.22% to 1801.6 points on 20 October 1987, a fall of 250.7 points.

GREATEST PERCENTAGE RISE OF THE FTSE 100

The greatest percentage rise in a day of the Financial Times Stock Exchange (FTSE) 100 share index was 7.89% to 1943.8 points on 21 October 1987, a rise of 142.2 points.

LARGEST GOLD RESERVES

The United States Treasury had approximately 262 million fine ounces of gold during 1996, equivalent to $100 billion (£65 billion) at the June 1996 price of $382 (£249) per fine ounce.

MOST CORPORATE DEBT FAILURES

In 2001 a record 211 companies defaulted on $115.4 billion (£79.5 billion) of debt, setting the record in both number of defaults and total amount. This is an increase of more than 120% from 2000 when 132 companies defaulted on $42.3 billion (£39.1 billion) of debt.

LARGEST DOLLAR VOLUME STOCK EXCHANGE

The largest stock exchange in terms of the total value of share trading in one year is the New York Stock Exchange, which in 2002 reached $10.3 trillion (£6.2 trillion). In comparison, the National Association of Securities Dealers Automated Quotation System (NASDAQ, a dealer shown right) was second with $7.2 trillion (£4.3 trillion) and the London Stock Exchange was third with $3.9 trillion (£2.3 trillion).

LARGEST CORPORATION

Based on revenues, the largest corporation in the world as of April 2002 was Wal-Mart Stores (USA), which had revenues of $219,812 million (£154,264 million), almost $30 billion (£21 billion) more than Exxon Mobil, which held the top spot the previous year.

LARGEST STOCK MARKET FLOTATION

The stock market launch of ENEL, Italy's state-owned electricity generator and distributor, on 31 October 1999 became the world's largest ever initial public offering after the Italian government sold €18-billion-worth (£11.8-billion or $19.26-billion) of shares.

LARGEST ANNUAL TRADING VOLUME BY SHARES

The largest annual trading volume at the New York Stock Exchange, New York City, USA, was achieved in 2002, when 363,135,930,000 shares were traded.

LARGEST CORPORATE BANKRUPTCY

The largest corporate bankruptcy in terms of assets amounted to $103.9 billion (£65.8 billion) filed by the telecommunications company WorldCom, Inc. (USA) on 21 July 2002.

LARGEST CHEQUE BY VALUE

The greatest amount paid by a single cheque in the history of banking was £2,474,655,000 ($3,971,821,324). Issued on 30 March 1995 and signed by Nicholas Morris (UK), Company Secretary of Glaxo plc, the cheque represented a payment by Glaxo plc to Wellcome Trust Nominees Limited in respect of the Trust's share in Wellcome plc. The Lloyds Bank Registrars computer system could not generate a cheque this large and so it was completed by a Lloyds employee using a typewriter. The typist was so overawed by the responsibility that she took three attempts to produce the cheque.

LARGEST HOSTILE TAKEOVER BID

British mobile phone company Vodafone AirTouch Plc launched a hostile £85-billion ($137.7-billion) takeover bid for German telecommunications and engineering rival Mannesmann in November 1999. The bid ultimately resulted in a £103.4-billion ($171.1-billion) merger completed after EU Phase 1 clearance on 12 April 2000. The company's name changed to Vodafone Group Plc on 11 August 2000.

LARGEST COMMERCIAL AND SAVINGS BANK

The world's largest commercial and savings bank is Mizuho Holdings, Inc. (Japan), with revenues of $40,074 million (£28,110 million), profits of $7,358 million (£5,161 million) and a workforce of 30,262. Mizuho Holdings, Inc. was created in September 2000 by the consolidation of the Dai-Ichi Kangyo Bank, the Fuji Bank Ltd and the Industrial Bank of Japan. It is the first bank to have over $1 trillion in assets (£600 billion).

LARGEST COMPANY MERGER

America Online (USA), the world's largest internet company, announced a $350,000-million (£213,000-million) merger with media corporation Time Warner on 10 January 2000. The completed merger created the world's largest media company.

GREATEST ANNUAL LOSS

The greatest annual net loss by a company is the $98.7-billion (£60-billion) loss reported by AOL Time Warner (USA) on 30 January 2003. This figure is about the same size as the gross domestic product of Israel. It works out at a loss of $10.10 (£6.10) per share, much higher than the company's 2001 losses of $4.9 billion (£2.9 billion) or $1.10 (£1.70) a share.

EARLIEST CASH DISPENSER

The world's first cash dispenser was installed at Barclays Bank, Enfield, Middlesex, UK, on 27 June 1967. Customers were issued paper vouchers that they fed into the machine, which retained the voucher and dispensed a single £10 ($28) note. Within a year there were machines in France, Sweden and Switzerland. In 1969 both the USA and Japan installed their first machines.

LARGEST FINE IMPOSED ON AN INDIVIDUAL

The record for an individual fine is $200 million (£122 million), which Michael Milken (USA) agreed to pay on 24 April 1990 in settlement of a criminal racketeering and securities fraud suit brought by the US government. In addition, he agreed to settle civil charges filed by the Securities and Exchange Commision. He was released from a 10-year prison sentence in 1993.

LONGEST CONTINUOUS ISSUER OF BANKNOTES

The Bank of England (UK) has been issuing banknotes without interruption since 1694 when it was first established to raise money for King William III's war against the French.

LOWEST INFLATION

Hong Kong had the lowest inflation at -3.6% according to the Economist Intelligence Unit in 2000. Hong Kong experienced what is known as 'deflation' – that is, a fall in the general price level or a contraction of credit and available money. A freeze in government fees and the ongoing stagnating property market and existing excess capacities have been blamed.

LARGEST BANK BY BRANCHES

The bank with most branches is the State Bank of India, which had 13,542 outlets on 31 March 2002 and assets of $92 billion (£64 billion).

MONARCH ON THE MOST CURRENCIES

The image of Her Majesty Queen Elizabeth II (b. 1926) appears on the coinage of at least 35 countries – more than any other living monarch. Elizabeth II is Queen of the United Kingdom and Head of the Commonwealth.

COUNTRY WITH MOST HIGHER EDUCATION INSTITUTIONS

Mexico has the greatest number of tertiary-level institutions (universities, colleges and other comparable institutions), with a total of 10,341.

OLDEST DOCTORATE

At the age of 90 years 58 days, Elizabeth Eichelbaum (USA) became the oldest person to receive a doctorate (PhD). She received her doctorate in Education on 12 May 2000 from the University of Tennessee, USA.

LARGEST EMPLOYMENT AGENCY

The world's largest employment agency is Adecco SA (Switzerland) with 250,000 clients in more than 5,800 offices in 63 countries. Adecco found employment for nearly four million people around the world in 2002.

MOST EMPLOYERS

The greatest number of different paid jobs recorded in a working life is the 110 accumulated by D H 'Nobby' Clarke (UK).

The female record is held by Anna Petty (USA), who worked for 67 companies during her working career.

HIGHEST COST OF LIVING

According to the Economist Intelligence Unit's twice-yearly report, Tokyo and Osaka/Kobe in Japan are the most expensive cities in the world, jointly holding the top spot. Five of the world's most expensive locations are in Asia: Tokyo, Osaka/Kobe, Hong Kong, Singapore and Taipei.

LOWEST COST OF LIVING

According to the Economist Intelligence Unit's twice-yearly report, Tehran in Iran became the cheapest city in the world in June 2001. It displaced New Delhi and Mumbai (Bombay) that had jointly held the top spot the previous year.

HIGHEST DEFENCE BUDGET

The USA has the world's highest government defence budget with $362 billion (£220 billion) approved for the financial year of 2002.

LARGEST SCHOOL BY PUPILS

In September 2002 the City Montessori School, Lucknow, India, had a record enrolment of 26,312.

LARGEST COMPANY BY EMPLOYEES

The largest federal company employer in the world is the US Postal Service (below), based in Washington DC, USA, which had 750,000 employees as of the end of 2001.

HIGHEST CONSUMPTION OF CALORIES

The country with the highest daily consumption of calories is the Republic of Ireland, where the average intake is 3,952 calories per day.

COUNTRY WITH THE LARGEST ENERGY CONSUMPTION

The USA is the world's largest consumer of both fossil fuels (coal, oil and natural gas) and of commercial energy (fossil fuels plus nuclear and hydro power). In 1998 the USA consumed a total of 1,937 million tonnes of oil equivalent (Mtoe) of fossil fuels and 2,147 Mtoe of commercial energy.

FROZEN FOOD CONSUMPTION

According to studies conducted in 1999, Norway annually consumes 35.6 kg (78 lb) of frozen food per person. This is followed by Denmark with 32.5 kg (71 lb 9.6 oz) per person and the UK with 30.9 kg (68 lb). In comparison, the USA consumes only 16.3 kg (35 lb) of frozen food per person.

LARGEST DONATION TO EDUCATION

The greatest single gift in the history of education was the $365 million (£256 million) donated by philanthropist, publisher and diplomat Walter H Annenberg (USA) in December 1993.

BIGGEST ELECTRICITY CONSUMPTION

The world's greatest consumer of electricity is the USA, which used 3,235.9 billion kilowatts per hour in 1999 – almost a quarter of the total net electricity consumption of the whole world, which came to 12,832.7 billion kilowatts per hour.

HIGHEST CONSUMPTION OF CIGARETTES

South Korea has the highest per capita consumption of cigarettes anywhere in the world, at 4,153 units per annum. Japan comes second with 2,739 and Hungary third with 2,689. US consumption for 1999 was 1,836 per capita. An estimated 4.6 trillion cigarettes were smoked in the world in 1999.

LARGEST SIMULTANEOUS LESSON

The world's largest simultaneous lesson involved 28,101 people each learning phrases in a new language. It was part of the 'Learning Day' organized by Birmingham City Council, Birmingham, UK, on 21 March 2002.

GREATEST FAST FOOD EXPENDITURE

In 2000, Americans spent over $110 billion (£67.1 billion) on fast food, more than on higher education, personal computers or new cars. On any one day approximately 25% of US adults visit a fast food outlet. A typical American eats roughly three burgers and four orders of fries a week.

MOST CHEWING GUM CONSUMED PER CAPITA

In Andorra each person consumed an average of 900 g (2 lb) of chewing gum in the year 2000.

HIGHEST BREAKFAST CEREAL CONSUMPTION

The country with the largest per capita breakfast cereal consumption is Sweden with 10.4 kg (22 lb) per person according to studies done in 2000. This is followed by Canada with 7.8 kg (17 lb) per person.

HIGHEST ICE CREAM CONSUMPTION

The country that consumes the most ice cream per capita is Australia where, on average, 16.6 litres (29.2 pints) of ice cream were consumed per person in 2000.

HIGHEST ALCOHOL CONSUMPTION

The country with the largest per capita consumption of alcohol is the Republic of Ireland with 12.3 litres (21.6 pints) of pure alcohol per person according to surveys done in 2000. This intake is based on the amount of pure alcohol consumed (wine, beer, and spirits). Luxembourg comes in at second place with 12.1 litres (21.2 pints) per person, followed by Romania with 11.7 litres (20.5 pints).

HIGHEST CHOCOLATE CONSUMPTION

In Switzerland the average person consumed 11.5 kg (25 lb 6 oz) of chocolate during 2000.

HIGHEST EDUCATION BUDGET PERCENT

New Caledonia in the South Pacific Ocean has the largest expenditure for education as a percentage, spending 13.5% of its GNP on primary, secondary and tertiary education according to the latest figures recorded in *Britannica Book of the Year 2002*. St Lucia is second with 9.8% (1998) of GNP. The UK spends 5.3% (1997) and the USA 5.4% (1998).

HIGHEST PAPER RECYCLING RATE

Germany recycles between 70 and 80% of its consumption of paper and cardboard per year.

LONGEST TEACHING CAREER

Medarda de Jesus Leon de Uzcategui (Venezuela) taught in Caracas, Venezuela, for over 80 years from 1911.

LOWEST EDUCATION BUDGET PERCENT

As of 2002, Somalia spends least on education, allocating just 0.4% of its GNP to primary, secondary and tertiary education. This is followed by Nigeria (0.7%) and Sierra Leone (0.9%, students below).

RELIGION & BELIEFS

LARGEST RELIGION
Christianity is the world's predominant religion, with approximately 1,999,560,000 adherents in 2000, or 33% of the world's population.

FASTEST GROWING RELIGION
Islam is the fastest growing religion in the world. In 1990, 935 million of the world's population were Muslim. This grew to 1,188,242,000 in 2000, which means that approximately 20% of the world's population follows Islam.

LARGEST GATHERING OF RELIGIOUS LEADERS
The Millennuim World Peace Summit of Religious and Spiritual Leaders involved 1,000 people. It was held at the United Nations headquarters in New York, USA, between 28 and 31 August 2000. Amongst the attendees were: Pope John Paul II, The Dalai Lama (below right, with an admirer) and Dr Abdullah Salehal-Obaid, the Secretary of the World Muslim League. The aim of the meeting was to create a commitment to achieving world peace.

MOST THREATENED RELIGION
Only six members of the United Society of Believers in Christ's Second Appearance (Shakers) remain. They live in a small community near New Gloucester, Maine, USA. The religion was founded in Manchester, UK, by Ann Lee (UK) in 1772. At its peak of popularity (c. 1830–40) there were around 6,000 members scattered over 19 communities. The drop in numbers is partly due to their belief in celibacy.

LARGEST ANNUAL GATHERING OF WOMEN
In February or March each year, over one million women gather at the Attukal Bhagavathy Temple, Thiruvananthapram, Kerala, India, for the 'Pongala' offering. The women, who come from all religions and communities in Kerala, gather with their cooking pots to perform a ritual for the health and prosperity of their families. The highest attendance recorded was on 23 February 1997, when 1.5 million women took part in the festival. The ceremonial duties, which involve cooking rice as an offering to the deity, last six hours.

EARLIEST PLACES OF WORSHIP
Many archaeologists think that the decorated Upper Palaeolithic caves of Europe (dating from c. 30,000–10,000 BC) were used as places of worship or religious ritual.

LARGEST PAPAL CROWD
On 15 January 1995 Pope John Paul II offered Mass to a crowd of between four and five million people at Luneta Park, Manila, during his visit to the Philippines.

YOUNGEST ELECTED POPE
Pope Benedict IX was just 11 years old when he became Pope in 1032.

LONGEST LIVED POPE
Of all the popes whose ages can be proved, the longest-lived was Leo XIII (Gioacchino Pecci, Italy, 1810–1903), who died aged 93 years 140 days.

LONGEST PAPAL REIGN
The longest papal reign was that of Pius IX (Giovanni Maria Mastai-Ferretti, Italy), who was pope for 31 years 236 days between 1846 and 1878. St Peter, the first pope (c. 33-67), is said to have been head of the Church for 34 years although this cannot be dated accurately.

POPE TO CREATE MOST SAINTS
By 1998 Pope John Paul II (Poland), who ascended the papal throne in 1978, had canonized (declared to be a saint) and beatified (declared worthy of public religious veneration) just over 1,000 people – ten times as many people as all his 20th-century predecessors put together and the largest number of any pontiff. On 6 October 2002 Josemaria Escriva de Balaguer (Spain) became the 468th person to be canonized by Pope John Paul II. A crowd of over 300,000 gathered at St Peter's Square to witness the founder of Opus Dei (a personal prelature of the Catholic Church) become a saint.

MOST INACCESSIBLE RELIC
The relic believed by the Ethiopian Orthodox Church to be the Ark of the Covenant is kept in a chapel in Axum, Ethiopia, where it is guarded by a single priest, and he alone is allowed to see it or enter its presence. A representation of the relic (above), rather than the relic itself, is carried in procession.

LONGEST PERIOD OF STIGMATISM
Father Pio (Francesco Forgione, Italy), a devout Italian Capuchin friar, bore the stigmata (the wounds received by Christ on the Cross) from 1918 until his death in 1968. The wounds were seen by thousands of pilgrims. He was canonized on 16 June 2002.

LARGEST WOODEN CHURCH
The world's largest wooden Christian church is the Kerimäki church in Kerimäki, Finland. It measures 45 x 42 x 27 m (147 x 137 x 88 ft) and its dome is 37 m (121 ft) high. It seats 3,000 people and standing capacity is 5,000.

LARGEST RELIGIOUS THEME PARK

The world's largest religious theme park is The Holy Land Experience. The 6.07-ha (15-acre) site in Orlando, Florida, USA, opened on 5 February 2001 and is a recreation of Jerusalem, Israel, from 1450 BC to 66 AD. Created and funded by Reverend Marvin Rosenthal (USA) and Zion's Hope Inc., a Christian organization, the $16-million (£9.8-million) project averages 900 visitors per day. Amongst the attractions are the Jerusalem Street Market, The Wilderness Tabernacle, Cavalry's Garden Tomb, authentically costumed people, music and even a library for research and biblical study.

LONGEST CHURCH

The crypt of the underground Civil War Memorial Church in the Guadarrama Mountains, in the Valley of the Fallen 45 km (28 miles) from Madrid, Spain, is 260 m (853 ft) in length, making it the longest church in the world. It took 21 years (1937–58) to build, at a reported cost of £140 million ($229 million or €211 million).

MOST MUSLIM PILGRIMS

The annual pilgrimage (hajj) to Mecca, Saudi Arabia, attracts greater numbers than any other Islamic mission, with an average of two million people a year.

LONGEST LAW ENFORCEMENT STANDOFF WITH A CULT

The longest standoff between members of law enforcement agencies and a cult was for 51 days at the Mount Carmel Compound in Waco, Texas, USA, in 1993. The cult involved was the Branch Davidians, led by the failed rock star David Koresh (USA). The standoff began on 28 February 1993 when federal agents tried to enter the compound, and ended on 19 April when police stormed the building and fire broke out. Over 80 people died inside, including 17 children and the leader himself. Federal agents were also killed in the standoff.

LARGEST UNDERGROUND TEMPLE

The world's largest underground temple has been excavated over 16 years by members of the 800-strong Damanhur religious community living in Baldissero near Turin, Italy. Dug into the side of a hill, it takes up a total volume of 6,000 m^3 (211,888 ft^3). The Damanhur or 'City of Light' was founded by Oberto Airaudi, the son of a Turin policeman, in 1978. They have dug out their temple, known as the Temple of Humankind, using only pick-axes and buckets.

LONGEST IRREGULAR RELIGIOUS WAR

The Reconquista – the series of campaigns in the Iberian Peninsula to recover the region from the Islamic Moors – began in 718 and continued intermittently for 774 years until 1492, when Granada, the last Moorish stronghold, was finally conquered.

MOST PROLIFIC 'CRYING' STATUE

On 14 days between 2 February and 17 March 1995, a 40-cm (15.75-in) plaster statue of the Virgin Mary, standing at the Marian shrine at Medjugorje, Bosnia and Herzegovina, apparently wept tears of blood. One such manifestation was witnessed by the diocesan bishop. Unlike this occasion, most reports of weeping statues do not receive any form of recognition from the Roman Catholic Church.

MOST RECENT APPARITION OF MARY

The most recent apparition of the Virgin Mary recognized by the Roman Catholic Church was at the cave of Betania, Cau, in Venezuela. This has been seen at intervals since March 1976 by Maria Esperanza Medrano Bianchini (Spain), and later by hundreds of other people. The apparitions were officially recognized by the Roman Catholic Church in 1987.

MOST WITNESSES TO AN APPARITION

On the occasion of the sixth, and last, apparition of the Virgin Mary to three children at Fatima, Portugal, on 13 October 1915, some 70,000 people witnessed the Sun appear to 'dance' in the sky immediately after the children received the vision. The Fatima apparitions were officially recognized by the Roman Catholic Church in 1930.

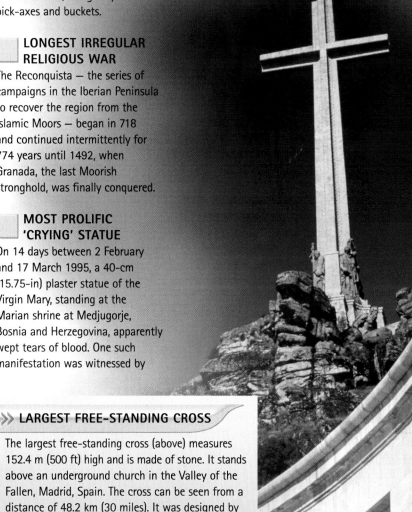

LARGEST FREE-STANDING CROSS

The largest free-standing cross (above) measures 152.4 m (500 ft) high and is made of stone. It stands above an underground church in the Valley of the Fallen, Madrid, Spain. The cross can be seen from a distance of 48.2 km (30 miles). It was designed by Juan de Avalos (Spain) and was built as a memorial to all those who died in the Spanish Civil War.

WEDDINGS

MOST COUPLES MARRIED UNDERWATER

On 14 February 2001 (Valentine's Day) 34 couples from 22 countries simultaneously exchanged wedding vows 10 m (32 ft 9.6 in) underwater off Kradan Island, southern Thailand (above). Couples received waterproof certificates before removing their mouthpieces for a watery kiss.

LONGEST ENGAGEMENT

The longest engagement on record is between Octavio Guillan and Adriana Martinez (both Mexico). They finally took the plunge after 67 years in June 1969 in Mexico City. Both were aged 82.

BRIDE WITH THE MOST BRIDESMAIDS

There is a tie for the record of bride with the most bridesmaids. Accompanied by 28 bridesmaids aged 2 to 40, bride Jane Williams married Julian Davis (both UK) at Priory Church in Depping St James, Lincolnshire, UK, in 2001.

Debbie-Jane 'DJ' Hunt (UK) had 28 bridesmaids when she married Jason Clark (UK) at St Mary's Church, Southampton, Hampshire, UK, in summer 2000.

CITY WITH THE MOST WEDDINGS

Regarded as the wedding capital of the world, Las Vegas, Nevada, USA, has over 100 chapels performing approximately 8,400 marriage ceremonies per month – 280 per day or one wedding every 5 min 17 sec. Of these, 12% are between couples from outside the USA. The appeal of a Vegas wedding may be that there is no blood test (a legal requirement in some US states) and a waiting period of only 15–30 minutes to obtain a marriage licence at a cost of $50 (£30) from the Clark County Courthouse.

LONGEST MARRIAGE

The longest marriages on record were both for 86 years. Sir Temulji Bhicaji Nariman and Lady Nariman (both India), who were married from 1853 to 1940, were cousins and the marriage took place when both were aged five. Sir Temulji died aged 91 years 11 months in August 1940.

Lazarus Rowe and Molly Webber (both USA), both born in 1725, were recorded as marrying in 1743. Molly died first, in June 1829, also after 86 years of marriage.

The longest-married living couple are Yung-Yang Liu (b. 7 October 1900) who married Yang-Wan Yang (b. 18 February 1901) in Kweishan Hsiang, Taoyan County, Taiwan, on 10 March 1917. Aged 102 and 101 respectively, they have been married over 85 years.

MOST COUPLES MARRIED SIMULTANEOUSLY

Some 35,000 couples officiated over by Sun Myung Moon (South Korea) of the Holy Spirit Association for the Unification of World Christianity were married in the Olympic Stadium in Seoul, South Korea, on 25 August 1995. A further 325,000 couples around the world took part in the ceremony through a satellite link.

COUNTRY WITH THE HIGHEST MARRIAGE RATE

Antigua and Barbuda was the sovereign country with the highest marriage rate in the world with 22.1 per 1,000 population in 1998.

COUNTRY WITH THE HIGHEST DIVORCE RATE

As of September 2002 the country with the highest divorce rate in the world is the Maldives with 10.97 divorces per 1,000 inhabitants per year. The Maldives is followed by Belarus with 4.63 and the USA with 4.34 per 1,000.

MOST EXPENSIVE WEDDING DRESS

A wedding outfit created by Hélène Gainville with jewels by Alexander Reza (both France) was estimated to be worth £4,269,934 ($7,301,587) when the dress, embroidered with diamonds mounted on platinum, was unveiled in Paris, France, on 23 March 1989.

LONGEST WEDDING VEIL

Katsura Yumi Bridal House of Tokyo, Japan, created the world's longest bridal veil measuring 2,023.86 m (6,639 ft 11.5 in). It was used in a civil wedding ceremony at the Takarazuka Hotel, Takarazuka, Hyogo, Japan, on 31 December 2000. Around 10,000 people helped the bride with her veil.

LONGEST WEDDING DRESS TRAIN

On 16 February 2002, newlyweds Ernst Boekhorst and Jorien Schuit (both Netherlands) walked hand-in-hand through Haastrecht, Netherlands, with a wedding train measuring 776 m (2,545 ft) trailing behind Jorien's gown. The 250 guests helped carry the train through the village.

LARGEST WEDDING BOUQUET

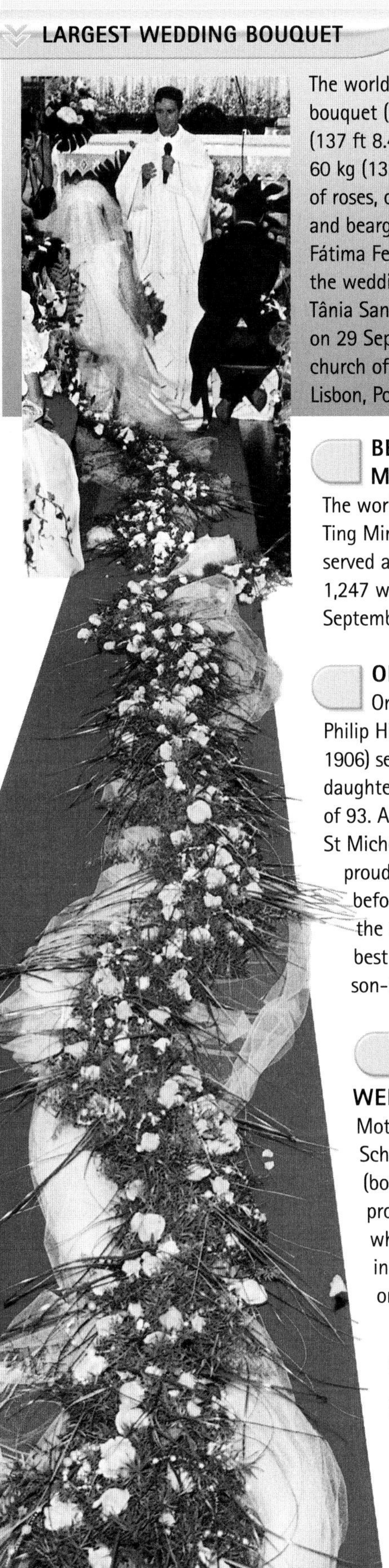

The world's largest wedding bouquet (left) measured 42 m (137 ft 8.4 in) long, weighed 60 kg (132 lb) and was made up of roses, orchids, asparagus stems and beargrass. It was created by Fátima Fernandes (Portugal) for the wedding of Mal Carlos and Tânia Santos (both Portugal) on 29 September 2002 at the church of Almargem do Bispo, Lisbon, Portugal.

BEST MAN AT THE MOST WEDDINGS

The world champion best man is Ting Ming Siong (Malaysia) who served as best man at a record 1,247 weddings between September 1975 and 1 April 2001.

OLDEST BEST MAN

On 14 August 1999, Philip Hicks (UK, b. 26 March 1906) served as best man at his daughter's wedding at the age of 93. At the civil ceremony in St Michel de Vax, France, Philip proudly gave his daughter away before promptly moving to the right to become the best man of his future son-in-law.

LARGEST MOTORCYCLE WEDDING PROCESSION

Motorcycle enthusiasts Peter Schmidl and Anna Turceková (both Slovakia) had a wedding procession of 597 motorcycles when they tied the knot in Bratislava, Slovakia, on 6 May 2000.

LARGEST MASS PRISON WEDDING

On 14 June 2000, 120 inmates of Carandiru prison, São Paulo, Brazil, married their fiancées in a mass ceremony.

MOST MARRIAGES

The greatest number of monogamous marriages by a woman is 23, by Linda Essex (USA).

The greatest number of marriages contracted by one man in the monogamous world is 29, by former Baptist minister Glynn 'Scotty' Wolfe (USA) who first married in 1927 and believed he had a total of 41 children. In June 1996, Wolfe and Essex married – for a publicity stunt, some have said – but Wolfe died 10 days before their first anniversary.

MOST MARRIAGE VOWS REAFFIRMED BY THE SAME COUPLE

Lauren Lubeck Blair and David E Hough Blair (both USA) married each other for the 66th time on 26 April 2002 in Loxwood, Westfield, Woking, Surrey, UK. The Blairs have married each other a total of 66 times since they first got hitched in 1984; all the wedding ceremonies have been in separate locations.

FASTEST WEDDING VIDEO PRODUCTION

Videotapes of the royal wedding of HRH Prince Andrew and Sarah Ferguson (both UK) on 23 July 1986 were produced in record time by Thames Video Collection (UK). Live filming ended with the departure of the honeymoon couple from Chelsea Hospital by helicopter at 4:42 pm, and the first fully edited and packaged VHS tapes were bought at 10:23 pm, 5 hr 41 min later, from the Virgin Megastore in Oxford Street, London, UK.

OLDEST COUPLE TO MARRY

On 1 February 2002 French couple François Frenandez (b. 17 April 1906) and Madeleine Francineau (b. 15 July 1907) exchanged vows at the rest home Le Foyer du Romarin, Clapiers, France, at the age of 96 and 94 respectively. The total aggregate years between them at the time of wedding ceremony was a record 190.

The oldest recorded bride is Minnie Munro (Australia), aged 102, who married fellow Australian Dudley Reid, aged 83, at Point Clare, New South Wales, Australia on 31 May 1991.

LARGEST INFLATABLE CHURCH

The world's largest inflatable church (below) is owned by InnovationsUK.com Ltd (UK). It is 14.3 m (47 ft) long, 7.6 m (25 ft) wide and has a 14.3-m (47-ft) high spire, plus stained glass windows, an altar and a pulpit. The church can be hired or bought for any occasion.

LONGEST RUNNING ROCK GROUP FAN CLUB

The Official Queen Fan Club was set up by EMI after the 1973 launch of the band's first album, *Queen*, in 1973, because of the unprecedented amount of fan mail the group was receiving. At its peak, the club had more than 20,000 members, although this number has now dropped to 9,500.

LONGEST RUNNING SOLO ARTIST FAN CLUB

The Club Crosby, celebrating the work of singer/actor Bing Crosby (USA), was founded in 1936 and currently has 450 members worldwide. Its official magazine, *Bingang*, is published twice a year.

MOST FAN MAIL

Although fan mail is traditionally associated with film stars, no actor or actress has received in the course of a career the number of letters delivered to Charles Lindbergh following his solo non-stop transatlantic flight in May 1927 – a total of 3.5 million. He took off in *Spirit of St Louis* from Roosevelt Field, Long Island, USA, on 20 May 1927 and landed on 21 May at Le Bourget, near Paris, France, after flying 5,793 km (3,600 miles) in 33 hr 30 min.

MOST FAN MAIL RECEIVED IN ONE YEAR

According to the US Postal Department, the highest confirmed volume of mail received by any private citizen in one year is 900,000 letters sent to the baseball star Hank Aaron (USA) in June 1974.

MOST FAN CLUBS FOR A SINGER

There are more than 613 active Elvis Presley fan clubs worldwide, with a total membership of 510,489 as of March 2000. The longest running of these is the French *La Voix d'Elvis* (The Voice of Elvis), founded in January 1956 by Evelyne Bellemin (France).

MOST WIDELY SUPPORTED FOOTBALL CLUB

The Official Supporters Club of Manchester United (UK, a fan shown below) has 152,000 paid-up members in addition to 45,000 season ticket holders. There are 108 UK branches, 78 Irish and 24 worldwide including countries as far afield as Mauritius and Australia.

MOST HOLLYWOOD FAN MAIL

Cartoon character Mickey Mouse was reported to have received 800,000 fan letters in 1933, an average of 66,000 a month.

In 1936 seven-year-old actress Shirley Temple (USA) was receiving just over 60,000 letters a month.

Charlie Chaplin (UK) created a fan-mail record when he received 73,000 letters in the first three days of his return home to London, UK, in 1921.

Clara Bow (USA) received 33,727 items of mail during the month of April 1928. Three full-time secretaries were employed to reply, costing the modern equivalent of $26,763 (£16,975).

In 1926, 32,250,000 fan letters were sent to various Hollywood studios, with Paramount receiving the most, according to a report by *Variety* in April 1927.

LARGEST SAME-NAME GATHERING

The world's largest same-name gathering occurred on 22 September 2001 at the Australasian Shirley Club's inaugural 'Shirley Conference' in the Rydges Plaza Resort, Alice Springs, Northern Territory, Australia. There were 122 Shirleys in attendance, all of whom produced birth certificates to prove their authenticity.

MOST POPULAR POLITICAL CAT

Socks, a stray cat rescued by a neighbour of Bill and Hillary Clinton (both USA) when they lived at the governor's mansion in Little Rock, Arkansas, USA, was adopted by the future First Family in 1991. At the height of his fame, Socks is said to have received 75,000 letters and parcels a week. The popular tabby answered every piece of fan mail with help from his personal correspondence staff.

MOST CONDOLENCES ON THE NET

Messages were left by 580,000 people on the memorial page of the official website of the British monarchy in September 1997, following the death of Diana, Princess of Wales (UK).

LARGEST FREE ROCK CONCERT ATTENDANCE

Rod Stewart's (UK) free concert at Copacabana Beach, Rio de Janeiro, Brazil, on New Year's Eve 1994, reportedly attracted an audience of 3.5 million.

LARGEST INTERNET POP CONCERT

On 28 November 2000 Madonna (USA) performed a concert at the Brixton Academy, London, UK, which was also broadcast live on the internet by Microsoft Network and watched by 11 million people online. MSN emailed their 75 million Hotmail users to advertise the event in addition to homepage promotions in 17 different languages on more than 30 internet sites worldwide.

LARGEST MAGIC SOCIETY

Founded in 1968 in New York, USA, The International Magicians' Society boasts 23,000 members worldwide. These include David Copperfield (USA), the world's highest paid magician.

LARGEST STAMP COLLECTING ORGANIZATION

With over 55,000 members in more than 110 countries, the American Philatelic Society is the largest non-profit society in the world for stamp collectors and postal historians. It is supported entirely by membership dues, gifts and the sale of its publications and services. The APS was founded in 1886.

LARGEST FOOTBALL MATCH ATTENDANCE

The greatest recorded crowd at any football match was 199,854 for the Brazil v. Uruguay World Cup match in the Maracanã Municipal Stadium, Rio de Janeiro, Brazil on 16 July 1950.

MOST RODEOS ATTENDED

James Newland (USA) has annually attended every performance of the Black Hills Roundup Rodeo since it was founded in 1918 when he was seven years old. This represents 82 years of uninterrupted rodeo attendance.

LARGEST STAR TREK FAN CLUB

Starfleet: the International *Star Trek* Fan Association, founded in 1974 and based in Maryland, USA, boasts over 4,100 annual members dedicated to t[illegible] ideals of the *Star Trek* television series. Two 'Trekkies' are pictured (right).

LARGEST BEER FESTIVAL

Munich's (Germany) Oktoberfest 99 (18 September to 5 October) stood on a site as large as 50 football pitches and was visited by seven million people who consumed a record 5.8 million litres (1,275,820 gal) of beer (above) in 11 beer tents.

OLDEST ROTARY CLUB

Paul Harris (USA), together with three friends, started the first Rotary Club on 23 February 1905. The club had a total of 30 members by the end of the year. Rotary International now consists of 29,500 clubs in 162 countries. The USA has the most rotary clubs with 7,485 followed by Japan with 2,280.

LONGEST CAREER AS AN ELVIS IMPERSONATOR

Victor Beasley (Belgium) has been appearing and performing as 'The King' since 1955, a total of 47 years. On 6 July 2002 Beasley gave his 48th annual show. During the course of his distinguished career, Beasley has also been made Honorary Citizen of Tupelo, Mississippi, USA, birthplace of the legendary Elvis Presley.

MOST VIEWERS FOR A SIMULTANEOUS CHARITY ROCK CONCERT

Live Aid, the world's largest simultaneous charity rock concert in terms of viewers, was organized by Bob Geldof (Ireland). Held in London, UK, and Philadelphia, USA, on 13 July 1985, over 60 of rock music's biggest acts played for free to an estimated 1.5 billion TV viewers watching via satellite throughout the world to raise money for African famine relief.

MOST SUCCESSFUL TOUR

The Rolling Stones' 1989 'Steel Wheels' North American tour earned an estimated £185 million ($310 million) and was attended by 3.2 million people in 30 cities.

LARGEST TAMALE FESTIVAL

A tamale is a popular Mexican dish that usually consists of spiced meat wrapped in a layer of cornmeal dough. The annual Indio International Tamale Festival that takes place in Indio, California, USA, had an attendance of over 154,000 people at its eleventh event in December 2000.

LARGEST TRUCKING COMPANY FAN CLUB

The Eddie Stobart Ltd (UK) haulage company has a fan club with over 25,000 members, including some in Australia and the USA. Founded in 1970, the green, red and gold trucks (each given a girl's name) driven by polite, tie-wearing, uniformed drivers, soon attracted the attention of other road users. Club members, or 'Eddie Spotters', as they are known, receive a 'fleet manual' detailing the name, number and type of each of the 800 trucks that members can spot.

LARGEST GNOME AND PIXIE COLLECTION

Since 1978 Ann Atkin (UK) has collected a total of 2,010 gnomes and pixies, all of which live in her 1.6-ha (4-acre) Gnome Reserve. The reserve enjoys an average of 25,000 visitors per year, who are encouraged to don hats and temporarily turn into gnomes for their magical journey through the woodland.

MOST PERIPATETIC FOOTBALL FAN

Ken Ferris (UK) watched a League match at all 92 League grounds in England and Wales (including Berwick Rangers) in just 237 days – from 10 September 1994 until 6 May 1995. He began at Brunton Park (Carlisle Utd) and finished at Goodison Park (Everton).

TRAVEL & TOURISM

LARGEST CARNIVAL

Rio de Janeiro's (Brazil) annual carnival, held during the first week of March, attracts an approximate daily crowd of two million people, 300,000 of whom are tourists. In 1998 the four-day event generated £100 million ($165 million).

FASTEST CIRCUMNAVIGATION BY SCHEDULED FLIGHTS, VISITING SIX CONTINENTS

Michael Bartlett and David J Springbett (both UK) circumnavigated the globe on scheduled flights from 18 to 21 October 1999, setting foot on all six continents in 68 hr 5 min. Their journey began in London and took them via Cairo, Singapore, Sydney, San Francisco, Dallas and Caracas back to their starting point.

MOST POPULAR TOURIST DESTINATION

According to the World Tourism Organization (WTO), France attracted 76.5 million international visitors in 2001 – 11% of all international travellers that year – making it the world's most popular tourist destination. Spain was second, with 49.5 million visitors, and the USA third, with 45.5 million.

LARGEST EXPORT INDUSTRY

Tourism is widely regarded as the largest export industry in the world, with a massive $555 billion (£343 billion) flowing into countries through the selling of services to visiting foreign tourists in 1999. The automotive industry (cars and car parts) is the second largest, accounting for $549 billion (£340 billion) of exports in that year.

MOST SCHEDULED FLIGHTS IN 24 HOURS

Michael Bartlett (UK) made 42 scheduled passenger flights with Heli Transport of Nice, southern France, between Nice, Sophia-Antipolis, Monaco and Cannes in 13 hr 33 min on 13 June 1990.

MOST SCHEDULED FLIGHTS IN A WEEK

Tae Oka (Japan) completed 70 scheduled flights in seven days on Thai Airways International between 14 and 20 February 2001. The flights were all internal flights between the Thai cities of Chiang Mai, Chiang Rai and Mae Hong Son and all lasted 70 minutes. All flights were on Boeing 747-400s, and the total value of the flights was THB69,960 (£1,135 or $1,642 at 2001 rates).

SHORTEST TIME TO VISIT 15 EU COUNTRIES

David Beaumont (UK) visited all (then) 15 European Union countries as a passenger on scheduled flights in a time of 35 hr 8 min between 2 and 3 May 1995.

BIGGEST TOURIST SPENDERS

The biggest overseas travel spenders are US citizens, who in 2001 spent a massive $58.9 billion (£40.87 billion) whilst on holiday in foreign countries (excluding airfares) according to the WTO. Germany and the UK were second and third respectively, spending $45.9 billion (£31.85 billion) and $36.9 billion (£25.6 billion).

BUSIEST AIRPORT FOR DOMESTIC AND INTERNATIONAL PASSENGERS

Hartsfield International Airport, serving Atlanta, Georgia, USA, was the world's busiest in terms of passengers in 2001, with 75.8 million people using it that year. The 2001 statistics reveal a fall of 5.4% on the previous year, the result of the 11 September attacks in New York and economic slowdown.

BUSIEST AIRPORT FOR INTERNATIONAL PASSENGERS

According to the Airports Council International (ACI), London's Heathrow Airport handled 53.79 million passengers arriving from, or departing to, destinations outside of the UK during 2001, making it the world's busiest airport for international passengers. However, it is only the fourth busiest airport overall.

BUSIEST AIRPORT FOR CARGO

Memphis International Airport, Tennessee, USA, is the world's busiest airport in terms of the amount of cargo passing through it, according to the ACI. In 2001, 2.631 million tonnes (5.8 billion lb) of freight was handled, with around 95% belonging to international express transport company FedEx, which has its main overnight sorting facility at the airport.

BUSIEST INTERNATIONAL AIRLINE

According to IATA, the German carrier Lufthansa is the biggest carrier of international passengers. In 2001 the airline carried 29.1 million passengers to and from destinations outside of Germany on regular scheduled flights. British Airways (UK), the former champion, took the number two spot with 28.1 million passengers.

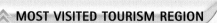

MOST VISITED TOURISM REGION

According to the WTO, the region that received the most international tourists in 2001 was Europe (the popular destination of Florence, Italy, shown above), with 400.3 million arrivals. Although its market share is gradually shrinking, the continent still attracts 57.8% of all international travellers.

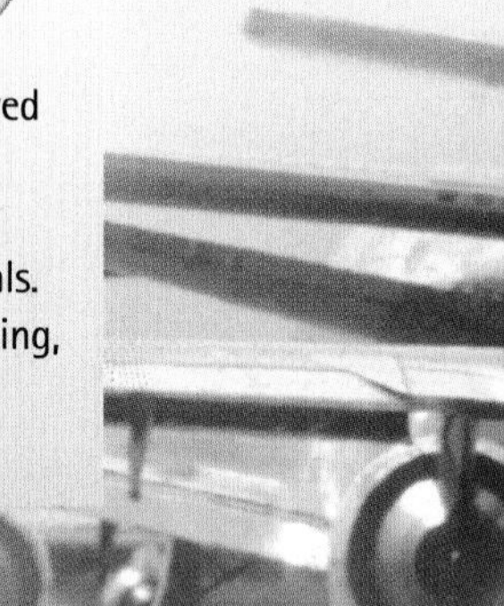

LARGEST AIRPORT BY ACREAGE

The £2.1-billion ($3.17-billion) King Khalid international airport outside Riyadh, Saudi Arabia, covers an area of 22,273 ha (55,040 acres). It was opened on 14 November 1983.

LONGEST HIKING TRAIL

The world's longest complete designated hiking trail is the Pacific Crest Trail, which runs for 4,260 km (2,650 miles) along the west coast of the USA between the Mexican and Canadian borders.

LONGEST WILDERNESS HORSE TRAIL

The Australian Bicentennial National Trail is the longest marked horse-trekking trail in the world at 5,330 km (3,312 miles). It winds through wilderness areas from Cooktown in North Queensland to Healesville in Victoria, following historic coach and stock routes, pack-horse trails and country roads.

LONGEST SINGLE AIR TICKET

A 12-m (39-ft 4.4-in) single air ticket was issued to Bruno Leunen (Belgium) in December 1984 for a 85,623-km (53,203-mile) round trip on 80 airlines, with 109 stopovers.

MOST EXPENSIVE TRIP BY A TOURIST

American businessman Dennis Tito and South African internet millionaire Mark Shuttleworth each paid Russia a reported $20 million (£14 million) for their trips to the International Space Station (ISS). Tito's trip lasted from 28 April to 6 May 2001, and Shuttleworth's from 25 April to 5 May 2002.

FASTEST TRANS-ATLANTIC FLIGHT

A British Airways (UK) Concorde took 2 hr 52 min 59 sec to travel the 6,035 km (3,750 miles) between JFK airport, New York, USA, and Luton Airport, Bedfordshire, UK, on 7 February 1996, breaking its own record (set in April 1990) by 1 min 30 sec. The plane, piloted by Captain Leslie Scott (UK), flew at an average speed of over 2,011 km/h (1,250 mph).

YOUNGEST PERSON TO HAVE TRAVELLED TO ALL SEVEN CONTINENTS

The youngest person ever to have travelled to all seven continents is Tanya Daniella Donkin (South Africa, b. 2 January 1997) who, on 16 November 2000, landed in Dubai, United Arab Emirates (Asia) at the age of 3 years 319 days, thereby visiting her seventh continent. All her travels were with her parents Dave and Irene Donkin.

SAFEST AIR TRAVEL YEAR ON RECORD

Despite the attacks on the World Trade Center in New York, USA, which are regarded as acts of terrorism and not accidents, 2001 was the safest year in modern times for travel on scheduled air services, according to International Civil Aviation Organization data. In this year there was, on average, one fatal accident for every 2 billion km (1.2 billion miles) flown by passenger aircraft, and one fatality for every 5 billion km (3.1 billion miles) flown.

YOUNGEST PERSON TO VISIT BOTH POLES

Jonathan Silverman (USA, b. 13 June 1990) reached the North Pole on 25 July 1999 and the South Pole on 10 January 2002, aged 11 years 211 days. He travelled as part of tourist expeditions.

BUSIEST SCHEDULED AIRLINE OVERALL

According to the International Air Transport Association (IATA), Delta Air Lines (USA) carried 93.4 million passengers on scheduled services during 2001, making it the world's largest airline. Delta operates a fleet of around 820 aircraft and carries most of its passengers within the USA. American Airlines (USA) was in second place, with 78.1 million passengers.

HIGHEST EARNINGS FROM TOURISM

Despite a fall of nearly 12% in 2001, the USA remains the world leader in terms of earnings from international tourism, taking $72.3 billion (£50.1 billion) in that year. This is equivalent to a world market share of 15.6%. The nearest rivals, Spain and France, have 7.1% and 6.4% of market share respectively.

LONGEST RING-ROAD

Work on the 195.5-km-long (121.8-mile) M25 London Orbital Motorway (mostly six lanes), UK, commenced in 1972 and was completed on 29 October 1986 at an estimated cost of £909 million ($1,333 million), or £4.6 million ($7 million) per km.

LONGEST MOTORABLE ROAD

The Pan-American Highway, from Fairbanks, Alaska, USA, to Santiago, Chile, and thence eastward via Buenos Aires, Argentina, to Brasîlia, Brazil, is over 24,140 km (15,000 miles) long. However, there is an incomplete section in Panama and Colombia known as the Darién Gap. This 110-km (70-mile) stretch of rainforest is the subject of debate between those who want the road completed and those who oppose it for environmental reasons.

BUSIEST AIRPORT FOR NUMBER OF AIRCRAFT

A total of 909,535 take-offs and landings by aircraft were made during 2001 at O'Hare International Airport (below), Chicago, Illinois, USA, making it the world's busiest in terms of the number of aircraft using it. However, O'Hare is still in second place behind Atlanta's Hartsfield International in terms of the number of passengers being served.

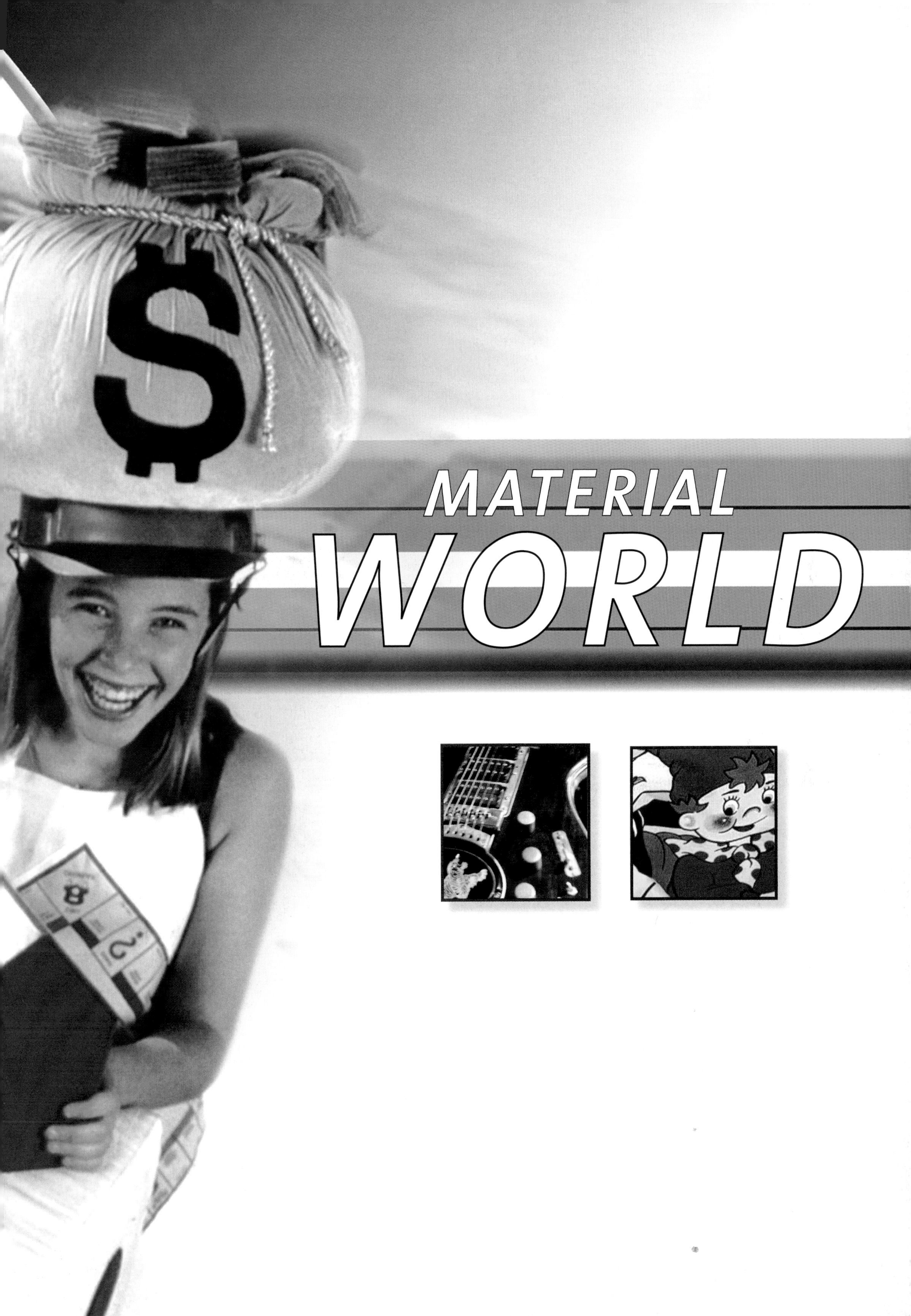
MATERIAL
WORLD

SPENDING POWER

MOST VALUABLE GUITAR

Jerry Garcia's 'Tiger' guitar (above) sold for $957,500 (£657,850) to an anonymous bidder at a Guernsey's auction in New York, USA, on 9 May 2002. Garcia died in 1995 and left his guitars to guitar maker Doug Irwin, who settled a lawsuit against The Grateful Dead in November 2001 and put the instruments up for sale.

MOST VALUABLE BASEBALL

A baseball was sold at Guernsey's auction house, New York, USA, for $3,054,000 (£1,874,655) including commission to Todd McFarlane (USA) on 12 January 1999. The ball had been hit by Mark McGwire (USA) of the St Louis Cardinals for his 70th and final home run in his record-setting season in 1998.

MOST VALUABLE BASEBALL GLOVE

Former New York Yankee Lou Gehrig's (USA) glove from his final baseball game on 30 April 1939 was sold for $389,500 (£236,778) at Sotheby's, New York, USA, on 29 September 1999.

MOST VALUABLE CIGARS

On 16 November 1997 at Christie's, London, UK, a record £9,980 ($16,877) was paid for 25 Trinidad cigars made by the Cuban National Factory.

MOST EXPENSIVE MEAL PER HEAD

On 5 July 2001 six diners at Pétrus, London, UK, spent £44,007 ($61,941) on one meal. The bill consisted mainly of five bottles of wine as, once the bill had been added up, the £300 ($422) charge for food was taken off. The most expensive bottle was a 1947 Chateau Pétrus vintage claret worth £12,300 ($17,312), followed by the slightly cheaper 1945 Chateau Pétrus at £11,600 ($16,327). A 1946 Chateau Pétrus cost £9,400 ($13,230) apparently due to this being a poor year. A 1900 Château d'Yquem dessert wine cost £9,200 ($12,949) and 1982 bottle of Montrachet was a snip at £1,400 ($1,970). The remaining £107 ($150) consisted of water, a fruit juice, cigarettes and six glasses of champagne.

LARGEST AUCTION OF COMIC BOOKS

The world's largest auction of comic books, comic art, movie posters and related memorabilia took place on 13 October 2002. The four-day auction, conducted by Heritage Comic Auctions of Dallas, Texas, USA, realized $5,207,430.65 (£3,335,958).

MOST VALUABLE COIN

The most valuable coin in the world is the 1933 'Double Eagle', a $20 gold coin which was auctioned at Sotheby's, New York, USA, on 30 July 2002 and fetched a massive $7,590,020 (£4,856,370) including buyer's premium.

MOST VALUABLE CAMERA

The prototype Phantom Camera Unit, designed by the eccentric British inventor and MP Noel Pemberton Billing, was sold for £146,750 ($216,826) at auction by Christie's, London, UK, on 16 January 2001. The buyer was a private photographic museum. The final bid for the Phantom was more than 12 times its original estimated value (£8,000–£12,000), an incredible amount considering it was never fully finished.

MOST VALUABLE MANUSCRIPT

On 6 December 1983 Hans Kraus (Germany), acting for the Hermann Abs consortium, paid £8.14 million ($11.7 million) for the 226-leaf manuscript *The Gospel Book of Henry the Lion, Duke of Saxony* at Sotheby's, London, UK. The book, which measures 34.3 x 25.4 cm (13.5 x 10 in), was illuminated with 41 full-page illustrations c.1170 by Herimann, a monk at Helmarshausen Abbey, Germany.

MOST VALUABLE CELLO

The highest ever auction price for a violoncello is £682,000 ($1,217,711) paid at Sotheby's, London, UK, on 22 June 1988 for a Stradivarius known as 'The Cholmondeley', which was made in Cremona, Italy, around 1698.

MOST VALUABLE HAIR

The most valuable hair clippings sold at auction are a mass of dark black cuttings from the head of Elvis Presley (USA), which were sold by his personal barber for $115,120 (£72,791) to an anonymous buyer during an online auction held by MastroNet Inc. on 15 November 2002.

MOST VALUABLE BEER CAN

A Rosalie Pilsner and a Tiger beer can each sold for $6,000 (£2,760) in the USA in April 1981. The beer was brewed in the 1930s by the Manhattan Brewing Company of Chicago and the cans have become collectors' items. Vintage beer can collecting is very popular with the Beer Can Collectors of America: there are over 5,000 members who make beer cans their passion.

MOST VALUABLE CIGARETTE CARD

The most valuable cigarette card is one of the six known baseball series cards of Honus Wagner (USA), who was a non-smoker, which was sold during an online eBay auction for $1,263,000 (£842,781) to an anonymous buyer on 15 July 2000.

MOST VALUABLE ATLAS

A version of ancient Greek astronomer Ptolemy's *Cosmographia* (below) dating from 1492 was sold for $1,144,947 (£1,666,666) at Sotheby's, New York City, USA, on 31 January 1990.

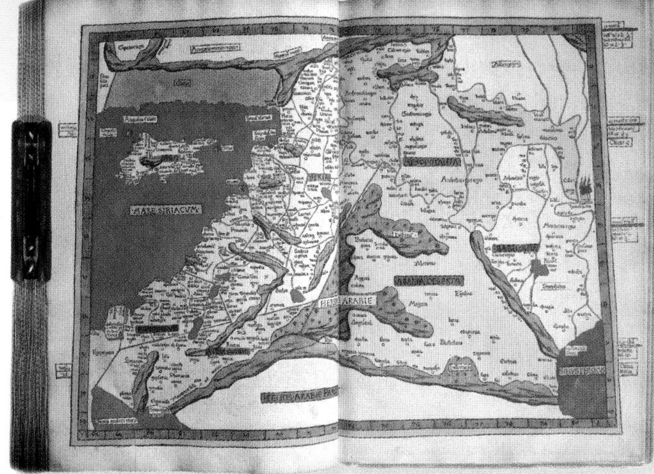

MOST VALUABLE FLAG

The Royal Standard rescued by Sir Ernest Shackleton (UK) from his doomed ship *Endurance* in 1915 went to an anonymous buyer in September 2002 for £116,000 ($180,635) at Christie's in London, UK.

MOST VALUABLE JACKET

The most valuable jacket sold at auction belonged to Jimi Hendrix (USA) and was sold to the Hard Rock Cafe chain for £35,000 ($49,185) at a Sotheby's sale at the London branch of the Hard Rock Cafe on 19 September 2000.

MOST VALUABLE BOXING MEMORABILIA

A black and white robe worn by Muhammad Ali (USA) before the 1974 'Rumble in the Jungle' fight against George Foreman (USA) fetched $157,947 (£94,000) at a sale in Los Angeles, USA, in October 1997.

MOST VALUABLE CHRISTMAS CARD

The world's most valuable Christmas card was sold at auction in Devizes, Wiltshire, UK, on 24 November 2001 for £20,000 ($28,158) to an anonymous bidder. Measuring 13 x 8 cm (5 x 3 in), it was sent by Sir Henry Cole (UK) to his grandmother in 1843 and is hand-coloured by the London illustrator John Calcott Horsley. It is considered to be the world's first Christmas card.

MOST VALUABLE CARPET

A 16th-century tabriz medallion carpet from northwest Persia was sold for £1,596,500 ($2,487,178) at the Rothschild Sale, Christie's, London, UK, on 8 July 1999.

MOST VALUABLE BOOK

An original four-volume subscriber set of J J Audubon's (Haiti) *The Birds of America* was auctioned for $8,802,500 (£5,567,573) by Christie's, New York, USA, on 10 March 2000.

MOST VALUABLE POP MEMORABILIA

John Lennon's (UK) 1965 Phantom V Rolls Royce (below) was bought for $2,229,000 (£1,702,827) by Jim Pattison, Chairman of the Expo 86 World Fair in Vancouver, Canada, at Sotheby's, New York, USA, on 29 June 1985.

LARGER THAN LIFE

LARGEST FAN

A hand-painted fan made of chintz and wood measuring 8 m (26 ft 3 in) when unfolded and 4.5 m (14 ft 8 in) high was made by Víctor Troyas Osés (Spain) in October 1994.

LARGEST CHRISTMAS BAUBLE ORNAMENT

The largest Christmas bauble ornament in the world measures 4.2 m (13 ft 9 in) in diameter and was made of galvanized steel by Sergio Rodríguez (Mexico) in December 2000.

LARGEST CRAYON

A red crayon standing 3 m (10 ft) tall and weighing 150.6 kg (332 lb) was unveiled on 28 May 1997. Made as part of a promotional campaign by the Dixon Ticonderoga Company, Heathrow, Florida, USA, it contained enough soya bean to make 34,527 standard-sized crayons.

LARGEST CONTAINER OF BODY CREAM

The world's largest container of body cream is 2 m (6 ft 6.75 in) in diameter, 53 cm (1 ft 8.75 in) high and holds 1,124.49 litres (323.48 gallons) of NIVEA Creme (below). It was created by Beiersdorf Hellas (Greece) and unveiled in Athens, Greece, on 15 December 2001.

LARGEST PESTLE AND MORTAR

The largest pestle and mortar on record was manufactured by Neftalí Maldonado (Puerto Rico). The mortar (base) was carved out of a single mahogany log and is 3.14 m (10 ft 4 in) high, with a mouth diameter of 1.82 m (6 ft). It weighs 1.8 tonnes (4,000 lb). The pestle is 3.6 m (12 ft) long with a diameter of 60 cm (2 ft) and weighs around 360 kg (800 lb). Maldonado says it took him 12 hours a day over four months to complete this project, using only hand tools.

LONGEST PENCIL

The world's longest pencil was created by Faber-Castell of Selangor, Malaysia, in November 2002. It measures 19.75 m (64 ft 9.5 in) long and 80 cm (2 ft 7.5 in) in diameter, and encases a lead 15 cm (6 in) in diameter. The giant pencil stands vertically within a protective glass structure on the new Malaysian premises of Faber-Castell. The company has been manufacturing writing instruments since 1761.

LARGEST MAILBOX

Canada Post Corporation erected a postbox 5.43 x 2.64 x 1.98 m (17 ft 10 in x 7 ft 2 in x 6 ft 6 in) in downtown Vancouver, British Columbia, Canada, in December 2000. The scaled-up version of a standard Canada Post postbox was made of steel and over 40,000 children used it to post their letters to Santa, by climbing a set of stairs to reach the slot at the top of the box. Many other regular letters were posted in the box and delivered as usual.

LONGEST HAMMOCK

On 22 June 2002 The Hessenstam Hattem of the Voerman Scouting Group unveiled a giant hand-knotted hammock measuring 2.5 m (8 ft 2 in) wide and 129.29 m (424 ft 2 in) long in Hattem, The Netherlands. The hammock was so huge it had to be hung between two cranes.

LARGEST WOODEN COAT HANGER

The largest wooden coat hanger ever made weighs 721 kg (1,589 lb) and was manufactured for H&L Russel Ltd (UK). The solid pine hanger, featuring a steel hook, is 5.51 m (18 ft) long, 2.5 m (8 ft) high, and 0.42 m (1 ft 4.5 in) wide.

LARGEST CHESS PIECE

The largest chess piece is a king made by Mats Allanson (Sweden). It is 4 m (13 ft) high and 1.4 m (4 ft 6 in) in diameter at the base.

LARGEST SLEEPING BAG

On 27 July 2002 in Salt Lake City, Utah, USA, Slumberjack (USA) unveiled the world's largest sleeping bag measuring 7.51 x 16.52 m (24 ft 8 in x 54 ft 2.5 in) and weighing 79 kg (175 lb).

LONGEST SOFA

In September 2001 Industrie Natuzzi SPA (Italy) created the world's longest sofa (which was crescent-shaped) measuring a length of 35.11 m (115 ft 2 in) on the outside edge, 24.86 m (81 ft 6 in) on the inside edge and with a height varying between 1 and 2 m (3 and 6 ft).

LARGEST BRA

In September 1990 Triumph International Japan Ltd developed a bra with an underbust measurement of 24 m (78 ft 8 in) and a bust measurement of 28 m (91 ft 10 in). The bra is based on the Tyrolean Cut (underwired three-quarter cup), which Triumph introduced in 1970. It was made from 70 m (230 ft) of fabric – enough to make 1,000 'regular' bras.

LARGEST ELECTRIC GUITAR

The largest playable guitar in the world is 13.29 m (43 ft 7.5 in) tall, 5.01 m (16 ft 5.5 in) wide and weighs 907 kg (2,000 lb). Modelled on a 1967 Gibson Flying V and built to a scale of 1:12, it was made by students from Conroe Independent School District Academy of Science and Technology, Conroe, Texas, USA, at a cost of $3,000 (£1,975). Construction began in October 1999 and the guitar was finally played at the Cynthia Woods Mitchell Pavilion, Texas, USA, on 6 June 2000 with the opening chord of The Beatles' 'A Hard Day's Night'.

LARGEST BEER MAT

The world's largest beer mat (below) was created by Carlsberg (Denmark) in Fredericia, Denmark, on 15 September 2002. It measured 15 m (49 ft 3 in) in diameter and had a thickness of 6 cm (2.5 in).

LARGEST BOX OF FACIAL TISSUES

The world's largest box of facial tissues measures 2.45 x 1.22 x 0.73 m (8 x 4 ft x 2 ft 4.75 in) and was constructed by FINE Hygienic Paper FZE and unveiled in Amman, Jordan, on 31 October 2002. The box was filled with giant sized tissues.

LARGEST CHAMPAGNE BOTTLE

Seven glass blowers from Demptos Glass, Jihlava, Czech Republic, created a champagne bottle 1.39 m (4 ft 6.5 in) tall and 1.32 m (4 ft 4 in) in circumference with a capacity of 117 litres (25.7 gal) on 15 October 1998. The bottle can hold enough champagne to fill 1,000 glasses.

LARGEST CIGAR

Jose Castelar Cairo (Cuba) took nine days to hand-roll a cigar measuring 11.04 m (36 ft 2.5 in). He presented his creation on 18 April 2001 at 'La Triada', Tiendas Habana Universo Cubanacan SA, Havana, Cuba.

LARGEST WORKING LIGHT SWITCH

The largest working light switch has a switch plate measuring 12.2 x 7.3 m (40 x 24 ft) with a mechanical toggle base approximately 2.45 m (8 ft) in height which moves through 2.3 m (7 ft 6 in) in either the 'on' or 'off' position. It is on the Broadway-facing façade of the Marriott Marquis Hotel in Times Square, New York City, USA.

LARGEST MODEL OF DNA

The largest model of DNA contained 300 base pairs and over 1,800 atoms and was roughly 12 m (40 ft) tall. Constructed of molymod, the base pairs were assembled by more than 3,000 British school children as well as celebrities from science, politics and the arts. The model was first assembled at the Potteries Shopping Centre in Stoke-on-Trent (UK) on 9 March 2002. Its current full length was created on 10 July 2002 in Earl's Court, London, UK.

LARGEST REVOLVER

The world's largest revolver weighs 45 kg (99.2 lb), has a length of 1.26 m (4 ft 1.5 in), a height of 40 cm (15.75 in) and is a working, scaled-up copy of a Remington 1859. It was built by Ryszard Tobys (Poland) and test-fired on 15 July 2002. The gun holds six bullets, each weighing 136 g (4.7 oz), and with a calibre of 28 mm (1.1 in).

LONGEST SURFBOARD

Tim Mellors' (UK) surfboard is 11.13 m (36 ft 6.5 in) long. He first used it on 11 August 1999.

LARGEST BASKET

The world's largest hand-woven basket (below) was made on behalf of the Cultural Centre in Nowy Tomysl, Poland, between 28 and 30 August 2000. The basket measured 17.29 x 9.46 x 7.71 m (56 ft 8.5 in x 31 ft 0.5 in x 25 ft 3.5 in) and was large enough to contain trees as well as flowers.

COLLECTIONS

LARGEST NODDY COLLECTION

Betty and Johnny Hopton (UK, left) have collected 1,351 different Noddy items, devoting every room in their home to the Enid Blyton character. Their most valuable item, a Noddy car, is worth about £1,100 ($1,725).

LARGEST UNOPENED BEER BOTTLE COLLECTION

Peter Broeker (Germany) has a collection of 8,131 unduplicated full beer bottles from 110 countries.

LARGEST AUTOGRAPHED DRUMSTICK COLLECTION

Peter Lavinger (USA) has collected over 1,300 drumsticks since 1980, all of which have been played and handed to him by drummers from various popular bands including Ringo Starr (UK) of The Beatles. His collection has been valued at over $1 million (£635,700).

LARGEST COLLECTION OF HOTEL BAGGAGE LABELS

Over the past 40 years, Robert Henin (USA) has collected 1,067 hotel baggage labels from different countries around the world. Hotel labels date back to the 19th century when fewer people travelled abroad. Labels were created as a means of advertising each hotel and they were stuck to travellers' suitcases as a testimony to places they had visited.

LARGEST AEROPLANE SICK BAG COLLECTION

Niek Vermeulen (Netherlands) has 3,240 airline sickness bags from 740 different airlines, topping a list of over 50 serious airsickness bag collectors. Legend has it that the airsickness bag was invented sometime in the 1920s after a particularly turbulent flight from Moscow to Berlin.

LARGEST COLLECTION OF HATS

The record for the largest collection of hats is 20,422 and is held by residents of the Tustumena Lodge, Kasilof, Alaska, USA.

LARGEST AIRLINE TAG COLLECTION

Raghav Somani (India) has a collection of 469 airline tags from 115 airlines around the world which he has been collecting since 1994.

LARGEST COLLECTION OF BUMPER STICKERS

The largest collection of car bumper stickers is owned by Bill Heermann (USA), who has amassed 3,230 since 1984.

LARGEST COLLECTION OF SAME BRAND SOFT DRINK CANS

Christian Cavaletti (Italy) has a collection of 3,284 different Pepsi cans from 71 different countries, which he has been collecting since 1989.

LARGEST MODEL AEROPLANE COLLECTION

The largest collection of hand-made m aeroplanes is owned by Robert Humph (USA). Robert's collection consists of 1 plastic aeroplane models, all of which has assembled himself.

LARGEST PENCIL COLLECTION

Emilio Arenas (Uruguay) has a collection of 6,885 different pencils, each printed with a distinct design, logo or brand. He also owns impressive collections of key rings, ashtrays, soft drink cans, beer cans, perfume bottles, pencil sharpeners, pins, matchboxes and phone cards.

LARGEST FRUIT STICKER COLLECTION

Antoine Secco (France) has collected over 26,875 different fruit stickers.

LARGEST BOTTLED WATER LABEL COLLECTION

Lorenzo Pescini (Italy) has a collection of 3,709 different bottled water labels that he has amassed since 1992. The oldest label in Lorenzo's collection is from a bottle of Acqua Roveta (1922) and his favourite is a rare label from a bottle of Acqua di Carnia (1971) produced for export to Saudi Arabia.

LARGEST MUG COLLECTION

The largest collection of mugs is owned by Harold Swauger (USA), who has amassed 4,567 since 1972.

LARGEST PLASTER COLLECTION

Brian Viner (UK) has 3,750 different types of unused first-aid plasters varying in colour, shape and size.

LARGEST COLLECTION OF 'DO NOT DISTURB' SIGNS

Jean Francois Vernetti (Switzerland) has collected 2,915 'Do Not Disturb' signs from hotels in 131 different countries across the world since 1985. His objective is to cover 191 countries.

LARGEST PRIVATE COLLECTION OF SPORTS PHOTOGRAPHS

The record for the largest private collection of sporting photographs belongs to Alex McFadyen (Canada). All of his 11,811 photos relate to ice hockey and are kept in a book of 678 pages, weighing a total of 74 kg (165 lb). The collection began in October 1977 and is still growing.

LARGEST STAR WARS MEMORABILIA COLLECTION

Jason Joiner (UK), a special effects expert who worked on the recent *Star Wars* films, has a collection of over 20,000 *Star Wars* toys. In addition, Joiner has one of the original C-3PO robots, an original R2-D2 and an original Darth Vader costume.

LARGEST DRAGON COLLECTION

Charlene Leatherman (USA) has a collection of 793 dragon items that she has been collecting since 1991, when she received one as a Christmas gift.

LARGEST COLLECTION OF MODEL COACHES AND BUSES

Geoff Price (UK) has been collecting model coaches and buses since 1959 and now has a total of 7,143 (right). Because of his huge collection, Geoff and his wife have had to move house three times.

LARGEST COLLECTION OF NAIL CLIPPERS

Andrè Ludwick (South Africa) has collected 505 different nail clippers since 1971. His collection began on a visit to Israel, when he bought some as souvenirs, and is now housed in a massive display cabinet. His favourite clipper is also one of the oldest as it was handmade by a blacksmith in 1935.

LARGEST LIPSTICK PRINT COLLECTION

The largest collection of lipstick prints was accumulated by Breakthrough Breast Cancer and Avon Cosmetics. A total of 39,537 prints were collected in aid of the 'Kiss Goodbye to Breast Cancer' campaign between July and October 2001.

LARGEST HOBBY-HORSE COLLECTION

Dan Cavanah (USA) has amassed 381 hobby-horses since 1990.

LARGEST MATCHBOOK COVER COLLECTION

Ed Brassard (USA) has a collection of 3,159,119 matchbook covers.

LARGEST PIG COLLECTION

Anne Langton (UK) has a collection of 9,130 pig items which she has been collecting for the past 20 years.

TOYS

SMALLEST RADIO-CONTROLLED CAR

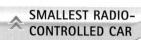

The record for the smallest radio-controlled car is held by a 25-mm-long (0.98-in) model (above, 1:90 perfect scale) of a Smart car developed by Michihiro Hino, Tokyo, Japan, in 2002.

LARGEST KITE FLOWN

The largest kite ever flown has a total area (when laid flat) of 680 m² (7,320 ft²). Called the 'Megabite', it was designed by Peter Lynn (New Zealand) and is 64 m (210 ft) long, including its tails, and 22 m (72 ft) wide.

FASTEST TIME TO SOLVE A RUBIK'S CUBE WHEN BLINDFOLDED

Ralf Laue (Germany) solved a Rubik's Cube puzzle whilst blindfolded in a time of 5 min 42 sec on the set of *Guinness World Records: Primetime*, Los Angeles, USA, on 11 March 2001.

LARGEST KALEIDOSCOPE

Glassblower Kazuhiko Kamiya (Japan) constructed a kaleidoscope that measured 7.36 x 3.1 x 2.55 m (24 ft 1 in x 10 ft 2 in x 8 ft 4 in) on 11 February 2000.

MOST HOOPS WHEN HULA-HOOPING

The record for hula-hooping the most hoops simultaneously is 83, set by Cia Grangér (Finland) at the studios of *Guinness World Records*, Helsinki, Finland, on 25 October 1999. She sustained three full revolutions of the standard size and weight hula-hoops between her shoulders and her hips.

LARGEST HULA-HOOP

The largest hula-hoop had a diameter of 3.6 m (11 ft 10 in) and Laura Rico Rodriguez (Spain) successfully rotated it three times around her waist on the set of *El Show de los Records* in Madrid, Spain, on 14 December 2001.

LARGEST TIN SOLDIER

The largest tin soldier measures 9.75 m (32 ft) in height and weighs approximately 4.5 tonnes (9,900 lb). It was constructed by the Sheet Metal Workers International Association and the British Columbia Sheet Metal Association (Canada). It is now on permanent display at New Westminster, British Columbia, Canada.

LONGEST LEGO STRUCTURE

The longest LEGO structure, built in the shape of a millipede, was 1,014.8 m (3,329 ft 4.68 in) long and consisted of over 2,000,000 bricks. It was assembled by pupils from 23 local primary schools at Myer, Westfield Southlands, Melbourne, Australia, between 21 and 22 September 2002.

LARGEST LEGO LOGO

The largest LEGO logo in the world measures 7.72 x 10.4 m (25 ft 4 in x 34 ft 1.5 in) and was made at The Franklin Institute Science Museum on 22 August 2001 in celebration of hosting the ESPN X Games in Philadelphia, Pennsylvania, USA. The logo consisted of nearly 180,000 LEGO bricks and took members of the public five days to make from start to finish.

LONGEST SWING

A wooden swing measuring 133.99 m (439 ft 7 in) long was constructed from 132 poles and 1,500 m (4,921 ft) of rope in two days by eight volunteers from the village of Havelte, The Netherlands. The swing can accommodate 288 children seated individually and was especially made for the Havelte village fête held on 2 September 1998. The children sat in special safety jackets to prevent them falling off.

MOST VALUABLE ANTIQUE TOY

A hand-painted tin-plate replica of the 'Charles' hose reel, a piece of fire-fighting equipment, measuring 38.1 x 58.4 cm (15 x 23 in) was sold at auction for $231,000 (£128,333) to a telephone bidder at Christie's, New York City, USA, on 14 December 1991. It was built c. 1870 by George Brown & Co. (USA).

SMALLEST HAND-MADE TEDDY BEAR

The record for the smallest hand-made teddy bear is held by Utaho Imaoka (Japan) who made a 6-mm-tall (0.25-in) bear on 31 July 2001 in Fuji, Shizuoka, Japan. The bear has six main body parts, moveable joints and is made of ultra-suede filled with a polyester/cotton stuffing.

SMALLEST SOUND-ACTIVATED SELF-POWERED TOY

The record for the smallest sound-activated self-powered toy is held by TOMY (Japan) who launched MicroPets at the Tokyo Toy Fair, Japan, in May 2002. Micropets are a range of different characters measuring up to 3.5 cm (1.37 in) tall, which react to sound.

LARGEST YO-YO

A yo-yo measuring 3.17 m (10 ft 4 in) in diameter and weighing 407 kg (897 lb) was devised by J N Nichols (Vimto) Ltd and made by students at Stockport College, Stockport, Greater Manchester, UK. It was launched from a crane at a height of 57.5 m (188 ft 7 in) at Wythenshawe, Greater Manchester, UK, on 1 August 1993 and yo-yoed four times.

LONGEST POOL TOY

The longest pool toy ever made was a 1,609.34-m-long (5,280-ft) 'pool noodle' produced by Industrial Thermo Polymers Ltd of Brampton, Ontario, Canada, on 1 July 2001.

LONGEST SKATEBOARD

Rhyn Noll (USA, left) built a 6.17-m-long (20-ft 3-in) skateboard called the 'Super Streetsurfer' and rode it for a distance of 1.1 km (0.7 miles) at Crescent City, California, USA, on 16 May 2002. The board was built to a standard, albeit lengthened, design.

FASTEST RADIO-CONTROLLED MODEL CAR

The top speed ever reached by a radio-controlled model car is 178.63 km/h (111 mph), set by the 1:10 scale Team Associated RC10L3 Oval Racer car at the Irwindale Speedway, California, USA, on 13 January 2001. The car was driven and built by Cliff Lett (USA) of Associated Electronics.

MOST VALUABLE TOY SOLDIER

A 1963 prototype G.I. Joe action figure, made by Hasbro (USA), was purchased by Matt Babek (USA) on an eBay online auction on 3 December 1999 for $14,000 (£8,747). This particular G.I. Joe is the only one ever made from resin, with hands and feet of diecast metal. His camouflage clothing is hand painted. Matt now keeps the figure locked up in a bank vault.

LONGEST HOT WHEELS TRACK

The longest Hot Wheels track measured 502.92 m (1,650 ft) and consisted of 2,100 pieces of track, held together by 2,150 connectors. The attempt was organized by Mattel Canada Inc. for Big Brothers Big Sisters of Canada and was completed on 7 July 2002 at Thunder Alley, Toronto, Ontario, Canada. A car successfully completed the full length of the track.

HIGHEST HOT WHEELS GRAVITY SPEED

The greatest speed reached under the power of gravity by a Hot Wheels car on a standard track is 45.811 km/h (28.465 mph) by Denis Yüksek (Germany) at Toys 'R' Us, Hamburg, Germany, on 5 October 2002.

MOST VALUABLE TEDDY BEAR

A Steiff bear named Teddy Girl was sold for £110,000 ($170,830) – more than 18 times the estimated value and twice the previous world record – at Christie's, London, UK, on 5 December 1994 to Japanese businessman Yoshihiro Sekiguchi. The bear was made in 1904, a year after Steiff (Germany) made the first jointed plush teddy bear, and had a particularly well-documented history. She had previously belonged to prominent collector Col. Bob Henderson (UK), who took her everywhere with him – even to his landing on the D-Day (6 June 1944) beaches during World War II, where he was a small arms adviser to Field Marshal Montgomery (UK).

MOST STUNT KITES SIMULTANEOUSLY FLOWN BY ONE PERSON

Mix McGraw (USA) flew 219 stunt kites simultaneously at Caesar Chavez Park, Berkeley, California, USA, on 27 July 2002. McGraw was unanchored, and managed to keep the dual-control kites airborne for a period of eight minutes.

LARGEST MODEL RAILWAY ENGINE

The largest model railway engine is a model of the *Thomas the Tank Engine* character 'James' (below), which measures 2.64 x 1.50 x 6.52 m (104.05 x 58.59 x 256.69 in) and weighs nearly 1.5 tonnes (3,300 lb). The electric, battery-powered model was built by BBC Visual Effects (UK) for a *Thomas the Tank Engine* tour in 2003.

GAMES & PASTIMES

LARGEST PERMANENT MONOPOLY BOARD

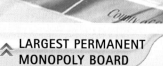

The largest permanent *Monopoly* board (above) measures 9.44 x 9.44 m (31 x 31 ft). Made of granite, it is located in San Jose, California, USA. It was opened to the public on 26 July 2002. The tokens, dice, houses and hotels are all scaled-up proportionally.

HIGHEST TOTAL SCRABBLE SCORE IN 24 HOURS

The record for the highest *Scrabble* score in 24 hours by two players is 162,171 and is held by Chris Hawkins and Austin Shin (both UK). It was set on 17–18 August 2002 in Milton Keynes, Buckinghamshire, UK.

YOUNGEST SCRABBLE WORLD CHAMPION

The youngest person to win a World *Scrabble* Championships is Mark Nyman (UK), who was 26 years 320 days when he won in 1993.

HIGHEST OVERALL SCRABBLE SCORE

The highest *Scrabble* score is 1,049 accomplished by Phil Appleby (UK). The winning match was played on 25 June 1989, at Wormley, Hertfordshire, UK. His opponent scored 253 and the margin of victory, 796 points, is also a record.

MOST CONSECUTIVE FOOTBAG SINGLES

The world record for footbag singles is 63,326 consecutive kicks in 8 hr 50 min 42 sec by Ted Martin (USA) at Lions Park, Mount Prospect, Illinois, USA, on 14 June 1997.

FASTEST 100-M MEN'S SPACE-HOPPER RACE

The men's record for the fastest 100-m space-hopper race is 45.1 seconds and was set by William Sadler (UK) at Framptons, Kings Langley, Hertfordshire, UK, on 1 September 2002.

MOST DOMINOES TOPPLED BY A GROUP

The record for the most dominoes toppled by a group is 3,847,295 (from a possible 4,000,000). The attempt was organised by Endemol Netherlands and took place at the FEC EXPO exhibition centre, Leeuwarden, The Netherlands, on 15 November 2002.

LARGEST BRIDGE TOURNAMENT

The Epson World Bridge Championship, held between 20 and 21 June 1992, was contested by more than 102,000 players playing the same hands at over 2,000 centres worldwide.

LARGEST TWISTER BOARD

The largest single *Twister* sheet measured 18.28 x 6 m (60 x 20 ft) and was manufactured by Vision International of Salt Lake City, Utah, USA, in February 1998.

MOST PARTICIPANTS IN A GAME OF TWISTER

The greatest-ever number of participants in a game of *Twister* is 4,160, at the University of Massachusetts at Amherst, USA, on 2 May 1987. Allison Culler (USA) won the game.

FASTEST GAME OF OPERATION

At an event held by the British Association of Urological Surgeons, Isa Isaa (Ireland) completed a game of *Operation* in 1 min 2 sec on 28 June 2001 in Dublin, Ireland.

FASTEST JENGA TOWER TO 30 LEVELS

The fastest time to build a *Jenga* tower 30 levels high, within the rules of the game, is 11 min 55 sec by Sabrina Ibrahim, John Chua and Alex Agboola (all UK) on the BBC's 'Big Toe Radio Show', London, UK, on 28 January 2003.

LARGEST COMMERCIALLY AVAILABLE BOARD GAME

The biggest commercially available board game is *Galaxion*, created by Cerebe Design International of Hong Kong. The board measures 83.8 x 83.8 cm (33 x 33 in).

MOST EXPENSIVE BOARD GAME

The most expensive commercially available board game is the deluxe version of *Outrage!* first produced by Imperial Games of Southport, Merseyside, UK, in 1995. The game, which is based on stealing the Crown Jewels from the Tower of London, currently retails at £7,995 ($12,590).

LARGEST GAME OF LEAPFROG

The largest game of leapfrog involved 675 participants from various local primary and secondary schools at the Flora Hill Stadium, Bendigo, Victoria, Australia, and took place on 4 December 2002.

LARGEST SACK RACE COMPETITION

The largest sack race involved 2,095 students from Agnieton College and primary school pupils from Zwolle, Wezep and Hattem on 11 October 2002 in Zwolle, The Netherlands.

MOST OPPONENTS IN CONSECUTIVE GAMES OF CHESS

The record for most consecutive games played with different opponents is 1,102 by Anna-Maria Botsari (Greece) at Kalavryta, Greece, on 27–28 February 2001.

YOUNGEST WORLD CHESS CHAMPION

Gary Kimovich Kasparov (USSR, now Russia, b. 13 April 1963) won the title on 9 November 1985 at 22 years 210 days.

Maya Grigoryevna Chiburdanidze (USSR, now Georgia, b. 17 January 1961) won the women's title in 1978 when 17.

LONGEST RUNNING CORRESPONDENCE CHESS RIVALRY

Reinhart Straszacker and Hendrik Roelof van Huyssteen (both South Africa) played their first game of correspondence chess in 1946. After 112 matches, with both men having won half the games, their record play of over 53 years ended with the death of Straszaker on 13 October 1999.

LONGEST TRADING-CARD-GAME MARATHON

The record for the longest trading card game playing marathon is held by Kyle Heuer, Joe Alread, Dan Bojanowski and Kevin Reitzel (all USA) who played *The Lord of the Rings* trading card game for 32 hr 1 min at Virginia Beach, Virginia, USA, on 25–27 May 2002.

LARGEST GAME OF KINGYOSUKUI

The largest game of kingyosukui involved a tank 100.8 m (331 ft) long containing 60,000 goldfish and 15,000 medaka (Japanese killifish) which are caught using a paper net. It was held on 4 August 2002 and organized by Maasaki Tanaka of Guild of Fujisawa Ginza Doyokai, Kanagawa, Japan.

MOST POINTS SCORED IN CRIBBAGE IN 24 HOURS

The most points scored in a cribbage game by a team of four people, playing singles in two pairs, is 139,454 by Colin Cooper, John Dunk, Peter Hyam and John Wilson (all UK) at HM Prison Doncaster, South Yorkshire, UK, between 16 and 17 September 1995.

LARGEST NON-COMMERCIAL JIGSAW PUZZLE

The largest non-commercial jigsaw puzzle measured 4,783 m^2 (51,484 ft^2) and consisted of 43,924 pieces. Assembled on 8 July 1992, it was devised by Centre Socio-Culturel d'Endoume in Marseille, France, and was designed with an environmental theme.

FASTEST TIDDLYWINK MILE

The record for the fastest tiddlywink mile is 52 min 10 sec and was set by Edward Wynn and James Cullingham (both UK) in Stradbroke, Suffolk, UK, on 31 August 2002.

LONGEST CARD PLAYING MARATHON

Rolando Fasani, Ivano Pancera, Claudio Zanelli, Andrea Zanelli, Mauro Rossi, Armando von Bürer, Eros Zanelli and Daniele Fiore played the card game *Jass* for 28 hours continuously at the Bellavista Restaurant, Sant'Abbondio, Switzerland, from 17 to 18 March 2001.

MOST BINGO NUMBERS CALLED IN ONE HOUR

The most numbers called in one hour by an individual is 2,668 by Paul Scott (UK) at The Riva Bingo Club, Brighton, East Sussex, UK, on 16 February 1997. A total of 140 lines were completed and the games were played by over 800 people.

MOST PIECES IN A JIGSAW PUZZLE

Ravensburger (Germany) make a commerically available puzzle consisting of 18,000 pieces (right). It depicts four world maps and measures 2.76 x 1.92 m (9 ft 1 in x 6 ft 3 in), which also makes it the largest puzzle by area on sale.

FOOD & DRINK

LARGEST PIECE OF TOFFEE

Weighing 1,333.5 kg (2,940 lb), the largest piece of toffee (left) was created by Susie's South Forty Confections Inc., USA, on 17 September 2002. The pecan toffee was made in the shape of Texas and contained a total of 7,056,000 calories. At its widest points, the toffee measured 3.2 x 2.5 x 0.6 m (10 ft 6 in x 8 ft 6 in x 2 ft).

LARGEST BOWL OF PASTA

The largest bowl of pasta weighed 1,480 kg (3,265 lb). The record was set by Nintendo of America Inc. on 22 August 2002 in Washington Square, San Francisco, California, USA. The bowl itself was made of fibreglass and was 91 cm (3 ft) high and 3.05 m (10 ft) wide.

LARGEST BOX OF CHOCOLATES

A Frango mint chocolate box weighing 1,463 kg (3,226 lb) was created by Marshall Field's, Chicago, Illinois, USA, on 14 November 2002. The box was 2.03 m (7 ft) wide, 4.39 m (14 ft) long, 48 cm (19 in) deep and contained 90,090 individual chocolates.

LARGEST LOLLIPOP

Staff of the Hershey Foods Company (USA) made a cherry-flavoured lollipop weighing 1,821.63 kg (4,016 lb) at the Hershey factory, Smithsfalls, Ontario, Canada, on 25 June 2002. The lollipop was 48 cm (18.9 in) thick, 159.5 cm (62.8 in) in diameter and 483.8 cm (190.5 in) long including the stick.

LARGEST ICE-CREAM SCOOP PYRAMID

The Carvel Corporation (USA) made the world's largest ice-cream scoop pyramid using 3,894 scoops of ice-cream in New York, USA, on 28 August 2002.

LARGEST ITEM ON A MENU

The largest item on any menu in the world is a particularly special roasted camel, which is prepared very occasionally for Bedouin wedding feasts. Cooked eggs are stuffed into fish, the fish are then stuffed into cooked chickens, the chickens in turn stuffed into a roasted sheep's carcass and the sheep finally stuffed into a whole camel.

LARGEST DOUGHNUT

Staff from Hemstroughts Bakeries, Donatos Bakery and the radio station WKLL-FM (all USA) made the largest American-style jelly doughnut weighing 1.7 tonnes (3,739 lb), and measuring 4.9 m (16 ft) in diameter and 40.6 cm (16 in) high, at Utica, New York, USA, on 21 January 1993.

LARGEST JELLY

Pool Fab (Australia) organized the creation of a 35,000-litre (7,700-gal) watermelon-flavoured pink jelly. It was made by Paul Squires and Geoff Ross (both Australia) at Roma Street Forum, Brisbane, Queensland, Australia, on 5 February 1981.

LARGEST PANCAKE

The Co-operative Union Ltd (UK) organized the making of a pancake 15.01 m (49 ft 3 in) in diameter and 2.5 cm (1 in) deep, and weighing an incredible 3 tonnes (6,614 lb) at Rochdale, Greater Manchester, UK, on 13 August 1994.

LARGEST PIZZA COMMERCIALLY AVAILABLE

Paul Revere's Pizza, Mount Pleasant, Iowa, USA, bake and deliver a pizza with a diameter of 1.21 m (4 ft) and area of 1.17 m² (13 ft²) making it the world's largest commercially available pizza. The pizza – named the 'Ultimate Party Pizza' – retails at $99.99 (£61).

LONGEST BANANA SPLIT

The residents of Selinsgrove, Pennsylvania, USA, made a banana split measuring 7.32 km (4.55 miles) in length along Market Street, Selinsgrove, on 30 April 1988. Ingredients included 24,000 bananas and 24,000 cherries.

LONGEST HOT DOG

The longest hot dog, made by Berks Packing Company Inc., USA, measured 4.64 m (15 ft 3 in) and was displayed at the Feeser's 100th Anniversary Food Show at Harrisburg, Pennsylvania, USA, from 16–17 October 2001.

LARGEST ALUMINIUM DRINKS CAN

The largest aluminium drinks can measured 4.67 m (15 ft 3 in) tall, 2.32 m (7 ft 6 in) wide and weighed 4,400 kg (9,700 lb) when empty. The can was made by the Vitalon Food Co. Ltd and was displayed at the Chiang Kai-Shek Memorial Hall Plaza, Taipei, Taiwan, on 2 June 2002.

LARGEST COCKTAIL

The world's largest cocktail was a margarita measuring a staggering 26,645 litres (7,038 gal). It was made on 17 May 2001 at Jimmy Buffett's Margaritaville and Mott's Inc., Universal City Walk, Orlando, Florida, USA.

LARGEST CHOCOLATE BAR

Elah-Dufour United Food Co. Ltd made a scaled-up version of a Novi chocolate bar that weighed 2,280 kg (5,026 lb) at the Eurochocolate 2000 confectionary exhibition in Turin, Italy, from 16–19 March, 2000. The chocolate bar measured 315 cm (124 in) long, 150 cm (59 in) wide and 45 cm (17.7 in) deep. It was made using approximately 850 kg (1,874 lb) of Gianduia chocolate, 850 kg (1,874 lb) of milk chocolate and 600 kg (1,323 lb) of whole Piedmont hazelnuts.

LARGEST HOT CROSS BUN

The largest hot cross bun (right) was made by staff at Pegrums Bakery, Rustington, West Sussex, UK, on 28 March 2002. The bun weighed 42.8 kg (94.35 lb), with a diameter of 1.303 m (4 ft 3 in) and a height of 13 cm (5 in).

LARGEST CURRY

Abdul Salam (UK), owner and chef of the Eastern Eye restaurant, Lichfield, Staffordshire, UK, cooked a vegetable curry weighing 3,106.5 kg (6,848 lb 11 oz) at Whittington Barracks, near Lichfield, on 17 July 2000. The curry fed about 7,500 people and the event raised an estimated £4,500 ($6,700) for charity.

LARGEST ICE-CREAM BOAT

The largest ice-cream boat weighed 594.5 kg (1,310 lb 8 oz) and was made by SIA Glass AB, Sweden, on 25 August 2001. The ingredients consisted of 135 kg (298 lb) of cream, 74 kg (163 lb) of sugar, 72 kg (159 lb) of strawberry cream, 54 kg (119 lb) of chocolate, 252 kg (555 lb) of milk and 7.5 kg (16 lb 8 oz) of wafers and biscuits.

LARGEST TEA BAG

The world's largest tea bag was made by Lipton Yellow Label of Lever Brothers Pakistan Ltd on 22 June 2002. It measured 3.18 m (10 ft 5 in) long and 2.21 m (7 ft 3 in) wide, and weighed 8.9 kg (19 lb 10 oz). Attached to the bag was a string measuring 4.26 m (14 ft) long. The giant bag was made from original filter paper and contained 7 kg (15 lb 7 oz) of black tea. It is estimated that 3,500 cups of tea can be made using it. It was displayed at the Avari Towers Hotel, Karachi, Pakistan.

LARGEST SERVING OF FISH AND CHIPS

The largest serving of fish and chips combined weighed 12.72 kg (28 lb 1 oz) and was made in conjunction with Asda Stores Ltd, Simpsons Seafish and McCain Foods Ltd (all UK) on 4 October 2002. Individually, the fish weighed 6.06 kg (13 lb 6 oz) and the chips weighed 6.66 kg (14 lb 11 oz).

TALLEST CHAMPAGNE PYRAMID

A 56-storey champagne fountain using 30,856 traditional glasses was constructed and successfully filled with champagne from the top at the Steigenberger Kurhaus Hotel, Scheveningen, The Netherlands. The record was achieved by Luuk Broos (The Netherlands) between 28 and 30 December 1999.

LARGEST BAG OF COOKIES

Loblaws Supermarkets Ltd (Canada) made a bag 3.29 m (10 ft 8 in) high, 2.13 m (7 ft) deep and 114.3 cm (45 in) wide (right). The bag contained a total of 100,152 cookies. It was presented at Loblaws Wonderland Market, London, Ontario, Canada, from 6–7 September 2001.

LARGEST MILKSHAKE

The Comfort Diners, Parmalat USA, and the American Dairy Association (all USA) made the world's largest milkshake at 22,712 litres (4,995 gal) in New York, USA, on 1 August 2000. The holders of this record chose to make a Black and White Shake – vanilla with chocolate syrup – as it is a classic New York flavour.

LARGEST SLAB OF FUDGE

Northwest Fudge Factory.Com, Ontario, Canada, created a slab of fudge that weighed 908.09 kg (2,002 lb). The chocolate-and-vanilla-swirl fudge was displayed at the New Sudbury Mall, Ontario, Canada, on 4 May 2002. The fudge measured 50.5 m (166 ft) in length, 23 cm (9 in) wide and 7.5 cm (3 in) high. It took 86 hours to prepare and mould the fudge.

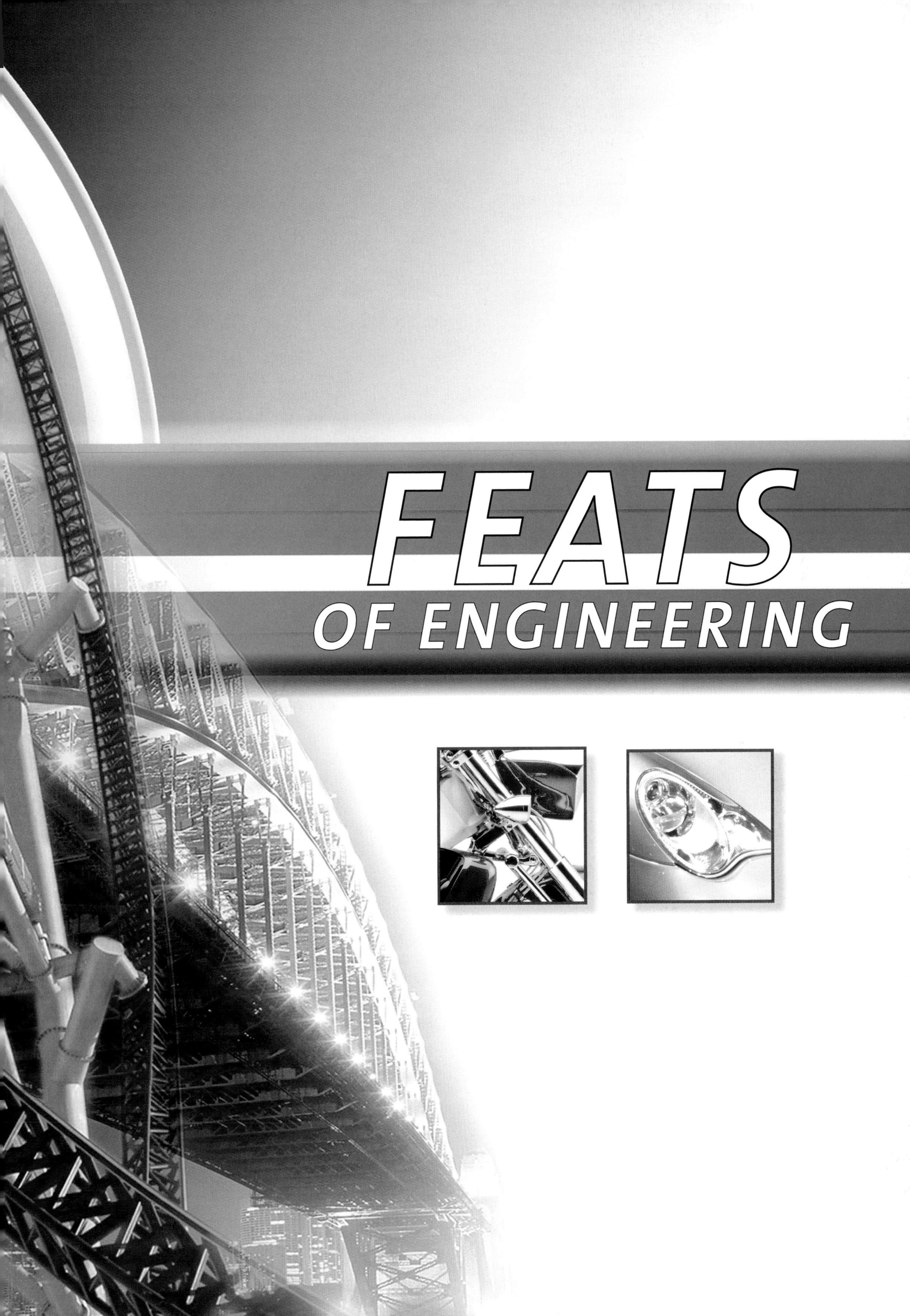
FEATS
OF ENGINEERING

TALL TALES

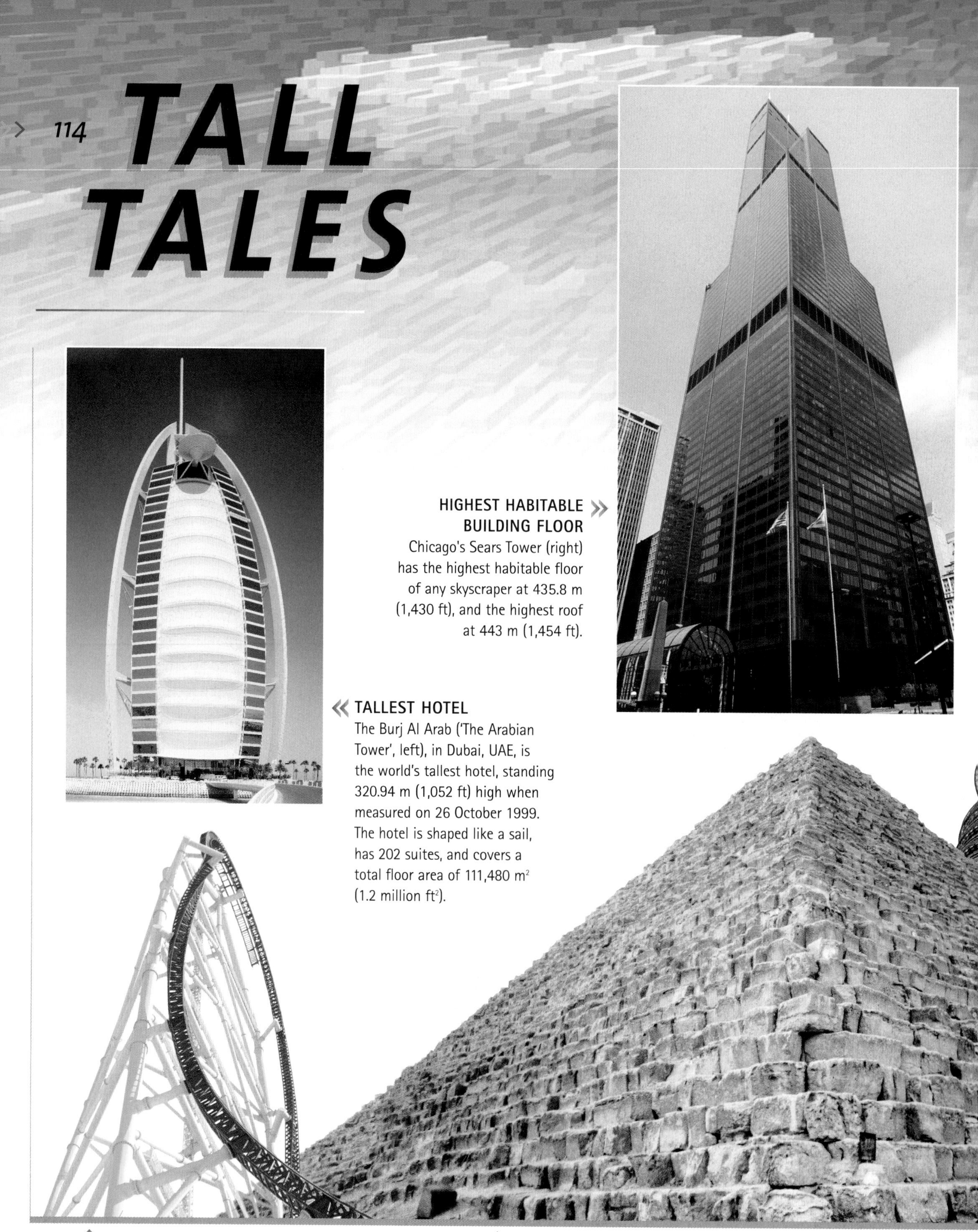

HIGHEST HABITABLE BUILDING FLOOR
Chicago's Sears Tower (right) has the highest habitable floor of any skyscraper at 435.8 m (1,430 ft), and the highest roof at 443 m (1,454 ft).

TALLEST HOTEL
The Burj Al Arab ('The Arabian Tower', left), in Dubai, UAE, is the world's tallest hotel, standing 320.94 m (1,052 ft) high when measured on 26 October 1999. The hotel is shaped like a sail, has 202 suites, and covers a total floor area of 111,480 m^2 (1.2 million ft^2).

TALLEST ROLLER COASTER
Top Thrill Dragster (above), a hydraulically launched out-and-back 'strata-coaster' at Cedar Point, Sandusky, Ohio, USA, reaches a height of 128 m (420 ft) and has a maximum design speed of 193 km/h (120 mph). It opened in 2003 and cost $25 million (£16.6 million).

TALLEST PYRAMID
The Pyramid of Khufu (above, also known as the Great Pyramid) at Giza, Egypt, is the world's tallest. It was 146.7 m (481 ft 4.8 in) high when completed around 4,500 years ago, but erosion and vandalism have reduced its height to 137.5 m (451 ft 4.8 in) today.

TALLEST OBELISK
The world's tallest obelisk (a tapered four-sided column) is the Washington Monument (right) in Washington DC, USA. It stands 169 m (555 ft) tall and was completed in 1884 to honour George Washington.

TALLEST FREE-STANDING TOWER
The tallest free-standing tower (as opposed to a guyed mast) is the $63-million (£28-million at 1975 rate) CN Tower (right) in Toronto, Ontario, Canada, which rises to 553.34 m (1,815 ft 5 in). Work began on 12 February 1973 and it was 'topped out' on 2 April 1975.

TALLEST OFFICE BUILDING
In March 1996 the Petronas Towers in Kuala Lumpur, Malaysia (above), overtook the Sears Tower's record as the world's tallest office building. Stainless steel pinnacles 73.5 m (241 ft) long placed atop the 88-storey towers brought their height to 451.9 m (1,482 ft 8 in).

BIG BUILDINGS

LARGEST PLANT CONSERVATORY

The Eden Project (right), near St Austell, Cornwall, UK, consists of two giant transparent domes ('biomes'), the larger of which (the humid tropics biome, on the left in the photo) is 55 m (180 ft) tall, covers 25,390 m^2 (273,295 ft^2) and has a total volume of 415,730 m^3 (14.681 million ft^3). The smaller warm-temperate biome has 6,540 m^2 (70,395 ft^2) of floor space and a volume of 85,620 m^3 (3.02 million ft^3). The full project – which aims to tell the story of humankind's dependence on plants – has been open to the public since 2001.

LARGEST AMPHITHEATRE

The Flavian amphitheatre or Colosseum of Rome, Italy, completed in 80 AD, covers 2 ha (5 acres) and has a capacity of 87,000 people. It has a maximum length of 187 m (612 ft) and a maximum width of 157 m (515 ft).

LARGEST THEATRE

The world's largest building used for theatre is the National People's Congress Building (*Ren min da hui tang*) on the west side of Tiananmen Square, Beijing, China. Completed in 1959, it covers an area of 5.2 ha (12.9 acres). When used as a theatre, the building seats 10,000, as it did in 1964 for the play *The East is Red*.

The most capacious purpose-built theatre is the Perth Entertainment Centre, Western Australia, with 8,500 seats and a main stage area measuring 21.3 x 13.7 m (70 x 45 ft). It was opened on 26 December 1974.

LARGEST TRAIN STATION BUILDING

With 410,000 m^2 (4.413 million ft^2) of floor space the JR Central Towers, Nagoya, Japan, is the world's largest train station building. The complex was completed on 20 December 1999, and was built by the Central Japan Railway Company to replace the existing Nagoya Station.

LARGEST THEATRE STAGE

The world's largest stage is in the Hilton Theatre at the Reno Hilton, Reno, Nevada, USA. It measures 53.3 x 73.4 m (175 x 241 ft). The stage has three main lifts, each capable of raising 1,200 performers, and two turntables each with a circumference of 19.1 m (62 ft 6 in).

LARGEST 'LIVING' ROOF

The roof of the Ford Motor Company's Rouge factory in Dearborn, Michigan, USA, has had 42,180 m^2 (454,000 ft^2) of low-growing vegetation called sedum planted on it, making it the world's largest 'living' roof. Planted in a 7.6-cm-thick (3-in) mat-like material, the vegetation insulates the roof, saving on heating costs. It also lasts longer than conventional roofing as it doesn't expand or contract when temperatures change.

LARGEST MOUND

The largest artificial mound (above) was built as a memorial to the Seleucid King Antiochus I (reigned 69-34 BC). It stands on the summit of Nemrut Daği (2,306 m or 7,565 ft), southeast of Malatya, Turkey. It is 59.8 m (197 ft) tall and covers an area of 3 ha (7.5 acres).

LARGEST STADIUM ROOF

The transparent acrylic glass 'tent' roof over the Munich Olympic Stadium, Germany, covers an area of 85,000m^2 (915,000 ft^2) and rests on a steel net supported by masts.

LARGEST FOOTBALL STADIUM

The Maracanã Municipal Stadium in Rio de Janeiro, Brazil, has a normal capacity for 205,000 spectators, of whom 155,000 can be seated. It was built for the 1950 World Cup and a record crowd of 199,854 was accommodated for the Brazil v. Uruguay final match on 16 July 1950. The oval stadium is 32 m (105 ft) high and the distance between the middle of the field and the furthest spectator is 126 m (413 ft). A dry moat, 2.13 m (7 ft) wide and more than 1.5 m (5 ft) deep, protects players from spectators and vice versa.

LARGEST ADMINISTRATIVE BUILDING

The largest ground area covered by any office building is that of the Pentagon in Arlington, Virginia, USA. Built to house the US Defense Department's offices, each of the outermost sides is 281 m (921 ft) long and the perimeter is about 1,405 m (4,610 ft). Its five storeys enclose a floor area of 604,000 m^2 (6.5 million ft^2), the corridors total 28 km (17.5 miles) in length and there are 7,754 windows to be cleaned. It was completed on 15 January 1943 at an estimated cost of $83 million (£20.5 million).

between 750 and 842 AD. The 60,000-m² (645,835-ft²) stone structure is 34.5 m (113 ft) tall and its base measures 123 x 123 m (403 x 403 ft).

LARGEST SYNAGOGUE

Temple Emanu-El on Fifth Avenue at 65th Street, New York City, USA, has an area of 3,523 m² (37,922 ft²). Up to 5,500 people can be accommodated when all sanctuaries are in use.

LARGEST MOSQUE

The Shah Faisal Mosque, near Islamabad, Pakistan, has a total area of 18.97 ha (46.87 acres), with the covered area of the prayer hall covering 0.48 ha (1.19 acres). It can accommodate 100,000 worshippers in the prayer hall and courtyard, and a further 200,000 in the adjacent grounds.

LARGEST RELIGIOUS STRUCTURE

Angkor Wat (City Temple) in Cambodia covers a 162.6-ha (401-acre) site. Its curtain wall measures 1,280 m (4,200 ft), and, before it was abandoned in 1432, its population was 80,000. Begun c. 900, the whole complex of 72 major monuments extends over 24.8 km (15.4 miles).

LARGEST SHOPPING CENTRE

West Edmonton Mall in Edmonton, Alberta, Canada, covers an area of 492,386 m² (5.3 million ft²). The mall cost CAN$1.2 billion (£700 million or $927 million) to build and features over 800 stores and services, as well as 11 major department stores. Over 20,000 vehicles can be accommodated in its car park – the world's largest.

LARGEST CATHEDRAL

St John the Divine, the gothic cathedral church of the Diocese of New York, USA, has a floor area of 11,240 m² (121,000 ft²), equivalent to 43 tennis courts or more than two American football fields. The nave is the world's longest at 183.2 m (601 ft) and the vaulted roof is 37.8 m (124 ft) – around 10 storeys – above floor level. Although construction began in 1892, the building is only two-thirds complete.

LARGEST HINDU TEMPLE

Srirangam Temple at Tiruchirappalli, Tamil Nadu, India, is the world's largest Hindu temple. Dedicated to the Hindu god Vishnu, the temple covers an area of 63.1 ha (156 acres) with a perimeter of 9,934 m (32,592 ft). This is nearly 50% larger than the Vatican City, which at 44 ha (108.73 acres) is the world's smallest country and the centre of Roman Catholicism.

LARGEST SURVIVING ZIGGURAT

The largest partially surviving ziggurat (rectangular stepped pyramid) is the Ziggurat of Ur (now Muqayyar, Iraq) which has a base measuring 61 x 45.7 m (200 x 150 ft). It had three storeys and was probably surmounted by a temple. The first storey and part of the second storey now survive to a height of 18 m (60 ft). Ziggurats were the dominant form of religious building of the Mesopotamian civilization between the fourth millennium and 600 BC.

LARGEST BUDDHIST TEMPLE

The largest Buddhist temple is Borobudur, near Yogyakarta, Central Java, Indonesia, built

LARGEST UNIVERSITY BUILDING

The largest existing university building is the MV Lomonosov Moscow State University, Moscow, Russia (above), which was built between 1949 and 1953. It is 240 m (787.5 ft) high, has 32 storeys and 40,000 rooms.

CONSTRUCTIONS

LONGEST WOODEN FOOTBRIDGE

The Hōrai Bridge, a wooden toll bridge across the Oi River in the middle of Shizuoka Prefecture, Japan, measures 897.42 m (2,944 ft 3 in). It was built in 1867 and rebuilt in the 1960s because of flooding.

WIDEST BRIDGE

The widest long-span bridge is the 503-m-long (1,650-ft) Sydney Harbour Bridge, Australia (below), which is 48.8 m (160 ft) wide. It carries two electric overhead railway tracks, eight lanes of roadway, a cycle track and a footway. It was officially opened on 19 March 1932.

HIGHEST CAUSEWAY

The Bailey bridge erected in August 1982 over the Khardungla Pass, Ladakh, India, was, at 5,602 m (18,380 ft), the road bridge at the highest altitude in the world. It was replaced by a causeway in the mid 1990s because of constant damage from avalanches.

LONGEST CANTILEVER BRIDGE

The Québec Bridge (Pont de Québec) over the St Lawrence River in Canada has the longest cantilever truss span of any in the world, measuring 549 m (1,800 ft) between the piers and 987 m (3,239 ft) overall. It carries a railway track and two carriageways. Work began in 1900, and it was finally opened to traffic on 3 December 1917, having cost CAN$ 22.5 million (£4.7 million or US$ 22.5 million) and 87 lives.

OLDEST ELECTRIC-OPENING BRIDGE

The Pyrmont Bridge over Cockle Bay in Sydney, Australia, opened in 1902 and is still in use today. Nineteen levers have to be pulled to open the 1,000-tonne (2.2 million lb) swinging section of the 368.8-m-long (1,210-ft) bridge.

LONGEST SPAN SUSPENSION BRIDGE

The Tsing Ma Bridge in Hong Kong, China, has a main span of 1,377 m (4,518 ft), a width of 40 m (131 ft) and a length of 2.2 km (1.36 miles). Its shipping clearance reaches 62 m (203 ft) and the tower height is 206 m (675 ft). The bridge carries both road and rail traffic.

LONGEST STEEL ARCH BRIDGE

The New River Gorge Bridge, near Fayetteville, West Virginia, USA, was completed in 1977 and has a span of 518 m (1,700 ft).

DEEPEST RAILWAY LINE

The Seikan Tunnel, which crosses the Tsugaro Strait between Honshū and Hokkaidō, Japan, reaches a depth of 240 m (786 ft) below sea level. Opened on 13 March 1988, the tunnel is a record 53.85 km (33.46 miles) long. Trains stop in the middle so that passengers can take photos through windows on the tunnel walls. By comparison, the Channel Tunnel linking Dover, UK, to Calais, France, is at an average depth of 45 m (148 ft) below the sea floor.

LONGEST FLOATING BRIDGE

Second Lake Washington Bridge, Seattle, Washington, USA, has a total length of 3,839 m (2.39 miles), with its floating section measuring 2,291 m (1.42 miles). The bridge cost $15 million (£5.35 million) to build and was completed in August 1963.

LONGEST BRIDGING

The Second Lake Pontchartrain Causeway, which joins Mandeville and Metairie, Louisiana, USA, is 38.42 km (23.87 miles) long. It was completed in 1969.

HIGHEST BRIDGE

The world's highest bridge is over the Royal Gorge of the Arkansas River in Colorado, USA, at 321 m (1,053 ft) above the water level. It is a suspension bridge with a main span of 268 m (880 ft) and construction took six months, ending on 6 December 1929.

LONGEST BRIDGE-TUNNEL

The Chesapeake Bay bridge-tunnel, which opened to traffic on 15 April 1964, extends 28.4 km (17.65 miles) from the Eastern Shore region of the Virginia Peninsula to Virginia Beach, Virginia, USA. The longest bridged section is Trestle C at 7.34 km (4.56 miles) long, and the longest tunnel is the Thimble Shoal Channel Tunnel, at 1.75 km (1.09 miles).

LONGEST SEWAGE TUNNEL

The Chicago TARP (Tunnels and Reservoir Plan) in Illinois, USA, when complete, will involve 211 km (131 miles) of machine-bored sewer tunnels between 2.7 and 10 m (9 and 33 ft) in diameter. Phase I comprises 175.4 km (109 miles), and as of June 2002, 148 km (92 miles) were operational, 12 km (8 miles) are under construction, and the rest are unfunded. The system provides pollution control (Phase I) and flood control (Phase II) and will service 3.9 million people in 52 communities over an area of 971 km^2 (375 miles^2). The estimated cost for the project is $3.7 billion. (£2.3 billion).

» LARGEST ROTATING BOAT LIFT

The Falkirk Wheel, Falkirk, UK, (right), is the largest rotating boat lift in the world. It is 35 m (114 ft) high, 35 m (114 ft) wide and 30 m (98 ft) long. It was officially opened by Queen Elizabeth II on 24 May 2002. The boat lift can transfer more than eight boats at a time from the Forth and Clyde Canal to the Union Canal. The journey takes around 15 minutes.

DEEPEST ROAD TUNNEL

The Hitra Tunnel, Norway, links the mainland to the island of Hitra and reaches a depth of 264 m (866 ft) below sea level. It is 5.6 km (3.4 miles) long, with three lanes, and was opened in December 1994.

LARGEST ROAD TUNNEL BY DIAMETER

The largest diameter road tunnel is that blasted through Yerba Buena Island, San Francisco, California, USA. It is 24 m (79 ft) wide, 17 m (56 ft) high and 165 m (541 ft) long. More than 280,000 vehicles pass along its two decks each day.

» FURTHEST DISTANCE TO MOVE A BRIDGE

London Bridge (right), unable to handle London's increasing traffic volume, was auctioned in 1962 to Robert McCulloch (USA) for $2,460,000 (£876,000). It was dismantled and moved brick-by-brick to Lake Havasu City, Arizona, USA, where it was reassembled and opened in 1971. The bridge was moved 8,530 km (5,300 miles) in total. It turned out that McCulloch had bought the wrong bridge: he thought he was buying Tower Bridge.

LARGEST TUNNEL-BORING MACHINE

The largest tunnel-boring machine in the world measures 14.87 m (48 ft 9.4 in) in diameter by 120 m (393 ft) long, and weighs 3,520 tonnes (7,760,200 lb). It is being used to carve the 7-km (4.3-mile) Groene Hart Tunnel from Amsterdam to Rotterdam, The Netherlands, which will be completed in February 2005.

LONGEST ROAD TUNNEL

The tunnel between Aurland and Lærdal on the main road between Bergen and Oslo, Norway, measures 24.5 km (15.2 miles) in length. The two-lane Lærdal Tunnel was ceremonially opened by King Harald on 27 November 2000, and opened to the public in 2001. It cost a reported $113.1 million (£78.5 million) to construct.

LARGEST CANAL SYSTEM

The seawater cooling system associated with the Madinat Al-Jubail Al-Sinaiyah construction project in Saudi Arabia is believed to be the world's largest canal system. It currently carries 11 million m^3 (388 million ft^3) of seawater per day to cool the industrial establishments and ultimately will bring 19.5 million m^3 (689 million ft^3) of water when industry consumption peaks.

LONGEST CANAL

The Belomorsko-Baltiysky Kanal, also known as the White Sea-Baltic Canal, from Belomorsk to Povenets, Russia, is 227 km (141 miles) long and has 19 locks. It was made using forced labour between 1930 and 1933.

OLDEST NAVIGABLE CANAL TUNNEL

The Malpas Tunnel on the Canal du Midi in south-west France was completed in 1681 and is 161 m (528 ft) long. Its completion enabled vessels to navigate from the Atlantic Ocean to the Mediterranean Sea.

LONGEST WALL

The Great Wall of China is the longest in the world and has a main-line length of 3,460 km (2,150 miles) – nearly three times the length of the UK – plus 3,530 km (2,195 miles) of branches and spurs. Construction of the wall began during the reign of Qin Shi Huangdi (221–210 BC). The wall runs from Shanhaiguan, on the Gulf of Bohai, to Yumenguan and Yangguan.

HOMES, HOUSES, HOTELS

HIGHEST ALTITUDE HOTEL

The Hotel Everest View above Namche Bazar, Nepal – the village closest to Mt Everest's base camp – is at a record height of 3,962 m (13,000 ft).

TALLEST RESIDENTIAL BUILDING

The Trump World Tower in New York City, USA, is the world's tallest purely residential building, standing 262.5 m (861 ft) tall. It has 72 storeys, although the luxuriously high ceilings make it taller than most other buildings with a similar number of floors.

MOST THEME HOTELS

There are more than 16 theme hotels on the Strip in Las Vegas, Nevada, USA. Luxor has a sphinx, a black pyramid and an obelisk; New York-New York features a one-third-scale New York skyline; and Paris Las Vegas has a half-scale Eiffel Tower. Other themes include Treasure Island and Venice. Las Vegas boasts an incredible 120,000 hotel rooms, nearly one for every four of its inhabitants. The city accounts for roughly one-thirtieth of all hotel rooms in the USA and has the highest density of hotel rooms in the world.

« HIGHEST HOTEL

The Grand Hyatt Shanghai (left) in Pudong, China, is the highest hotel in the world. It occupies floors 53 to 87 of the 88-storey Jin Mao Tower, the tallest building in China and at 420 m (1,377 ft 10.8 in) is one of the tallest buildings in the world. The hotel, is around 90 m (295 ft) higher than the pinnacle of the Burj Al Arab in Dubai (UAE) – the world's tallest hotel.

LARGEST HOTEL

The MGM Grand Hotel and Casino in Las Vegas, Nevada, USA, consists of four 30-storey towers on a site covering 45.3 ha (112 acres). The hotel has 5,005 rooms, with suites of up to 560 m^2 (6,000 ft^2), a 15,200-seat arena, and a 13.3-ha (33-acre) theme park.

LARGEST HOTEL PRESIDENTIAL SUITE

The largest hotel presidential suite is the Villa Salaambo attached to the Hasdrubal Thalassa Hotel, Yasmine Hammamet, Tunisia. It has a total floorspace of 1,542 m^2 (16,597 ft^2).

LARGEST INHABITED CASTLE

The royal residence of Windsor Castle at Windsor, Berkshire, UK, is originally of 12th-century construction and measures 576 x 164 m (1,890 x 540 ft).

LARGEST HOTEL CHAIN

Best Western International Inc. is the world's biggest hotel chain, with more than 4,000 hotels in 81 countries and territories. The company, which is based in Phoenix, Arizona, USA, says it has 308,627 rooms available in its establishments which, although part of the Best Western group, are independently owned and operated.

MOST EXPENSIVE HOTEL SUITE

The Imperial Suite at the President Wilson Hotel in Geneva, Switzerland, can be reserved for CHF 45,000 (£20,907 or $33,000) per night.

LARGEST HOTEL ROOMS

Standard suites at the Venetian, Las Vegas, Nevada, USA, measure on average 65 m^2 (700 ft^2).

» LARGEST ICE HOTEL

In the winter of 2002/03 The Ice Hotel (right) in Jukkasjärvi, Sweden, had a total floor area of 5,000 m^2 (54,000 ft^2) with 25 suites and 60 bedrooms. Lying 200 km (120 miles) north of the Arctic Circle, it has been rebuilt every December since 1990 and increases in size each year. It featured ice sculptures, a cinema, a pillared ice hall, an ice bar and an ice chapel. Guests' ice beds are covered with thick reindeer pelts, and the interior temperature is around -6°C (20°F).

NORTHERNMOST HOTEL

The world's most northerly hotel is the Radisson SAS Polar Hotel in Longyearbyen, Svalbard, Norway. Svalbard consists of several islands from Bjørnøya in the south to Rossøya in the north, Europe's northernmost point. About 60% of the archipelago is covered by ice.

HIGHEST HABITATION

In April 1961 a three-roomed dwelling believed to date from the late pre-Columbian period c. 1480 was discovered perched at 6,600 m (21,650 ft) on Cerro Llullaillaco. This 6,723-m (22,057-ft) active volcano sits on the Argentine-Chile border.

NORTHERNMOST INHABITED PLACE

The Canadian Forces Station Alert on Ellesmere Island, Northwest Territories, Canada, lies at Lat 82°30'N, Long 62°W. Set up in 1950, it is around 800 km (500 miles) from the geographic North Pole, and was an important 'listening post' for spying on the former USSR (now Russia).

The Danish scientific station set up in 1952 in Pearyland, northern Greenland, is over 1,450 km (900 miles) north of the Arctic Circle and is manned every summer, making this site the northernmost habitation.

SOUTHERNMOST INHABITED PLACE

The most southerly permanent human habitation is the USA's Amundsen-Scott South Pole Station, completed in 1957 and replaced in 1975. Currently undergoing further expansion, the base, open to tourists during the summer months, now has a shop, bank and a post office.

LONGEST CONTINUOUS HOUSE CONSTRUCTION

Winchester House in San Jose, California, USA, was under continuous construction for 38 years. Originally an eight-room farmhouse on a 65-ha (161-acre) estate, its transformation into a mansion was begun in 1886 by the widowed Sarah Winchester (USA), heiress to the Winchester rifle fortune. It is also called the Winchester Mystery House because of its many oddities, such as closets opening into blank walls, a window in the floor, and staircases leading nowhere. Some believe that after the death of her husband, the widow was convinced by a medium that endless remodelling would confuse and appease the ghosts of all the people killed by the 'gun that won the West'. The house has 13 bathrooms, 52 skylights, 47 fireplaces, 10,000 windows, 40 staircases, 2,000 doorways and trapdoors, and three lifts.

HIGHEST INHABITED BUILDING

The highest inhabited buildings in the world are those in the Indo-Tibetan border fort of Basisi by the Mana Pass (Lat 31°04'N, Long 79°24'E) at c. 6,000 m (19,700 ft). Because of lower air pressures at high altitudes and the corresponding decrease in the amount of oxygen in each breath taken, many people begin to feel the effects of altitude sickness at heights above 2,500 m (8,200 ft). It would take several days to acclimatize to the altitude at Basisi and most people would become very ill if they were airlifted directly to that height.

OLDEST HOTEL

The Hōshi Ryokan at the village of Awazu in Japan is reputed to be the world's oldest hotel. It dates back to 717, when Taicho Daishi built an inn near a hot-water spring that was said to have miraculous healing powers. The waters are still celebrated for their recuperative effects, and the Ryokan now has 100 bedrooms.

MOST EXPENSIVE HOUSE SALE

The home belonging to Hong Kong businessman and philanthropist Eric Hotung at 6-10 Black's Link, Hong Kong, sold for HK$778.88 million (£62,767,500 or $101,909,312) on 12 May 1997. It was bought by an anonymous buyer.

LONGEST RESIDENCY

Virginia Hopkins Phillips (USA) resided in the same house at Onancock, Virginia, USA, from the time of her birth in 1891 until shortly after her 102nd birthday in 1993.

LARGEST HOTEL LOBBY

The lobby at the Hyatt Regency in San Francisco, California, USA, is 107 m (350 ft) long, 49 m (160 ft) wide and, at 52 m (170 ft) tall, is the height of a 15-storey building.

MOST EXPENSIVE NON-PALATIAL HOUSE BUILT

Hearst Castle at San Simeon, California, USA, was built between 1922 and 1939 for William Randolph Hearst (USA) at a total cost of more than $30 million (then £6.5 million), which is the equivalent today of $350 million (£250 million). It has more than 100 rooms, a heated swimming pool 32 m (104 ft) long, an assembly hall 25 m (83 ft) long and a garage for 25 limousines. The house required 60 servants to maintain it.

LARGEST CASINO

Foxwoods Resort Casino in Ledyard, Connecticut, USA, includes a total gaming area of 17,900 m^2 (193,000 ft^2). The complete complex covers an area of 436,000 m^2 (4.7 million ft^2) and includes three separate hotels, 24 restaurants, a theatre and a performance arena. The casino itself features more than 5,800 slot machines, 17 different table games and a 3,200-seat bingo hall. Foxwoods employs more than 8,000 people.

LARGEST AREA OF POLISHED MARBLE FLOOR TILES

The Venetian Resort-Hotel-Casino, Las Vegas, Nevada, USA, has a total floor area of 139,354 m^3 (1.5 million ft^3) covered in marble tiles shipped over from Italy and Spain. This is equivalent to the area of 535 tennis courts.

LARGEST PALACE

The Imperial Palace in the centre of Beijing, China (above) covers a rectangular area measuring 960 x 750 m (3,150 x 2,460 ft) within its 72-ha (178-acre) site. The outline dates from the beginning of the 15th century, but owing to constant reconstruction work, most of the intra-mural buildings (five halls and 17 palaces) are from the 18th century.

CARS

EARLIEST FULL-SCALE AUTOMOBILE

The earliest full-scale automobile was a military steam tractor made by Nicolas-Joseph Cugnot (France) at the Paris Arsenal in October 1769. It had a maximum speed of 4 km/h (2.5 mph). Cugnot's second, larger tractor, completed in May 1771, survives in the Conservatoire Nationale des Arts et Métiers in Paris, France.

EARLIEST PASSENGER CAR

The world's first passenger-carrying automobile was a steam-powered road vehicle carrying eight passengers, built by Richard Trevithick (UK). The car made its first run at Camborne, Cornwall, UK, on 24 December 1801.

EARLIEST INTERNAL COMBUSTION CAR

The first successful petrol-driven car, the Motorwagen, built by Karl Friedrich Benz (Germany), ran at Mannheim in late 1885. The three-wheeler weighed 254 kg (560 lb) and could reach 13–16 km/h (8–10 mph). Its single-cylinder engine delivered 0.63 kW (0.85 hp) at 400 rpm. It was patented on 29 January 1886.

LARGEST PRODUCTION CAR

Of cars produced for private use, the largest was the Bugatti 'Royale' Type 41, known in the UK as the 'Golden Bugatti', which was assembled at Molsheim, France, by the Italian Ettore Bugatti. First built in 1927, it measured over 6.7 m (22 ft) in length. The hood was over 2.13 m (7 ft) long.

LONGEST CAR

A 30.5-m-long (100-ft), 26-wheeled limo was designed by Jay Ohrberg (USA). It has many unique features, including a swimming pool with diving board and a king-sized water bed. It is designed to drive as a rigid vehicle but it can be changed to bend in the middle. It was designed for use in films and displays.

BIGGEST VEHICLE PRODUCER

In 2002 the General Motors Corpora (USA, right) produced an estimated 8,274,000 motor vehicles, making it world's largest automobile producer. company, whose brands include Buic Cadillac, Chevrolet, Opel (Vauxhall), Isuzu and Saab, made profits of $1.7 billion (£1.1 billion) that year, u from $600 million (£416 million) in 2(

LARGEST AUTOMOTIVE SHOW

The biennial International Motor Show for Passenger Cars (IAA), held in Frankfurt, Germany, is the world's largest automotive exhibition. The 2001 event, held from 13 to 23 September, attracted over 1,000 exhibitors (including Porsche, right) from 39 countries and covered an area of 235,000 m^2 (2.5 million ft^2). The show was attended by around 13,600 journalists from 75 countries and over 800,000 other visitors.

MOST POWERFUL PRODUCTION CAR

The Koenigsegg CC (Sweden) has a maximum power output of 488 kW (655 hp), making it the most powerful car ever to enter series production. The car has a claimed top speed of 392 km/h (243.5 mph) and a 0–100 km/h (0–60 mph) acceleration time of under 3.5 seconds. The Bugatti Veyron, with a claimed power output of 736 kW (987 hp), was due to be launched in 2003 but had not entered production at the time of going to press.

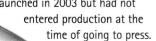

LARGEST ENGINE OF A PRODUCTION CAR

The greatest engine capacity of a production car was 13.5 litres (823.8 in^3), for the US Pierce-Arrow 6-66 Raceabout of 1912–18, the US Peerless 6-60 of 1912–14 and the Fageol of 1918.

FASTEST PRODUCTION CAR

The highest speed ever attained by a standard production car is 386.7 km/h (240.1 mph) for a McLaren F1, driven by Andy Wallace (UK) at the Volkswagen Proving Ground, Wolfsburg, Germany, on 31 March 1998.

FASTEST REVERSE DRIVING

Darren Manning (UK) reached a speed of 165.08 km/h (102.58 mph) going backwards in a Caterham 7 Fireblade at Kemble airfield, Gloucester, UK, on 22 October 2001.

BLINDFOLD LAND-SPEED RECORD

Alistair Weaver (UK) reached a speed of 226.91 km/h (141 mph) while driving an Audi S8 blindfolded and guided by radio at Elvington airfield, N Yorks, UK, on 8 April 2002.

FASTEST ELECTRIC CAR

The highest speed achieved for an electric vehicle over a two-way flying kilometre is 395.821 km/h (245.523 mph), by Dempsey's World Record Associates *White Lightning Electric Streamliner*. The car was driven by Patrick Rummerfield (USA) at the Bonneville Salt Flats, Utah, USA, on 22 October 1999.

GREATEST DISTANCE DRIVEN IN ONE HOUR USING AN INTERNAL COMBUSTION ENGINE

The greatest distance driven in one hour by a car with an internal combustion engine is 353.409 km (219.598 miles), by Helmut Henzler (Germany) and Keke Rosberg (Finland) in a prototype Volkswagen diesel-powered car on 18 October 1980, at the Nardo circuit in Italy.

GREATEST DISTANCE DRIVEN IN ONE HOUR BY AN ELECTRIC VEHICLE

The greatest distance covered in one hour by an electric car is 199.881 km (124.2 miles), by Oscar De Vita (Italy) driving the Bertone *ZER* (Zero Emission Record) prototype at the Nardo circuit, Italy, on 2 October 1994. The streamlined car was also the first electric vehicle to break the 300-km/h (186-mph) barrier.

HIGHEST CAR MILEAGE

The highest recorded mileage for a car is in excess of 3.2 million km (2 million miles) for a 1966 Volvo P-1800S owned by Irvin Gordon (USA). He reached the 2-million-mile mark in the NBC Studios at Times Square, New York, USA, on 27 March 2002.

MOST FUEL-EFFICIENT VEHICLE

The best fuel consumption ever recorded is 3,624.5 km/litre (10,240 mpg) for a vehicle by team Fancy Carol-Nok (Japan) in the Scottish Eco Marathon on 12 August, 2001. The minimum speed allowed was 16.1 km/hr (10 mph).

FASTEST ROCKET CAR

The highest speed attained in a rocket-powered four-wheeled vehicle over a measured kilometre is 1,016.086 km/h (631.367 mph). This was achieved by *The Blue Flame*, driven by Gary Gabelich (USA) on the Bonneville Salt Flats, Utah, USA, on 23 October 1970. Momentarily, Gabelich exceeded 1,046 km/h (650 mph).

FASTEST ROAD RACE

The fastest road race in the world is the Silver State Classic on Route 318, Nevada, USA, in which drivers maintain average speeds in excess of 305 km/h (190 mph) over the 145-km (90-mile) course. The highest ever average speed was 334.38 km/h (207.78 mph), set by Chuck Shafer and Gary Brockman (both USA) in May 2000.

LONGEST OWNERSHIP OF VEHICLE FROM NEW

Eugene Stenger (USA) bought his white 1954 Chevrolet Corvette on 5 April 1954 and has owned it ever since. The original price was $3,577.85 (then £1,270).

SMALLEST PRODUCTION CAR

Smaller than a fairground 'dodgem' car, the Peel P50 (above) was 134 cm (53 in) long, 99 cm (39 in) wide and 134 cm (53 in) high, and weighed just 59 kg (130 lb). The vehicle was made by Peel Engineering Co., Peel, Isle of Man, UK, between 1962 and 1965.

TRAINS, TRAMS & BUSES

FASTEST TRAIN IN REGULAR PUBLIC SERVICE

The magnetically levitated (maglev) train linking China's Shanghai International Airport to the city's financial district reaches a top speed of 431 km/h (267.8 mph) on each 30-km (18-mile) run. The train (right), built by Germany's Transrapid International, had its maiden run on 31 December 2002.

FASTEST SPEED ON A RAIL SYSTEM

The highest speed recorded on any national rail system is 515.3 km/h (320.2 mph) by a French SNCF high-speed TGV (Train à Grande Vitesse) 'Atlantique' train between Courtalain and Tours, France, on 18 May 1990.

FASTEST AVERAGE-SPEED TRAIN JOURNEY

The West Japan Railway Company operates its 500-Series Nozomi bullet trains or *shinkansen* at an average speed of 261.8 km/h (162.7 mph) on the 192-km (119-mile) line between Hiroshima and Kokura on the island of Honshu, Japan.

FASTEST STEAM LOCOMOTIVE

The highest speed ever ratified for a steam locomotive is 201 km/h (125 mph) over 402 m (1,319 ft) by the London North Eastern Railway 'Class A4' (4–6–2) No. 4468 *Mallard* (later numbered 60022), which hauled seven coaches weighing 243 tonnes (535,722 lb) gross down Stoke Bank, near Essendine, (now) Rutland, UK, on 3 July 1938.

MOST POWERFUL STEAM LOCOMOTIVE

The world's most powerful steam locomotive measured by tractive effort (the force exerted at the rim of the driving wheel) was No. 700, a triple-articulated or triplex six-cylinder 2-8-8-8-4 tank engine built by the Baldwin Locomotive Works in 1916 for the Virginian Railway, USA. It had a tractive force of 75,433 kg (166,300 lb) when working compound and 90,519 kg (199,560 lb) when working simple.

FASTEST DIESEL TRAIN

The former British Rail (UK) inaugurated its HST (High Speed Train) daily service between London, Bristol and South Wales on 4 October 1976 using InterCity 125 trains. One of these holds the world speed record for diesel trains, at 238 km/h (148 mph), set on a test run between Darlington, Durham, and York, N Yorks, UK, on 1 November 1987.

FASTEST MAGLEV TRAIN

The highest speed attained by a manned magnetically levitated vehicle (Maglev) is 552 km/h (343 mph) by the MLX01, run by the Central Japan Railway Company and Railway Technical Research Institute on a test line between Otsuki and Tsuru, Japan, on 14 April 1999.

EARLIEST PUBLIC ELECTRIC RAILWAY

The first public electric railway was opened on 12 May 1881, at Lichtervelde near Berlin, Germany. It was 2.5 km (1.5 miles) long, ran on 100V current and carried 26 passengers at up to 48 km/h (30 mph).

LARGEST STEAM LOCOMOTIVE

The largest steam locomotives are generally considered to be the 4-8-8-4 'Big Boys', built by the American Locomotive Company from 1941 to 1944. They are 39.852 m (130 ft 9 in) long and weigh 508.02 tonnes (1.12 million lb) with their tenders.

LONGEST PASSENGER TRAIN

A passenger train created by the National Belgian Railway Company (NMBS) in aid of a Belgian cancer research charity measured 1.73 km (1.07 miles) and consisted of 70 coaches. The train, which weighed 2,786 tonnes (6.14 million lb), was pulled by one electric locomotive and travelled 62.5 km (38.9 miles) from Ghent to Ostend on 27 April 1991. It made the journey in 1 hr 11 min at an average speed of 52.8 km/h (32.8 mph).

OLDEST STEAM LOCOMOTIVE IN USE

The *Fairy Queen* was built in 1855 by Kitson Thompson Hewitson of Leeds, West Yorkshire, UK. Between October 1997 and February 1998 she was put into service hauling a twin-coach train between Delhi Cantonment, Delhi, and Alwar, Rajasthan, India.

HIGHEST RAILWAY LINE

At La Cima, Peru, the standard-gauge (1,435-mm or 56.5-in) track on the main line between Lima and La Oroya reaches 4,818 m (15,806 ft) above sea level as it crosses the Andes, making it the highest in the world. There are 67 tunnels and 59 bridges on the line. However, in 2001, China began building the Qinghai–Tibet railway, which is planned to reach a height of 5,072 m (16,640 ft).

COUNTRY WITH SHORTEST RAILWAY

The country with the shortest length of railway track is the Vatican City. It only has an 862-m (2,828-ft) spur, which is used just for goods and supplies, that enters the Holy See from Italy.

LARGEST RAILWAY STATION BY PLATFORMS

The world's largest station by number of platforms is Grand Central Terminal, Park Avenue and 42nd Street, New York, USA, which was built from 1903 to 1913 and has 44 platforms. They are situated on two underground levels with 41 tracks on the upper level and 26 on the lower. The station covers 19 ha (47 acres) and some 550 trains and 200,000 commuters use it daily.

MOST TRAINS 'SPOTTED'

Bill Curtis (UK) is acknowledged as the world champion 'train spotter'. His totals include some 85,000 locomotives, clocked up over a period of 40 years in 31 different countries.

LONGEST MODEL TRAIN

The longest model train consisted of 650 1:87-(HO) scale wagons hauled by four locomotives and measured 70.2 m (228 ft) in length. It was run by the Arid Australia model railway group in Perth, Australia, on 3 June 1996.

LONGEST MINIATURE HOBBY RAILWAY

Train Mountain Railroad Museum near Chiloquin, Oregon, USA, has a total of 35,847 m (117,610 ft) of 19-cm (7.5-in) gauge track, with 20,533 m (67,366 ft) of 'mainline' track, and the remainder comprising yards and sidings.

LONGEST MONORAIL

The Osaka Monorail, Osaka, Japan, has a total operational length of 22.2 km (13.8 miles). Fully operational since August 1997, it runs between Osaka International Airport and Hankyu Railway Minami Ibaraki Station, with the second stage running between Hankyu and Keihan Railway Kadomashi Station. The Chiba Urban Monorail near Tokyo, Japan, is the longest suspended monorail train system in the world, measuring 15.2 km (9.45 miles). The first 3.2 km (1.99 mile) stretch opened on 20 March 1979 and the line has been expanded three times since.

MOST EXTENSIVE UNDERGROUND RAIL SYSTEM

America's New York City subway system is the most extensive in the world, with a total track distance of 1,355 km (842 miles) and some 468 stations.

LEAST EXTENSIVE UNDERGROUND RAIL SYSTEM

The shortest operating underground system is the Carmelit in Haifa, Israel. Opened in 1959, the Carmelit is just 1,800 m (1.12 miles) long. The only subway/metro in Israel, the Carmelit is a funicular running at a gradient of 12 degrees. Running from Paris Square to Carmel Central, it has six stations.

OLDEST TRAMS IN REVENUE SERVICE

The oldest trams in revenue service in the world are cars 1 and 2 of the Manx Electric Railway, dating from 1893. These still run regularly on the 28.5-km (17.75-mile) railway between Douglas and Ramsey, Isle of Man, UK.

MOST EXTENSIVE TRAM SYSTEM

The city of St Petersburg, Russia, has the most extensive tramway system (below) with approximately 2,400 cars on routes with over 690 km (430 miles) of track. The first electric locomotive in Russia was tested in St Petersburg in 1880, and the first electrical tramlines on the city streets were opened in September 1907.

LARGEST BUS FLEET

The largest fleet of buses is owned by the Andhra Pradesh State Road Transport Corporation (India). As of 31 October 1999 the company owned a total of 18,397 buses. The bus network comprises 8,745 routes between 209 depots, 703 stations and 1,801 bus stops spread over the 275,068-km² (106,204-mile²) state.

LONGEST BUS

The articulated DAF Super CityTrain buses of the Democratic Republic of the Congo are 32.2 m (105 ft 8 in) long and can carry 350 passengers comfortably (sitting and standing). They weigh 28 tonnes (61,729 lb) unladen.

EARLIEST BUSES

The first municipal motor omnibus service in the world was inaugurated on 12 April 1903 and ran between Eastbourne railway station and Meads, East Sussex, UK (below).

BIKES & MOTORBIKES

EARLIEST BICYCLE

The earliest machine propelled by cranks and pedals with connecting rods was built between 1839 and 1840 by Kirkpatrick Macmillan (UK). A copy of the machine is now in the Science Museum, London, UK.

LONGEST UNICYCLE RIDE

Lars Clausen (USA, left) covered a distance of 14,686.82 km (9,125.97 miles) by unicycle between 22 April and 12 November 2002. His double crossing of the USA started in Tillamook, Oregon, and finished in Los Angeles, California, taking in 39 states. The 326.34 km (202.78 miles) covered in a 24-hour period, from Martin, South Dakota, to a point near Highmore, South Dakota, from 5–6 June 2002, was also a record. He used a 91-cm (36-in) Coker unicycle.

LARGEST BICYCLE

The largest rideable bicycle, as measured by the wheel diameter, is *Frankencycle*, built by David Moore (USA) and first ridden by Steve Gordon (USA) on 4 June 1989. The giant penny-farthing has a front wheel diameter of 3.05 m (10 ft) and is 3.4 m (11 ft 2 in) high.

PRODUCTION MOTORCYCLE WITH LARGEST ENGINE

Honda's Goldwing GL1800 and Valkyrie Rune (below) models both have a horizontally-opposed 6-cylinder engine with a capacity of 1832 cc (111.7 in³) – the largest available on any standard production motorcycle. However, at the time of going to press, Triumph had an even larger three-cylinder c. 2200 cc (134.25 in³) motorcycle planned for production.

SMALLEST BICYCLE

The world's smallest-wheeled rideable bicycle is one with wheels of a diameter of 11 mm (0.43 in) at the front and 13 mm (0.51 in) at the rear. The bicycle was ridden by its constructor Zbigniew Rózanek (Poland) for a distance of 5 m (16 ft) on 11 August 1999.

LARGEST PEDAL-POWERED VEHICLE

Roger Dumas (USA) created a 55-seater 'bicycle' 42.875 m (140 ft 8 in) long, consisting of multiple bicycle frames welded together and supported by wheels at regular intervals along its length. It was pedalled by 52 people for 986 m (3,236 ft) in Augusta, Maine, USA, on 29 July 2000 (although there were 55 seats, three were for children who were unable to pedal).

LONGEST BICYCLE

The longest true bicycle ever built (ie with only two wheels) is 25.88 m (84 ft 11 in) long and was built by Super Tandem Club Ceparana (Italy). Forty club members cycled a distance of 112.2 m (368 ft) at Ceparana, Italy, on 20 September 1998. Cornering proved a problem.

LARGEST TRICYCLE

The world's largest rideable tricycle was constructed at Bay de Noc Community College, Escabana, Michigan, USA, in July 1998. The trike was 7.13 m (23 ft 4 in) high, had a front wheel 4.67 m (15 ft 4 in) in diameter and back wheels 2.23 m (7 ft 4 in) in diameter.

LIGHTEST FULL-SIZE RACING BICYCLE

Dionisio Coronado (Spain) constructed a full-size racing bicycle weighing just 4.492 kg (9.903 lb) in 2001. The secret behind the hi-tech machine's weight is its beryl-alloy frame, which measures 50 x 60 x 48 cm (19.6 x 23.6 x 18.9 in).

PENNY-FARTHING STACK

The Colorado chapter of bicycle historians 'The Wheelmen' created a self-supporting line of 83 penny-farthing bicycles and riders at Clear Creek History Park near Golden, Colorado, USA, on 27 July 2002.

FASTEST 100 MILES ON A UNICYCLE

Takayuki Koike (Japan) set the unicycle record for 100 miles (160.9 km) in 6 hr 44 min 21.84 sec on 9 August 1987 – an average speed of 23.87 km/h (14.83 mph).

FASTEST HUMAN-POWERED VEHICLE

Sam Whittingham (Canada) reached a speed of 130.36 km/h (80 mph) on his streamlined recumbent bike *Varna Diablo* at the World Human Powered Speed Challenge near Battle Mountain, Nevada, USA, on 5 October 2002.

LONGEST FRONT-WHEEL WHEELIE ON A MOTORCYCLE

Craig Jones (UK) covered 225 m (738 ft) on the front wheel of his Buell XB9S motorcycle at Naples, Florida, USA, on 23 November 2002.

BLINDFOLD MOTORCYCLE SPEED RECORD

Blind motorcyclist Mike Newman (UK) reached a speed of 143.2 km/h (89 mph) at Elvington airfield, N Yorks, UK, on 7 August 2001.

FASTEST MOTORCYCLE SPEED

Dave Campos (USA), riding a 7-m (23-ft) streamliner named *Easyriders* powered by two 1500-cc (91.5-in^3) Ruxton Harley-Davidson engines, set American Motorcyclist Association (AMA) and Fédération Internationale de Motorcyclisme (FIM) absolute records with an average speed of 518.45 km/h (322.15 mph) over two 1-mile (1.6-km) runs at Bonneville Salt Flats, Utah, USA, on 14 July 1990.

GREATEST DISTANCE ON A MOTORCYCLE IN 24 HOURS

A team of 19 riders from Suzuki and Metzeler covered a total distance of 5,900.426 km (3,666.355 miles) in 24 hours on a Suzuki RF900R at Nardo racetrack, Italy, from 4 to 5 June 1994.

HIGHEST SPEED ON A QUADBIKE

Graham 'G-Force' Hicks, a deaf-blind daredevil from Peterborough, Cambs, UK, reached a speed of 167.4 km/h (104.02 mph) on a quadbike at Bruntingthorpe Proving Ground, Leics, UK, on 22 June 2002. Hicks received instructions from his pillion rider, Rob Hall, who told him where to steer using a system of touch-based commands. The quadbike was a custom-built machine powered by an 1100-cc (67-in^3) Honda Blackbird motorcycle engine.

LONGEST MOTORCYCLE

Douglas and Roger Bell (both Australia) designed and built *Big Ben*, a 7.6-m-long (24-ft 11-in) motorcycle weighing nearly 2,000 kg (4,400 lb). It is powered by three 5.2-litre (317-in^3) V12 Jaguar car engines, connected by a solid crankshaft to synchronize their running. *Big Ben* is so large that it needs power steering to manoeuvre it.

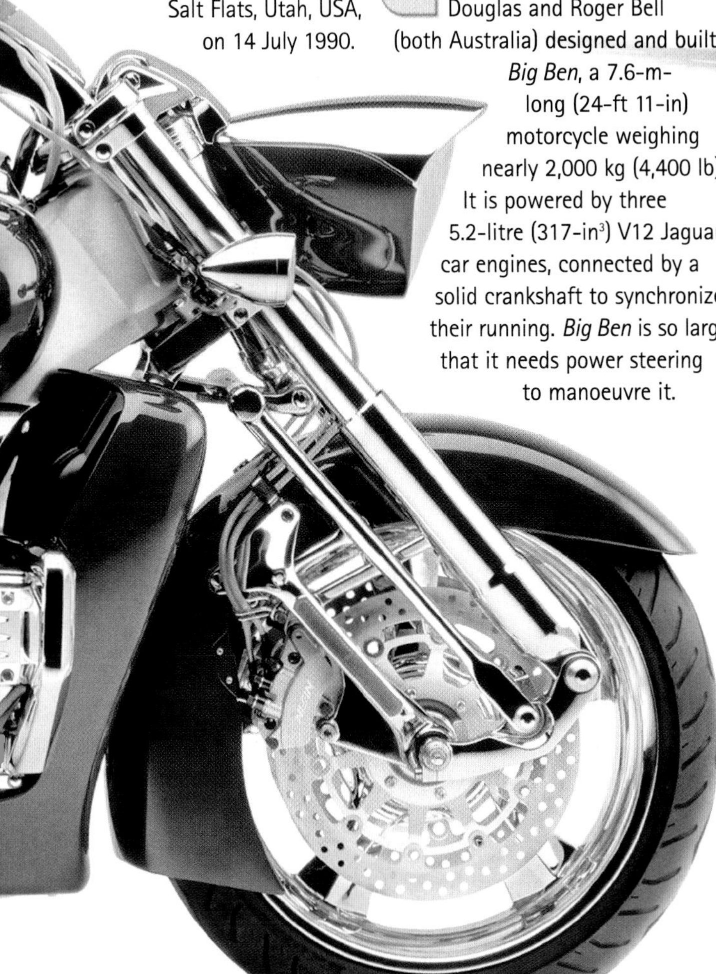

TALLEST RIDEABLE MOTORCYCLE

The tallest rideable motorcycle is *Bigtoe*, built by Tom Wiberg (Sweden), which at its highest point is 2.3 m (7 ft 6 in) tall. The bike has a top speed of 100 km/h (60 mph) and is powered by a Jaguar V12 engine. *Bigtoe* cost £50,000 ($80,000) to build and features hydraulic steering and a 500-W stereo.

FASTEST BACKWARDS MOTORCYCLING

Szabolcs Borsay (Hungary, below) reached a speed of 200.726 km/h (124.725 mph) riding his Suzuki GSX-R 1000 sitting backwards at Balaton Airport, Sármellék, Hungary, on 2 July 2002. Borsay started by riding forwards, then turned around so he was sitting on the petrol tank holding the handlebars behind him. Once through the speed trap, he turned back around to brake.

LONGEST MOTORCYCLE WHEELIE

Yasuyuki Kudo (Japan) covered 331 km (205.7 miles) non-stop on the rear wheel of his Honda TLM220R motorcycle at the Japan Automobile Research Institute proving ground, Tsukuba, near Tsuchiura, Japan, on 5 May 1991.

LARGEST SCOOTER BY ENGINE CAPACITY

The Suzuki Burgman 650 scooter has a 638-cc (40-in3) four-stroke, two-cylinder engine, the largest available on a production model today. The 238-kg (524-lb) Burgman went on sale in 2003.

LONGEST SNOWMOBILE JOURNEY

Tony Lenzini (USA) drove his 1986 Arctic Cat Cougar snowmobile a total of 11,604.6 km (7,211 miles) in 60 riding days between 28 December 1985 and 20 March 1986.

GREATEST DISTANCE ON A SNOWMOBILE IN 24 HOURS

The greatest distance covered on a snowmobile in 24 hours is 2,262.2 km (1,405.67 miles), by Vince Lofquist (USA) from 9 to 10 January 2001. Lofquist completed 304 laps of a 7.44-km (4.624-mile) course at an average speed of 94.2 km/h (58.57 mph).

FURTHEST DISTANCE TRAVELLED ON A SNOWMOBILE ON WATER

On 18 June 2000, Jani Anttila (Finland) travelled a distance of 18 km (11.18 miles) along a lake near Toivakka, Finland, on his standard snowmobile.

BOATS, YACHTS & FERRIES

LARGEST FLOATING CRANE SHIP

The world's largest floating crane ship is *Thialf*, a 201.6-m-long (661.5-ft) semi-submersible barge which has two 95-m (311-ft) cranes that, when operating in tandem, have a lifting capacity of 14,200 tonnes (31.3 million lb).

LARGEST HOSPITAL SHIP

United States Navy Ship (USNS) *Mercy* and her sister ship USNS *Comfort* each have a total patient capacity of 1,000, with 80 intensive-care beds and 12 operating rooms, making them the largest floating hospitals in the world. They are 272.5 m (894 ft) long, 32.2 m (105 ft 8 in) across, and have a full-load displacement of 62,922 tonnes (138.72 million lb).

LARGEST SAILING SHIP BY WEIGHT

The largest vessel ever built in the era of sail was the *France II*, a steel-hulled, five-masted barque launched at Bordeaux, France, in 1911. Her hull measured 127.4 m (418 ft) overall and she had a deadweight tonnage (cargo-carrying capacity) of 8000 tonnes (17.6 million lb). Although principally designed as a sailing vessel, she was also fitted with two auxiliary engines. However, these were removed in 1919 and she became a pure sailing vessel. *France II* was wrecked off the island of New Caledonia on 12 July 1922.

TALLEST MAST ON A SAILING SHIP

The 75.2-m-long (246-ft 8-in) luxury yacht *Mirabella V*, which was due to be commissioned in the second half of 2003, has a single carbon-fibre mast 90 m (295 ft) tall. The largest ever single-masted yacht, *Mirabella V* was built by Vosper Thornycroft in Southampton, UK, and is available for hire at a reported rate of £200,000 ($300,000) per week.

LONGEST SAILING SHIP

The French-owned sister ships *Club Med I* and *II* are the largest sailing ships afloat, with a length of 187 m (613 ft). They have five aluminium masts and 2,800 m^2 (30,100 ft^2) of computer-controlled sails. Each caters for around 400 passengers, with roughly 200 crew members. With their relatively small sail area and powerful engines, the ships are strictly motor-sailers.

MOST POWERFUL TUG

The 20,800-kW (27,900-hp) tug/supply vessel *Normand Progress* achieved a bollard pull (a test of a ship's pulling power) of 304 tonnes (670,200 lb) – believed to be the greatest ever – on 15 October 1999 at Osneset, Norway. The 95-m-long (311-ft) vessel was built by Ulstein Verft (Norway) in 1999 and is owned by Solstad Rederi AS (Norway).

FASTEST PROPELLER-DRIVEN BOAT

Russ Wicks (USA) achieved a speed of 178.61 knots (330.79 km/h or 205.494 mph) in his hydroplane *Miss Freei* on 15 June 2000, at Lake Washington, Seattle, USA, the highest ever speed in a propeller-driven boat. *Miss Freei* was powered by a Lycoming L-7C turbine engine taken from a Chinook helicopter, generating 2,237 kW (3,000 hp) at 10,000 rpm. Featuring a canopy from an F-16 jet fighter, the 8.5-m (28-ft), 3-tonne (6,600-lb) boat shoots a 60-m (200-ft) jet of water out behind it at speed.

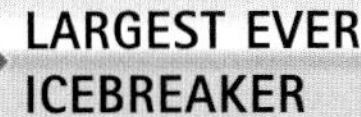

LARGEST EVER ICEBREAKER

The largest icebreaker was the SS *Manhattan*, a 306.9-m-long (1,007-ft) oil tanker specially converted in 1968 (right). Fitted with protective steel armour 2.7 m (9 ft) thick, 9.1 m (30 ft) deep and 204 m (670 ft) long, she weighed 152,407 tonnes (335 million lb).

FASTEST SAILING VESSEL

On 26 October 1993 the trifoiler (three-hulled hydrofoil) *Yellow Pages Endeavour* reached a speed of 46.52 knots (86.21 km/h or 53.57 mph) while on a timed run of 500 m (1,640 ft) at Sandy Point near Melbourne, Victoria, Australia.

FASTEST TRANS-ATLANTIC SAILING

The fastest ever Atlantic crossing, made between Ambrose Light Tower, New York, USA, and Lizard Point, Cornwall, UK, is 4 days 17 hr 28 min 6 sec by the catamaran *Playstation*, captained by Steve Fossett (USA) in October 2001.

FASTEST ATLANTIC CROSSING

The fastest crossing of the Atlantic is 2 days 10 hr 34 min 47 sec by the 68-m (222-ft) luxury yacht *Destriero*, skippered by Cesare Fiorio (Italy), from 6 to 9 August 1992. The gas-turbine-propelled vessel maintained an average speed of 45.7 knots (84.6 km/h or 52.6 mph) despite weighing nearly 400 tonnes (882,000 lb). The turbines, which generate 13,420 kW (18,000 hp) each and burn nearly 10 tonnes (21,700 lb) of fuel per hour, suck water in beneath the vessel and expel it from the rear at a rate of 60,000 litres (13,200 gal) per second.

GREATEST DISTANCE SAILED IN 24 HOURS

The greatest distance ever covered under sail in 24 hours is 694.78 nautical miles (1,286.73 km or 799.5 miles) by the 33.5-m (110-ft) maxi catamaran *Maiden 2*, in the North Atlantic on 12 and 13 June 2002. The yacht was sailed by Brian Thompson, Helena Darvelid, Adrienne Cahalan (all UK) and a crew of seven. The average speed was 28.95 knots (53.61 km/h or 33.31 mph).

FASTEST CIRCUMNAVIGATION IN A POWERED BOAT

On 3 July 1998 the *Cable & Wireless Adventurer* (left) circumnavigated the world in 74 days 20 hr 58 min 30 sec. The powered, 35.05-m-long (115-ft) stabilized monohull vessel, equipped with state-of-the-art navigation and communications equipment, travelled more than 41,841 km (26,000 miles).

FASTEST CIRCUMNAVIGATION BY A CREWED YACHT

The fastest ever circumnavigation by crewed yacht is 64 days 8 hr 37 min by the 33-m (108-ft) catamaran *Orange*, skippered by Bruno Peyron (France). The record voyage, which ended on 5 May 2002, started and finished at Brest, France, and took the 12-man crew into the South Atlantic and around Antarctica.

LARGEST CARGO VESSEL

The world's largest ship of any kind is the oil tanker *Jahre Viking* (formerly the *Happy Giant* and *Seawise Giant*), with a deadweight tonnage (cargo-carrying capacity) of 564,763 tonnes (1.24 billion lb). The tanker is 458.45 m (1,504 ft) long, has a beam of 68.8 m (226 ft) and a draught of 24.61 m (80 ft 9 in).

LARGEST CAR FERRY

The ferry with the greatest car-carrying capacity is Irish Ferries' *Ulysses*, launched on 1 September 2000. The ship can carry 1,342 cars or 240 trucks, is 209 m (685 ft 8 in) long and 31.84 m (104 ft 6 in) wide and has full-load displacement of 27,425 tonnes (60.46 million lb).

FASTEST CAR FERRY

Designed in Australia by Advanced Multi-Hull Designs PTY Ltd, the *Luciano Federico L* is powered by two 16,000-kW (21,500-hp) gas turbines and has a loaded speed of 57 knots (105.5 km/h or 65.5 mph), with a top speed of 60 knots (111 km/h or 69 mph). She sails between Buenos Aires, Argentina, and Montevideo, Uruguay.

LARGEST PASSENGER SHIP

The Cunard Line's *Queen Mary II*, which is due to make her maiden voyage in January 2004, is 345 m (1,132 ft) long and 41 m (135 ft) wide. At approximately 150,000 grt (gross registered tons), *Queen Mary II* is nearly three times larger than *Titanic* (46,000 grt), and has space for 2,620 passengers and 1,253 crew. She is estimated to have cost around £498 million ($800 million) to build.

EARLIEST SCHEDULED PUBLIC HOVERCRAFT SERVICE

The first public hovercraft service was run across the Dee estuary between Rhyl (Wales) and Wallasey (England), UK, by the 60-knot (111-km/h or 69-mph) 24-passenger Vickers-Armstrong VA-3 from July to September 1962.

LARGEST CIVILIAN HOVERCRAFT

The SRN4 Mk III, a British-built civil hovercraft formerly employed for ferrying passengers and cars across the English Channel, weighs 310 tonnes (683,400 lb) and can hold 418 passengers and 60 cars. It is 56.38 m (185 ft) in length, and is powered by four Bristol-Siddeley Marine Proteus engines, giving a maximum speed in excess of 65 knots (120 km/h or 75 mph).

OLDEST ACTIVE SAILING SHIP

The oldest square-rigged sailing vessel that is still sea-going is thought to be the 1,200-tonne (2,645,544-lb) iron barque *Star of India*, built at Ramsey, Isle of Man, UK, in 1863 as the full-rigged ship *Euterpe*. She is now preserved as a museum ship in San Diego, California, USA, but makes occasional day-trips under sail.

AIRCRAFT

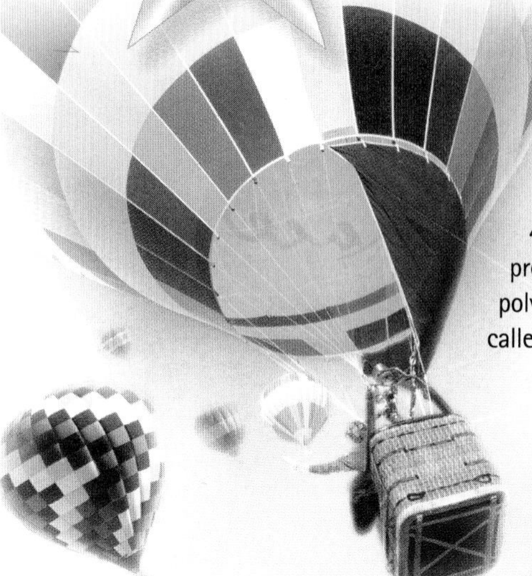

Commander Victor A Prather (both USA) of the US Navy over the Gulf of Mexico, USA, on 4 May 1961. Their non-pressurized, gas-filled polyethylene balloon was called *Lee Lewis Memorial*.

LARGEST BALLOON

The largest balloon ever made, known by its model number of SF3-579.49-035-NSC-01, had an inflatable volume of 2,003,192 m³ (70,732,718 ft³) and was 239.49 m (785 ft 9.36 in) in gore length. The unmanned balloon, manufactured by Winzen Research, Inc. (now Winzen Engineering, Inc.) of South St Paul, Minnesota, USA, was prepared for flight at the National Scientific Balloon facility in Palestine, Texas, USA, on 1 October 1975. There were no photographs of the attempt and, unfortunately, due to problems, the launch was 'aborted on launch pad'.

GREATEST MASS BALLOON ASCENT

The greatest mass ascent of hot-air balloons took place on 7 October 2000 when 329 balloons were launched in one hour at the 2000 Albuquerque International Balloon Fiesta in New Mexico, USA (above).

FASTEST CIRCUMNAVIGATION BY BALLOON

Steve Fossett (USA) flew around the world alone in 13 days 8 hr 33 min in *Bud Light Spirit of Freedom* from 19 June to 2 July 2002. He took off from Northam, Western Australia, and landed at Eromanga, Queensland, Australia. This was only the second ever non-stop circumnavigation of the globe by balloon, and the first ever solo.

HIGHEST ALTITUDE IN A HOT-AIR BALLOON

Per Lindstrand (Sweden) achieved the altitude record of 19,811 m (64,997 ft) in a Colt 600 hot-air balloon over Laredo, Texas, USA, on 6 June 1988.

HIGHEST BALLOON ALTITUDE RECORD

The greatest altitude ever reached by a manned balloon is 34,668 m (113,740 ft), by Commander Malcolm D Ross and Lieutenant

LONGEST HELICOPTER FLIGHT

On 6 April 1966 Robert Ferry (USA), in accordance with Fédération Aéronautique Internationale (FAI) rules, piloted his Hughes YOH-6A helicopter from Culver City, California, to Ormond Beach, Florida, USA, without refuelling – a distance of 3,561.6 km (2,213.1 miles).

HIGHEST ALTITUDE FOR A HELICOPTER

The highest recorded altitude in a helicopter is 12,442 m (40,820 ft) by Jean Bouletan (France) flying an Aérospatiale SA315B Lama over Istres, France, on 21 June 1972.

HELICOPTER SPEED RECORD

Under FAI rules, the world speed record for helicopters was set by John Trevor Eggington with co-pilot Derek J Clews (UK), who averaged 400.87 km/h (249.09 mph) over Glastonbury, Somerset, UK, on 11 August 1986 in a Westland Lynx demonstrator.

LARGEST HELICOPTER

The Russian Mil Mi-12 was powered by four 4,847-kW (6,500-hp) turboshaft engines. It had a rotor diameter of 67 m (219 ft 10 in), with a length of 37 m (121 ft 4.8 in) and a weight of 103.3 tonnes (227,737 lb). A prototype was shown in 1971 at the Paris Air Show but it never went into production.

LARGEST HELICOPTER IN PRODUCTION

The largest helicopter currently produced is the five-man-crewed Russian Mil Mi-26, which has a maximum take-off weight of 56,000 kg (123,460 lb). Unladen, it weighs 28,200 kg (62,170 lb) and its overall length is 40 m (131 ft). The eight-bladed main rotor has a diameter of 32 m (105 ft) and is powered by two 8500-kW (11,240-hp) turbine engines.

FASTEST AERIAL CIRCUMNAVIGATION

The fastest flight under Fédération Aéronautique Internationale (FAI) rules, which permit flights that exceed the length of the Tropic of Cancer or Capricorn (36,787.6 km or 22,858.8 miles), was one of 31 hr 27 min 49 sec by an Air France Concorde flown by Captains Michel Dupont and Claude Hetru (both France) from JFK airport in New York, USA, eastbound via Toulouse, Dubai, Bangkok, Guam, Honolulu and Acapulco, from 15–16 August 1995. In total, there were 80 passengers and 18 crew on board flight AF1995.

LIGHTEST AEROPLANE TO CROSS THE SOUTH ATLANTIC

The lightest aeroplane to cross the South Atlantic is the RWD-5bis, powered by a De Havilland Gipsy Moth engine. It set the Fédération Aéronautique Internationale (FAI) world record for straight line distance in Category II (single-seater aircraft with a maximum weight of 450 kg) on 7 May 1933, travelling 3,582 km (2,226 miles). The plane was flown by Captain Stanislaw Skarzynski (Poland) from St Louis, Senegal, to Maceio, Brazil, in 20 hr 30 min.

FASTEST PROPELLER-DRIVEN AIRCRAFT

The former Soviet Tu-95/142 (NATO code-name Bear) long-range bomber is the fastest propeller-driven aircraft in standard production, with a maximum speed of Mach 0.82 or 925 km/h (575 mph). First produced in the 1950s, it remains in service with several air forces around the world. It has four 11,033-kW (14,795-hp) engines driving eight-blade contra-rotating propellers.

HEAVIEST AIRCRAFT

The aircraft with the highest standard maximum take-off weight is the Antonov An-225 Mriya (Dream, below) at 600 tonnes (1.32 million lb). The An-225 also has the longest wingspan of any aircraft to have flown more than once, at 88.4 m (290 ft), but only one was ever built. Another Antonov aircraft, the An-124, has the largest wing span of any series-produced aircraft, measuring 73.3 m (240 ft 6 in).

HIGHEST FLYING PROPELLER-DRIVEN AIRCRAFT

The highest ever altitude reached by a propeller-driven aircraft is 29,413 m (96,500 ft), by the unmanned, solar-powered *Helios* prototype flying wing over the Hawaiian Island of Kauai on 13 August 2001. Commissioned by NASA and developed by AeroVironment Inc. of Monrovia, California, USA, *Helios* is one of a new breed of slow-flying, high-altitude aircraft that experts believe may offer a viable alternative to communications satellites in the future.

LARGEST AEROPLANE PROPELLER

The largest aeroplane propeller ever to fly was the 6.9-m-diameter (22-ft 7.5-in) Garuda propeller, fitted to the Linke-Hofmann R II, which was built in Breslau, Germany (now Wroclaw, Poland) and flown in 1919. It was driven by four 195-kW (260-hp) Mercedes engines and turned at only 545 rpm. Today, typical single-engine aircraft have propellers of roughly 2 m (7 ft) diameter that turn at 2,500 rpm.

LARGEST PROPELLER-DRIVEN AIRCRAFT

The largest propeller-driven aircraft ever to enter production is the Russian Antonov An-22. It has a wing span of 64.4 m (211 ft) and a maximum take-off weight of 250 tonnes (550,000 lb). Still in service with the Russian military, the An-22 is powered by four 11,030-kW (14,791-hp) contra-rotating turboprop engines and has a cruising speed of 680 km/h (422 mph).

FASTEST AIRLINER

On 31 December 1968 the Tupolev Tu-144, Russia's version of Concorde, became the first airliner to fly supersonic. It was reported to have reached Mach 2.4 (2,587 km/h or 1,600 mph) – the fastest speed of any airliner – although its normal cruising speed was Mach 2.2. The aircraft was retired in 1978.

LARGEST PASSENGER AIRCRAFT

The Boeing 747-400 is the largest passenger aircraft flying today, with a wingspan of 64.4 m (211 ft 4 in), a length of 70.6 m (231 ft 7 in) and a maximum take-off weight of 396.89 tonnes (875,000 lb). Thanks to the trademark 'bubble' above its nose, the 747 also has a higher capacity than its nearest competitor, the Airbus A340-600 – typically 524 passengers, compared with 419 in the A340.

LONGEST PASSENGER AIRCRAFT IN SERVICE

At 75.3 m (246 ft 11 in) the Airbus A340-600 is the longest passenger aircraft currently in service. It has a maximum take-off weight of 365 tonnes (804,700 lb), a wingspan of 63.45 m (208 ft 2 in), and a passenger capacity of 419.

LARGEST VOLUME CARGO AIRCRAFT

The aircraft with the largest cargo hold by volume is the Airbus Beluga A300-600ST Super Transporter. The cargo deck has a volume of 1,400 m^3 (49,440 ft^3). It is 37.7 m (123 ft 8 in) long, with a maximum height and widlth of 7.1 m (23 ft 3 in). Its maximum payload weight is 47 tonnes (103,616 lb).

« GREATEST SPEED IN A MANNED AIRCRAFT

The greatest speed ever reached by an air-launched manned aircraft is 7,274 km/h (4,520 mph), or Mach 6.7, by the X-15A-2 rocket plane flown by USAF test pilot Major William 'Pete' Knight (left) over California, USA, on 3 October 1967. Although this is is nearly twice the official FAI air speed record, the X-15's flights are not eligible because the aircraft did not take off using its own power.

FASTEST JET

The USAF Lockheed SR-71 'Blackbird', a reconnaissance aircraft, is the world's fastest non-experimental aeroplane, with a top speed in excess of Mach 3. First flown in its definitive form on 22 December 1964, it is capable of attaining an altitude of close to 30,000 m (100,000 ft). Its range at Mach 3 is 4,800 km (3,000 miles) at 24,000 m (79,000 ft).

FIRST SUPERSONIC FLIGHT

The first ever supersonic flight was achieved on 14 October 1947 by Captain (later Brigadier General) Charles 'Chuck' Elwood Yeager (USA) over Lake Muroc, California, USA, in a Bell XS-1 rocket aircraft. Yeager reached Mach 1.015 (1,078 km/h or 670 mph) at an altitude of 12,800 m (42,000 ft). The XS-1 is now in the Smithsonian Institution, Washington DC, USA.

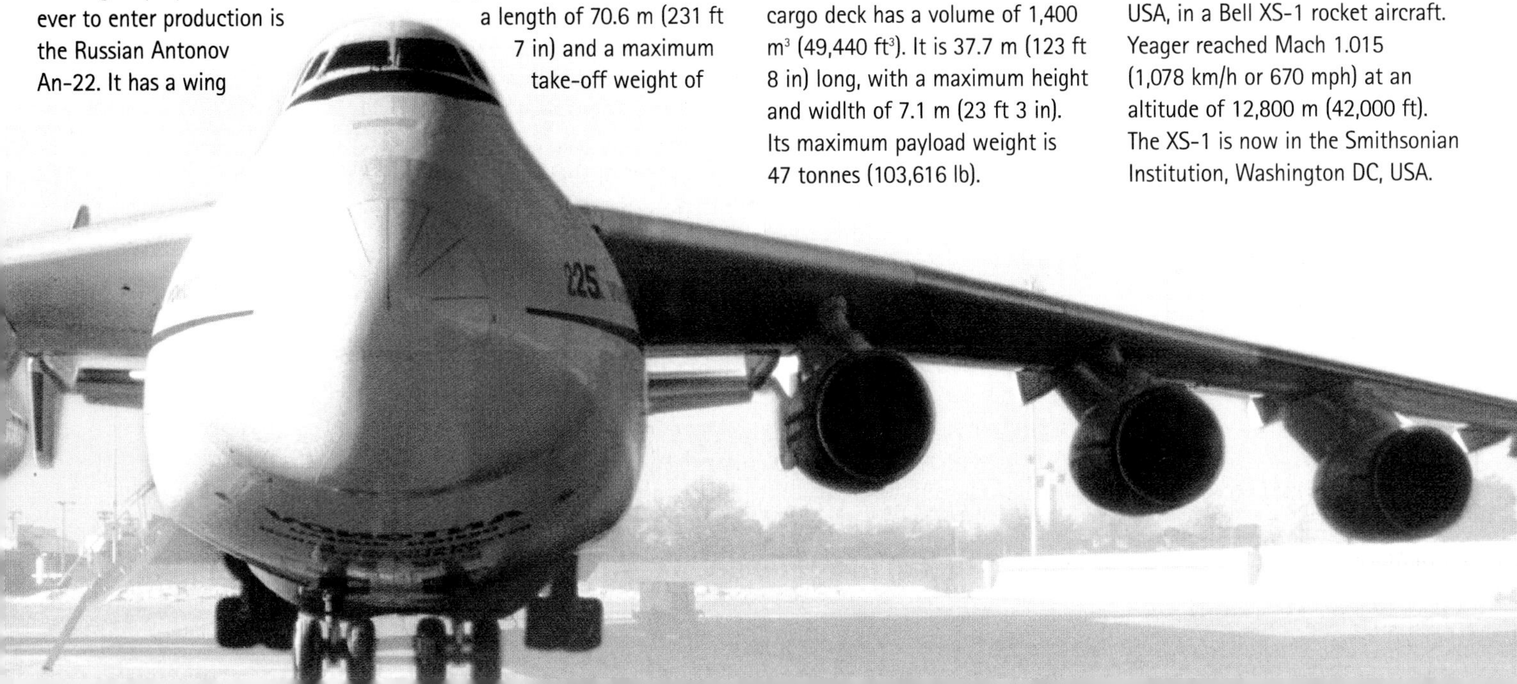

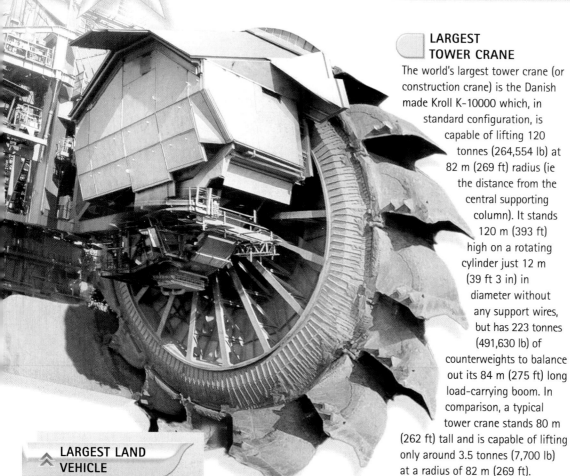

LARGE VEHICLES

LARGEST TOWER CRANE

The world's largest tower crane (or construction crane) is the Danish made Kroll K-10000 which, in standard configuration, is capable of lifting 120 tonnes (264,554 lb) at 82 m (269 ft) radius (ie the distance from the central supporting column). It stands 120 m (393 ft) high on a rotating cylinder just 12 m (39 ft 3 in) in diameter without any support wires, but has 223 tonnes (491,630 lb) of counterweights to balance out its 84 m (275 ft) long load-carrying boom. In comparison, a typical tower crane stands 80 m (262 ft) tall and is capable of lifting only around 3.5 tonnes (7,700 lb) at a radius of 82 m (269 ft).

LARGEST DUMPER TRUCK

The T-282, manufactured by the Liebherr Mining Equipment Co. of Virginia, USA, is the world's largest two-axle dump truck, with a payload capacity of 327 tonnes (720,900 lb). The diesel-electric-powered vehicle is 14.47 m (47 ft 6 in) long, 8.7 m (28 ft 7 in) wide and 7.3 m (24 ft) high, and weighs 201 tonnes (443,100 lb).

LARGEST MONSTER TRUCK

'Bigfoot 5' is 4.7-m tall (15 ft 6 in) with 3-m-tall (10-ft) tyres and weighs 17.23 tonnes (38,000 lb). It is one of a fleet of 17 Bigfoot trucks created by Bob Chandler (USA), and was built in the summer of 1986. Now parked in St Louis, Missouri, USA, it makes occasional appearances at local shows.

FASTEST MONSTER TRUCK

On 11 September 1999 at Smyrna Airport, Nashville, Tennessee, USA, Dan Runte reached a speed of 111.5 km/h (69.3 mph) in 'Bigfoot 14', the highest ever recorded speed in a monster truck. The speed was clocked during the run-up to the longest ever monster truck jump of 61.57 m (202 ft).

LARGEST LAND VEHICLE

The largest machine capable of moving under its own power is the 14,196-tonne (31.3-million-lb) RB293 bucket wheel excavator, an earthmoving machine manufactured by MAN TAKRAF of Leipzig, Germany. It is 220 m (722 ft) long, 94.5 m (310 ft) tall, and is capable of shifting 240,000 m^3 (8.475 million ft^3) of earth per day. The bucket wheel, (above) is 21.6 m (71 ft) in diameter, which means it stands as tall as a five-storey building.

LARGEST BULLDOZER

The Komatsu D575A 'Super Dozer' is the world's largest bulldozer weighing in at 152.6 tonnes (336,000 lb). Its 7.4 x 3.25-m (24.27 x 10.66-ft) blade has a capacity of 69 m^3 (2,437 ft^3). The 11.72-m-long (38-ft 5-in) pusher moves on tank-style tracks and is powered by an 858-kW (1,150-hp) turbocharged diesel engine.

LARGEST REVOLVING PEDESTAL CRANE

The revolving pedestal crane at the Yantai Raffles shipyard in Yantai, China, is thought to be the most powerful of its kind. It can lift 2,000 tonnes (4.4 million lb) to a height of 95 m (311 ft) from its main hook, and 200 tonnes (44,000 lb) to 135 m (443 ft) from its secondary arm. It was designed for use in the construction of oil rigs.

TALLEST MOBILE CRANE

The Demag CC 12600, made by Mannesmann Dematic, is 198 m (649 ft 7 in) high. It has a 120-m (393 ft 8 in) 'fixed jib' attached to a 114-m (374-ft) near-vertical boom and has a maximum lifting capacity of 1,600 tonnes (3.53 million lb) at 22 m (72 ft) radius. This monster crane requires 100 trucks to transport all its different parts to a site.

LONGEST TRUCKS ON PUBLIC ROADS

Australian road trains, which consist of powerful semi-trucks pulling up to three trailers, are permitted by national legislation to be up to 53.5 m (175.5 ft) long and weigh up to 125.2 tonnes (276,000 lb), although some states set the limits lower. Such vehicles, which are the main form of freight transportation in remote areas of the country, are only permitted to travel on designated routes.

LARGEST FORK-LIFT TRUCK

In 1991 Kalmar LMV of Lidhult, Sweden, manufactured three counterbalanced fork-lift trucks capable of lifting loads up to 90 tonnes (198,415 lb) at a load centre of 2.4 m (7 ft 6 in). They were built to handle the great manmade river project comprising two separate pipelines, one 998 km (620 miles) long from Sarir to the Gulf of Sirte, and the other 897 km (557 miles) from Tazirbu to Benghazi, Libya.

LARGEST HYDRAULIC SHOVEL EXCAVATOR

The RH 400-2000 hydraulic shovel excavator manufactured by O & K Mining (Germany, right) is the largest of its kind in the world. The giant crawler weighs 900 tonnes (1.984 million lb) and is capable of filling the world's largest dumper truck in just six passes. It has a shovel capacity of 51.7 m³ (1,825.7 ft³). The top of the driver's cab is 10.2 m (33.5 ft) high and the machine is powered by a 2,984-kW (4,002-hp) Cummins diesel engine fed by a 16,000-litre (3,520-gal) fuel tank.

FASTEST TRUCK WHEELIE

Patrick Bourny (France) drove his modified truck cab in a wheelie at 90 km/h (55.92 mph) at Lure on 21 October 2000 for *L'Émission des Records*, Paris, France.

LARGEST CARAVAN

The largest caravan was built in 1990 for HE Sheik Hamad Bin Hamdan Al Nahyan of Abu Dhabi, UAE. A two-wheeled five-storey vehicle, it is 20 m (66 ft) long, 12 m (39 ft) wide and weighs 109 tonnes (240,303 lb). There are eight bedrooms and bathrooms, four garages and water storage for 24,000 litres (5,279 gal).

LARGEST DRAGLINE EXCAVATOR

'Big Muskie', a walking earthmoving machine weighing 13,200 tonnes (29.1 million lb) was the largest ever dragline excavator and among the largest mobile machines ever made, weighing as much as nearly 10,000 saloon cars. It stood at Central Ohio Coal Co.'s Muskingham open-cast coal mine in Ohio, USA, but was dismantled in 1999.

LARGEST LAND TRANSPORT VEHICLE

The two 2,721-tonne (6-million-lb) crawler-transporters used to move Space Shuttles to their launch pad at Kennedy Space Center, Florida, USA, are the largest vehicles used to transport other objects. Each crawler is 40 m (131 ft) wide and 35 m (114 ft) long and runs on eight tank-style tracks. Each of the 57 links that make up these tracks weigh around 900 kg (2,000 lb).

LONGEST VEHICLE

The longest land vehicles ever made are the overland supply trains built by R G Le Tourneau Inc. of Longview, Texas, USA, for the US Army. One example, the *Arctic Snow Train*, later owned by the famous wire-walker Steve McPeak (USA), had 54 wheels and was 174.3 m (572 ft) long. Its gross train weight was 400 tonnes (880,000 lb), with a top speed of 32 km/h (20 mph).

LARGEST TYRE

Standing 4 m (13 ft 1 in) tall and weighing over 4 tonnes (8,800 lb), the world's largest tyres are built by Michelin to fit on to specialized dump trucks, including Caterpillar's largest model, the 797.

HEAVIEST LOAD TRANSPORTED BY ROAD

Between 14 and 15 July 1984, John Brown Engineers & Contractors BV moved the Conoco Kotter Field oil production deck, which has a roll-out weight of 3,805 tonnes, (8,38 million lb) for the Continental Netherlands Oil Co. of Leidsenhage, The Netherlands.

LARGEST FRONT-END LOADER

The largest wheel-driven front-end loader is the LeTourneau L-2350 (below), which weighs 262,176 kg (578,000 lb) and can lift up to 72,574 kg (160,000 lb) in its 40.52-m³ (1,431-ft³) capacity bucket. This massive earthmover is powered by a giant diesel engine that develops 1,715 kW (2,300 hp).

SCIENCE
& TECHNOLOGY

SCIENCE ADVANCES

SMALLEST LASER SCULPTURE

On 15 August 2001 researchers at Osaka University, Japan, made a three-dimensional bull (below) measuring seven thousandths of a millimetre high and ten thousandths of a millimetre long – the same size as a single red blood cell. The bull was sculpted from resin with two focused laser beams using a technique called two-photon micropolymerization. The bull is so small that 30 of them could be placed side by side across the full stop at the end of this sentence.

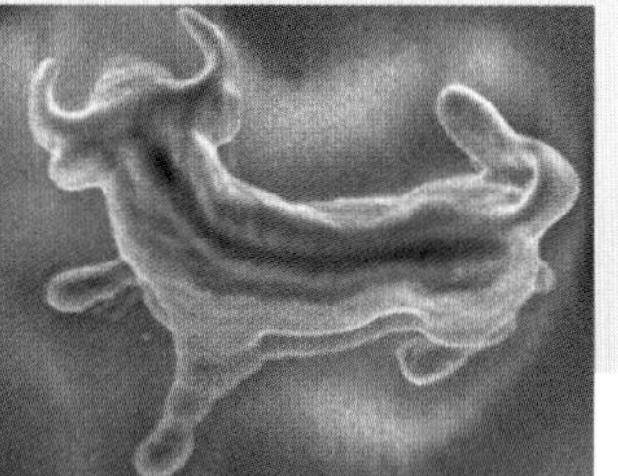

DARKEST MANMADE SUBSTANCE

The darkest manmade substance is a black coating composed of a nickel-phosphorus alloy. It reflects just 0.16% of visible light, around 25 times less than conventional black paint. The principle was first developed by researchers in the USA and India in 1980. In 1990 Anritsu (Japan) further refined this method to produce the darkest version so far.

SMALLEST PIECE OF ICE

The smallest piece of ice was created by Roger Miller and Klaus Nauta of the University of North Carolina, USA, in 1999. Consisting of just six water molecules arranged in a hexagon, the ice crystal is the smallest theoretically possible, as a minimum of six molecules are required for the formation of ice. In comparison, the average water droplet contains around 100,000,000,000,000,000,000 molecules of water.

LARGEST VACUUM CHAMBER

The Space Power Facility at NASA's Glenn Research Center, Plum Brook Station, Sandusky, Ohio, USA, measures 30.4 m (100 ft) in diameter and 37 m (122 ft) in height. It can sustain a high vacuum of 10^{-6} torr and simulate solar radiation using a 4 megawatt quartz heat-lamp array, as well as temperatures as low as -195.5°C (-320°F). It is used to test the performance of spacecraft and space hardware prior to launch.

SMALLEST THERMOMETER

On 7 February 2002, Yihua Gao and Yoshio Bando (both Japan) of the National Institute for Materials Science announced that they had created a thermometer from a single carbon nanotube. Measuring just 75 nanometres wide (one nanometre equals one billionth of a metre) and with a length of around 10,000 nanometers, the tube contains liquid gallium with linear expansion properties that allow the measurement of a wide range of temperatures, from 50–500°C (122–932°F).

SHORTEST FLASH OF LIGHT

On 16 August 2002, a team of European physicists, led by Ferenc Krausz at the Vienna Institute of Technology, Austria, announced that they had created bursts of X-ray light lasting just 500 billion billionths of a second (or 500 attoseconds). The technique will allow detailed studies of how electrons behave within atoms.

HEAVIEST ELEMENT

The undisputed heaviest chemical element discovered to date is 110. Its 'discovery' was reported on 19 November 1994 by researchers at the Heavy Ion Research Centre at Darmstadt, Germany. They used an ion accelerator to bombard lead atoms with nickel nuclei to create the new element, which existed for less than one thousandth of a second before decaying into lighter elements. The name darmstadtium (with the symbol Ds) has been proposed, following the tradition of naming elements after their place of discovery.

LONGEST RUNNING AGRICULTURAL EXPERIMENT

The Broadbalk Experiment, Rothamsted, Hertfordshire, UK, which aims to measure the effects of fertilizer on crops, has continuous data from 1843 to the present day.

MOST POWERFUL PULSED NEUTRON SOURCE

ISIS, at the Rutherford Appleton Laboratory, Chilton, Oxfordshire, UK, is the world's most powerful pulsed neutron source. Covering the size of a football field, it produces 4×10^{16} fast neutrons per second. These are focused into beams in a 'neutron microscope', allowing scientists to study, at a microscopic scale, the atomic and molecular arrangements that give materials their unique properties.

DEEPEST OPERATING NEUTRINO OBSERVATORY

The Sudbury Neutrino Observatory (above) is located 2,072 m (6,800 ft) below ground in the Inco Creighton Mine, Ontario, Canada. It consists of a 12-m-diameter (39-ft) vessel containing around 900 tonnes (1.9 million lb) of heavy water. It is designed to detect neutrinos, the neutral particles produced by nuclear fusion in the Sun. The depth of the observatory facilitates detection.

LOWEST MANMADE TEMPERATURE

The lowest manmade temperature achieved to date is 0.000000003 Kelvin, or 3 nanoKelvin above absolute zero, the coldest temperature theoretically possible. It was reached using rarified gas composed of atoms of 85 rubidium which, at these low temperatures, form a Bose-Einstein condensate – where the atoms behave as one 'superatom'. It was achieved by a team of scientists led by Elizabeth Donley from the University of Colorado, Boulder, Colorado, USA, and the National Institute of Science & Technology, Boulder, Colorado, USA.

LARGEST GRAVITATIONAL WAVE DETECTOR

The largest gravitational detector is the Laser Interferometry Gravitational Wave Observatory (LIGO) in the USA, which is 4 km (2.4 miles) long. LIGO consists of two almost identical L-shaped structures based in Louisiana and Washington (USA), almost 3,200 km (2,000 miles) apart. The 4-km-long (2.4-mile) arms of the facility provide LIGO with the extreme sensitivity required for the detection of gravitational waves.

SLOWEST LIGHT

In January 2001 two groups of US scientists announced that they had slowed down light itself to a dead stop. Light usually travels at 300,000 km/sec (186,000 miles /sec).

HIGHEST-INTENSITY FOCUSED LASER

The Vulcan laser at the Rutherford Appleton Laboratory, Chilton, Oxfordshire, UK, is the highest-intensity focused laser in the world. Following its 2002 upgrade, it is now capable of producing a laser beam with an irradiance (focused intensity) of 10^{21} watts per cm^2.

LONGEST LASER RANGING EXPERIMENT

The McDonald Laser Ranging Station near Fort Davis, Texas, USA, uses a laser to measure the distance between the Earth and the Moon to an accuracy of 1 cm (0.39 in). It bounces a laser off the reflective targets left on the lunar surface by five US and Soviet missions. The distance between the centres of the Earth and the Moon is 385,000 km (239,000 miles), and the laser ranging has shown that the Moon is receding from us at a rate of 3.8 cm (1.5 in) per year. This is one of the most accurate distance measurements ever made.

MOST ACCURATE VALUE OF PI

As continuation of a long-running project, mathematician Yasumasa Kanada (Japan) of the University of Tokyo has calculated the number pi to 1,241,100,000,000 decimal places. This calculation has been achieved using a HITACHI SR8000/MPP computer.

LEAST DENSE SOLID

The least dense solid in the world is an aerogel with a density of just 1.9 mg/cm^3 (0.47 grains/inch^3). It is made by Lawrence Livermore National Laboratory (USA).

LARGEST LENS

The largest refracting optical lens in the world measures 1.827 m (5 ft 11.93 in) in diameter. It was constructed by a team led by Thomas Peck (USA) at the Optics Shop of the Optical Sciences Center of the University of Arizona in Tucson, Arizona, USA, and completed in January 2000. It was built as a test for the secondary mirror of the 6.5-m-diameter (21-ft 3.9-in) MMT Telescope on Mt Hopkins, Arizona, USA.

MOST POWERFUL X-RAY GENERATOR

The Z Machine at the Sandia National Laboratories, USA (below), can, very briefly, give out X-rays with a power output roughly the same as 80 times that of all the world's electrical generators. The Z machine is used by scientists to study extreme conditions in physics, such as the nature of black holes.

AMAZING SCIENCE

WEAKEST FORCE

Of the four fundamental forces in the universe – the strong nuclear, the weak nuclear, electromagnetic, and gravitational forces – the weakest is gravity, with a strength of 10^{-40} compared to electromagnetism which is given the value of 1. Every single atom in the universe is 'gravitationally aware' of every other atom. The gravity of this bright cluster of galaxies (above), for example, is acting like a huge lens in space, bending the light from more distant galaxies into distorted arcs.

LARGEST BACTERIUM

According to a study published in the journal *Science* in April 1999, the bacterium *Thiomargarita namibiensis* ('Sulphur Pearl of Namibia') is the largest prokaryotic organism yet known, and is visible to the naked eye at around the size of the full stop at the end of this sentence. A typical bacterial cell is about 750 times smaller than this. Biologist Heide Schulz (Germany) from the Max Planck Institute for Marine Microbiology in Bremen, Germany, found these up-to-0.75-mm-wide (0.029-in) microorganisms in sediments off the Namibian coast during a cruise in 1997 with the Russian research vessel *Petr Kottsov*.

SIMPLEST GENOME

Mycoplasma genitalium has the smallest number of genes of any organism on Earth. Its genome was sequenced in 1995 and found to have just 480 genes compared with around 40,000 for humans. This organism lives in the genital tracts of humans.

HEAVIEST AND LIGHTEST QUARK

Of the six 'flavours' of quarks – known as 'up', 'down', 'top', 'bottom', 'strange' and 'charmed' – the 'top' is the heaviest at 170 giga-electron-volts (GeV). The lightest are the 'up' and 'down' quarks, both at 0.15 GeV.

SMALLEST ENTITY

The smallest of the known free-living organisms are the pleuro-pneumonia-like organisms (PPLO) of the genus *Mycoplasma*. One of these, *Mycoplasma laidlawii*, first discovered in sewage in 1936, has a diameter during its early existence of only 10^{-7} m. Examples of the strain known as H.39 have a maximum diameter of 3×10^{-7} m and weigh an estimated 10^{-16} g. Thus an average 190-tonne (420,000-lb) blue whale would weigh 1.9×10^{24} times as much.

MOST POWERFUL REACTION

When normal matter reacts with antimatter, the result is the complete annihilation of both. All mass is converted to energy as in Einstein's famous equation $E=MC^2$. Weight for weight, matter/antimatter reactions are 300 times more powerful than fusion reactions, and a thousand times more powerful than fission (as used in nuclear plants). They are also 10 billion times more powerful than conventional chemical reactions such as burning hydrogen and oxygen.

RAREST ELEMENT ON EARTH

The element astatine (At) is the rarest element in the Earth's crust, with around 25 g (0.9 oz) in total occurring naturally.

HIGHEST MICROBE

In April 1967 NASA reported that bacteria had been discovered at an altitude of 41 km (25 miles).

MOST STABLE HADRON

Hadrons are sub-atomic particles made up of quarks. The most stable hadron is the proton, with a lifetime of at least 10^{25} years. This carbon nucleus (right) show protons made up of one 'down' and two 'up' quarks, and neutrons made up of two 'downs' and one 'up'. Quarks exist in three 'colours' – red, green and blue – and one of each colour is required to make a hadron.

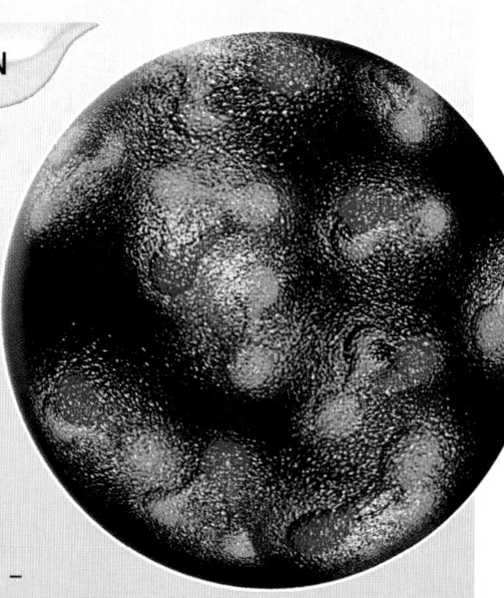

LOWEST TEMPERATURE POSSIBLE

Temperature is a direct result of the vibrations of the atoms or molecules that make up matter. The coldest that any substance can theoretically be is when there is no vibration in its atoms or molecules. This is referred to as absolute zero, and is at 0 K (zero Kelvin) or -273.15°C (-459.67°F. Absolute zero has never been achieved in an Earth laboratory, and even in the coldest parts of deep space, the temperature is slightly above absolute zero.

OLDEST LIVING BACTERIA

Bacteria trapped in suspended animation inside salt crystals for 250 million years have been revived and cultured by US scientists. Designated Bacillus 2-9-3, this species is ten times older than the previous oldest revived bacteria.

DEADLIEST NATURAL TOXIN

The anaerobic bacterium of spoiled food which causes botulism (*Clostridium botulinum)* is so deadly (more so than strychnine, arsenic or even snake venom) that 30 g (1 oz) could theoretically kill 30 million tonnes of living matter, and 0.5 kg (1 lb) could kill the entire human population.

TOUGHEST MICROBE

The bacterium *Deinococcus radiodurans* (formerly *Micrococcus radiodurans*) can withstand atomic radiation of 6.5 million roentgens, or 10,000 times the level fatal to the average human. In March 1983, John Barras (USA) of the University of Oregon, USA, reported bacteria from sulphurous seabed vents thriving at 306°C (583°F) in the East Pacific Rise at Lat 21°N.

LARGEST MICROBE

The largest known protozoans in terms of volume are the extinct *Calcareous foraminifera* (Foraminiferida) of the genus *Nummulites*. Individuals measuring up to 150 mm (6 in) wide were found in the Middle Eocene rocks of Turkey.

The largest existing protozoan is a species of the fan-shaped *Stannophyllum* (Xenophyophora). This is also the longest known microbe, with one example found measuring 25 cm (9.8 in).

FASTEST SPEED POSSIBLE

The fastest speed possible in the universe is the speed of light. This is achieved only by light and other forms of electromagnetic radiation, ie radio waves, infrared radiation, X-rays, etc. The speed of light varies depending on what it is travelling through. It is fastest when travelling through a vacuum, where its velocity is 299,792,458 m/s (around 300,000 km/s or 186,000 mps). This means that when you look at the Moon, you see it as it was about 1.3 seconds ago, and the Sun around 8.3 minutes ago.

LARGEST VIRUS

The world's largest virus is 'Mimivirus', which contains 900 genes. It was discovered in 1992 in a sample from a water cooling tower in Bradford, UK. It was examined by researchers at the National Centre for Scientific Research in Paris, France, who released their results on 27 March 2003 in the journal *Science*.

LONGEST TIME SURVIVED IN SPACE BY BACTERIA

From 7 April 1984 to 11 January 1990 *E. coli* bacteria cells survived unshielded onboard NASA's Long Duration Exposure Facility satellite, in low Earth Orbit.

Hardware samples removed from the US unmanned lunar probe *Surveyor 3* were returned to Earth by the crew of *Apollo 12* in November 1969. Upon analysis it was discovered that bacterial organisms (*Streptococcus mitis*) – that had contaminated *Surveyor 3* before its launch on 17 April 1967 – had survived more than two-and-a-half years in space.

LIGHTEST KNOWN PARTICLE

The lightest known particles in the universe are neutrinos which have a maximum mass of 0.00000000000000000000000000000000000018 kg. Neutrinos come in three varieties – electron, muon and tau neutrinos. The mass is an average of the three types. Neutrinos are created by radioactive decay and nuclear fusion (the same process that powers the Sun).

SMALLEST UNIT OF LENGTH

The smallest possible size for anything in the universe is the Planck length -1.6 x 10^{-35} m across (equivalent to around a millionth of a billionth of a billionth of a billionth of a cm across). This is the scale at which the quantum foam (representation below) is believed to exist. The laws of quantum physics cause minute wormholes to open and close constantly, giving space a rapidly changing, foam-like structure. If it were possible to exploit the tremendous energy of the quantum foam, then the power contained within one cubic centimetre of empty space would be enough to boil the Earth's oceans.

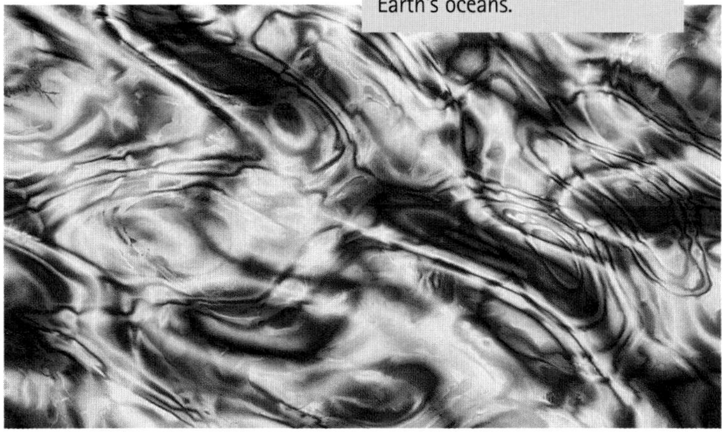

MEDICAL MILESTONES

MOST EYE OPERATIONS PERFORMED

Dr Murugappa Chennaveerappa Modi (India), a pioneer of mass eye surgery, performed a total of 610,564 cataract, squint correction and cornea transplant operations between 1943 and 1993 – an average of 12,211 a year.

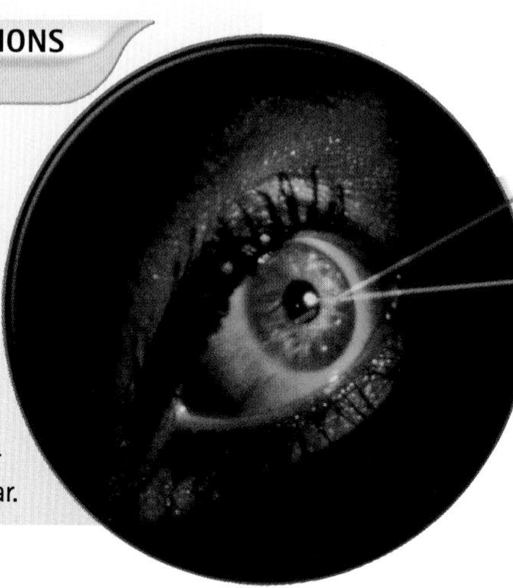

FIRST SUCCESSFUL KIDNEY TRANSPLANT

The first successful human kidney transplant was performed by RH Lawler (USA) at Little Company of Mary Hospital, Chicago, Illinois, USA, on 17 June 1950.

FIRST HEART TRANSPLANT PATIENT

The first heart transplant operation was performed on 55-year-old Louis Washkansky (South Africa) at the Groote Schuur Hospital, Cape Town, South Africa. The operation lasted from 1 am to 6 am on 3 December 1967 and was performed by a team led by Prof Christiaan Barnard (South Africa). Washkansky survived for 18 days.

FIRST HEART-LUNG-LIVER TRANSPLANT PATIENT

The first triple-transplant patient was Davina Thompson (UK). On 17 December 1986 at Papworth Hospital, Cambridge, UK, she underwent seven hours of surgery performed by a team of 15, headed by chest surgeon Mr John Wallwork and Prof Sir Roy Calne (both UK).

LONGEST SURVIVING KIDNEY TRANSPLANT PATIENT

The longest surviving kidney transplant patient is Johanna Leanora Rempel (Canada), who was given a kidney from her identical twin sister Lana Blatz on 28 December 1960. The operation was performed at the Peter Bent Brigham Hospital, Boston, Massachusetts, USA. Both Johanna and her sister have continued to enjoy excellent health and both have had healthy children.

LONGEST SURVIVING HEART TRANSPLANT PATIENT

Dirk van Zyl (South Africa) survived 23 years 57 days having received an unnamed person's heart at the Groote Schuur Hospital, University of Cape Town, South Africa, on 10 May 1971.

FIRST RECIPIENT OF AN ARTIFICIAL HEART

On 2 December 1982 at the Utah Medical Center, Salt Lake City, Utah, USA, Dr Barney B Clark (USA) was the first recipient of an artificial heart. The surgeon was Dr William C DeVries and the heart was a Jarvik 7 designed by Dr Robert K Jarvik. Dr Clark died on 23 March 1983, 112 days later.

YOUNGEST PERSON WITH A PACEMAKER

Stephanie Gardiner (UK) was four hours old when she was fitted with a tiny pacemaker the size of a postage stamp on 11 March 1995 at Bristol Children's Hospital, Bristol, UK.

LONGEST ARTIFICIAL HEART TRANSPLANT SURVIVAL

The longest surviving recipient of an artificial heart was William J Schroeder (USA) who lived for 620 days after his operation at Louisville, Kentucky, USA, from 25 November 1984 to 7 August 1986.

LONGEST-WORKING PACEMAKER

The longest-working pacemaker was a lithium-battery-powered Biotec 777 fitted into János Szilágyi (Hungary) on 18 January 1979. It was last confirmed to be operating as normal on 2 September 2002.

MOST ORGANS TRANSPLANTED IN A SINGLE OPERATION

Dr Andreas Tzakis (USA) transplanted seven organs – a liver, pancreas, stomach, large and small intestines and two kidneys – into a 10-month-old Italian girl during 16 hours of surgery at Jackson Children's Hospital in Miami, Florida, USA, on 23 March 1997. The girl suffered from megacystis microcolon syndrome, a rare congenital defect that interferes with the body's ability to absorb nutrients.

YOUNGEST MULTI-ORGAN TRANSPLANT PATIENT

Sarah Marshall (Canada) became the youngest person to receive a multi-organ transplant when, on 7 August 1997, aged 174 days, she was given a liver, a bowel, a stomach and a pancreas at London's Children's Hospital of Western Ontario, Canada. Sarah was born with the rare condition known as megacystis microcolon intestinal hypoperistalis syndrome. She had an enlarged bladder, a small colon and an abnormal bowel.

LEAST INVASIVE COCHLEAR IMPLANT SURGICAL TECHNIQUE

A minimally invasive surgical technique to perform cochlear implants in children was pioneered by Prof Gerry O'Donoghue at the Queen's Medical Centre, Nottingham, UK. Instead of cutting a long incision in the scalp, a simple 3-cm-long (1.2-in) incision is made behind the ear and a well drilled in the skull into which the implant is then inserted. This new method to treat children with profound deafness results in less scarring, a reduced chance of infection and significantly less trauma to the child.

MOST DETAILED HUMAN DISSECTION

The 'Visible Woman' is a real cadaver that was sliced into 5,189 slices 330 microns thick by Dr Victor Spitzer and his team at the University of Colorado (USA). Each slice was photographed (below) and stored in a computer to form a minutely detailed 3-D virtual human body. The team have also created a 'Visible Man'.

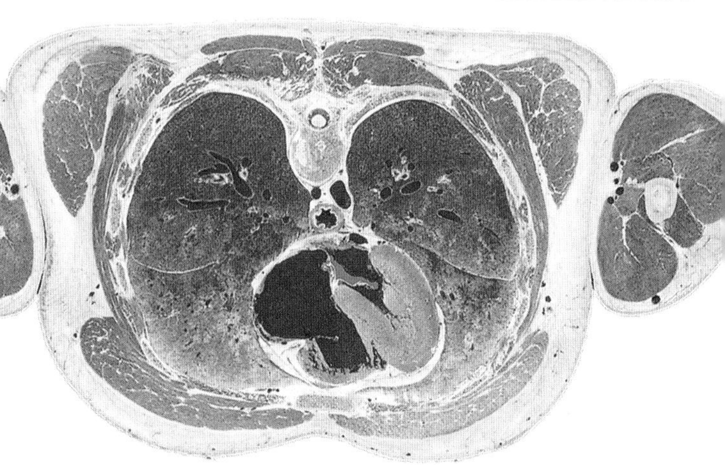

YOUNGEST PERSON FITTED WITH A PAIR OF BIONIC ARMS

Kyle Barton (UK) was eight years old when he was fitted with his second bionic arm by Dr Dipak Datta, a consultant at the Northern General Hospital, Sheffield, UK, in February 2002. Kyle had to have both his legs and arms amputated after he contracted meningitis in 1998, and was fitted with his first bionic arm in 2001. The arms, equipped with electrodes, can sense impulses from the brain and have a grip action in each hand.

YOUNGEST PERSON TO HAVE A FULL LIMB TRANSPLANTED

Chong Lih Ying (Malaysia) was only four weeks old when doctors transplanted her twin sister's left arm to her body on 18 May 2000. Chong was born with a deformed left arm and no hand. The donor arm came from Lih Ying's twin sister, who was born with the severe brain abnormality meningoencephalocele and had no hope of survival.

FIRST BIONIC ARM

In 1993, Scottish hotel owner Campbell Aird, who had his right arm amputated in 1982 after doctors diagnosed muscle cancer, was fitted with the first working bionic arm, created by a team of five bioengineers at the Margaret Rose Hospital, Edinburgh, UK.

FIRST BRAIN CELL TRANSPLANT

The first ever brain cell transplant was performed by a team of doctors from the University of Pittsburgh Medical Center, Pennsylvania, USA, on 23 June 1998. The aim of the operation was to reverse the damage that had been caused by a stroke to 62-year-old Alma Cerasini, who had suffered paralysis of her right arm and leg as well as the loss of most of her speech. The team has subsequently performed a further 11 operations of this type.

MOST RECONSTRUCTIVE SURGERIES BY A TEAM OF TRAVELLING DOCTORS

A team of volunteer doctors visited 18 countries and treated 5,139 patients as part of Operation Smile's 'World Journey of Hope', which took place from 5 February to 14 April 1999. The doctors repaired cleft lips and cleft palates, as well as performing surgery on facial tumours, burns and facial injuries.

FIRST SUCCESSFUL SEPARATION OF CONJOINED TWINS

The earliest successful separation of Siamese twins was performed on xiphopagus (joined at the sternum) girls at Mount Sinai Hospital, Cleveland, Ohio, USA, by Dr Jac S Geller (USA) on 14 December 1952.

LONGEST-LIVING HUMAN CELLS

The cells of Henrietta Lacks (USA) are still alive and being grown in laboratories worldwide decades after her death in October 1951. In February of that year doctors had removed cells from a malignant tumour in the 31-year-old, and found them to to lack chromosome 11 – now known as the 'tumour suppressor'. As a result, 'HeLa' cells have become 'immortal' and are one of the most helpful tools in biomedical research.

FIRST TEST-TUBE BABY

Louise Brown (UK) was delivered by Caesarean section in Oldham General Hospital, Lancashire, UK, at 11.47 pm on 25 July 1978. She was externally conceived on 10 November 1977 and weighed 2.6 kg (5 lb 12 oz) at birth. Louise's birth was the result of the work of UK gynaecologist Patrick Steptoe and two Cambridge doctors, Robert Edwards and Barry Bavister. The trio pioneered a new technique by which an egg could be taken from a woman's ovary, fertilized in a laboratory (*in vitro* fertilization), and then returned to the womb to develop normally. The technique has since helped thousands of women throughout the world with fertility problems to have children.

EARLIEST KIDNEYS CREATED BY CLONING

In January 2001 scientists from Advanced Cell Technologies, Massachusetts, USA, announced that they had for the first time successfully grown kidneys using cloning technology. The technique took a DNA-containing nucleus from a single cow skin cell and fused it with a host egg. The egg multiplied into an embryo rich in stem cells. These cells were chemically manipulated to grow into kidney cells, using an artificial kidney-shaped scaffold. Several of these miniature kidneys were grown in this way and transplanted back into the cow, where they began to produce urine.

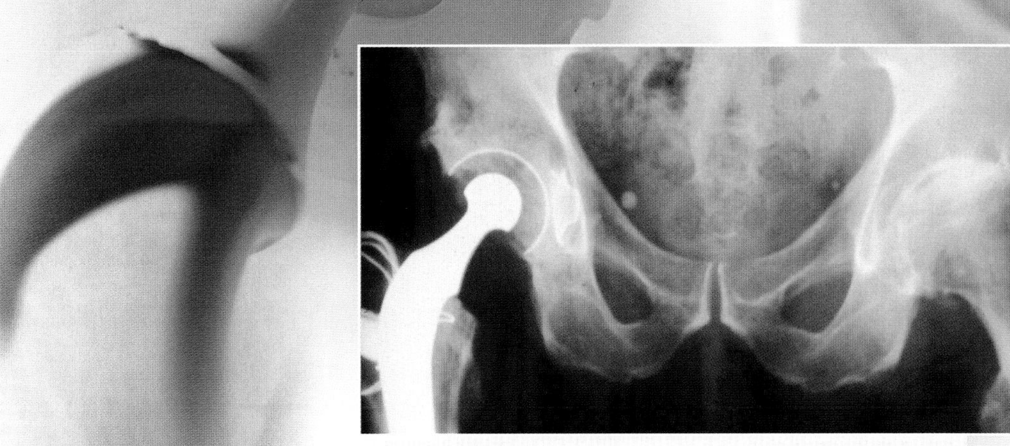

LONGEST LASTING HIP REPLACEMENT

In September 1970, when aged 32, Denise Poole (UK) received a complete hip replacement (shown in x-ray photo above). The hip is still in place today – almost 34 years later.

INTERNET

FIRST HYPERTEXT BROWSER

In October 1990 Tim Berners-Lee (UK, below) started work on a global hypertext browser. The result – the World Wide Web – was made available on the internet in the summer of 1991. Berners-Lee had originally proposed a global hypertext project to allow people to combine their knowledge in a web of hypertext documents in 1989.

LARGEST INTERNET CAFÉ

The easyEverything internet café (above), Times Square, New York, USA, opened on 28 November 2000. It has a record 648 computer terminals.

LARGEST FINE FOR AN INTERNET CRIME

US anti-abortion activists who operated a site called 'The Nuremberg Files', which contained 'wanted' posters listing the names and addresses of doctors who perform abortions, were ordered to pay more than $107.7 million (£65 million) in damages on 3 February 1999.

LARGEST INTERNET ADVERTISER BY SECTOR

According to Competitive Media Reporting/TNS Media Intelligence, in 2002 the largest internet advertisers by sector were the business and finance sectors which, between them, spent a massive $1,216,879,196 (£810,940,465) worldwide.

LARGEST INTERNET SEARCH ENGINE

Google, with over three billion pages, has the largest continually refreshed index of webpages of all the world's search engines. The company was founded by Larry Page and Sergey Brin (both USA). Their first office was a garage in Menlo Park, California (USA), which opened in September 1998 with a staff of four people.

MOST COMPREHENSIVE CYBERSPACE MAP

American researchers Bill Cheswick and Hal Burch, working out of the Bell Laboratories, Murray Hill, New Jersey, USA, created a map of cyberspace featuring 88,000 endpoints. Colours are used to represent different Internet Service Providers (ISPs). To create the map, Cheswick sent out electronic tracers from his New Jersey-based computer, which 'died' when they reached way points of terminal destinations. On the point of expiry, the messages sent back a death notice, enabling Burch's program to create the map.

MOST POPULAR COUNTRY-LEVEL DOMAIN

According to NetNames Ltd, as of March 2001, the most popular country level domain is .uk (Britain), with over two million domain registrations. Britain is closely followed by Germany (.de). Although America has the most internet sites, few of them use .us in their url.

LARGEST INTERNET JOKE VOTE

Laughlab, an internet experiment into humour, was conducted by psychologist Richard Wiseman (UK) from the University of Hertfordshire, UK, and the British Association for the Advancement of Science. Running from September 2001 to October 2002, around 40,000 jokes were submitted from people all over the world, and over two million votes cast for the funniest (which can be read at: www.laughlab.co.uk/winner).

EARLIEST COMPUTER VIRUS

The first computer programme that replicates itself surreptitiously was demonstrated by Fred Cohen, a student at the Massachusetts Institute of Technology, USA, on 11 November 1983.

LARGEST WIRELESS INTERNET PROVIDER

NTT DoCoMo (Japan) is the world's largest wireless internet provider, with 36,931,000 subscribers to their imode service as of February 2003.

INTERNET2 LAND SPEED RECORD

Internet2 is a consortium of 202 universities working to develop the next generation of the internet. In November 2002 an international team sent 6.7 gigabytes of data – equivalent to nearly two feature-length DVD movies – across 10,978 km (6,821 miles) of network, from Sunnyvale, California, USA, to Amsterdam, The Netherlands, in less than one minute. The team consisted of the Nationaal Instituut voor Kernfysica en Hoge-Energiefysica (NIKHEF), the Stanford Linear Accelerator Center (SLAC), the California Institute of Technology (Caltech) and the Faculty of Science of the Universiteit van Amsterdam (UvA). This ongoing competition is judged on a combination of bandwidth and distance, using standard internet protocols.

EARLIEST EMAIL

In 1971 Ray Tomlinson (USA), an engineer at computer company Bolt, Beranek and Newman, Cambridge, Massachusetts, USA, sent the first ever email in an experiment to see if he could get two computers to exchange a message. It was Ray who decided to use the @ symbol to separate the recipient's name from their location. The first ever email message was: 'QWERTYUIOP'.

OLDEST ELECTRONIC 'SPAM'

The world's first 'spam' (unsolicited mass email) was sent at 12:33 EDT on 3 May 1978 by Gary Thuerk (USA) who worked for Digital Equipment Corp. (USA). It was sent to 397 email accounts on the ARPAnet (Advanced Research Projects Agency Network) of the US Defense Deptartment, inviting them to a product demonstration of the DECSYSTEM-2020, 2020T, 2060 and 2060T computers. ARPAnet is regarded as the predecessor to the internet.

COUNTRY WITH THE MOST INTERNET USERS

In December 2002 the USA had over 160 million internet users out of a world total of around 665 million users.

HIGHEST CAPACITY INTERCONTINENTAL INTERNET ROUTE

In 2001, the internet routes between Europe and USA/Canada had a bandwidth capacity of 162,250.1 Mbps (megabits per second). In second place was the combined routes connecting USA/Canada and Asia and Pacific, with a bandwidth capacity of 41,820.1 Mbps. The lowest capacity was between Africa and Europe, with a bandwidth capacity of 444.8 Mbps.

MOST INTERNET USERS PER CAPITA

At year-end 2001, the Computer Industry Almanac released figures that showed Sweden with the highest proportion of internet users, with 554.18 people online for every 1,000 of the population. Iceland was in second place with 552.04 per 1,000. The USA came sixth with 522.1.

CONTINENT WITH THE MOST INTERNET USERS

According to analysts Nua, as of September 2002, of the 605.6 million people online worldwide, 190.91 million were online in Europe. Asia/Pacific was second with 187.24 million users.

LARGEST FREE WEB-BASED EMAIL PROVIDER

Microsoft's Hotmail is the world's largest free web-based email service provider, with more than 110 million subscribers as of September 2002.

HIGHEST INTERNET BANDWIDTH CONNECTION FROM A COMMERCIAL PLANE

On 15 January 2003 the first ever commercial airline flight with a broadband internet connection left Frankfurt, Germany, and flew to Washington DC, USA. The data transfer rates on this flight, operated by Lufthansa (Germany), was 3 Mbps (download) and 128 Kbits per second (upload). Lufthansa is the first airline to offer this service.

LONGEST BROADBAND WIRELESS CONNECTION

The longest wireless broadband connection to date, using Wi-Fi (wireless fidelity) technology, was 310 km (192.6 miles) and was achieved on 25 November 2002 by the Swedish Space Corporation. The link was between a stratospheric balloon, launched from Esrange, Sweden, and a base station near Esrange. The balloon's antenna was provided by Alvarion (Israel). A data rate of at least 1 Mbps was sustained throughout the link.

LARGEST ONLINE DATING SERVICE

Match.com has logged more than 17 million registrations since its launch in April 1995. As of August 2002, there were more than 3.5 million members worldwide with profiles posted on the site. Founded in the USA, Match.com is a subscription-based site that registers more than 800,000 new members each month.

MOST GLOBALLY CONNECTED CITY ON THE INTERNET

New York City, USA, has direct internet connections to 71 other countries and can handle almost 150 Gbps of internet traffic at any time. London, UK, comes second with direct connections to 61 other countries.

OLDEST INTERNET BENCH

On 6 August 2001 the world's first park bench with free access to the internet (right) was opened in Bury St Edmunds, Suffolk, UK. The standard park bench was converted by msn.co.uk to allow four people to connect their laptops simultaneously, in an attempt to change how people use the internet.

COMMUNICATIONS

BUSIEST INTERNATIONAL TELEPHONE ROUTE

The busiest international telephone route is between the USA and Canada. In 2001 there were some 10.4 billion minutes of two-way traffic between the two countries.

FIRST POLE-TO-POLE TELEPHONE CALL

On 28 April 1999 at 10:30 am (GMT) the first ever phone call took place between people at the North and the South Poles. The call was made by Mike Comberiate and Andre Fortin (both NASA, USA) and lasted 45 minutes.

COUNTRY WITH THE MOST TELEPHONES

The country with the greatest number of telephones is the USA, with 165 million. The USA also makes the greatest number of calls of any country, with 550 billion a year.

MOST TELEPHONES PER HEAD OF POPULATION

Monaco has the most telephones per head of population with 1,994 per 1,000.

LARGEST TELEPHONE VOTE

The record for the largest TV telephone vote belongs to Thames Television and 19 Television's (both UK) *Pop Idol*, which was broadcast on ITV on 9 February 2002. The communications firm Telescope (UK) registered 9,006,025 votes, as viewers decided who of the two finalist singers should win.

LONGEST TELEPHONE CABLE

The world's longest submarine telephone cable is Fibre-optic Link Around the Globe (FLAG), which runs for 27,000 km (16,800 miles) from Japan to the UK. It links three continents (Europe, Africa and Asia) and 11 countries, and can support 600,000 simultaneous phone calls.

LARGEST SWITCHBOARD

The switchboard at the Pentagon, Arlington, Virginia, USA, has 34,500 lines handling nearly one million calls per day through 161,000 km (100,000 miles) of telephone cable. Its busiest ever day was 6 June 1994 – the 50th anniversary of D-Day – when there were 1,502,415 calls.

SMALLEST TELEPHONE

The smallest operational telephone was created by Jan Piotr Krutewicz (USA) on 16 September 1996. It measured just 47.5 x 10 x 21 mm (1.8 x 0.3 x 0.8 in).

LOUDEST SIGNALLING DEVICE

The Chrysler air raid sirens (being demonstrated right) are the loudest sirens ever made and are capable of producing 138 dB at a distance of 30 (100 ft). They are so loud that a norm person would be deafened within 60 (200 ft) of one during operation.

LARGEST CARRIER OF INTERNATIONAL TELEPHONE CALLS

In 2001 the largest carrier of international telephone calls, in terms of outgoing traffic, was AT&T Corp. (USA), with 12 billion minutes of communications.

COUNTRY WITH THE MOST MOBILE PHONES

The country with the greatest number of cellular telephone subscribers is China, with 170 million in mid 2001.

MOST MOBILE PHONE SUBSCRIBERS

Vodafone Group Plc has the world's largest mobile phone subscriber base, with more than 100 million subscribers worldwide as of February 2002.

MOST DISTANT RADIO SIGNAL FROM ANOTHER WORLD

In August 1989 some of the 27 dishes of the Very Large Array (above), New Mexico, USA, joined the efforts of the Deep Space Network of radio antennae in order to boost the reception of NASA's *Voyager 2* spacecraft during its encounter with the planet Neptune, 4,496.7 million km (2,794.1 million miles) from the Sun.

LARGEST TELECOMS COMPANY MERGER

A merger between British cellular communications company Vodafone Group Plc, formerly known as Vodafone Airtouch Plc, and German telecoms company Mannesmann AG, valued at £103.4 billion ($171.1 billion), was completed on 12 April 2000.

LARGEST TELECOM COMPANY

In 2002 Nippon Telegraph and Telephone Corporation (NTT) based in Tokyo, Japan, had revenues of £60,870 million ($86,734 million), a recorded loss of £6,276 million ($4,404 million) and had a workforce of 213,000 employees.

LARGEST DIGITAL SATELLITE RADIO BROADCASTER

From its two geosynchronous satellites, WorldSpace (USA) broadcasts digital radio channels to Africa, Asia and Europe, covering a total surface area (footprint) of 80 million km^2 (30.8 million miles^2). Its first satellite, Afristar, began broadcasting in October 1999 and Asiastar was launched in March 2000. Its third satellite, Ameristar, is due for launch in the near future.

LARGEST CIVIL COMMUNICATIONS SATELLITE

The Astra 1-K was built by Alcatel Space (France). It had a mass of 5,250 kg (11,576 lb) and, fully deployed, would have been 37 m (121 ft 4 in) in length and 6.6 m (21 ft 7 in) in height. Upon its launch on 26 November 2002 its Russian Proton booster failed, leaving the satellite stranded in low Earth orbit. It was safely deorbited on 10 December 2002, over the Pacific Ocean.

MOST POWERFUL RADIO SIGNAL BEAMED INTO SPACE

On 16 November 1974 scientists at the Arecibo Radio Telescope, Puerto Rico, transmitted a binary radio signal to the M13 globular cluster in the constellation of Hercules. The message, which shows basic data on humanity, lasts for 169 seconds at 2,380 MHz. When the message arrives, in around 25,000 years, any advanced alien civilization will receive the signal at a strength 10 million times the intensity of the normal radio signals from our Sun. Of course, if anyone replies, it will take another 25,000 years for us to receive it.

MOST POWERFUL COMMUNICATIONS SATELLITE

The Hughes Space and Communications HS702 satellite is capable of emitting a 15-kW signal, making it the most powerful commercial communications satellite in the world. To achieve such a high output, the satellite draws upon twin high-efficiency solar cells.

LONGEST TRANSMISSION USING OPTICAL FIBRE

As reported in September 1994, the longest transmission distance at a data rate of 20 gigabits per second over a fibre path containing repeaters is 125,000 km (78,000 miles). This was achieved using a recirculating fibre loop at BT laboratories at Martlesham, Suffolk, UK.

NARROWEST OPTICAL FIBRE CHANNELS

Physicists at the University of Bath, UK, have produced a material called photonic crystal fibre that has a regular array of holes that run the fibre's entire length. These tubes are the basis for the world's narrowest optical fibre channels for communications. The fibres could stretch to 10 km (6.2 miles) with cores just 0.00000001 mm (1/400000000 in) thick. The core length-to-width ratio is equivalent of the Channel Tunnel extended all the way from the Earth to Jupiter.

FASTEST MULTIMODE OPTICAL FIBRE TRANSMISSION

A team of scientists at Essex University, UK, led by Stuart Walker (UK), transmitted 1.02 terabits per second of data down a single 3-km (1.86-mile) strand of multimode optical fibre in March 2002. This is equivalent to around 15.9 million simultaneous phone calls.

EARLIEST RADIO TRANSMISSION

The earliest description of a radio transmission system was written by Mahlon Loomis (USA) on 21 July 1864 and demonstrated between two kites that were 22 km (14 miles) apart at Bear's Den, Loudoun County, Virginia, USA, in October 1866. Loomis received US patent No. 129,971 on 20 July 1872.

FASTEST AROUND-THE-WORLD TEXT MESSAGE

On 20 February 2002 at the 3GSM World Congress in Cannes, France, Logica sent a text message around the world by forwarding it to mobile phones in six countries in six continents. The message finally came back to the original mobile phone in Cannes after 3 min 17.53 sec.

FASTEST MORSE CODE TRANSMITTER

The highest speed recorded for hand-key transmitting Morse Code (above) is 175 symbols a minute (equivalent to 35 wpm) by Harry A Turner (USA) of the US Army Signal Corps on 9 November 1942.

ROCKETS

LARGEST SOLID ROCKET BOOSTER

The two reusable boosters (above) that assist the launch of the US space shuttle use solid fuel. Each booster measures 45.4 m (149 ft) long and 3.6 m (12 ft) wide and contains over 450,000 kg (1,000,000 lb) of propellant.

HEAVIEST PAYLOAD LAUNCHED TO THE OUTER SOLAR SYSTEM

On 15 October 1997 a Titan IV rocket with a Centaur upper stage launched the 5,655-kg (12,467-lb) NASA/ESA *Cassini-Huygens* spacecraft (above). This robotic probe will explore Saturn and its moons in July 2004.

MOST SUCCESSFUL COMMERCIAL ROCKET LAUNCHER

From March 1995 to February 2003 Arianespace's (France) family of *Ariane 4* rockets (above) had 74 consecutive commercial rocket launches. Its final launch occurred on 15 February 2003.

SMALLEST ROCKET

Pegasus (left), a three-stage booster, is 15.5 m (50 ft 10 in) long. It was first air-launched from a B-52 aircraft in 1990. It is designed to place light payloads into low-level orbit.

MOST POWERFUL ROCKET

The NI booster (below) from the former USSR launched on 21 February 1969 with a thrust of 4,620 tonnes (10.1 million lb), but exploded 70 seconds after take-off.

LARGEST SPACECRAFT TO ORBIT AND LAND UNMANNED

Buran (right) was the Soviet answer to the US space shuttle. It was only launched into Earth orbit once on 15 November 1988 before its budget was cut. As there were no cosmonauts on board, this two-orbit flight and landing was computer-controlled. The *Buran* orbiter measured 36.37 m (119.3 ft) long and had a mass of 105,000 kg (231,000 lb).

ᴅST POWERFUL COMMERCIAL ᴅCKET LAUNCHER

ane 5-ESCA (above), is capable of cing a 10-tonne (22,000-lb) ᴅload into geosynchronous ᴅit 36,000 km (22,000 miles) ᴅve Earth.

SPACE EXPLORATION

FIRST MEN ON THE MOON

Neil Armstrong (USA, above), commander of the *Apollo 11* mission, became the first man to set foot on the Moon when he stepped on to the Sea of Tranquillity at 02:56:15 GMT on 21 July 1969 (or 22:56:15 EDT on 20 July 1969). He was followed out of the lunar module *Eagle* by Edwin 'Buzz' Aldrin (USA) while the command module *Columbia*, piloted by Michael Collins (USA), orbited above.

MOST DISTANT IMAGE OF EARTH

On 4 February 1990 NASA's *Voyager 1* spacecraft turned its camera back towards the Sun and the planets. After 12.5 years in space, travelling away from Earth, *Voyager 1*'s camera took a picture of our home planet from a distance of almost 6.5 billion km (4 billion miles).

LONGEST EXTRATERRESTRIAL BALLOON FLIGHT

The twin Soviet spacecraft *Vega 1* and *Vega 2* were launched on 15 and 20 December 1984. Both probes encountered Venus in June 1985, where they dropped packages into the Venusian atmosphere. Each package split into a lander and a balloon. The *Vega 2* balloon transmitted data on the Venusian atmosphere for 46.5 hours, before contact was lost. *The Vega 1* balloon transmitted data for 56 minutes. After dropping their packages at Venus, both *Vega* spacecraft continued on their course to successful fly-bys of Halley's Comet, in March 1986.

LONGEST ORBITAL SURVEY OF AN OUTER PLANET

NASA's Galileo spacecraft arrived at the planet Jupiter on 7 December 1995. This survey was the first time a probe has orbited an outer-Solar-System body. Galileo is destined to burn up in the atmosphere of Jupiter in September 2003.

GREATEST SPACECRAFT COLLISION

On 25 June 1997 an unmanned *Progress* supply vehicle weighing 7 tonnes (15,000 lb) collided with the Russian *Mir* Space Station. Cosmonauts Vasily Tsibliev and Alexander Lazutkin (both USSR) on board *Mir* had to work quickly to seal a breach in the hull of *Mir*'s *Spektr* module, while US astronaut Michael Foale prepared *Mir*'s *Soyuz* capsule for a possible evacuation. Although loss of life was avoided, the station was left dangerously low on power and oxygen and temporarily tumbled out of control.

MOST PLANETS VISITED BY ONE SPACECRAFT

NASA's *Voyager 2* spacecraft, launched in 1977, visited all four of the outer gas giants, Jupiter, Saturn, Uranus and Neptune, between 1979 and 1989.

SMALLEST MANNED SPACECRAFT

The Manned Manoeuvring Unit (MMU) used by astronauts working outside the space shuttle is 1.24 m (4 ft) tall, 0.83 m (2 ft 8 in) wide, 1.12 m (3 ft 8 in) deep and weighs just 109 kg (240 lb). Powered by nitrogren thrusters, it was first used on shuttle mission STS-41-B in February 1984 when astronaut Bruce McCandless (USA) manoeuvered up to 100 m (328 ft) away from *Challenger.*

MOST DISTANT SOLAR-POWERED SPACECRAFT

On 18 April 2002 NASA's *Stardust* spacecraft, en route to sample comet Wild 2 in January 2004, was a distance of 407 million km (253 million miles) from the Sun. Solar-powered spacecraft are usually used to explore the inner Solar System, as the more distant planets do not receive enough sunlight to efficiently power spacecraft at those distances from the Sun.

CLOSEST COMET FLY-BY BY A SPACECRAFT

On 13 March 1986 the European Space Agency's *Giotto* probe passed the icy nucleus of Halley's Comet at a distance of just 596 km (370 miles).

MOST REMOTE MANMADE OBJECT

Voyager 1, launched from Cape Canaveral, Florida, USA, on 5 September 1977, is now the furthest manmade object from the Earth. On 17 February 1998 it surpassed the slower *Pioneer 10,* which was launched on 2 March 1972. As of 25 February 2003, *Voyager 1*, was over 13.091 billion km (8.134 billion miles) from Earth.

MOST ACCURATE MEASURE OF THE AGE OF THE UNIVERSE

Just as a map of Earth can be show as an oval, these results from NASA Wilkinson Microwave Anisotropy Pro (WMAP, below) show the whole universe. The colours show temperat differences of just a few millionths a degree in the microwave 'heat ec of the 'Big Bang'. They provide a sna shot of the universe when it was ju 380,000 years old, and have allowe astronomers to calculate its current age to be 13.7 billion years, with a uncertainty of only 1%.

MOST SPACE FLIGHTS BY AN ASTRONAUT

On 8 April 2002 US astronaut Jerry Ross began his seventh space mission, setting the record for the most space flights. He was a crew member on the STS 110 mission of the space shuttle *Atlantis*, on a construction flight to the International Space Station. All Ross's flights have been on the space shuttle. His record has since been equalled by NASA astronaut Franklin Chang-Diaz (USA), who flew his seventh mission between 5 and 19 June 2002 on the space shuttle *Endeavour.*

LONGEST SURVIVING INTERPLANETARY SPACECRAFT

The unmanned space probe *Pioneer 6* was launched on 16 December 1965. After achieving its Solar orbit between Earth and Venus, it was able to successfully determine the structure and flow of the Solar wind – the million-mile-an-hour stream of charged particles from the Sun. Although no longer used to collect science data, *Pioneer 6* is still functioning more than 37 years on.

MOST PROBED PLANET

To date there have been 28 missions to Venus. The most recent spacecraft to encounter Venus was the *Cassini-Huygens* spacecraft, which flew by the planet twice (in 1998 and 1999) to pick up speed from gravitational slingshots. *Cassini-Huygens* is now en route to Saturn and will get there in July 2004.

MOST COMETS DISCOVERED BY A SPACECRAFT

The Solar and Heliospheric Observatory (SOHO) was launched on 2 December 1995. It orbits between the Sun and the Earth where it constantly monitors solar activity. As of 15 February 2003 SOHO had discovered 587 comets by chance, as they appeared close to the Sun and were imaged by the spacecraft.

LONGEST TIME SURVIVED ON VENUS

Of the nine successful and partially successful robotic probes that have landed on Venus, the one that lasted the longest was *Venera 11.* This Soviet spacecraft, launched on 9 September 1978, landed on 25 December 1978. Following touchdown, it transmitted data back to Earth for 95 minutes before being crushed or incinerated by the harsh Venusian atmosphere.

OLDEST OPERATING MANNED SPACECRAFT

Discovery, the third of NASA's fleet of space shuttle orbiters, was first launched into space on 30 August 1984. With the losses of *Challenger* in 1986 and *Columbia* during re-entry on 1 February 2003, *Discovery* is now the world's oldest operating manned spacecraft.

FIRST SPACEWALK

On 18 March 1965, Lieutenant-Colonel Alexei Arkhipovich Leonov (USSR) became the first person to engage in EVA or extra-vehicular activity, commonly known as a 'spacewalk'.

MOST SPACEWALKS

The greatest number of spacewalks is ten, totalling 31 hr 37 min by Russian cosmonaut Aleksandr Serebrov. The first five spacewalks took place in January/February 1990 during Soyuz TM-8 (launched 5 September 1989). The second five took place in September/October 1993 during Soyuz TM-17 (launched 1 July 1993).

MOST REUSED SPACECRAFT

NASA's space shuttle *Discovery* was first launched on 30 August 1984. It has since completed 30 space missions, more than any other spacecraft. Shown in the picture below is astronaut Steven L Smith (USA) standing on the shuttle's robot arm, preparing to replace a transmitter in the Hubble Space Telescope on *Discovery*'s 27th mission in December 1999.

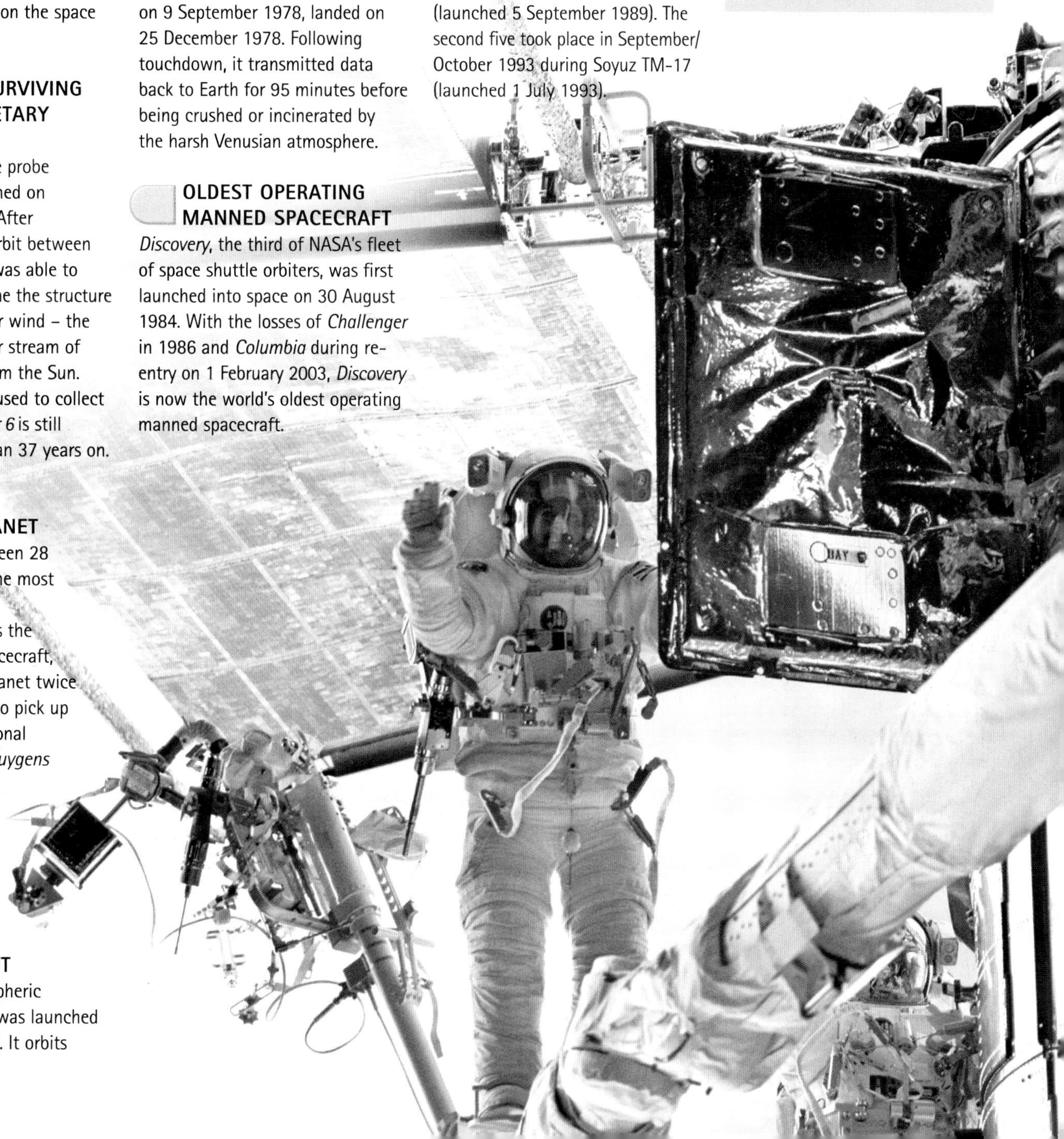

SMALLEST COLOUR TELEVISION SCREEN

Microemissive Displays Ltd, Edinburgh (UK) have developed a tiny colour TV/video screen that measures just 3.84 x 2.88 mm (0.15 x 0.11 in). The ME1602 (above), which can be linked to video cameras and DVD players, has a resolution of 160 x 120 pixels. It works using organic light-emitting diode technology.

SMALLEST TRANSISTOR

On 9 December 2002 IBM (USA) announced the development of a 6-nanometre-long transistor. This breakthrough could allow the creation of computer chips with 100 times more transistors than currently possible.

LARGEST LCD TELEVISION SCREEN

The largest liquid display crystal (LCD) television has been built by Samsung (South Korea). It has a diagonal viewing area of 137 cm (54 in) and was revealed as a prototype at the Consumer Electronics Show, Las Vegas, Nevada, USA, on 9 January 2003.

EARLIEST JPEG

Jpeg, standing for Joint Photographic Experts Group, is one of the best known digital image formats. Developed in order to standardize the techniques for digital image compression, the format is used particularly for the internet and by digital cameras. The earliest images to use Jpeg compression are four digital test images called 'Boats', 'Barbara', 'Toys' and 'Zelda' created by the Jpeg Group on 18 June 1987 in Copenhagen, Denmark.

HIGHEST RESOLUTION DIGITAL CAMERA

The highest resolution digital camera is MegaCam, which has a resolution of 320 million pixels. An astronomical camera, it has been used on the 3.6-m (11-ft 10-in) Canada-France-Hawaii Telescope, Hawaii, USA, since 28 June 2002.

HIGHEST-CAPACITY DVD DISC

Blu-ray, the new format for DVDs, uses a blue laser instead of the traditional red laser seen in current CD and DVD players. The blue laser allows up to 27 gigabytes of data to be stored on a single layer of a single-sided DVD. This new format was jointly established by nine of the largest electronics companies, and announced in February 2002. DVD players using the Blu-ray format are now under development.

SMALLEST BIOLOGICAL COMPUTING DEVICE

A team of scientists from the Weizmann Institute of Science (Israel) has adapted molecules of DNA to act as tiny molecular computing devices. Two DNA molecules and an enzyme molecule react together, acting as input, software, hardware and power supply. Experiments have shown that a microlitre of salt solution containing 3 trillion self-contained DNA computing devices can perform 66 billion operations per second, with the necessary power/fuel for the computations provided by the DNA itself as it is cleaved by the hardware enzyme. The results were announced on 24 February 2003 in the Proceedings of the National Academy of Sciences. The team consisted of Rivka Adar, Yaakov Benenson, Zvi Livneh, Tamar Paz-Elizur and Ehud Shapiro (all Israel).

SMALLEST PC

On 16 April 2002, OQO (USA) unveiled a fully functioning PC measuring just 10.4 x 7.3 x 2.2 cm (4.1 x 2.9 x 0.9 in) and weighing less than 225 g (9 oz). Described as an ultra personal computer, it runs with a 1 GHz processor, 10 or 20 GB hard drive and 256 MB of RAM and is capable of running the full version of Microsoft's Windows XP.

LARGEST PLASMA SCREEN

The largest plasma screen produced to date is the PPM63H1 produced by Samsung (South Korea), which measures 160 cm (63 in) diagonally. Plasma screen technology (above) uses charged gas between two layers of glass which operates under the same principles as fluorescent lights and neon tubes. The result is a perfectly flat, uniformly focussed, high-quality image on a slim screen.

MOST POWERFUL QUANTUM COMPUTER

Whereas normal computers use a string of zeros and ones (bytes) to represent data, experimental quantum computers use qubits, which can be a zero, one or both simultaneously. On 20 December 2001, IBM's Almaden Research Center in San Jose, California, USA, announced that they had used a 7-qubit quantum computer to calculate the factors of the number 15. They used a billion billion molecules that have seven nuclear spins for the calculation. Consisting of the nuclei of five atoms of fluorine and two of carbon, these molecules are able to interact with each other as qubits.

FASTEST DIGITAL SIGNAL PROCESSOR

The fastest digital signal processor (DSP) is the TMS320C6416, made by Texas Instruments (USA). On 12 March 2003 a clock speed of 1 GHz was demonstrated at the Texas Instruments Laboratories, Stafford, Texas, USA. DSPs are used for real-time processing of data where no time lag is acceptable. Applications include audio signal processing, video signal processing and telecommunications.

MOST SOPHISTICATED BATTLEFIELD SIMULATOR

The most sophisticated battlefield computer simulator is the Combined Arms Tactical Trainer. Situated at Warminster, UK, and Sennelager, Germany, it is capable of training more than 850 military personnel at once in an integrated, realistic combat scenario involving vehicles, aircraft, soldiers and commanders. Simulated combat arenas of more than 10,000 km² (3,800 miles²) are used. It was constructed for the UK's Ministry of Defence by Lockheed Martin, and became operational on 1 September 2002.

MOST EMOTIONALLY RESPONSIVE ROBOT

Kismet, created by Cynthia Breazeal at the Massachusetts Institute of Technology, USA, is a robotic head powered by 15 networked computers and 21 motors. It is designed to recognize and respond to different emotions while interacting with humans. Nine of the computers are used to control Kismet's vision alone.

LARGEST CONSUMER ELECTRONICS SHOW

The International Consumers Electronics Show (CES) 2003, which ran from 9 to 12 January 2003 in Las Vegas, Nevada, USA, was the largest ever consumer electronics show. A total of 116,687 people attended the event, which had 2,283 exhibitors and 11,600 m² (124,800 million ft²) of exhibition space.

LARGEST-DISTRIBUTED COMPUTING PROJECT

SETI@home, launched on 17 May 1999 by the University of California at Berkeley, California, USA, is a free downloadable software package that activates instead of a screen-saver when a computer is idle. It uses the computer's processor to analyse radio radiation data from the universe (downloaded when the user logs on to the internet) in the search for extraterrestrial intelligence. The astronomical data is collected from the Arecibo radio telescope, Puerto Rico. As of 18 March 2003 there were a total of 4,320,471 users around the world. Since its launch, SETI@home has amassed more than one million years of computing time.

» MOST GENDER-AWARE ROBOT

Artificial intelligence company Intelligent Earth, Kirkcaldy, UK, have developed visual gender recognition software for its robotic head Doki (below). Based on visual data alone, Doki can recognize the gender of women with an accuracy of 100%, and men with an accuracy of 96%. Doki is also able to scientifically rate the attractiveness of women, using visual data.

INVENTIONS

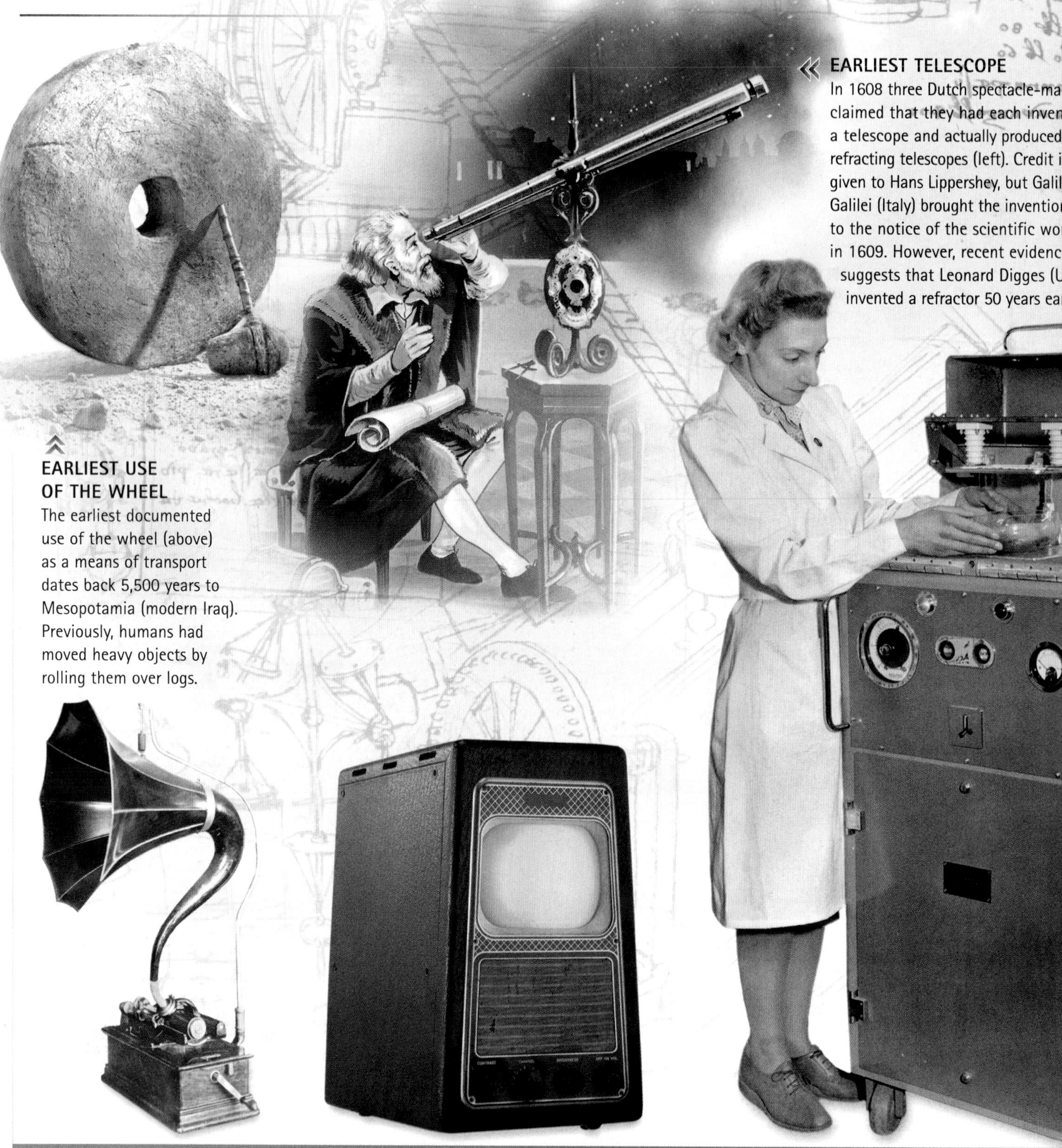

EARLIEST TELESCOPE

In 1608 three Dutch spectacle-ma
claimed that they had each inven
a telescope and actually produced
refracting telescopes (left). Credit i
given to Hans Lippershey, but Galil
Galilei (Italy) brought the inventio
to the notice of the scientific wor
in 1609. However, recent evidenc
suggests that Leonard Digges (U
invented a refractor 50 years ea

EARLIEST USE OF THE WHEEL

The earliest documented use of the wheel (above) as a means of transport dates back 5,500 years to Mesopotamia (modern Iraq). Previously, humans had moved heavy objects by rolling them over logs.

EARLIEST GRAMOPHONE

The gramophone or phonograph was first conceived by Charles Cros (France), who described his idea in papers deposited in the French Academy of Sciences on 30 April 1877. Thomas Edison (USA) achieved the first practical device. The picture above shows an Edison Standard Phonograph.

EARLIEST COLOUR TELEVISION TRANSMISSION

On 3 July 1928 John Logie Baird (UK) demonstrated colour television transmission for the first time at his studios in London, UK. The picture above shows an early portable television.

EARLIEST MICROWAVE

In 1946 Percy Spencer (USA), an enginee
at the Raytheon Company, Lexington,
Massachusetts, USA, demonstrated the fi
microwave, named a Radarange. Shown at
is an early microwave at the 1947 Ideal
Home Exhibition at Olympia, London UK.

MOST PATENTS

Thomas Edison (USA) holds the record for the most patents held by a single person with 1,093, either on his own or jointly. They include the microphone, the motion-picture projector and the incandescent electric lamp (left).

EARLIEST COMPACT DISC

The standard for the compact disc (DVD shown above) was first proposed by Philips (Netherlands) and Sony (Japan) in 1980, and agreed upon in 1981 by the Compact Disc Standard Digital Audio Disc Committee. The first CDs became available to the public in Europe and Japan in the autumn of 1982, and the USA in 1983 – where 800,000 discs were sold in the first year alone.

EARLIEST PORTABLE PHONE

The concept of a portable telephone (a radio-telephone from the early 1970s shown right) first appeared in 1947 at Lucent Technologies' Bell Labs, New Jersey, USA. The first actual portable telephone handset was invented by Martin Cooper (USA), of Motorola, who made the first call on 3 April 1973 to his rival, Joel Engel, head of research at Bell Labs.

EARLIEST 'CLAMSHELL' LAPTOP

Regarded as the first 'true' laptop, the GRiD Compass was designed in 1979 by William Moggridge (UK) for GRiD Systems Corporation (USA). It was introduced in 1982 with a RAM of 512K. The picture above shows a 2003 Apple Mac Titanium G4.

WEAPONS

EARLIEST USE OF A CROSSBOW

The earliest reliable record of the use of a crossbow is from 341 BC at the Battle of Ma-Ling, Linyi, China. Historians believe these weapons were single-shot and held with a pistol-style grip. The earliest (non-recorded) use of crossbows was probably by the Stone Age people in Africa and southeast Asia.

LARGEST-CALIBRE CANNON

The largest-calibre cannon ever constructed is the *Tsar Pushka* (Emperor of Cannons), used by the Turks against the walls of Constantinople (now Istanbul, Turkey) in 1453 and now housed in the Kremlin, Moscow, Russia. This 39.3-tonne (86,641-lb) cannon has a barrel 5.34 m (17 ft 6 in) long with a bore of 89 cm (35 in) and fires a 540-kg (1,200-lb) stone shot. The cannon was pulled by 60 oxen and 200 men.

LARGEST GUN

In the siege of Sevastopol, USSR (now Ukraine), in July 1942, the Germans used a gun of a calibre of 80 cm (31 in) with a barrel 28.87 m (94 ft 8.5 in) long. It was named *Schwerer Gustav*, and was built by Krupp (Germany). The whole assembly of the gun was 42.9 m (141 ft) long and weighed 1,344 tonnes (2,963,000 lb).

GREATEST RANGE OF A GUN

The famous long-range gun that shelled Paris, France, in World War I (1914–18), the *Paris-Geschütz*, or Paris Gun, had a calibre of 21 cm (8.25 in) and a range of 122 km (76 miles). The little-known V3 static underground firing tubes built in 50 shafts during World War II (1939–45) near Mimoyecques, not far from Calais, France, to bombard London, UK, never actually became operative; but they would have fired projectiles a distance of some 150 km (95 miles).

HIGHEST RATE OF FIRE OF A MACHINE GUN IN SERVICE

Designed for use in helicopters and armoured vehicles in the late 1960s, the 7.62-mm-calibre (0.3-in) M134 Minigun is based on the multiple-barrelled Gatling design. It has six barrels revolved by an electric motor and fed by a 4,000-round link belt. This allows for a firing rate of 6,000 rounds per minute, or 100 per second – about ten times that of an ordinary machine gun.

HIGHEST RATE OF FIRE FOR A BALLISTIC WEAPON

The fastest firing ballistic weapon is a prototype 36-barrel gun built by Metal Storm of Brisbane, Australia, which has a firing rate in excess of one million rounds per minute. This is possible because the gun has no moving parts. Instead, numerous bullets are stacked in the barrels of the gun, separated by packages of primer and propellant (gunpowder) connected to a computer-controlled firing system. Although the weapon's rate of fire is in excess of one million rounds per minute, the magazine has a capacity of just 540 rounds. This means that when fired at its maximum rate the weapon will be out of ammunition in a fraction of a second.

EARLIEST TANK

The first tank was No. 1 Lincoln, modified to become *Little Willie*, built by William Foster Co. Ltd of Lincoln, Lincolnshire, UK. It first ran on 6 September 1915. Tanks first saw action with the Heavy Section, Machine Gun Corps (later the Tank Corps), at the Battle of Flers-Courcelette, France, on 15 September 1916. The Mark I 'Male' tank, armed with a pair of 6-pounder guns and four machine guns, weighed 28.4 tonnes (62,611 lb) and was powered by a 105-hp (78.2-kW) motor, giving a maximum speed of 4.8–6.4 km/h (3–4 mph).

MOST HEAVILY ARMED TANK

The most heavily armed tanks in recent times have been the Russian T-64, T-72, T-80 (above) and T-90 tanks, all of which have a 12.5-cm (4.92-in) gun-missile system. The American Sheridan light tank mounts a 15.2-cm (6-in) weapon which is both a gun and a missile launcher combined, but this is not a long-barrelled, high-velocity gun of the conventional type. The British AVRE (Armoured Vehicle Royal Engineers) Centurion tank had a 16.5-cm (6.5-in) low-velocity demolition gun.

LIGHTEST TANK

The entire hull of the Advanced Composite Armoured Vehicle Platform (ACAVP) tank is manufactured from E-glass epoxy, a plastic/fibreglass composite material strong enough to protect its crew from rifle fire and shrapnel while making it 10% lighter than an equivalent metal-hulled tank. To provide protection from heavier fire, additional metal armour can be mounted. The ACAVP was developed by the British Defence Evaluation and Research Agency (DERA) and first demonstrated in March 2000.

FIRST ATOMIC BOMB USED IN BATTLE

The first atom bomb was dropped on Hiroshima, Japan, by the United States at 8:16 am on 6 August 1945. It had an explosive power equivalent to that of 15 kilotons of trinitrotoluene (TNT). Code-named *Little Boy*, the bomb was 3.04 m (10 ft) long and weighed 4,080 kg (9,000 lb).

HEAVIEST CONVENTIONAL BOMB

The heaviest conventional bomb ever used operationally was the British Royal Air Force's Grand Slam, which weighed 9,980 kg (22,000 lb) and measured 7.74 m (25 ft 4 in) long. It was first dropped on Bielefeld railway viaduct, Germany, on 14 March 1945. The US Air Force tested an even larger bomb, weighing 19,050 kg (42,000 lb), in 1949.

LARGEST NON-NUCLEAR CONVENTIONAL BOMB IN EXISTENCE

The world's largest non-nuclear conventional bomb is the Massive Ordnance Air Blast (MOAB), a precision-guided weapon weighing 9,752 kg (21,500 lb). It was first tested by the US Air Force at the Eglin Air Force Armament Center, Florida, USA, on 11 March 2003. Rather than exploding on impact with the ground, the bomb deploys a parachute and detonates just above the ground, directing its blast more effectively into the enemy target.

EARLIEST SUCCESSFUL TEST OF A HIGH-POWERED MICROWAVE WEAPON

High-powered microwave (HPM) weapons are designed to disable electrical systems. The earliest recorded successful testing of an HPM occurred in April 1999 under the observation of the Joint Command and Control Warfare Center of San Antonio, Texas, USA. HPMs discharge a powerful energy pulse of around two billion watts, which destroys any electronics within a 300-m (984-ft) range. Their aim is to cause maximum destruction to any military or civilian power and electrical systems and thereby partially disable the enemy.

EARLIEST USE OF A GRAPHITE BOMB

The earliest use of a graphite bomb (G-bomb) in battle occurred in 1991 when Allied forces used it to disable 85% of Iraq's power supplies during the Gulf War. The bomb explodes a cloud of ultra-fine carbon-fibre wires over electrical installations, short-circuiting electrical systems.

EARLIEST USE OF INFRARED EQUIPMENT IN BATTLE

The earliest use of infrared technology in battle was during World War II (1939–45), when the USA, the UK and Germany were all developing the new technology. Electric sniperscopes mounted on top of rifles converted the infrared light of enemy soldiers into visible light, enabling accurate night-time firing. However, few of these early sniperscopes were actually used in battle as they had heavy batteries and a low range.

MOST ACCURATE BOMB

The US-built Joint Direct Attack Munition (JDAM) is the world's most accurate air-drop munition. JDAMs are steerable tailkits attached to existing 'dumb bombs' (above, nearest on wing). The tailkits have internal navigation systems that continually check the bomb's position by satellites. Upon impact JDAMs are accurate to plus/minus 2 m (6 ft 7 in).

MOST POWERFUL NERVE GAS

S-2-(diisopropylamino)ethyl O-ethyl methylphosponothioate, or VX, developed at the Chemical Defence Experimental Establishment, Porton Down, Wiltshire, UK, in 1952, is lethal with an airborne dosage of 10 mg-minute/m^3, or an oral dosage of 0.3 mg – about one fifth the size of a raindrop. VX gas affects the nervous system by bonding with the chemicals that transmit signals to the nerves and disrupting them. Symptoms of VX begin to occur two hours after contact and include loss of muscle control, slurred speech, convulsions and then death.

SMALLEST NUCLEAR WEAPON

The W54 fission bomb (right), deployed by the USA in the 1960s, is the smallest confirmed nuclear weapon ever made. Its warhead was 76 cm (30 in) long, 27 cm (11 in) in diameter at its widest point, weighed 23.13 kg (51 lb) and had a yield of 0.1 kilotons. It was designed to be used by commando teams to destroy harbours or bridges, or else deployed as a battlefield weapon, shot from a purpose-built bazooka.

LARGEST TORPEDO

The Russian Type 65, a 65-cm-diameter (25.5-in) torpedo, carries a warhead of nearly 1 tonne (2,200 lb) of conventional explosive, or a 15-kiloton nuclear warhead – slightly less powerful than the bombs that destroyed Hiroshima and Nagasaki in 1945. It can home in on a ship more than 80 km (50 miles) away and close at 43.5 knots (80 km/h or 50 mph) – far in excess of the speed of the fastest surface ships.

AIR & SEA WARFARE

OLDEST AIR FORCE

The earliest autonomous air force is the UK's RAF (Royal Air Force, above), whose origins date back to 1878 when the War Office commissioned a military balloon. The RAF itself came into existence on 1 April 1918, to take on a growing flying role previously undertaken by the army.

LARGEST BATTLESHIP EVER

The largest battleships ever commissioned were the Japanese vessels *Yamato* (commissioned in December 1941 and sunk south-west of Kyushu, Japan, on 7 April 1945) and *Musashi* (commissioned in August 1942 and sunk in the Philippine Sea on 24 October 1944). The Imperial Japanese Navy's super battleships, they were designed to be the most heavily armed in the world. Both ships had a full-load displacement of 71,111 tonnes (156.7 million lb), an overall length of 263 m (863 ft), and a full-load draught of 10.8 m (35.5 ft). They were armed with nine 460-mm (18.1-in) guns.

FASTEST DESTROYER

The highest speed attained by a destroyer was 45.25 knots (83.42 km/h or 52 mph) by the 2,900-tonne (6.4 million-lb) French ship *Le Terrible* in 1935. Built in Blainville, France, and powered by four Yarrow small tube boilers and two Rateau geared turbines giving 74,570 kW (100,000 hp), she was decommissioned at the end of 1957.

LARGEST AIRCRAFT CARRIER

The nine US Navy Nimitz class nuclear-powered aircraft carriers are the largest warships afloat. Fully loaded, each ship displaces 98,550 tonnes (217.2 million lb) and, when battle-ready, can carry around 5,680 personnel and 80 aircraft.

FASTEST WARSHIP

The world's fastest ever warship was the US Navy's 23.7-m-long (78-ft), 100-tonne (220,000-lb) experimental surface-effect ship SES-100B. The hovercraft attained a world record 91.9 knots (170 km/h or 105 mph) on 25 January 1980 on Chesapeake Bay, Maryland, USA.

LARGEST NAVY

The largest navy in the world in terms of manpower is the United States Navy. In March 2003 there were 383,427 uniformed personnel on active duty, supported by 185,371 civilian employees. This does not include the 170,000 uniformed members of the US Marine Corps which is, strictly speaking, a separate part of the armed forces.

EARLIEST AIRCRAFT CARRIER

Although platforms for take-offs and landings had been fitted to warships as early as 1910, the first ship with a runway running the full length of its deck was the British Royal Navy's HMS *Argus*, launched in 1918. She had a flight deck 172 m (565 ft) long and space for 20 aircraft.

EARLIEST STEALTH SHIP

The earliest known ship incorporating stealth technology is the US Navy's *Sea Shadow*, which was completed in the mid 1980s but only revealed to the public in 1993. The bizarre-looking twin-hulled ship is 49.98 m (164 ft) long, 20.72 m (68 ft) wide and has a full-load displacement of 569 tonnes (1.25 million lb). It has a crew of ten and a top speed of 18.52 km/h (11.5 mph).

LARGEST AMPHIBIOUS SHIP

With a full-load displacement of 36,500 tonnes (80.47 million lb) and a length of 257.3 m (844 ft), the US Navy's Wasp-class vessels are the largest amphibious ships afloat today. Primarily designed for landing troops on shore, they are also capable of carrying aircraft, and various smaller landing vessels.

EARLIEST NUCLEAR SUBMARINE

The world's first nuclear-powered submarine was USS *Nautilus* of the United States Navy (left), launched on 21 January 1954. *Nautilus* was 98.7 m (324 ft) long, with a beam of 26.8 m (88 ft). She had a crew of 95 enlisted men and 10 officers, and was capable of reaching speeds of over 20 knots (37 km/h or 23 mph).

LARGEST SURFACE-EFFECT SHIP

Similar to hovercraft, surface-effect ships travel on a cushion of air, but also have two sharp, rigid hulls that remain in the water. The largest surface-effect ships currently in operation are two Russian Bora-class guided-missile corvettes, which have a displacement of around 1,050 tonnes (2.31 million lb) and a claimed cruising speed of 54 knots (100 km/h or 62 mph). The Bora are 65.6 m (215 ft) long, 18 m (59 ft) wide, and have a crew of 68.

LARGEST SUBMARINE

The world's largest submarines are those of the Russian 941-Akula class (code-named Typhoon by NATO). The launch of the first Akula submarine, at the secret covered shipyard at Severodvinsk in the White Sea, was announced by NATO on 23 September 1980. The vessels are believed to have a submerged displacement of 26,500 tonnes (58.4 million lb), to measure 171.5 m (562.6 ft) overall and to be armed with 20 multiple-warhead SS-N-20 missiles with a range of 8,300 km (4,500 nautical miles). It is thought that less than five remain in service.

MOST SUBMARINES

The United States Navy has 74 armed submarines, the greatest number of any country. The entire submarine fleet is nuclear-powered, and includes more than 50 Seawolf- and Los Angeles-class attack ships, as well as 18 Ohio-class ballistic missile carriers.

EARLIEST SINKING OF A SHIP BY A SUBMARINE

The US Civil War Confederate ship H.L. *Hunley* became the first submarine ever to sink another vessel during wartime, when she successfully 'torpedoed' the Union Navy's *Housatonic* off Charleston Harbour, South Carolina, USA, on 17 February 1864. The 12-m-long (40-ft) sub was powered by a propeller turned by a crew of seven, who endured claustrophobic conditions in a cabin just 1.2 m (4 ft) tall and 1.06 m (3 ft 6 in) wide. The 'torpedo' consisted of a barrel of gunpowder attached to a 6-m (20-ft) spear at the front of *Hunley*. The sub would ram an enemy ship, embedding the spear, then back off and detonate the charge remotely by pulling a rope.

LARGEST NAVAL HOVERCRAFT

The largest naval hovercraft, and the largest hovercraft currently in operation anywhere, are the Russian Zubr ships (code-named Pomornik by NATO), which are 57 m (187 ft) long, 22.3 m (73.1 ft) wide and have a full-load displacement of 535 tonnes (1.17 million lb). Zubr ships are amphibious landing craft able to deliver 360 troops or three battle tanks onto beaches at speeds of up to 60 knots (111 km/h or 69 mph). They have a crew of between 21 and 31 and are heavily armed, with two multiple-rocket launchers, four portable air-defence missile systems, and two 30-mm machine guns.

GREATEST WINGSPAN FOR A BOMBER

The American ten-engined Convair B-36J 'Peacemaker' had a wingspan of 70.1 m (230 ft), the longest ever for a bomber. The aircraft, which had a maximum take-off weight of 185 tonnes (410,000 lb), has been out of service since the late 1950s, when it was replaced by the Boeing B-52. Its top speed was 700 km/h (435 mph).

MOST WIDELY USED MILITARY HELICOPTER

Over 16,000 Bell Helicopter Textron (USA) UH-1 Iroquoise ('Huey') helicopters have been produced since 1959, making it the most widely used military helicopter in the world. The general-purpose UH-1 became the workhorse of the US forces during the Vietnam War (1959–75), and it is claimed that over 5,000 UH-1s still remain in service in over 45 countries.

FASTEST COMBAT JET

The fastest combat jet is the Russian Mikoyan MiG-25 fighter (code-named 'Foxbat' by NATO), which has been tracked by radar at about Mach 3.2 (3,395 km/h or 2,110 mph). The MiG-25 was designed as a high-altitude interceptor but is also used as a reconnaissance aircraft. A MiG-25 can take off and climb to an altitude of 35,000 m (114,000 ft) in a little over four minutes.

GREATEST AIRBORNE ASSAULT

The largest airborne assault was the World War II Anglo-American Operation Market Garden, when three divisions (34,000 men) landed near Arnhem, The Netherlands, starting on 17 September 1944. The operation involved 2,800 aircraft and 1,600 gliders, but failed in its objectives.

LARGEST AIR FORCE EVER

The largest air force of all time was the United States Army Air Corps (now the United States Air Force), which had 79,908 aircraft in July 1944 and 2,411,294 personnel in March 1944.

NAVY WITH THE LARGEST NUMBER OF AIRCRAFT

The United States Navy (below) currently has over 4,000 aircraft in service, the greatest number of any world navy. It operates around 20 different types of fixed-wing aircraft, including carrier-based F-14 Tomcat and F/A-18 Hornet fighters, and reconnaissance, transport, anti-submarine and airborne-command-post aircraft. It also has six different types of helicopter.

ART
& MEDIA

ART & INSTALLATIONS

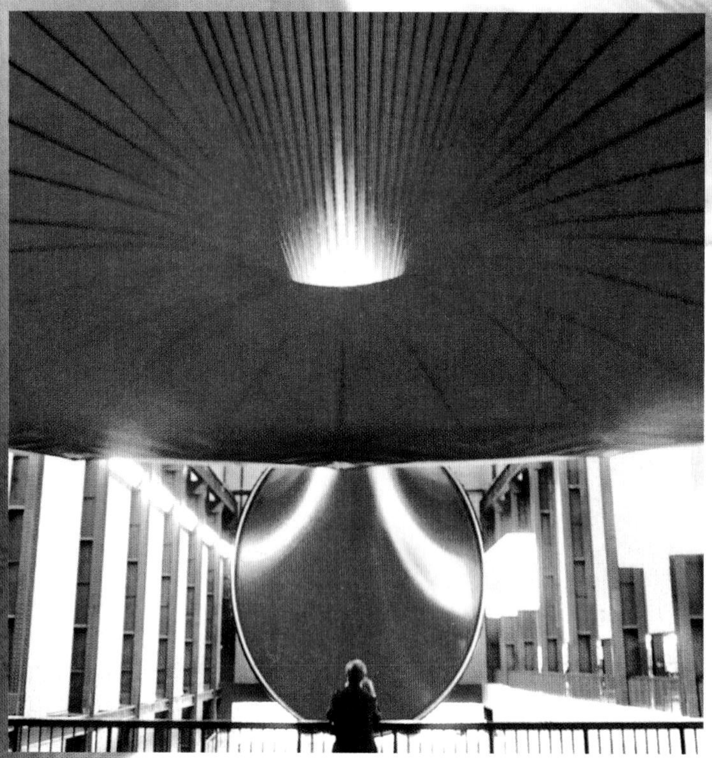

LONGEST MODERN ART SCULPTURE

The longest modern art sculpture is *Marsyas* (above), which measures 150 m (492 ft) long and approximately 10 storeys high. It was created by Turner Prize-winning artist Anish Kapoor (India). The giant sculpture was displayed in the Turbine Hall of the Tate Modern, London, UK, from 2002 to 2003. *Marsyas* comprises three steel rings joined together by a single span of red PVC membrane.

LARGEST MATCHSTICK MOSAIC

In 1998 M Schumann (Netherlands) constructed a mosaic of the Town Hall in Haarlem, The Netherlands, comprising 80,000 wooden matchsticks. The finished picture measured 110 x 75 cm (3 ft 6 in x 2 ft 4 in). Schumann spends hours constructing the world's famous buildings out of thousands of matchsticks.

LARGEST FINGER PAINTING

The largest finger painting in the world measures 257 m² (2,766.5 ft²) and was created by students from Lawrence Technological University, Southfield, Michigan, USA, on 10 September 2002. The final image was that of an American flag in memory of those lost in the 11 September 2001 tragedy.

MOST VISITED MODERN ART GALLERY

The Tate Modern, London, UK, is the world's favourite modern art museum with 5.25 million visitors in the year 2000. This is more than double the visitors to the Museum of Modern Art in New York, USA, and Paris's Pompidou Centre, France.

LARGEST BATIK

The largest batik painting measures 13.93 m² (150 ft²) and was created by Satish Ryali (India) in April 2002. It took Satish around 206 hours over 35 days to complete the batik. The batik's theme is derived from Indian mythology in the Hoysala art tradition.

LARGEST MANMADE CROP PICTURE

Crop artist Stan Herd's (USA) largest work to date was a 65-ha (160-acre) portrait of the 1930s Hollywood star Will Rogers (USA) created on the plains of southwest Kansas, USA, in 1983.

LARGEST NEEDLEPOINT

Beginning in August 2000, Vahid Saadati (Canada), along with a team of 650 volunteers, created the largest needlepoint, measuring 4.44 x 7.49 m (14 ft 7 in x 24 ft 7 in). It depicts the word 'welcome' in 103 languages.

MOST VALUABLE SCULPTURE BY A LIVING ARTIST

Michael Jackson and Bubbles, a porcelain sculpture created by the artist Jeff Koons (USA) in 1988, sold for $5,616,750 (£3,945,344) at Sotheby's, New York, USA, on 15 May 2001. The piece measures 106.7 x 179.1 x 82.6 cm (42 x 70.5 x 32.5 in) and is described as a mix of pop culture and high art that perfectly captures the decade of the eighties. The gold-and-white-coloured sculpture shows Michael Jackson (USA) reclining with his arm around his pet primate.

LARGEST PERMANENT COIN MURAL

Eduardo D Henriques (Portugal) has produced a number of permanent 'nautical' murals made from Portuguese coins, the largest of which, *Império Português*, measures 1.83 x 5 m (6 x 16 ft 4 in) and uses 37,121 coins. An admiration for the tradition of Portuguese naval adventurers inspired Eduardo's artwork.

LARGEST PAINTING BY NUMBERS

The largest painting by numbers measures 88.95 m² (957 ft²) and was created by nearly 300 students and staff from Portmead Primary School, Swansea, UK, on 24 July 2002. The giant painting depicts an underwater scene.

MOST VISITED TRAVELLING ART EXHIBITION

Since it opened in Japan in 1996, *Body Worlds*, an exhibition of posed, plastinated (plastic-preserved) human bodies by Gunther von Hagens (Germany), has travelled to 11 major cities. As of September 2002, the exhibition had received more than 9.57 million vistors.

TALLEST SCULPTURE

The *Windwand*, at Canary Wharf, London, UK, is a 50.7-m-tall (166-ft 4-in) red flexible wand made from glass-fibre composite with an outer layer of carbon-fibre. Designed by Ron Arad Associates, it was built by Carbospars Ltd (UK). Weighing 700 kg (1,543 lb), it measures 40 cm (15 in) in diameter at its base and narrows to 8 cm (3.1 in) with red high-density LED lights at the tips, making it visible from 3.21 km (2 miles) away.

LARGEST ICE SCULPTURE

An ice palace completed in January 1992 during the Winter Carnival at St Paul, Minnesota, USA, used 18,000 blocks of ice. Built by TMK Construction Specialties Inc. (USA), it was 50.8 m (166 ft 8 in) high and contained 4,900 tonnes (10.8 million lb) of ice.

LARGEST LINOPRINT

The world's largest linoprint measures 40.7 m² (438 ft²) and was created by the Stiching Grafisch Collectief Thoets (Netherlands), on 28 October 2000.

LARGEST SAND PAINTING

The world's largest sand painting measures 9.9 x 8.3 m (32 ft 6 in x 27 ft 2 in) and was created by a team from Procter & Gamble on 23 October 2002 at the Le Meridien Limassol Spa & Resort, Cyprus. The design depicts the company's logo.

LARGEST SIMULTANEOUS PHOTOGRAPHY EXHIBITION

A photography exhibition showing photographer Martin Parr's (UK) work entitled *Common Sense* was held simultaneously in 44 venues around the world, with 41 of them opening on 1 April 1999. The aim of the exhibition, which had already toured the world, was to highlight details of day-to-day life. Although the intensely colourful pictures were taken with a 35-mm camera, their high quality meant they could be successfully reproduced by a laser copier. This meant that Parr's work could be shown in a number of public spaces simultaneously.

GREATEST ART ROBBERY

On 14 April 1991, 20 paintings, estimated to be worth £280 million ($500 million), were stolen from the Van Gogh Museum in Amsterdam, The Netherlands. However, only 35 minutes later they were found in an abandoned car not far from the museum.

LARGEST 3D BALLOON SCULPTURE

The world's largest three-dimensional balloon sculpture used 58,942 balloons and was constructed by a team from the Balloon Express Shop, Rovigo, Italy, in the shape of a giant diplodocus dinosaur named 'DinoBigo.' The sculpture was 27 m (88 ft 6 in) long and displayed in La Fattoria shopping centre, Rovigo, Italy, in November and December 2001.

LARGEST PICTURE MOSAIC

The world's largest picture mosaic was created by 15,550 British children as part of Persil's *Big Mummy* project. It measured 643.65 m² (6,928 ft 2 in²), and was completed on 30 August 2002, at Alexandra Palace, London, UK.

LARGEST SCRAP-METAL SCULPTURE

The world's largest scrap-metal sculpture, completed by Gary Greff (USA) in August 2001, stands 33.5 m (110 ft) tall, is 46.9 m (154 ft) wide and weighs 71,513 kg (157,659 lb). Entitled *Geese in Flight*, the sculpture resembles Canadian geese flying against a backdrop of sky and prairie and is one of a series of metal sculptures located along the Enchanted Highway between Gladstone and Regent, North Dakota, USA.

LARGEST BRICK SCULPTURE

Entitled *Train*, the world's biggest brick sculpture cost £760,000 to build and used more than 180,000 housebricks by the time it was unveiled on 23 June 1997, just a few steps from where the world's first train passenger service ran 170 years ago. The life-size structure depicting the *Mallard* steam engine is 39.6 m (130 ft) long and was made in Darlington, Co Durham, by David Mach (UK) and a team of 20 apprentice bricklayers.

LARGEST TOAST MOSAIC

The largest toast mosaic was created by Maurice Bennett (New Zealand, below with a mosaic depicting Elvis Presley). It measured 12 x 4.1 m (39 ft 4 in x 13 ft 5 in) and used 2,724 slices of bread, toasted to different tones to create skin colour and shadow. It portrayed Mark Blumsky, former mayor of Wellington, and was displayed in Wellington, New Zealand, from February to March 1999.

FASHION

MOST EXPENSIVE TIARA

The world's most expensive tiara was designed by Italian fashion designer Gianni Versace and had an estimated retail value of £3.2 million ($5 million) in 1996. The tiara was decorated with 100-carat diamonds, set in yellow gold, and weighed approximately 300 g (10.5 oz).

LARGEST NECK TIE

A tie measuring 80.46 m (264 ft) and made from 354 m (1,161 ft) of fabric using 125,128 stitches was displayed at Shoppers Stop, Bangalore, India, from 15 November to 14 December 1997. The tie took 12 men 120 hours to make.

MOST POPULAR SUNGLASSES

Ray-Ban sunglasses sold 10 million units worldwide in 1998. Ray-Ban's best-known model, the Wayfarer, has been available since 1953 and is reported to be the best-selling style in history. The Luxottica Group, the Italian company that acquired Ray-Ban in 1999, reported for the fiscal year ending December 2002 an increased net income of 18% to €372.1 million (£242.7 million or $390.7 million).

LARGEST JEANS

The world's largest pair of jeans are 28.6 m (94 ft) long and 18.8 m (62 ft) wide and were constructed by Levi Strauss Co. Inc. (Canada). The giant jeans were unveiled on 30 July 2001 and were inflated by a hot-air device to raise them to their full three-dimensional height. They are based on a pattern for a size 32 waist and 36 leg – yet enlarged to more than 20 times the normal pattern size. The jeans weigh 246.3 kg (543 lb), use more than 725 m^2 (7,805 ft^2) of 10-oz denim and have a working 3.96-m-long (13-ft) zipper and embossed metal button.

HIGHEST ANNUAL EARNINGS FOR A MODEL

The world's top-earning model is currently Gisele Bundchen (Brazil), who earned £8.3 million ($12.5 million) in 2001, according to the *Forbes* Celebrity 100 list released on 21 June 2002.

LONGEST SAREE

A silk saree created by Vikas Chajjer (India) in May 1998 measured 121 m (396 ft 11 in) long and 114 cm (45 in) wide. Taking 19 days to complete (11 to weave, three to hand-paint and one day each to bleach, spray, print, embroider and finish) the saree has two hand-painted designs: one with the seven wonders of the world and the other portraying Mahatma Gandhi.

LARGEST G-STRING

The world's largest g-string was unveiled at the Body Shop's UK headquarters in Littlehampton, West Sussex, on 15 March 2001. The giant white and red cotton thong, measuring approximately 9.2 x 4.6 m (30 ft 2 in x 15 ft), was presented by the Body Shop in conjunction with the charity Comic Relief's 'Pants to Poverty' fundraising campaign.

HIGHEST HEELED SHOES COMMERCIALLY AVAILABLE

The highest heels commercially available boast a combination of 27.9-cm (11-in) platforms and 40.6-cm (16-in) heels. Available in red or black leather, these 'Vertigo' shoes sell for £725 ($1,092). Produced by Leatherwork London Ltd (UK), they are sold by LadyBWear (UK). The company take no responsibility for anyone who falls whilst wearing the shoes.

FASTEST SHEEP TO JUMPER

The Exeter Spinners Audrey Felton, Christine Heap, Eileen Lancaster, Marjorie Mellis, Ann Sandercock and Maria Scott (all UK) produced a jumper by hand from raw fleece in 1 hr 55 min 50.2 sec on 25 September 1983, at BBC Television Centre, London, UK.

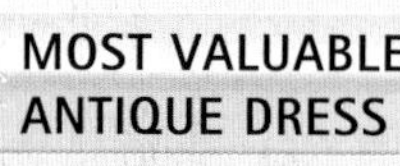

MOST VALUABLE ANTIQUE DRESS

An 1888 court dress (above) designed by Charles Frederick Worth (UK) was sold at auction by Monica Seggos and Robert von Kampen (both USA) on 3 May 2001 at Doyle New York, USA, to an anonymous buyer for $101,500 (£70,894). It was worn by Esther Maria Lewis Chapin (USA) when presented to Queen Victoria in 1889. The gown has a 58.4-cm (23-in) waist and a 3.1-m (10-ft 6-in) train.

MOST EXPENSIVE BIKINI

The jewellers Prestons of Windsor, Berkshire, UK, made a diamond-encrusted bikini valued at £123,409.90 ($194,458.97) and unveiled it on 22 March 2000 at Windsor Fashion Week. Modelled by Naomi Campbell look-alike Susan Sangster, the plain black bikini was hand-sewn with individual pieces of jewellery to form a design that used a staggering total of 66 carats' worth of diamonds.

LARGEST KNICKERS

The largest pair of knickers were manufactured by Cunning Stunts (UK) from acrylic and lace, and measured 4.26 x 8.97 m (14 ft x 29 ft 7 in). The giant pair of pants was devised by advertising agency Bartle Bogle Hegarty (UK) to promote *FHM* magazine's lingerie special, and hung across Oxford Street, London, UK, in October 1999.

LONGEST MODELLING CONTRACT

The Japanese actress and model Shima Iwashita has been a house model for the Japanese cosmetic company Menard since she first signed with them on 1 April 1972. Her contract is renewed every year.

LARGEST BERET

José Antonio Basteguieta (Spain) made a beret (*boina*) measuring 3.5 m (11 ft 5.76 in) in diameter, which was displayed on *El Show de los Récords*, Madrid, Spain, on 13 October 2001.

LONGEST WORKING CAREER FOR A CATWALK MODEL

Born in 1931, model Carmen Dell'Orefice (USA, left) has been modelling for the Ford Agency (USA) since the 1940s. At the age of 72 she is still in demand for contracts and international shows. Daphne Self (UK) is 73 years old but has had an intermittent modelling career. She is signed to Models 1 in London, UK, and has been photographed for *Vogue* and *Marie Claire*.

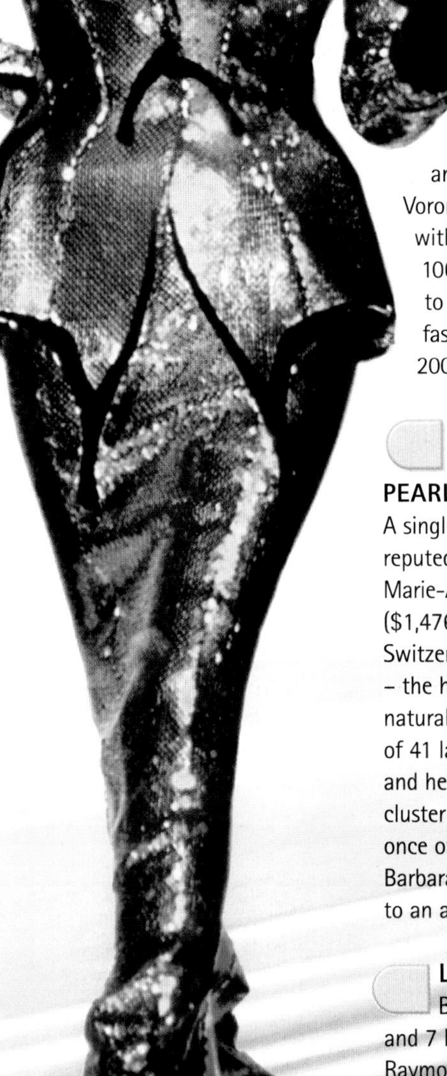

LARGEST EVENING JACKET

The world's largest evening jacket is 9.9 m (32 ft 6 in) long and 5.4 m (17 ft 9 in) wide, and was created by Michael Voronin (Ukraine). Constructed with the help of 26 people in 106 hours, the jacket was made to celebrate the Ukrainian fashion holiday on 8 September 2002 in Kiev, Ukraine.

MOST VALUABLE NATURAL PEARL NECKLACE

A single-strand pearl necklace reputedly worn by French queen Marie-Antoinette fetched £910,313 ($1,476,345) at Christie's, Geneva, Switzerland, on 16 November 1999 – the highest price ever paid for a natural pearl necklace. Consisting of 41 large and graduated pearls and held together by a diamond cluster clasp, the necklace was once owned by Woolworth heiress Barbara Hutton (USA). It was sold to an anonymous European buyer.

LARGEST MEN'S SUIT

Between 14 February and 7 March 2001 tailors from Raymond Ltd (India) constructed the world's largest men's suit at their factory in Mumbai (Bombay), India. From shoulder to trouser hem the suit measured 19.5 m (64 ft) long. The suit was made from 385 m (1,263 ft) of polywool sapphire fabric, 240 m (787 ft) of polyester lining and a total of 7.8 km (4.8 miles) of thread.

LARGEST DRESS

A dress measuring 9.6 m (39 ft 6 in) long with a diameter of 20 m (65 ft 6 in) was made for the 1998 Junta Central Fallera de Valencia in Spain. The dress was made from 700 m² (7,532 ft²) of fabric and was an exact, scaled-up replica of a dress worn by the first Miss Spain in 1929.

MOST VALUABLE DRESS

A flesh-coloured, beaded, silk Jean Louis gown, worn by the actress Marilyn Monroe (USA) when she sang 'Happy Birthday' to President Kennedy (USA) on 19 May 1962, was sold at auction on 27 October 1999 for $1,267,000 (£782,340) at Christie's, New York, USA, to New York dealers Robert Schagrin and Peter Siegel (both USA) of Gotta Have It! Collectibles. The dress originally cost $12,000 (£7,410) and was such a tight fit for the actress that she had to be sewn into it.

LARGEST CANVAS SPORTS SHOE

The world's largest canvas sports shoe measures 3.9 x 1.5 x 1.2 m (13 x 5 x 4 ft) and was made by Michelle Nagy (Canada) in conjunction with the Juvenile Diabetes Research Foundation and Shopper's Drug Mart in Toronto, Ontario, Canada, on 16 September 2001. The shoe is made of canvas with cotton stitching, aluminium grommets and a rubber sole. The shoe's lace is 15.2 m (50 ft) long.

MOST OSCAR DRESSES SOLD AT A CHARITY AUCTION

A record 56 dresses and evening gowns that had been worn to Academy Awards ceremonies by actresses such as Elizabeth Taylor, Sharon Stone and Uma Thurman were auctioned at 'Unforgettable: Fashion of the Oscars' at Christie's, New York, USA, on 18 March 1999. A total of $786,120 (£488,820) was donated to the American Foundation for Aids Research (AmFAR). The most valuable item was a blue and violet faille-crepe dress worn by Elizabeth Taylor to the 1969 Academy Awards. It sold for $167,500 (£104,154).

LARGEST LEATHER BOOT

In 2001, Pasquale Tramontana (Italy) completed the largest leather boot (below), which measures 4.16 x 2.7 m (13 ft 7 in x 8 ft 10 in ft) and is 80 cm (31 in) wide. The boot took five years to make at a cost of 25 million lire (£8,884 or $11,416). It weighs 280 kg (617 lb), and used 40 hides of leather.

MOVIE CLASSICS

EARLIEST MOTION PICTURE
Louis Aimé Augustin Le Prince (France) was attested to have achieved dim moving outlines on a whitewashed wall at the Institute for the Deaf, Washington Heights, New York, USA, as early as 1885–87.

FIRST TALKIE
The earliest sound-on-film motion picture was achieved by Eugene Augustin Lauste (France), who patented his process on 11 August 1906 and produced a workable system using a string galvanometer in 1910 at Benedict Road, Stockwell, London, UK.

HIGHEST GROSS FOR A FILM SERIES
The 20 James Bond movies made by Eon Productions Ltd (UK), from *Dr No* (UK, 1962) to *Die Another Day* (UK/USA, 2002), have grossed over $3.6 billion (£2.25 billion) worldwide. *Die Another Day*, starring Pierce Brosnan (Rep. of Ireland) as James Bond, is the highest earner of the series, with a worldwide gross of over $393 million (£246 million).

MOST APPEARANCES AS JAMES BOND
Sean Connery (above) and Roger Moore (both UK) have both starred as British secret agent '007' seven times. Connery starred in the first Bond movie, *Dr No* (UK, 1962), and Moore made his debut as Bond in *Live and Let Die* (UK, 1973).

MOST EXPENSIVE FILM
Paramount's *Titanic* (USA, 1997) cost just over $200 million (then £118.9 million) to make. Originally given a $125-million (£74.3-million) budget, it was due for release in July 1997, but post-production problems set the date back to December 1997 and added to the cost.

With production costs adjusted for inflation, the most expensive film ever made was *Cleopatra* (USA, 1963), whose $44-million (then £15.7-million) budget would be equivalent to $307 million (£175.4 million) today.

HIGHEST BOX-OFFICE GROSS
The film with the highest box-office earnings is *Titanic* (Paramount, USA) which was released on 19 December 1997. It became the first film ever to take $1 billion at the international box office, with a total gross of $1.8 billion (£1.3 billion).

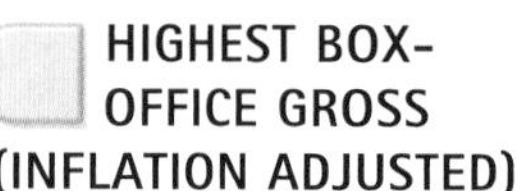

HIGHEST BOX-OFFICE GROSS (INFLATION ADJUSTED)
Rising cinema ticket prices mean that the all-time top-grossing movies are nearly all recent films. However, *Gone with the Wind* (USA, 1939), based on the best selling novel by Margaret Mitchell (USA), took a massive $393.4 million (then £88 million) at the international box office – a sum which, accounting for inflation, places the film top with a total gross equivalent to $3,785,107,801 (£2,365,692,376) today. In the USA alone, *Gone with the Wind* had 283,100,000 admissions compared to 130,900,000 for *Titanic* (USA, 1997) – the film with the highest box-office gross to date.

HIGHEST BOX-OFFICE GROSS FOR AN ANIMATED MOVIE (INFLATION ADJUSTED)
Walt Disney's (USA) first full-length feature film, *Snow White and the Seven Dwarfs* (USA, 1937), took $184.9 million (£37.4 million) at the box office worldwide, equivalent to $1.6 billion (£1 billion) today. The film took four years to make at a cost of $1.5 million (then £303,398) – equivalent to $13.3 million (£8.3 million) today.

HIGHEST BOX-OFFICE GROSS FOR A WESTERN
Dances with Wolves (USA, 1990), directed by and starring Kevin Costner (USA), has grossed $424.2 million (£297.6 million) at the international box office. The film won seven Oscars from 12 nominations in 1991, including Best Director for Costner.

HIGHEST BOX-OFFICE GROSS FOR A SILENT FILM
King Vidor's (USA) *The Big Parade* (USA, 1925), set during World War I and starring John Gilbert (USA), had a box-office gross of $22 million (then £4.6 million).

HIGHEST BOX-OFFICE GROSS FOR A HORROR MOVIE
The Exorcist (USA, 1973), directed by William Friedkin (USA) with a budget of $12 million (then £4.89 million), has taken $292.7 million (£205.3 million) at the international box office to date.

MOST EXTENSIVE SCREEN TEST

To find the actress to play the role of Scarlett O'Hara in *Gone with the Wind* (USA, 1939), film makers MGM shot 45,415 m (149,000 ft) of black-and-white test film and another 3,962 m (13,000 ft) of colour film with 60 actresses, none of whom got the part. Vivien Leigh's (UK, left with Clark Gable) successful test was actually made after the movie shoot had commenced – perhaps the only instance of a major motion picture going into production before the star role had been cast.

HIGHEST BOX-OFFICE GROSS FOR A SCIENCE FICTION FILM (INFLATION ADJUSTED)

In an inflation-adjusted list, *Star Wars* (USA, 1977) has an international box-office gross of $2.65 billion (£1.62 billion). The film originally took $513.7 million (£294.29 million) worldwide before its re-issue in 1997.

MOST OSCARS WON BY A FILM

Two films have both won a record 11 Oscars (American Academy Awards). The first to achieve the record was *Ben Hur* (USA, 1959) which won its Oscars from 12 nominations in 1960. *Titanic* (USA, 1997) won its Oscars from 14 nominations in 1998.

MOST FILM OSCAR NOMINATIONS WITHOUT WINNING

The Turning Point (USA, 1977) starring Shirley MacLaine and Anne Bancroft (both USA) and *The Color Purple* (USA, 1986) starring Danny Glover and Whoopi Goldberg (both USA) were each nominated 11 times for an Academy Award, but neither film won an Oscar.

MOST BEST DIRECTOR OSCAR WINS

John Ford (USA) won an Oscar for Best Director on four occasions, for *The Informer* (USA, 1936), *The Grapes of Wrath* (USA, 1940), *How Green was My Valley* (USA, 1941) and *The Quiet Man* (USA, 1952).

MOST EDITED SINGLE SEQUENCE IN A MOVIE

The chariot-race scene in *Ben Hur* (USA, 1925), starring Ramon Novarro (Mexico), for which editor Lloyd Nosler (USA) had to compress 60,960 m (200,000 ft) of film into a sparse 228.6 m (750 ft), was the most edited scene in cinema history, with a ratio of 267:1.

LONGEST SCREEN PARTNERSHIP FOR A COMEDY DUO

Actors Stan Laurel (UK) and Oliver Hardy (USA) starred in 106 films together (including 50 shorts) between 1917 and 1950. They first appeared together in *Lucky Dog* (USA, 1917 – released 1922) and starred together for the last time in *Atoll K* (France/Italy, 1950).

MOST PROLIFIC ACTOR/ SINGER FILM STAR

Bing Crosby (b. Harry Lillis Crosby, USA) made 104 films for cinema and was producer to six during his singing and acting career, which began in 1930. For ten years Bing was continually among the top ten box-office stars, and for five consecutive years (1944–49) he remained at the No.1 spot – a feat no other film star has bettered. He won the Oscar for Best Actor in 1944 for the film *Going My Way* (USA, 1943) and was nominated for Best Actor in *The Country Girl* (USA, 1954) and *Man on Fire* (USA, 1957).

MOST LEADING ROLES

John Wayne (b. Marion Michael Morrison, USA) acted in 153 movies from *The Drop Kick* (USA, 1927) to *The Shootist* (USA, 1976). In 142 of these he played the lead.

MOST FILM EXTRAS

It is believed that over 300,000 extras appeared in the funeral scene of *Gandhi* (UK, 1982), the epic film directed by Richard Attenborough (UK). Eleven camera crews shot 6,096 m (20,000 ft) of film for that scene, more than the total footage of the 188-minute released film. The edited funeral sequence ran for only 125 seconds of screen time.

LONGEST INTERVAL BETWEEN AN ORIGINAL FILM AND A SEQUEL

A record 46 years elapsed before Walt Disney Production's *Return to Oz* (USA, 1985) was made, which resumed the story six months after Dorothy's return to Kansas in MGM's *The Wizard of Oz* (USA, 1939).

FILM STAR WITH THE MOST BIOGRAPHIES

Charlie Chaplin (UK) has had his life and art expounded in 259 book-length works. He began his career on the music-hall stage, and while a member of a troupe touring the USA he was recruited by Mack Sennet to create his Little Tramp character for the big screen. Chaplin refused to use sound until 1940.

MOST FILMS BY A DANCING PARTNERSHIP

Fred Astaire (USA, below) and Ginger Rogers (USA) appeared as a dancing partnership in ten films, starting with *Flying Down to Rio* (USA, 1933) in which they had a brief dance number called the Carioca, and ending with *The Berkleys of Broadway* (USA, 1949).

MOST NOMINATIONS FOR BEST FOREIGN LANGUAGE FILM

France has been nominated for the Best Foreign Language Film Oscar 34 times between 1948 and 2002. The last nomination in this category was for *Le Fabuleux destin d'Amélie Poulain* (*Amélie from Montmartre*, France, 2001) in 2002. France has won the category 12 times.

LONGEST FILM COMMERCIALLY SHOWN IN ITS ENTIRETY

Edgar Reitz's *Die Zweite Heimat* (*The Second Homeland*, Germany, 1992), lasted 25 hr 32 min and premiered in Munich, Germany, in September 1992.

LONGEST FILM TITLE

The official title of Lina Wertmüller's (Italy) film is *Un Fatto di sangue nel commune di Sculiana fra due uomini per causa di una vedova si sospetano moventi politici. Amore-Morte-Shimmy. Lugano belle. Tarantelle. Tarallucci é vino* (Italy, 1979). It has 179 characters, including punctuation. The English language title was simply *Revenge*.

HIGHEST BOX-OFFICE GROSS FOR A FOREIGN LANGUAGE FILM

The martial arts film *Wo hu zang long* (*Crouching Tiger, Hidden Dragon*, Taiwan, 2000) was first released on 30 June 2000. Directed by Ang Lee (Taiwan) and starring Yun-Fat Chow (Hong Kong) and Michelle Yeoh (Malaysia, right), it became the highest grossing foreign language film, taking £144,501,285 ($209,136,710) by April 2002 in the UK and USA.

HIGHEST BOX-OFFICE GROSS FOR A FRENCH FILM

Directed by Jean-Pierre Jeunet and starring Audrey Tautou (both France), *Le Fabuleux destin d'Amélie Poulain* (*Amélie from Montmartre*, France, 2001), first released in France on 25 April 2001, took the foreign box office by storm and amassed a total of £101,005,911 ($144,488,955).

HIGHEST BOX-OFFICE GROSS FOR AN ITALIAN FILM

La Vita è Bella (*Life is Beautiful*, Italy, 1997), released by Miramax and starring Roberto Benigni (Italy), had a worldwide gross of £143 million ($229 million). It also became the highest grossing foreign language film in North America, making $57.6 million (£36 million), and overtaking the previous record of $21.8 million (£13.62 million) set by *Il Postino* (*The Postman*, Italy, 1994).

« LARGEST ANNUAL FILM OUTPUT

India produces more feature-length films than any other country. A record 948 films were produced in 1990, and in 1994 a total of 754 films were produced in a record 16 languages at its three major centres of production: Bombay (Mumbai), Calcutta and Madras. Actress Aishwarya Rai (left) is one of India's biggest film stars.

HIGHEST BOX-OFFICE GROSS FOR AN AUSTRALIAN FILM

Directed by Peter Fairman, *Crocodile Dundee* (Australia, 1986), starring Paul Hogan (Australia) and Linda Kozlowski (USA), grossed £218 million ($328 million).

HIGHEST BOX-OFFICE GROSS FOR A BOLLYWOOD FILM

Hum Aapke Hain Koun . . . ! (*Who Am I To You?*, India, 1994), starring Madhuri Dixit and Salman Khan (both India), is the highest grossing Bollywood film of all time taking more than £40.4 million ($63.8 million) in its first year, and breaking the record set by the curry western, *Sholay* (*Embers*, India, 1975).

HIGHEST BOX-OFFICE GROSS FOR A GERMAN FILM

Das Boot (*The Boat*, Germany, 1981), the story of a WW II U-boat crew, is the highest grossing German film in cinema history. The film took £41.933 million ($84.915 million) at the international box office.

MOST OSCAR NOMINATIONS FOR A FOREIGN LANGUAGE FILM

The martial arts film *Wo hu zang long* (*Crouching Tiger, Hidden Dragon*, Taiwan, 2000, left) was nominated for a record ten Oscars in 2001, including Best Picture, Best Director, Music (Song), Costume Design, Film Editing and Writing (Adapted Screenplay). It won Oscars for Best Foreign Language Film, Art Direction, Music (Score) and Cinematography.

OLDEST FILM DIRECTOR

Manoel de Oliveira (Portugal), who began directing films in 1931, made his most recent film, *O Princípio da Incerteza* (*The Principle of Uncertainty*, Portugal, 2002), at the age of 94. The film was presented at the Cannes film festival, France, on 18 May 2002.

LARGEST PRODUCTION CREW FOR A FEATURE FILM

The largest number of craftsmen and technicians employed on a dramatic feature was 532 for the WW I flying story *Gunbus* (*Sky Bandits*, UK, 1986), directed by Zoran Perisic (Yugoslavia) and starring Nicholas Lyndhurst (UK).

LONGEST FILM SHOT ON A SINGLE CAMERA

Written and directed by Fabrizio Prada (Mexico), *A Day in Paradise* (Mexico, 2001) was shot in real time at 15 different locations on 16 December 2001 on a single camera for 82 minutes. The final running time was 88 minutes and the film was shown without any cuts on 5 July 2002 at the El Ágora de Xalapa, Xalapa, Veracruz, Mexico.

FASTEST MOVIE PRODUCED FROM SCRIPT TO SCREEN

The shortest time ever taken to make a feature-length film from scripting to screening is 13 days for *The Fastest Forward* (UK, 1990), produced by Russ Malkin and directed by John Gore (both UK). The cast, crew, technicians and cinemagraphic suppliers accepted a charity challenge and the 75-minute thriller was given a gala première at the Dominion Theatre, London, UK, on 27 May 1990.

LONGEST FILM SERIES WITH THE SAME STAR

Kiyoshi Atsumi (Japan) appeared in the lead role of all the Torajiro Kuruma (more commonly known as Tora-san) comedy movies produced by Shockiki studios, Japan, between August 1969 and December 1995.

MOST OSCARS WON FOR BEST FOREIGN LANGUAGE FILM

Italy has won 13 Oscars for Best Foreign Language Film, the most recent being for *La Vita è Bella* (*Life is Beautiful*, 1997) in 1999, at the 71st Academy Awards. *Cinema Paradiso* (1989, right) won an Oscar in 1990.

LONGEST SCREEN PARTNERSHIP

The stars of India's Malayalam cinema, Prem Nazir and Sheela (both India), played opposite each other in a total of 130 movies until Sheela retired in 1975. Prem Nazir, who was the quintessential male lead, starred in over 700 films in total, while the actress Sheela starred in 370.

LONGEST CLOSE-UP ON FILM

Daera (*The Division*, India, 1953), has a close-up of actress Meena Kumari (India), who plays the lead female character Sheetal, that lasts for 6 min 30 sec. Written and directed by Kamaal Amrohi (India), the film was made in black and white, and has a running time of 139 minutes.

LONGEST WORKING CAREER OF A FILM ACTOR

The German comedian and character actor Curt Bois (1901–91), who made his film debut at the age of seven in *Der Fidele Bauer* (*The Jolly Peasant*, Germany, 1908), had a film career lasting 79 years, with his final role being as Homer in *Der Himmel über Berlin* (*Wings of Desire*, Germany, 1987). Bois left Germany in 1933 on the accession of the Nazis and made his way to the USA via Prague, Vienna, Paris and London, arriving in Hollywood in 1938. He appeared in such films as *Caught* (USA, 1949) and *Casablanca* (USA, 1942), before returning to Germany in the early 1950s.

LONGEST WORKING CAREER OF A FILM ACTRESS

Maxine Elliott Hicks (USA) made her debut in *The Borrowed Finery* (USA, 1914) for the Thomas Edison Company, leading to a career spanning 78 years. Her last film for the big screen was *Beethoven* (USA, 1992).

BUSIEST HOLLYWOOD STAR

In terms of the most movies completed during a limited period of time, comedienne Joan Blondell (USA) starred in 32 feature films in 27 months between 1930 and 1933.

HIGHEST ANNUAL EARNINGS FOR A FILM ACTOR

According to the 2002 *Forbes* Celebrity 100 list, the top-earning actor is currently Adam Sandler (USA) who earned an estimated $47 million (£31.3 million) in 2001.

HIGHEST ANNUAL EARNINGS FOR A FILM PRODUCER

Screenwriter, film director, producer and media entrepreneur George Lucas (USA) topped the 2002 *Forbes* Celebrity 100 list having earned an estimated $200 million (£133.5 million) in 2001.

>> MOST GENERATIONS OF PRINTS AT MANN'S CHINESE THEATRE

Actor Kirk Douglas (USA) left his mark on Hollywood Boulevard, Los Angeles, USA, in 1962, when his footprints were set in stone. His actor/producer son Michael (USA, right) left his handprints in September 1997. Their prints sit side by side – the first time one family has had two generations of prints at the famous cinema.

HIGHEST SALARY PER FILM FOR AN ACTRESS

For her roles in both *Erin Brockovich* (USA, 2000) and *The Mexican* (USA, 2001) Julia Roberts (USA) commanded a fee of $20,000,000 (then £12,500,000 and £13,750,430 respectively).

HIGHEST SALARY PER FILM FOR AN ACTOR

Arnold Schwarzenegger (USA, b. Austria) was paid a basic wage of $30 million (then £20.9 million) in 2001 for his role as 'The Terminator' in *Terminator 3: Rise of the Machines* (USA, 2003).

MOST GOLDEN GLOBE FILM AWARDS

The Golden Globe Awards have been presented annually since 1944 by the Hollywood Foreign Press Association. The most Golden Globes awarded to a single film is five, and five films share this record: *Doctor Zhivago* (USA, 1965), *Love Story* (USA, 1970); *The Godfather* (USA, 1972); *One Flew Over the Cuckoo's Nest* (USA, 1975); and *A Star is Born* (USA, 1976).

<< MOST GOLDEN GLOBE AWARDS WON BY AN ACTOR

The most Golden Globes won by an individual is six, achieved by Jack Nicholson (left, USA) between 1975 and 2003. His most recent win was for *About Schmidt* (USA, 2002).

MOST OSCAR NOMINATIONS FOR AN ACTOR

Since beginning his career in the film *The Cry Baby Killer* (USA, 1958), Jack Nicholson (USA) has been nominated for 12 Oscars, four as Best Supporting Actor and the rest as Best Actor. His first nomination was in 1970 for Best Supporting Actor in *Easy Rider* (USA, 1969).

MOST GOLDEN GLOBE AWARDS WON BY AN ACTRESS

Shirley MacLaine (USA) won six Golden Globe awards between 1955 and 2003, as well as a Special Award in 1959 for most versatile actress, and a Cecil B DeMille Award in 1998 for outstanding contribution in the entertainment world.

MOST OSCARS WON IN A YEAR BY AN INDIVIDUAL

Walt Disney (USA) won the most Oscars at a single presentation with four in 1953 for Best Cartoon: *Toot, Whistle, Plunk and Boom*; Best Documentary Short: *The Alaskan Eskimo*; Best Documentary Feature: *The Living Desert*; and Best Two-Reel Short: *Bear Country*.

MOST OSCAR NOMINATIONS FOR A LIVING PERSON

Between 1968 and 2003 the composer John Williams (USA) received 42 Oscar nominations. His first nomination was for Best Music, Scoring of Music, Adaptation or Treatment for *Valley of the Dolls* (USA, 1967), and his most recent for Best Original Score for *Catch Me If You Can* (USA, 2002).

EARLIEST POSTHUMOUS OSCAR AWARDED

The first posthumous Oscar was awarded at the 1939 Academy Awards on 29 February 1940 to Sidney Howard (USA, d. 23 August 1939) for his screenplay of *Gone With The Wind* (USA, 1939).

MOST OSCARS WON FOR INDIVIDUAL CREATIVE ACHIEVEMENT

MGM filmmaker Cedric Gibbons (USA) won 11 Oscars for Art Direction from a total of 40 nominations from 1930 to 1957. The most won by a woman is eight, by costume designer Edith Head (USA).

MOST OSCAR NOMINATIONS FOR AN ACTRESS

Between 1979 and 2003 Meryl Streep (USA) was nominated for 13 Oscars, three as Best Actress in a Supporting Role and the rest for Best Actress. She won the Best Actress in a Supporting Role Oscar in 1980 for *Kramer vs. Kramer* (USA, 1979) and Best Actress in 1983 for *Sophie's Choice* (USA, 1982).

ONLY TIE FOR BEST ACTRESS OSCAR

The only tie for Best Actress was between Barbra Streisand (USA), honoured for *Funny Girl* (USA, 1968), and Katharine Hepburn (USA), for *The Lion in Winter* (UK, 1968), at the 1969 Academy Awards.

MOST OSCARS WON FOR BEST ACTRESS

With four Best Actress Oscars, Katharine Hepburn (USA) holds the record. She won for *Morning Glory* (USA, 1933), *Guess Who's Coming to Dinner* (USA, 1967), *The Lion in Winter* (UK, 1968) and *On Golden Pond* (USA, 1981).

MOST OSCAR NOMINATIONS FOR AN ACTOR WITHOUT WINNING

Both Richard Burton (UK) and Peter O'Toole (Rep. of Ireland) have been nominated seven times for the Best Actor award, but neither has won. Richard Burton's span lasted 25 years: the first nomination was in 1953 for *My Cousin Rachel* (USA, 1952) and the last for *Equus* (UK, 1977) in 1978. Peter O'Toole's no-win span has so far lasted 20 years, from a nomination for *Lawrence of Arabia* (UK, 1962) in 1973 to one for *My Favourite Year* (USA, 1982) in 1983. In 2003 he was presented with an Honorary Award.

MOST OSCARS FOR BEST SUPPORTING ACTOR

Walter Brennan (USA) won three Oscars for Best Actor in a Supporting Role, for *Come and Get It* (USA, 1936), *Kentucky* (USA, 1938) and *The Westerner* (USA, 1940). He also gained a fourth nomination in the same category for *Sergeant York* (USA, 1941).

MOST OSCARS WON FOR BEST SUPPORTING ACTRESS

The record is shared by two actresses: Shelley Winters (USA), who won Oscars for her roles in *The Diary of Anne Frank* (USA, 1959) and *A Patch of Blue* (USA, 1965); and Dianne Weist (USA), who won for *Hannah and Her Sisters* (USA, 1986) and *Bullets Over Broadway* (USA, 1994).

YOUNGEST OSCAR WINNER

The youngest Oscar winner is Tatum O'Neal (USA) who was 10 years 148 days on 2 April 1974 when she received the Best Supporting Actress award for *Paper Moon* (USA, 1973).

In 1934 Shirley Temple (USA) was awarded an honorary Oscar for her achievements at the age of 6 years 310 days.

YOUNGEST BEST ACTOR OSCAR WINNER

Richard Dreyfuss (b. 29 October 1947, USA) won the Best Actor Oscar on 13 April 1978, aged 29 years 166 days, for his performance as Elliot Garfield in *The Goodbye Girl* (USA, 1977).

YOUNGEST BEST ACTRESS OSCAR WINNER

Marlee Matlin (b. 24 August 1965, USA) won the Best Actress award on 31 March 1987, aged 21 years 219 days, for her role as Sarah Norman in *Children of a Lesser God* (USA, 1986)

MOST TONY AND OSCAR AWARD WINS FOR THE SAME ROLE

A total of eight performers have won the Tony and the Oscar for the same role: José Ferrer (USA) in the title role of *Cyrano de Bergerac* (Tony in 1947 and the Oscar in 1950); Shirley Booth (USA) in *Come Back, Little Sheba* (1950/1953); Yul Brynner (Russia) in *The King and I* (1952/1956); Rex Harrison (UK) in *My Fair Lady* (1957/1964); Anne Bancroft (USA) in *The Miracle Worker* (1960/1962); Paul Schofield (UK) in *A Man for All Seasons* (1962/1966); and Joel Grey (USA) in *Cabaret* (1967/1973). The American Theatre Wing's Tony Awards are given in recognition of achievement in a theatre performance. The Tony was named after Broadway actress and director Antoinette Perry (USA, d. 1946).

« HIGHEST ANNUAL EARNINGS FOR A FILM ACTRESS

The world's top-earning actress is currently Cameron Diaz (USA, left) who earned an estimated $40 million (£26.7 million) in 2001, according to the 2002 Forbes Celebrity 100 list.

AT THE MOVIES

THE GOOD
The grooviest movie of the summer has a secret, baby!
AUSTIN POWERS IN
GOLDMEMBER

HIGHEST OPENING WEEKEND BOX-OFFICE GROSS FOR A COMEDY

Austin Powers in Goldmember (USA, 2002), starring Mike Myers (Canada, in the poster above as Austin Powers), opened at 3,613 cinemas in the USA on 26 July 2002, taking $71.5 million (£45.7 million) over its first three days. In comparison, the original 'Austin' debuted with $9.5 million (£5.7 million) in May 1997 and the first sequel opened at $54.92 million (£33.14 million) in June 1999.

LARGEST CURRENT CINEMA ATTENDANCE

In India, 1999 figures show cinema admissions reaching 3.1 billion, over twice as much as the USA, which in 2001 had 1.48 billion admissions. In third place is France, with 185.4 million admissions in 2001. The largest cinema audience ever in one given year was 4.49 billion in the USA in 1929.

CINEMA COMPLEX WITH MOST SCREENS

The largest cinema multiplexes have 30 screens and are known within the industry as 'megaplexes'. There are currently around a dozen such complexes in the world, operated by several cinema companies, mostly in North America and Western Europe. The first megaplex theatre (defined as 16 screens or more) – an AMC Grand - opened in May 1995 in Dallas, Texas, USA.

LARGEST CINEMA BY SEATING CAPACITY

The Roxy, on 7th Avenue and 50th Street, New York City, USA, was built at a cost of $12 million (then £2.4 million) and had an original seating capacity of 6,214 when it opened on 11 March 1927. It employed 16 projectionists, an orchestra of 110 musicians led by four conductors, and three organists who played simultaneously on Kimball organ consoles rising from the orchestra pit. It closed on 29 March 1960 and was demolished later that year.

The largest cinema in the world today by seating capacity is the Radio City Music Hall, New York City, USA, which opened on 27 December 1932 with 5,945 (now 5,910) seats.

LARGEST CINEMA COMPLEX BY SEATS

Kinepolis Madrid, which opened in Madrid, Spain, on 17 September 1998, is the world's largest cinema complex, with a seating capacity of 9,200 in its 25 screens, which each seat between 211 and 996 people.

OLDEST CONTINUOUSLY RUNNING CINEMA

The Duke of York's Cinema in Brighton, East Sussex, UK, has been running continuously as a cinema since it first opened as The Duke of York Premier Picture House on 22 September 1910. When new, it seated an audience of 800 but it only seats 330 today.

OLDEST PURPOSE-BUILT CINEMA IN OPERATION

The oldest purpose-built cinema still in operation is the Electric on Portobello Road in London, UK. It first opened on 24 February 1911 as a 600-seater. It was closed in the 1980s but re-opened on 22 February 2001 with a seating capacity of 240.

OLDEST DRIVE-IN CINEMA

The oldest drive-in cinema still in operation is Shankweiler's Drive-in Theater, Orefield, Pennsylvania, USA, which has opened for every season (April to September) since 15 April 1934. It was only the second drive-in cinema to open in the USA and then held 275 cars. It now has a 300-car capacity.

FIRST DRIVE-IN CINEMA

The first patent for the Drive-in Theater (US Patent no. 1909537) was issued on 16 May 1933 to Richard Hollingshead (USA). He opened the first drive-in on 6 June 1933 on a 400-car site in Camden, New Jersey, USA. The film shown was *Wife Beware* (USA, 1933).

EARLIEST PUBLIC SCREENING OF SOUND ON FILM

The earliest showing of a 'talkie' was *The Arsonist,* (Germany/USA, 1922), which was screened at the Alhambra cinema, Berlin, Germany, on 17 September 1922.

LONGEST CINEMATIC RELEASE

Titanic (USA, 1997) stayed in the US movie charts from 19 December 1997 to 25 September 1998, a duration of 281 days.

WIDEST FILM RELEASE

Heyday Films and Warner Bros' *Harry Potter and the Chamber of Secrets* (USA/Germany 2002) had the widest release of any film in history when it opened on 17 November 2002 in the USA on 8,500 screens (3,682 cinemas).

LONGEST FIRST RUN OF A FILM IN ONE CINEMA

Romance in Lushan (China, 1980) first opened at the Jiangxi Movie Circulation & Screening Company, Lushan, China, on 12 July 1980, and has been shown four times a day ever since. As of 8 December 2001, the film had been seen by 1,336,638 movie-goers.

LONGEST COMMERCIALLY MADE FILM ON GENERAL RELEASE

The Burning of the Red Lotus Temple (China, 1928–31), adapted by the Star Film Co. from the newspaper serial *Strange Tales of the Adventurer in the Wild Country* by Shang K'ai-jan, was released in 18 feature-length parts over a period of three years. Although never shown publicly in its 27-hour entirety, some cinemas put on all-day performances of six parts in sequence.

HIGHEST BOX-OFFICE GROSS FOR AN OPENING DAY

Spider-Man (USA, 2002) took a record $43.6 million (£29.8 million) in box-office receipts on its opening day in the USA on 3 May 2002 and a record-breaking $114.8 million (£78 million) for its opening weekend from a total of 3,615 screens.

MOST VALUABLE FILM POSTER

A one-sheet poster for the Universal film *The Mummy* (USA, 1932), starring Boris Karloff (UK), sold for $453,500 (then £282,431) at Sotheby's, New York, USA, on 1 March 1997. The sale of this poster surpassed the previous high of $198,000 for a *Frankenstein* (USA, 1931) one-sheet in 1993.

FIRST IN-FLIGHT MOVIE

The first in-flight movie was First National's *The Lost World* (USA, 1925), shown during an Imperial Airways flight in a converted Handley-Page bomber, from London, UK, to Paris, France, in April 1925.

FASTEST BOX-OFFICE GROSS OF $100 MILLION

Spider-Man (USA, 2002, above) opened on 3 May 2002 at 3,615 cinemas. It passed the $100 million (£62.244 million) mark faster than any other movie, in just three days.

LARGEST DRIVE-IN CINEMA

The largest drive-in cinema measured by capacity was the All-Weather Drive-In (left) of Copiague, New York, USA. It had space for 2,500 cars plus an indoor 1,200-seat viewing area on its 11.33-ha (28-acre) site. The largest drive-in cinemas by car capacity were the Troy Drive-in, Detroit, Michigan, USA, and the Panther Drive-in, Lufkin, Texas, USA, which were each able to hold 3,000 cars.

STUNTS & SPECIAL EFFECTS

LARGEST 'BREAKAWAY GLASS' STRUCTURE MADE FOR A FILM

Eight panels of 'breakaway glass', each measuring 2.525 x 1.635 x 0.03 m (8 ft 3.5 in x 5 ft 4.5 in x 1.125 in), were built for the stunt sequence in *Die Another Day* (UK/USA, 2002) in which James Bond drives his Aston Martin car through the closed doors of an ice palace (above). Created at Pinewood Studios (UK), each panel weighed 160 kg (352.7 lb) and was made of SMASH! urethane liquid plastic.

MOST PROLIFIC MOVIE STUNTMAN

Vic Armstrong (UK) has doubled for every actor playing James Bond, and in a career spanning three decades has performed stunts in more than 200 films, including *Superman* (USA, 1978) and *Raiders of the Lost Ark* (USA, 1981). He has also coordinated stunts for movies such as *Tomorrow Never Dies* (UK/USA, 1997). Armstrong was awarded the Oscar for Technical Achievement in 2001 for 'the refinement and application to the film industry of the Fan Descender for accurately and safely arresting the descent of stunt persons in high freefalls'.

MOST STUNTS BY A LIVING ACTOR

Jackie Chan, the Hong Kong actor, director, writer, producer and stunt co-ordinator, has appeared in more than 90 films, including *The Big Brawl* (USA, 1980) and *Highbinders* (HK/USA, 2002). He made his debut in *Big and Little Wong Tin Bar* (HK, 1962) at the age of eight. No insurance company will underwrite Chan's productions, in which he performs all his own stunts.

HIGHEST FREE FALL ON FILM

The greatest height from which a stuntman has leaped in a free fall was 335 m (1,100 ft), a stunt performed for *Highpoint* (Canada, 1979) by Dar Robinson (USA) from a ledge at the summit of the CN Tower, Toronto, Canada. His parachute opened just 91 m (300 ft) from the ground after six seconds of free falling.

HIGHEST JUMP WITHOUT A PARACHUTE ON FILM

The highest jump without a parachute by a movie stuntman was 70.71 m (232 ft) by AJ Bakunas (USA) doubling for Burt Reynolds in *Hooper* (USA, 1978). He fell onto an air mattress. A specialist in such dangerous high falls, Bakunas tragically died on 9 September 1980 doing a stunt for the film *Steel* (USA, 1980).

HIGHEST SKI BASE JUMP ON FILM

For the pre-title sequence of *The Spy Who Loved Me* (UK, 1977), Rick Sylvester (USA) skied off the edge of a 610-m (2,000-ft) cliff on Asgard Peak, Baffin Island, Canada, before opening his Union Jack round canopy.

HIGHEST BUNGEE JUMP FROM A STRUCTURE IN A MOVIE

James Bond's bungee jump off a dam during the opening sequence of *GoldenEye* (UK/USA, 1995), performed by Wayne Michaels (UK), was a drop of over 220 m (722 ft). The sequence, orchestrated by Michaels, Simon Crane and the Oxford Stunt Factory (all UK), took place at the Verzasca hydroelectric dam in Switzerland. Taking two weeks to prepare, Michaels jumped from a suspended platform to avoid banging into the steel-peg-studded face of the dam.

MOST EXPENSIVE AERIAL STUNT

Simon Crane (UK) performed one of the most dangerous ever aerial stunts when he moved between two jets at an altitude of 4,572 m (15,000 ft) for *Cliffhanger* (USA, 1993). The stunt, performed only once because it was so risky, cost a record $1 million (£568,000). Sylvester Stallone (USA), the film's star, is said to have offered to reduce his fee by the same amount to ensure that the stunt was made.

LARGEST CO-ORDINATOR OF FILMED AERIAL STUNTS

Flying Pictures of Surrey, UK, has planned and co-ordinated aerial stunts for more than 200 feature films, including *Cliffhanger* (USA, 1993) and *GoldenEye* (UK/USA, 1995), as well as co-ordinating stunts for hundreds of television shows and commercials.

LONGEST LEAP IN A CAR

The longest leap in a car propelled by its own engine was performed by stunt driver Gary Davis (USA) in *Smokey and the Bandit II* (USA, 1980). Davis raced a stripped-down Plymouth at 128 km/h (80 mph) up a ramp placed against the back of a double-tiered car carrier and described a trajectory of 49.6 m (163 ft) before landing safely on the desert floor.

LONGEST SPEEDBOAT JUMP IN A MOVIE

A stunt sequence by Jerry Comeaux (USA) in *Live and Let Die* (UK, 1973), in which James Bond is chased through a Louisiana bayou in a Glastron GT-150 speedboat and leaps over a road, set a then world-record distance of 36.5 m (120 ft).

LARGEST CAR PILE-UP ON FILM

The climax of the film *Blues Brothers 2000* (USA,1998) is marked by a car chase resulting in a pile-up that involves 50 cars. The crash sequence lasts just over two minutes but took four months to film.

LARGEST FILM STUNT EXPLOSION

An explosion staged for the movie *Blown Away* (USA, 1994) on 24 September 1993 incorporated a scuttled ship beside an old wharf in East Boston, USA, filled with 2,727 litres (600 gal) of fuel and 32 bombs each weighing 453 g (16 oz). The explosion lasted nine seconds.

MOST EXPENSIVE EXPLOSION SEQUENCE IN A MOVIE

An explosion sequence involving the destruction of six ships during the bombing scene at the end of the film *Pearl Harbor* (USA, 2001) cost $5.5 million (then £3,850,000). The blast used 700 sticks of dynamite, 610 m (2,000 ft) of primer cord and 18,185 litres (4,000 gal) of gasoline.

HIGHEST SPECIAL-EFFECTS BUDGET

A total of $6.5 million (then £2,246,023) was budgeted for the special effects in *2001: A Space Odyssey* (UK/USA, 1968), which represented over 60% of the total production cost of $10.5 million (then £3,628,191). At today's exchange rates, this figure is more like $33.1 million (£23 million).

MOST COMPUTER-GENERATED EFFECTS IN A MOVIE

The film *Pleasantville* (USA, 1998, right) had 1,700 digital visual-effect shots, compared with the average Hollywood film, which has 50.

LARGEST FILM STUNT BUDGET

More than $3 million (then £1.87 million) of the $200-million (then £125-million) budget for *Titanic* (USA, 1997) went towards stunts.

LARGEST CAMERA CRANE USED ON A FILM

To be able to cover all angles of the 236.22-m-long (775-ft) set of the film *Titanic* (USA, 1997), an Akela Crane with a normal reach of 24.38 m (80 ft) was adapted to have an expanded reach of almost 61 m (200 ft). A gyro-stabilized camera was then mounted on the crane basket and the crane was moved along the side of the set on tracks.

MOST DIGITAL ARTISTS ON A FILM

Sony Pictures Imageworks (USA) had a team of 200 visual-effect artists working on *Spider-Man* (USA, 2002). During the 121 minutes of film, 450 digital shots were produced.

MOST OSCARS WON FOR VISUAL EFFECTS

Dennis Muren (USA) won a total of six Oscars for Visual Effects between 1983 and 1994. He also won a Technical Achievement Award in 1982 and two Special Achievement Awards: one in 1981 for *Star Wars: Episode V – The Empire Strikes Back* (USA, 1980) and another in 1984 for *Star Wars: Episode VI – Return of the Jedi* (USA, 1983).

MOST DEVELOPED DIGITAL CHARACTER ON FILM

The character Gollum (left) in *The Lord of the Rings: The Two Towers* (NZ/USA, 2002) was created by WETA Digital (NZ) to have 250 facial expressions and 300 moving muscles. His body movements were based on those of the actor Andy Serkis (UK), who, to facilitate the creation of the computer graphics, was filmed wearing both a body stocking and a motion-capture suit for every scene in which Gollum appears.

ALL-TIME BEST SELLING BOOK

Excluding non-copyright works such as the Bible and the Koran, the world's all-time best selling book is *Guinness World Records* (formerly *The Guinness Book of Records*). Since it was first published in October 1955, global sales in some 37 languages have exceeded 94,767,083 copies (to 30 June 2002).

MOST SYNDICATED COMIC STRIP

'Garfield' (right), created by Jim Davis (USA) and circulated by Universal Press Syndicate, is the world's most syndicated comic strip, appearing in 2,570 journals throughout the world.

BEST SELLING DIARY

The Diary of Anne Frank (1947) has sold more than 25 million copies worldwide and has been translated into 67 languages. It is the true autobiographical account of events that took place whilst the Frank family hid in an attic in Amsterdam, The Netherlands, to escape Nazi persecution during World War II.

BEST SELLING WORK OF NON-FICTION

Although it is impossible to obtain exact figures, there is little doubt that the Bible is the world's best selling and most widely distributed book. A survey by the Bible Society concluded that around 2.5 billion copies were printed between 1815 and 1975, but more recent estimates put the number at more than 5 billion.

BEST SELLING CHILDREN'S BOOK SERIES IN A SINGLE YEAR

In 1999 the *Harry Potter* series by JK Rowling (UK) sold more than 18.5 million copies in the USA and over 4.5 million copies in the UK and Commonwealth. In the same year, Rowling became the first novelist to have three titles occupying the top four slots (both hardback and paperback) of the *New York Times* bestseller list for 16 weeks (*Harry Potter and the Philosopher's Stone, Harry Potter and the Chamber of Secrets* and *Harry Potter and the Prisoner of Azkaban*). The first title hit the bestseller list on 27 September 1999 and was still there in April 2000. The second and third books in the series both debuted at number one on the list and by April 2000 were still in the top five.

BEST SELLING AUTHOR

The world's best selling fiction writer is the late Agatha Christie (UK), whose 78 crime novels have sold an estimated two billion copies in 44 languages. She also wrote 19 plays and penned six romantic novels under the pseudonym Mary Westmacott. Annual royalty earnings from her works are estimated to be in the millions.

FASTEST SELLING BOOKER PRIZE-WINNING NOVEL

In 1993, on the day after the Booker Prize was announced, Roddy Doyle's (Republic of Ireland) winning novel *Paddy Clarke Ha Ha Ha* sold 27,000 copies in hardback within half an hour of bookshops opening.

MOST BOOKER PRIZE NOMINATIONS

Iris Murdoch (UK) was nominated for the Booker Prize six times over 18 years for *The Nice and the Good* (1969), *Bruno's Dream* (1970), *The Black Prince* (1973), *The Good Apprentice* (1985) and *The Book and the Brotherhood* (1987). She won in 1978 with *The Sea, the Sea*. Both JM Coetzee (South Africa) and Peter Carey (Australia) have won a record two Booker Prizes.

LARGEST ADVANCE FOR A NON-FICTION BOOK

Former US President Bill Clinton (USA) sold the worldwide publishing rights to his memoirs to Alfred A Knopf Inc. (USA) for an advance of more than $10 million (£7.1 million) – the largest ever advance for a non-fiction book.

LONGEST NOVEL

A la Recherche du Temps Perdu (*Remembrance of Things Past*) by Marcel Proust (France) contains an estimated 9,609,000 characters (every letter and space counts as one character). Proust produced the first volume of his 13-volume masterpiece in 1912 (it was first published in 1913). His second volume won international awards as soon as it was published. This long novel explores the power of the unconscious and the nature of writing itself.

LARGEST ENCYCLOPAEDIA

The largest encyclopaedia in current use is *The Arabic Legislations Encyclopaedia* compiled by Mohamed Abu Baker Ben Younis (Libya). Its 164,000 pages are contained in 200 volumes weighing 420 kg (925 lb). The general index is contained in a further six volumes and there are also additional annexes. It claims to contain every piece of legislation from all Arab countries.

LARGEST BOOK

The *Super Book* measures 2.74 x 3.07 m (9 ft x 10 ft 0.84 in) and weighs 252.6 kg (557 lb). Consisting of 300 pages, it was published in Denver, Colorado, USA, in 1976.

LARGEST POP-UP BOOK

The largest pop-up book is a revised edition of *Aesop's Fables* (right) measuring 122 x 76 cm (48 x 30 in) and weighing 13 kg (28.5 lb). The book was designed by Roger Culbertson (USA) using the original illustrations by Peter de Sève (USA). Published in 1993, the original book was 10 x 6 cm (4 x 2.5 in). It is now out of print.

LARGEST DICTIONARY

Deutsches Wörterbuch (German Dictionary), begun in 1854 by German brothers Jacob and Wilhelm Grimm (best known for their collection of fairy tales), was completed in 1971 and consists of 34,519 pages in 33 volumes. It is available as a special order at Amazon.com for $1,695 (£1,200).

EARLIEST CARTOON STRIP

The first cartoon strip ever printed was 'The Yellow Kid', which first appeared in the *New York Journal* on 18 October 1896. He was a New York character who excelled at making fun of upper-class customs and who wore a characteristic yellow gown. Although it was the first comic strip to be published, single satirical cartoons had been published in journals for many years.

LONGEST RUNNING COMIC BOOK

The Dandy comic has been published by DC Thomson & Co. (UK) continuously since its first edition on 4 December 1937. The weekly comic's best known character is Desperate Dan, an unshaven cowboy whose favourite food is cow pie. The only time publication varied from its weekly schedule was during World War II, when it was published fortnightly.

MAGAZINE WITH THE LARGEST CIRCULATION

Parade, the syndicated colour magazine, is distributed with 330 newspapers across the USA every Sunday and currently has a circulation of around 35.9 million. It has a readership of 77.6 million and in 2001 had advertising revenues of $570 million (£400 million). *Parade*'s first issue was published on 31 May 1941 with an initial print run of 125,000 copies.

LARGEST WEEKLY MAGAZINE SALES

In 1974 the US *TV Guide* became the first weekly periodical to sell a billion copies in a year. It has the highest circulation of any weekly magazine with 11.8 million copies per week and an estimated reach of 35 million readers.

MOST TRANSLATED DOCUMENT

A six-page document entitled *Universal Declaration of Human Rights*, produced by the United Nations (UN) in 1948, has been translated into 321 languages and dialects from Abkhaz to Zulu. The revelations after the horrors of World War II prompted the newly formed UN to produce a document in recognition 'of the inherent dignity and of the equal and inalienable rights of the human family' and to guarantee peace, justice, dignity, respect, tolerance, equality and freedom to all individuals.

MOST LETTERS TO EDITORS PUBLISHED IN ONE YEAR

Ehud Buch (Israel, left) had 131 of his letters published by four prominent Israeli national newspapers – namely *Ma'ariv*, *Yediot Achronot*, *Ha'aretz* and *Globes* – during the year 2001.

TV SHOWS & PEOPLE

LONGEST TIME IN SAME TV SERIES ROLE

The record for the longest time playing the same role in a television series is held by William Roache (UK). He has been playing the character Ken Barlow in ITV's *Coronation Street* continuously since the first episode of the British soap on 9 December 1960. The character was first seen as a student and since then has had three wives and numerous girlfriends, been a newspaper editor and a teacher, and survived a suicide attempt.

MOST ENDURING TV PRESENTER

The monthly *Sky at Night* (BBC, UK) has been presented by Patrick Moore (UK) without a break or a miss since 24 April 1957. By December 2002 a total of 600 shows had been broadcast. This makes the *Sky At Night* the world's longest running TV programme with the same presenter.

MOST TV VARIETY SHOWS HOSTED BY THE SAME PRESENTER

As of 5 April 2002 the record for the highest number of live variety TV shows hosted by the same presenter is 5,000. Fuji Television Network Inc.'s (Japan) *Waratte Iitomo!* has been hosted by Kazuyoshi Morita, aka Tamori (Japan), since its first episode on 4 October 1982.

LONGEST CAREER AS A CARTOON VOICE-OVER ARTIST

In its first few weeks, the original cinema series *Popeye* was voiced by William Costello (USA), but in 1934, for the film *Let You and Him Fight* (USA), Jack Mercer (USA) took over the role, and continued in it for the next 45 years and 294 productions – also recording the voice-overs for the TV cartoons.

MOST ENDURING COMMERCIAL STARS

The PG Tips tea advertising campaign starring chimpanzees began in December 1956, the second year of commercial television in the UK. Since the first instalment (voiced by Peter Sellers, UK) was televised, the campaign ran to more than 100 adverts, with the final one made in 1994. The chimpanzees, who are said to have earned more than £1,000 ($1,530) each per commercial, have a retirement fund set up by the company. PG Tips teabags came on the market in 1930.

MOST PROLIFIC TV SCRIPTWRITER

The most prolific television writer in the world was Ted (later Lord) Willis (UK), whose total output since 1942 is estimated to be 20 million words. From 1949 until his death in 1992 he wrote 41 TV series, including the first seven years and 2.25 million words of *Dixon of Dock Green*, which ran on BBC television (UK) from 1955 to 1976. He also wrote 37 stage plays and 39 feature films.

MOST CELEBRITIES FEATURED IN A CARTOON TV SERIES

Since first appearing in 1987 as a series of 30-second spots produced by Matt Groening (USA) for the FOX network's *The Tracey Ullman Show* (USA), *The Simpsons* cartoon series has featured 340 guests as of episode 300, 'Barting Over'. Celebrities have included Barry White, Elizabeth Taylor, Britney Spears and U2.

HIGHEST ANNUAL EARNINGS FOR A TV NEWS BROADCASTER

The world's highest paid TV news broadcaster is Katie Couric (USA), who earns $13 million (£8 million) per year as the host of NBC's *Today* (USA) news programme. She signed a 4.5-year contract in December 2001 that is reported to be worth $65 million (£40 million). Katie overtook fellow newsreader Barbara Walters (USA) on the *Forbes* list of 2002.

« HIGHEST PAID TV GUEST STAR

The world record for the highest amount paid to an actor to guest star on a TV show is £500,000 ($765,900), paid to Matthew Perry (USA, left) for appearing in an episode of *Ally McBeal* (FOX, USA). In the 2-hour show, broadcast on 15 April 2002, Perry played the character of Todd Merrick. The record is based on money earned per minute.

MOST PRIME-TIME EMMY AWARD NOMINATIONS IN A SEASON

The world record for the most Prime-time Emmy Award nominations in a season is 23, for HBO's *Six Feet Under* (USA, right) in 2002. *Six Feet Under* is a dark comedy-drama series about brothers running a funeral home.

HIGHEST EARNINGS BY A CHILD TV ACTOR

The child TV actors with the highest earnings are the twins Mary-Kate and Ashley Olsen (USA). Their TV career began when they were just 9 months old when they appeared in *Full House* (ABC, USA). By the age of 9 they could command a total of £56,000 ($79,000) per episode. Now aged 17, they are currently staring in ABC Family Channel's *So Little Time*.

HIGHEST PAID TV ACTOR PER EPISODE

Kesley Grammer (USA) was paid a salary of $1.6 million (£1.1 million) per show for playing psychoanalyst Frasier Crane in the 2002–03 series of *Frasier* (NBC, USA). Grammer is also executive producer on the show and on occasion has directed episodes.

HIGHEST-PAID TV DRAMA ACTOR PER EPISODE

The world's highest-paid actor in a TV drama series is Noah Wyle (USA), who will earn approximately $400,000 (£258,530) per episode of *ER* (NBC, USA) for the 2003–04 series. Wyle plays the character of the head doctor, Dr John Carter.

HIGHEST EARNINGS FOR AN ACTRESS FOR A CURRENT TV SERIES

Jennifer Aniston, Lisa Kudrow and Courteney Cox Arquette (all USA), who have played the female leads in NBC's *Friends* (USA) since 1994, were earning $1 million (£703,330) each per episode of the 2002/03 series. At the time of going to press the series was still running. There are typically 24 episodes in a series, meaning that each of the actresses will earn $24 million (£16.88 million) overall.

MOST EMMY AWARDS WON BY A TV SERIES IN A SEASON

NBC's (USA) drama series *The West Wing*, which is set behind the scenes at the White House, won a record nine awards for a single season at the 52nd Annual Prime-time Emmy Awards held on 9 and 10 September 2000.

MOST AWARDS WON BY A TV COMMERCIAL

The international commercial that has won the most awards is the 1995 Levi 'Drugstore' 501 jeans television advertisement, which won a total of 33 awards. It was directed by Michel Gondry (France) who won a Lion D'Or for this at Cannes in 1994.

FIRST VIRTUAL TV PRESENTER

The world's first virtual TV presenter is Maddy, who on 27 March 2002 co-presented *Tomorrow's World* (BBC, UK) for the first time and in real-time alongside the human presenters. Maddy was created by Digital Animations Group, Glasgow, UK.

MOST TV QUIZ APPEARANCES BY A CONTESTANT

Since March 1986 Marc Vanacker, of Kortrijk-Heule, Belgium, has appeared on an impressive 29 television quiz shows, broadcast in Belgium, Germany, The Netherlands and the UK. As a result of appearing on these shows, which included *Going for Gold* (Grundy Television), *Risiko* (ZDF) and *Einstein* (NCRV), he won BFr 1,520,326, (£23,721 or $ 34,577), trips to the USA, Paris and Vienna, a car, and two encyclopaedias.

MOST TV LINKS HIJACKED BY A CAMPAIGNER

As of 28 March 2002 the record for the most television links hijacked is 16,335 and belongs to Gabriele Paolini (Italy). He regularly sabotages presenter links on national TV in Italy, encouraging the use of condoms as part of his personal battle against the spread of the disease AIDS.

LONGEST WORKING CAREER OF A TV NATURALIST

The longest working career as a writer and presenter of TV nature programmes belongs to Sir David Attenborough (UK, right), whose first series, *Zoo Quest* (BBC), was broadcast in 1954. He most recently presented the BBC's *The Life of Mammals* in 2003.

LARGEST MUSIC TV NETWORK

MTV is beamed into 340 million households in 140 countries around the globe, which means it can be seen by one in three of the world's total TV audience. MTV began broadcasting in the USA in 1981. The most watched and highest rated show in the history of MTV is *The Osbournes*, a 'reality TV' show that follows the bizarre real life of rock star Ozzy Osbourne (UK) and his family (above).

LONGEST RUNNING CHILDREN'S MAGAZINE PROGRAMME

Blue Peter, the BBC's (UK) magazine programme for children, was first transmitted from London's Lime Grove Studios on 16 October 1958 and is still broadcast today. Originally presented by Christopher Trace and Leila Williams (both UK), it has so far seen 29 presenters, the longest serving being John Noakes (1965–78). As of 28 March 2003, 3,682 shows have been broadcast.

LONGEST RUNNING REALITY TV SHOW

The world's longest running reality TV show is *The Real World*, which first aired on MTV (USA) in May 1992. The series follows the lives of seven strangers living together for six months. The first series was set in Chicago, USA. The show is now in its 12th season and set in Las Vegas. This 'live soap-opera' style of television, in which cameras have no limits, led to many other shows, including *Survivor*, *Big Brother* and *The Osbournes*.

LONGEST RUNNING TV DRAMA

Procter & Gamble Productions' *Guiding Light* (USA), which was first aired on CBS on 30 June 1952, and is currently aired each weekday, is the longest running TV drama. Originally a 15-minute radio serial on WLW Radio in Cincinnati, USA, it was first broadcast on 25 January 1937. The show celebrated its 50th anniversary in June 2002.

LONGEST RUNNING PRIME-TIME ANIMATED SERIES

The Simpsons, created by cartoonist Matt Groening (USA), is the longest running prime-time animated television show, with 300 episodes having been aired on the FOX network (USA) as of 16 February 2003. *The Simpsons* originally featured as a series of 30-second spots for FOX's *The Tracey Ullman Show* in 1987. After 50 cartoons were aired on the show, Groening was offered his own series, which premiered as a half-hour Christmas special on 17 December 1989 and began as a regular series on 14 January 1990. The show has won 17 Emmy awards and is watched in over 70 countries worldwide. It is also the longest running prime-time series still releasing new episodes.

MOST WATCHED TV NETWORK

The state-owned station China Central Television (CCTV) is transmitted to 90% of all Chinese viewers in China. It is estimated that more than 1.1 billion people have access to television in China. The total broadcasting time of its 12 channels each day is 240 hours, in Mandarin, Fujian dialect and English. The single most watched show is the daily *Xin Wen Lian Bo* news programme, which attracts 315 million viewers.

LARGEST TV AUDIENCE FOR A WEDDING

On 29 July 1981 the marriage of HRH Prince Charles to Lady Diana Spencer was seen by an estimated 750 million people in 74 countries. At the time the largest outside broadcast in British history, it had an audience in the UK of 39 million.

LARGEST TV AUDIENCE FOR A SERIES

At its peak of popularity, *Baywatch* (USA) was the most widely viewed TV series in the world ever, with an estimated weekly audience of more than 1.1 billion in 142 countries in 1996. Shown in every continent bar Antarctica, the show has since been seen in 148 countries and translated into 44 languages.

LONGEST RUNNING TV CHAT SHOW

NBC's *The Tonight Show* (USA) was first aired on 27 September 1954. In 1992 the show was renamed *The Tonight Show With Jay Leno*, and has been hosted continually since then by Jay Leno (USA), pictured below with guest Steve Irwin (Australia). Although the show's name and presenters have changed over the years, the essential format of late-night celebrtity interviews, with the presenter behind a desk has remained the same.

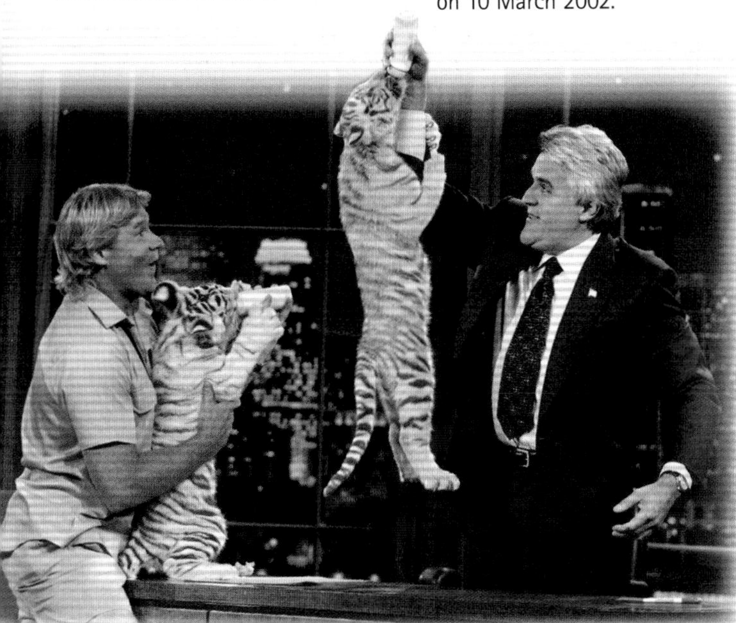

LARGEST TV AUDIENCE FOR A LIVE BROADCAST

The broadcast of the funeral of Diana, Princess of Wales (1961–97) on 6 September 1997 had the largest worldwide audience for a live broadcast with 2.5 billion viewers. The event was simultaneously shown by six television stations in the UK as well as by many other stations around the world.

LARGEST TV AUDIENCE FOR A COMEDY PROGRAMME

The final episode of the US TV comedy series *Seinfeld*, starring Jerry Seinfeld (USA), was screened on 14 May 1998 and attracted 108 million viewers. Described commonly as being about nothing in particular, the show offered weekly vignettes from the lives of four New Yorkers.

LARGEST AUDIENCE FOR A TV DOCUMENTARY

The world's highest audience for a TV documentary is 39 million, for CBS's (USA) programme *9/11* about the 11 September 2001 terrorist attacks in America, which was shown in the USA on 10 March 2002.

MOST SUCCESSFUL TV SOAP

The American TV series *Dallas* began quietly in 1978 with just five episodes. By 1980, it was watched by an estimated 83 million Americans, giving it a then record 76% share of the television audience. It was also seen in more than 90 other countries, often in locally dubbed versions.

LARGEST NUMBER OF TV PROGRAMME EPISODES SOLD

The greatest number of episodes from one TV programme ever sold was 1,144 episodes of *Coronation Street* sold by Granada Television (UK) to CBKST (Canada) on 31 May 1971. This constituted 20 days 15 hr 44 min of continuous viewing.

LONGEST TV TALK-SHOW MARATHON

The world record for the longest TV talk-show marathon is 30 hours, held by Vador Lladó (Spain) of Flaix TV, who continually interviewed and presented from 3 to 4 May 2002 in Barcelona, Spain.

DEEPEST LIVE TV BROADCAST BY A PRESENTER

The world's deepest underwater live TV broadcast was presented by Alastair Fothergill (UK) at a depth of 2.4 km (1.5 miles) on the BBC's *Abyss Live*. The dive was broadcast on 29 September 2002 from inside a MIR submersible off the east coast of the USA.

LONGEST TV DOCUMENTARY ON A SINGLE SUBJECT

The six-part documentary film series *7 Up* shown on ITV (UK) has followed, every seven years, the lives of 14 children who were selected in 1963 at the age of seven from different social groups in the UK. The first film in the series, *7 Up* (1963), was followed by *7 times 7* (1970) which filmed the children aged 14, and by a further four instalments so far. The most recent was *42 Up* (1998).

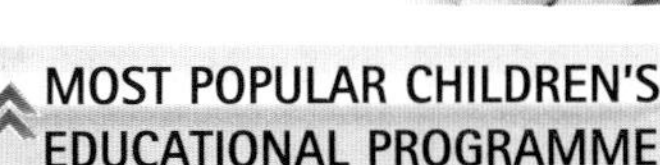

MOST POPULAR CHILDREN'S EDUCATIONAL PROGRAMME

Sesame Street (above), produced since 10 November 1969 by the Children's Television Workshop, New York, USA, is sold to 180 countries around the world. *Sesame Street* was created as an experiment in 1968, designed to use the medium of television to reach and teach preschoolers. *Sesame Street* has received the most Emmys in television history.

MOST EXPENSIVE TV PROGRAMME

In January 1998 Warner Brothers (USA), the makers of the hospital drama *ER* – America's number one prime-time show, with a then weekly audience of 33 million – agreed to a three-year deal with NBC (USA), who paid a record $13.1 million (£8.2 million) per episode for 22 of the one-hour shows.

MOST EXPENSIVE TV DOCUMENTARY SERIES PER MINUTE

Depicting how dinosaurs lived, reproduced and became extinct, the BBC's (UK) documentary series *Walking with Dinosaurs* (1999) cost over £37,654 ($61,112) per minute to produce. The six-part series took over two years to make and cost a total of £6.1 million ($9.9 million).

BRANDS & ADVERTISING

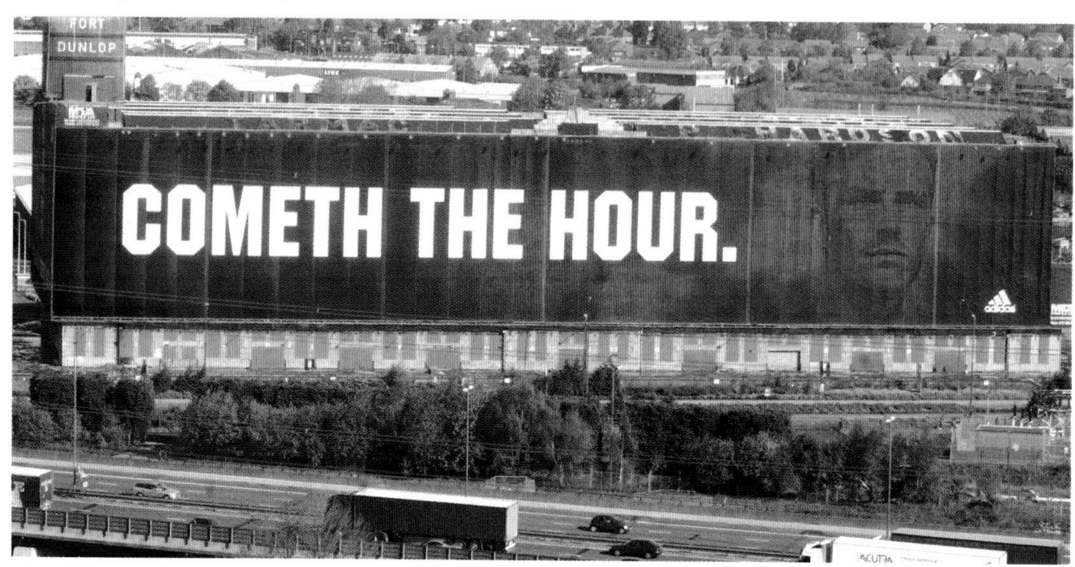

LARGEST ADVERTISING HOARDING

The largest advertising hoarding (left) measures 23.7 m (77.7 ft) high and 132 m (433 ft) long, has a surface area of 3,128.4 m² (33,673.8 ft²) and weighs 2 tonnes (4,400 lb). The hoarding, owned by Mega Profile Ltd (UK), is on the side of Fort Dunlop next to the M6 motorway near Birmingham, West Midlands, UK.

LARGEST GLOBAL BRAND

According to a recent study by leading market research company AC Nielsen, the largest global brand based on sales is Coca-Cola, which in 2002 had sales of over $19 billion (£13 billion). The Coca-Cola Company, which has its global headquarters in Atlanta, Georgia, USA, is the world's foremost manufacturer, marketer, and distributor of non-alcoholic beverage concentrates and syrups, with markets in nearly 200 countries worldwide.

BEST SELLING BRAND OF CLOTHING

Levi Strauss & Co. (USA) is the world's biggest brand-named clothing manufacturer and sells under the Levis, Dockers and Slates brands in more than 30,000 retail outlets in 100 countries. As of November 2002 the company's sales had totalled $4.1 billion (£2.6 billion).

BEST SELLING UNDERWEAR

Marks & Spencer (UK) sells more underwear globally than anyone else, selling 50 million pairs (counting multi-packs as a pair) of their own-brand women's knickers each year alone. The company operates almost 700 stores in some 30 countries worldwide.

LARGEST BRA MANUFACTURER

In 2002 US clothing and food giant Sara Lee controlled 30% of the US bra market. The company, which had total sales of $17,628 million (£11,504 million) and profits of over $1,010 million (£659 million), owns the Wonderbra, Playtex, Berlei and Gossard brands.

EARLIEST EXISTING ADVERTISING

The earliest existing advertisement to be found was discovered in the ruins of Pompeii, near Naples, Italy, and is for a bookseller. It dates from around AD 79.

EARLIEST PUBLIC TV ADVERTISEMENT

The first public TV advertisement ever broadcast was shown on 27 June 1941 on NBC's WNBT station in New York, USA. The advert was for a Bulova watch.

EARLIEST ADVERTISING AGENCY

James White's advertising agency was established in London, UK, in 1800.

MOST EXPENSIVE ADVERTISING CAMPAIGN

The most expensive advertising campaigns are to be found in the pharmaceutical industry. Both Johnson & Johnson-Merck Consumer Pharmaceuticals Co. (USA) and SmithKline Beecham (UK) unleashed $100-million-plus (£62.3 million) marketing campaigns to introduce Pepcid AC and Tagamet HB respectively, which act as acid reducers. The advertising category for heartburn, acid indigestion and sour stomach remedies is worth $1.12 billion (£700 million).

BEST SELLING DESIGNER UNDERWEAR

The most popular designer underwear brand is Calvin Klein (USA, Calvin Klein model Travis, also USA, shown above and right). In 1998 the company sold 30 million pairs of ladies' and gentlemen's briefs with a total retail value of $425 million (£256 million).

MOST EXPENSIVE TV ADVERTISING CAMPAIGN

The most expensive TV advertising campaign cost $8.1 million (£5.7 million) and was produced for Pepsi-Cola (USA) in 2002. The 90-second commercials cost $90,000 (£63,333) per second and starred the pop star Britney Spears (USA). The adverts were first aired during Super Bowl XXXVI, held on 3 February 2002.

LARGEST SIMULTANEOUS TV ADVERT PREMIERE

On 1 November 1999, at 9pm local time, the Ford Motor Company (USA) aired their 2-minute 'Global Anthem' advertisement on over 140 pan-regional or local market networks in 190 countries. The commercial was shot in nine countries and featured singer Charlotte Church (UK) and all seven of Ford's automobile brands.

HIGHEST TV ADVERTISING RATE

The highest TV advertising rate was $2.4 million (£1.6 million), paid for each 30-second slot of NBC network's (USA) prime airtime during the transmission of Super Bowl XXXV on 28 January 2001.

FIRST ADVERTISEMENT FILMED IN SPACE

An advertising campaign for Tnuva Milk, showing cosmonaut Vasily Tsibliyev (Russia) drinking milk aboard the Russian Mir space station, was first broadcast on 22 August 1997.

SHORTEST TV COMMERCIAL

The world's shortest TV commercial is half a frame (one field) long and lasts for $^1/_{60}$ of a second. Twelve different versions of the commercial were produced, all advertising MuchMusic (a Canadian music and video TV channel), and the first was aired on 2 January 2002. The creator, producer and editor of the commercial was Tharanga Ramanayake (Canada).

LARGEST ADVERTISING BUDGET

General Motors Corporation (USA) spent $2,876,242,400, (£1,810,369,345) on advertising within the media industry in 1999, according to marketing information company CMR's report released in March 2000.

LARGEST ADVERT ON A ROOF

A logo for The Big Fresh Company (NZ) measuring 48 m (157 ft 5 in) wide and 145 m (475 ft 8 in) long was put on the roof of the Woolworths Distribution Centre, Manukau City, New Zealand, in March 1998. The sign, with each capital letter measuring 30 m (98 ft 5 in) high, is visible to 2.5 million people annually sitting at window seats in planes landing at and taking off from Auckland Airport.

LARGEST ADVERT ON A BUILDING

An advertisement measuring 4,402 m^2 (47,385 ft^2) was erected on a building next to the M4 motorway near Chiswick, London, UK, to promote international airline Gulf Air. It was displayed during May and June 1995.

LARGEST ILLUMINATED ADVERTISING SIGN

The Las Vegas Hilton Hotel in Nevada, USA, has a sign that is 60 m (197 ft) in length and 10 m (32 ft 10 in) high. Lit by 16,000-W metal-halide projectors, it was constructed by Abudi Signs Industry Ltd at Ramat Gan, Israel.

LONGEST MOVING ADVERTISING BILLBOARD

To launch the South African Broadcasting Corporation's Channel 2 on 11 May 1998, a 268.2-m (880-ft 1-in) billboard covering an area of 1072.19 m^2 (11,541 ft^2) was created along the sides of a train which then travelled between cities in Gauteng province.

LARGEST FREESTANDING ADVERTISING SIGN

The largest and tallest freestanding advertising sign is at the Hilton Hotel and Casino in Las Vegas, Nevada, USA, and was unveiled in November 1996. Its two faces have a total area of 6,512.3 m^2 (70,100 ft^2), and it is 85.03 m (279 ft) high. It also features more than 9.65 km (6 miles) of lights.

BIGGEST SELLING DESIGNER CLOTHING LABEL

The biggest selling designer clothing brand in the world is Ralph Lauren (USA, above) which had annual global sales of $2.3 billion (£1.4 billion) in the 2002 fiscal year. The company has 236 Polo shops worldwide, and also sells its designs through approximately 1,600 department stores and speciality shops.

MUSIC & ENTERTAINMENT

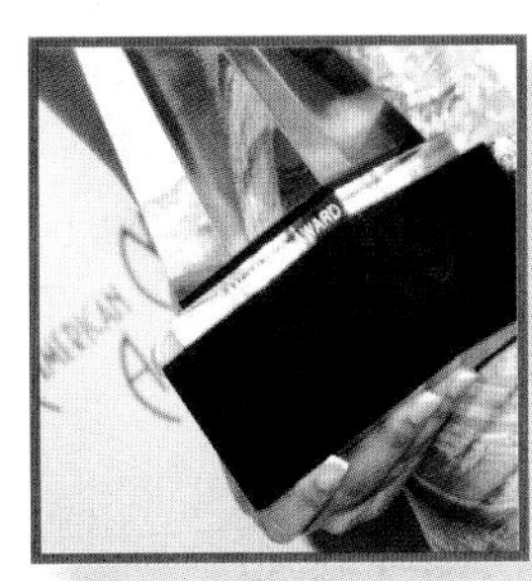

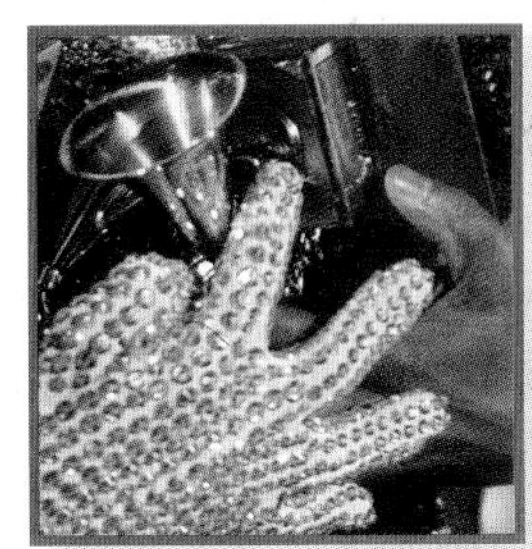

POP MUSIC

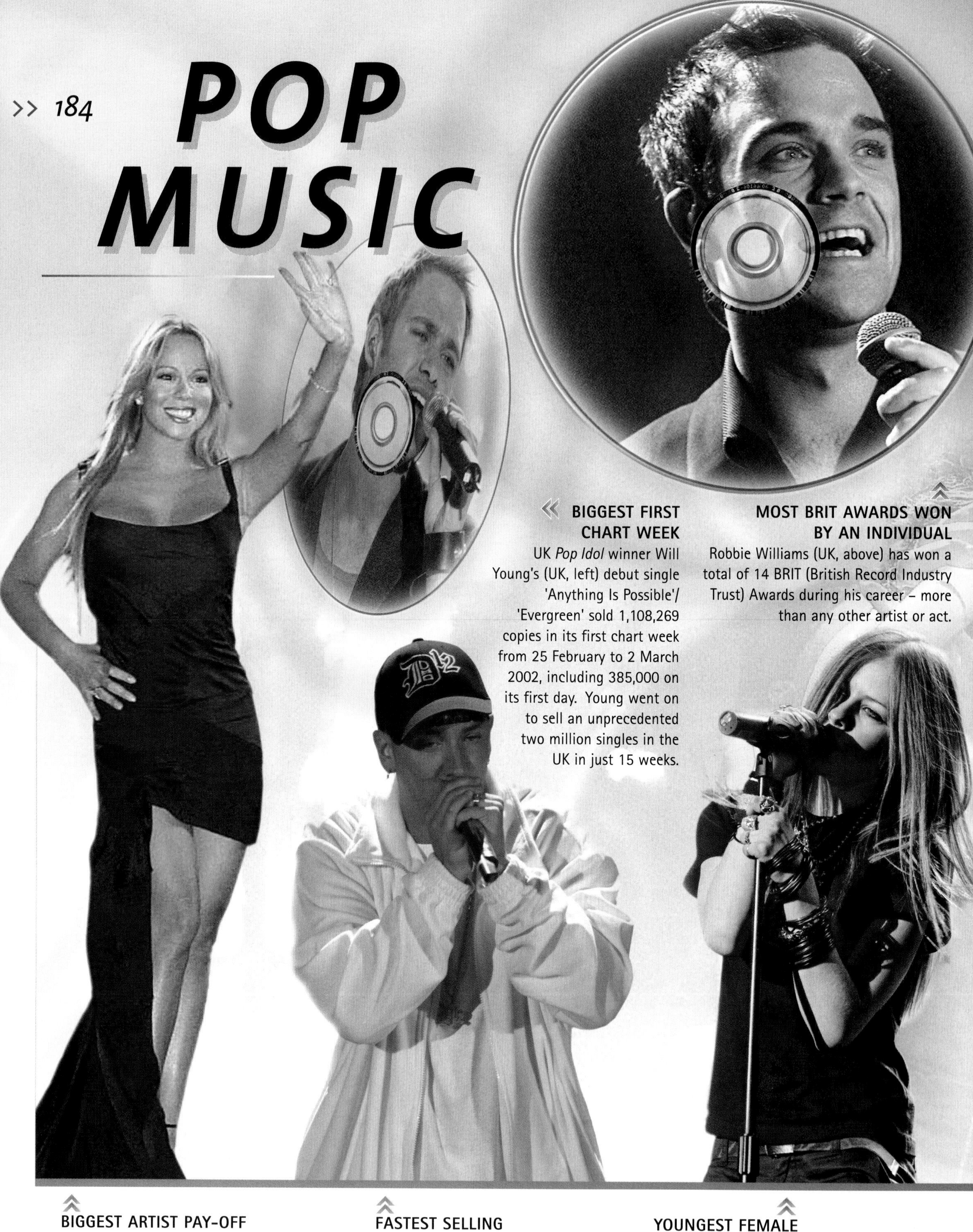

BIGGEST FIRST CHART WEEK

UK *Pop Idol* winner Will Young's (UK, left) debut single 'Anything Is Possible'/ 'Evergreen' sold 1,108,269 copies in its first chart week from 25 February to 2 March 2002, including 385,000 on its first day. Young went on to sell an unprecedented two million singles in the UK in just 15 weeks.

MOST BRIT AWARDS WON BY AN INDIVIDUAL

Robbie Williams (UK, above) has won a total of 14 BRIT (British Record Industry Trust) Awards during his career – more than any other artist or act.

BIGGEST ARTIST PAY-OFF

Mariah Carey (USA, above) received a reported $28-million (£17.3-million) pay-off to end her recording contract with EMI/Virgin (UK) in January 2002. The company lost an estimated $54.3 million (£33.5 million) on the deal.

FASTEST SELLING RAP ARTIST

Eminem's (USA, above) album *The Marshall Mathers LP* sold a record 1.76 million copies in its first week on release in the USA in May 2000.

YOUNGEST FEMALE TO TOP UK ALBUM CHART

Canadian singer/songwriter Avril Lavigne (above, b. 27 September 1984) topped the UK album chart 11 January 2003 when aged 18 years 106 days. The album *Let Go* reached No.1 in its 18th chart week.

« BIGGEST ALBUM ACT IN JAPAN

Utada Hikaru (Japan, left) is the only Japanese act to sell over two million copies of three consecutive albums.

MOST PERFORMERS ON ONE SINGLE

The largest number of people to sing on one single is 275,000 on S Club 7's (UK, above) 'Have You Ever'. The single was released on 19 November 2001 as part of BBC's Children in Need appeal, and features contributions from 3,616 schools in the UK.

YOUNGEST MALE SOLO ARTIST TO ENTER THE UK SINGLES CHART AT NO.1

Gareth Gates (UK, below, b. 12 July 1984) was 17 years 262 days old when his single 'Unchained Melody' entered the chart at No.1 on 30 March 2002.

« MOST SUCCESSFUL REMIX ALBUM

In February 2002 Jennifer Lopez's (USA, left) album *J To Tha Lo!: The Remixes* became the first album solely featuring remixes to top the US charts, with sales over 156,000 in its first week.

POP CLASSICS

MOST GRAMMY AWARDS WON IN A SINGLE YEAR BY AN INDIVIDUAL

The record for the most Grammy Awards won in a year is eight, by Michael Jackson (USA, above) in 1984. He won Best New R&B Song and Best Male R&B Vocal Performance with 'Billie Jean'; Best Male Rock Vocal Performance and Record of the Year with 'Beat It'; and Best Recording for Children with 'E.T. The Extra-Terrestrial'. He also won Album of the Year and Best Male Pop Vocal Performance with *Thriller*, as well as jointly winning Producer of the Year with Quincy Jones (USA).

BIGGEST SELLING GROUP

The Beatles (UK) recorded the greatest sales for any group, with all-time sales estimated by EMI at over one billion discs and tapes to date. In 2001 the band was certified for album sales of 163.5 million in the USA alone.

MOST NO.1 ALBUMS BY A GROUP ON THE US CHARTS

The Beatles (UK) have had a record 19 No.1 albums on the US album charts – more than double that of Elvis Presley (USA) and the Rolling Stones (UK), who have both had nine albums at the top spot.

BIGGEST SELLING ALBUM SERIES

As of November 2002 the *Now!* series was the biggest selling album series with worldwide sales of over 60 million. It was first launched in the UK in 1984, where 52 of the 53 albums released made No.1.

BIGGEST SELLING DEBUT ALBUM

Boston by Boston (USA), released in 1976, has sold over 16 million copies worldwide, making it the best selling debut album of all time.

BIGGEST SELLING ALBUM ON UK CHART

The biggest selling album on the UK chart is *Sgt. Pepper's Lonely Hearts Club Band* by The Beatles (UK), with a reported 4.5 million sales since its release in June 1967.

MOST ALBUMS SIMULTANEOUSLY ON THE US CHARTS

The most albums in the US Top 200 at the same time by the same artist is seven. The Beatles (UK), The Monkees (USA) and U2 (Rep. of Ireland) all share the record.

GREATEST ADVANCE SALES FOR A SINGLE

'Can't Buy Me Love' by The Beatles (UK) had 2.7 million advance orders before its release on 21 March 1964.

FASTEST SELLING ALBUM

The Beatles' (UK) album entitled *1*, released on 13 November 2000, sold a record 13.5 million copies around the world in its first month – 3.6 million on the first day alone. It was No.1 in 35 countries, earning over 100 platinum albums around the globe.

MOST NO.1 ALBUMS BY A MALE SOLOIST ON THE US CHARTS

Elvis Presley (US) had a record nine No.1 solo albums. They were: *Elvis Presley* (1956), *Elvis* (1956), *Loving You* (1957), *Elvis Christmas Album* (1957), *GI Blues* (1960), *Something For Everybody* (1961), *Blue Hawaii* (1961), *Roustabout* (1964) and *Elvis – Aloha From Hawaii* (1973).

MOST CONSECUTIVE UK NO.1 SINGLES

The Beatles (UK) hold the record for the most consecutive No.1 hits. They had 11 in a row between 1963 and 1966 (from 'From Me to You' through to 'Yellow Submarine').

LONGEST TIME ON THE UK SINGLES CHARTS

'My Way' by Frank Sinatra (USA) spent 124 weeks on the UK charts. It entered and re-entered the charts no fewer than 10 times between 2 April 1969 and April 1994.

MOST SUCCESSFUL FAMILY POP GROUP

The Bee Gees – brothers Maurice (1949–2003), Robin and Barry Gibb (all UK, left) – had 24 Top 20 singles in the USA and the UK between 1968 and 2000, plus 13 Top 20 albums in the USA and 12 in the UK, including the best selling film soundtrack ever – *Saturday Night Fever*. They were inducted into the Rock and Roll Hall of Fame in 1996 and won a BRIT award for Lifetime Achievement the following year.

MOST HIT SINGLES ON THE UK CHARTS

Cliff Richard (UK) holds the record for the most UK chart hit singles, with 126 to March 2003.

MOST NO.1 SINGLES ON THE US CHARTS

The Beatles (UK) have had the most No.1 hits on the US singles charts, with 20.

MOST CONSECUTIVE WEEKS ON THE UK SINGLES CHARTS

Elvis Presley (USA) spent the most consecutive weeks on the UK singles charts. His 13 hit singles from 'A Mess of Blues' in 1960 to 'One More Broken Heart for Sale' in 1963 spent an unbroken 144 weeks on the charts.

BIGGEST SELLING SINGLE BY A FEMALE GROUP

The best selling single by a female group is 'Wannabe' by The Spice Girls (UK) in July 1996. It topped the charts in the UK for seven weeks, selling over 1.2 million copies, and hit No.1 in 31 other countries, selling a reported 4 million worldwide.

BIGGEST SELLING CHRISTMAS SONG

The 1942 recording of 'White Christmas' by Bing Crosby (USA) has sold over 100 million units around the world, with about half the sales being singles. The song has been reissued annually since 1942. Its latest chart success was in December 1998, when it charted for four consecutive weeks in the UK, reaching No.29.

MOST HITS BY A SOLO ARTIST

Bing Crosby (USA) started his solo career in 1931 and accumulated 396 chart entries, including 38 No.1s, in the USA alone. During his lifetime he recorded an estimated 2,600 songs.

MOST GRAMMY AWARDS WON BY A SOLO POP PERFORMER

Stevie Wonder (USA) has won 19 Grammy Awards since 1973 including Best Male R&B Vocal Performance six times. Stevie Wonder's career was launched by his first hit, the US No.1 'Fingertips - Part 2' in 1963, and he remains one of pop and soul's top artists.

CITY WITH THE MOST UK NO.1 HITS PER CAPITA

According to *Guinness World Records Book of BRITISH HIT SINGLES*, the city that has provided the most No.1 hit singles, (from Lita Roza in 1953 to Atomic Kitten in 2002) on the UK chart per head of population is Liverpool (pop 439,473) with local acts achieving 56 hits – 1 per 7,847 of the city's population.

MOST US TOP 40 SINGLES ENTRIES BY A FEMALE ARTIST

In November 2002 Madonna (USA, right) made the US Top 40 for a record 44th time with the James Bond theme, 'Die Another Day' – overtaking Aretha Franklin (USA) as the female with the most US Top 40 entries. The same single was also her 35th US Top 10 entry – thus overtaking The Beatles (UK) who were on 34, and just one short of Elvis Presley's (USA) record 36 entries.

ROCK & COUNTRY

LARGEST PAYING ROCK-BAND CONCERT ATTENDANCE

An estimated 195,000 people paid £10 (then $16.50) each to attend a performance by A-Ha at the Rock In Rio festival, Maracanã Stadium, Brazil, in April 1990.

MOST PERFORMERS IN A CONCERT

The largest single rock concert, in terms of participants and organization, was Roger Waters' production of Pink Floyd's *The Wall* staged on 21 July 1990 in Potsdamer Platz, straddling East and West Berlin, Germany. Over 600 people performed on stage and an estimated 200,000 others made up the production crew.

LARGEST ROCK-STAR BENEFIT CONCERT

A concert held at Wembley Stadium, London, UK, on 20 April 1992 in memory of Freddie Mercury (UK) of Queen, raised £20.1 million (then $35 million) for AIDS charities. The concert was attended by 75,000 people and is estimated to have been seen by almost 1 billion people in more than 70 countries. It featured artists such as U2 (Rep. of Ireland), David Bowie (UK), and Liza Minnelli (USA).

LONGEST STAY AT NO.1 IN US ROCK SINGLES CHART

Canadian band Nickelback's single 'Too Bad' held top spot on the US Mainstream Rock chart for a record-breaking 20 weeks between January and May 2002. Lead singer Chad Kroeger is shown above.

MOST CONCERTS BY A GROUP IN 50 DAYS

The most musical performances by a group in 50 days is 101, by the rock band Jackyl (USA) as they toured the USA from 12 September to 31 October 1998. The band appeared in 59 cities in 26 states.

MOST CONCERTS PERFORMED IN 12 HOURS

The Bus Station Loonies (UK), a four-piece punk act, played twenty five 15-minute gigs in 12 hours at venues in and around Plymouth, Devon, UK, on 29 September 2001. The band, supported by two road crews, raised £1,200 ($1,894) for charity.

HIGHEST GROSSING COUNTRY MUSIC TOUR

Garth Brooks' (USA) three-year 'Sevens' tour starting in March 1997 grossed $105 million (then £65.6 million), playing 350 shows in 100 cities with an average attendance of 55,000 people per show.

HIGHEST GROSSING COUNTRY MUSIC TOUR PER SHOW

George Strait's (USA) 45-date 1998 to 2000 tour grossed $90 million (then £56.25 million) – an average of $2 million (£1.25 million) per show. The final ten dates in 2000 grossed $24 million (£15 million) – an average of $2.4 million (£1.5 million) per show – and were attended by 475,000 people.

HIGHEST ANNUAL EARNINGS BY A COUNTRY MUSIC ARTIST

Shania Twain (Canada) earned $36.6 million (then £23.2 million) for her tours during 1999, more than any other country performer and $3.1 million (£2 million) more than she earned from touring in 1998. Overall in the 1990s, the top-earning act on the road was George Strait (USA), who grossed $158 million (then £100.1 million). The most popular live act, Garth Brooks (USA) always kept his seat prices lower and therefore did not out-earn George Strait.

MOST NO.1 ALBUMS BY A COUNTRY MUSIC ARTIST

Since 1981 George Strait (USA) has had 15 of his 26 released albums go to No.1 in the charts – a total unbeaten by any other act. In terms of box-set editions, his *Strait Out of the Box* has sold 7 million copies, more than any other artist.

BIGGEST SELLING COUNTRY ALBUM IN USA BY A SOLO ARTIST

The best selling country album in the USA by a solo artist is Shania Twain's (Canada) *Come On Over,* which sold a record 19 million copies after its release on 4 November 1997. The sales of Shania Twain's album overtook those of Garth Brooks' (USA) album *No Fences* (1990), which had sold just over 16 million copies as of 15 June 2000.

MOST SUCCESSFUL MALE COUNTRY ARTIST IN THE USA

Garth Brooks is the most successful country recording artist of all time, with album sales of over 100 million since 1989. He also has the highest certified album sales of any solo artist in the USA. Brooks has won many awards, including Entertainer of the Year at the 1997 Country Music Awards.

MOST PLATINUM RIAA ALBUMS FOR A COUNTRY MUSIC ARTIST

Since 1981 George Strait (USA) has released 26 albums, with all but one of them (a Christmas album) earning RIAA (Recording Industry Association of America) platinum certificates for sales of over one million copies in the USA. In all, his albums have sold over 55 million copies.

MOST MULTI-PLATINUM RIAA CERTIFICATES

The recording artist with the most multi-platinum RIAA certificates is Elvis Presley (USA), who has a total of 33. This figure excludes certificates for videos.

BIGGEST SELLING LIVE ALBUM

Double Live by Garth Brooks (USA) is the top-selling live album in the USA with certified sales of 14 million (7 million double LPs) since its release on 17 November 1998.

BIGGEST SELLING SINGLE ALBUM IN THE USA BY A BRITISH ACT

The best-selling album in the USA by a British group is *Led Zeppelin IV* by Led Zeppelin, with estimated sales of 22 million. In the world's biggest album market, the USA, *The Wall* by Pink Floyd has certified sales of 23 million (11.5 double albums) and *The Dark Side of the Moon* (also Pink Floyd) 15 million single albums. The latter continues to sell well worldwide and may well have outsold the other two on a global basis – its accredited world sale being 23 million – the same figure claimed by The Beatles' *1.*

BIGGEST SELLING ALBUM IN USA FOR A FEMALE SOLO ARTIST

Canadian country singer Shania Twain's album *Come On Over* has sold 19 million copies in the USA and 30 million worldwide since its release on 4 November 1997.

BIGGEST SELLING AUSTRALIAN ALBUM

Back in Black by AC/DC (Australia) has had estimated global sales of 19 million copies since 1980. The band – currently Bon Scott (UK), Angus and Malcolm Young (UK), Cliff Williams (UK) and Phil Rudd (Australia) – formed in 1973 in Sydney, NSW, Australia, and took their name at the suggestion of Angus and Malcolm's sister, who saw it on a vacuum cleaner.

EARLIEST MILLION-SELLING CD

The first CD to sell one million copies worldwide was Dire Straits' (UK) *Brothers in Arms* album in 1986. It went on to sell more than a million in Europe alone, including over 250,000 in Britain.

MOST SIMULTANEOUS ALBUM ENTRIES IN A WEEK IN THE US CHART

Rock group Pearl Jam (USA) had seven different albums enter the US Top 200 chart on 17 March 2001. They were part of a series of 23 albums recorded live at different venues around the USA, breaking their own record of five entries from a series of 25 simultaneously released live albums from previous concerts held during their highly successful world tour.

LONGEST STAY IN A SINGLES CHART

'How Do I Live' by LeAnn Rimes (USA, below) entered the Top 25 US Country singles sales chart on 21 June 1997 and was still there in February 2003, a record 291 weeks (five and a half years) later.

URBAN BEATS

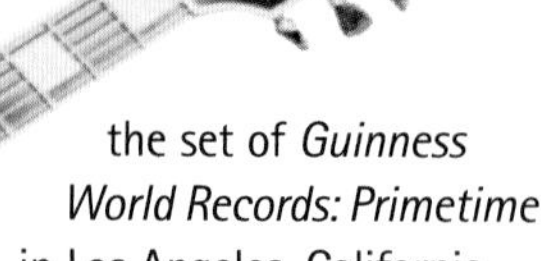

OLDEST MOBO WINNER

The oldest MOBO (Music Of Black Origin) award winner is BB King (USA, above) who was 73 in 1998 when he picked up the Lifetime Achievement award.

RAPPER WITH THE MOST US NO.1 ALBUMS

When *The Blueprint 2* topped the US album charts in November 2002, Jay-Z (USA) became the only rap act to have scored five No.1 albums. Eminem (USA) is the only MC to have sold more albums.

BEST SELLING RAP/R&B ALBUM IN THE USA

The best selling rap/R&B album ever in the USA is *CrazySexyCool* by TLC (USA), which has recorded 11 million sales. This surpasses MC Hammer's *Please Hammer Don't Hurt 'Em* album, which has sold 10 million.

BIGGEST SELLING RAP ARTIST

Rap legend 2Pac (born Tupac Shakur, USA) has certified US album sales of 33.5 million, and has now had more hits after his death (at the age of 25 in September 1996) than he achieved while he was alive. His posthumous hits include two US No.1 albums, *The Don Killuminati* (1997) and *Until the End of Time* (2001) (both produced after his death), and a dozen US R&B chart singles.

LARGEST RAP GROUP

Hip-Hop outfit Minority Militia (USA) is the world's largest rap group, with 124 members. Each member either raps, sings, plays an instrument or produces on the group's 2001 album *The People's Army*, released on Low Town Records.

YOUNGEST SOLO RAP ARTIST

Jordy (Lemoine, France) was at No.1 in the French singles chart with techno/house rap 'Dur dur d'être bébé' (It's Hard to be a Baby) at the age of four years six months in September 1993. The song later entered the US Billboard chart.

FASTEST RAP ARTIST

Rebel XD (Seandale Price) from Chicago, Illinois, USA, beat his own record when he rapped 683 syllables in 54.501 seconds on the set of *Guinness World Records: Primetime* in Los Angeles, California, USA, on 24 June 1998.

LONGEST STAY ON THE US RAP SINGLES CHART

'Hot Boyz' by Missy 'Misdemeanor' Elliott, featuring Nas, Eve and Q-Tip (all USA), spent a record 18 weeks at the top of the US Rap Chart in 1999/2000.

YOUNGEST SOLO RAP ARTIST AT NO.1 ON THE US R&B AND RAP CHARTS

In July 2000 Lil' Bow Wow (aka Shad Lamar Moss, USA), aged 13 years 4 months, went to No.1 on the US rap and R&B charts with 'Bounce with Me' (featuring Xscape).

YOUNGEST R&B CHART ENTRANT

Hailie Jade Mathers (USA) became the youngest performer to be credited with an R&B hit when, aged 6 years 210 days, 'My Dad's Gone Crazy' charted in August 2002. She performed on the track with her father, Eminem (USA).

LONGEST SPAN ON THE US R&B CHART

Ray Charles (USA) has appeared on the US R&B Singles Chart for seven decades. He first charted as leader of the Maxine Trio with 'Confession Blues' in April 1949, and his latest entry came in July 2002 with 'Mother', making a span of 53 years.

BEST SELLING DRUM 'N' BASS ALBUM

The best selling drum 'n' bass album is *New Forms* by Reprazent (UK), which has sold a total of 763,910 albums around the world. The band sold 250,000 albums in the UK and 513,910 worldwide.

BEST SELLING BIG-BEAT ALBUM

The best selling big-beat album is Fatboy Slim's (UK) *You've Come a Long Way Baby*, which was released in October 1998 and has sold over three million copies worldwide, one million in the UK alone.

BEST SELLING REGGAE ALBUM

Legend (1984), by the late Bob Marley (Jamaica), is the biggest selling reggae album of all time. In the UK, where it topped the album charts, it has had certified sales of 1.8 million, and although it never reached the Top 40 in the USA, it sold more than 10 million copies there.

BEST SELLING RAÏ ARTIST

Algerian raï singer Khaled has sold over 3 million albums worldwide, including *Khaled* (1992), which featured his first international hit 'Didi'. Khaled also appeared in concert with fellow Algerian stars Rachid Taha and Faudel in 1999. Their live album, *1, 2, 3 Soleils*, sold one million copies worldwide.

BEST SELLING WORLD MUSIC ALBUM

The 1998 Grammy-award-winning album *Buena Vista Social Club* (1997) has sold over four million copies, with 1.5 million sold in the USA alone. The album brought some of Cuba's best musicians together, including Rubén González, Ibrahím Ferrer and Compay Segundo.

FASTEST SELLING FEMALE DEBUT ALBUM

Ashanti's (USA, right) debut album *Ashanti* sold 503,000 copies in its firs[t] week on release in the USA in April 2002. In the same week, she became th[e] first female performer to simultaneous[ly] hold the top two places on the Hot 100 Singles Chart with 'Foolish' and 'What's Luv' (with Fat Joe).

BIGGEST SELLING ALBUM BY A LATIN ARTIST

Mexican-born Carlos Santana's *Supernatural* album (1999) has sold 14 million copies in the USA alone, and many millions more worldwide.

BIGGEST SELLING SOLO BHANGRA ARTIST

Malkit Singh (India) has sold an average of 260,000 copies of each of his albums, totalling sales of over 4.9 million records since he began his career in 1985.

FASTEST SELLING RAP ALBUM

Rap artist Eminem's (USA) album *The Marshall Mathers LP* sold a record 1.76 million copies in its first week in the USA when it was released in June 2000.

OLDEST ARTIST AT NO.1 ON THE US CHARTS

Louis Armstrong (USA) was almost 63 years old when his single 'Hello Dolly!' reached No.1 in 1964.

OLDEST ARTIST TO HAVE A MILLION-SELLER

Cuban singer/guitarist Compay Segundo (born Francisco Repilado) has sold over one million albums around the world since his 88th birthday in 1995. The entertainer, who first recorded in the 1930s, found new fame as a member of the group Buena Vista Social Club in 1996.

MOST SIMULTANEOUS R&B HITS

In 2001 US R&B artists R Kelly and Jay-Z (above) equalled the record set by both DMX and Juvenile (both USA) in 1999 of achieving six simultaneous entries on the Billboard Hot R&B/Hip-Hop Singles and Tracks chart.

MOST CONSECUTIVE WEEKS AT NO.1 BY THE SAME PRODUCER

Hip-Hop producer Irv Gotti (USA) produced the No.1 single on the US Hot 100 Pop Chart for a record 19 successive weeks between 23 February and 22 June 2002. Some of the major artists Gotti has worked with include Ja Rule, Ashanti, Jay-Z, DMX and Fat Joe (all USA).

MOST MUSIC VIDEOS MADE FOR ONE SONG

Five different videos were made for the track 'Timber' (1998) by UK dance act Coldcut: the original mix, the EBN remix (New York), the LPC remix (Sweden), the Clifford Gilberto remix (Germany) and the Gnomadic remix (UK).

LARGEST INTERNATIONAL MUSIC FESTIVAL

The largest international music festival is WOMAD (World of Music, Arts and Dance), which has staged more than 90 events in 20 different countries since 1982. Originally inspired by musician Peter Gabriel (UK), WOMAD's worldwide profile has grown quickly, with annual events in Australia, North America, Japan and Europe. The central aim of WOMAD is to bring together and celebrate music, arts and dance drawn from all over the world.

CLASSICAL & JAZZ

LONGEST OPERA

The longest of the commonly performed operas is *Die Meistersinger von Nürnberg* by Richard Wagner (Germany). A normal uncut version as performed by the Sadler's Wells company (UK) between 24 August and 19 September 1968 entailed 5 hr 15 min of music. The photo shows John Tomlinson and Thomas Allen (both UK) in a recent production at the Royal Opera House, Covent Garden, London, UK.

MOST PROLIFIC CONDUCTOR

Herbert von Karajan (Austria) made over 800 recordings encompassing all the major works. During his career, he conducted the London Philharmonia Orchestra, the Vienna State Opera and La Scala Opera Orchestra of Milan, and founded the Salzburg Festival in 1967. He was principal conductor of the Berlin Philharmonic Orchestra for 35 years before his retirement, which was shortly before his death in 1989.

LONGEST CAREER AS A CONDUCTOR

As of September 2002, Torstein Grythe (Norway, b. 24 November 1918), aged 84, had been conducting the Silver Boys Choir of Oslo, Norway, for 62 years, since he started in 1940.

OLDEST ORCHESTRA

The first modern symphony orchestra – four sections consisting of woodwind, brass, percussion and string instruments – played at the court of Duke Karl Theodor (Germany) at Mannheim, Germany, in 1743. The oldest existing symphony orchestra, the Gewandhaus Orchestra of Leipzig, Germany, was also established in 1743. Originally known as the Grosses Concert and later as the Musik bende Gesellschaft, its current name dates from 1781.

MOST PROLIFIC COMPOSER

Georg Philipp Telemann (Germany) wrote 12 complete sets of services for the church year (with one cantata for every Sunday), 78 services for special occasions, 40 operas, between 600 and 700 orchestral suites, 44 passions, plus concertos, sonatas and other pieces of chamber music.

LONGEST OPERATIC ENCORE

The longest encore listed in the *Concise Oxford Dictionary of Opera* was the whole of Domenico Cimarosa's (Italy) opera *Il Matrimonio Segreto* at its premiere in 1792. This was at the command of the Austro-Hungarian Emperor Leopold II.

SHORTEST OPERA

The shortest published opera is *The Sands of Time* by Simon Rees and Peter Reynolds (both UK), which was 3 min 34 sec long when performed under Reynolds' direction at BBC TV Centre, London, UK, on 14 September 1993.

YOUNGEST OPERA SINGER

On 24 March 1950 Ginetta Gloria La Bianca (USA, b. 12 May 1934) sang Gilda in *Rigoletto* at Velletri, Italy, aged 15 years 316 days.

OLDEST OPERA SINGER

The Ukrainian bass Mark Reizen sang the role of Prince Gremin in Tchaikovsky's *Eugene Onegin* at the Bolshoi Theatre in Moscow, Russia, on his 90th birthday in 1985.

MOST COSTUME CHANGES IN A LIVE OPERATIC PERFORMANCE

On 2 November 1997 Natalie Choquette (Canada) wore a total of 15 costumes during a recital at the Wilfred-Pelletier Hall, Montreal, Canada. During the first part of the show she wore seven costumes and after the interval, she donned a further eight.

LARGEST OPERA HOUSE

The Metropolitan Opera House (right) at the Lincoln Center, New York City, USA, has a combined seating and standing capacity of 4,065. The auditorium, which seats 3,800, is 137 m (451 ft) deep, and the stage measures 70 m (230 ft) wide by 45 m (148 ft) deep. It was completed in September 1966 at a cost of $45.7 million (then £16.3 million).

BIGGEST SELLING CLASSICAL ALBUM

The best selling classical album is *In Concert*, with global sales of 10.5 million to date. It was recorded by José Carreras, Placido Domingo (both Spain) and Luciano Pavarotti (Italy) in Rome, Italy, on 7 July 1990. The recording was made for the football World Cup finals, held that year in Italy.

LONGEST INTERVAL BETWEEN COMPOSITION AND PERFORMANCE

The longest interval between a composer writing a piece of music and its performance in the manner intended is from 3 March 1791 until 9 October 1982 (over 191 years). Mozart's *Organ Piece for a Clock* was finally performed at Glyndebourne, East Sussex, UK, with the assistance of organ builders William Hill & Son and Norman & Beard Ltd.

MOST PEOPLE TO SHARE A GRAMMY AWARD

The greatest number of people to share a Grammy award is 46, by the Chicago Symphony Orchestra. (CSO). The CSO won the first of its Grammy awards in February 1978 for Best Choral Performance – Classical with its recording of Verdi's *Requiem*. The Orchestra has been involved in 56 wins since, including 24 by conductor Sir Georg Solti (UK) and nine by chorus director Margaret Hillis (USA).

YOUNGEST PERSON AT NO.1 IN THE CLASSICAL CHARTS

In November 1998 Charlotte Church (UK, b. 21 February 1986) entered the UK classical album charts with her debut *Voice of an Angel* at the age of 12 years 9 months. The album went double platinum in the UK within four weeks of its release.

MOST VALUABLE JAZZ INSTRUMENT

The most valuable jazz instrument is a saxophone once owned by Charlie Parker (USA) which sold for £93,500 ($144,500) at Christie's, London, UK, on 7 September 1994.

BEST SELLING JAZZ ARTIST

The best selling jazz artist is Kenny G (USA), who has sold an estimated 55 million albums worldwide to date. This includes 12 million copies of *Breathless*, the best selling jazz album of all time, which was released in 1992.

LONGEST WORKING CAREER AS A RECORDING ARTIST

Adelaide Hall (USA) is the artist with the longest recording career, having released material over eight consecutive decades. The jazz singer's first record, *Creole Love Call*, was recorded with Duke Ellington (USA) on 26 October 1927, and her last was made on 16 June 1991 at the Cole Porter Centennial Gala.

MOST EXPENSIVE HIT

The most expensive hit was the CD set *Miles Davis at Montreux* (Miles Davis, USA, right) which entered the US Top 20 Jazz Chart in November 2002, and was priced at $250 (£154).

EARLIEST JAZZ RECORD MADE

The first jazz record made was of *Indiana* and *The Dark Town Strutters' Ball*, recorded for the Columbia label in New York, USA, on or about 30 January 1917, by the Original Dixieland Jazz Band. It was released on 31 May 1917.

LARGEST PIPES AND DRUMS BAND

The Millennium Pipes event, held in aid of Marie Curie Cancer Care, took place in Edinburgh, UK, on 5 August 2000, with 10,000 bagpipers and drummers from around the world playing many pipe music classics.

LARGEST DRUM ENSEMBLE

A drum ensemble numbering 2,208 participants gathered to play at Mydonose Showland, Istanbul, Turkey, on 17 March 2002. The ensemble consisted of members of Türk Otomobil Fabrikasi AS (TOFAS) and was led by the popular Turkish rhythm band Harem.

LARGEST EHRU ENSEMBLE

Conducted by Yan Huichang (China), 938 ehru (a Chinese stringed instrument) players aged between 6 and 76 years performed with the Hong Kong Chinese Orchestra at the opening of the Huqin Festival of Hong Kong at Hong Kong's Cultural Festival Centre on 11 February 2001.

OLDEST PIANO

The earliest pianoforte in existence is one built in Florence, Italy, in 1720 by Bartolommeo Cristofori (Italy) and now preserved in the Metropolitan Museum of Art, New York City, USA.

PERFORMANCE ARTS

« THICKEST MAKE-UP

The thickest three-dimensional make-up is Chutti (left), unique to the southwest Indian Kathakali dance-theatre tradition. The villainous redbeard characters have mask-li attachments, built up using rice paste and paper, that exte 15 cm (6 in) from the face. The make-up takes hours to apply and the colours and costume styles used denote th different nature of each of the characters.

LARGEST DANCE FESTIVAL

The Festival de Dança de Joinville in Santa Catarina, Brazil, is the world's largest dance festival. First produced in 1983, the festival is held over a minimum of 10 days and is attended by 4,000 national and international dancers from 140 amateur and professional dance groups. It is watched by more than 200,000 people annually.

LARGEST CHORUS LINE

On 28 September 1997, 593 people from The Roy Castle Foundation (UK) performed a routine for the finale of *The Roy Castle Record Breaking Extravaganza* at the Royal Liverpool Philharmonic Hall, Liverpool, UK.

MOST GRANDS JETÉS

On 28 November 1988 Wayne Sleep (UK) completed 158 grands jetés along the length of Dunston Staiths, Gateshead, Tyne & Wear, UK, in 2 minutes.

MOST BALLET KICKS

Emma Smith (USA) performed 587 continuous *grand battements* on alternating legs on 26 February 2002 at the New Hanover County Senior Center, Wilmington, N. Carolina, USA.

MOST FLAMENCO TAPS IN A MINUTE

The most flamenco taps in a minute is 734, achieved by Alberto Hidalgo (Germany) at the JHQ Rheindahlen International Golden Jubilee Show, Monchengladbach, Germany, on 9 June 2002.

OLDEST SURVIVING BALLET

The Whims of Cupid and the Ballet Master was choreographed in 1786 by Vincenzo Galeotti (Italy) for the Royal Danish Ballet. La Fille Mal Gardée is sometimes regarded to be the oldest, but it appeared three years later and the original choreography is lost.

» FASTEST THEATRICAL PRODUCTION

Velvet Jacket Ltd's musical production of *Oklahoma!* (right), performed by Act 24 at The Playhouse, Edinburgh, UK, at 8pm on 6 May 2000, was produced in a time of 23 hr 55 min from first receiving the script. The time in production includes auditions, casting, rehearsals, publicity design, rigging, stage and set design and construction.

LONGEST PLAY

The longest recorded theatrical production has been *The Warp* by Neil Oram (UK) directed by Ken Campbell (UK), a ten-part play cycle performed at the Institue of Contemporary Art, The Mall, London, UK, between 18 and 20 January 1979. Russell Denton (USA) was on stage for all but 5 min of the 18 hr 5 min play.

LONGEST SHAKESPEARE PLAY

Of William Shakespeare's (UK) 37 plays, *Hamlet* (1604), comprising 4,042 lines and 29,551 words, is the longest. Within the play is the longest speech of Shakespeare's 1,277 speaking parts, with Hamlet having 1,569 lines containing 11,610 words.

LARGEST SIMULTANEOUS PERFORMANCE OF ONE SHOW

The children's musical *The Rainbow Juggler* was performed in 56 different theatres across the UK, Ireland, Germany, USA and Australia by 4,568 Stagecoach Theatre Arts students on 20 November 1999.

LONGEST RUNNING OFF-BROADWAY MUSICAL

The Fantasticks by Tom Jones and Harvey Schmidt (both USA) opened on 3 May 1960 and finally closed on 13 January 2002 having been performed a record 17,162 times at the Sullivan Street Playhouse, Greenwich Village, New York, USA.

LONGEST THEATRICAL RUN

The longest continuous run of any show in the world is *The Mousetrap* by Agatha Christie (UK), with its 50th anniversary and the 20,807th performance held on 25 November 2002 at the St Martin's Theatre, London, UK. The thriller opened on 25 November 1952 at the Ambassadors Theatre, London, UK, and moved after 8,862 performances to the St Martins Theatre next door on 25 March 1974. The box office has grossed £20 million ($33.3 million) from more than ten million theatre-goers in its 50 years.

LONGEST PERIOD AS AN UNDERSTUDY IN THE SAME ROLE

On 12 March 1994 Nancy Seabrooke (UK) retired from the Company of *The Mousetrap* at the age of 79 after having understudied the part of Mrs Boyle for 15 years and 6,240 performances. She performed the part on 72 occasions.

MOST EXPENSIVE STAGE PROP

For the musical stage version of *Chitty Chitty Bang Bang*, which opened on 16 April 2002 at the London Palladium, London, UK, the magical flying car of the title (above) cost an estimated £750,000 ($1.07 million) to make. The complete set, designed by set designer Anthony Ward (UK), cost an estimated £6.2 million ($8.9 million) to stage. The show is the most expensive British production ever seen in the West End.

MOST EXPENSIVE STAGE PRODUCTION

The stage adaptation of Disney's 1994 film *The Lion King* is the most expensive theatrical production ever, with the Broadway production, which opened on 13 November 1997, costing an estimated $15 million (£9.3 million).

LONGEST THEATRICAL RUN FOR A COMEDY

The longest running comedy was *No Sex, Please, We're British*, written by Anthony Marriott and Alistair Foot (both UK) and presented by John Gale. It opened at the Strand Theatre, London, UK, on 3 June 1971, transferred to the Duchess Theatre on 2 August 1986 and finally ended on 5 September 1987 after 16 years 3 months and 6,761 performances.

GREATEST THEATRICAL LOSS

The largest loss sustained by a theatrical show was borne by the American producers of the Royal Shakespeare Company's musical *Carrie*, which closed after five performances on Broadway on 17 May 1988 at a cost of $7million (then £3,744,516).

LONGEST THEATRICAL RUN FOR A REVUE

The greatest number of performances of any theatrical presentation is 47,250 (to April 1986) for *The Golden Horseshoe Revue*, a show staged at Disneyland Park, Anaheim, California, USA, from 16 July 1955 to 12 October 1986. It was seen by over 16 million people.

LONGEST RUNNING MUSICAL

Andrew Lloyd Webber's *Cats* is the longest running musical in the history of both London's West End and Broadway, New York, USA. In London it opened in 1981 at the New London Theatre, Drury Lane, and when it closed after its 8,950th and final West End performance on 11 May 2002 – its 21st birthday – it had been seen by over eight million people. On Broadway, it opened at the Winter Garden Theatre on 7 October 1982 and the 7,485th and final performance was held on 10 September 2000.

MOST THEATRE PERFORMANCES IN THE SAME ROLE

Kanbi Fujiyama (Japan) played the lead role in 10,288 performances by the comedy company Sochiku Shikigeki from November 1966 to June 1983.

LONGEST THEATRE PERFORMANCE

A team of 15 people from Thisaigal Cultural Troupe (India) performed 12 plays on a stage outside Karuna Hospital, Madurai, India, from 9 to 11 July 1999 for a total of 57 hr 30 min.

ASF
94

SPORT

AMERICAN FOOTBALL

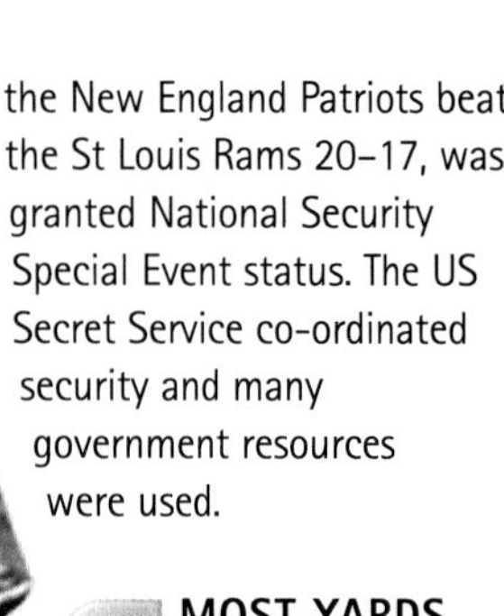
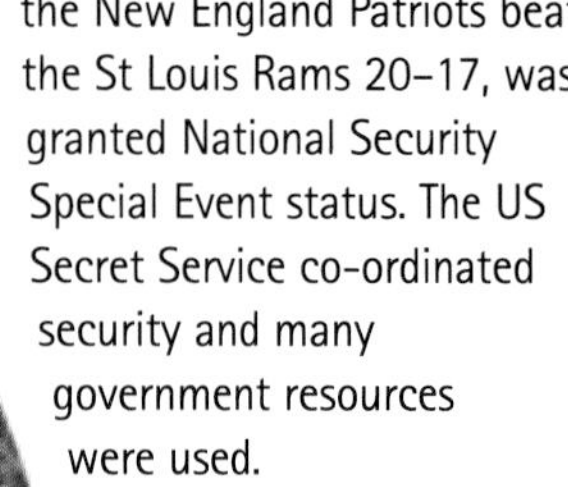

MOST POINTS IN A SUPER BOWL CAREER

Jerry Rice (USA) has scored 48 points in Super Bowl games, in 1989-90, 1995 and 2003 for the San Francisco 49ers and the Oakland Raiders.

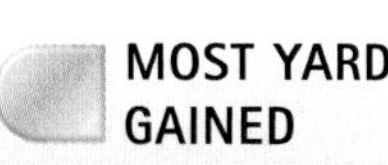

MOST TEAM INTERCEPTIONS IN A SUPER BOWL

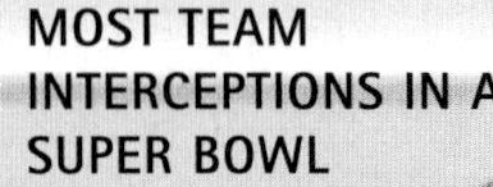

In Super Bowl XXXVII, played in San Diego, California, USA, on 26 January 2003, the Tampa Bay Buccaneers (player Dexter Jackson, above) made a record five interceptions, returning them 172 yards for three touchdowns.

YOUNGEST COACH TO WIN A SUPER BOWL

At age 39 years 161 days, Jon Gruden (USA) led the Tampa Bay Buccaneers to victory at Super Bowl XXXVII in San Diego, California, USA, on 26 January 2003.

HIGHEST SUPER BOWL AGGREGATE SCORE

The highest aggregate score in a Super Bowl was 75, when the San Francisco 49ers beat the San Diego Chargers 49–26 at the Super Bowl XXIX in 1995.

MOST SECURE SUPER BOWL

Super Bowl XXXVI at the Louisiana Superdome in New Orleans, USA, on 3 February 2002 had the tightest security measures ever for a Super Bowl. The match, in which the New England Patriots beat the St Louis Rams 20–17, was granted National Security Special Event status. The US Secret Service co-ordinated security and many government resources were used.

MOST YARDS GAINED RECEIVING IN A SUPER BOWL CAREER

Jerry Rice (USA) has caught passes for a record 589 yards over four Super Bowl appearances in 1989, 1990, 1995 and 2003, playing for the San Francisco 49ers and the Oakland Raiders.

Jerry Rice also holds the record for the most receiving yards at a single Super Bowl, with 215 yards for the San Francisco 49ers against the Denver Broncos in 1989.

MOST YARDS GAINED RUSHING IN AN NFL CAREER

Emmitt Smith (USA) of the Dallas Cowboys rushed for a total of 17,162 yards over his NFL career, between 1990 and 2002.

MOST YARDS GAINED RECEIVING IN AN NFL CAREER

Jerry Rice (USA) of the San Francisco 49ers and the Oakland Raiders gained 21,597 yards pass receiving between 1985 and 2002.

In addition to the career record, Jerry Rice also holds the record for the most yards earned receiving in an NFL season, with 1,848 yards for the San Francisco 49ers in 1995.

MOST INTERCEPTIONS IN AN NFL SEASON

The most interceptions made in an NFL season is 14 by Dick 'Night Train' Lane (USA) playing for the Los Angeles Rams in the first fully professional season in 1952. He returned them for 298 yards and two touchdowns.

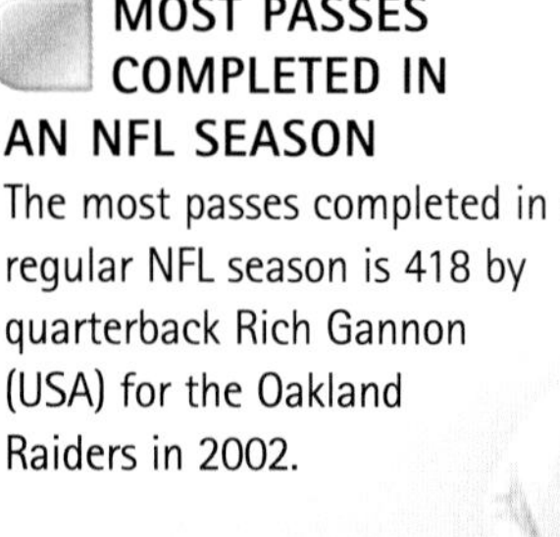

MOST PASSES COMPLETED IN AN NFL SEASON

The most passes completed in a regular NFL season is 418 by quarterback Rich Gannon (USA) for the Oakland Raiders in 2002.

MOST PASSES RECEIVED IN AN NFL SEASON

Marvin Harrison (USA) of the Indianapolis Colts caught a record 143 passes in 2002.

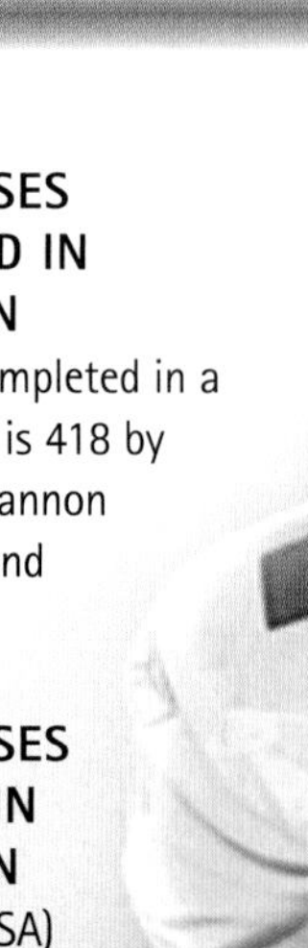

MOST PASSES COMPLETED IN AN NFL CAREER

Dan Marino (USA) of the Miami Dolphins completed a total of 4,967 passes between 1983 and his retirement from the game in 2000. He holds many other records, including most yards gained passing in both a career (61,631) and a season (5,084 in 1984).

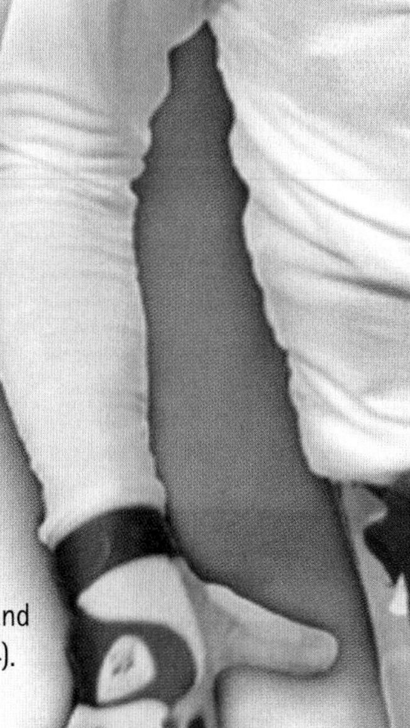

MOST TOUCHDOWNS IN AN NFL CAREER

Multiple NFL record holder Jerry Rice (USA) has scored 192 touchdowns in his career to date, playing for the San Francisco 49ers and the Oakland Raiders since 1985.

HIGHEST COMBINED KICK-OFF RETURN YARDAGE IN AN NFL SEASON

Michael Lewis (USA) of the New Orleans Saints set an NFL combined punt/kick-off return record with 2,432 yards in the 2002 season.

LONGEST FIELD GOAL

The longest ever field goal in an NFL game is 63 yards by Tom Dempsey (USA) of the New Orleans Saints on 8 November 1970 against the Detroit Lions; and by Jason Elam (USA) of the Denver Broncos against the Jacksonville Jaguars on 25 October 1998.

LONGEST RUN FROM SCRIMMAGE

Tony Dorsett (USA) scored on a touchdown run of 99 yards playing for the Dallas Cowboys against the Minnesota Vikings on 3 January 1983.

MOST RUSHING YARDS MADE BY A QUARTERBACK IN AN NFL GAME

Quarterback Michael Vick (USA, left) rushed a record 173 yards in a single NFL game playing for the Atlanta Falcons against the Minnesota Vikings at Minneapolis, Minnesota, USA, on 1 December 2002.

LONGEST RETURN OF A MISSED FIELD GOAL

The longest return of a missed field goal for a touchdown is 107 yards by Chris McAlister (USA) playing for the Baltimore Ravens against the Denver Broncos on 30 September 2002.

MOST FIELD GOALS IN AN NFL CAREER

Gary Anderson (USA) scored 494 field goals during his NFL career (Pittsburgh Steelers, 1982–94; Philadelphia Eagles, 1995–96; San Francisco 49ers, 1997; Minnesota Vikings, 1999–2002).

MOST SAFETIES IN AN NFL GAME

Fred Dryer (USA) made two safeties in a single game, playing for the Los Angeles Rams against the Green Bay Packers on 21 October 1973.

HIGHEST SCORE IN AN NFL GAME

The highest score in any NFL game is 73 by the Chicago Bears against the Washington Redskins (0) in the 1940 NFL Championship game at Washington DC, USA, on 8 December.

MOST NFL TITLES

The Green Bay Packers have won a record 12 NFL titles – in 1929–31, 1936, 1939, 1944, 1961–62, 1965–67 and 1996.

MOST CONSECUTIVE NFL GAMES PLAYED

Jim Marshall (USA) played 282 consecutive NFL games, for the Cleveland Browns in 1960 and the Minnesota Vikings in 1961–79.

MOST NFL GAMES

Quarterback George Blanda (USA) played a record 340 games in a record 26 seasons. He played for the Chicago Bears in 1949–58, the Baltimore Colts in 1950, the Houston Oilers in 1960–66, and the Oakland Raiders in 1967–75, and was the first player to score more than 500 points for three different teams. He was voted player of the year in 1961.

MOST CONSECUTIVE NFL WINS

The Chicago Bears achieved a record 17 consecutive NFL wins in 1933–34. The most consecutive games without defeat is 25 by Canton Bulldogs (22 wins and 3 ties) from 1921–23.

LARGEST ATTENDANCE AT AN NFL REGULAR SEASON GAME

The largest crowd numbered 102,368 for the Los Angeles Rams against the San Francisco 49ers at the LA Coliseum, Los Angeles, California, USA, on 10 November 1957.

SHORTEST NFL PLAYER

Jack Shapiro (USA), who played for the Staten Island Stapletons in 1929, was 1.54 m (5 ft 0.5 in) tall. He played just one game at halfback, rushing for seven yards (in two attempts) and returning a punt 12 yards.

MOST PASSES RECEIVED IN AN NFL CAREER

The most pass receptions in an NFL career is 1,456 by Jerry Rice (USA, right) of the San Francisco 49ers and the Oakland Raiders (1985–2002).

BASEBALL

LONGEST HIT FOR A HOME RUN IN AN MLB GAME

The longest measured hit for a home run in a Major League Baseball (MLB) game is 193 m (634 ft) by Mickey Mantle (USA) on 10 September 1960 for the New York Yankees against the Detroit Tigers at Briggs Stadium, Detroit, USA.

MOST CONSECUTIVE MAJOR LEAGUE GAMES BATTED SAFELY

The most consecutive Major League games batted safely is 56 by Joe DiMaggio (USA, above) between 15 May and 16 July 1941.

MOST BASE HITS IN AN MLB SEASON

The most base hits in a Major League Baseball season is 257 by George Sisler (USA) playing for the St Louis Browns in 1920.

HIGHEST BATTING AVERAGE IN AN MLB SEASON

The highest batting average in a Major League season is .438 by Hugh Duffy (USA) playing for the Boston Beaneaters in 1894.

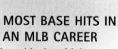

MOST BASE HITS IN AN MLB CAREER

The most base hits in a Major League career is 4,256 by Peter Rose (USA) who played for the Cincinnati Reds, the Philadelphia Phillies and the Montreal Expos between 1963 and 1986.

MOST CY YOUNG PITCHING AWARDS

The Cy Young Award is presented each season to the League's outstanding pitcher. Roger Clemens (USA, above, with the New York Yankees) has received the award six times, with the Boston Red Sox (1986–87 and 1991), the Toronto Blue Jays (1997–98) and the New York Yankees (2001).

MOST CONSECUTIVE HITS IN THE MLB

The most consecutive hits in the Major League is 12, and the record is shared by two players. The first to achieve the feat was Pinky Higgins (USA) of the Boston Red Sox in June 1938. He was followed by Walt Dropo (USA) playing for the Detroit Tigers in July 1952.

MOST HITS BY AN MLB ROOKIE IN A SEASON

The most hits by a rookie (a first year player) in an MLB season is 242 by Ichiro Suzuki (Japan) playing for the Seattle Mariners in 2001. Ichiro broke the 90-year record set by 'Shoeless' Joe Jackson (USA) for the Cleveland Naps (later renamed the Cleveland Indians) in 1911.

MOST RUNS IN AN MLB CAREER

The most runs scored in a Major League career is 2,288 by Rickey Henderson (USA) up to the end of the 2002 season. He began the first of his 28 seasons to date on 24 June 1979 with the Oakland Athletics. He then played for a further eight franchises before finishing the 2002 season with the Boston Red Sox.

MOST RBIs IN AN MLB CAREER

The most runs batted in (RBIs) in an MLB career is 2,297 by Hank Aaron (USA), between 1954 and 1976.

MOST DOUBLES HIT IN AN MLB CAREER

The most doubles hit in a Major League career is 792 by Tris Speaker (USA) who played for the Boston Red Sox, the Cleveland Indians, the Washington Senators and the Philadelphia Athletics from 1907 to 1928.

MOST TRIPLES HIT IN AN MLB CAREER

The most triples hit in a Major League career is 309 by Sam Crawford (USA) for the Cincinnati Reds and the Detroit Tigers from 1899 to 1917.

MOST GRAND SLAM HOME RUNS IN THE SAME INNINGS

On 23 April 1999 Fernando Tatis (Dominican Republic), batting for the St Louis Cardinals, became the first player in Major League history to hit two grand slam home runs in the same innings. He set the record against the Los Angeles Dodgers' pitcher Chan Ho Park (South Korea) in the 3rd inning of the game, which was won by the Cardinals 12-5.

MOST STRIKEOUTS IN AN MLB CAREER

Nolan Ryan (USA) pitched a total of 5,714 strikeouts during his Major League career with the New York Mets, the California Angels, the Houston Astros and the Texas Rangers from 1966 to 1993. In 1979 Ryan became the first player in Major League history to sign a contract worth $1 million (then £472,660) when he joined the Houston Astros.

MOST STRIKEOUTS IN AN MLB GAME

Roger Clemens (USA) playing for the Boston Red Sox, pitched a record 20 strikeouts in one game (nine innings) against the Seattle Mariners on 29 April 1986 and the Detroit Tigers on 18 September 1996. Kerry Wood (USA) playing for the Chicago Cubs equalled this record on 6 May 1998 against the Houston Astros.

MOST STRIKEOUTS IN AN MLB SEASON

The most strikeouts in a Major League season is 383, pitched by Nolan Ryan (USA) of the California Angels in 1973. The record for American League baseball is 513 strikeouts in one season, by Matt Kilroy (USA) for the Baltimore Orioles in 1886.

MOST SHUTOUTS IN AN MLB SEASON

The most shutouts achieved by a pitcher in one season is 16, by George Bradley (USA) for the St Louis Brown Stockings in 1876 and Pete Alexander (USA) for the Philadelphia Phillies in 1916.

MOST TOTAL BASES IN AN MLB SEASON

The most total bases in a season is 457 by Babe Ruth (USA) for the New York Yankees in 1921.

MOST STOLEN BASES IN AN MLB SEASON

The most stolen bases in a season is 130 by Rickey Henderson (USA) playing for the Oakland Athletics in 1982.

MOST CONSECUTIVE MLB GAMES

Cal Ripken Jr (USA) of the Baltimore Orioles played a record 2,632 consecutive Major League games between 30 May 1982 and 19 September 1998.

MOST MLB MVP AWARDS

Barry Bonds (USA) has won a record five Major League Most Valuable Player (MVP) awards. He won his fifth while playing with the San Francisco Giants in the 2002 season. Bonds won his previous awards in 1990, 1992, 1993 and 2001.

MOST WORLD SERIES MVP AWARDS

The most World Series Most Valuable Player (MVP) Awards received by a player is two. Several people have won this award twice: Sandy Koufax (USA) of the Los Angeles Dodgers in 1963 and 1965; Bob Gibson (USA) of the St Louis Cardinals in 1964 and 1967; and Reggie Jackson (USA) with the Oakland Athletics in 1973 and the New York Yankees in 1977.

MOST HOME RUNS IN A MINOR LEAGUE SEASON

Joe Bauman (USA) of the Roswell Rockets scored a record 72 home runs in one season in 1954.

YOUNGEST WORLD SERIES PLAYER

Fred Lindstrom (USA) played for the New York Giants on 24 October 1924 aged 18 years and 339 days.

LONGEST BASEBALL THROW

Glen Gorbous (Canada) threw a baseball a record 135.88 m (445 ft 10 in) on 1 August 1957.

LARGEST BASEBALL GAME ATTENDANCE

An estimated 114,000 spectators watched a game between Australia and an American Services team in a demonstration event during the Olympic Games at Melbourne, Australia, on 1 December 1956.

LARGEST WOODEN BASEBALL BAT

The largest wooden baseball bat is 4.089 m (13 ft 5 in) long with a circumference of 1.016 m (3 ft 4 in) and is owned by the Fargo-Moorhead RedHawks baseball club (Fargo Baseball LLC) of Fargo, North Dakota, USA.

MOST STOLEN BASES IN A CAREER

The most bases stolen in a career is 1,403 by Rickey Henderson, (USA, below, playing for the Boston Red Sox), known as the 'Man of Steal', from 1979–2002.

BASKETBALL

MOST NBA CHAMPIONSHIP TITLES

The most NBA Championship titles won is 16 by the Boston Celtics, in 1957, 1959–66, 1968–69, 1974, 1976, 1981, 1984 and 1986.

MOST WINS IN AN NBA SEASON

The most wins in an NBA season is 72 by the Chicago Bulls in the 1995/96 season.

MOST POINTS IN AN NBA SEASON

The most points scored in an NBA season is 4,029 by Wilt 'The Stilt' Chamberlain (USA) for the Philadelphia Warriors in 1961–62.

MOST POINTS SCORED BY A PLAYER IN AN NBA GAME

The most points scored by one player in an NBA game is 100 by Wilt Chamberlain (USA) playing for the Philadelphia Warriors against the New York Knicks on 2 March 1962.

MOST POINTS BY A TEAM IN AN NBA GAME

The highest team score in an NBA game is 186 by the Detroit Pistons against the Denver Nuggets (184) at Denver, Colorado, USA, on 13 December 1983.

MOST FIELD GOALS IN AN NBA SEASON

The most field goals scored by one player in an NBA season is 1,597 by Wilt Chamberlain (USA) in 1961-62 for the Philadelphia Warriors.

MOST FREE THROWS IN AN NBA CAREER

The most free throws in an NBA career is 9,443 in 1,405 games by Karl Malone (USA, right) playing for the Utah Jazz from 1985 to 2003.

MOST FIELD GOALS IN AN NBA GAME

The most field goals scored by an individual in an NBA game is 36 by Wilt Chamberlain (USA) when he played for the Philadelphia Warriors against the New York Knicks on 2 March 1962.

MOST THREE-POINT FIELD GOALS IN AN NBA SEASON

The most three-point field goals scored by an individual in an NBA season is 267 by Dennis Scott (USA) for the Orlando Magic in 1996 to 1997.

HIGHEST SCORING AVERAGE IN AN NBA SEASON

The highest scoring average in a NBA season is 50.4 points per game by Wilt Chamberlain (USA) for the Philadelphia Warriors in 1961 to 1962.

HIGHEST AGGREGATE SCORE IN AN NBA MATCH

The highest aggregate score in an NBA match is 370, when the Detroit Pistons (186) beat the Denver Nuggets (184) at Denver, USA, on 13 December 1983.

HIGHEST POINTS-SCORING AVERAGE IN AN NBA CAREER

The highest points-per-game scoring average for players exceeding 10,000 points is 30.1 by Michael Jordan (USA, right), who scored 32,292 points in 1,072 games for the Chicago Bulls (1984–98) and the Washington Wizards (2001–03).

Overtime was played after a 145–145 tie in regulation time.

The record for the highest aggregate score in regulation time is 320, when the Golden State Warriors beat Denver 162–158 on 2 November 1990.

GREATEST NBA GAME-WINNING MARGIN

The greatest winning margin in an NBA game is 68 points, when the Cleveland Cavaliers beat Miami Heat 148–80 on 17 December 1991.

MOST POINTS IN NBA ALL-STAR GAMES

The most points scored in NBA All-Star games is 262 by Michael Jordan (USA). He scored 20 points in his 14th appearance in Atlanta, Georgia, USA on 9 February 2003.

MOST POINTS SCORED IN AN NBA CAREER

The most points scored in an NBA career is 38,387 (at an average of 24.6 points per game) by Kareem Abdul-Jabbar (USA) from 1969 to 1989. This includes 15,837 field goals scored in regular season games and 5,762 points, including 2,356 field goals, scored in playoff games.

MOST CONSECUTIVE NBA GAMES PLAYED

The most consecutive NBA games played is 1,177 by AC Green (USA) for the Los Angeles Lakers, Phoenix Suns, Dallas Mavericks and Miami Heat from 19 November 1986 to 20 March 2001.

LONGEST BASKETBALL MARATHON

The longest basketball marathon lasted for 26 hr 42 min. The record was set by Warwick Academy (Bermuda) at the Bermuda College gym, Paget, Bermuda, from 15 to 16 March 2003. In total, 27 games were played.

MOST CONSECUTIVE FREE THROWS

Ted St Martin (USA) scored 5,221 consecutive free throws at Jacksonville, Florida, USA, on 28 April 1996.

MOST CONSECUTIVE FREE THROWS IN AN NBA SEASON

Mike Williams (USA), of the Minnesota Timberwolves, made 97 consecutive free throws in NBA matches between 24 March and 9 November 1993.

FURTHEST HEADED BASKETBALL SHOT

Eyal Horn (Israel) shot a basketball with his head while standing a distance of 7.62 m (25 ft) from the backboard in Los Angeles, USA, on 10 November 2000.

FURTHEST BASKETBALL DRIBBLE

The greatest distance covered in 24 hours while dribbling a basketball is 156.71 km (97.37 miles) by Suresh Joachim (Australia) at Vulkanhallen, Oslo, Norway, from 30 to 31 March 2001.

MOST BASKETBALLS DRIBBLED SIMULTANEOUSLY

On 15 August 2000 at his home in Mesa, Arizona, USA, Joseph Odhiambo (USA) dribbled six basketballs simultaneously, beating his previous record of five.

MOST ASSISTS IN AN NBA CAREER

The most assists in an NBA career is 15,585 in 1,475 games by John Stockton (USA) playing for the Utah Jazz from 1984 to 2003.

MOST REBOUNDS IN AN NBA CAREER

The most rebounds in an NBA career is 23,924 in 1,045 games by Wilt Chamberlain (USA) playing for the Philadelphia Warriors (1959–62), San Francisco Warriors (1962–65), Philadelphia 76ers (1965–68) and Los Angeles Lakers (1968–73).

MOST BLOCKS IN AN NBA CAREER

The most blocks in an NBA career is 3,830 in 1,238 games by Hakeem Olajuwon (USA) playing for the Houston Rockets (1984–2001) and the Toronto Raptors (2001–02).

TALLEST NBA PLAYER

The tallest ever NBA player was Gheorghe Muresan (Romania) of the Washington Bullets, who was 2.31 m (7 ft 7 in). His first game was in 1994.

YOUNGEST NBA PLAYER TO START A GAME

The youngest player to start an NBA game is Kobe Bryant (USA), who played for the Los Angeles Lakers against the Dallas Mavericks on 28 January 1997 aged 18 years 158 days.

MOST STEALS IN AN NBA CAREER

The most steals in an NBA career is 3,216 in 1,475 games by John Stockton (USA, above) playing for the Utah Jazz from 1984 to 2003.

ICE HOCKEY

MOST HAT-TRICKS IN A CAREER

The greatest number of hat-tricks scored in a National Hockey League (NHL) career is 50, by Wayne Gretzky (Canada, right, with the 1999 All-Star trophy). He played in the NHL between 1979 and 1999.

MOST POINTS SCORED IN AN NHL CAREER

The most points scored in an NHL career is 2,857, by Wayne Gretzky (Canada) for the Edmonton Oilers, Los Angeles Kings, St Louis Blues and New York Rangers between 1979 and 1999. The points total comprises 894 goals and 1,963 assists achieved in 1,487 games.

MOST POINTS SCORED IN THE STANLEY CUP

The most points scored in the Stanley Cup is 47, by Wayne Gretzky (Canada) for the Edmonton Oilers in 1985. The points scored comprise 17 goals and 30 assists, which are in themselves records.

MOST MEN'S OLYMPIC ICE HOCKEY WINS

The most men's Olympic ice hockey titles won is eight by the USSR in 1956, 1964, 1968, 1972, 1976, 1984, 1988 and 1992 (as the CIS).

MOST WINS IN AN NHL SEASON

The most wins in an NHL season is 62 by the Detroit Red Wings (USA) in the 1995/96 season.

MOST LOSSES IN AN NHL SEASON

The most losses in an NHL season is 71 by the San Jose Sharks (USA), who managed this in the 1992/93 season, despite playing a record 32 games at home.

LONGEST NHL WINNING STREAK

The longest run of winning games home and away in NHL history is 17 by the Pittsburgh Penguins (USA) between 9 March and 10 April 1993.

LONGEST ICE HOCKEY GAME

The longest game of ice hockey lasted 62 hr 15 min and was played by the Moosomin Moose Hockey Team, at Moosomin Communiplex, Saskatchewan, Canada, from 9 to 12 January 2003.

MOST TEAM GOALS IN AN NHL SEASON

The most goals scored by a team in an NHL season is 446 by the Edmonton Oilers (Canada) in 1983/84. In the same season they also achieved a record 1,182 points.

MOST GOALS IN AN NHL SEASON BY A ROOKIE

Teemu Selanne (Finland) scored a total of 76 goals in his first season for the Winnipeg Jets in 1992/93.

MOST GAMES IN A PROFESSIONAL ICE HOCKEY CAREER

The most games played in a professional career is 2,421 by Gordon 'Gordie' Howe (Canada) from 1946 to 1979. This includes 1,767 regular season games and 157 playoff games for the Detroit Red Wings and the Hartford Whalers in the NHL, and 419 regular season games and 78 playoff games for the Houston Aeros and the New England Whalers in the World Hockey Association.

QUICKEST NHL GOAL

The fastest time for a goal to be scored in an NHL match is five seconds. This record is shared by three players: Doug Smail (Canada) for the Winnipeg Jets against the St Louis Blues in Winnipeg, Manitoba, Canada, on 20 December 1981; Bryan John Trottier (Canada) for the New York Islanders against the Boston Bruins in Boston, Massachusetts, USA, on 22 March 1984; and Alexander Mogilny (Russia) for the Buffalo Sabres against the Toronto Maple Leafs in Toronto, Ontario, Canada, on 21 December 1991.

QUICKEST ICE HOCKEY GOAL

Per Olsen (Denmark) scored two seconds after the start of the match for Rungsted against Odense in the Danish First Division at Hørsholm, Denmark, on 14 January 1990. Jørgen Palmgren Erichsen (Norway) scored three goals in 10 seconds for Frisk against Holmen in a junior league match in Norway on 17 March 1991.

MOST ICE HOCKEY TARGETS SHOT IN 30 SECONDS

Daniel Wågström (Sweden) hit four goal targets in 30 seconds on the set of the *Guinness Rekord TV* programme in Stockholm, Sweden, on 5 November 2001.

MOST WOMEN'S ICE HOCKEY WORLD CHAMPIONSHIPS

The women's ice hockey World Championships have been held since 1990 and have been won on each occasion – a total of seven times – by Canada (in 1990, 1992, 1994, 1997, 1999, 2000 and 2001). In winning the seven titles, Canada (below, winning Olympic gold in 2002) have not lost a single game.

MOST ASSISTS IN AN NHL CAREER

The most assists in an NHL career is 1,963 by Wayne Gretzky (Canada), for the Edmonton Oilers, the Los Angeles Kings, the St Louis Blues and the New York Rangers between 1979 and 1999.

MOST GOALTENDING SHUTOUTS IN AN NHL CAREER

The most goaltending shutouts in an NHL career is 103 achieved by Terry Sawchuk (USA) for the Detroit Red Wings, the Boston Bruins, the Toronto Maple Leafs, the Los Angeles Kings and the New York Rangers between 1949 and 1970.

MOST GOALTENDING SHUTOUTS IN NHL PLAYOFFS

The most shutouts by a goaltender in NHL playoff history is 22 by Patrick Roy (Canada) playing for the Montreal Canadiens and the Colorado Avalanche between 1985 and 2002.

MOST CAREER WINS BY AN NHL GOALTENDER

At the end of the 2002 regular season, the most NHL career wins by a goaltender was 516 by Patrick Roy (Canada) of the Colorado Avalanche. Roy began his NHL career with the Montreal Canadiens in 1985.

MOST CONSECUTIVE NHL GAMES PLAYED

The most consecutive NHL games played is 964 by Doug Jarvis (Canada) playing for the Montreal Canadiens, the Washington Capitals and the Hartford Whalers from 8 October 1975 to 10 October 1987.

MOST NHL PLAYOFF PENALTY MINUTES

The most penalty minutes amassed in NHL playoff games is 729 by Dale Hunter (Canada) playing for the Quebec Nordiques, Washington Capitals and Colorado Avalanche from 1980 to 1999.

MOST PENALTY MINUTES IN AN NHL CAREER

The player with the most penalty minutes in NHL history is Dave 'Tiger' Williams (Canada) with 3,966, amassed over 17 seasons between 1971 and 1988, playing for the Toronto Maple Leafs, the Vancouver Canucks, the Detroit Red Wings, the Los Angeles Kings and the now defunct Hartford Whalers.

MOST PENALTIES IN AN NHL GAME

The most penalties awarded in an NHL game is 85 when the Edmonton Oilers played the Los Angeles Kings in Los Angeles, California, USA on 28 February 1990.

LONGEST NHL INFRACTION SUSPENSION

The longest suspension handed to a player for an on-ice incident is 23 games to Marty McSorley (Canada) of the Boston Bruins in February 2000. McSorley had struck Vancouver Canucks' Donald Brashear (Canada) on the head with his stick during a game at Vancouver, British Columbia, Canada on 21 February 2000.

MOST OVERALL GOALS IN A WINTER PARALYMPICS ICE SLEDGE HOCKEY COMPETITION

The most goals scored overall in the ice sledge hockey competition at the Winter Paralympics is 16 by Jens Kask (Sweden); four in 1994, seven in 1998 and five in 2002.

MOST OVERALL ASSISTS IN A WINTER PARALYMPICS ICE SLEDGE HOCKEY COMPETITION

The most overall assists in an ice sledge hockey competition at the Winter Paralympics is 16 by Helge Bjoernstad (Norway); one in 1994, five in 1998 and ten in 2002. The total for 2002 is a record for a single Games.

MOST NHL ALL-STAR SELECTIONS

Gordie Howe (Canada, below) was selected 21 times for National Hockey League All-Star games while playing for the Detroit Red Wings between 1946 and 1979. He was selected for the first team on 12 occasions and the second team nine times.

SOCCER

MOST COUNTRIES IN FIFA WORLD CUP QUALIFIERS
A record 198 federations registered to play in the qualifiers for the 2002 FIFA World Cup, held jointly in South Korea and Japan. The football federations of Afghanistan, Burundi, New Guinea, Niger and North Korea were the exceptions.

MOST GOALS IN A WORLD CUP FINALS
The most goals scored by a player in a single World Cup Finals tournament is 13 by Just Fontaine (France) in Sweden in 1958.

MOST WORLD CUP CLEAN SHEETS
The goalkeeper to have kept the most clean sheets in World Cup Finals matches is Peter Shilton (UK), who played for England in a total of 10 matches in three tournaments between 1982 and 1990 without conceding a single goal.

FASTEST WORLD CUP RED CARD
The fastest time to be sent off in a World Cup Finals soccer match is 3 minutes by Ion Vladoiu (Romania) playing against Switzerland on 22 June 1994 at the Pontiac Silverdome, Detroit, Michigan, USA.

MOST WORLD CUP WINS
The Fédération Internationale de Football Association (FIFA), which was founded on 21 May 1904, instituted the first World Cup on 13 July 1930, in Montevideo, Uruguay. The tournament is held quadrennially. Brazil has won five times, in 1958, 1962, 1970, 1994 and 2002. Brazil's captain Cafu (left) lifted the trophy in 2002 in Yokohama, Japan.

MOST OLYMPIC TITLES WON
The most Olympic soccer titles won is three, by Great Britain in 1900 (unofficial competition), 1908, 1912; and Hungary, in 1952, 1964, 1968.

MOST WOMEN'S OLYMPIC SOCCER TITLES
Women's soccer was introduced to the Olympic Games in 1996. The winners have been the USA in 1996 and Norway in 2000.

MOST FUTSAL WORLD CUP TITLES
Since it was first held in 1989, the Futsal (indoor soccer) World Cup has been won three times by Brazil, in 1989, 1992 and 1996. The fourth tournament, held in 2000 in Guatemala, was won by Spain, who beat Brazil in the final.

MOST EUROPEAN CUP WINS
The most European Champions Cup (instituted 1956) wins is nine by Real Madrid (Spain), in 1956–60, 1966, 1998, 2000 and 2002.

MOST AFRICAN CUP OF NATIONS WINS
The record for the most wins at the African Cup of Nations is four, held jointly by Ghana (1963, 1965, 1978, 1982), Egypt (1957, 1959, 1986, 1998) and Cameroon (1984, 1998, 2000, 2002).

MOST WORLD CUP FINALS GOALS
The most goals scored in World Cup Finals tournaments is 14 by Gerd Müller (West Germany, right), who scored ten in 1970 in Mexico and four in West Germany in 1974, when the host nation went on to lift the trophy.

MOST ASIAN CUP WINS
The most wins in the Asian Cup is three, by Iran in 1968, 1972 and 1976, and Saudi Arabia in 1984, 1988 and 1996.

HIGHEST SCORE IN AN INTERNATIONAL SOCCER MATCH
The highest score ever achieved in an international match is 31–0 by Australia against American Samoa. It occurred in a World Cup qualifying match at Coffs Harbour, New South Wales, Australia, on 11 April 2001. During the match, Archie Thompson (Australia) scored an international record 13 goals.

MOST EXPENSIVE SOCCER PLAYER
The highest transfer fee quoted for a player is a reported 13 billion Spanish pesetas (£47 million or $66.36 million) for Zinedine Zidane (France) for his transfer from Juventus (Italy) to Real Madrid (Spain) on 9 July 2001.

OLDEST SOCCER GROUND
The first competitive game was played on 26 December 1860 at Sandygate, owned by Hallam FC, Sheffield, South Yorkshire, UK.

OLDEST CUP COMPETITION
The oldest soccer trophy is the Youdan Cup, first won in 1867 by Hallam FC in Sheffield, South Yorkshire, UK.

HIGHEST SCORE IN A WOMEN'S INTERNATIONAL MATCH

In a women's international, the record score is 21–0 and has occurred on four occasions: Japan against Guam at Guangzhou, China, on 5 December 1997; Canada against Puerto Rico at Centennial Park, Toronto, Canada, on 28 August 1998; and Australia against American Samoa and New Zealand against Samoa, both at Mt Smart Stadium, Auckland, New Zealand, on 9 October 1998.

MOST LEAGUE TITLES

The record number of successive national league championships is eleven by Al-Ansar Sporting Club of Lebanon, who were top of their league between 1988 and 1999.

FASTEST HAT-TRICK

The fastest time to score three goals is 2 min 13 sec by Jimmy O'Connor (Ireland) for Shelbourne against Bohemians at Dallymount Park, Dublin, on 19 November 1967.

FASTEST HAT-TRICK IN AN INTERNATIONAL

Japanese international Masashi 'Gon' Nakayama scored a hat-trick in 3 min 15 sec against Brunei during an Asian Cup qualifying match on 16 February 2000. Nakayama netted on 1 min, 2 min and 3 min 15 sec, bettering the 62-year-old mark set by England's George Hall, who scored three goals in 3 min 30 sec against Ireland.

MOST WORLD CUP HAT-TRICKS

Four players have scored two hat-tricks in World Cup tournaments: Sándor Kocsis (Hungary) at the 1954 tournament in Switzerland; Just Fontaine (France) in Sweden in 1958; Gerd Müller (West Germany) at the 1970 tournament in Mexico; and Gabriel Batistuta (Argentina) on his World Cup debut against Greece in the USA in 1994, and against Jamaica in France in 1998.

MOST GOALS IN A CAREER

The most goals scored in a specified period is 1,279 by Edson Arantes do Nascimento (known as Pelé, Brazil), from 7 September 1956 to 1 October 1977 in 1,363 games. His best year was 1959 with 126 goals, and the Milésimo (1,000th) came from a penalty for his club Santos at the Maracanã Stadium, Rio de Janeiro, Brazil, on 19 November 1969 when playing his 909th first-class match. He later added two more goals in special appearances.

MOST GOALS SCORED DIRECT FROM CORNER KICKS

The most goals scored in a single match by an individual direct from corners is three by Steve Cromey (UK) for Ashgreen Utd against Dunlop FC on 24 February 2002 at Bedworth, Warwickshire, UK, and by Daniel White (UK) for Street and Glastonbury under-11s against Westfield Boys on 7 April 2002.

MOST PENALTIES MISSED BY A PLAYER IN AN INTERNATIONAL

Martín Palermo (Argentina) missed three penalties during his team's defeat by Colombia in the 1999 Copa América in Paraguay. His first shot hit the crossbar, the second landed in the stands and the third was saved.

FASTEST SOCCER KICK

The fastest soccer kick is 129 km/h (80.1 mph) achieved by Francisco Javier Galan Màrin (Spain) at the studios of *El Show de los Récords*, Madrid, Spain, on 29 October 2001.

FASTEST GOAL IN A WORLD CUP FINALS MATCH

The quickest goal scored in a World Cup Finals match, as recognized by FIFA, is 11 seconds, by Hakan Sukur (right) for Turkey against South Korea at Daegu, South Korea, on 29 June 2002.

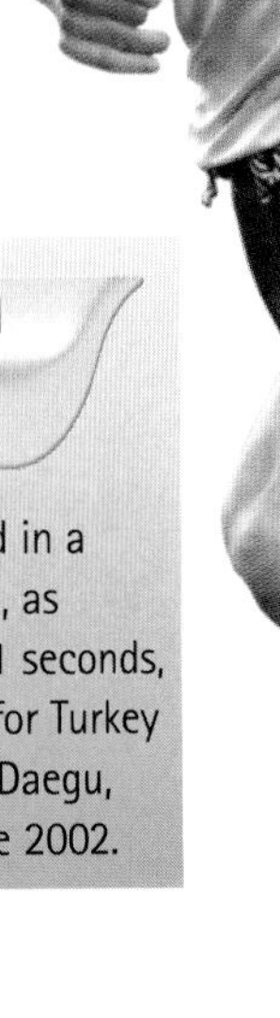

MOST UNDISCIPLINED SOCCER MATCH

In the local cup match between Tongham Youth Club, Surrey, UK, and Hawley, Hampshire, UK, on 3 November 1969, the referee booked all 22 players, including one who went to hospital, and one of the linesmen. The match, won by Tongham 2-0, was described by a player as 'a good, hard game'.

FASTEST GOAL

Goals scored in three seconds and under, following kick-off, have been claimed by a number of players. From video evidence, Ricardo Olivera (Uruguay) scored in 2.8 seconds for Río Negro against Soriano at the José Enrique Rodó stadium, Soriano, Uruguay, on 26 December 1998.

SOCCER

MOST GOALS IN A MAJOR LEAGUE SOCCER GAME

The most goals scored in a Major League Soccer (MLS) game by a player is five by Clint Mathis (USA) for the MetroStars against the Dallas Burn on 26 August 2000. Mathis' team went on to win the game with a final score of 6–4.

MOST ASSISTS IN A MAJOR LEAGUE SOCCER SEASON

The most assists by one player in an MLS season is 26 by Carlos Valderama (Colombia) for the Tampa Bay Mutiny in 2000.

MOST MAJOR LEAGUE SOCCER GOALS

The most goals scored in MLS is 88 by Ray Lassiter (USA) for the Tampa Bay Mutiny, DC United, Miami Fusion and Kansas City Wizards in 1996–2001.

MOST MAJOR LEAGUE SOCCER TITLES

DC United of Washington DC, USA, has won three MLS titles, in 1996, 1997 and 1999.

MOST GOALS SCORED BY A GOALKEEPER IN ONE GAME

Paraguayan José Luis Chilavert scored a hat-trick of penalties for Vélez Sarsfield in their 6–1 defeat of Ferro Carril Oeste in the Argentine professional league. A penalty and free kick specialist, Chilavert also holds the record for the most goals scored by a goalkeeper, with 56 league and international goals from July 1992 to October 2001 for Paraguay and Strasbourg, France. He is the only goalkeeper to score in a World Cup qualifier.

YOUNGEST PLAYER IN ALL FOUR ENGLISH SOCCER DIVISIONS

The youngest person to play in all four divisions of the soccer league is Melvyn John Rees (UK, b. 25 January 1967). Rees achieved this feat during the 1987/88 season, at just 20 years of age, playing for Watford. The goalkeeper previously turned out for Cardiff City and went on to play in the inaugural season of the Premiership in 1992/93 for Sheffield United, following a spell at West Bromwich Albion. Having already fought off one attack of cancer, he succumbed to a recurrence in 1993, aged 26.

MOST EXPENSIVE DEFENDER

Rio Ferdinand (UK, left in picture) continued to be the world's most expensive defender in July 2002 after joining Manchester United from Leeds United (both UK) in a deal worth a reported £30 million ($46.9 million).

FASTEST CHAMPIONS LEAGUE GOAL

The fastest goal in a Champions League match was scored by Gilberto Silva (Brazil, left) in 20.07 seconds playing for UK club Arsenal against Dutch side PSV Eindhoven in Eindhoven, The Netherlands, on 25 September 2002. Arsenal went on to win the game 4–0.

HIGHEST SCORE IN A NATIONAL SOCCER CUP FINAL

In 1935 Lausanne-Sports beat Nordstern Basel 10–0 in the Swiss Cup Final. Two years later they were beaten by an identical margin by Grasshopper-Club (Zurich) in the same Cup Final.

MOST SOCCER MATCHES PLAYED

Peter Shilton (UK) made a record 1,389 senior appearances, including a record 1,005 league appearances – comprising 286 for Leicester City (1966–74), 110 for Stoke City (1974–77), 202 for Nottingham Forest (1977–82), 188 for Southampton (1982–87), 175 for Derby County (1987–92), 34 for Plymouth Argyle (1992–94), one for Bolton Wanderers (1995) and nine for Leyton Orient (1996–97) – one League play-off, 86 FA Cups, 102 League Cups, 125 internationals, 13 Under-23s, four Football League XIs and 53 various European and other club competitions.

LONGEST CLEAN SHEET

The longest that any goalkeeper has succeeded in preventing goals being scored past him in top class competition is 1,275 minutes (just over 14 matches) by Abel Resino (Spain) of Atlético Madrid. The record in international matches is 1,142 minutes (nearly 13 matches) by Dino Zoff (Italy) from September 1972 to June 1974.

MOST EUROPEAN CHAMPIONSHIPS

Germany has won the European Championship three times, in 1972, 1980 and 1996 (the first two as West Germany). A women's version was first held in 1984 and the most wins is four by Germany, in 1989, 1991, 1995 and 1997.

MOST CHAMPIONS LEAGUE VICTORIES

Real Madrid (Spain) has won the most UEFA Champions League matches with 49 victories between 1992 and 2003, scoring a record 176 goals in the process. With 46 wins and 162 goals, Manchester United (UK) is second.

MOST CHAMPIONS LEAGUE APPEARANCES

The most UEFA Champions League appearances by an individual player is 76 by Gary Neville (UK) for Manchester United between 1993 and 2003, having made his debut against Galatasaray in Istanbul, Turkey, in a second round tie.

MOST CHAMPIONS LEAGUE GOALS

Raúl González Blanco (Spain) has scored 39 goals in UEFA Champions League matches, playing for Real Madrid from 1992 to date.

LARGEST SOCCER BALL

A soccer ball made from artificial leather PV-PVC and sewn by hand, made by Ihsan Sports (Pakistan), had a diameter of 4 m (13 ft 1 in) when measured on 30 June 2002.

MOST CONSECUTIVE SOCCER PASSES

The most consecutive soccer passes is 557 by members of the McDonald's Youth Football Scheme at Tsing Yi, Hong Kong, China, on 4 May 2002. The event lasted four and a half hours, and 1,250 children aged 6 to 14 took part.

LONGEST TIME SPINNING A SOCCER BALL ON THE FOREHEAD

On 25 November 2001 Tommy Baker (UK) spun a FIFA-approved soccer ball on his forehead for a record 11.9 seconds after transferring it from his finger at the studios of *Guinness Rekord TV* in Stockholm, Sweden.

LONGEST TIME HEADING A BALL

The world record for heading a soccer ball without it dropping is 8 hr 12 min 25 sec by Goderdzi Makharadze (Georgia) at the Boris Paichadze National Stadium, Tbilisi, Georgia, on 26 May 1996.

FURTHEST DISTANCE TRAVELLED KEEPING A SOCCER BALL IN THE AIR

Jan Skorkovsky (Czechoslovakia) kept a soccer ball in the air without it dropping while travelling 42.195 km (26.219 miles) as a competitor in the Prague City marathon on 8 July 1990. He finished the marathon in a time of 7 hr 18 min 55 sec.

MOST PEOPLE JUGGLING A SOCCER BALL SIMULTANEOUSLY

The most individuals each keeping a soccer ball in the air at the same time is 446 by teams of girls taking part in the Football Association National Centres of Excellence Festival at the University of Warwick, Coventry, UK, on 19 June 1999.

MOST TOUCHES OF A SOCCER BALL IN 30 SECONDS

The most touches of a soccer ball in 30 seconds, whilst keeping the ball in the air, is 136 by Ferdie Adoboe (USA) at Fort Lowell Park, Tucson, Arizona, USA, on 22 January 1999. He also completed 262 touches in one minute, a record which he subsequently went on to break with 266 touches in July 2000.

MOST INTERNATIONAL CAPS

The most international appearances for a national team by a player is 170 by Claudio Suarez (Mexico, below) between 1992 and 2002.

RUGBY

MOST INTERNATIONAL APPEARANCES BY A RUGBY UNION FORWARD

Jason Leonard (UK, above) has played 102 times for England. The prop was awarded his first cap in July 1990 against Argentina in Buenos Aires and he won his 100th against France in the Six Nations Championship at Twickenham, UK, in February 2003.

MOST CONVERSIONS IN 12 HOURS

The most rugby conversions kicked in 12 hours is 1,782 by members of Braintree (UK) under-15s rugby squad on 13 July 2002 at Braintree Rugby Club, Braintree, Essex, UK. The kicks were taken from three positions along the 22-metre line.

MOST CONSECUTIVE RUGBY LEAGUE APPEARANCES

Keith Elwell (UK) played in 239 consecutive games for Widnes from 5 May 1977 to 5 September 1982.

MOST CONSECUTIVE HAT-TRICKS IN RUGBY LEAGUE

The most consecutive matches in which an individual player has scored a hat-trick of tries is 12 by Richard Lopag of Deighton New Saracens, Huddersfield, West Yorkshire, UK, during the 2000/01 season.

MOST RUGBY LEAGUE WORLD CUP WINS

Australia has won the World Cup eight times, in 1957, 1968, 1970, 1977, 1988, 1992, 1995 and 2000, as well as a win in the International Championship of 1975. The competition was first held in 1954.

MOST RUGBY LEAGUE CHALLENGE CUP WINS

The Rugby League Challenge Cup (inaugurated 1896/97 season) has been won 17 times by Wigan, in 1924, 1929, 1948, 1951, 1958-59, 1965, 1985, 1988-95 and 2002.

HIGHEST SCORE IN AN INTERNATIONAL RUGBY LEAGUE MATCH

The highest score in an international league match is Australia's 110–4 defeat of Russia during the Rugby League World Cup at Hull, East Yorkshire, UK, on 4 November 2000.

MOST POINTS SCORED BY AN INDIVIDUAL IN AN INTERNATIONAL RUGBY LEAGUE MATCH

Hazem El Masri (Lebanon) scored a record 48 points (16 goals, 4 tries) against Morocco in a World Cup qualifying match at Avignon, France, on 17 November 1999.

MOST SUPER LEAGUE TITLES

The most Super League titles won by a team is four by St Helens, in 1996, 1999, 2000 and 2002. The Super League is the UK's premier rugby league competition, instituted in 1996.

HIGHEST ATTENDANCE AT A RUGBY UNION MATCH

The largest paying attendance for an international match is 109,874 on 15 July 2000 for New Zealand's 39–35 Tri-Nations victory over Australia at Stadium Australia, Sydney, NSW, Australia.

MOST POINTS SCORED BY AN INDIVIDUAL IN A RUGBY UNION SEASON

The first class season scoring record is 581 points by Samuel Arthur Doble (UK) for Moseley, in 52 matches in 1971/72. He also scored 47 points for England in South Africa out of season.

MOST INTERNATIONAL RUGBY UNION APPEARANCES

Philippe Sella (France) played in 111 internationals for France, between 1982 and 1995.

MOST RUGBY UNION WORLD CUP WINS

The most wins of the Webb Ellis Trophy (instituted 1987) is two by Australia, in 1991 and 1999.

MOST WORLD SEVENS SERIES TITLES

The World Sevens Series, which began in 1999, has been won every year by New Zealand (team captain Eric Rush pictured above) in 2000, 2001 and 2002. The series is a competition consisting of between nine and eleven separate sevens tournaments played around the world each season.

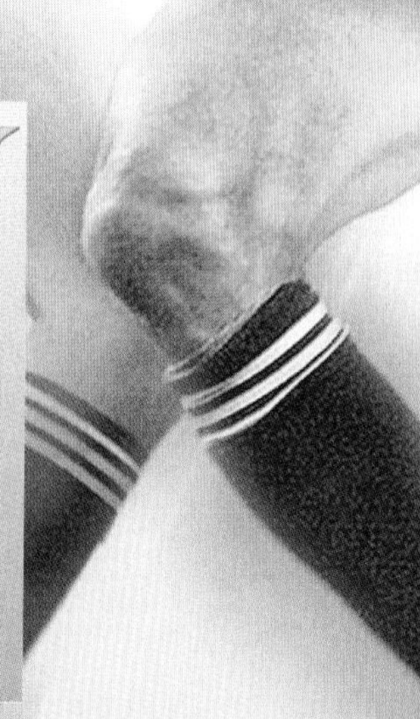

HIGHEST COMBINED SCORE IN A PROFESSIONAL CROSS-CODE RUGBY MATCH

The highest combined points score in a professional cross-code rugby match is 80 points scored between St Helens (Rugby League) and Sale Sharks (Rugby Union) at Knowsley Road, St Helens, Merseyside, UK, on 27 January 2003. Sale Sharks won the match 41–39.

MOST WOMEN'S RUGBY UNION WORLD CUP TITLES

The women's World Cup has been contested four times (1991, 1994, 1998 and 2002). New Zealand has won the title twice, in 1998 and 2002, while USA and England have one win apiece.

MOST POINTS IN AN INTERNATIONAL RUGBY UNION CAREER

Neil Jenkins (UK) has scored 1,052 points in 86 matches for Wales (1,011 points in 83 matches) and the British Lions (41 points in three matches), between 1991 and March 2001.

MOST TRI-NATIONS TITLES

The Tri-Nations, inaugurated in 1996 and played annually between Australia, New Zealand and South Africa, has been won a record four times by New Zealand, in 1996-97, 1999 and 2002.

MOST CONSECUTIVE INTERNATIONAL RUGBY UNION APPEARANCES

The most consecutive international appearances is 63 by hooker Sean Fitzpatrick (New Zealand) between 1986 and 1995.

MOST POINTS SCORED BY A TEAM IN THE SIX NATIONS TOURNAMENT

England scored a record 229 points in their five games in 2001.

MOST SIX NATIONS CHAMPIONSHIPS

England have won more Six Nations Championships than any other country with three, in 2000 2001 and 2003. Their 2003 campaign was also a grand slam win. The Six Nations replaced the Five Nations tournament in 2000 when Italy were invited to join the historic competition.

MOST INTERNATIONAL GRAND SLAMS

The most grand slams – winning all matches in what was the Five and is now the Six Nations Championship – is 12 by England between 1913 and 2003.

HIGHEST RUGBY UNION POSTS

The posts at the Roan Antelope Rugby Union Club, Luanshya, Zambia, are the world's highest, at 33.54 m (110 ft 0.5 in).

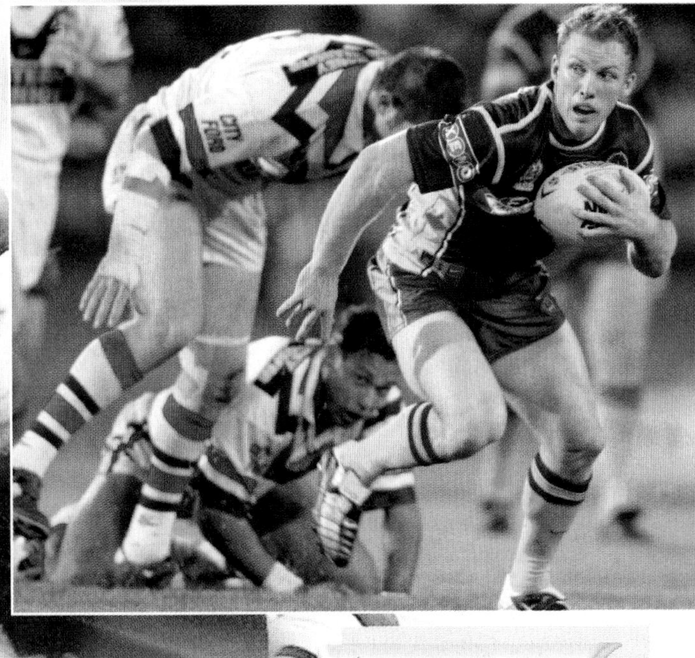

MOST NRL TITLES

The most National Rugby League (NRL) titles won by a team is two by the Brisbane Broncos, in 1998 and 2000. The NRL is Australia's premier rugby league competition, instituted in 1998. Broncos fullback Darren Lockyer (Australia) is pictured above.

CRICKET

HIGHEST BATTING AVERAGE IN TEST CRICKET

Don Bradman (Australia, pictured on right of photo with Australian captain Bill Woodfull), holds the record for the highest batting average with 99.94, playing for Australia in 52 Tests (6,996 runs in 80 innings) in 1928–48.

FASTEST TEST DOUBLE CENTURY

The fastest 200 scored in a Test match was by Nathan Astle (New Zealand) playing against England in the first Test at Jade Stadium, Christchurch, New Zealand, on 17 March 2002. He reached the 200 mark in 153 balls and proceeded to score 222 off 168, including 28 fours and 11 sixes. England, however, went on to win the game by 98 runs, making Astle's effort the highest individual innings in a lost game.

MOST RUNS IN TEST CRICKET

Allan Border (Australia) scored 11,174 runs in 156 Tests (av 50.56) between 1978 and 1994.

MOST CENTURIES IN TEST CRICKET

Sunil Gavaskar (India) scored 34 centuries (in 214 innings) playing for India between 1971 and 1987.

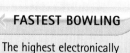

FASTEST BOWLING

The highest electronically measured speed for a ball bowled by any bowler is 161.3 km/h (100.23 mph) by Shoaib Akhtar (Pakistan, above) against England on 22 February 2003 in a World Cup match at Newlands, Cape Town, South Africa.

HIGHEST INDIVIDUAL TEST INNINGS

Brian Lara (Trinidad) scored 375 in 12 hr 48 min for the West Indies against England at Recreation Ground, St John's, Antigua, between 16 and 18 April 1994.

MOST CATCHES IN TEST CRICKET

Mark Waugh (Australia) made 181 catches in 128 Tests for Australia between 1991 and 2002.

MOST EXTRAS CONCEDED IN A TEST INNINGS

The West Indies conceded a total of 71 sundries in Pakistan's first innings at Georgetown, Guyana, on 3–4 April 1988. This figure was made up of 21 byes, eight leg byes, four wides and 38 no-balls.

HIGHEST TEST SCORE

Sri Lanka scored 952 for 6 against India at Colombo, Sri Lanka, between 4 and 6 August 1997.

HIGHEST MAIDEN TEST CENTURY SCORE

Garfield Sobers (Barbados) scored 365 not out for the West Indies against Pakistan at Kingston, Jamaica, on 27–28 February and 1 March 1958.

BIGGEST TEST PARTNERSHIP

On 4–6 August 1997, Sanath Jayasuriya (340) and Roshan Mahanama (225) scored 576 for the second wicket for Sri Lanka against India at Colombo, Sri Lanka.

LOWEST INNINGS TOTAL

The lowest innings total in Test cricket is 26 by New Zealand against England at Auckland, New Zealand, on 28 March 1955.

LOWEST TEST BOWLING AVERAGE

George Lohmann (England) had a bowling average of 10.75 playing for England. He appeared in 18 tests between 1886 and 1896 and took 112 wickets.

MOST CATCHES BY A WICKETKEEPER

Ian Healy (Australia) made 366 catches in 119 Tests playing for Australia between 1988 and 1999.

OLDEST TEST CRICKET PLAYER

The oldest man to play in a Test match was Wilfred Rhodes (UK), aged 52 years 165 days, for England against the West Indies at Kingston, Jamaica, on 12 April 1930. Rhodes made his debut in the last Test captained by WG Grace (UK) who, at 50 years 320 days old on 3 June 1899, was the oldest ever Test captain.

MOST 'DUCKS' IN TEST MATCHES

The player who has the dubious honour of scoring the most 'ducks' (or zeros) in Test cricket is Courtney Walsh (Jamaica) with 43 in 185 innings for the West Indies, between November 1984 and April 2001.

BEST ONE-DAY INTERNATIONAL BOWLING START

The best bowling start to a match was made by Chaminda Vass (Sri Lanka) playing in a World Cup game for Sri Lanka against Canada at Pietermaritzburg, South Africa, on 15 February 2003. He took a hat-trick with the first three balls of the game and then claimed a fourth victim in his opening over before finishing with 6 for 25. Sri Lanka went on to win the match by 10 wickets.

LOWEST ONE-DAY INTERNATIONAL TEAM SCORE

The lowest completed innings total is 36 by Canada against Sri Lanka at Boland Park, Paarl, South Africa, on 19 February 2003.

MOST WICKETS IN A ONE-DAY INTERNATIONAL CAREER

The most wickets taken in a one-day career is 502 (at an average of 23.52) by Wasim Akram (Pakistan) in 356 matches between 1985 and 2003.

HIGHEST BATTING AVERAGE IN A SEASON

The highest batting average for a season is 330 by Colin Gill (UK) for Plymstock 2nd XI playing in the Devon Cricket League in 1998. Gill batted 10 times and was dismissed just once in the season.

HIGHEST INDIVIDUAL INNINGS SCORE

Brian Lara (Trinidad) scored 501 not out in 7 hr 54 min for Warwickshire against Durham at Edgbaston, West Midlands, UK, between 3 and 6 June 1994. His innings included the most runs in a day (390 on 6 June) and the most runs from boundaries (308 – 62 fours and 10 sixes).

HIGHEST INNINGS IN A LIMITED OVERS MATCH

The highest innings by an individual in a limited overs match is 268 by Surrey's Alistair Brown (UK) against Glamorgan on 19 June 2002 at The Oval, London, UK, in a Cheltenham and Gloucester Trophy match. During his stay at the wicket, Brown hit 12 sixes and 30 fours.

The highest scored by a team in a limited overs match is 438 by Surrey against Glamorgan in the same match.

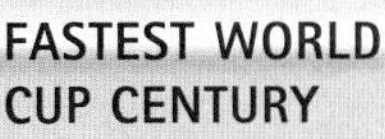

FASTEST WORLD CUP CENTURY

The fastest World Cup 100 runs scored by an individual was made in 67 balls by John Davison (Canada, above) playing against the West Indies at Centurion Park, Northern Transvaal, South Africa, on 23 February 2003. The innings contained eight fours and six sixes.

LONGEST INDIVIDUAL INNINGS

Rajiv Nayyar (India) batted for 16 hr 55 min when scoring 271 for Himachal Pradesh against Jammu and Kashmir at Chamba, India, between 1 and 3 November 1999.

MOST WORLD CUP WINS

The most tournament wins is three by Australia in 1987, 1999 and 2003.

HIGHEST AND LOWEST WORLD CUP TEAM SCORES

The highest innings total in a cricket World Cup match is 398-5 by Sri Lanka against Kenya at Kandy, Sri Lanka, on 6 March 1996.

The lowest cricket World Cup score is 36 by Canada against Sri Lanka at Boland Park, Paarl, South Africa, on 19 February 2003.

MOST RUNS OFF A BALL

Garry Chapman (Australia) scored 17 (all run, with no overthrows) off a single delivery for Banyule against Macleod at Windsor Reserve, Victoria, Australia, on 13 October 1990. Chapman had pulled the ball to mid-wicket where it disappeared into 25-cm-high (10-in) grass.

YOUNGEST TEST PLAYER

Hasan Raza (Pakistan, b. 11 March 1982) made his debut aged 14 years 227 days, against Zimbabwe at Faisalabad, Pakistan, on 24 October 1996.

BALL SPORTS

HOCKEY

MOST APPEARANCES IN MEN'S HOCKEY

By January 2001 Jacques Brinkman had represented The Netherlands 337 times since his debut in 1985.

MOST APPEARANCES IN WOMEN'S HOCKEY

Karen Brown made a record 355 international appearances for England and Great Britain between 1984 and 1999.

MOST GOALS SCORED IN A HOCKEY CAREER

David Ashman (UK) scored a record 2,326 goals in hockey, having played for UK sides Hampshire, Southampton, Southampton Kestrals and Hamble Old Boys (for whom he scored 2,165 goals, a record for one club) between 1958 and 1999.

MOST GOALS SCORED BY A PLAYER IN A HOCKEY GAME

MC Marckx (UK) scored 19 goals playing for Bowdon 2nd XI against Brooklands 2nd XI (final score 23–0) on 31 December 1910. He was selected for the England team in March 1912 but declined owing to business priorities.

HIGHEST SCORE IN INTERNATIONAL MEN'S HOCKEY

The highest score in a men's international hockey match was achieved when India defeated the USA 24–1 in Los Angeles, California, USA, in the 1932 Olympic Games.

HIGHEST SCORE IN INTERNATIONAL WOMEN'S HOCKEY

The highest score in an international women's hockey match was by England when they beat France 23–0 at Merton, Greater London, UK, on 3 February 1923.

MOST WINS IN WORLD CUP WOMEN'S HOCKEY

The *Fédération Internationale de Hockey* (FIH) World Cup for women was first held in 1974. The most wins is five by The Netherlands, in 1974, 1978, 1983, 1986 and 1990.

MOST MEN'S OLYMPIC BEACH VOLLEYBALL WINS

Beach volleyball has been part of the Olympic Games since 1996, and the USA has won the men's competition on both occasions. Karch Kiraly and Kent Steffes won in Atlanta in 1996 and Dain Blanton and Eric Fonoimoana (right) won in Sydney in 2000.

HANDBALL

MOST HANDBALL TARGETS HIT IN 30 SECONDS

Jonas Källman (Sweden) hit a record eight handball targets in 30 seconds on the set of *Guinness Rekord TV* in Stockholm, Sweden, on 27 November 2001.

HIGHEST SCORE IN AN INTERNATIONAL HANDBALL MATCH

The highest score in an international handball match was recorded when the USSR beat Afghanistan 86–2 in the 'Friendly Army Tournament' at Miskolc, Hungary, in August 1981.

HIGHEST MEN'S OLYMPIC HANDBALL SCORE

The highest handball score in a match at the Olympic Games is 44 by Yugoslavia against Kuwait in 1980 and by Sweden against Australia in 2000.

MOST MEN'S WORLD CUP HOCKEY WINS

The FIH hockey World Cup for men was first held in 1971. The most wins by a team is four by Pakistan, in 1971, 1978, 1982 and 1994. Pakistan's current captain, Muhammad Nadeem, is shown left.

HIGHEST WOMEN'S OLYMPIC HANDBALL SCORE

The highest score by a women's handball team in an Olympic match is 45 by Austria against Brazil at Sydney, Australia, in 2000.

MOST MEN'S OLYMPIC HANDBALL TITLES

The USSR has won the men's Olympic handball title three times, in 1976, 1988 and 1992 as the Unified Team from the republics of the former USSR.

MOST MEN'S EUROPEAN CUP HANDBALL TITLES

Two teams have won the men's European Cup five times: Vfl Gummersbach (West Germany) in 1969–71, 1974 and 1983; and Barcelona (Spain) in 1991 and 1996–99. Vfl Gummersbach is the only club team to win all three European trophies: the European Champions' Cup, the European Cup Winners' Cup and the IHF Cup.

KORFBALL

LARGEST KORFBALL TOURNAMENT

On 12 June 1999 a total of 1,796 players participated in the *Kom Keukens/Ten Donck* international youth korfball tournament in Ridderkerk, The Netherlands. The games were played by the rules of the Royal Dutch Korfball Association.

MOST KORFBALL WORLD GAMES TITLES

First held as part of the World Games in 1985, the korfball World Games title has been won five times (the total number of times that the event has been held) by The Netherlands, in 1985, 1989, 1993, 1997 and 2001. In winning these five titles, the Dutch team has never lost a match.

HIGHEST FINAL SCORE IN WORLD CHAMPIONSHIP KORFBALL

The highest team score in the final of the Korfball World Championships is 23 by The Netherlands against Belgium (11) in 1999. The margin of victory was the greatest in a final.

LACROSSE

MOST WOMEN'S INTERNATIONAL LACROSSE APPEARANCES

Vivien Jones (UK) played in 97 internationals (85 for Wales, 9 for the Celts and 3 for Great Britain) between 1977 and 2001.

MOST WOMEN'S LACROSSE WORLD CUP TITLES

The women's lacrosse World Cup replaced the World Championships in 1982. The USA has won six times, in 1974, 1982, 1989, 1993, 1997 and 2001.

MOST MEN'S LACROSSE WORLD CHAMPIONSHIPS

The USA has won eight of the nine men's lacrosse World Championships, in 1967, 1974, 1982, 1986, 1990, 1994, 1998 and 2002.

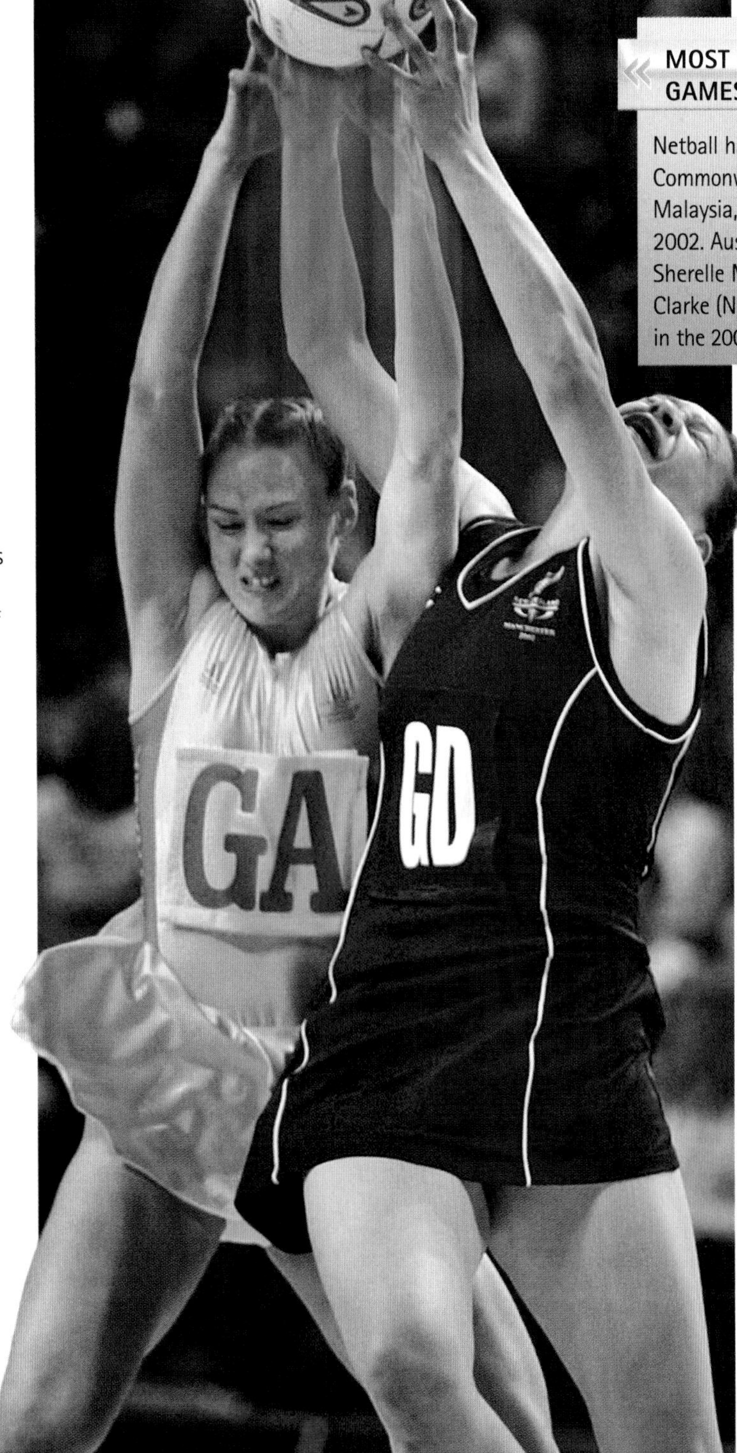

MOST COMMONWEALTH GAMES NETBALL TITLES

Netball has been contested twice at the Commonwealth Games – first in Kuala Lumpur, Malaysia, in 1998 and in Manchester, UK, in 2002. Australia won on both occasions. Sherelle McMahon (Australia) battles Sherly Clarke (New Zealand, on the right) for the ball in the 2002, New Zealand v. Australia final, left.

STICKBALL

LONGEST STICKBALL HIT

Josue Rodriguez (USA) hit a self-pitched ball a distance of 96 m (315 ft) with a stickball bat in New York, USA, on 30 September 2000.

VOLLEYBALL

MOST MEN'S OLYMPIC VOLLEYBALL TITLES

Introduced into the Olympic Games in 1964 for men and women, volleyball has been dominated by teams from the former USSR, the men's team winning a record three titles, in 1964, 1968 and 1980.

MOST WOMEN'S OLYMPIC VOLLEYBALL TITLES

The USSR women's volleyball team has won four gold Olympic medals, in 1968, 1972, 1980 and 1988.

MOST MEN'S WORLD VOLLEYBALL TITLES

The USSR won six World Championship titles, in 1949, 1952, 1960, 1962, 1978 and 1982.

HIGHEST BEACH VOLLEYBALL CAREER EARNINGS

Karch Kiraly (USA) amassed a record $2,929,158 (£1,872,708) in official AVP Tour earnings through to the end of the 2002 season.

BALL SPORTS

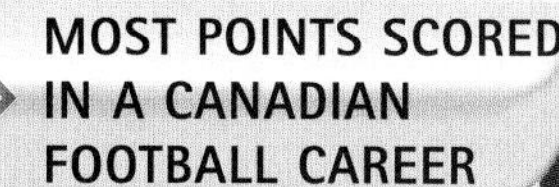

MOST POINTS SCORED IN A CANADIAN FOOTBALL CAREER

Lui Passaglia (Canada, far right, receiving the 88th Grey Cup), who played for the BC Lions, scored a record 3,984 points in his career, which lasted from 1976 to 2000.

CANADIAN FOOTBALL

MOST TOUCHDOWNS SCORED IN A CFL SEASON

Cory Philpot (USA) scored a record 22 touchdowns for the BC Lions in the 1995 Canadian Football League season.

MOST TOUCHDOWNS SCORED IN A CFL CAREER

George Reed (USA) scored 137 touchdowns for the Saskatchewan Roughriders from 1963 to 75.

MOST CFL GAMES PLAYED

Lui Passaglia (Canada) played a record 408 Canadian Football League games for the BC Lions between 1976 and 2000.

MOST POINTS SCORED

The most points scored in a game is 36 by Bob McNamara (Canada) for the Winnipeg Blue Bombers versus the BC Lions on 13 October 1956.

LONGEST RUSH IN CANADIAN FOOTBALL

Two players have gained 109 yards rushing from the line of scrimmage: George Dixon (Canada) for the Montreal Alouettes against the Ottawa Roughriders on 2 September 1963; and Willie Fleming (Canada) for the BC Lions against the Edmonton Eskimos on 17 October 1964.

LONGEST FIELD GOAL

The longest field goal was 60 yards by Dave Ridgeway (UK) for the Saskatchewan Roughriders against the Winnipeg Blue Bombers on 6 September 1987.

MOST YARDS RECEIVING IN A SEASON

Allen Pitts (Canada) gained a record 2,036 yards receiving for the Calgary Stampeders in the 1994 season.

MOST YARDS RUSHING IN A GAME

The most yards gained rushing in a game is 287 by Ron Stewart (Canada) for the Ottawa Roughriders against the Montreal Alouettes on 10 October 1960.

MOST INTERCEPTIONS IN A CAREER

The most interceptions made in a Canadian football career is 396 by Ron Lancaster (Canada) for Ottawa and Saskatchewan in 1960–78.

AUSTRALIAN FOOTBALL

HIGHEST TEAM SCORE IN AN AFL MATCH

The record score by one team in an Australian Football League game is 239 (37–17) by Geelong against Brisbane on 2 May 1992.

MOST AFL GRAND FINAL GOALS

The Australian Football League Grand Final scoring record is nine goals. This has been achieved by two players: Gordon Coventry (Australia) for Collingwood versus Richmond in 1928, and Gary Ablett (Australia) for Geelong versus Hawthorn in 1989.

MOST GOALS IN AN AFL CAREER

The most goals scored in an Australian Football League career is 1,357, by Tony Lockett (Australia), between 1983 and 1999.

Peter Hudson (Australia) holds the senior career goal-scoring record with 2,191, scored from 1963 to 1981 in the Victorian Football League (VFL) and in Tasmania.

MOST AFL GAMES PLAYED

The career record for the greatest number of Australian Football League games played is 426, by Michael Tuck (Australia), who played for Hawthorn between 1972 and 1991.

LONGEST AFL WINNING STREAK

The most consecutive games won in the Australian Football League Premiership is 23 by Geelong between 1952 and 1953.

HIGHEST ATTENDANCE AT AN AFL LEAGUE GRAND FINAL

A record 121,696 spectators attended the Melbourne Cricket Ground, Melboure, Victoria, to see Carlton versus Collingwood in the Grand Final on 26 September 1970.

SHINTY

HIGHEST INDIVIDUAL SCORE IN A SHINTY CUP FINAL

In 1938 John Macmillan Mactaggart (UK) scored ten hails, or goals, for Mid Argyll in a Camanachd Cup match.

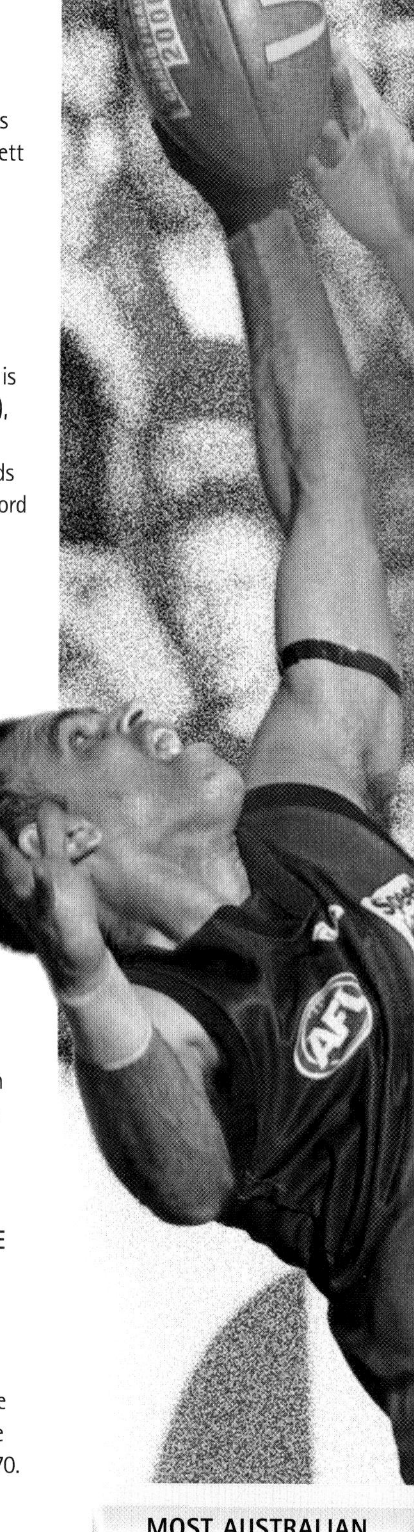

MOST AUSTRALIAN FOOTBALL LEAGUE PREMIERSHIP TITLES

The greatest number of AFL Premiership titles won is 16 – Carlton between 1906 and 19 and Essendon between 1897 a 2000. (Near right: Essendon player Michael Long in the 20 Grand Final versus Melbourne.)

MOST SHINTY CHALLENGE CUP INDIVIDUAL WINS

David Ritchie and Hugh Chisholm (both UK) of Newtonmore have won a record 12 Challenge Cup winners' medals each.

HURLING

LONGEST HIT IN A HURLING CONTEST

The greatest distance for a 'lift and stroke' hit is 118 m (129 yds) credited to Tom Murphy of Three Castles, Kilkenny, Ireland, in a 'long puck' contest held in 1906.

MOST WINS OF THE ALL-IRELAND HURLING CHAMPIONSHIP

The greatest number of All-Ireland Championships won by one team is 28. These were won by Cork between 1890 and 1999.

LARGEST ATTENDANCE FOR A HURLING MATCH

The largest crowd ever to attend a hurling match was 84,865 for the All-Ireland final between Cork and Wexford at Croke Park, Dublin, in 1954.

OTHER BALL SPORTS

MOST PELOTA VASCA WORLD CHAMPIONSHIP TITLES

The *Federación Internacional de Pelota Vasca* holds world championships every four years. The most world titles won is 13 by Aaron Sehter (Argentina) from 1952 to 1982. The most successful pair has been Roberto Elías and Juan Labat (both Argentina), who won the *Trinquete Share* four times – in 1952, 1958, 1962 and 1970. The most wins in the long court game, Cesta Punta, is three, by José Hamuy (Mexico) with two different partners, in 1958, 1962 and 1966.

FASTEST MOVING BALL IN A SPORT

On 3 August 1979, at a game of jai-alai at Newport Jai-Alai, Rhode Island, USA, a throw from Jose Ramon Areitio was measured at a speed of 302 km/h (188 mph) – the fastest projectile speed in any ball sport.

LARGEST ATTENDANCE AT A GAELIC FOOTBALL MATCH

The record crowd for a Gaelic Football game is 90,556, for the Down v. Offaly final at Croke Park, Dublin, Ireland, in 1961. The ground, as it is today, is shown below.

TENNIS

YOUNGEST MALE WIMBLEDON CHAMPION

The youngest male Wimbledon champion is Boris Becker (West Germany, above) who won the men's singles title in 1985 at the age of 17 years 227 days. He was also the first unseeded player and the first German to become champion.

LONGEST TENNIS MATCH

The longest competitive tennis match, lasting 24 hr 24 min, was played between Paul Jessop and Lee Marks (both UK) on 22–23 June 2002 at the David Lloyd Leisure Club in Birmingham, West Midlands, UK.

MOST DAVIS CUP TIES IN A SEASON

In reaching the Challenge Round in 1965, Spain played a record eight Davis Cup ties in a single year, more than any other nation.

MOST DAVIS CUP APPEARANCES

The most Davis Cup appearances by an individual player is 164 matches in 66 ties by Nicola Pietrangeli (Italy) between 1954 and 1972. His win-loss record for singles is 78-32 and 42-12 for doubles.

MOST DAVIS CUP FINAL APPEARANCES

The most Davis Cup final appearances by a player is 11 by Bill Tilden (USA) between 1920 and 1930. He played 28 matches with a win-loss record of 21-7.

MOST CONSECUTIVE DAVIS CUP WINS

The most consecutive Davis Cup tournament wins is seven by the USA between 1920 and 1926. Their reign was brought to an end in 1927 by France, who went on to keep the title for six years. Theirs was the second longest winning streak before losing to Great Britain in 1933.

OLDEST TENNIS PLAYER

The oldest tennis player is José Guadalupe Leal Lemus (Mexico), who began playing tennis in 1925 and has been playing regularly ever since. At the age of 99 he continues to play every week at the Club Campestre Morelia, Morelia, Mexico, with a group of players over 20 years his junior.

LONGEST RALLY

The longest contrived tennis rally is one of 17,062 strokes between Ray Miller and Rob Peterson (both USA) at Alameda, California, USA, as part of the United States Tennis Association's Tennis Festival on 4 July 2001. The attempt lasted 9 hr 6 min.

MOST WIMBLEDON WOMEN'S SINGLES TITLES

The most Wimbledon singles titles won by a woman is nine by Martina Navrátilová (USA) in 1978-79, 1982-87 and 1990.

MOST WIMBLEDON MEN'S SINGLES TITLES

The most Wimbledon men's singles titles won is seven by Pete Sampras (USA) in 1993-95 and 1997-2000.

OLDEST WIMBLEDON CHAMPION

The oldest Wimbledon tennis champion is Margaret Evelyn Du Pont (USA). She won the mixed doubles with Neale Fraser (Australia) in 1962 at the age of 44 years 125 days.

YOUNGEST FEMALE WIMBLEDON CHAMPION

The youngest female Wimbledon champion is Martina Hingis (Switzerland), who was 15 years 282 days old when she won the women's doubles in 1996.

BEST WILDCARD PERFORMANCE AT WIMBLEDON

The best performance by a wildcard entrant at Wimbledon is that of Goran Ivanisevic (Croatia) in 2001. Invited to play in the competition by the All England Club, Ivanisevic was ranked 125th in the world. He won the Men's singles title, beating Pat Rafter (Australia) 6-3, 3-6, 6-3, 2-6, 9-7 in the final. It was his fourth Wimbledon final. He also served a record 213 aces throughout the tournament, including 27 in the final.

WOMEN'S GRAND SLAM WINNERS

Four women have achieved the grand slam, and the first three won six successive grand slam tournaments: Maureen Connolly (USA), in 1953; Margaret Court (Australia) in 1970; and Martina Navrátilová (USA) in 1983-84. The fourth was Steffi Graf (Germany) in 1988, when she also won the women's singles Olympic gold medal. Pam Shriver (USA), with Navrátilová, won a record eight successive grand slam tournament women's doubles titles and 109 successive matches in all events from April 1983 to July 1985.

EARLIEST MEN'S GRAND SLAM WINNER

The first man to have won all four of the world's major singles championships – Wimbledon and the US, Australian and French Opens – was Fred Perry (UK), when he won the French title in 1935.

The first man to hold all four championships simultaneously was Don Budge (USA) in 1938. He also won Wimbledon and the US Open in 1937, giving him six successive grand slam wins.

The first man to win the grand slam twice was Rod Laver (Australia) as an amateur in 1962 and again in 1969, when the tournaments were opened to professionals.

MOST GRAND SLAM SINGLES TITLES

Margaret Court (Australia) won 24 grand slam singles titles between 1960 and 1973.

YOUNGEST MALE NUMBER ONE TENNIS PLAYER

Marat Mikhailovich Safin (Russia, right) was 20 years 234 days old when his victory at the President's Cup Tournament in Tashkent, Uzbekistan, on 17 September 2000, made him the number one ranked player in the world.

MOST GRAND SLAM MEN'S SINGLES TITLES

The most grand slam singles tennis titles won by a man is 14 by Pete Sampras (USA) between 1990 and 2002.

MOST US OPEN MEN'S SINGLES TITLES

The most US Open singles titles won by a man is seven. The record is shared by three players: Richard Sears (USA) in 1881-87; William Larned (USA) in 1901, 1902 and 1907-11; and Bill Tilden (USA) in 1920-25 and 1929.

MOST US OPEN WOMEN'S SINGLES TITLES

Molla Mallory (Norway, *née* Bjurstedt) won eight US Open women's singles titles in 1915-18, 1920-22 and 1926.

MOST US OPEN TITLES WON BY A MAN

The most US Open titles won by a man is 16, by Bill Tilden (USA), including seven men's singles, in 1920-25 and 1929.

MOST US OPEN TITLES WON BY A WOMAN

Margaret Du Pont (USA) won 25 US Open titles. She won 13 women's doubles, nine mixed doubles and three singles titles between 1941 and 1960.

MOST CONSECUTIVE SERVES

The most consecutive 'good' serves (without a double fault) is 8,017 by Rob Peterson (USA) at Port Aransas, Texas, USA, on 5 December 1998. The attempt lasted 10 hrs 7 min.

MOST FRENCH OPEN MEN'S SINGLES TITLES

The most French Open singles tennis titles won by a man is six by Björn Borg (Sweden) in 1974-75 and 1978-81.

MOST FRENCH OPEN WOMEN'S SINGLES TITLES

The most French Open singles titles won by a woman is seven, by Chris Evert (USA) in 1974-75, 1979-80, 1983 and 1985-86.

LONGEST TENNIS COACHING MARATHON

Butch Heffernan (Australia) coached tennis for a record 52 hours on 23-25 November 2001 at the Next Generation Club in Brierley Hill, Dudley, West Midlands, UK.

MOST FEDERATION CUP WINS

The most wins in the Federation Cup, the women's international team championship instituted in 1963 and known as the Fed Cup from 1995, is 17 by the USA between 1963 and 2000. Virginia Wade (UK) played each year from 1967 to 1983 in a record 57 ties, playing 100 rubbers. Her win-loss record for singles is 36-20 and 30-14 for doubles.

YOUNGEST WIMBLEDON MATCH WINNER

The youngest person to win a match at Wimbledon is Jennifer Capriati (USA, below) who was 14 years 89 days old when she played her first match on 26 June 1990. She was also the youngest seeded Wimbledon player.

RACKET SPORTS

MOST OLYMPIC MEN'S TABLE TENNIS GOLDS

The most Olympic table tennis gold medals won by a man is two by Liu Guoliang (China, below). He won in the singles and doubles in 1996.

TABLE TENNIS

MOST MEN'S TEAM WORLD CHAMPIONSHIPS

The Chinese men's table tennis team has won the most World Championship titles. They have taken home the coveted Swaythling Cup a record 13 times between 1961 and 2001.

MOST WOMEN'S TEAM WORLD CHAMPIONSHIPS

China has won the most women's team table tennis world titles, with 15 Marcel Corbillon Cup victories. They first won in 1965, then had eight successive biennial wins from 1975 to 1989 and more victories in 1993, 1995, 1997 and 1999-2001.

MOST WOMEN'S OLYMPIC GOLD MEDALS

Deng Yaping (China) has won a record four Olympic table tennis titles. She won the women's singles in 1992 and 1996, and the women's doubles (both with Qiao Hang) in 1992 and 1996. A naturally attacking player, Yaping was widely acclaimed as the greatest female player in table tennis history. She was the top-ranked woman in the world for eight consecutive years from 1991.

LONGEST TABLE TENNIS RALLY

On 5 November 1977 John Duffy and Kevin Schick (both New Zealand) achieved a contrived table tennis rally lasting a record time of 5 hr 2 min 18.5 sec at Whangarei, New Zealand.

YOUNGEST TABLE TENNIS INTERNATIONAL

The youngest age at which any person has won international honours is eight, in the case of Joy Foster, the Jamaican singles and mixed doubles table tennis champion in 1958.

SQUASH

LONGEST SQUASH MATCH

The longest squash match in competition lasted 2 hr 45 min, when Jahangir Khan (Pakistan) beat Gamal Awad (Egypt) 9-10, 9-5, 9-7, 9-2 in the final of the Patrick International Festival at Chichester, West Sussex, UK, on 30 March 1983. The first game of the match lasted a record 1 hr 11 min.

MOST WORLD CHAMPIONSHIPS

Jahangir Khan (Pakistan) has won a record nine squash world championships. He began by winning the International Squash Rackets Federation world title (then amateur) three times, in 1979, 1983 and 1985. When the tournament became professional and renamed the World Open, Khan went on to win a further six titles, in 1981-85 and in 1988. He is considered the most successful player in the history of the sport.

Jansher Khan (Pakistan, not related) has won eight squash World Open titles in 1987, 1989, 1990 and from 1992 to 1996.

MOST MEN'S TEAM WORLD CHAMPIONSHIPS

The most World Championship men's squash team titles won is seven by Australia in 1967, 1969, 1971, 1973, 1989, 1991 and 2001.

MOST WOMEN'S TEAM WORLD CHAMPIONSHIPS

The Australian women's team has won the most squash World Championships, with a seven victories in 1981, 1983, 1992, 1994, 1996, 1998 and 2002.

FASTEST SQUASH BALL

In tests at Wimbledon Squash and Badminton Club, London, UK, in January 1988, Roy Buckland (UK) hit a squash ball with an overhead serve at a measured speed of 232.7 km/h (144.6 mph) over the distance to the front wall. This is equivalent to an initial speed at the racket of 242.6 km/h (150.8 mph).

MOST WOMEN'S SQUASH WORLD CHAMPIONSHIPS

The most women's squash World Open titles won is five by Sarah Fitzgerald Australia, left in the picture on the left) in 1996-98 and 2001-02.

FASTEST SHUTTLECOCK SPEED

Simon Archer (UK, left) hit a shuttlecock at a speed of 260 km/h (162 mph) at Warwickshire Racquets and Health Club, Coventry, Warwickshire, UK, on 5 November 1996.

BADMINTON

MOST OLYMPIC MEDALS

Badminton was first contested at the 1992 Barcelona Olympics and no individual has won more than one gold medal. The most medals won is three by Gil Young Ah (South Korea): gold in the mixed doubles and silver in the women's doubles in 1996, and bronze in the women's doubles in 1992.

MOST WORLD CHAMPIONSHIP SINGLES TITLES

Four Chinese players have won two individual world titles. Yang Yang won the men's singles in 1987 and 1989. The women's singles have been won twice by Li Lingwei in 1983 and 1989; Han Aiping in 1985 and 1987 and Ye Zhaoying in 1995 and 1997.

MOST WORLD CHAMPIONSHIP TITLES

A record five World Championship badminton titles have been won by Park Joo-bong (South Korea). He won the men's doubles in 1985 and 1991, and the mixed doubles in 1985, 1989 and 1991.

MOST THOMAS CUP TEAM WINS

The most wins at the men's World Team Championships for the Thomas Cup is 13 by Indonesia between 1958 and 2002.

MOST UBER CUP TEAM WINS

The record number of wins at the women's World Team Badminton Championships for the Uber Cup is eight by China between 1984 and 2002.

LONGEST BADMINTON MATCH

At the badminton World Championship men's singles final in Glasgow, UK, on 1 June 1997, Peter Rasmussen (Denmark) beat Sun Jun (China) 16–17, 18–13, 15–10 in a match that lasted a record 2 hr 4 min.

LONGEST BADMINTON RALLY

In the men's singles final of the 1987 All-England Championships between Morten Frost (Denmark) and Icuk Sugiarto (Indonesia) there were two rallies of over 90 strokes.

SHORTEST BADMINTON MATCH

Ra Kyung-min (South Korea) beat Julia Mann (England) 11-2, 11-1 in 6 minutes at the 1996 Uber Cupin Hong Kong on 19 May 1996.

RACKETBALL

MOST MEN'S TEAM WORLD CHAMPIONSHIP WINS

The racketball world championships have been held biennially since 1984. The USA has won ten combined team titles between 1981 and 2002.

MOST WOMEN'S TEAM WORLD CHAMPIONSHIP WINS

The USA has won a record nine women's team titles in 1986, 1988, 1990, 1992, 1994, 1996, 1998, 2000 and 2002.

MOST WOMEN'S WORLD CHAMPIONSHIPS

Michelle Gould (USA) has won a record three individual women's racketball World Championships in 1992, 1994 and 1996.

ATHLETICS

FASTEST WOMEN'S 2,000 M

Sonia O'Sullivan (Ireland, below front) ran the fastest women's 2,000 m on 8 July 1994 with a time of 5:25.36. She set the record in Edinburgh, Lothian, UK.

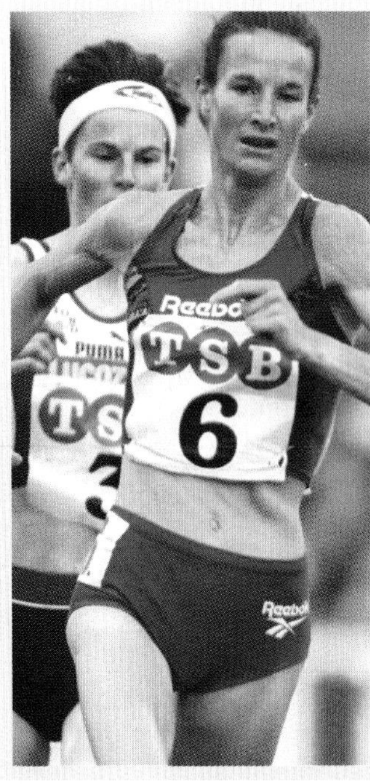

FASTEST MEN'S 100 M

The men's 100-m record stands at 9.78 seconds and is held by Tim Montgomery (USA, below – far left of photo). The record was set in Paris, France, on 14 September 2002.

LONGEST WINNING SEQUENCE IN A TRACK EVENT

Ed Moses (USA) achieved 122 wins in the 400-m hurdles between his losses to Harald Schmid (West Germany) in Berlin, Germany, on 26 August 1977, and Danny Lee Harris (USA) in Madrid, Spain on 4 June 1987.

LONGEST WINNING SEQUENCE IN A FIELD EVENT

Iolanda Balas (Romania) won a record 150 consecutive high jump competitions from 1956 to 1967.

OLDEST ATHLETICS OLYMPIC GOLD MEDALLIST

The oldest athlete to win an Olympic title was Irish-born Patrick Joseph 'Babe' McDonald (USA, 1878–1954) who was aged 42 years 26 days when he won the 56-lb weight throw at Antwerp, Belgium, on 21 August 1920.

YOUNGEST ATHLETICS OLYMPIC GOLD MEDALLIST

The youngest Olympic athletics gold medallist was Barbara Pearl Jones (USA, b. 26 March 1937) who at 15 years 123 days was a member of the winning 4 x 100-m relay team, at Helsinki, Finland, on 27 July 1952.

MOST OLYMPICS GOLD MEDALS AT ONE GAMES

Paavo Nurmi (Finland) won five golds at the 1924 games for the 1,500 m, 5,000 m, 10,000-m cross-country, 3,000-m team and cross-country team.

The most Olympic gold medals at individual events is four by Alvin Kraenzlein (USA) in 1900 for the 60 m, 110-m hurdles, 200-m hurdles and long jump.

MOST MEN'S OLYMPIC GOLD MEDALS

The most Olympic gold medals won is ten by athlete Ray Ewry (USA) in the standing high, long and triple jumps in 1900, 1904, 1906 and 1908.

MOST WOMEN'S ATHLETICS OLYMPIC GOLD MEDALS

The most gold medals won by a woman is four, shared by: Fanny Blankers-Koen (Netherlands) for the 100 m, 200 m, 80-m hurdles and 4 x 100-m relay, in 1948; Betty Cuthbert (Australia) for the 100 m, 200 m, 4 x 100-m relay in 1956 and 400 m in 1964; Bärbel Wöckel (née Eckert, GDR) for the 200 m and 4 x 100-m relay in 1976 and 1980; and Evelyn Ashford (USA) for the 100 m in 1984 and 4 x 100-m relay in 1984, 1988 and 1992.

MOST MEN'S ATHLETICS OLYMPIC MEDALS

The most medals won is 12 (nine gold and three silver) by Paavo Nurmi (Finland), nicknamed 'The Flying Finn', in the Games of 1920, 1924 and 1928.

MOST WOMEN'S OLYMPIC MEDALS

Three women athletes have each won seven gold medals. Shirley de la Hunty (Australia) won three gold, one silver and three bronze in the 1948, 1952 and 1956 Games. A re-read of the photo-finish indicates that she finished third, not fourth, in the 1948 200-m event, thus unofficially increasing her medal haul to eight. Irena Szewinska (Poland) won three gold, two silver and two bronze in 1964, 1968, 1972 and 1976, and is the only woman athlete to win a medal in four successive Games. Merlene Ottey (Jamaica) has also won seven medals – two silver and five bronze – in 1980, 1984, 1992 and 1996.

MOST SUCCESSFUL INDIVIDUAL IN THE IAAF GOLDEN LEAGUE

Hicham El Guerrouj (Morocco) is the only athlete to have twice won a share of the jackpot in the IAAF (International Amateur Athletics Federation) Golden League. For the jackpot, an athlete must win five of the seven IAAF Grand Prix meetings in a season and remain undefeated.

FASTEST MEN'S 100 X 1-MILE RELAY

The record for 100 miles by 100 runners is 7 hr 35 min 55.4 sec by the Canadian Milers Athletic Club set at York University, Toronto, Canada, on 20 December 1998.

The same record for women was set by the Canadian Women's Miler's Club, who ran the 100 x 1-mile relay in a time of 9 hr 23 min 39 sec on 27 December 1999.

FASTEST 100 X 100-M MASS RELAY

The record for a 100 x 100-m relay is 19 min 14.19 sec by a team from Antwerp who set the record at Merksem, Belgium, on 23 September 1989.

FASTEST BACKWARDS MILE

The time for the fastest backwards mile is 6 min 2.35 sec and was set by D Joseph James (India) at Nehru Stadium Athletics Track, Coimbatore, Tamil Nadu, India, on 10 August 2002.

FASTEST 10-KM RUN WEARING A PANTOMIME COSTUME

Simon Wiles and Les Morton (both UK) ran the Percy Pud 10-km race in Loxley, Sheffield, South Yorkshire, UK, on 2 December 2001 in a time of 44 min 2 sec. They wore their pantomime camel costume for the whole race.

FASTEST 110-M HURDLES

Colin Jackson (GB, left) set a new 110-m hurdle record with a time of 12.91 seconds in Stuttgart, Germany, on 20 August 1993. He has competed at this event in four Olympic Games, winning silver in 1988. At the World Championships, Jackson won in 1993 and 1999, came second in 1997 and third in 1987. He was European champion in 1990, 1994 and 1998, and Commonwealth champion in 1990 and 1994.

★ MEN'S OUTDOOR WORLD RECORDS ★

EVENT	RECORD	NAME AND COUNTRY	VENUE	DATE
100 m	9.78	Tim Montgomery (USA)	Paris, France	14 September 2002
200 m	19.32	Michael Johnson (USA)	Atlanta, USA	1 August 1996
400 m	43.18	Michael Johnson (USA)	Seville, Spain,	26 August 1999
800 m	1:41.11	Wilson Kipketer (Denmark)	Cologne, Germany	24 August 1997
1,000 m	2:11.96	Noah Ngeny (Kenya)	Rieti, Italy	5 September 1999
1,500 m	3:26.00	Hicham El Guerrouj (Morocco)	Rome, Italy	14 July 1998
1 mile	3:43.13	Hicham El Guerrouj (Morocco)	Rome, Italy	7 July 1999
2,000 m	4:44.79	Hicham El Guerrouj (Morocco)	Berlin, Germany	7 September 1999
3,000 m	7:20.67	Daniel Komen (Kenya)	Rieti, Italy	1 September 1996
5,000 m	12:39.36	Haile Gebrselassie (Ethiopia)	Helsinki, Finland	13 June 1998
10,000 m	26:22.75	Haile Gebrselassie (Ethiopia)	Hengelo, Netherlands	1 June 1998
20,000 m	56:55.60	Arturo Barrios (Mexico, now USA)	La Flèche, France	30 March 1991
25,000 m	1:13:55.80	Toshihiko Seko (Japan)	Christchurch, New Zealand	22 March 1981
30,000 m	1:29:18.80	Toshihiko Seko (Japan)	Christchurch, New Zealand	22 March 1981
1 hour distance	21,101 m	Arturo Barrios (Mexico, now USA)	La Flèche, France	30 March 1991
110-m hurdles	12.91	Colin Jackson (GB)	Stuttgart, Germany	20 August 1993
400-m hurdles	46.78	Kevin Young (USA)	Barcelona, Spain	6 August 1992
3,000-m steeplechase	7:53.17	Brahim Boulami (Morocco)	Zürich, Switzerland	16 August 2002
4 x 100-m relay	37.40	USA (Michael Marsh, Leroy Burrell, Dennis Mitchell, Carl Lewis)	Barcelona, Spain	8 August 1992
		USA (John Drummond Jr, Andre Cason, Dennis Mitchell, Leroy Burrell)	Stuttgart, Germany	21 August 1993
4 x 200-m relay	1:18.68	Santa Monica Track Club (Michael Marsh, Leroy Burrell, Floyd Heard, Carl Lewis, all USA)	Walnut, USA	17 April 1994
4 x 400-m relay	2:54.20	USA (Jerome Young, Antonio Pettigrew, Tyree Washington, Michael Johnson)	New York City, USA	23 July 1998
4 x 800-m relay	7:03.89	Great Britain (Peter Elliott, Garry Cook, Steve Cram, Sebastian Coe)	London, UK	30 August 1982
4 x 1,500-m relay	14:38.80	West Germany (Thomas Wessinghage, Harald Hudak, Michael Lederer, Karl Fleschen)	Cologne, Germany	17 August 1977
High jump	2.45 m (8 ft 0.25 in)	Javier Sotomayor (Cuba)	Salamanca, Spain	27 July 1993
Pole vault	6.14 m (20 ft 1.75 in)	Sergei Bubka (Ukraine)	Sestriere, Italy	31 July 1994
Long jump	8.95 m (29 ft 4.5 in)	Mike Powell (USA)	Tokyo, Japan	30 August 1991
Triple jump	18.29 m (60 ft 0.25 in)	Jonathan Edwards (GB)	Gothenburg, Sweden	7 August 1995
Shot	23.12 m (75 ft 10.25 in)	Randy Barnes (USA)	Los Angeles, USA	20 May 1990
Discus	74.08 m (243 ft)	Jürgen Schult (GDR)	Neubrandenburg, Germany	6 June 1986
Hammer	86.74 m (284 ft 7 in)	Yuriy Sedykh (USSR)	Stuttgart, Germany	30 August 1986
Javelin	98.48 m (323 ft 1 in)	Jan Zelezny (Czech Republic)	Jena, Germany	25 May 1996
Decathlon★	9,026 points	Roman Šebrle (Czech Republic)	Götzis, Austria	26–27 May 2001

★ Day 1: 100 m: 10.64; Long jump: 8.11 m (26 ft 7.25 in); Shot: 15.33 m (50 ft 3.5 in); High jump: 2.12 m (6 ft 11.5 in)
Day 2 110-m hurdles: 13.92; Discus: 47.92 m (157 ft 2.5 in); Pole vault: 4.80 m (15 ft 9 in); Javelin: 70.16 m (230 ft 2 in); 1,500 m: 4:21.98

ATHLETICS

LONGEST INDOOR TRIPLE JUMP

Ashia Hansen (GB, right), holds the indoor record for the triple jump with a distance of 15.16 m (49 ft 8 in). The record was set in Valencia, Spain, on 28 February 1998.

HIGHEST STANDING HIGH JUMP

The best high jump from a standing position is 1.90 m (6 ft 2.75 in) by Rune Almen (Sweden) at Karlstad, Sweden, on 3 May 1980.

The women's best is 1.52 m (4 ft 11.75 in) by Grete Bjordalsbakka (Norway) in 1984.

LONGEST STANDING LONG JUMP

The longest long jump from a standing position is 3.71 m (12 ft 2 in) by Arne Tvervaag (Norway) in 1968.

The women's best is 2.92 m (9 ft 7 in) by Annelin Mannes (Norway) at Flisa, Norway, on 7 March 1981.

MOST PARTICIPANTS IN A RELAY RACE

The most participants in a relay race is 7,175, (287 teams of 25), for the Batavieren race which was run between Nijmegen and Enschede, The Netherlands, on 24 April 1999.

FASTEST 1,000-MILE RELAY BY TEAM OF TEN

The record for the fastest 1,000-mile relay by a team of ten is 99 hr 3 min 27 sec. It was run by Willie Mtolo, Graham Meyer, Jan van Rooyen, Dimitri Grishine, Daniel Radebe, Pio Mpolokeng, Oliver Kandiero, Frans Moyo, Simon Mele and Philip Molefi (all South Africa) who ran from Cape Town to Johannesburg, South Africa, from 14 to 18 August 2002.

MOST ATHLETICS WORLD RECORDS SET ON ONE DAY

Athlete Jesse Owens (USA) set six world records in 45 minutes at Ann Arbor, Michigan, USA, on 25 May 1935 with a 9.4-sec 100 yd at 3:15 pm, a 8.13-m-long (26-ft 8.25-in) jump at 3:25 pm, a 20.3-sec 220 yd (and 200 m) at 3:45 pm, and a 22.6-sec 220 yd low hurdles (and 200 m) at 4 pm.

MOST INDOOR WORLD CHAMPIONSHIP MEDALS

First held as the World Indoor Games in 1985, the Indoor World Championships are now staged biennially. The most medals won in an individual event is six by Merlene Ottey (Jamaica) who won three gold (60 m 1995, 200 m 1989, 1991), two silver (60 m 1991, 200 m 1987) and one bronze (60 m 1989).

The men's record is five by Ivan Pedroso (Cuba) in the long jump (gold 1993, 1995, 1997, 1999 2001) and Javier Sotomayor (Cuba) for the high jump (gold 1989, 1993, 1995, 1999; bronze 1991).

★ MEN'S TRACK WALKING ★

EVENT	RECORD	NAME AND COUNTRY	VENUE	DATE
20 km	1:17:25.60	Bernardo Segura (Mexico)	Fana, Norway	7 May 1994
30 km	2:01:44.10	Maurizio Damilano (Italy)	Cuneo, Italy	4 October 1992
50 km	3:40:57.90	Thierry Toutain (France)	Héricourt, France	29 September 1997
2 hours	29,572 m	Maurizio Damilano (Italy)	Cuneo, Italy	4 October 1992

★ WOMEN'S TRACK WALKING ★

EVENT	RECORD	NAME AND COUNTRY	VENUE	DATE
5 km	20:02.60	Gillian O'Sullivan (Ireland)	Dublin, Ireland	13 July 2002
10 km	41:56.23	Nadezhda Ryashkina (USSR)	Seattle, USA	24 July 1990
20 km	1:26:52.30	Olimpiada Ivanova (Russia)	Brisbane, Australia	6 September 2001

MOST MEDALS WON IN THE WORLD CHAMPIONSHIPS

The athletics World Championships were inaugurated in 1983 in Helsinki, Finland. The most medals won is ten by Carl Lewis (USA) with eight gold medals, (100 m, long jump and 4 x 100-m relay 1983; 100 m, long jump and 4 x 100-m relay 1987; 100 m and 4 x 100-m relay 1991); silver medals for long jump in 1991 and bronze for 200 m in 1993.

The women's record is 14 medals won by Merlene Ottey (Jamaica), who won three gold, four silver, seven bronze, between 1983 and 1997.

MOST WORLD CHAMPIONSHIP GOLD MEDALS

The most golds won to date is nine by Michael Johnson (USA), for the 200 m (1991, 1995), 400 m (1993, 1995, 1997, 1999) and 4 x 400-m relay (1993, 1995, 1999).

The most gold medals won by a woman is five by Gail Devers (USA), for the 100 m (1993), 100-m hurdles (1993, 1995, 1999) and 4 x 100-m relay (1997).

MOST CONSECUTIVE WINS IN THE WORLD CHAMPIONSHIPS

The most successive wins in the same event at the World Championships is six by Sergey Bubka (Ukraine), who won the pole vault title from 1983 to 1997.

In track events the record is four by Michael Johnson (USA) for 400 m between 1993 and 1999, and Haile Gebrselassie (Ethiopia), who won the 10,000 m between 1993 and 1999.

MOST PARTICIPANTS AT AN ATHLETICS CHAMPIONSHIPS

A record 11,475 participants (9,328 men, 2,147 women) attended the 1993 World Veterans' Athletic Championships in Miyazaki, Japan.

★ MEN'S ULTRA LONG DISTANCE WORLD RECORDS ★

EVENT	RECORD	NAME AND COUNTRY	VENUE	DATE
100 km	6:10:20	Don Ritchie (GB)	London, UK	28 October 1978
100 miles	11:30:51	Don Ritchie (GB)	London, UK	15 October 1977
1,000 km	5 days 16:17:00	Yiannis Kouros (Greece)	Colac, Australia	26 November–1 December 1984
1,000 miles	11 days 13:54:58	Piotr Silikin (Lithuania)	Nanango, Australia	11–23 March 1998
24 hours	303.506 km (188 miles 1,038 yards)	Yiannis Kouros (Australia)	Adelaide, Australia	4–5 October 1997
6 days	1,022.068 km (635 miles 147 yards)	Yiannis Kouros (Greece)	New York, USA	2–8 July 1984

★ WOMEN'S ULTRA LONG DISTANCE WORLD RECORDS ★

EVENT	RECORD	NAME AND COUNTRY	VENUE	DATE
100 km	7:23:28	Valentina Liakhova (Russia)	Nantes, France	28 September 1996
100 miles	14:29:44	Ann Trason (USA)	Santa Rosa, USA	18–19 March 1989
1,000 km	8 days 00:27:06	Eleanor Robinson (GB)	Nanango, Australia	11–18 March 1998
1,000 miles	13 days 01:54:02	Eleanor Robinson (GB)	Nanango, Australia	11–24 March 1998
24 hours	240.169 km (149 miles 412 yards)	Eleanor Adams (GB)	Melbourne, Australia	19–20 August 1989
6 days	883.631 km (549 miles 110 yards)	Sandra Barwick (New Zealand)	Campbelltown, Australia	18–24 November 1990

★ WOMEN'S OUTDOOR WORLD RECORDS ★

EVENT	RECORD	NAME AND COUNTRY	VENUE	DATE
100 m	10.49	Florence Griffith-Joyner (USA)	Indianapolis, USA	16 July 1998
200 m	21.34	Florence Griffith-Joyner (USA)	Seoul, South Korea	29 September 1988
400 m	47.60	Marita Koch (GDR)	Canberra, Australia	6 October 1985
800 m	1:53.28	Jarmila Kratochvílová (Czechoslovakia)	Munich, Germany	26 July 1983
1,000 m	2:28.98	Svetlana Masterkova (Russia)	Brussels, Belgium	23 August 1996
1,500 m	3:50.46	Qu Yunxia (China)	Beijing, China	11 September 1993
1 mile	4:12.56	Svetlana Masterkova (Russia)	Zürich, Switzerland	14 August 1996
2,000 m	5:25.36	Sonia O'Sullivan (Ireland)	Edinburgh, UK	8 July 1994
3,000 m	8:06.11	Wang Junxia (China)	Beijing, China	13 September 1993
5,000 m	14:28.09	Jiang Bo (China)	Beijing, China	23 October 1997
10,000 m	29:31.78	Wang Junxia (China)	Beijing, China	8 September 1993
20,000 m	1:05:26.60	Tegla Loroupe (Kenya)	Borgholzhausen, Germany	3 September 2000
25,000 m	1:27:05.90	Tegla Loroupe (Kenya)	Megerkirchen, Germany	21 September, 2002
30,000 m	1:47:05.60	Karolina Szabó (Hungary)	Budapest, Hungary	22 April 1988
1 hour distance	18,340 m	Tegla Loroupe (Kenya)	Borgholzhausen, Germany	7 August 1998
100-m hurdles	12.21	Yordanka Donkova (Bulgaria)	Stara Zagora, Bulgaria	20 August 1988
400-m hurdles	52.61	Kim Batten (USA)	Gothenburg, Sweden	11 August 1995
3,000-m steeplechase	9:16:51	Aleysa Turova (Belarus)	Gdansk, Poland	27 July 2002
4 x 100-m relay	41.37	GDR (Silke Gladisch, Sabine Rieger, Ingrid Auerswald and Marlies Göhr)	Canberra, Australia	6 October 1985
4 x 200-m relay	1:27.46	United States 'Blue' (LaTasha Jenkins, Latasha Colander Richardson, Nanceen Perry and Marion Jones)	Philadelphia, USA	29 April 2000
4 x 400-m relay	3:15.17	USSR (Tatyana Ledovskaya, Olga Nazarova, Maria Pinigina and Olga Bryzgina)	Seoul, South Korea	1 October 1988
4 x 800-m relay	7:50.17	USSR (Nadezhda Olizarenko, Lyubov Gurina, Lyudmila Borisova and Irina Podyalovskaya)	Moscow, Russia	5 August 1984
High jump	2.09 m (6 ft 10.25 in)	Stefka Kostadinova (Bulgaria)	Rome, Italy	30 August 1987
Pole vault	4.81 m (15 ft 9.25 in)	Stacy Dragila (USA)	Palo Alto, USA	9 June 2001
Long jump	7.52 m (24 ft 8.25 in)	Galina Chistyakova (USSR)	St Petersburg, Russia	1 June 1988
Triple jump	15.50 m (50 ft 10.25 in)	Inessa Kravets (Ukraine)	Gothenburg, Sweden	10 August 1995
Shot	22.63 m (74 ft 3 in)	Natalya Lisovskaya (USSR)	Moscow, Russia	7 June 1987
Javelin	71.54 m (234 ft 8 in)	Osleidys Menédez (Cuba)	Réthymno, Greece	1 July 2001
Discus	76.80 m (252 ft)	Gabriele Reinsch (GDR)	Neubrandenburg, Germany	9 July 1988
Hammer	76.07 m (249 ft 6 in)	Mihaela Melinte (Romania)	Rüdlingen, Germany	29 August 1999
Heptathlon★	7,291 points	Jacqueline Joyner-Kersee (USA)	Seoul, South Korea	23-24 September 1988

★ Day 1: 100-m hurdles: 12.69; High jump: 1.86 m (6 ft 1.25 in); Shot: 15.80 m (51 ft 10 in); 200 m: 22.56
Day 2: Long jump: 7.27 m (23 ft 10.25 in); Javelin: 45.66 m (149 ft 10 in); 800 m: 2:08.51

ATHLETICS

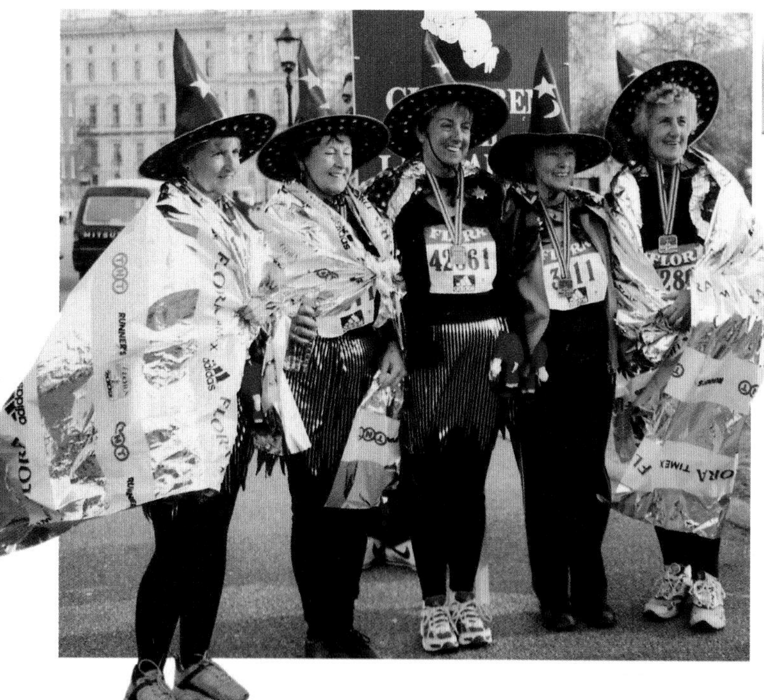

LONGEST DISTANCE BACKWARDS WALKING IN 24 HOURS

The longest distance recorded for walking backwards in 24 hours is 153.52 km (95.4 miles) by Anthony Thornton (USA) in Minneapolis, Minnesota, USA, from 31 December 1988 to 1 January 1989. His average speed was 6.4 km/h (3.9 mph).

FASTEST MARATHON

The men's world marathon best is 2 hr 5 min 38 sec set by Khalid Khannouchi (USA) at the London Marathon, London, UK, on 14 April 2002.

The women's world best is 2 hr 15 min 25 sec by Paula Radcliffe (UK), also at the London Marathon, on 13 April 2003.

FASTEST AGGREGATE TIME TO RUN A MARATHON ON EACH CONTINENT

The fastest aggregate time to complete a marathon on each of the seven continents is 34 hr 23 min 8 sec by Tim Rogers (UK) who ran them all between 13 February and 23 May 1999.

The women's record is 37 hr 20 sec by Kimi Puntillo (USA), who ran them all between 3 November 1996 and 4 October 1998.

MOST SIBLINGS TO COMPLETE THE SAME MARATHON

Five sisters – Valerie Lewis, Audrey Kenniford, Frederica Maguire, Sandra Hubbard and Denise Wilson (all UK, all née Mason, left) – ran the London Marathon, UK, on 14 April 2002. They all finished within two seconds of each other, in under 6:35.20.

FASTEST TIME TO COMPLETE THREE MARATHONS IN THREE DAYS

The fastest combined time for three marathons in three days is 8 hr 22 min 31 sec set by Raymond Hubbard (UK). The marathons were run in Belfast (2 hr 45 min 55 sec), London (2 hr 48 min 45 sec) and Boston (2 hr 47 min 51 sec), and all were run between 16 and 18 April 1988.

FASTEST HALF MARATHON

The world best time on a properly measured course is 59 min 5 sec by Paul Tergat (Kenya) at Lisbon, Portugal, on 26 March 2000. However, the official world best as recognized by the International Amateur Athletics Federation (IAAF) is 59 min 17 sec, also by Paul Tergat, at Milan, Italy, on 4 April 1998.

The women's official half marathon best is 66 min 43 sec by Masako Chiba (Japan) at Tokyo, Japan, on 19 January 1997.

MOST INDIVIDUAL WINS IN THE HALF MARATHON AT THE WORLD CHAMPIONSHIPS

Tegla Loroupe (Kenya) has won the IAAF Half Marathon World Championship three times – in 1997, 1998 and 1999.

The same record for the men's event is two by Paul Tergat (Kenya) in 1999 and 2000.

★ MEN'S INDOOR WORLD RECORDS ★

EVENT	RECORD	NAME AND COUNTRY	VENUE	DATE
50 m	5.56	Donovan Bailey (Canada)	Reno, USA	9 February 1996
		Maurice Greene (USA)	Los Angeles, USA	3 February 1999
60 m	6.39	Maurice Greene (USA)	Madrid, Spain	3 February 1998
			Atlanta, USA	3 March 2001
200 m	19.92	Frank Fredericks (Namibia)	Liévin, France,	18 February 1996
400 m	44.63	Michael Johnson (USA)	Atlanta, USA	4 March 1995
800 m	1:42.67	Wilson Kipketer (Denmark)	Paris, France	9 March 1997
1,000 m	2:14.36	Wilson Kipketer (Denmark)	Birmingham, UK	20 February 2000
1,500 m	3:31.18	Hicham El Guerrouj (Morocco)	Stuttgart, Germany	2 February 1997
1 mile	3:48.45	Hicham El Guerrouj (Morocco)	Ghent, Belgium	12 February 1997
3,000 m	7:24.90	Daniel Komen (Kenya)	Budapest, Hungary	6 February 1998
5,000 m	12:50.38	Haile Gebrselassie (Ethiopia)	Birmingham, UK	14 February 1999
50-m hurdles	6.25	Mark McCoy (Canada)	Kobe, Japan	5 March 1986
60-m hurdles	7.30	Colin Jackson (GB)	Sindelfingen, Germany	6 March 1994
4 x 200-m relay	1:22.11	Great Britain (Linford Christie, Darren Braithwaite, Ade Mafe and John Regis)	Glasgow, UK	3 March 1991
4 x 400-m relay	3:02.83	USA (Andre Morris, Dameon Johnson, Deon Minor and Milton Campbell)	Maebashi, Japan	7 March 1999
5,000-m walk	18:07.08	Mikhail Shchennikov (Russia)	Moscow, Russia	14 February 1995
High jump	2.43 m (7 ft 11.5 in)	Javier Sotomayor (Cuba)	Budapest, Hungary	4 March 1989
Pole vault	6.15 m (20 ft 2 in)	Sergei Bubka (Ukraine)	Donets'k, Ukraine	21 February 1993
Long jump	8.79 m (28 ft 10.25 in)	Carl Lewis (USA)	New York City, USA	27 January 1984
Triple jump	17.83 m (58 ft 6 in)	Aliecer Urrutia (Cuba)	Sindelfingen, Germany	1 March 1997
Shot	22.66 m (74 ft 4.5 in)	Randy Barnes (USA)	Los Angeles, USA	20 January 1989
Heptathlon★	6,476 points	Dan O'Brien (USA)	Toronto, Canada	13–14 March 1993

★ Events: 60 m: 6.67; Long jump: 7.84 m (25 ft 8.75 in); Shot: 16.02 m (52 ft 6.75 in); High jump: 2.13 m (6ft 11.75 in); 60-m hurdles: 7.85; Pole vault: 5.20 m (17 ft 0.75 in); 1,000 m: 2:57.96

LARGEST HALF MARATHON

The world's largest half marathon is The BUPA Great North Run, which is run between Newcastle upon Tyne and South Shields, Tyne & Wear, UK. The 2000 event, held on 22 October, had 36,822 finishers out of 50,173 entries.

FASTEST MARATHON SPEED MARCH TEAM WITHOUT RIFLES

The fastest time for a team to complete a marathon whilst carrying 40-lb backpacks is 4 hr 19 min 7 sec by eight members of 29 Commando Regiment Royal Artillery at the Luton Marathon, Bedfordshire, UK, on 29 November 1998.

GREATEST AVERAGE DAILY MILEAGE RUN

During the year from 1 August 1996 to 31 July 1997, Tirtha Kumar Phani (India) ran every day, running 22,565.76 km (14,021.7 miles) in total – an average of 61.824 km (38.41 miles) a day.

LONGEST DISTANCE RUN ON A TREADMILL IN 24 HOURS

Scott Eppelman (USA) ran 186.74 km (116.04 miles) over 24 hours on a treadmill in Addison, Texas, USA, on 1-2 November 2002. He also ran the fastest 100 miles on a treadmill.

FASTEST PRAM-PUSHING MARATHON

The fastest time to run a marathon while pushing a pram is 4 hr 6 min 30 sec by Patrick Read (UK) at the Abingdon Marathon, Oxfordshire, UK, on 20 October 2002.

MOST INDIVIDUAL MEDALS WON AT THE IAAF HALF MARATHON WORLD CHAMPIONSHIPS

The most individual medals won at the IAAF Half Marathon World Championships is eight by Lidia Simon-Slavuteanu (Romania, below), who won three team gold, one team silver, one individual silver and three individual bronze medals between 1996 and 2000.

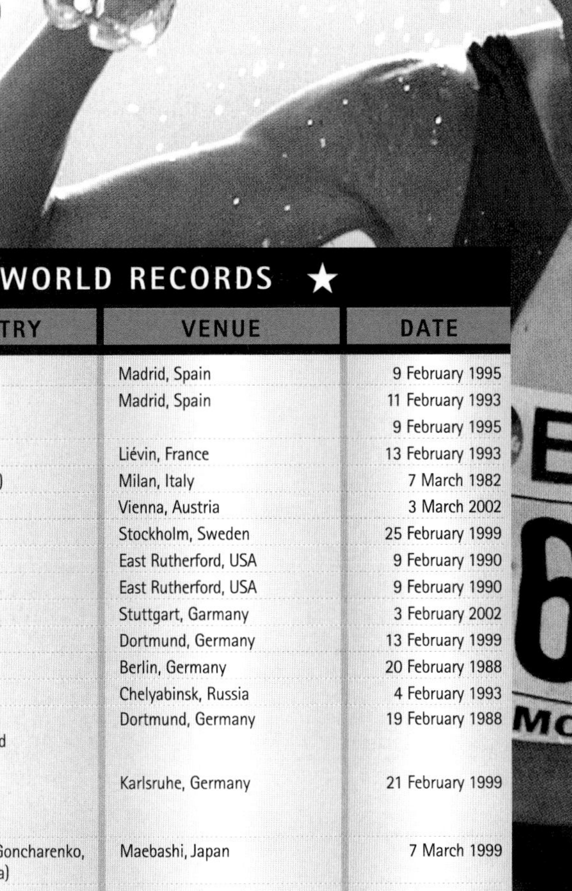

★ WOMEN'S INDOOR WORLD RECORDS ★

EVENT	RECORD	NAME AND COUNTRY	VENUE	DATE
50 m	5.96	Irina Privalova (Russia)	Madrid, Spain	9 February 1995
60 m	6.92	Irina Privalova (Russia)	Madrid, Spain	11 February 1993 9 February 1995
200 m	21.87	Merlene Ottey (Jamaica)	Liévin, France	13 February 1993
400 m	49.59	Jarmila Kratochvílovà (Czechoslovakia)	Milan, Italy	7 March 1982
800 m	1:55.82	Jolanda Ceplak (Slovenia)	Vienna, Austria	3 March 2002
1,000 m	2:30.94	Maria Mutola (Mozambique)	Stockholm, Sweden	25 February 1999
1,500 m	4:00.27	Doina Melinte (Romania)	East Rutherford, USA	9 February 1990
1 mile	4:17.14	Doina Melinte (Romania)	East Rutherford, USA	9 February 1990
3,000 m	8:29.15	Berhane Adere (Ethiopia)	Stuttgart, Garmany	3 February 2002
5,000 m	14:47.35	Gabriela Szabo (Romania)	Dortmund, Germany	13 February 1999
50-m hurdles	6.58	Cornelia Oschkenat (GDR)	Berlin, Germany	20 February 1988
60-m hurdles	7.69	Lyudmila Engquist (Russia)	Chelyabinsk, Russia	4 February 1993
4 x 200-m relay	1:32.55	SC Eintracht Hamm (Helga Arendt, Silke-Beate Knoll, Mechthild Kluth and Gisela Kinzel, all West Germany)	Dortmund, Germany	19 February 1988
		LG Olympia Dortmund (Esther Möller, Gabi Rockmeier, Birgit Rockmeier and Andrea Philipp, all Germany)	Karlsruhe, Germany	21 February 1999
4 x 400-m relay	3:24.25	Russia (Tatyana Chebykina, Svetlana Goncharenko, Olga Kotlyarova and Natalya Nazarova)	Maebashi, Japan	7 March 1999
3,000-m walk	11:40.33	Claudia Iovan (Romania)	Bucharest, Romania	30 January 1999
High jump	2.07 m (6 ft 9.5 in)	Heike Henkel (Germany)	Karlsruhe, Germany	9 February 1992
Pole vault	4.80 m (15 ft 9 in)	Svetlana Feofanova (Russia)	Birmingham, UK	16 March 2003
Long jump	7.37 m (24 ft 2.25 in)	Heike Drechsler (GDR)	Vienna, Austria	13 February 1988
Triple jump	15.16 m (49 ft 9 in)	Ashia Hansen (GB)	Valencia, Spain	28 February 1998
Shot	22.50 m (73 ft 10 in)	Helena Fibingerová (Czechoslovakia)	Jablonec, Czechoslovakia	19 February 1977
Pentathlon★	4,991 points	Irina Belova (Russia)	Berlin, Germany	14–15 February 1992

★ Events: 60-m hurdles: 8.22; High jump: 1.93 m (6 ft 4in); Shot: 13.25 m (43 ft 5.75 in); Long jump 6.67 m (21 ft 10.75 in); 800 m: 2:10.26.

OLYMPICS

GREATEST ATTENDANCE AT AN OLYMPIC GAMES

The greatest ever total spectator attendance at an Olympic Games was 5,797,923, at the Los Angeles games in California, USA, in 1984.

BEST OLYMPICS ATTENDANCE BY A COUNTRY

Five countries have been represented at all of the 25 Summer Olympic Games that have been held (1896–2000): Australia, France, Greece, Great Britain and Switzerland (in 1956 Switzerland only contested the equestrian events, held in Stockholm, Sweden, and, therefore, did not attend the main Games in Melbourne, Australia). Of these countries, only France, Great Britain and Switzerland have been present at all the Winter Olympic Games (1924–2002) as well.

MOST COUNTRIES REPRESENTED AT AN OLYMPICS

The most countries ever to be represented at an Olympic Games is 199 at the Sydney games in Australia, between 15 September and 1 October 2000.

MOST PARTICIPANTS AT AN OLYMPIC GAMES

The Summer Olympic Games held from 15 September to 1 October 2000 in Sydney, Australia, hold the record for the greatest number of participants. In total, 11,084 athletes attended the games, of which a record 4,245 were women.

MOST PARTICIPANTS AT A PARALYMPIC GAMES

The most participants in a Paralympic Games is 3,824 for the games held in 2000 in Sydney, Australia. The participants came from 125 different countries, also a Paralympic Games record.

LONGEST TIME AS AN OLYMPIC COMPETITOR

Four Olympic competitors have participated in games over a period of 40 years: Ivan Joseph Martin Osiier (Denmark) in fencing (1908–32 and 1948); Magnus Andreas Thulstrup Clasen Konow (Norway) in yachting (1908–20, 1928 and 1936–48); Paul Elvstrøm (Denmark) in yachting (1948–60, 1968–72 and 1984–88); and Durward Randolph Knowles (UK then Bahamas) in yachting (1948–72 and 1988).

MOST PARTICIPANTS AT A WINTER OLYMPIC GAMES

The 2002 Winter Olympic Games, held at Salt Lake City, Utah, USA (below), were attended by a record 2,550 competitors from 77 different countries.

MOST GOLD MEDALS WON BY A COUNTRY

The USA has won a record 931 gold medals in the history of the Olympic Games, which have been held from 1896 to 2000. Below, the USA's Women's 4 x 200-m freestyle swimming team celebrate with their gold medals after victory at the 2000 Olympic Games in Sydney, Australia.

MOST CONSECUTIVE OLYMPIC GOLD MEDALS WON

The most gold medal wins at successive Olympic games is six by Aladár Gerevich (Hungary), who was a member of the winning sabre team from 1932 to 1960.

MOST CONSECUTIVE GOLD MEDALS WON IN AN INDIVIDUAL EVENT

The only Olympians to win four consecutive individual titles in the same event are Al Oerter (USA) in the discus (1956–68) and Carl Lewis (USA) in the long jump (1984–96). Paul Elvstrøm (Denmark) also won four successive gold medals, at monotype yachting events (1948–60), but there was a class change (1948 Firefly class, 1952–60 Finn class).

However, if the Intercalated Games of 1906 (which were staged officially by the International Olympic Committee) are included, Raymond Clarence Ewry (USA) won both the standing long jump and the standing high jump in four consecutive games (1900, 1904, 1906 and 1908).

MOST CONSECUTIVE OLYMPIC GOLD MEDALS WON BY A WOMAN

The most consecutive Olympic gold medals won by a woman is four by Birgit Fischer (formerly Birgit Schmidt, Germany) at the Seoul games in 1988 and the Sydney Olympics in 2000. Fischer's medals were all won in canoeing.

MOST CONSECUTIVE ENDURANCE EVENT OLYMPIC GOLD MEDALS WON

The most Olympic gold medals won in an endurance event is five by Steven Redgrave (UK), who won a gold medal for rowing at five consecutive Olympic Games from 1984 to 2000.

MOST MEDAL-WINNING COUNTRIES AT THE OLYMPIC GAMES

The 2000 Olympic Games in Sydney, Australia, saw the most medal-winning countries ever at an Olympics, with 80 countries winning at least one medal.

MOST WINTER OLYMPIC GOLD MEDALS WON BY AN INDIVIDUAL

Bjørn Dæhlie (Norway) won eight Olympic gold medals in Nordic skiing between 1992 and 1998. The women's record is six by Lidya Skoblikova (USSR) in speed skating from 1960 to 1964, and Lyubov Yegerova (Russia) in Nordic skiing from 1992 to 1994.

MOST WINTER OLYMPIC GOLD MEDALS WON BY A COUNTRY

Norway has won a record 94 gold medals in the history of the Winter Olympic Games, from 1924–2002.

MOST MEDAL WINNING COUNTRIES AT A WINTER OLYMPIC GAMES

The most countries to win medals at a single Winter Olympic Games is 25 in 2002 at Salt Lake City, Utah, USA. Below, the German (silver), Norwegian (gold) and French (bronze) medal winners celebrate after the Men's 4 x 7.5-km biathlon relay.

COMBAT

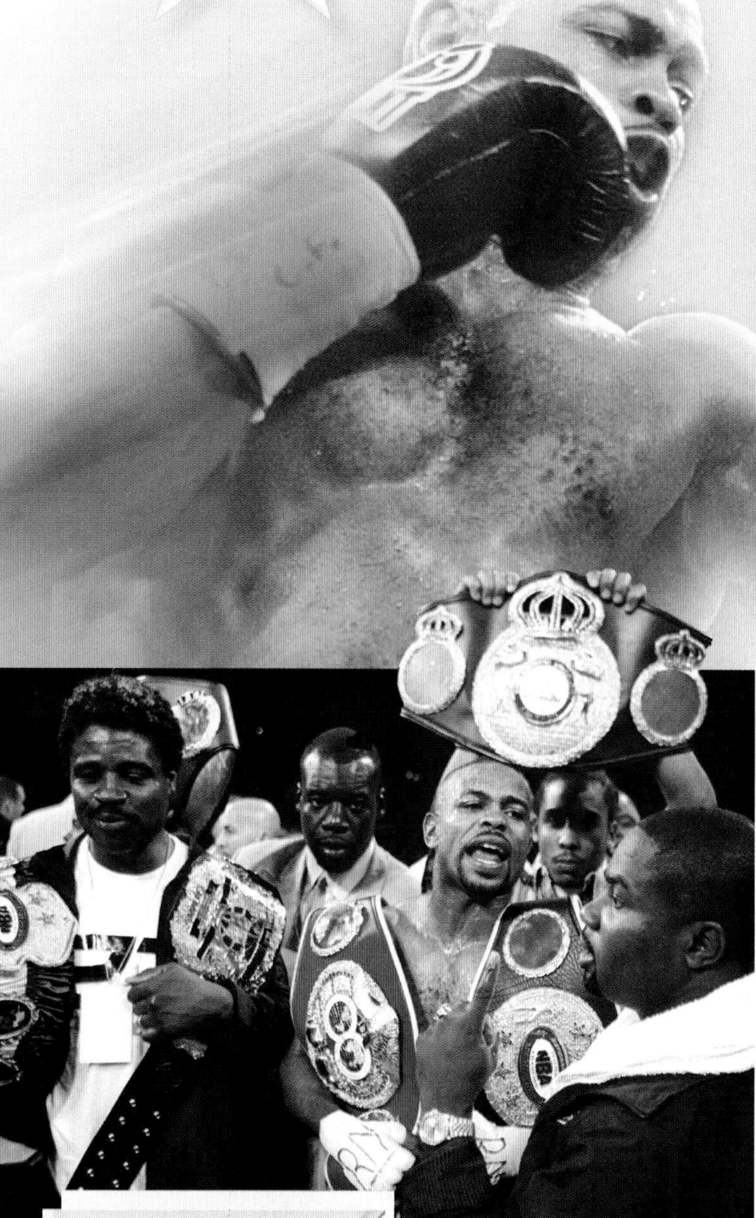

MOST HEAVYWEIGHT TITLES BY A FORMER MIDDLEWEIGHT

This remarkable feat has been achieved only twice in 106 years. The first time was by Robert James 'Bob' Fitzsimmons (UK) when the former middleweight knocked out James J Corbett (USA) at Carson City, Nevada, USA, on 17 March 1897. Roy Jones Jnr (USA, above) matched this when he beat John Ruiz (USA) for the World Boxing Association heavyweight title by unanimous decision on 2 March 2003 at Las Vegas, Nevada, USA.

BOXING

MOST FIGHTS UNDEFEATED

From 1916 to 1923 Edward Henry 'Harry' Greb (USA) was unbeaten in a sequence of 178 bouts including 117 ruled 'no decision', of which five were unofficial losses. Of boxers with complete records, Packey McFarland (USA) had 97 fights from 1905 to 1915 without a defeat, five of which were draws. Pedro Carrasco (Spain) won 83 consecutive fights from 22 April 1964 to 3 September 1970, drew once and had a further nine wins before his loss to Armando Ramos (Mexico) in a World Boxing Council (WBC) lightweight contest on 18 February 1972.

MOST WORLD TITLE RECAPTURES

The only boxer to win a world title five times at one weight is 'Sugar' Ray Robinson (USA) who beat Carmen Basilio (USA) in Chicago, USA, on 25 March 1958, to regain the world middleweight title for the fourth time.

MOST CONSECUTIVE KNOCK-OUTS

The record for most consecutive knock-outs is held by Lamar Clark (USA), who achieved 44 consecutive knock-outs from 1958 to January 1960. He knocked out six opponents in one night (five in the first round) at Bingham, Utah, USA, on 1 December 1958.

LONGEST REIGNING WORLD HEAVYWEIGHT CHAMPION

Joe Louis (USA) was champion for 11 years 252 days, from 22 June 1937, when he knocked out James Joseph Braddock (USA) in the eighth round at Chicago, Illinois, USA, until his retirement on 1 March 1949. During his reign, Louis made a record 25 defences of his title. This record is also the longest reign of any champion in any weight division.

MOST WORLD TITLES AT DIFFERENT WEIGHTS

Henry 'Homicide Hank' Armstrong (USA) held world titles at three different weights – featherweight, lightweight and welterweight – simultaneously between August and December 1938. It is claimed that Barney Ross (USA) held the world lightweight, junior welterweight and welterweight titles at the same time from 28 May to 17 September 1934, but the date when he relinquished his lightweight title is disputed.

MOST SPEEDBALL HITS IN ONE MINUTE

The greatest number of hits of a speedball in one minute is 366 by Wayne Harbinson (Australia) at the GTV9 Studios, Melbourne, Australia, on 14 October 1996.

JUDO

MOST MEN'S JUDO WORLD TITLES

David Douillet (France) has won five world and Olympic titles: in the Over 95-kg class in 1993, 1995 and 1997; in the Open in 1995; and in the Olympic Over 95-kg class in 1996. Yasuhiro Yamashita (Japan) has also won five world and Olympic titles: three in the Over 95-kg class, and one each in the Open and the Olympic Over 95-kg class.

MOST WOMEN'S JUDO WORLD CHAMPIONSHIPS

Ingrid Berghmans (Belgium) has won six women's world titles (first held 1980) – in the Open category in 1980, 1982, 1984 and 1986, and in the Under-72 kg class in 1984 and 1989.

MOST JUDO THROWS IN 10 HOURS

Patrick Hurley and Tony Cox (both UK) of the Leeds Central Aikido Club completed 46,261 judo and aikido throwing techniques in a ten-hour period at the Aireborough Leisure Centre, Leeds, West Yorkshire, UK, on 30 May 1998.

FENCING

MOST MEN'S OLYMPIC MEDALS

Edoardo Mangiarotti (Italy) holds the record for the most men's Olympic medals with 13: six gold, five silver and two bronze. He won them for foil and epée from 1936 to 1960.

MOST MEN'S TEAM WORLD CHAMPIONSHIPS

The greatest number of fencing team World Championships won is 34 by Italy, a record 16 foil, 13 epée and five sabre titles, between 1929 and 1994. France have won nine foil titles (1924–80), and a record 14 epée titles, (1904–2002). The record number of wins for sabre is 20 by Hungary between 1908 and 1998.

MOST OLYMPIC GOLDS

The most men's individual Olympic fencing gold medals won is three by Nedo Nadi (Italy), who won in 1912 and 1920 (two) and Ramón Fonst (Cuba) who won in 1900 and 1904 (two). Nadi also won three team gold medals in 1920, making five golds at one games – the record for fencing and at the time a record for any sport.

The most fencing gold medals won by a woman at the Olympic Games is four (one individual, three team) by Yelena Dmitryevna Novikova (USSR), who won her titles between 1968 and 1976.

MOST MEN'S WORLD TITLES

The greatest number of individual fencing world titles won is five by Aleksandr Romankov (USSR) for foil in 1974, 1977, 1979, 1982 and 1983.

MARTIAL ARTS

MOST CONCRETE BLOCKS BROKEN IN A MINUTE

The most concrete blocks smashed by hand in one minute is 55 by Dan Netherland (USA) at Ripley's Aquarium of the Smokies, Gatlinburg, Tennessee, USA, on 26 February 2003. Each block, measuring 76.2 x 20.3 x 7.3 cm (30 x 8 x 2.9 in) was stacked in piles of one, two, three, four, five, six, seven, eight, nine and finally ten high.

MOST CONCRETE BLOCKS BROKEN USING THE ROUNDHOUSE KICK METHOD

Mikael Birgersson (Sweden) holds the record for the most concrete blocks broken using the roundhouse kick method. In one minute he smashed 33 blocks at the studios of *Guinness Rekord TV* in Stockholm, Sweden, on 28 November 2001.

HIGHEST MARTIAL ARTS KICK

The highest martial arts kick measured is 2.94 m (9 ft 8 in) by Jessie Frankson (USA), who kicked a target with a pin attached, which in turn burst a balloon on the set of *Guinness World Records; Primetime*, Los Angeles, California, USA, on 21 December 2000.

MOST KARATE KICKS IN ONE MINUTE

The most karate kicks in one minute using only one leg is 128 by Fabian Cuenca Pirroti (Spain) on 11 November 2001 on the set of *El Show de los Récords* in Madrid, Spain.

SUMO

MOST CONSECUTIVE SUMO TOURNAMENTS WON

Yokozuna (grand champion) Mitsugu Akimoto (Japan, sumo name Chiyonofuji) won one of the six annual tournaments – the Kyushu Basho – for eight years in a row from 1981 to 1988. He also holds the record for the most career wins, with 1,045, and *Makunouchi* (top division) wins, with 807.

LARGEST YOKOZUNA SUMO WRESTLER

Hawaiian-born Chad Rowan, alias Akebono (USA, right facing out), became the first foreign rikishi to be promoted to the top rank of *yokozuna* in January 1993. He is the tallest *yokozuna* in sumo history at 2.04 m (6 ft 8 in) high. He is also the heaviest, weighing 227 kg (501 lb).

MOST SUMO YOKOZUNA CONSECUTIVE WINS

Yokozuna Sadji Akiyoshi (Japan), alias Futabayama, had a record 69 consecutive wins between 1937 and 1939.

MOST RIKISHI BOUTS WON IN A YEAR

Toshimitsu Ogata (Japan), alias Kitanoumi, set a record in 1978 winning 82 of the 90 bouts that top *rikishi* fight annually.

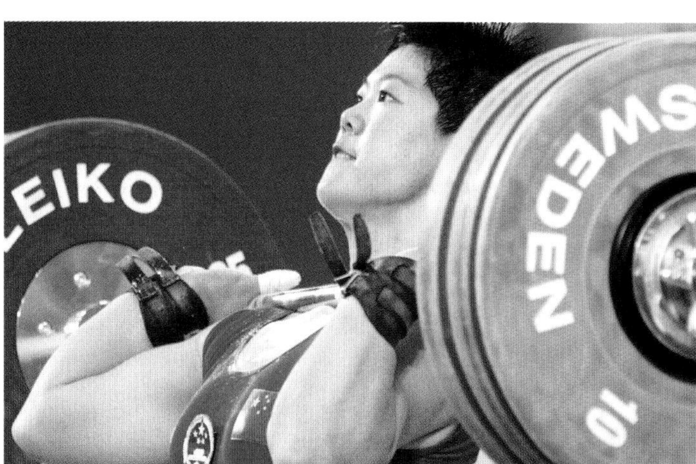

WOMEN'S 69-KG CLEAN AND JERK

The record for the women's 69-kg clean and jerk is held by Chunhong Liu (China, above), who lifted 148 kg at Busan, South Korea, on 3 October 2002.

STAMINA EVENTS

MOST SKIPS IN 24 HOURS BY A TEAM

The record for the most skips in 24 hours by a team of six is 260,307 and was set by Jim Payne, Neil Gough, Larry O'Brien, Christy O'Reilly, Deirdre Hearne and Martin Murphy (all Ireland) in Waterford, Ireland, on 24–25 May 2002. Each skipper skipped for an hour at a time in relay fashion.

MOST PUSH-UPS IN ONE HOUR

Roy Berger (Canada) achieved 3,416 push-ups in one hour at the Central Canada Exhibition, Ottawa, Ontario, Canada, on 30 August 1998.

MOST PUSH-UPS IN ONE MINUTE

The record for the most push-ups in one minute is 124, set by Campbell Pentney (New Zealand) at Takapuna Athletic Club, New Zealand, on 3 August 2002.

MOST ONE-ARM PUSH-UPS IN ONE MINUTE

Yvan de Weber (Switzerland) completed 120 one-arm push-ups in one minute at the studios of *El Show de los Récords*, Madrid, Spain, on 23 October 2001.

MOST PUSH-UPS USING BACK OF HANDS IN ONE HOUR

The record for the most push-ups using the backs of the hands in one hour is 1,584 and was set by Kevin Jefferson (UK) at Stanley Central Working Men's Club, Stanley, Durham, UK, on 20 October 2002.

MOST PARALLEL BAR DIPS IN ONE HOUR

Simon Kent (UK) achieved 3,989 parallel bar dips in one hour at Farrah's Health Centre, Lincoln, UK, on 5 September 1998.

Simon Kent also holds the record for the most parallel bar dips in one minute with 140. This was set at Lincoln College, Lincoln, UK, on 17 July 2002.

MOST ABDOMINAL FRAME SIT-UPS IN ONE HOUR

The record for the most sit-ups in one hour using an abdominal frame is 5,633 and was set by Guillermo Subiela (Argentina) at Synergy Fitness Club, Astoria, New York, USA, on 5 October 2002.

MOST SQUATS IN ONE HOUR

On 30 January 2002 Attila Horvàth (Hungary) completed 4,656 squats in one hour at the Centre of Sports Gym, University of Debrecen, Hungary.

MOST ROTATIONS ON A POMMEL HORSE IN ONE MINUTE

The record for the most rotations on a pommel horse in one minute is 59 by Andreu Vivo Tomas (Spain). The record was set on *El Show de los Récords* in Madrid, Spain, on 4 October 2001.

WEIGHTLIFTING

MOST OLYMPIC WEIGHTLIFTING APPEARANCES

The most Olympic weightlifting appearances is five by Imre Földi (Hungary) between 1960 and 1976.

MOST OLYMPIC WEIGHTLIFTING MEDALS WON

The most Olympic weightlifting medals won is four by Norbert Schemansky (USA) between 1948 and 1964. Schemansky won gold at middle-heavyweight class in 1952; silver at heavyweight class in 1948; and bronze at heavyweight class in 1960 and 1964.

MOST WOMEN'S WEIGHTLIFTING WORLD CHAMPIONSHIPS

The most gold medals won at the women's weightlifting World Championships is 13 by Chunhong Liu (China) in the 60/64 kg class in 1992–96.

MOST MEN'S WORLD WEIGHTLIFTING TITLES

The most world weightlifting title wins, including Olympic Games, is 10 by Naim Suleymanoglü (Turkey) in 1985–86, 1988–89 and 1991–96.

YOUNGEST WEIGHTLIFTING WORLD RECORD HOLDER

Naim Suleymanoglü (b. 23 January 1967, Turkey) was 16 years 62 days old when he set world records for clean and jerk at 160 kg (353 lb) and a combined total of 285 kg (628 lb) at Allentown, New Jersey, USA, on 26 March 1983.

OLDEST WEIGHTLIFTING WORLD RECORD HOLDER

The oldest weightlifting world record holder is Norbert Schemansky (b. 30 May 1924, USA) who, aged 37 years 333 days, snatched 164.2 kg (362 lb) in the then unlimited heavyweight class at Detroit, Michigan, USA, on 28 April 1962.

MOST POWERLIFTING WORLD CHAMPIONSHIPS

Hideaki Inaba (Japan) holds the most powerlifting world titles with 17 at 52 kg, in 1974–83 and 1985–91.

FASTEST BACKFLIP OVER 50 M

On 31 August 1995, at Makuhar Messe Event Hall, Chiba, Japan, Vitaliy Scherbo (Belarus, left) backflipped 50 m (164 ft) along the ground in 10.22 seconds.

MOST OLYMPIC WEIGHTLIFTING GOLD MEDALS

The most Olympic weightlifting gold medals won is three by Naim Suleymanoglü (Turkey) in 1988, 1992 and 1996; Pyrros Dimas (Greece) in 1992, 1996 and 2000; and Akakios Kakiasvili (Greece, left) in 1992, 1996 and 2000. In 1992 Kakiasvili was known as Kakhi Kakhiachbili and he represented EUN/CIS, the Unified team of the former Soviet Republics.

★ WEIGHTLIFTING WORLD RECORDS ★

EVENT	WEIGHT	NAME AND COUNTRY	VENUE	DATE
Men's 56-kg clean and jerk	168.0 kg	Halil Mutlu (Turkey)	Trencín, Slovakia	24 April 2001
Men's 56-kg snatch	138.5 kg	Halil Mutlu (Turkey)	Antalya, Turkey	4 November 2001
Men's 56-kg total	305.0 kg	Halil Mutlu (Turkey)	Sydney, Australia	16 September 2000
Men's 62-kg clean and jerk	182.5 kg	Maosheng Le (China)	Busan, South Korea	2 October 2002
Men's 62-kg snatch	153.0 kg	Shi Zhiyong (China)	Izmir, Turkey	28 June 2002
Men's 62-kg total		No record yet set		
Men's 69-kg clean and jerk	196.5 kg	Galabin Boevski (Bulgaria)	Sydney, Australia	20 September 2000
Men's 69-kg snatch	165.0 kg	Georgi Markov (Bulgaria)	Sydney, Australia	20 September 2000
Men's 69-kg total	357.5 kg	Galabin Boevski (Bulgaria)	Athens, Greece	24 November 1999
Men's 77-kg clean and jerk	210.0 kg	Oleg Perepetchenov (Russia)	Trencín, Slovakia	27 April 2001
Men's 77-kg snatch	173.0 kg	Sergey Filimonov (Kazakhstan)	Busan, South Korea	4 October 2002
Men's 77-kg total	377.5 kg	Plamen Zhelyazkov (Bulgaria)	Doha, Qatar	27 March 2002
Men's 85-kg clean and jerk	218.0 kg	Zhang Yong (China)	Tel Aviv, Israel	25 April 1998
Men's 85-kg snatch	182.5 kg	Andrei Ribakov (Bulgaria)	Havirov, Czech Republic	2 June 2002
Men's 85-kg total		No record yet set		
Men's 94-kg clean and jerk	232.5 kg	Szymon Kolecki (Poland)	Sofia, Bulgaria	29 April 2000
Men's 94-kg snatch	188.0 kg	Akakios Kakiasvili (Greece)	Athens, Greece	27 November 1999
Men's 94-kg total		No record yet set		
Men's 105-kg clean and jerk		No record yet set		
Men's 105-kg snatch	198.5 kg	Marcin Dolega (Poland)	Havirov, Czech Republic	4 June 2002
Men's 105-kg total		No record yet set		
Men's over-105-kg clean and jerk	263.0 kg	Hossein Rezazadeh (Iran)	Warsaw, Poland	26 November 2002
Men's over-105-kg snatch	212.5 kg	Hossein Rezazadeh (Iran)	Sydney, Australia	26 September 2000
Men's over-105-kg total	472.5 kg	Hossein Rezazadeh (Iran)	Sydney, Australia	26 September 2000
Women's 48-kg clean and jerk	115.5 kg	Mingjuan Wang (China)	Warsaw, Poland	19 November 2002
Women's 48-kg snatch	92.5 kg	Mingjuan Wang (China)	Warsaw, Poland	19 November 2002
Women's 48-kg total	207.5 kg	Mingjuan Wang (China)	Warsaw, Poland	19 November 2002
Women's 53-kg clean and jerk	127.5 kg	Xueju Li (China)	Busan, South Korea	20 November 2002
Women's 53-kg snatch	102.5 kg	Ri Song-hui (North Korea)	Warsaw, Poland	1 October 2002
Women's 53-kg total	225.0 kg	Yang Xia (China)	Sydney, Australia	18 September 2000
Women's 58-kg clean and jerk	133.0 kg	Caiyan Sun (China)	Izmir, Turkey	28 June 2002
Women's 58-kg snatch	106.0 kg	Zhijuan Song (China)	Kazincbarcika, Hungary	5 October 2002
Women's 58-kg total	237.5 kg	Caiyan Sun (China)	Izmir, Turkey	28 June 2002
Women's 63-kg clean and jerk	136.0 kg	Anastasia Tsakiri (Greece)	Warsaw, Poland	21 November 2002
Women's 63-kg snatch	112.5 kg	Chen Xiaomin (China)	Sydney, Australia	19 September 2000
Women's 63-kg total	242.5 kg	Chen Xiaomin (China)	Sydney, Australia	19 September 2000
Women's 69-kg clean and jerk	148.0 kg	Chunhong Liu (China)	Busan, South Korea	2 October 2002
Women's 69-kg snatch	115.5 kg	Chunhong Liu (China)	Busan, South Korea	6 October 2002
Women's 69-kg total	262.5 kg	Chunhong Liu (China)	Busan, South Korea	3 October 2002
Women's 75-kg clean and jerk	152.5 kg	Ruiping Sun (China)	Busan, South Korea	7 October 2002
Women's 75-kg snatch	118.5 kg	Ruiping Sun (China)	Busan, South Korea	7 October 2002
Women's 75-kg total	270.0 kg	Ruiping Sun (China)	Busan, South Korea	7 October 2002
Women's over-75-kg clean and jerk	167.5 kg	Tang Gonghong (China)	Busan, South Korea	8 October 2002
Women's over-75-kg snatch	135.0 kg	Ding Meiyuan (China)	Sydney, Australia	22 September 2000
Women's over-75-kg total	300.0 kg	Ding Meiyuan (China)	Sydney, Australia	22 September 2000

From 1 January 1998 the International Weightlifting Federation (IWF) introduced modified bodyweight categories, thereby making the existing world records redundant. This is the new listing with the world standards for the new bodyweight categories. Results achieved at IWF-approved competitions exceeding the world standards by 0.5 kg for snatch or clean and jerk, or by 2.5 kg for the total, will be recognized as world records.

HIGHEST SPEED IN AN OLYMPIC DOWNHILL RACE

The highest average speed achieved in an Olympic downhill race was 107.53 km/h (66.81 mph) by Jean-Luc Cretier (France, left) at Nagano, Japan, on 13 February 1998.

ALPINE SKIING

MOST WORLD CUP INDIVIDUAL RACE WINS

The most World Cup individual event wins is 86 (46 giant slalom and 40 slalom from a total of 287 races) by Ingemar Stenmark (Sweden) between 1974 and 1989. Stenmark also holds the men's record of 13 wins in one season (1978/79), of which 10 were part of a record 14 successive giant slalom wins from 18 March 1978 (his 22nd birthday) to 21 January 1980. The women's record is held by Annemarie Moser (Austria), who won 62 individual events between 1970 and 1979. She had a record 11 consecutive downhill wins from December 1972 to January 1974. She has also claimed the World Cup Overall Champion (downhill and slalom events combined) title a record six times since the tour began in 1967.

MOST BIATHLON OLYMPIC MEDALS

The most Olympic medals won in the men's biathlon is seven by Ricco Gross (Germany, right in the picture below). He won three gold for the 4 x 7.5 km in 1992, 1994 and 1998; three silver for the 10 km in 1992 and 1994, and the 4 x 7.5 km in 2002, and a bronze for pursuit in 2002.

HIGHEST SPEED IN WORLD CUP SKIING

Armin Assinger (Austria) reached a record speed of 112.4 km/h (69.8 mph) at Sierra Nevada, Spain, on 15 March 1993.

MOST ALPINE SKIING OLYMPIC GOLD MEDALS

The most men's Olympic gold medals won is three. Four skiers share the record: Anton 'Toni' Sailer (Austria) won gold in the downhill, slalom and giant slalom events in 1956; Jean-Claude Killy (France) took home gold in the same events in 1968; Alberto Tomba (Italy) won in the slalom in 1988 and the giant slalom in 1988 and 1992; and Kjetil André Aamodt (Norway) won in the super giant slalom in 1992 and 2002, and in the combined event at the 2002 Games.

The most Olympic gold medals won by a woman is three, a record also shared by four skiers: Vreni Schneider (Switzerland) in the giant slalom in 1988 and the slalom in 1988 and 1994; Janica Kostelic (Croatia) in the combined event, the giant slalom and slalom in 2002; Katja Seizinger (Germany) for downhill in 1994 and 1998 and combined in 1998; and Deborah Campagnoni (Italy) in the super giant slalom in 1992 and the giant slalom in 1994 and 1998.

MOST ALPINE SKIING OLYMPIC MEDALS

The most Olympic Games medals won by a male is seven by Kjetil André Aamodt (Norway) who, in addition to his record three gold medals, has won two silver (downhill, combined 1994) and two bronze (giant slalom 1992, super giant slalom 1994).

The most Olympic medals won by a woman is five. Vreni Schneider (Switzerland), in addition to her record three gold medals, won silver in the combined and bronze in the giant slalom in 1994. Katja Seizinger (Germany) also has five Olympic medals. As well as her three golds, she won bronze in 1992 and 1998 in the super giant slalom.

MOST WORLD ALPINE SKIING CHAMPIONSHIP TITLES

The greatest number of World Alpine Championship titles won by a man is seven by Anton 'Toni' Sailer (Austria), who won all four events (giant slalom, slalom, downhill and the non-Olympic Alpine combination) in 1956 and the downhill, giant slalom and combined in 1958.

The greatest number of World Alpine Championship titles won by a woman is 12 by Christl Cranz (Germany). She has won seven individual titles (four slalom in 1934, 1937–39 and three downhill in 1935, 1937 and 1939), and five combined in 1934–35 and 1937–39. She also won the gold medal for the combined event in the 1936 Olympics.

MOST WORLD CUP SKI WINS IN A SEASON

Vreni Schneider (Switzerland) won 13 events (and a combined event), including all seven slalom events, in the 1988/89 season.

GREATEST VERTICAL DISTANCE SKIED IN ONE DAY

On 29 April 1998, Edi Podivinsky, Luke Sauder, Chris Kent (all Canada) and Dominique Perret (Switzerland) skied a record total of 107,777 m (353,600 ft) in 14 hr 30 min on a slope at Blue River, British Columbia, Canada. They made the run 73 times and were helicoptered back to the summit each time.

Jennifer Hughes (USA) holds the women's vertical skiing distance record. On 20 April 1998 she skied 93,124 m (305,525 ft) at Atlin, British Columbia, Canada. Hughes was accompanied by Tammy McMinn (USA), who broke the snowboarding record for the same feat.

GREATEST VERTICAL DISTANCE SKIED IN ONE DAY USING T-BAR LIFT

Neal Weisenberg skied a total of 46,920 m (153,937 ft) in one day, from 27 to 28 February 1999 at Kimberley Alpine Resort, Kimberley, British Columbia, Canada. He used a t-bar ski lift to return to the top of the slope.

MOST EXTENSIVE SKIERS

In 1994, Arnie Wilson and Lucy Dicker (both UK) skied every day in a round-the-world expedition. In total they covered 5,919 km (3,678 miles) and 1,263,972 vertical metres (4,146,890 vertical feet) at 237 resorts in 13 countries in five continents.

The first person to ski in all seven continents was Tom Hayes (USA) and the first woman was Norma Rowlerson (UK).

MOST WORLD CUP DOWNHILL WINS

Franz Klammer (Austria) won a record 25 World Cup downhill races between 1974 and 1984.

LONGEST RUN IN DOWNHILL SKIING

The Weissfluhjoch-Küblis Parsenn course, near Davos, Switzerland is 12.23 km (7.6 miles) long.

LONGEST DOWNHILL RACE

The Inferno in Switzerland is 15.8 km (9.8 miles) from the top of the Schilthorn to Lauterbrunnen. The record time for completing the course is 13 min 53.40 sec by Urs von Allmen (Switzerland) in 1992. The women's record time for the race is 17 min 8.42 sec by Christine Sonderegger (Switzerland) in the same year.

HIGHEST SPEED SKIING

Harry Egger (Austria) skied at 248.105 km/h (154.165 mph), at Les Arcs, France, on 2 May 1999.

On the same day at Les Arcs, Karine Dubouchet (France) achieved a women's record speed of 234.528 km/h (145.728 mph).

FREESTYLE SKIING

MOST SOMERSAULT AND TWIST COMBINATIONS IN A FREESTYLE JUMP

Matt Chojnacki (USA), completed a quadruple-twisting quadruple back flip at Colorado, USA, on 4 April 2001.

MOST FREESTYLE SKIING WORLD CHAMPIONSHIP TITLES

The first freestyle World Championships were held at Tignes, France, in 1986. Edgar Grospiron (France) has won a record three titles, for moguls in 1989 and 1991 and aerials in 1995. He also won an Olympic title in 1992.

The most women's skiing freestyle world titles won is also three by Candice Gilg (France) for moguls in 1993, 1995 and 1997.

MOST FREESTYLE WORLD CUP WINS

Eric Laboureix (France) achieved five freestyle World Cup wins, winning the overall title in 1986-88 and 1990-91.

The same record for women is ten by Connie Kissling (Switzerland) in 1983-92.

MOST ALPINE NATIONS CUP WINS

The Nations Cup, awarded on the combined results of the men and women in the World Cup, has been won a record 22 times by Austria in 1969, 1973–80, 1982 and 1990–2001. Alexandra Meissnitzer (right) has helped Austria to Nations Cup victory on several occasions.

WINTER SPORTS

NORDIC SKIING

MOST NORDIC SKIING WORLD TITLES

The 1924 Winter Olympics in Chamonix, France, was the first skiing World Nordic Championships. The greatest number of titles (including Olympics) won is 17 by Bjørn Dæhlie (Norway) (12 individual and 5 relay) in 1991–98. Dæhlie has won a record 29 medals in total.

The most women's titles won is 17 by Yelena Välbe (Russia) (10 individual and 7 relay) in 1989-98. She has won a record total of 24 medals.

MOST NORDIC SKIING OLYMPIC GOLD MEDALS

The most Nordic skiing Olympic gold medals won by a man is eight by Bjørn Dæhlie (Norway) for the 15 km, 50 km and 4 x 10-km relay in 1992, the 10 km and 15 km in 1994, and the 10 km, 50 km and 4 x 10-km relay in 1998.

Lyubov Yegorova (Russia) holds the women's record with six wins for the 10 km, 15 km and 4 x 5-km relay in 1992, and the 5 km, 10 km and 4 x 5-km relay in 1994.

MOST NORDIC COMBINED SKIING OLYMPIC GOLD MEDALS

Ulrich Wehling (Germany) has won three gold medals in the individual event in 1972, 1976 and 1980. Sampaa Lajunen (Finland) shares the record, with golds in the individual, sprint and relay in 2002. Lajunen also won silver in the individual and relay events in 1998 for a record total of five medals.

HIGHEST AVERAGE SPEED IN A NORDIC SKIING 50-KM RACE

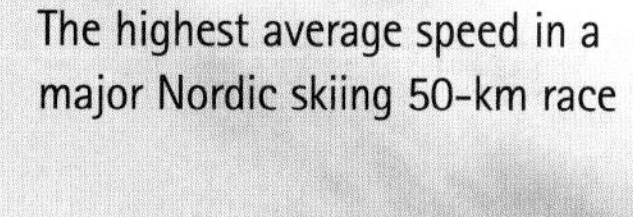

The highest average speed in a major Nordic skiing 50-km race is 26.14 km/h (16.24 mph). The race was completed in a record time of 1 hr 54 min 46 sec by Aleksey Prokurorov (Russia) at Thunder Bay, Canada, on 19 March 1994.

GREATEST DISTANCE NORDIC SKIING IN 24 HOURS

Seppo-Juhani Savolainen (Finland) covered 415.5 km (258.2 miles) in 24 hours at Saariselk, Finland, on 8–9 April 1988.

Kamila Horakova (Czech Republic) is the women's record holder, with 333 km (206.91 miles), achieved on 12–13 April 2000.

LONGEST SKI JUMP BY A WOMAN

The longest ski-jump performed by a woman is 112 m (367 ft) by Eva Ganster (Austria), who achieved the distance at Bischofshofen, Austria, on 7 January 1994.

LONGEST SKI JUMP ON A DRY SKI SLOPE

The longest dry ski-jump is 92 m (302 ft) by Hubert Schwarz (Germany) at Berchtesgarten, Germany, on 30 June 1981.

MOST GOLD WORLDLOPPETT MASTERS TITLES

By the end of the 2001 season, the most times an individual had qualified as a Worldloppett Gold Master is nine, by Jan Jasiewicz (Switzerland). To qualify as a Gold Master you must have completed 10 races in the Worldloppett series, all in different countries and at least two different continents.

« LONGEST COMPETITIVE MEN'S SKI JUMP

The longest competitive ski jump made by a man is 225 m (738 ft) by Andreas Goldberger (Austria, left) at Planica, Slovenia, on 18 March 2000.

SNOWBOARDING

MOST SNOWBOARDING WORLD CUP TITLES

The most snowboarding World Cup titles won is 16 by Karine Ruby (France). She won overall titles in 1996–98 and 2001–2002; slalom/ parallel slalom titles in 1996–98 and 2002; giant slalom titles in 1995–98 and 2001; and snowboard cross titles in 1997 and 2001. The most men's titles won is six, by Mathieu Bozzetto (France). He won the overall title in 1999 and 2000, and the slalom and parallel slalom titles between 1999 and 2002.

» MOST SNOWBOARDING CHAMPIONSHIP TITLES

The most snowboarding titles won (including Olympic titles) is three, by Karine Ruby (France, right). She won the giant slalom in 1996, the Olympic title in 1998, and the snowboard cross in 1997.

MOST OLYMPIC SNOWBOARDING MEDALS

The most Olympic snowboarding medals won is two. Ross Powers (USA, left), won bronze in 1998 and gold in 2002 for the halfpipe. Karine Ruby (France) shares the record with a gold in 1998 and a silver in 2002 for the parallel giant slalom.

MOST MEN'S X-GAMES SNOWBOARDING MEDALS

Shaun Palmer (USA) has won a record three gold medals at the Winter ESPN X-Games for the boarder X discipline (1997-99) since the inaugural X-Games in 1997. Additionally, across all the disciplines, he has won a total of six gold medals at the X-Games. This is as well as a gold in the 1997 X-Games snow mountain biking dual downhill event.

MOST WOMEN'S X-GAMES SNOWBOARDING MEDALS

The most X-Games snowboarding medals won by a woman is six, by Barrett Christy (USA). Christy took the gold medal in the big air event and the silver medal in the slopestyle discipline at the 1999 Winter X-Games. She also won silver for both events in 1998, and golds at the first X-Games in 1997.

FASTEST SNOWBOARD ON A BOBSLEIGH RUN

In November 1998 at Königssee, Germany, Reto Lamm (Switzerland) managed to surf down a complete bobsleigh run on his snowboard at a speed of 80 km/h (49.7 mph).

GREATEST VERTICAL DISTANCE SNOWBOARDED IN ONE DAY

On 20 April 1998, Tammy McMinn (USA) snowboarded down a slope at Atlin, British Columbia, Canada, 101 times, making a total vertical descent of 93,124 m (305,525 ft). She was lifted back to the top each time by helicopter. She performed her feat alongside skier Jennifer Hughes (USA). The total duration of the event was 14 hr 50 min.

HIGHEST SPEED SNOWBOARDING

On 2 May 1999 at Les Arcs, France, Darren Powell (Australia) achieved a record snowboarding speed of 201.907 km/h (125.459 mph).

YOUNGEST PRO SNOWBOARDING HALFPIPE COMPETITOR

Born 3 September 1986, Shaun White (USA) began competing as a professional snowboarder in 1999 at 13 years of age.

BOBSLEIGH AND TOBOGGANING

OLDEST RIDER OF THE CRESTA RUN

The oldest person to have ridden the Cresta Run successfully is Prince Constantin von Liechtenstein aged 88 years 54 days, on 15 February 2000. The Cresta Run at St Moritz, Switzerland, is one of winter sport's legendary challenges. It is an ice run similar to those found in the sport of bobsledding, but with crucial differences. In bobsledding the tracks are manmade and the corners are banked high, whereas the Cresta is natural ice and uses the contours of the land to form its curves.

FASTEST CRESTA RUN COMPLETION TIME

The Cresta run course, which dates from 1884, is 1,212 m (3,977 ft) long with a drop of 157 m (514 ft). The record for completing the course is 50.09 seconds by James Sunley (UK) on 13 February 1999. His average speed on the run was 87.11 km/h (54.13 mph).

FASTEST CRESTA RUN TIME FROM JUNCTION

On 17 January 1999 Johannes Badrutt (Switzerland) set a fastest Cresta Run record, beginning at the Junction, the second point of the run from which competitors can officially start. He made a time of 41.02 seconds, covering a total distance of 890 m (2,921 ft).

WINTER SPORTS

YOUNGEST OLYMPIC BOBSLEIGH CHAMPION
William Guy Fiske (USA) was 16 years 260 days old when he won gold with the five-man team at the Winter Olympic Games in Switzerland in 1928.

MOST WOMEN'S WORLD LUGE CHAMPIONSHIP TITLES
The most World Luge Championship titles won by a woman is four by Margit Schumann (GDR), from 1973 to 1975 and in 1977. She also won the gold medal at the 1976 Olympic Games.

FASTEST LUGEING SPEED
Tony Benshoof (USA) reached a record speed of 139.39 km/h (86.6 mph) on the 2002 Olympic luge track at Park City, Utah, USA, on 16 October 2001. The speed was reached during training for the 2001 Luge World Cup Series.

MOST OLYMPIC BOBSLEIGH MEDALS
The most individual Olympic bobsleigh medals won is seven (one gold, five silver and one bronze) by Bogdan Musiol (GDR) between 1980 and 1992.

MOST OLYMPIC GOLD BOBSLEIGH MEDALS
The most Olympic gold bobsleigh medals won by an individual is three by Meinhard Neher and Bernard Germeshausen (both GDR). They won the two-man event and the four-man event in 1976, and the four-man event in 1980.

MOST WORLD CHAMPIONSHIP AND OLYMPIC GAMES FOUR-MAN BOBSLEIGH WINS
Switzerland has won the world four-man bob title 20 times, in 1924, 1936, 1939, 1947, 1954–57, 1971–73, 1975, 1982–83, 1986–90 and 1993. They also have a record five Olympic victories, in 1924, 1936, 1956, 1972 and 1988.

MOST WORLD CHAMPIONSHIP BOBSLEIGH TITLES
Eugenio Monti (Italy) won a record 11 world championship bobsleigh titles between 1957 and 1968. He won three four-man titles and eight two-man titles.

OLDEST OLYMPIC BOBSLEIGH CHAMPION
Jay O'Brien (USA) was 47 years 357 days old when he won gold with the four-man bobsleigh team at the 1932 Winter Olympics at Lake Placid, New York, USA.

MOST SKELETON WORLD TITLES
Alex Coomber (UK, above) has won a record four world skeleton titles. He won the World Cup in 2000, 2001 and 2002, and the World Championships in 2000.

MOST MEN'S WORLD CHAMPIONSHIP AND OLYMPIC LUGE WINS
The most World Championship and Olympic Games luge titles won by a man is six by Georg Hackl (GDR and Germany), who won single-seater titles in 1989, 1990, 1992, 1994, 1997 and 1998.

Stefan Krausse and Jan Behrendt (both GDR and Germany) have won a record six two-seater titles, in 1989, 1991-93, 1995 and 1998.

SKI-BOB

MOST INDIVIDUAL WOMEN'S COMBINED WORLD SKI-BOB CHAMPIONSHIP TITLES
The most individual combined World Ski-bob Championship titles won by a woman is four by Petra Tschach-Wlezcek (Austria), who won between 1988 and 1991.

FASTEST SKI-BOB SPEED
The fastest speed on a ski-bob is 184.9 km/h (114.89 mph) by Romuald Bonvin (Switzerland) on 21 March 2000 at Les Arcs, France.

CURLING

LARGEST CURLING TOURNAMENT
The world's largest bonspiel (curling tournament) is the Manitoba Curling Association Bonspiel held annually in Winnipeg, Canada. In 1988 there were 1,424 teams of four men, a total of 5,696 curlers, using 187 sheets of curling ice.

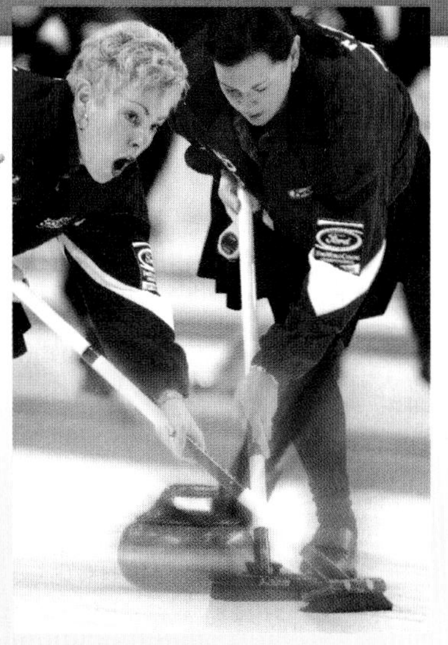

MOST WOMEN'S WORLD CURLING CHAMPIONSHIP TITLES

The Canadian women's team (Kim Kelly, left, and Mary Ann Wayne from the 2002 team pictured right) has won more curling World Championships than any other team, with a record 12 titles, won in 1980, 1984–87, 1989, 1993–94, 1996–97 and 2000–01.

FASTEST EIGHT-ENDER

Eight curlers from the Burlington Golf and Country Club, Canada, curled the fastest ever eight-end game in a time of 47 min 24 sec, with time penalties of 5 min 30 sec, at Burlington, Ontario, Canada, on 4 April 1986, following rules agreed with the Ontario Curling Association. The time is taken from when the first stone crosses the near hogline until the game's last stone comes to a complete stop.

MOST STRATHCONA CUP WINS

The most wins of the Strathcona Cup (instituted in 1903) is seven, by Canada against Scotland in 1903, 1909, 1912, 1923, 1938, 1957 and 1965.

MOST MEN'S WORLD CURLING CHAMPIONSHIP TITLES

The Canadian men's team has won the World Curling Championship 27 times, in 1959–64, 1966, 1968–72, 1980, 1982–83, 1985–87, 1989–90, 1993–96, 1998, 2000 and 2002.

LONGEST THROW

The longest throw of a curling stone was 175.66 m (576 ft 4 in) by Eddie Kulbacki (Canada) at Park Lake, Neepawa, Manitoba, Canada, on 29 January 1989. The attempt took place on a specially prepared sheet of curling ice 365.76 m (1,200 ft) long.

LARGEST CURLING RINK

The world's largest ever curling rink was the Big Four Curling Rink in Calgary, Alberta, Canada, which opened in 1959 and closed in 1989. It accommodated 96 teams and 384 players on two floors, each with 24 sheets of ice.

FIGURE SKATING

MOST WOMEN'S OLYMPIC GOLD FIGURE SKATING MEDALS

The most Olympic gold figure skating medals won by a woman is three by Sonja Henie (Norway) at the Winter Olympic Games of 1928, 1932 and 1936. Henie also holds the record for the most women's individual World Championship figure skating titles, having won 10 times from 1927 to 1936.

MOST MEN'S OLYMPIC GOLD FIGURE SKATING MEDALS

Gillis Grafstrom (Sweden) has won three golds, in 1920, 1924 and 1928. He also won silver in 1932.

MOST MEN'S WORLD CHAMPIONSHIP FIGURE SKATING TITLES

Ulrich Salchow (Sweden) won 10 individual world figure skating titles in 1901–05 and 1907–11.

MOST FIGURE SKATING GRAND SLAMS WON

The most figure skating grand slams, which comprise the European, World and Olympic titles, won by a man is two by Karl Schäfer (Austria) in 1932 and 1936. Two women have won a record two figure skating grand slams: Sonja Henie (Norway) in 1932 and 1936, and Katarina Witt (West Germany) in 1984 and 1988.

YOUNGEST FIGURE SKATING WORLD CHAMPION

The youngest female winner of a world figure skating title is Tara Lipinski (USA), when she won the individual title aged 14 years 286 days on 22 March 1997.

LONGEST FIGURE SKATING JUMP-FLIP

The longest figure skating jump-flip was completed by Robin John Cousins (UK) with a 5.81-m (19-ft 1-in) axel jump and a 5.48-m (18-ft) back-flip at Richmond Ice Rink, Surrey, UK, on 16 November 1983.

MOST WORLD CHAMPIONSHIP AND OLYMPIC GAMES TWO-MAN BOBSLEIGH WINS

Switzerland (current team pictured right) has won the two-man bobsleigh title 17 times, in 1935, 1947–50, 1953, 1955, 1977–80, 1982–83, 1987, 1990, 1992 and 1994. They have also had a record four Olympic successes in 1948, 1980, 1992 and 1994.

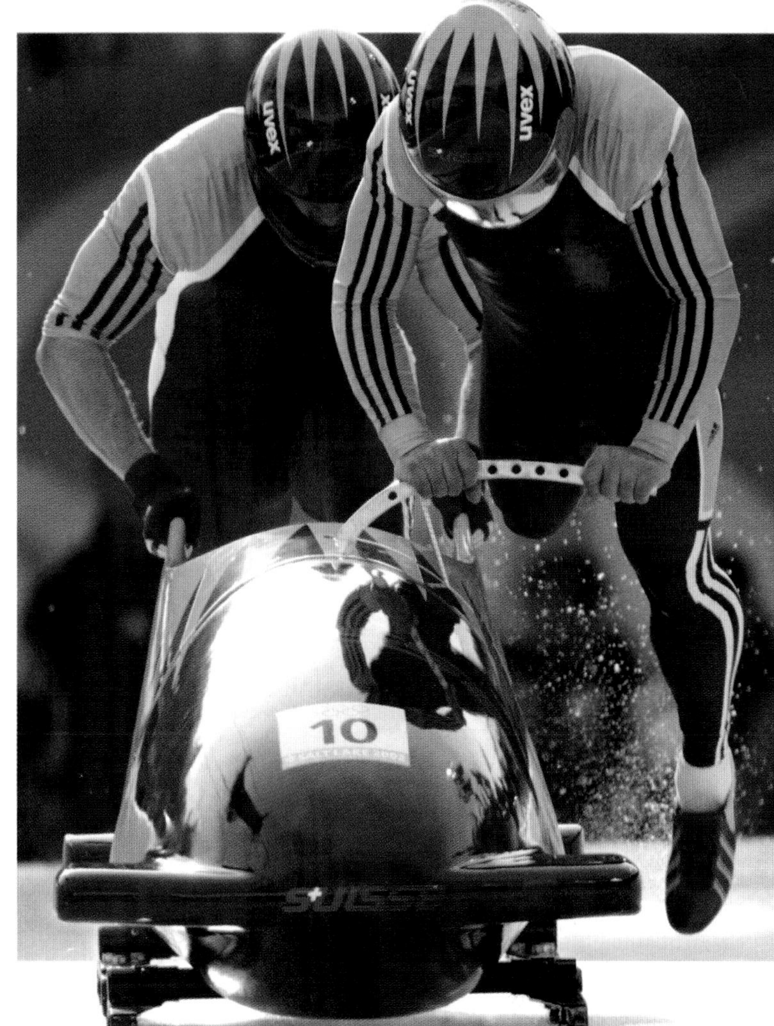

MOST FIGURE SKATING PAIRS WORLD CHAMPIONSHIPS

Irina Rodnina (USSR) has won 10 pairs titles: four with Aleksey Nikolayevich Ulanov (USSR) in 1969-72, and six with her husband Aleksandr Gennadyevich Zaitsev (USSR) in 1973-78. The most ice dance titles won is six by Lyudmila Alekseyevna Pakhomova (USSR) and her husband Aleksandr Georgiyevich Gorshkov (USSR), from 1970 to 1974 and in 1976.

MOST WOMEN'S OLYMPIC GOLD SPEED SKATING MEDALS

The most Olympic gold medals won by a woman speed skater is six by Lidiya Pavlovna Skoblikova (USSR). She won two in 1960 and four in 1964.

FASTEST WOMEN'S 1,500 M SHORT-TRACK SPEED SKATING

The women's short-track speed skating record is held by Choi Eun-kyung (South Korea, far left in picture) with a time of 2:21.069 at Salt Lake City, Utah, USA, on 13 February 2002.

SPEED SKATING

MOST MEN'S OLYMPIC SPEED SKATING MEDALS

The most Olympic speed skating medals won by a man is seven. Clas Thunberg (1893–1973, Finland) won five gold, one silver and one tied bronze. Ivar Ballangrud (Norway) shares the record, with four gold, two silver and one bronze between 1928 and 1936.

MOST WOMEN'S OLYMPIC SPEED SKATING MEDALS

Karin Kania (born Enke, GDR) has won eight medals. She won three gold, four silver and one bronze between 1980 and 1988.

MOST MEN'S OLYMPIC GOLD SPEED SKATING MEDALS

Clas Thunberg (Finland) won five golds in 1924 and 1928. Eric Arthur Heiden (USA) shares the record. He won all of his five medals at one Games, at Lake Placid, New York, USA, in 1980.

MOST SHORT-TRACK SPEED SKATING WORLD CHAMPIONSHIPS WON

The most successful skater in the World Championships (instituted in 1978) is Marc Gagnon (Canada), who has been the men's overall champion four times in 1993, 1994, 1996 and 1998.

MOST OLYMPIC SHORT-TRACK GOLD MEDALS

The most gold medals won in men's short-track speed skating at the Olympics Games is three. Kim Ki-hoon (South Korea) won gold medals in the 1,000 m race in 1992 for both the solo and relay events. He also won a 1,000 m gold in 1994. Marc Gagnon (Canada) shares the record. He won gold in the 500-m relay in 1998, as well as the 500 m relay and solo races in 2002.

The most short-track gold medals won by a woman is four by Chun Lee-kyung (South Korea). She won both the solo and relay 1,000 m finals in 1994 and 1998.

★ MEN'S SPEED SKATING WORLD RECORDS ★

EVENT	MIN:SEC	NAME AND COUNTRY	VENUE	DATE
500 m	34.32	Hiroyasu Shimizu (Japan)	Salt Lake City, USA	10 March 2001
1,000 m	1:07.18	Gerard van Velde (Netherlands)	Salt Lake City, USA	16 February 2002
1,500 m	1:43.95	Derek Parra (USA)	Salt Lake City, USA	19 February 2002
3,000 m	3:42.75	Gianne Romme (Netherlands)	Calgary, Canada	11 August 2000
5,000 m	6:14.66	Jochem Uytdehaage (Netherlands)	Salt Lake City, USA	9 February 2002
10,000 m	12:58.92	Jochem Uytdehaage (Netherlands)	Salt Lake City, USA	22 February 2002
500 m short-track	41.514	Jeffrey Scholten (Canada)	Calgary, Canada	13 October 2001
1,000 m short-track	1:25.985	Steve Robillard (Canada)	Calgary, Canada	14 October 2001
1,500 m short-track	2:12.234	Steve Robillard (Canada)	Calgary, Canada	13 November 2002
3,000 m short-track	4:38.061	Steve Robillard (Canada)	Calgary, Canada	13 November 2002
5,000 m short-rack relay	6:43.73	Eric Bédard, Marc Gagnon, Jean-Francois Monette, Mathieu Turcotte (Canada)	Calgary, Canada	14 October 2001

★ WOMEN'S SPEED SKATING WORLD RECORDS ★

EVENT	MIN:SEC	NAME AND COUNTRY	VENUE	DATE
500 m	37.22	Catriona LeMay Doan (Canada)	Calgary, Canada	9 December 2001
1,000 m	1:13.83	Christine Witty (USA)	Salt Lake City, USA	17 February 2002
1,500 m	1:54.02	Anni Friesinger (Germany)	Salt Lake City, USA	20 February 2002
3,000 m	3:57.7	Claudia Pechstein (Germany)	Salt Lake City, USA	10 February 2002
5,000 m	6:46.91	Claudia Pechstein (Germany)	Salt Lake City, USA	23 February 2002
500 m short-track	43.671	Evgenia Radanova (Bulgaria)	Calgary, Canada	19 October 2001
1,000 m short-track	1:30.483	Byun Chun-sa (South Korea)	Budapest, Hungary	12 January 2003
1,500 m short-track	2:21.069	Choi Eun-kyung (South Korea)	Salt Lake City, USA	13 February 2002
3,000 m short-track	5:01.976	Choi Eun-kyung (South Korea)	Calgary, Canada	22 October 2000
3,000 m short-track relay	4:12.793	Park Hye-won, Joo Min-jin, Choi Min-kyung, Choi Eun-kyung (South Korea)	Salt Lake City, USA	20 February 2002

MOST OLYMPIC SHORT-TRACK MEDALS

The most Olympic medals won by a man in short-track speed skating is five by Marc Gagnon (Canada). He has won three gold, in the 500 m in 2002 and the relay in 1998 and 2002, as well as two bronze, in the 1,000 m in 1994 and the 1,500 m in 2002.

The most Olympic medals won by a woman in short-track speed skating is five. Chun Lee-kyung (South Korea) has won four gold, in the 1,000 m solo and relay in 1994 and 1998, and one bronze in the 500 m in 1998. Yang Yang (China) shares the women's record. She won four silver, in the 500 m, the 1,000 m and the relay in 1998, and the relay in 2002, and one bronze in the 1,000 m in 2002.

LONGEST ICE SKATING RACE

The *Elfstedentocht* ('Tour of the Eleven Towns'), which originated in the 17th century, was held in The Netherlands in 1909-63, 1985-86 and again in 1997. It covers 200 km (124 miles 483 yds). As the weather does not always permit an annual race in The Netherlands, alternative Elfstedentocht races take place at other suitable sites throughout the world. These have included Lake Vesijrvi, near Lahti, Finland, and Ottawa River in Canada.

MOST WORLD CHAMPIONSHIP SPEED SKATING TITLES

The most World Championship speed skating titles won by a man is five by Oscar Mathisen (Norway) in 1908–09 and 1912–14. Clas Thunberg (Finland) shares the record with wins in 1923, 1925, 1928–29 and 1931.

The record for the most World Championship speed skating titles won by a woman is eight, by Gunda Niemann-Stirnemann (Germany). She took the title in 1991–93 and 1995–99.

MOST SINGLE DISTANCE SPEED SKATING WORLD CHAMPIONSHIP TITLES

The most titles won at the World Single Distance Championships (instituted in 1996) is 11 by Gunda Niemann-Stirnemann (Germany) in the 1,500 m, 3,000 m and 5,000 m between 1996 and 2001.

The most titles won by a man is seven by Gianni Romme (Netherlands) in the 5,000 m and 10,000 m from 1996 to 2000.

BEST WORLD CHAMPIONSHIP SPEED SKATING SCORE

The lowest, and therefore best, score in men's World Championship speed skating is 152.651 points, achieved by Rintje Ritsma (Netherlands) in Hamar, Norway, on 6–7 February 1999.

The same record by a woman is 161.479 points by Gunda Niemann-Stirnemann (Germany) at Hamar, Norway on 6–7 February 1999.

FASTEST WOMEN'S 1,500 M SPEED SKATING

The fastest women's 1,500 m in speed skating was achieved by Anni Friesinger (Germany, above) with a time of 1:54.02 in Salt Lake City, Utah, USA, on 20 February 2002.

GOLF

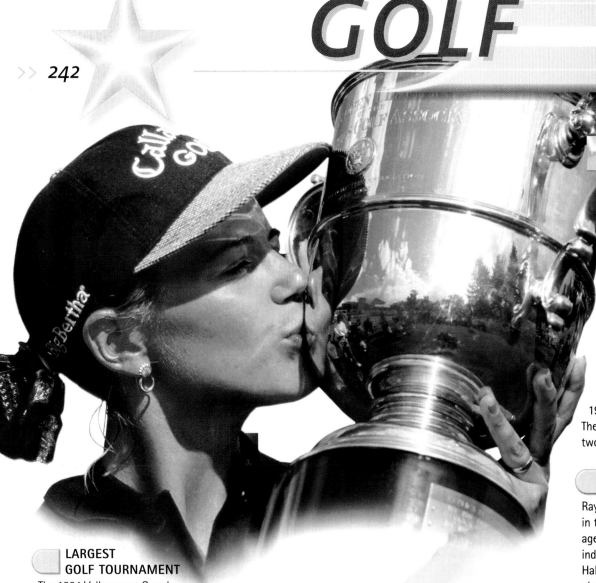

HIGHEST US LPGA CAREER EARNINGS

The record career earnings for a woman on the US LPGA Tour is by Annika Sorenstam (Sweden, left), who earned $11,217,687 (£7,124,884) between 1993 and the end of 2002.

MOST RYDER CUP WINS

The biennial Ryder Cup professional match between the USA and Europe (British Isles or Great Britain prior to 1979) was instituted in 1927. The USA has won 24 to 8 (with two draws) to 2002.

OLDEST RYDER CUP PLAYER

Raymond Floyd (USA) competed in the Ryder Cup in 1993 when aged 51 years 20 days. Floyd was inducted into the World Golf Hall of Fame in 1989 and still plays on the Senior PGA tour.

LARGEST GOLF TOURNAMENT

The 1984 Volkswagen Grand Prix Open Amateur Championship, held in the UK, attracted a record 321,778 competitors – 206,820 men and 114,958 women.

MOST BRITISH OPEN TITLES

Harry Vardon (UK) won six British Open Titles, in 1896, 1898, 1899, 1903, 1911 and 1914.

MOST US OPEN TITLES

Willie Anderson (UK), Bobby Jones Jr, Ben Hogan and Jack Nicklaus (all USA) have all won the US Open four times. Willie Anderson won in 1901 and 1903–05; Bobby Jones Jr in 1923, 1926, 1929 and 1930; Ben Hogan in 1948, 1950-51 and 1953; and Jack Nicklaus in 1962, 1967, 1972 and 1980.

MOST SUCCESSFUL RYDER CUP CAPTAIN

Walter Hagen (USA) captained the US team to victory a record four times – in 1927, 1931, 1935 and 1937. One of the most colourful sports personalities of his time, Hagen is credited with doing more than any other golfer to influence the perception of the game.

MOST INDIVIDUAL WINS IN THE RYDER CUP

Nick Faldo (UK) holds the record for match wins, with 23 from 46 played, and points scored with 25, having halved four other matches.

NORTHERNMOST GOLF COURSE

The island of Uummannaq, west of Greenland at a longitude of 70°N, hosts the annual World Ice Golf Championship (the 2002 competition shown right). The course varies annually with the variations in ice floes and snow distribution. Frostbite is a constant hazard for competitors.

MOST RYDER CUP TOURNAMENT MATCHES PLAYED

Nick Faldo (UK) played in a record 11 Ryder Cup contests between 1977 and 1997. The equivalent US record is eight by three players: Billy Casper in 1961-75, Ray Floyd in 1969, 1975-85, 1991-93, and Lanny Wadkins in 1977-79, 1983-93.

MOST TEAM SOLHEIM CUP WINS

The female equivalent of the Ryder Cup is contested biennially between the top professional players of Europe and the USA and was first held in 1990. The USA has won five times, 1990, 1994, 1996, 1998 and 2002.

MOST WALKER CUP WINS

Formerly known as the International Trophy, the Walker Cup has been held biennally since 1922. The USA have won 31, Great Britain & Ireland six (in 1938, 1971, 1989, 1995, 1999, 2001), and the 1965 match was tied.

MOST WORLD CUP SUCCESSES

The only men to have been on six winning World Cup teams are Arnold Palmer (USA) in 1960, 1962–64 and 1966–67 and Jack Nicklaus (USA) in 1963–64, 1966–67, 1971 and 1973. Nicklaus has taken the individual title a record three times – in 1963–64 and 1971.

HIGHEST US PGA CAREER EARNINGS

The all-time career earnings record on the US PGA circuit is held by Tiger Woods (USA) who earned $35,944,852 (£22,822,164) between August 1996 and March 2003.

HIGHEST US LPGA SEASON'S EARNINGS

The season's record for earnings on the US LPGA Tour is held by Annika Sorenstam (Sweden) who earned $2,863,904 (£1,817,467) in 2002.

HIGHEST US PGA SEASON'S EARNINGS

The season's record earnings for the US PGA Tour is $9,188,321 (£5,720,587) by Tiger Woods (USA) in 2000.

FASTEST ROUND OF GOLF BY A TEAM

The Fore Worcester's Children golf team completed 18 holes in 9 min 28 sec at the Tatnuck Country Club, Worcester, Massachusetts, USA, on 9 September 1996. They scored 70.

LOWEST SCORE OVER 18 HOLES BY A WOMAN

The lowest recorded score on an 18-hole course (over 5,120 m or 5,600 yd) for a woman is 59 by Annika Sorenstam (Sweden) in the 2001 Standard Register PING at Moon Valley Country Club, Phoenix, Arizona, USA, on 16 March 2001.

MOST NATIONS REPRESENTED IN A GOLF COMPETITION

A record 72 nations were involved in the 2000 Junior Open Championships, held at Crail Golf Club, Fife, UK, in July 2000. The event was organized by the Royal and Ancient Golf Club of St Andrews, Fife, UK.

LONGEST GOLF BALL CARRY

The greatest recorded carry of a golf ball is 458 yd (418.78 m) by Jack Hamm (USA) at Highlands Ranch, Colorado, USA, on 20 July 1993.

The longest golf drive at an altitude below 1,000 m is 408 yd (373 m) by Karl Woodward (UK) at Golf del Sur, Tenerife, Spain, on 30 June 1999.

MOST GOLF BALLS HIT IN 24 HOURS

The most balls driven in 24 hours over 100 yd (91.44 m) and into a target area is 10,392 by David Ogron (USA) at Raymore, Missouri, USA, on 21-22 June 2002. Ogron hit a total of 10,887 balls with a strike rate of 95.45%.

YOUNGEST TO PLAY IN A RYDER CUP

The youngest player to compete in the Ryder Cup is Sergio Garcia (Spain, b. 9 January 1980, right) who played for Europe in 1999 when aged 19 years 229 days.

MOST GOLF BALLS HIT IN ONE HOUR

The most balls driven in one hour over 100 yd (91.44 m) into a target area is 2,146 by Sean Murphy (Canada) at Swifts Practice Range, Carlisle, Cumbria, UK, on 30 June 1995.

MOST HOLES PLAYED IN 12 HOURS

Brennan F Robertson (USA) played 476 holes using a cart at Foxfire Golf Club, Sarasota, Florida, USA, on 19 August 2000.

The same record achieved when on foot is held by David Brett (UK), who played 218 holes in 12 hours at Didsbury Golf Club, Greater Manchester, UK, on 22 June 1990.

LONGEST GOLF PUTT

On 6 November 2001 Fergus Muir (UK) successfully sank a putt measuring 125 yd (114.3 m) on the Eden Course at St Andrews Links, Scotland, UK. The shot was made directly from the tee on the 5th hole using a hickory-shafted putter.

LONGEST GOLF HOLE

The longest hole in the world is the 7th hole (par 7) of the Satsuki Golf Club, Sano, Japan, which measures 964 yd (881 m).

GREATEST DISTANCE BETWEEN TWO ROUNDS OF GOLF PLAYED ON THE SAME DAY

The greatest distance between two rounds of golf played on the same day is 9,582 km (5,954 miles) by Nobby Orens (USA) who played at Stockley Park, Uxbridge, Greater London, UK, and Braemar Country Club, Tarzana, California, USA, on 20 July 1999.

YOUNGEST HOLE-IN-ONE GOLFER

The youngest golfer recorded to have shot a hole-in-one is Christian Carpenter (USA, b. 6 June 1995), who achieved this aged 4 years 195 days at the Mountain View Golf Club, Hickory, North Carolina, USA, on 18 December 1999.

YOUNGEST NATIONAL CHAMPION

Thuashni Selvaratnam (b. 9 June 1976) won the 1989 Sri Lankan Ladies Amateur Open Golf Championship aged 12 years 324 days at Nuwara Eliya Golf Club on 29 April 1989.

CANOEING

FASTEST 50-M CANOE DESCENT
The fastest time to descend a height of 50 m (164 ft) on a river by canoe is 4 min 53 sec by Shaun Baker (UK) in Snowdonia, Wales, UK, on 4 November 1994.

FASTEST 1000 M IN A CANOE
The German four-man kayak Olympic team covered 1,000 m (1,093 yards) in 2 min 51.52 sec to win gold in Atlanta, USA, on 3 August 1996. Their average speed was 20.98 km/h (13.04 mph).

FURTHEST DISTANCE IN 24 HOURS ON FLAT WATER IN A CANOE
Marinda Hartzenberg (South Africa) paddled 220.69 km (137.13 miles) without the benefit of current in a canoe on Loch Logan, Bloemfontein, South Africa, from 31 December 1990 to 1 January 1991.

LONGEST CANOE RACE
The Canadian Government Centennial Voyageur Canoe Pageant and Race from Rocky Mountain House, Alberta, to the Expo '67 site at Montreal, Quebec, was 5,283 km (3,283 miles) long. Ten canoes represented Canadian provinces and territories. The winner of the race, which took place from 24 May to 4 September 1967, was the Province of Manitoba canoe, *Radisson*.

MOST WORLD AND OLYMPIC MEN'S CANOEING TITLES
The record for the most World and Olympic men's canoeing titles is 13 and is held by three people: Gert Fredriksson (Sweden) in 1948–1960; Rüdiger Helm (GDR) in 1976–1983; and Ivan Patzaichin (Romania) in 1968–1984.

MOST CANOEING GOLD MEDALS WON AT A SINGLE OLYMPIC GAMES
The most canoeing gold medals won at one Olympic Games is three, by Vladimir Parfenovich (USSR) in 1980 and Ian Ferguson (New Zealand) in 1984.

MOST WOMEN'S CANOEING WORLD CHAMPIONSHIP TITLES
In addition to seven Olympic titles, Birgit Fischer (formerly Birgit Schmidt, GDR/Germany) has won 29 World Canoeing Championships from 1979 to 1998, making a record 34 titles overall.

MOST WOMEN'S OLYMPIC CANOEING GOLD MEDALS
The most Olympic gold canoeing medals won by a woman is seven by Birgit Fischer (formerly Birgit Schmidt, GDR/Germany) from 1980 to 2000.

MOST ESKIMO ROLLS DONE CONSECUTIVELY
Randy Fine (USA) completed 1,796 consecutive 'Eskimo' canoe rolls at Biscayne Bay, Florida, USA, on 8 June 1991.

« MOST WOMEN'S WAKEBOARDING WORLD TITLES
Two women share the record for the most women's World Championship wakeboarding titles. Tara Hamilton (USA, left) won in 1998 and 2002, and Meghan Major (USA) won in 1999 and 2000.

MOST CONSECUTIVE KAYAK CARTWHEELS
The record for the most consecutive cartwheels performed in a kayak is 35 and was set by Koyo Morita (Japan) at Yamanaka Lake, Yamanashi Prefecture, Japan, on 5 August 2002.

RAFTING

MOST WHITEWATER RAFTING WORLD CHAMPIONSHIPS WON
The World Rafting Challenge Championship has been held since 1995 and the most successful country is Slovenia, with five wins from 1995 to 1999.

WAKEBOARDING

MOST WAKEBOARDING INVERTS IN A MINUTE
On 30 August 1999 at the John Battleday Waterski Centre, Chertsey, Surrey, UK, Julz Heaney (UK) did 15 inverts (somersaults) in a minute on a wakeboard measuring 125 cm (49 in) long, 39.8 cm (15 in) wide and weighing 2.27 kg (5 lb). The attempt was recorded by the BBC's *Linford's Record Breakers* TV show.

★ WATER-SKIING WORLD RECORDS ★

MEN	WOMEN
SLALOM	
1 buoy on a 9.75-m line by Jeff Rogers (USA) at Charleston, South Carolina, USA, on 31 August 1997 and Andy Mapple (GB) at Miami, Florida, USA, on 4 October 1998.	1 buoy on a 10.25-m line by Kristi Overton Johnson (USA) at West Palm Beach, Florida, USA, on 14 September 1996.
TRICKS	
12,120 points by Nicolas Le Forestier (France) at the French Masters, Lancaneau, France, on 7 July 2001.	8,630 points by Tawn Larsen Hahn (USA) at Wilmington, Illinois, USA, on 11 July 1999.
JUMPING	
71 m (233 ft) by Freddy Kreuger (USA) at the Malibu Open, Rio Linda, California, USA, on 27 July 2002.	56.6 m (186 ft) by Elena Milakova (Russia) at the Malibu Open, Rio Linda, California, USA, on 27 July 2002.
SKI FLY	
91.1 m (298 ft 10 in) by Jaret Llewellyn (Canada) at the Big Air Challenge event at Orlando, Florida, USA, on 14 May 2000.	69.4 m (227 ft 7 in) by Elena Milakova (Russia) at the Masters event at Pine Mountain, Georgia, USA, on 26 May 2002.
OVERALL	
2,741.75 points by Patrice Martin (France) at Traver's Sunset Cup, Okahumpka, Florida, USA, on 20 May 2001.	2,854.01 points by Elena Milakova (Russia) at the Europe, Africa and Middle East (EAME) Championships, Lincolnshire, UK, on 29 July 2001.

MOST BODYBOARDING WORLD CHAMPIONSHIPS

Mike Stewart (USA, left) has won every bodyboarding competition he has entered in the last seven years, including nine bodyboarding World Championships, eight national tour titles and 21 pipeline titles. He has also won every *BodyBoarding Magazine* readers' poll.

BAREFOOT WATER SKIING

WORLD BAREFOOT WATER-SKIING SLALOM RECORD

The world barefoot water-skiing slalom record is 20.5 crossings of the wake in 15 seconds by Brian Fuchs (USA) in Liverpool, New South Wales, Australia, in April 1994.

WOMEN'S BAREFOOT WATER-SKIING SLALOM RECORD

The women's barefoot water-skiing slalom record is 17.0 crossings of the wake in 15 seconds by Nadine de Villiers (South Africa) on 5 January 2001 at the Gauteng Waterski Championships, Wolwekrans, South Africa.

HIGHEST MEN'S BAREFOOT WATER-SKIING TRICKS SCORE

The highest men's barefoot water-skiing tricks score is 9,400 points by Keith St Onge (USA) on 10 August 2002 at Arc sur Tilles, France.

HIGHEST WOMEN'S BAREFOOT WATER-SKIING TRICKS SCORE

The highest barefoot water-skiing tricks score for a woman is 4,400 points by Nadine de Villiers (South Africa) on 5 January 2001 at Gauteng Waterski Championships, Wolwekrans, South Africa.

WATER POLO

MOST WATER POLO OLYMPICS MEDALS

Five players share the record of three Olympic gold water polo medals: George Wilkinson (UK) in 1900, 1908 and 1912; Paulo 'Paul' Radmilovic and Charles Sidney Smith (both UK) in 1908, 1912 and 1920; and Desz Gyarmati and Gyrgy Krpti (both Hungary) in 1952, 1956 and 1964. Paul Radmilovic also won a gold medal for 4,200-m freestyle swimming in 1908.

MOST INTERNATIONAL WATER POLO GOALS

The greatest number of goals scored by an individual in an international water polo game is 13 by Debbie Handley for Australia (16) v Canada (10) at the World Championship in Guayaquil, Ecuador, in 1982.

MOST MEN'S OLYMPIC WATER POLO TITLES

Hungary has won the men's Olympic water polo title most often with six wins, in 1932, 1936, 1952, 1956, 1964 and 1976.

MOST WATER POLO WORLD CHAMPIONSHIPS

The first water polo World Championships were held at the World Swimming Championships in 1973. The most wins is two, by the USSR (1975 and 1982), Yugoslavia (1986 and 1991), Italy (1978 and 1994) and Spain (1998 and 2001).

MOST WOMEN'S OLYMPIC WATER POLO TITLES

Women's water polo was introduced at the 2000 Olympic Games in Sydney, Australia. The team from the host nation (below) won the first and only title to date in a final against the USA on 23 September.

WATER SPORTS

YOUNGEST DIVING WORLD CHAMPION

Fu Mingxia (China, right, b. 16 August 1978) won the women's world title for platform diving at Perth, Australia, on 4 January 1991, at the age of 12 years 141 days.

DIVING

MOST DIVING WORLD CHAMPIONSHIPS

Greg Louganis (USA) won a record five world diving titles. He won the highboard title in 1978, and both the highboard and springboard titles in 1982 and 1986. The most diving titles won in a single event is three by Phil Boggs (USA), who took three gold medals in the springboard, in 1973, 1975 and 1978.

MOST OLYMPIC DIVING MEDALS

The most medals won by a diver is five. Klaus Dibiasi (Italy) won three gold and two silver between 1964 and 1976, and Greg Louganis (USA) won four golds and one silver won between 1976 and 1988. Dibiasi is the only diver to win the same event (highboard) at three successive Games – in 1968, 1972 and 1976. Two divers have won the highboard and springboard doubles at two Games: Patricia McCormick (USA) in 1952 and 1956, and Louganis in 1984 and 1988.

ROWING

MOST OLYMPIC AND WORLD CHAMPIONSHIPS GOLD MEDALS

The most gold medals won at the World Championships and Olympic Games is 13 by Steve Redgrave (UK) who, in addition to his five Olympic successes – coxed fours (1984), coxless pairs (1988, 1992 and 1996) and coxless fours (2000) – won World titles at coxed pairs in 1986, coxless pairs in 1987, 1991 and 1993–95 and coxless fours in 1997–99.

Francesco Esposito (Italy) has won nine titles at lightweight events: coxless pairs in 1980–84, 1988 and 1994, and coxless fours in 1990 and 1992.

At women's events Yelena Tereshina (USSR) has won a record seven gold medals, all eights, in 1978–79, 1981–83 and 1985–86. The rowing World Championships, as distinct from the Olympic Games, were first held in 1962, at first four yearly, then from 1974 annually, except in Olympic years.

FASTEST EIGHT OVER 2,000 M

The men's eights record time for rowing 2,000 m on non-tidal water is 5 min 22.80 sec (22.30 km/h or 13.85 mph) by The Netherlands at the World Championships held at St Catharines, Ontario, Canada, on 28 August 1999.

The women's eights record time for 2,000 m on non-tidal water is 5 min 57.02 sec (20.16 km/h or 12.53 mph) by Romania at Lucerne, Switzerland, on 9 July 1999.

FASTEST SINGLE SCULLS OVER 2,000 M

The single sculls men's record is 6 min 31.67 sec (18.38 km/h or 11.42 mph) by Leonid Gulov (Estonia) during the Junior World Championships at Plovdiv, Bulgaria, on 5 August 1999.

The women's single sculls rowing record is 7 min 11.68 sec (16.68 km/h or 10.36 mph) by Ekaterina Karsten (Belarus) at St Catharines, Ontario, Canada, on 28 August 1999.

FASTEST INTERNATIONAL DRAGON BOAT RACE

The Dragon Boat Race is held annually in Hong Kong, China. The fastest time achieved for the 640-m (2,100-ft) course is 2 min 27.45 sec by the Chinese Shun De team (right) on 30 June 1985.

MOST UNIVERSITY BOAT RACE WINS

The earliest University Boat Race (won by Oxford) was raced on the River Thames from Hambledon Lock to Henley Bridge, Oxfordshire, UK, on 10 June 1829. In the 149 races to 2003, Cambridge have won 77 times, Oxford 71 times and there was a dead heat on 24 March 1877.

LONGEST ANNUAL ROWING RACE

The longest annual rowing race is the annual 160-km (100-mile) *Tour du Lac Leman* in Geneva, Switzerland, for coxed fours (the five-man crew taking turns as cox). The best time is 12 hr 22 min 29 sec by team RG Red Bull (Germany) on 2 October 1994.

YACHTING

MOST AMERICA'S CUP WINS

Since its beginnings at Cowes, Hampshire, UK, in 1851 there have been 31 challenges for the America's Cup. The USA has won the Cup every time except in 1983 (when Australia won), in 1995 (when New Zealand won), in 2000 (when New Zealand retained the Cup), and in 2003 (when Switzerland won).

MOST AMERICA'S CUP INDIVIDUAL APPEARANCES

Dennis Walter Conner (USA) has been in more cup races as a member of the afterguard than any other sailor. He has taken part six times since 1974, when he was starting helmsman with Ted Hood as skipper. He was winning skipper/helmsman in 1980, 1987 and 1989, and losing skipper in 1983 and 1995.

HIGHEST YACHTING SPEED

The highest speed reached under sail on water by any craft over a 500-m timed run is 46.52 knots (86.21 km/h or 53.56 mph) by trifoiler *Yellow Pages Endeavour*, piloted by Simon McKeon and Tim Daddo (both Australia) at Sandy Point near Melbourne, Victoria, Australia, on 26 October 1993.

The women's record for the highest speed reached under sail on water by any craft over a 500-m timed run is by boardsailer Babethe Coquelle (France), who achieved 40.38 knots (74.83 km/h or 46.5 mph) at Tarifa, Spain, on 7 July 1995.

SURFING

MOST MEN'S PROFESSIONAL WORLD CHAMPIONSHIPS

The men's title has been won six times by Kelly Slater (USA) in 1992 and 1994–98. The World Professional series started in 1975.

MOST AMATEUR WORLD CHAMPIONSHIPS

The most World Amateur Surfing Championships titles won is three, by Michael Novakov (Australia) who won the Kneeboard event in 1982, 1984 and 1986. The World Amateur Surfing Championships were inaugurated in May 1964 at Sydney, New South Wales, Australia.

MOST CONSECUTIVE DAYS SURFING

Dale Webster (USA) has gone surfing every day since 2 September 1975. He passed his 10,000th consecutive day of surfing on 1 January 2003. Webster set himself the condition that 'a surf' consists of catching at least three waves to shore each time.

LARGEST WAVE SURFED

The largest wave successfully surfed had a face measuring a massive 68 ft (20.7 m) in height, from crest to trough. The wave was ridden by Carlos Burle (Brazil) at Maverick's, Half Moon Bay, California, USA, on 22 November 2001. Burle was towed into the wave using a 155-hp wave runner.

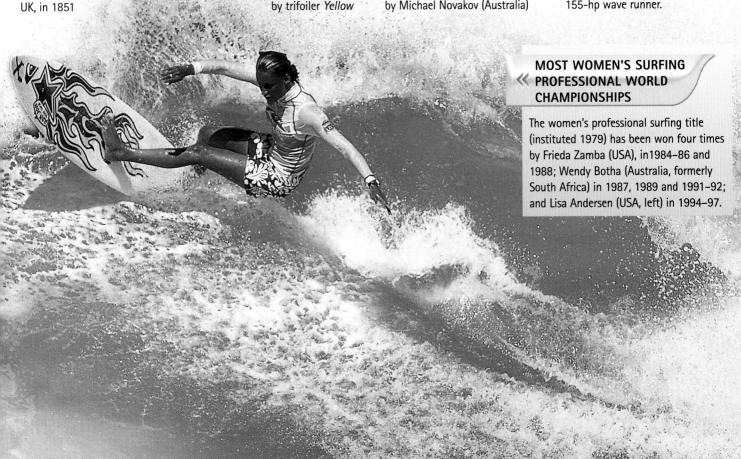

« MOST WOMEN'S SURFING PROFESSIONAL WORLD CHAMPIONSHIPS

The women's professional surfing title (instituted 1979) has been won four times by Frieda Zamba (USA), in1984–86 and 1988; Wendy Botha (Australia, formerly South Africa) in 1987, 1989 and 1991–92; and Lisa Andersen (USA, left) in 1994–97.

SWIMMING

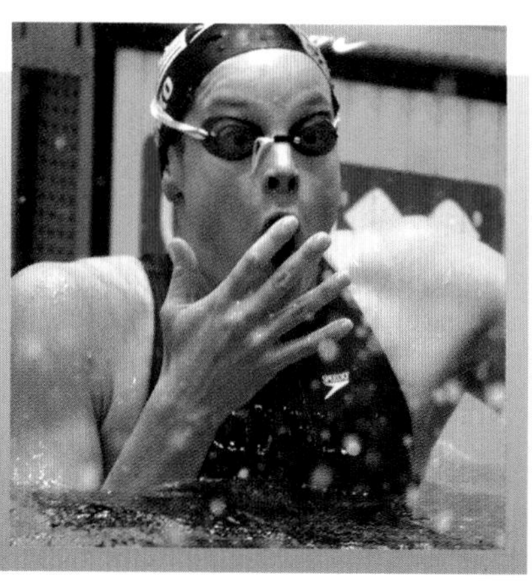

FASTEST WOMEN'S SHORT-COURSE 200-M FREESTYLE

Lindsay Benkso (USA, right) holds the women's short-course 200-m freestyle record, with a swim of 1 min 54.04 sec. She set the record in Moscow, Russia, on 7 April 2002.

GREATEST OVERALL SWIMMING DISTANCE

Between 25 June and 23 August 2000 (a total of 60 days), marathon swimmer Martin Strel (Slovenia) swam the length of the river Danube, and then three more stages of the river to complete a total distance of 3,004 km (1,866 miles). The river Danube flows from Germany to the Black Sea through eight countries, including Austria and Hungary.

FASTEST UNDERWATER 50-M SWIM

Maarten Sterck (Netherlands) swam 50 m (164 ft) underwater in a time of 38.98 seconds on 11 March 2001 at Valkenswaard, The Netherlands. No fins or any other swimming aids were worn during the attempt.

MOST CONTINUOUS ROTATIONS UNDER WATER WITH ONE BREATH

Marta Fernãndez Pèrez (Spain) completed 28 rotations with one breath, in a tank, at the studios of *El Show de los Récords* in Madrid, Spain, on 18 October 2001.

★ MEN'S LONG-COURSE SWIMMING WORLD RECORDS ★

EVENT	TIME	NAME AND COUNTRY	VENUE	DATE
50-m freestyle	21.64	Alexander Popov (Russia)	Moscow, Russia	16 June 2000
100-m freestyle	47.84	Pieter van den Hoogenband (Netherlands)	Sydney, Australia	19 September 2000
200-m freestyle	1:44.06	Ian Thorpe (Australia)	Fukuoka, Japan	25 July 2001
400-m freestyle	3:40.17	Ian Thorpe (Australia)	Fukuoka, Japan	22 July 2001
800-m freestyle	7:39.16	Ian Thorpe (Australia)	Fukuoka, Japan	24 July 2001
1,500-m freestyle	14:34.56	Grant Hackett (Australia)	Fukuoka, Japan	29 July 2001
4 x 100-m freestyle relay	3:13.67	Australia (Michael Klim, Chris Fydler, Ashley Callus, Ian Thorpe)	Sydney, Australia	16 September 2000
4 x 200-m freestyle relay	7:04.66	Australia (Grant Hackett, Michael Klim, William Kirby, Ian Thorpe)	Fukuoka, Japan	27 July 2001
50-m butterfly	23.44	Geoff Huegill (Australia)	Fukuoka, Japan	27 July 2001
100-m butterfly	51.81	Michael Klim (Australia)	Canberra, Australia	12 December 1999
200-m butterfly	1:54.58	Michael Phelps (USA)	Fukuoka, Japan	24 July 2001
50-m backstroke	24.99	Lenny Krayzelburg (USA)	Sydney, Australia	28 August 1999
100-m backstroke	53.60	Lenny Krayzelburg (USA)	Sydney, Australia	24 August 1999
200-m backstroke	1:55.15	Aaron Peirsol (USA)	Minneapolis, USA	20 March 2002
50-m breaststroke	27.18	Oleg Lisogor (Ukraine)	Berlin, Germany	2 August 2002
100-m breaststroke	59.94	Roman Sloudnov (Russia)	Fukuoka, Japan	23 July 2001
200-m breaststroke	2:10.16	Mike Barrowman (USA)	Barcelona, Spain	29 July 1992
200-m medley	1:58.16	Jani Sievinen (Finland)	Rome, Italy	11 September 1994
400-m medley	4:11.76	Tom Dolan (USA)	Sydney, Australia	17 September 2000
4 x 100-m medley relay	3:33.48	USA (Aaron Peirsol, Brendon Hanson, Michael Phelps, Jason Lezak)	Yokohama, Japan	29 August 2002

★ WOMEN'S LONG-COURSE SWIMMING WORLD RECORDS ★

EVENT	TIME	NAME AND COUNTRY	VENUE	DATE
50-m freestyle	24.13	Inge de Bruijn (Netherlands)	Sydney, Australia	22 September 2000
100-m freestyle	53.77	Inge de Bruijn (Netherlands)	Sydney, Australia	20 September 2000
200-m freestyle	1:56.64	Franziska van Almsick (Germany)	Berlin, Germany	3 August 2002
400-m freestyle	4:03.85	Janet Evans (USA)	Seoul, South Korea	22 September 1988
800-m freestyle	8:16.22	Janet Evans (USA)	Tokyo, Japan	20 August 1989
1,500-m freestyle	15:52.10	Janet Evans (USA)	Orlando, USA	26 March 1988
4 x 100-m freestyle relay	3:36.60	Germany (Franziska van Almsick, Petra Dallmann, Sandra Volker, Kathrin Meibner)	Berlin, Germany	29 July 2002
4 x 200-m freestyle relay	7:55.47	GDR (Manuela Stellmach, Astrid Strauss, Anke Möhring, Heike Friedrich)	Strasbourg, France	18 August 1987
50-m butterfly	25.64	Inge de Bruijn (Netherlands)	Sheffield, UK	26 May 2000
100-m butterfly	56.61	Inge de Bruijn (Netherlands)	Sydney, Australia	17 September 2000
200-m butterfly	2:05.78	Otylia Jedrejczak (Poland)	Berlin, Germany	2 August 2002
50-m backstroke	28.25	Sandra Voelker (Germany)	Berlin, Germany	17 June 2000
100-m backstroke	1:00.16	He Cihong (China)	Rome, Italy	10 September 1994
200-m backstroke	2:06.62	Krisztina Egerszegi (Hungary)	Athens, Greece	25 August 1991
50-m breaststroke	30.57	Zoe Baker (UK)	Manchester, UK	30 July 2002
100-m breaststroke	1:06.52	Penny Heyns (South Africa)	Sydney, Australia	23 August 1999
200-m breaststroke	2:22.99	Hui Qi (China)	Hangzhou, China	13 April 2001
200-m medley	2:09.72	Wu Yanyan (China)	Shanghai, China	17 October 1997
400-m medley	4:33.59	Yana Klochkova (Ukraine)	Sydney, Australia	16 September 2000
4 x 100-m medley relay	3:58.30	USA (Megan Quann, Jenny Thompson, BJ Bedford, Dara Torres)	Sydney, Australia	23 September 2000

FASTEST WOMEN'S 200-M FREESTYLE

The fastest women's 200-m freestyle is 1 min 56.64 sec by Franziska van Almsick (Germany, right) in Berlin, Germany, on 3 August 2002.

MOST SWIMMING WORLD RECORDS

The most swimming world records set by a woman is 42, by Ragnhild Hveger (Denmark) between 1936 and 1942. For currently recognized events (only metric distances in 50-m pools) the most is 23 by Kornelia Ender (GDR) between 1973 and 1976.

The most swimming world records set by a man is 32 by Arne Borg (Sweden) between 1921 and 1929. For currently recognized events the most is 26 by Mark Spitz (USA) between 1967 and 1972.

MOST CONSECUTIVE SWIMMING OLYMPIC GOLD MEDALS

Two swimmers have won the same event on three consecutive occasions: Dawn Fraser (Australia) in the 100-m freestyle in 1956, 1960 and 1964 and Krisztina Egerszegi (Hungary) in the 200-m backstroke in 1988, 1992 and 1996.

MOST OLYMPIC SWIMMING MEDALS

Mark Spitz (USA) won nine Olympic gold medals at the 1968 and 1972 Games. All but one of his wins were new world records. He also won a silver and a bronze in 1968, for a record overall 11 medals. He holds the record for the most medals won at one Games, with seven in 1972, as does Matt Biondi (USA), for seven medals at the 1998 Games.

The most medals won by a woman is eight by: Dawn Fraser (Australia), with four gold and four silver in 1956–64; Kornelia Ender (GDR) with four gold and four silver in 1972–76; and Shirley Babashoff (USA), with two gold and six silver in 1972–76.

★ MEN'S SHORT-COURSE SWIMMING WORLD RECORDS ★

EVENT	TIME	NAME AND COUNTRY	VENUE	DATE
50-m freestyle	21.13	Mark Foster (UK)	Paris, France	28 January 2001
100-m freestyle	46.74	Alexander Popov (Russia)	Gelsenkirchen, Germany	19 March 1994
200-m freestyle	1:41.10	Ian Thorpe (Australia)	Berlin, Germany	6 February 2000
400-m freestyle	3:34.58	Grant Hackett (Australia)	Sydney, Australia	18 July 2002
800-m freestyle	7:25.28	Grant Hackett (Australia)	Perth, Australia	3 August 2001
1,500-m freestyle	14:10.10	Grant Hackett (Australia)	Perth, Australia	7 August 2001
4 x 50-m freestyle relay	1:26.78	USA (Bryan Jones, Matt Ulricksson, Robert Bogart, Leffie Crawford)	Minneapolis, USA	23 March 2000
4 x 100-m freestyle relay	3:09.57	Sweden (Johan Nystrom, Lars Frolander, Mattias Ohlin, Stefan Nystrand)	Athens, Greece	16 March 2000
4 x 200-m freestyle relay	6:56.41	Australia (William Kirby, Ian Thorpe, Michael Klim, Grant Hackett)	Perth, Australia	7 August 2001
50-m butterfly	22.74	Geoff Huegill (Australia)	Berlin, Germany	26 January 2002
100-m butterfly	50.10	Thomas Rupprath (Germany)	Berlin, Germany	27 January 2002
200-m butterfly	1:50.73	Frank Esposito (France)	Antibes, France	8 December 2002
50-m backstroke	23.31	Matthew Welsh (Australia)	Melbourne, Australia	2 September 2002
100-m backstroke	50.58	Thomas Rupprath (Germany)	Melbourne, Australia	8 December 2002
200-m backstroke	1:51.17	Aaron Peirsol (USA)	Moscow, Russia	7 April 2002
50-m breaststroke	26.20	Oleg Lisogor (Ukraine)	Berlin, Germany	26 January 2002
100-m breaststroke	57.47	Ed Moses (USA)	Stockholm, Sweden	23 January 2002
200-m breaststroke	2:03.17	Ed Moses (USA)	Berlin, Germany	26 January 2002
100-m medley	52.58	Thomas Rupprath (Germany)	Berlin, Germany	25 January 2003
200-m medley	1:54.65	Jani Sievinen (Finland) Atilla Czene (Hungary)	Kuopio, Finland Minneapolis, USA	21 April 1994 23 March 2000
400-m medley	4:02.72	Brian Johns (Canada)	Victoria, Canada	21 February 2003
4 x 50-m medley relay	1:35.51	Germany (Thomas Rupprath, Mark Warnecke, Alexander Luderitz, Stephan Kunzelmann) Sweden (Daniel Carlsson, Patrik Isaksson, Jonas Akesson, Lars Frolander). (Achieved in same race)	Sheffield, UK	13 December 1998
4 x 100-m medley relay	3:29.00	USA (Aaron Peirsol, David Denniston, Peter Marshall, Jason Lezak)	Moscow, Russia	7 April 2002

★ WOMEN'S SHORT-COURSE SWIMMING WORLD RECORDS ★

EVENT	TIME	NAME AND COUNTRY	VENUE	DATE
50-m freestyle	23.59	Therese Alshammar (Sweden)	Athens, Greece	18 March 2000
100-m freestyle	52.17	Therese Alshammar (Sweden)	Athens, Greece	17 March 2000
200-m freestyle	1:54.04	Lindsay Benko (USA)	Moscow, Russia	7 April 2002
400-m freestyle	3:59.53	Lindsay Benko (USA)	Berlin, Germany	26 January 2003
800-m freestyle	8:14.35	Sachiko Yamada (Japan)	Tokyo, Japan	2 April 2002
4 x 50-m freestyle relay	1:38.21	Sweden (Annika Lofstedt, Therese Alshammar, Johanna Sjöberg, Anna-Karin Kammerling)	Valencia, Spain	15 December 2000
4 x 100-m freestyle relay	3:34.55	China (Le Jingyi, Na Chao, Shan Ying, Nian Yin)	Gothenburg, Sweden	19 April 1997
4 x 200-m freestyle relay	7:46.30	China (Xu Yanvei, Zhu Yingven, Tang Jingzhi, Yang Yu)	Moscow, Russia	3 April 2002
50-m butterfly	25.36	Anna-Karin Kammerling (Sweden)	Stockholm, Sweden	25 January 2001
100-m butterfly	56.34	Natalie Coughlin (USA)	New York City, USA	23 November 2002
200-m butterfly	2:04.16	Susan O'Neill (Australia)	Sydney, Australia	18 January 2000
50-m backstroke	26.83	Hui Li (China)	Shanghai, China	2 December 2001
100-m backstroke	56.71	Natalie Coughlin (USA)	New York City, USA	23 November 2002
200-m backstroke	2:03.62	Natalie Coughlin (USA)	New York City, USA	27 November 2001
50-m breaststroke	29.96	Emma Igelström (Sweden)	Moscow, Russia	4 April 2002
100-m breaststroke	1:05.11	Emma Igelström (Sweden)	Stockholm, Sweden	16 March 2003
200-m breaststroke	2:19.25	Hiu Qi (China)	Paris, France	28 January 2001
100-m medley	58.80	Natalie Coughlin (USA)	New York City, USA	23 November 2003
200-m medley	2:07.79	Allison Wagner (USA)	Palma de Mallorca, Spain	5 December 1993
400-m medley	4:27.83	Yana Klochkova (Ukraine)	Paris, France	19 January 2002
4 x 50-m medley relay	1:48.31	Sweden (Therese Alshammar, Emma Igelström, Anna-Karin Kammerling, Johanna Sjöberg)	Valencia, Spain	16 December 2000
4 x 100-m medley relay	3:55.78	Sweden (Therese Alshammar, Emma Igelström, Anna-Karin Kammerling, Johanna Sjöberg)	Moscow, Russia	5 April 2002

SADDLE SPORTS

HIGHEST RODEO CAREER EARNINGS

Ty Murray (USA, above) has record rodeo career earnings of $2,931,227 (£1,870,624) won between 1989 and 2002.

RODEO

HIGHEST ANNUAL RODEO EARNINGS

The record figure for prize money in a single rodeo season is $377,358 (£240,692) earned by Ty Murray (USA) in 1998.

Murray also holds the record for the most prize money won at a single rodeo with $124,821 (£79,716) won at the National Finals Rodeo in Las Vegas, Nevada, USA, in 1993.

LARGEST RODEO ATTENDANCE

The world's largest rodeo is the National Finals Rodeo organized by the Professional Rodeo Cowboys Association (PRCA) and the Women's Professional Rodeo Association (WPRA). The 1991 Finals, held at the Thomas and Mack Center, Las Vegas, Nevada, USA, had a paid attendance of 171,414 for ten performances.

POLO

MOST POLO WORLD CHAMPIONSHIP GOALS

Argentina have scored 35 goals during final matches of the Federation of International Polo (FIP) World Championships. Brazil are second, with 29.

MOST POLO WORLD CHAMPIONSHIPS

Of the five World Championships contested, three have been won by Argentina: in 1987 in Argentina, 1992 in Chile and 1998 in the USA. The contest is held every three years under the auspices of the FIP.

MOST POLO CHUKKAS

The greatest number of chukkas played on one ground in a day is 43. This was achieved by the Pony Club on the Number 3 Ground at Kirtlington Park, Oxfordshire, UK, on 31 July 1991.

HIGHEST POLO SCORE

The highest aggregate number of goals scored in an international match is 30, when Argentina beat the USA 21–9 at Meadowbrook, Long Island, New York, USA, in September 1936.

HORSERACING

GREATEST TOTAL PRIZE MONEY FOR A DAY'S RACING

The richest single day's racing was for a total of $15.25 million (£9.59 million) at the Dubai World Cup at Nad Al Sheba, Dubai, United Arab Emirates, in both 2002 and 2003. The seven races at the meeting are: the Dubai Kahayla Classic for Purebred Arabians, Godolphin Mile, UAE Derby, Dubai Sheema Classic, Dubai Golden Shaheen, Dubai Duty Free and the world's richest race, the Dubai World Cup.

LARGEST PRIZE FOR A SINGLE HORSE RACE

The largest prize for a single horse race is for the Dubai World Cup, held in Dubai, United Arab Emirates. The race carries a total purse of $6 million (£4 million), $3.6 million (£2.5 million) of which goes to the winner.

MOST WINS BY AN OWNER

The most wins in a racehorse owner's career is 4,775 by Marion H Van Berg (USA). He began his 35-year career in the 1930s and was the leading race-winning owner for 14 years, 11 of them consecutively from 1960 to 1970.

OLDEST RACE WINNING HORSE

Al Jabal, a purebred Arabian ridden by Brian Boulton (UK), is the oldest racehorse to have won on the flat. Al Jabal won the Horseshoes Handicap Stakes (6 furlongs) on 9 June 2002 at Barbury Castle, Wiltshire, UK, aged 19 years.

FASTEST 1,000 GUINEAS

Las Meninas, ridden to victory by John Reid (UK), achieved the time of 1 min 36.71 sec in the 1,000 Guineas horse race in 1994. The race was first held in 1814 at Newmarket, Suffolk, UK.

FASTEST 2,000 GUINEAS

Mister Baileys, ridden by Jason Weaver (UK), achieved the record time of 1 min 35.08 sec in 1994 at Newmarket, Suffolk, UK.

LONGEST ODDS IN THE DERBY

Three Derby winners have been returned at odds of 100–1: Jeddah in 1898, Signorinetta in 1908 and Aboyeur in 1913.

>> MOST OLYMPIC DRESSAGE TEAM GOLD MEDALS

Germany (West Germany 1968–90) have won a record ten team gold medals: 1928, 1936, 1964, 1968, 1976, 1984, 1988, 1992, 1996 and 2000. Ulrich Kirchhoff (on left of photo) and Franke Sloothaas are shown (right) celebrating their 1996 gold medals.

SHORTEST ODDS IN THE DERBY

The shortest-priced Derby winner was Ladas in 1894 at 2–9 and the hottest losing favourite was Surefoot, fourth at 40–95 in 1890.

FASTEST EPSOM DERBY TIME

Lammtarra, ridden by Walter Swinburn (UK), won the Derby at Epsom, Surrey, UK, in a time of 2 min 32.31 sec in 1995. The Derby Stakes, inaugurated on 4 May 1780 and named after Edward Stanley, 12th Earl of Derby, is the most prestigious of England's five Classics.

FASTEST ST LEGER WIN

In 1926 Coronach, ridden by Joe Childs (UK), achieved a record St Leger winning time of 3 min 1.6 sec. This time was equalled by Windsor Lad, ridden by Charlie Smirke (UK) in 1934. The St Leger is the oldest Classic race in the world, with its origins in 1776. It is held in September at Doncaster, South Yorkshire, UK.

FASTEST KENTUCKY DERBY

The fastest winning time for the Kentucky Derby is 1 min 59.4 sec by Secretariat, ridden by Ron Turcotte (Canada) on 5 May 1973 at Churchill Downs, Kentucky, USA.

MOST JOCKEY CAREER WINS

The most wins by a jockey in a horse racing career is 9,531 by Laffit Pincay Jr (USA), from his first winner on 16 May 1964 to 1 March 2003. He retired in April 2003 after a serious fall.

MOST STEEPLECHASE WINS IN A SEASON BY A JOCKEY

The most steeplechase wins in a season by a jockey is 289 in 2001/02 by Tony McCoy (UK).

MOST STEEPLECHASE WINS IN A CAREER BY A JOCKEY

The most steeplechase winners ridden in a career is 1,847 by Tony McCoy (UK) from 1992 to 2003.

MOST JOCKEY WINS IN A YEAR

The most races won in a year is 598 from 2,312 rides by Kent Desormeaux (USA) in 1989.

MOST RUNNERS IN A HORSE RACE

The most horses in a race was 66 in the Grand National at Aintree, Merseyside, UK, on 22 March 1929. The record for a flat race is 58 in the Lincolnshire Handicap at Lincoln, UK, on 13 March 1948.

DRESSAGE

MOST DRESSAGE WORLD CUP WINS

Instituted in 1986, the most World Cup wins in the dressage event is five by Anky van Grunsven (Netherlands) on Bonfire from 1995 to 1997 and 1999 to 2000.

MOST DRESSAGE OLYMPIC GOLD MEDALS

Dr Reiner Klimke (West Germany) has won a record six Olympic gold medals in the dressage event, taking five team golds between 1964 and 1988 and an individual gold in 1984. He also won individual bronze in 1976 for a record seven medals overall.

SHOW JUMPING

MOST OLYMPIC SHOW JUMPING GOLD MEDALS

The most Olympic show jumping gold medals won by a rider is five by Hans Günter Winkler (West Germany). He won four team medals in 1956, 1960, 1964 and 1972 and the individual Grand Prix in 1956. He also won team silver in 1976 and team bronze in 1968 for a record seven medals overall.

MOST WORLD CUP SHOW JUMPING WINS

The most World Cup show jumping wins is three by Hugo Simon (Austria) in 1979, 1996 and 1997, and Rodrigo Pessoa (Brazil, below) in 1998, 1999 and 2000.

AIR SPORTS

AEROBATICS

MOST WORLD AEROBATIC CHAMPIONSHIP TEAM WINS

The men's team aerobatics competition has been won six times by the USA in 1970, 1972, 1980, 1982, 1984 and 1988.

The women's team record is four wins: by the USSR, in 1978, 1982, 1984 and 1986, and Russia in 1996, 1998, 2000 and 2001. The world championships have been held biennially since 1960 (except 1974). Pilots are judged by a panel and scored on their accuracy while performing aerial manoeuvres.

MOST MEN'S AEROBATICS WORLD CHAMPIONSHIP WINS

Petr Jirmus (Czechoslovakia) is the only man to become world aerobatics champion twice, in 1984 and 1986.

MOST WOMEN'S AEROBATICS WORLD CHAMPIONSHIP WINS

Svetlana Kapanina (Russia) has won the women's aerobatics World Championships three times, in 1996, 1998 and 2001.

MOST HEIGHT GAINED IN A HANG GLIDER

The greatest height gain in a hang glider is 4,343 m (14,250 ft) by Larry Tudor (USA) over Owens Valley, California, USA, on 4 August 1985.

The greatest height gain in a hang glider by a woman is 3,970 m (13,025 ft) by Judy Leden (UK, pictured left being towed to altitude on a later flight) at Kuruman, South Africa, on 1 December 1992.

HANG GLIDING

MOST CONSECUTIVE HANG GLIDING LOOPS

Chad Elchin (USA) performed 95 consecutive loops with a hang glider at the Highland Aerosports flight park at Ridgely, Maryland, USA, on 16 July 2001. Elchin was towed to 4,846 m (15,900 ft) and looped his Aeros Stealth Combat non-stop down to 213 m (700 ft) at speeds of 28 to 128 km/h (18 to 80 mph).

LONGEST HANG GLIDER FLIGHT

The greatest distance flown when setting an official *Fédération Aéronautique International* (FAI) hang gliding record is 700.6 km (435.33 miles) by Manfred Ruhmer (Austria), starting from Zapata, Texas, USA, on 17 July 2001.

The FAI straight line distance record by a woman in a hang glider is 370.87 km (230.44 miles) by Tove Heaney (Australia), from Garnpung Lake, New South Wales, to Bealiba, Victoria, Australia, on 2 December 1998.

GREATEST DISTANCE IN TRIANGULAR HANG GLIDING

Tomas Suchanek (Czech Republic) flew the world-record triangular course distance of 357.12 km (221.9 miles) on a hang glider at Riverside, Australia, on 16 December 2000.

The equivalent women's record is 167.2 km (103.9 miles) by Nichola Hamilton (UK) at Croydon Hay, New South Wales, Australia, on 2 January 1997.

LARGEST FAI-APPROVED PARACHUTING FREEFALL FORMATION

A freefall formation consisting of 300 skydivers (right) was held for 7.02 seconds over Eloy, Arizona, USA, on 12 December 2002, at the World Record 300-Way event.

PARAGLIDING

LONGEST PARAGLIDER FLIGHT

The men's paragliding distance record is 423.4 km (263.08 miles) by William Gadd (Canada) who paraglided from Zapata to south of Ozona, Texas, USA, on 21 June 2002.

The women's record is 285 km (177.1 miles) by Kat Thurston (UK) at Kuruman, South Africa, on 25 December 1995.

MOST HEIGHT GAINED IN A PARAGLIDER

The height-gain world record in a paraglider is 4,526 m (14,849 ft) by Robbie Whittal (UK) at Brandvlei, South Africa, on 6 January 1993. In comparison, Boeing 747s cruise at 10,000 m (35,000 ft). At his record-breaking altitude, Whittal needed to use bottled oxygen, and ice formed on his clothing and the glider.

The women's record is 4,325 m (14,189 ft) by Kat Thurston (UK) over Kuruman, South Africa, on 1 January 1996.

PARACHUTING

LONGEST OFFICIAL FAI FREEFALL PARACHUTE JUMP

Eugene Andreev (USSR) holds the official FAI record for the longest freefall parachute jump, after falling for 24,500 m (80,380 ft) from an altitude of 25,458 m (83,523 ft) over Saratov, Russia, on 1 November 1962. He jumped from a balloon, opening his parachute at 958 m (3,143 ft).

LONGEST UNOFFICIAL FREEFALL PARACHUTE JUMP

The longest ever non-FAI approved parachute jump was by Captain Joseph W Kittinger (USA), who dropped 25,820 m (84,700 ft) from a balloon at 31,330 m (102,800 ft), at Tularosa, New Mexico, USA, on 16 August 1960. He reached a maximum speed of 1,006 km/h (625.25 mph) in rarified air at 27,400 m (90,000 ft) – just faster than the speed of sound. He fell for 4 min 37 sec before his parachute was deployed automatically.

FASTEST WOMEN'S SPEED SKYDIVING

The highest speed ever achieved by a woman in a speed skydiving competition is 432.12 km/h (268.5 mph) by Lucia Bottari (Italy) at Bottens, Switzerland, on 16 September 2002.

FASTEST MEN'S SPEED SKYDIVING

The highest speed ever reached in a speed skydiving competition is 524.13 km/h (325.67 mph) by Michael Brooke (France) at the Millennium Speed Skydiving Competition over Gap, France, on 19 September 1999. Speed skydiving involves jumping from an aircraft at 4,000 m (13,000 ft) and accelerating in a near-vertical head-first position into the 'measuring zone' that extends from an altitude of 2,700 m (8,850 ft) to 1,700 m (5,570 ft). Electronic altimeters are attached to the skydivers to measure their average speed as they cross the measuring zone. Below 1,700 m (5,570 ft) the jumper must change position to slow down sufficiently (to around 200 km/h or 120 mph) to allow the parachute to open safely above 800 m (2,620 ft).

MICROLIGHTING

HIGHEST MICROLIGHT SPEED

The highest average speed reached when setting an official FAI world microlight record is 168.55 km/h (104.73 mph) by Serge Ferrari (France) at Belley-Peyrieu, France, on 29 June 1996.

LARGEST CANOPY FORMATION

In 1996 a record 53 skydivers held the largest canopy formation (above) for six seconds over the skies of Kassel, Germany. A canopy stack formation is when sky divers hook their legs into the parachute directly beneath their feet to form an interlocking human structure.

TARGET SPORTS

SNOOKER

MOST SNOOKER CENTURY BREAKS IN A SEASON

The most century breaks made by an individual player in a snooker season is 53 by Stephen Hendry (UK) in 1994–95.

HIGHEST SNOOKER BREAK

Wally West (UK) recorded a break of 151 in a match at the Hounslow Lucania, Middlesex, UK, in October 1976. The break involved a free ball, which therefore created an 'extra' red, when all 15 reds were still on the table. In these very exceptional circumstances, the maximum break is 155.

LONGEST SNOOKER UNBEATEN RUN

From 17 March 1990 to his defeat by Jimmy White (UK) on 13 January 1991, Stephen Hendry (UK) won five successive titles and 36 consecutive matches in ranking snooker tournaments.

During the summer of 1992, Ronnie O'Sullivan (UK) won 38 consecutive matches but these were in qualifying competitions.

FASTEST SNOOKER 147 BREAK

The fastest ever 147 break (normally the maximum break possible) in a professional snooker tournament was made by Ronnie O'Sullivan (UK) in 5 min 20 sec during the World Championships at Sheffield, South Yorkshire, UK, on 21 April 1997.

YOUNGEST SNOOKER WORLD CHAMPION

Stephen Hendry (UK) was the youngest ever snooker world champion when he won the 1990 World Championship aged 21 years 106 days. He was also the youngest ever Scottish amateur champion, at the age of 15.

POOL

MOST POOL BALLS POCKETED IN 24 HOURS

Nick Nikolaidis (Canada) pocketed 16,723 balls in 24 hours at the Unison Bar, Montreal, Canada, on 13–14 August 2001. During the attempt he also broke the record for the fastest pool potting on two tables when he pocketed two consecutive racks in 1 min 33 sec.

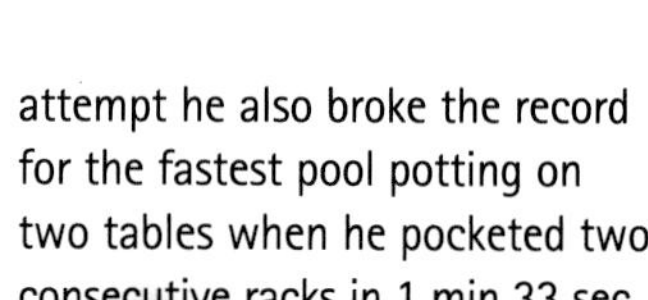

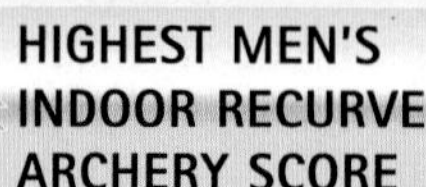

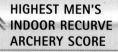

HIGHEST MEN'S INDOOR RECURVE ARCHERY SCORE

In November 2001 Michele Frangilli (Italy, above), scored 598 points from a possible 600 at the 25-m distance in the recurve bow category.

HIGHEST SCORE IN WOMEN'S TRAP-100 SHOOTING

Satu Pusila (Finland) and Delphine Racinet (France, left) have both scored 95 (71+24) in Women's Trap-100 targets clay shooting. Pusila set the record in Nicosia, Cyprus, on 13 June 1998, and Racinet equalled it in Sydney, Australia, on 26 March 2000.

FASTEST POOL POTTING

The record time for potting all 15 pool balls is 26.5 seconds by Dave Pearson (UK) at Pepper's Bar and Grill, Windsor, Ontario, Canada, on 4 April 1997.

MOST POOL WORLD CHAMPIONSHIPS

Pool, or championship pocket billiards, with numbered balls, began to become standardized around 1890. One of its greatest exponents was Ralph Greenleaf (USA), who won the world professional title 19 times between 1919 and 1937.

ARCHERY

HIGHEST FITA 18 ARCHERY SCORE IN 24 HOURS

The highest score in 24 hours shooting *Fédération Internationale de Tir à l'Arc* (FITA) 18 rounds is 26,064 by Michael Howson and Stephen Howard (both UK) at Oakbank Sports College, Keighley, West Yorkshire, UK, on 11–12 November 2000.

MOST ARROWS TRIGGERED BY A CROSSBOW SHOT

The most arrows triggered by a single crossbow shot, with the final arrows hitting a marked target, is nine. Ross and Elisa Hartzell (both USA) performed the feat on 18 December 1998 on the set of *Guinness World Records: Primetime* in Los Angeles, California, USA.

HIGHEST HORSEBACK KASSAI-STYLE ARCHERY SCORE

Kassai-style archery is inspired by ancient Hungarian and Asian horseback archers. The most points scored in kassai-style archery in 12 hours is 7,126.05 by Kassai Lajos (Hungary) at Kaposmero, Hungary, on 11 May 2002.

SHOOTING

CLOSEST GROUPING AT 1,000 YARDS BENCH REST SHOOTING

The smallest recorded group of 10 shots fired from a bench rest at 1,000 yards (914 m) is 8.003 cm (3.151 in) wide. The shots were fired by John Voneida (USA) at Williamsport, Pennsylvania, USA, on 8 July 1995.

MOST CONSECUTIVE BULLSEYES IN INDOOR SHOOTING

The most consecutive bullseyes scored in target shooting is 1,530 by Leonard Proteau (Canada) over a period of six months in 1967–68 at the Canadian Forces Station at Mont Apica, Quebec, Canada. He used a Dominion Marksman Model 190 S rifle, with a rear peep sight and hooded front sight, and shot from the prone position over 22.8 m (25 yd) on an indoor range.

DARTS

LARGEST ELECTRONIC DARTS TOURNAMENT

The largest electronic darts tournament took place in Benalmadena, Malaga, Spain, on 21–24 March 2002. The competition featured 617 teams from all over Spain and 3,622 individual players.

YOUNGEST DARTS PLAYER IN A MAJOR TOURNAMENT

The youngest player in a major competitive darts tournament is Nick Stoekenbroek (b. 11 May 1989, Netherlands), who played in the Dutch Open at Veldhoven, The Netherlands, on 5–7 February 2002 at the age of 12 years 270 days.

MOST DARTS WORLD CHAMPIONSHIP TITLES

Phil Taylor (UK, left) has won a record 10 darts world championship titles. He won the Embassy World Championship in 1990 and 1992 and the PDC (Professional Darts Corporation) World Championship from 1995 to 2002.

★ MEN'S RECURVE ARCHERY WORLD RECORDS ★

EVENT	SCORE	NAME AND COUNTRY	VENUE	DATE
Indoor 18 m	597	Michele Frangilli (Italy)	Nîmes, France	January 2001
Indoor 25 m	598	Michele Frangilli (Italy)	Gallarate, Italy	November 2001
Outdoor 30 m	360/17	Kye Dong-hyun (South Korea)	Cheongju, South Korea	September 2002
Outdoor 50 m	351	Kim Kyung-ho (South Korea)	Wonju, South Korea	September 1997
Outdoor 60 m	347	Choi Young-kwang (South Korea)	Hongseong, South Korea	August 2002
Outdoor 90 m	334	Choi Young-kwang (South Korea)	Yecheon, South Korea	March 2002
Outdoor FITA round	1,379	Oh Kyo-oon (South Korea)	Wonju, South Korea	November 2000
Outdoor FITA round team	4,053	Oh Kyo-oon, Lee Kyung-chul, KIm Jae-pak (South Korea)	Jakarta, Indonesia	August 1995

★ WOMEN'S RECURVE ARCHERY WORLD RECORDS ★

EVENT	SCORE	NAME AND COUNTRY	VENUE	DATE
Indoor 18 m	591	Lena Herasymenko (Ukraine)	Istanbul, Turkey	March 1997
Indoor 25 m	592	Petra Ericsson (Sweden)	Oulu, Finland	March 1991
Outdoor 50 m	345	Kim Moon-sun (South Korea)	Cheongju, South Korea	November 1996
Outdoor 60 m	350	Kim Jo-soon (South Korea)	Ye-chun, South Korea	September 1998
Outdoor 70 m	348	Lee Hee-Jeong (South Korea)	Cheongju, South Korea	October 2001
Outdoor FITA round	1,384	Chung Chang-sook (South Korea)	Wonju, South Korea	November 2000
Outdoor FITA round team	4,094	Cho Youn-jeong, Kim Soo-nyung, Lee Eun-kyung (South Korea)	Barcelona, Spain	August 1992

F1

GREATEST NUMBER OF POLE POSITIONS

Ayrton Senna (Brazil, 1960–1994, below) achieved 65 pole positions (and 41 wins) from 161 races between 1985 and 1994 for the Toleman, Lotus, McLaren and Williams teams. He also won the Monaco Grand Prix a record five consecutive times between 1989 and 1993.

MOST GRAND PRIX WINS BY A DRIVER

Michael Schumacher (Germany, below) won 64 Formula One Grand Prix between 1991 and 2002. He has scored a record 945 points in his career to date (1991–2002).

YOUNGEST FORMULA ONE WORLD CHAMPION

Emerson Fittipaldi (Brazil, b. 12 December 1946) won his first Formula One World Championship on 10 Septembe 1972 aged 25 years 273 days. (He is pictured below at the 1996 Rio 400 IndyCar race.)

MOST GRAND PRIX STARTS

The most Grand Prix starts by a driver is 256 by Ricardo Patrese (Italy, above, driving for Williams-Renault) between 1977 and 1993.

MOST RACES WITHOUT A WIN

Andrea de Cesaris (Italy, above) competed in 208 Formula One races without a victory between 1980 and 1994. He drove for Alfa Romeo (1980, 1982–83), McLaren (1981), Ligier (above, 1984–85), Minardi (1986), Brabham (1987), Rial (1988), Dallara (1989–90), Jordan (1991, 1994), Tyrell (1992–93) and Sauber (1994).

MOST CONSECUTIVE POLE POSITIONS

Alain Prost (France, below) achieved seven pole positions in the 1993 season, driving for the Williams-Renault team. Prost was also the World Champion that year.

MOST FORMULA ONE CONSTRUCTORS' WORLD CHAMPIONSHIP TITLES

The most Formula One Constructors' World Championship titles is 12 by Ferrari (Italy, team shown below) in 1961, 1964, 1975–77, 1979, 1982–83 and 1999–2002. In the 2002 season, the Ferrari team amassed a record 221 World Championship points. The team's drivers that year were Michael Schumacher (Germany) and Reubens Barichello (Brazil). The team won 15 races out of 17, wrapping up both the drivers' and the constructors' titles in record time.

MOST FORMULA ONE WORLD CHAMPIONSHIPS

The World Drivers' Championship inaugurated in 1950 has been won a record five times, by Juan Manuel Fangio (Argentina, above, driving for Maserati) in 1951 and 1954–57, and Michael Schumacher (Germany) in 1994–95 and 2000–02.

YOUNGEST DRIVER TO SCORE A WORLD CHAMPIONSHIP POINT

Jenson Button (UK, b. 19 January 1980, above) was aged 20 years 67 days when he finished in sixth place in the Brazilian Grand Prix on 26 March 2000, driving for the BMW WilliamsF1 team.

MOTORBIKE SPORTS

MOST WORLD SUPERBIKE CHAMPIONSHIP TITLES

The most World Superbike (WSB) championship titles won is four by Carl 'Foggy' Fogarty (UK, above), in 1994, 1995, 1998 and 1999.

MOST SUPERCROSS TITLES WON

The most supercross titles won is nine by Jeremy McGrath (USA). McGrath won the AMA (American Motorcycle Association) Supercross 250cc title from 1993 to 1996 and from 1998 to 2000. He also won the World Supercross title (also 250cc) in 1994 and 1995.

MOST 250cc SUPERCROSS RACE WINS IN A CAREER

The most 250cc supercross race wins in a professional career is 74 by Jeremy McGrath (USA) between 1989 and 2002.

MOST 250cc WORLD MOTOCROSS CHAMPIONSHIP WINS

Joël Robert (Belgium) won a record six 250cc World Motocross Championships, in 1964 and from 1968 to 1972. Between 25 April 1964 and 18 June 1972 he also won an unequalled fifty 250 cc World Motocross races.

MOST 125cc WORLD MOTOCROSS CHAMPIONSHIP WINS

The 125cc class of the World Motocross Championship has been won three times by three riders: Gaston Rahier (Belgium) in 1975–77; Harry Everts (Belgium) in 1979–81; and Alessio Chiodi (Italy) in 1997–99.

MOST MOTOCROSS DES NATIONS WINS

The *Motocross des Nations*, also known as the 'Olympics of Motocross', has been contested annually in different countries since 1947. The national team with the most wins is Great Britain, with 16 in 1947, 1949–50, 1952–54, 1956–57, 1959–60, 1963–67 and 1994.

MOST 50cc WORLD CHAMPIONSHIP TITLES WON

The most World Championship 50cc titles won is six by Angel Roldán Nieto (Spain) in 1969–70, 1972 and 1975–77.

MOST 125cc WORLD CHAMPIONSHIP TITLES WON

The most World Championship 125cc titles won is seven by Angel Roldán Nieto (Spain) in 1971–72, 1979 and 1981-1984.

MOST WORLD SUPERBIKE RACE WINS

The most World Superbike (WSB) Championship race wins is 59 by Carl Fogarty (UK) between 1992 and 1999.

MOST SUCCESSIVE ISLE OF MAN TT RACE WINS

James Redman (Rhodesia) won both the 250cc and 350cc events at the Isle of Man TT (Tourist Trophy) races three times in succession, from 1963 to 1965.

MOST ISLE OF MAN TT RACE WINS IN A CAREER

The most Isle of Man TT race wins in a career is 26 by Joey Dunlop (Ireland, 1952–2000) between 1977 and 2000.

MOST ISLE OF MAN TT RACE WINS BY A MANUFACTURER

The most wins by a manufacturer at the Isle of Man TT races is 176 by Yamaha (Japan) from 1965 to 2003.

MOST SUZUKA 8 HOURS RACE WINS BY A MANUFACTURER

The Japanese manufacturer Honda has provided the winning motorcycle for the Suzuka 8 Hours endurance race (held at Suzuka, Japan) a record 16 times between 1979 and 2002.

MOST INDOOR AND OUTDOOR WORLD TRIALS CHAMPIONSHIP WINS

Dougie Lampkin (UK, left) has won 11 Indoor and Outdoor World Trials Championships, claiming both titles every year between 1997 and 2001 and the outdoor title in 2002. Lampkin entered and won his first competition when he was only nine years old, and was awarded the MBE (Member of the British Empire) medal in 2002.

MOST SIDECAR WORLD CHAMPIONSHIP TITLES WON

The most Sidecar World Championship titles won is seven by Rolf Biland (Switzerland), in 1978, 1979, 1981, 1983, and 1992–94.

MOST WORLD CHAMPIONSHIP TITLES WON

The most World Championship motorcycling titles won is 15 by Giacomo Agostini (Italy), with seven 350cc titles from 1968 to 1974, and eight 500cc titles in 1966–1972 and 1975.

MOST WORLD CHAMPIONSHIP RACE WINS IN A CAREER

The most World Championship motorcycle race wins in a career is 122 by Giacomo Agostini (Italy). He achieved 68 race wins in the 500cc class and 54 race wins in the 350cc class between 24 April 1965 and 25 September 1977.

MOST ISLE OF MAN TT RACE WINS IN A YEAR

The most Isle of Man TT races won in one year is four (Formula One, Senior, Junior and Production classes) by Phillip McCallen (Ireland) in 1996. McCallen is shown, left, holding the Senior TT trophy.

MOST CAREER WINS IN A SINGLE WORLD CHAMPIONSHIP CLASS

The most World Championship career wins in a single class is 79 and was achieved by Rolf Biland (Switzerland) in the sidecar class.

FASTEST NHRA PRO STOCK BIKE

The highest terminal velocity for an NHRA (National Hot Rod Association) Pro Stock (petrol-powered piston-engine) drag bike is 312.37 km/h (194.1 mph) by Matt Hines (USA) on a Suzuki at Englishtown, New Jersey, USA, in May 2001.

FASTEST 440 YARDS ON AN NHRA PRO STOCK BIKE

The lowest elapsed time over 440 yards (402 m) on an NHRA Pro Stock drag bike is 7.049 seconds by Angelle Savoie (USA), riding a Suzuki at Matthews, Louisiana, USA, in May 2002.

FASTEST UNIMOTORCYCLE DRAG RACER

Unimotorcycles are one-wheeled machines with their riders sat on sleds behind the wheel and engine. William Nassau (USA) covered 30.48 m (100 ft) in 2.88 seconds on his unimotorcycle at the Volusia County Fairgrounds, Daytona Beach, Florida, USA, on 10 March 2000.

LONGEST MOTORCYCLE RACE CIRCUIT

The 60.72-km (37.73-mile) 'Mountain' circuit on the Isle of Man (UK), over which the principal TT (Tourist Trophy) races have been run since 1911 (with minor amendments in 1920), has 264 curves and corners and is the longest circuit used for any motorcycle race.

MOST PARIS-DAKAR RALLY MOTORCYCLE WINS

The most wins in the bike category of the Paris-Dakar Rally is six by Stéphane Peterhansel (France) in 1991–93, 1995 and 1997–98.

HIGHEST MOTORCYCLE JUMP

Tommy Clowers (USA) achieved a motorcycle jump height of 10.67 m (35 ft) from a steep take-off ramp at the X-Games Moto-X Step Up event in San Francisco, California, USA, on 18 August 2000.

HIGHEST ALTITUDE REACHED BY A MOTOR VEHICLE

The greatest altitude reached autonomously by a motor vehicle is 6,116 m (20,065 ft), by two Chinese-produced Jinlong motorcycles on the slopes of Mt Everest, Tibet, on 13 May 2002.

MOST 250cc WORLD CHAMPIONSHIP TITLES

The most 250cc World Championship titles won is four, by Phil Read (UK) in 1964, 1965, 1968 and 1971, and Max Biaggi (Italy, below, riding for Aprilia) between 1994 and 1997.

MOTORCAR RACING

MOST DAYTONA 500 RACE WINS

The most wins of the Daytona 500, the race with the most prize money in the NASCAR series, is seven by Richard Petty (USA), in 1964, 1966, 1971, 1973–74, 1979 and 1981.

MOST SOUTHERN 500 RACE WINS

The most wins of the Southern 500, the oldest race in the NASCAR series, is five by Cale Yarborough (USA), in 1968, 1973–74, 1978 and 1982.

LARGEST NASCAR SPEEDWAY TRACK

Talladega Superspeedway in Alabama, USA, is the largest NASCAR speedway. The tri-oval track is 4.28 km (2.66 miles) long with a banking angle of 33 degrees, and has seating for 143,000 spectators and space for thousands more in the 87-hectare (215-acre) infield.

MOST INDIVIDUAL WINS AT THE LE MANS 24-HOUR RACE

The most wins by an individual at the Le Mans 24-hour race is six by Jacky Ickx (Belgium, above), in 1969, 1975–77 and 1981–82.

MOST NASCAR TITLES WON

Since it was first held in 1949, the most titles won in the NASCAR (National Association for Stock Car Auto Racing) Championship is seven, by Richard Petty (USA) in 1964, 1967, 1971–72, 1974–75 and 1979, and Dale Earnhardt (USA) in 1980, 1986–87, 1990–91 and 1993–94.

MOST NASCAR RACE VICTORIES IN A CAREER

The most victories in a NASCAR career is 200 by Richard Petty (USA), between 1958 and 1992.

MOST COCA-COLA 600 RACE WINS

The most wins at the Coca-Cola 600, the longest race in the NASCAR series, is five by Darrell Waltrip (USA), in 1979–80, 1985 and 1988–89.

HIGHEST NASCAR CAREER EARNINGS

The highest earnings in a NASCAR career is $52,800,668 (£33,624,712) by Jeff Gordon (USA), between 1992 and 2003.

MOST WINS BY A TEAM AT THE LE MANS 24-HOUR RACE

The most wins by a team at the Le Mans 24-hour race is 16 by Porsche (Germany), in 1970–71, 1976–77, 1979, 1981–87, 1993 and 1996–98.

FASTEST 440 YARDS BY AN NHRA FUNNY CAR

The lowest elapsed time over 440 yards (402 m) in a National Hot Rod Association (NHRA) Funny Car dragster is 4.731 seconds by John Force (USA), driving a Ford Mustang (right) at Reading, Pennsylvania, USA, in October 2001.

FASTEST LAP IN THE LE MANS 24-HOUR RACE

The fastest lap in a Le Mans 24-hour race is 3 min 21.27 sec (average speed 242.093 km/h or 150.429 mph) by Alain Ferté (France) in a Jaguar XJR-9LM on 10 June 1989.

GREATEST DISTANCE COVERED IN A LE MANS 24-HOUR RACE

The greatest distance covered on the current Le Mans 24-hour race circuit is 5,331.998 km (3,313.15 miles) – at an average speed of 222.166 km/h (138.047 mph) – by Jan Lammers (Holland), Johnny Dumfries and Andy Wallace (both GB) in a Jaguar XJR-9LM from 11 to 12 June 1988.

MOST FORMULA NIPPON CHAMPIONSHIPS WON

The Japanese Formula Nippon Championship started in April 1996 as the replacement of the former Japanese Formula 3000 Championship which had existed for nine years from 1987. The most championships won by a driver is five by Satoru Nakajima (Japan) in 1981–82 and 1984–86. Many drivers have made their way from this championship to Formula One, among them Michael and Ralf Schumacher, Heinz-Harald Frentzen (all Germany) and Jacques Villeneuve (Canada).

FASTEST NHRA PRO STOCK DRAGSTER

The highest terminal velocity for an NHRA (National Hot Rod Association) Pro Stock (petrol-powered piston-engine) dragster is 329.77 km/h (204.91 mph) by Warren Johnson (USA) in a Pontiac Grand Am in Pomona, California, USA, in February 2003.

FASTEST 440 YARDS BY AN NHRA PRO STOCK DRAGSTER

The lowest elapsed time over 440 yards (402 m) in an NHRA Pro Stock dragster is 6.750 seconds by Jeg Couglin (USA), driving a Chevy Cavalier at Reading, Pennsylvania, USA, in October 2001.

FASTEST NHRA FUNNY CAR

Gary Densham (USA) reached a terminal velocity of 526.04 km/h (326.87 mph) over 440 yards (402 m) from a standing start in a Ford Mustang Funny Car at Pomona, California, USA, in February 2002.

MOST PARIS–DAKAR RALLY WINS IN A CAR

Ari Vatanen (Finland) has won the Paris–Dakar Rally in a car a record four times – first in 1987 and then three times from 1989 to 1991.

MOST CART CHAMPIONSHIP TITLES WON

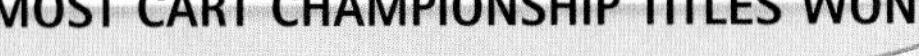

The most wins in the CART (Championship Auto Racing Teams) Series is seven by AJ Foyt (USA, below, racing a Lola T9000 in the 1990 Long Beach Grand Prix). Foyt won the series in 1960–61, 1963–64, 1967, 1975 and 1979. He also holds the record for the most race wins in a CART career, with 67 wins between 1958 and 1993.

MOST WORLD RALLY CHAMPIONSHIP RACE WINS

The most World Rally Championship race wins is 25 by Colin McRae (UK), in 1993–2002. McRae (b. August 5, 1968) was also the youngest World Rally champion when he won the title in 1995, aged 27 years 89 days.

MOST WORLD RALLY CHAMPIONSHIP RACE WINS IN A SEASON

The most World Rally Championship race wins in a season is six by Didier Auriol (France) in 1992, driving for Lancia.

MOST WORLD RALLY CHAMPIONSHIP MANUFACTURER WINS

The most World Rally Championship manfacturer titles won is 11 by Lancia (Italy), achieved between 1972 and 1992.

MOST INDIVIDUAL MONTE CARLO RALLY WINS

The Monte Carlo Rally, first staged in 1911, is the oldest and best known event in world rally. The most individual Monte Carlo Rally wins is four, by two drivers: Sandro Munari (Italy) in 1972 and 1975–77 driving a Lancia; and Walter Röhrl (with co-driver Christian Geistdorfer; both West Germany) in 1980 and 1982–84, each time in a different car.

LARGEST DEMOLITION DERBY

The largest ever demolition derby had 123 participants and took place at Todd & Pollock Speedway, Mount Maunganui, New Zealand, on 16 March 2002. It took 47 minutes before the winner – the last remaining mobile car – emerged.

OLDEST RACING DRIVER

On 6 and 7 February 2000 actor Paul Newman (USA, b. 26 January 1925), aged 75 years 11 days, along with 17-year old co-driver Gunnar Jeannette (USA) and two other members of his racing team, competed in a #75 Champion Racing Porsche 996-GT3 during the Rolex 24 race at the Daytona International Speedway, Florida, USA.

MOST CONSECUTIVE WORLD RALLY CHAMPIONSHIP TITLES WON

The most consecutive World Rally Championship titles won is four by Tommi Mäkinen (Finland) between 1996 and 1999. He won all his titles driving for the Mitsubishi Ralliart team (below).

CYCLING

spaced 2.95 m (9 ft 8 in) apart at the studio of *El Show de los Récords* in Madrid, Spain, on 23 October 2001. No ramps were used and the 1.7-m x 2-m platforms (5 ft 6 in x 6 ft 6 in) gave very little run up before the jumps.

MOST WOMEN'S DOWNHILL MOUNTAIN BIKING WORLD CHAMPIONSHIPS

The most mountain biking downhill World Championship wins by a woman is nine, by Anne-Caroline Chausson (France). She won three in the junior championship from 1993 to 1995 and six in the senior class from 1996 to 2001.

MOST MEN'S CROSS-COUNTRY MOUNTAIN BIKING WORLD CHAMPIONSHIPS

The most cross-country mountain biking World Championships won by a man is three, by Henrik Djernis (Denmark) in 1992–94.

LONGEST ONE-DAY CYCLE RACE

The longest one-day 'massed start' road race is the 551–620 km (342–385 mile) Bordeaux-Paris event held in France. Paced over all or part of the route, Herman van Springel (Belgium) is the fastest finisher, covering 584.5 km (363.1 miles) in a record 13 hr 35 min 18 sec in 1981. This gave him a highest average speed of 47.186 km/h (29.32 mph).

MOST TOUR DE FRANCE WINS

The greatest number of wins in the Tour de France is five and is shared by five riders: Jacques Anquetil (France), who won in 1957 and 1961–64; Eddy Merckx (Belgium) with triumphs in 1969–72 and 1974; Bernard Hinault (France), who was champion in 1978–79,1981–82 and 1985; and Miguel Induráin (Spain), the winner in 1991–95.

MOST TOUR DE FRANCE STAGE WINS

The rider with the most Tour de France stage wins is Eddie Merckx (Belgium) with 34.

OLDEST TOUR DE FRANCE WINNER

The oldest winner of the Tour de France was Firmin Lambot (Belgium), aged 36 years 4 months in 1922.

FASTEST GRAVITY SPEED BIKE

On 26 September 1998 Dwight Garland (USA) reached 103.03 km/h (64.02 mph) on a gravity speed bike. These bikes have tubular steel chassis and run on pneumatic racing slicks. They have front and rear brakes and fairings to increase aerodynamic efficiency.

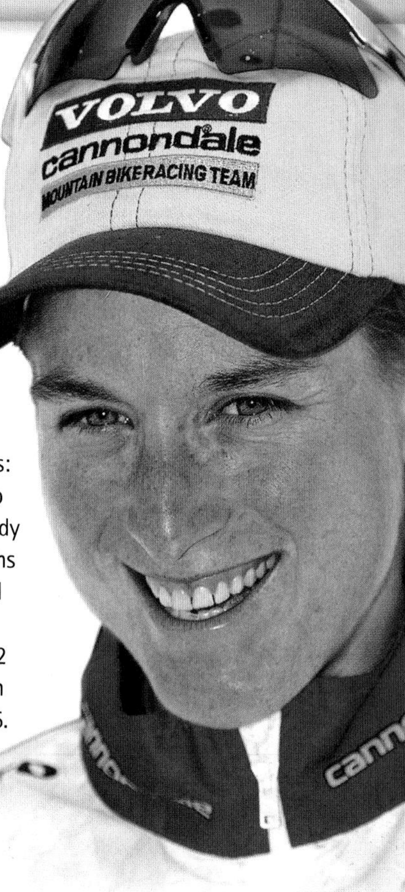

MOST MEN'S DOWNHILL MOUNTAIN BIKING WORLD CHAMPIONSHIPS

Nicolas Vouilloz (France, above) has won 10 men's mountain biking World Championships – three in the junior championships from 1992 to 1994 and seven in the senior class between 1995 and 2002.

LONGEST PLATFORM-TO-PLATFORM BICYCLE JUMP

César Canas and Otilio Pi Isern (both Spain) jumped their mountain bikes between two platforms

CLOSEST TOUR DE FRANCE RACE

The closest Tour de France race (below) was in 1989 when, after 23 days (from 1 to 23 July) and 3,267 km (2,030 miles), Greg LeMond (USA) crossed the finish line in Paris in 87 hr 38 min 35 sec, beating Laurent Fignon (France) by only 8 seconds.

MOST WOMEN'S CROSS-COUNTRY MOUNTAIN BIKING WORLD CHAMPIONSHIPS

The most mountain biking cross-country World Championships won by a woman is three, by Alison Sydor (Canada, left) from 1994 to 1996.

FASTEST SINGLE-RIDER HUMAN-POWERED VEHICLE SPEED

Sam Whittingham (Canada) reached 130.36 km/h (81 mph) on a flat road surface on his streamlined recumbent bicycle *Varna Diablo* at the World Human Powered Speed Challenge near Battle Mountain, Nevada, USA, on 5 October 2002.

FASTEST 'END-TO-END' CYCLE OF THE UK

Andy Wilkinson (UK) cycled from Land's End, Cornwall, to John O'Groats, Highland, UK, in 1 day 21 hr 2 min 18 sec from 29 September to 1 October 1990, covering around 1,600 km (1,000 miles).

GREATEST DISTANCE CYCLED IN 12 HOURS

Marko Baloh (Slovenia) cycled a record 452.196 km (280.9 miles), solo and unpaced, in 12 hours at the Novo Mesto Velodrome, Novo Mesto, Slovenia, on 31 August 2002.

MOST STEPS CLIMBED BY BICYCLE

The most steps ascended on a bicycle is 1,200 by Javier Zapata (Colombia) on 19 June 2001 at the Parque Central Tower in Caracas, Venezuela. The stair climb took Zapata 1 hr 5 min to complete.

LONGEST STATIC CYCLING MARATHON

The record for the longest static cycling marathon belongs to Eddy Kontelj (Australia), who cycled for 72 hours at the Geelong Showgrounds, Geelong, Victoria, Australia, on 16–19 October 2002.

GREATEST DISTANCE ON A STATIC CYCLE IN 24 HOURS

The greatest distance achieved on a spinning machine in 24 hours is 751.4 km (466.8 miles) by Ronald Martzloff (Germany) at the Maier Kitchen showroom, Bahlingen, Germany, on 8–9 June 2002.

LARGEST STATIC CYCLE EVENT

The world's largest static cycle event, comprising 300 people cycling simultaneously, took place at the Great Speed Stick Marathon in Bogotá, Colombia, on 10 March 2001.

MOST PROFESSIONAL WORLD CHAMPIONSHIP MEN'S CYCLING TITLES

Koichi Nakano (Japan) has won 10 professional World Championship cycling titles in the sprint event between 1977 and 1986.

FASTEST UNPACED 200-M CYCLE FROM A FLYING START

The world's fastest unpaced 200-m cycle from a flying start is 9.865 seconds by Curtis Harnett (Canada), in Bogotá, Colombia, on 28 September 1995. The women's record is 10.831 seconds by Olga Slyusareva (Russia), in Moscow, Russia, on 25 April 1993.

FASTEST UNPACED 500-M CYCLE FROM A FLYING START

On 20 October 1988 Aleksandr Kiritchenko (USSR) cycled the fastest unpaced 500 m from a flying start in 26.649 seconds in Moscow, Russia. Yong Hua Jiang (China) holds the women's record, with 34.000 seconds at Kunming, China, on 10 August 2002.

FASTEST WOMEN'S UNPACED 3-KM CYCLE FROM A STANDING START

The fastest women's unpaced 3-km cycle from a standing start, known as the Women's Individual Cycling Pursuit, is 3 min 30.816 sec by Leontien Zijlaard-Van Moorsel (Netherlands) on 17 September 2000 at the Olympic Games in Sydney, Australia.

FASTEST MEN'S UNPACED 4-KM CYCLE FROM A STANDING START

The fastest unpaced 4 km cycled from a standing start is 4 min 11.114 seconds by Chris Boardman (GB), at Manchester, UK, on 29 August 1996.

FASTEST MEN'S 4-KM TEAM PURSUIT

The fastest unpaced team pursuit over 4 km from a standing start is 3 min 59.583 sec, by Peter Dawson, Mark Renshaw, Luke Roberts and Graham Brown (all Australia), at the Commonwealth Games in Manchester, UK, on 1 August 2002.

FASTEST UNPACED 1-KM CYCLE FROM A STANDING START

Arnaud Tournant (France, bottom in picture below) cycled 1 km (0.62 mile), unpaced and from a standing start, in a record 58.875 seconds at La Paz, Bolivia, on 10 October 2001.

WHEEL SKILLS

HIGHEST BUNNY HOP ON A MOUNTAIN BIKE

Daniel Comas Riera (Spain) achieved the highest ever bunny hop on a mountain bike when he cleared a horizontal bar at a height of 1.16 m (45.6 in) without using a ramp at the studios of *El Show de los Récords* in Madrid, Spain, on 15 November 2001. Although the rules allow the bike to have front suspension, Daniel's bike had no suspension of any sort.

HIGHEST BUNNY HOP ON A MICRO SCOOTER

Marc Vinco (France) was able to bunny hop on his micro scooter to an 80-cm-high (31-in) platform, landing with both feet still on the scooter at the studios of *L'Émission des Records*, Paris, France, on 14 September 2000.

HIGHEST INDOOR BMX JUMP

Timo Pritzel (Germany) and Jesús Fuentes (Spain) cleared a bar at 5.12 m (16 ft 9.48 in) above floor level using BMX bikes on the set of *El Show de los Récords* in Madrid, Spain, on 21 September 2001.

LONGEST POWER-ASSISTED BICYCLE RAMP JUMP

Professional stunt rider Colin Winkelmann (USA) jumped his BMX bike 35.63 m (116 ft 11 in) after being towed to approximately 100 km/h (60 mph) behind a motorcycle at Agoura Hills, California, USA on 20 December 2000 on the set of *Guinness World Records: Primetime*.

FASTEST CYCLIST ON SNOW

The fastest cycling speed attained down a glacier is 212.139 km/h (132 mph), by downhill mountain bike racer Christian Taillefer (France, above) on a Peugeot Cycle at the Speed Ski Slope in Vars, France, in March 1998.

HIGHEST VERTICAL DROP ON A BICYCLE

Walter Belli (Italy) and David Cachón Labrador (Spain) both rode their BMX bikes off a platform 4 m (13 ft 1.4 in) high and continued to cycle upon landing without their feet touching the ground on the set of *El Show de los Récords* in Madrid, Spain, on 5 December 2001. In accordance with the rules, they were not allowed a run-up before dropping off the platform.

LONGEST DURATION BICYCLE WHEELIE ON A FRONT WHEEL

Martti Kuoppa (Finland) was able to maintain a wheelie on the front wheel of his BMX bike for 23.25 seconds, covering around 100 m (328 ft) on 26 June 2001 in Helsinki, Finland.

MOST GYRATOR SPINS IN ONE MINUTE

The record for the most gyrator spins in one minute is 29 by Sam Foakes (UK) on BBC1's *Blue Peter* TV programme in London, UK, on 11 March 2002.

MOST PINKY SQUEAKS

Andreas Lindqvist (Sweden) completed 98 continuous 360° rotations of his freestyle BMX bike whilst balancing on just the front wheel in Stockholm, Sweden, on 30 October 2001.

MOST SKIPS ON A UNICYCLE IN ONE MINUTE

The most skips (number of rope revolutions) on a unicycle in one minute is 209 by Amy Shields (USA) in St Paul, Minnesota, USA, on 23 February 2002.

TALLEST UNICYCLE RIDE

The tallest unicycle ever mastered is 31.01 m (101 ft 9 in) high and was ridden by Steve McPeak (USA) in Las Vegas, USA, in October 1980. He achieved a distance of 114.6 m (376 ft) using a safety wire suspended from an overhead crane.

FASTEST 100 M ON A UNICYCLE

On 25 March 1994 Peter Rosendahl (Sweden) unicyled 100 m from a standing start in 12.11 seconds – a speed of 29.72 km/h (18.47 mph) – at Las Vegas, Nevada, USA.

MOST BACKFLIPS ON A KICKSCOOTER FROM A SINGLE JUMP

Jarret Reid (USA) travelled from a ramp at a height of 5.48 m (18 ft) and achieved a single scooter back flip, landing with both feet on the scooter, at Van Nuys Airport, California, USA, for the *Guinness World Records: Primetime* TV show on 21 January 2001.

SKATEBOARDING HIGH JUMP

The skateboarding high jump record is 1.67 m (5 ft 5 in) by Trevor Baxter (UK) at Grenoble, France, on 14 September 1982. This record involves approaching a standard high-jump bar on a skateboard, clearing the bar, and successfully landing on the other side.

MOST CONTINUOUS SKATEBOARD REVOLUTIONS

Richard Carrasco (USA) completed a record 142 continuous 360° revolutions on a skateboard on 11 August 2000 in Santa Ana, California, USA.

HIGHEST BMX VERTICAL AIR

The highest air on a BMX is by Mat Hoffman (USA, left) who achieved a vertical height of 8.07 m (26 ft 6 in) jumping from a 7.31-m (24-ft) quarterpipe on 20 March 2001 in Oklahoma City, Oklahoma, USA. However, Hoffman was towed by a motorcycle in the run-up to the jump. The highest ever unassisted air is 5.8 m (19 ft) by Dave Mirra (USA) from a 5.4-m (18-ft) ramp in San Diego, California, USA, in January 2001.

HIGHEST SKATEBOARD DROP INTO A QUARTERPIPE

Adil Dyani (Norway, left) dropped into a quarterpipe ramp from a height of 9.03 m (29 ft 7.2 in) on a skateboard in Oslo, Norway, on 10 August 2002.

HIGHEST AIR ON A SKATEBOARD

Danny Way (USA) performed a 5.56-m (18-ft 3-in) method air off a 6-m (20-ft) quarterpipe at Point X Camp near Aguanga, California, USA, on 17 April 2002.

HIGHEST PRONE SKATEBOARD SPEED

The highest speed recorded on a skateboard, lying face down in a prone position, is 126.12 km/h (78.37 mph) by Roger Hickey (USA) on a course near Los Angeles, California, USA, on 15 March 1990.

HIGHEST STANDING SKATEBOARD SPEED

Gary Hardwick (USA) set a speed record, standing on a skateboard, of 100.66 km/h (62.55 mph) at Fountain Hills, Arizona, USA, on 26 September 1998.

LONGEST SKATEBOARD RAIL GRIND

Christian Pujola Herandez (Spain) performed a 6.5-m (21-ft 4-in) rail grind on a skateboard on the set of *El Show de los Récords* in Madrid, Spain, on 22 November 2001.

MOST SKATEBOARD ROTATIONS IN THE AIR OFF A HALFPIPE

The most airborne rotations off a skateboard ramp is two and a half, achieved by Tony Hawk (USA) at the X-Games in San Francisco, California, USA, on 27 June 1999. The so-called '900' (as in 900° spin) is regarded as one of the most difficult skateboarding tricks, with Hawk remaining the first and only person to have achieved it in competition.

HIGHEST OLLIE ON A SKATEBOARD

Danny Wainwright (UK) popped the highest ever ollie at 1.13 m (44.5 in) off flat ground on 6 February 2000 at the Action Sports Retailers (ASR) Show at Longbeach, California, USA.

HIGHEST INDOOR VERTICAL AIR ON INLINE SKATES

Taïg Khris (France) achieved an inline skate jump of 3.1 m (10 ft 2 in) from a halfpipe on the set of *L'Émission des Records* in Paris, France, on 6 December 2000.

FURTHEST INLINE SKATES DISTANCE IN ONE HOUR

Mauro Guenci (Italy) covered a distance of 36.83 km (22.88 miles) in one hour on inline skates at Senigallia, Italy, on 29 June 2002. He completed over 34 laps of a 1,063-m (3,487-ft) street course through the town.

FASTEST DOWNHILL INLINE SKATING SPEED

Graham Wilkie and Jeff Hamilton (both USA) set the inline skating speed record of 103.03 km/h (64.02 mph) in Arizona, USA, on 26 September 1998.

HIGHEST INLINE SKATE RAMP JUMP

José Félix Hormaetxe Henry (Spain) cleared a bar set at 4.5 m (14 ft 8.4 in) on inline skates at the studios of *El Show de los Récords* in Madrid, Spain, on 14 December 2001.

FURTHEST DISTANCE COVERED IN A 24-HOUR ROLLER SKIING RELAY

The greatest distance covered by a team of four roller skiers in 24 hours is 488.74 km (303.69 miles) by Simon Tinning, A Simpson, A Adamson and Mark Walker (all UK) at RAF Alconbury, Cambridgeshire, UK, on 23–24 May 1998.

LONGEST BMX BACKFLIP

Allan Cooke (USA, pictured left performing a tail whip) performed a 16.4-m (54-ft) backflip on his BMX bike between two specially constructed ramps at Point X Camp near Aguanga, California, USA, on 9 February 2002.

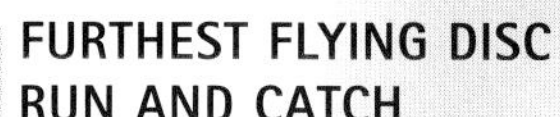

FURTHEST FLYING DISC RUN AND CATCH

The men's flying disc throw-run-and-catch record is 92.64 m (304 ft 11 in) by Hiroshi Oshima (Japan) at San Francisco, California, USA, on 20 July 1988.

The women's record is 60.02 m (196 ft 11 in) by Judy Horowitz (USA) at La Mirada, California, USA, on 29 June 1985.

FASTEST TIME TO MAKE, THROW AND CATCH A BOOMERANG

On 26 August 2001 Lawrence West (UK) cut out a boomerang from a sheet of material (where the shape had already been drawn) and then threw it and caught it in 1 min 11 sec at the Boomerang Championships held in Trefriw, Gwynedd, UK. Participants are given the same sized piece of sheet material with the outline of the boomerang drawn on it, and they can use whatever tools they wish to cut it out. They then run 20 m (65 ft) to a line where they have to throw and catch the boomerang.

FASTEST CROSSING OF THE ENGLISH CHANNEL BY KITE SURFER

Chris Calthrop, Jason Furness (right) and Andy Preston (all UK), from kite manufacturer Flexifoil International (UK), crossed the English Channel using kite surfers – custom-made boards with 4.9-m^2 (52-ft^2) traction kites. On 17 September 1999 they made the 23.2-nautical mile (42.9-km) Channel crossing from Hythe, Kent, UK, to Wissant, France, in a record time of 2 hr 30 min (2 members) and 3 hr respectively (1 member).

FURTHEST DYNO WALL CLIMB

The furthest distance acheived in Dyno climbing is 2.6 m (8 ft 6 in) by Matt Heason (UK) at the Bendcrete Dyno Competition held at the Edge Climbing Centre, Sheffield, South Yorkshire, UK, on 20 April 2002.

The furthest distance achieved by a woman is 1.9 m (6 ft 2 in) by Katherine Schirrmacher (UK) at the same competition. In this event competitiors leap from one set of handholds to a higher set (a move known as a dynamic manoeuvre or dyno) that would otherwise be out of reach.

LONGEST FOUR-FINGER HANG

José Antonio Burcio Enrique (Spain) was hoisted up to a bar housing two finger holds, from which he hung with just two fingers of each hand for 2 min 1 sec at the studios of *El Show de los Récords* in Madrid, Spain, on 5 December 2001.

GREATEST FLYING DISC DISTANCE

The record flying disc (formerly Frisbee) distance for men, officiated by the World Flying Disc Federation, is 250 m (820 ft) by Christian Sandstrom (Sweden, left) at El Mirage, California, USA, on 26 April 2002. Jennifer Griffin (USA) holds the women's record, throwing a distance of 138.56 m (454 ft 6 in) at Fredericksburg, Virginia, USA, on 8 April 2000.

MOST FOOTBAG KICKS IN FIVE MINUTES

The greatest number of kicks of a footbag in five minutes is 1,019 by Andy Linder (USA) at Mount Prospect, Illinois, USA, on 7 June 1996. The doubles record is 132,011 kicks by Gary Lautt and Tricia George (both USA) at Chico, California, USA, on 21 March 1998.

MOST FOOTBAG KICKS BY A WOMAN

The women's world record for keeping a footbag airborne is 24,713 consecutive kicks in a time of 4 hr 9 min 27 sec by Constance Constable (USA) at the California Athletic Club, Monterrey, California, USA, on 18 April 1998.

MOST FOOTBAG PARTICIPANTS

The greatest number of people playing footbag in a circle at one time is 964. The attempt was organized by Andy Linder (USA) and took place at the Cornerstone Festival, Bushnell, Illinois, USA, on 6 July 2001.

HIGHEST VERTICAL HEIGHT CLIMBING STAIRS

Russell Gill (USA) climbed the 835 steps of the Rhodes State Office Tower in Columbus, Ohio, USA, 53 times (a total of 44,255 steps) in 9 hr 16 min 24 sec on 20 February 1994. This was equivalent to a vertical height of 8,141.8 m (26,712 ft). He descended by lift each time.

DEEPEST CONSTANT-WEIGHT FREEDIVE

The world record for the deepest AIDA (Association Internationale pour le Développement de l'Apnée) approved constant-weight freedive is 87 m (285 ft) by Guillaume Néry (France) in Nice, France, on 31 August 2002.

The women's record is 70 m (229 ft) by Tanya Streeter (USA) in the waters off Guadeloupe on 11 May 2001.

DEEPEST VARIABLE-WEIGHT FREEDIVE

The deepest variable-weight freedive is a record 117 m (383 ft) by Benjamin Franz (Germany) off Safaga, Egypt, on 1 September 2001.

Deborah Andollo (Cuba) is the women's record holder, with a dive of 95 m (311 ft) off Parghalia, Italy, on 12 July 2000.

DEEPEST NO-LIMITS FREEDIVE

Using the no-limits freediving method, Tanya Streeter (USA) reached a record depth of 160 m (525 ft) in the waters off the Turks and Caicos Islands in the Caribbean on 17 August 2002.

The men's record is held by Loic Leferme (France), who reached a depth of 154 m (505 ft) off Saint-Jean-Cap-Ferrat, France, on 18 August 2001.

DEEPEST DYNAMIC APNEA FREEDIVE WITHOUT FINS

Herbert Nitsch (Austria) made a dynamic apnea freedive without the use of fins to a record depth of 134 m (439 ft) at Wiesbaden, Germany, on 24 November 2001.

Nathalie Desreac (France) holds the women's record, with a 95-m (311-ft) dive in the waters off Réunion in the Indian Ocean, on 7 February 1999.

FASTEST BUTT BOARDING

Darren Lott (USA, right) reached a record speed of 105 km/h (65.24 mph) on a butt board in Fountain Hills, Arizona, USA, on 26 September 1998.

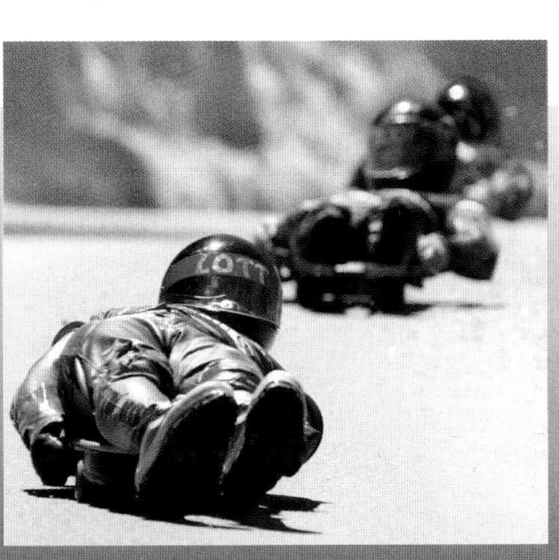

FASTEST FEMALE SANDBOARDER

Nancy Sutton (USA) was clocked at 71.94 km/h (44.7 mph) at Sand Mountain, Nevada, USA, on 19 September 1998.

LONGEST HORSESHOE PITCHING WINNING STREAK

The longest winning streak in the horseshoe pitching World Championships is 69 games by Fernando Isais (USA) in 1950–52. This outstanding run was finally broken when Isais was beaten by Jim Johnson (USA).

MOST MEN'S HORSESHOE PITCHING WORLD CHAMPIONSHIPS

The most horseshoe pitching World Championships won in the men's category is 10 by Ted Allen (USA) in 1933–35, 1940, 1946, 1953, 1955–1957 and 1959. The championships were not held between 1936 and 1939.

MOST WOMEN'S HORSESHOE PITCHING WORLD CHAMPIONSHIPS

The most horseshoe pitching World Championships won in the women's category is 10 by Vicki Chappelle-Winston (USA). She won in 1956, 1958–59, 1961, 1963, 1966–67, 1969, 1975 and 1981.

MOST RINGERS IN A WORLD CHAMPIONSHIP HORSESHOE PITCHING GAME

The most ringers scored by an individual in a World Championship game is 175 by Glen Henton (USA) in 1965. A ringer is a shoe that comes to rest encircling the stake.

MOST EWES SHORN IN EIGHT HOURS

Hayden Te Huia (New Zealand) sheared 495 ewes in eight hours, under World Shearing Record Committee rules, on 18 December 1999 at Marton, New Zealand.

HIGHEST SPEED ON A SANDBOARD

On 12 April 1999 Erik Johnson (USA, above) reached a top speed of 82 km/h (51 mph) at the Sand Master Jam at Dumont Dunes, California, USA.

MOST LAMBS SHORN IN EIGHT HOURS

Justin Bell (New Zealand) sheared a record 731 lambs in eight hours, following World Shearing Record Committee rules, on 16 December 2002 at Opepe Trust Farm, Hawkes Bay, New Zealand.

MOST MERINO EWES SHORN IN EIGHT HOURS

The most merino ewes shorn in eight hours, following World Shearing Record Committee rules, is 466 by Cartwright Terry (Australia) on 22 February 2003 at Westerndale Station, Western Australia, Australia.

FASTEST SHEEP SHEARING WITH A 'MUM AND DAD' MACHINE

Rod Search and Murray Moser (both Australia) sheared two merino sheep in 5 min 55.89 sec using a 'Mum and Dad' machine in Euroa, Victoria, Australia, on 30 October 1999.

BIZARRE SPORTS

MOST CONSECUTIVE PEA SHOOTING WORLD CHAMPIONSHIPS

The most consecutive pea shooting World Championships won is three by Mike Fordham (UK) in 1983–85. He shares the record with David Hollis (UK) who won in 1999–2001. Hollis was also the youngest world champion, aged just 13 when he scooped the title in 1999. The Championships are held every year in Witcham, Cambridgeshire, UK. The skill is to shoot a pea at a putty-smeared target the size of a dart-board from a distance of 3.2 m (10 ft 6 in). Contestants gain five points for hitting the target in the inner circle, three points for the middle circle and one point for the outer circle.

MOST PEA SHOOTING WORLD CHAMPIONSHIPS

The most pea shooting World Championships won by an individual is seven by Mike Fordham (UK) in 1977–78, 1981, 1983–85 and 1992.

MOST TOE WRESTLING WORLD CHAMPIONSHIPS

The most toe wrestling World Championships won in the men's category is five by Alan 'Nasty' Nash (UK) in 1994, 1996–97, 2000 and 2002.

The women's record is four Championships, won by Karen 'Kamikaze' Davies (UK) from 1999 to 2002. The Championships are held annually on the first Saturday in June at Ye Olde Royal Oak, Wetton, Derbyshire, UK. The aim of the contest, the barefoot equivalent of arm wrestling, is to push the opponent's foot to the other side of a specially constructed ring, called a 'toerack', using only the toes.

WORLD CHAMPIONSHIPS WITH THE HEAVIEST PARTICIPANTS

Founded in 1982, the World Elephant Polo Association (WEPA) hosts a championship tournament every year. Elephant polo is played by riders on elephants, four to a team. An adult male Asian elephant can weigh over 5 tonnes (11,000 lb) but the contest has no weight restrictions. Rules state that participants cannot lie down in front of the goal. The invitational tournament is held every December in Megauly, on the edge of Nepal's Royal Chitwan National Park.

MOST MEN'S COAL CARRYING TITLES

Terry Lyons (UK) holds the record for the most titles at the annual coal carrying championship race. He won eight times between 1977 and 1985 inclusive, with the exception of 1980 when Colin Claypole (UK) was the winner. The contest is held annually at Gawthorpe, West Yorkshire, UK. Contestants carry a 50-kg (110-lb) bag of coal over a 1,012.5-m (1,107.2-yd) course.

FASTEST WIFE CARRYING CHAMPION

The fastest ever time to complete the 235-m (771-ft) course of the World Wife Carrying Championships, held annually in Sonkajärvi, Finland, (first held in 1992) is 55.5 seconds, by Margo Uusorg and Birgit Ulricht (both Estonia) on 1 July 2000. Winners take home litres of beer equivalent to the wife's weight. The contest pits some 30 couples in a challenge to carry a female around the village school playground. She need not actually be a wife, but must be over 17 years of age and wear a crash helmet.

FURTHEST GRAPE SPITTING DISTANCE

On 21 May 2000 Robert Bonwell (UK) spat a grape a record distance of 6.82 m (22 ft 4 in) at Aston Tirrold Fete in Aston Tirrold, Oxfordshire, UK,

FASTEST INDIVIDUAL COAL CARRYING RACE

David Jones (UK) holds the men's record for the annual coal carrying championship race (below) at Gawthorpe, West Yorkshire, UK. He carried a 50-kg (110-lb) bag over a 1,012.5-m (1,107.2-yd) course in 4 min 6 sec on 1 April 1991.

Ruth Clegg (UK) holds the women's record, with a time of 5 min 4 sec on 6 April 2002.

MOST EXTREME IRONING WORLD CHAMPIONSHIPS

Organized by the German Extreme Ironing Section (GEIS) and first held in Munich, Germany, on 20–21 September 2002, the inaugural Extreme Ironing World Championship was won by Inga Kosak (Germany) with a score of 522. Participants (an extreme ironer in action is shown above) are scored on both style and textile, and against the clock, over five disciplines: Forest, Water, Rocky, Urban and Freestyle.

HIGHEST SHEAF TOSS

Glen Young (Australia) threw a 3.65-kg (8-lb) sheaf over a 18.25-m (59-ft 10.5-in) high crossbar at the Royal Canberra Show, Australian Capital Territory, Australia, on 22 February 1997.

MOST PEOPLE BUNGEE-JUMPING IN 24 HOURS

A record 505 people bungee-jumped in 24 hours on 26 October 2000 in Cairns, Queensland, Australia, averaging one bungee jump every 2.85 minutes. The mass bungee was organized by AJ Hackett Bungy.

LONGEST CANAL JUMP

In the sport of *Fierljeppen*, or canal jumping, the world record jump is 19.4 m (63 ft 7.6 in), using a 12.2-m (40-ft) aluminium pole, by Aart de Wit (Netherlands) at Winsam, Friesland, The Netherlands, in August 1991.

MOST TRAMPOLINING HULA HOOP SKIPS

On 25 May 1999 Ken Kovach (USA) set the world record for the most hula hoop skips while somersaulting and jumping on a trampoline in London, UK. Using a standard 91-cm (36-in) diameter hula hoop, Kovach passed completely through the hoop 122 times, landing on the trampoline between each jump.

GREATEST GUMBOOT THROWING DISTANCE

Often called 'Wellie Wanging', gumboot throwing is contested by tossing a size 8 Challenger Dunlop boot, and the throwing distance record is 63.98 m (209 ft 9 in) by Teppo Luoma (Finland) at Hmeenlinna, Finland, on 12 October 1996.

The women's distance record is 40.87 m (134 ft 1 in), thrown by Sari Tirkkonen (Finland) at Turku, Finland, on 19 April 1996.

LONGEST SUCCESSFULLY ROTATED KIIKING SWING

Kiiking (left) is a sport in Baltic and Scandinavian countries where the aim is to complete a 360° revolution on a swing. The platforms of Kiiking swings are suspended on rigid arms, or shafts, and the challenge is to make a full revolution on the longest shaft possible. The longest shafts on a swing to complete a successful rotation were 7.01 m (23 ft) long. The swinger was Andrus Aasamäe (Estonia) at Rakveres, Estonia, on 16 July 2000. The women's record is 5.86 m (19 ft 2.7 in) by Kätlin Kink (Estonia) at Pärnus, Estonia, on 2 September 2001.

MOST CONSECUTIVE WORLD BOG SNORKELLING CHAMPIONSHIPS

Steve Griffiths (UK) is the only person to have held the World Bog Snorkelling Championship title three times, winning consecutively from 1985 to 1987. Competitors have to complete two lengths of a 55-m (180-ft) trench cut through a peat bog in the quickest time possible, wearing snorkels and flippers, but without using any conventional swimming strokes.

MOST ENTRANTS AT A WORLD BOG SNORKELLING CHAMPIONSHIPS

The most entrants for a World Bog Snorkelling Championships is 93 on 26 August 2002 at Waen Rhydd Peat bog, Llanwrtyd Wells, Powys, UK. The title was won by Philip John (UK) in a time of 1 min 45.22 sec.

LARGEST WELLINGTON BOOT RACE

Held annually on New Year's Day since 1981, the Castlecomer Wellington Race at Castlecomer, County Kilkenny, Ireland, is run over a 6.4-km (4-mile) circuit and has a turnout of over 400 participants, all wearing standard Wellington boots.

LONGEST FOOTBALL PITCH

The annual Shrovetide football match has been played for more than 300 years in Ashbourne, Derbyshire, UK. It is a game short on rules and long on physical contact contested between the Up'ards (those born north of the River Henmore) and the Down'ards (those born south of the river). The goals are the waterwheels at Clifton (target for the Down'ards) and at Sturston (target for the Up'ards), 4.8 km (3 miles) apart. The pitch is all the water and land in between, excluding the churchyard, where ball games are forbidden. Players must be in the river to score a goal, which they do by banging the ball three times against the waterwheel.

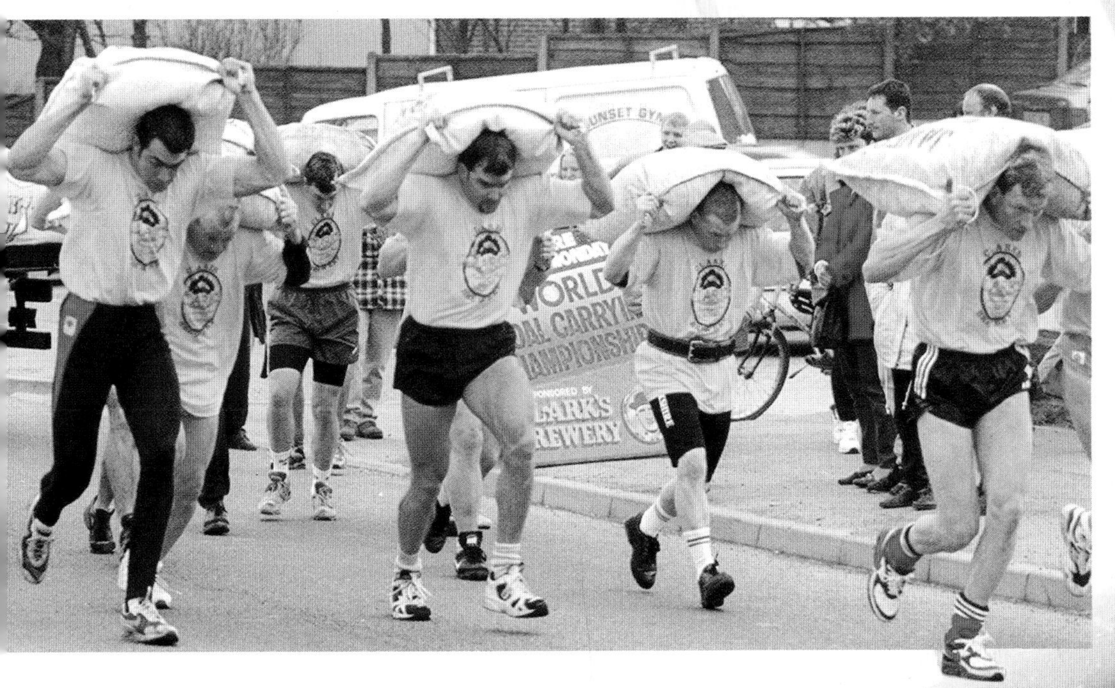

INDEX

This index concentrates on the subjects of the records (eg weddings, jellyfish, teddy bears) rather than the type of record (eg highest, widest, longest). Personal names of record holders are not included. Page numbers in bold type indicate the main entry on a topic.

A

B

GUINNESS
WORLD RECORDS

C

INDEX

D

INDEX

GUINNESS
WORLD RECORDS

INDEX

GUINNESS
WORLD RECORDS

INDEX

GUINNESS
WORLD RECORDS

INDEX

GUINNESS
WORLD RECORDS

PICTURE CREDITS

4 Science Photo Library
Oxford Scientific Films
Associated Press
Drew Gardner/Guinness World Records
Honda
c/o Microemissive Displays Ltd
c/o Maurice Bennett
Rex Features
Getty Images
6 PA Photos
Corbis
Getty Images
Associated Press
Simon Freshfield
Rex Features
8 Rex Features
c/o State Historical Society of North Dakota
Corbis
Science Photo Library
Corbis
10 Rex Features
11 Rex Features
c/o Fabien Pretou
12 Science Photo Library (9)
Corbis
14 Science Photo Library
Corbis
PA Photos
15 c/o Dr Katherine O'Hanlan
16 c/o Wilkins triplets
17 Corbis
Associated Press
18 KelownaPhotography.com
Corbis
19 c/o Noah Bryant/ Lakewood Sentinel
20 c/o Wimpy
21 Fox Broadcasting
Nikki Boertman
22 c/o Keith Friedman
c/o Michael Kettman
23 c/o Sandy Young
24 Associated Press
c/o State Historical Society of North Dakota
Peter Higby (2)
25 Environics Communications
26 c/o Hong Kong Federation of Youth Groups
c/o Power Cheer Training Center, Louisville
27 c/o Tomaz Ambroz
28 c/o Race City Corvette Gang (3)
National News & Pictures
29 c/o Antanas Kontrimas
30 Betty Halvagi
31 Tony Gay
c/o Northcliff Union Church
32 Arnold Newman/Getty Images
Rex Features
33 Corbis
34 Getty Images
35 c/o Emil & Liliana Schmid
Cambridge Newspapers Ltd 2001
Corbis
36 Associated Press
Rex Features
Kyodo Press
Rex Features
PA Photos
Mario A. Gentinetta/ bikeitsolo
Associated Press
Rex Features
Corbis
Corbis
38 Associated Press
Fernbank University
Ardea
Corbis
Oxford Scientific Films
40 Juerg Alean
Magnum
41 NASA
42 Corbis (2)
43 Corbis
44 Corbis(2)
45 Rex Features
46 Bob Lapree/Union Leader
47 Rex Features
c/oSher Singh Kanwal
48 Corbis (3)
Alamy
Corbis (3)
Rex Features
Alamy (2)
Corbis
Corbis
50 c/o Phil Jeffries
c/o Amilcar Reis Mendes
51 c/o Lucinda W. Fayrer-Hosken
52 Getty Images
Corbis (2)
Associated Press
Ardea
Rex Features
NHPA
Corbis
Illustration: Colin Brown
54 Ardea (2)
55 PA Photos
Corbis
56 Bruce Coleman
57 Oxford Scientific Films
Corbis
58 NHPA
Oxford Scientific Films
Science Photo Library
Corbis
Oxford Scientific Films
Science Photo Library
Corbis (2)
Natural History Museum
Corbis
Oxford Scientific Films
Corbis
60 Corbis
Ardea
61 Corbis
Oxford Scientific Films
62 Ardea
Oxford Scientific Films
63 Corbis
64 Fernbank University
Corbis
65 Dany Azar
Corbis
66 NASA/CXC
Regional Planetary Image Facility, UCL/NASA/JPL
67 NASA/N. Smith, J. Morse
68 Alamy (3)
70 Associated Press
71 Corbis
Associated Press
72 Corbis
73 Corbis
Magnum
74 Getty Images
Hiromitsu Toyosaki
75 c/o Anglogold
76 c/o Thai Airways International
Corbis
PA Photos
Associated Press
PA Photos
78 Corbis
Arte Wolfe
79 Corbis
80 Corbis
Getty Images
81 PA Photos
82 Associated Press
83 Corbis
Getty Images
84 Getty Images
Powerstock
85 Associated Press
86 c/o UBS
87 Getty Images
Corbis
88 NASA/GFSC
Getty Images
89 Corbis
90 Associated Press (2)
91 Corbis
92 c/o Thai Airways International
93 c/o Fátima Fernandes
Michael Gill/InnovationsUK.com (2)
94 Getty Images
95 PA Photos (2)
96 Alamy
Corbis
97 Corbis
98 c/o Pergrums Bakery
Pete Jones, Thomas and Friends, The Big Live Tour
Monopoly in the Park
Associated Press
Drew Gardner
100 Associated Press
Rex Features
101 Corbis
102 c/o Beiersdorf Hellas AE
103 c/o Carslberg/Pilsner
c/o The Cultures Centre, Poland
104 Drew Gardner/Guinness World Records
c/o Robert Humphrey (2)
c/o Geoff Price (2)
106 c/o Michihiro Hino
c/o Rhyn Noll
107 Pete Jones,Thomas and Friends, The Big Live Tour
108 Monopoly in the Park
109 c/o Masaaki Tanaka
c/o Ravensburger
Betty Halvagi
110 c/o Susie's South Forty Confections Inc. USA
111 c/o Pergrum's bakery
London Free Press
112 Peter Grant
Cedarpoint
Corbis
Honda
Auto Express
114 Corbis
Cedarpoint
Corbis (3)
Getty Images
Alamy
Illustration: Colin Brown
116 Rex Features
Corbis
117 Corbis

118 Corbis
119 Rex Features (2)
120 Alamy
121 Peter Grant
Getty Images
122 AutoExpress
123 Corbis
Hulton Archive/Getty Images
124 Reuters/Popperfoto
PA Photos
125 Eastbourne Central Library
126 c/o Lars Clausen
Honda
127 c/o Szabolcs Borsay
128 Getty Images
129 Corbis
130 AIBF/Raymond Watts
131 Justin Cedarholm
NASA
132 MAN TAKRAF
133 Le Tourneau, Inc.
O & K Mining
134 Reuters/Popperfoto
NASA/JSC
Rex Features
c/o Microemissive Displays Ltd
136 Satoshi Kawata
Sudbury Neutrino Observatory Institute
137 Sandia National Laboratories
138 NASA/ESA
139 Science Photo Library (2)
140 Science Photo Library (2)
141 Science Photo Library (2)
142 Getty Images
Associated Press
143 Bury Free Press
144 Corbis
145 Corbis
Rex Features
146 Kennedy Space Center (2)
Science Photo Library
Kennedy Space Center
ESA
Novosti
Energia/Genesis Space Library
Corbis
148 Corbis
NASA/GSFC
149 NASA/JSC
150 c/o Microemissive Displays Ltd
Reuters/Popperfoto
151 Steve Lindridge/Ideal Images
152 Corbis
Hulton Archive/Getty Images (2)
Corbis
Hulton Archive/Getty Images
Corbis
Hulton Archive/Getty Images
Rex Features
Getty Images
Bridgeman Art Library
154 Getty Images
155 Hulton Archive/Getty Images
Rex Features
156 PA Photos
Associated Press
USAF
157 Rex Features
158 Big Pictures
Rex Features
Associated Press
c/o Maurice Bennett
PA Photos
160 PA Photos (2)
161 c/o Maurice Bennett
162 Doyle New York
163 Rex Features
c/o Marikina Colossal Footwear
164 Rex Features (2)
165 Ronald Grant Archive
166 PA Photos
Ronald Grant Archive
167 Ronald Grant Archive
168 Getty Images
Rex Features
169 Associated Press
170 Ronald Grant Archive
Rex Features
171 Big Pictures
172 c/o Pinewood Studios
173 "The Lord of the Rings: The Two Towers" © MMII NLP. All rights reserved. Photo by Pierre Vinet. Photo appears courtesy of New Line Productions, Inc.
Ronald Grant Archive
174 2003 Paws Inc./ UPS
c/o Udi Buch
175 c/o Roger Culbertson
176 Associated Press
177 Getty Images
Rex Features
178 c/o MTV
179 Getty Images
PA Photos
180 PA Photos (2)
181 Associated Press
182 Rex Features
Mark Douet
Rex Features
Rex Features
Associated Press
184 Rex Features (9)
Corbis
186 Associated Press
Rex Features
187 Live Photography
188 Redferns
189 Rex Features
190 Rex Features
191 Rex Features
Redferns
192 Rex Features
193 Corbis (2)
194 Corbis
Scotsman Publications
195 Mark Douet
196 Getty Images (5)
198 Getty Images (2)
199 Getty Images
200 Getty Images
Corbis
201 Getty Images
202 Corbis
Reuters/Popperfoto
203 Getty Images
204 Getty Images (2)
205 Corbis
206 Getty Images
207 Reuters/Popperfoto
Popperfoto
208 Getty Images
209 Getty Images (2)
210 Getty Images
PA Photos
211 Getty Images
212 Corbis
Reuters/Popperfoto
213 Getty Images
214 Getty Images (2)
215 Getty Images
216 Associated Press
Getty Images
217 Reuters/Popperfoto
218 Getty Images
219 Getty Images (2)
220 Associated Press
Getty Images
221 Getty Images
222 Getty Images (3)
223 Getty Images
224 Getty Images (2)
225 Getty Images
226 Getty Images
228 c/o Valerie Lewis
229 Getty Images
230 Getty Images (2)
231 PA Photos
232 Reuters/Popperfoto
Associated Press
233 Associated Press
234 Getty Images (3)
235 Getty Images
236 Reuters/Popperfoto
Getty Images
237 Associated Press
238 Getty Images
239 Getty Images (2)
240 Getty Images
241 Getty Images
242 Getty Images (3)
243 Getty Images
244 Getty Images
245 Buzz Pictures
Getty Images
246 Associated Press (2)
247 Buzz Pictures
248 Associated Press (2)
250 Getty Images
Empics
251 Getty Images
252 Rex Features
Willy Boeykens
253 Bryan Scott
254 Associated Press
255 Getty Images
PA Photos
256 Empics (4)
Getty Images
LAT photographic
Empics (2)
Getty Images
Corbis
Powerstock
258 Empics (2)
259 Empics (2)
260 Empics
Getty Images
261 Getty Images
Empics
262 Getty Images
Rex Features
Getty Images
263 Getty Images
264 Michael Castillo/Hoffmann Bikes
Actionplus
265 Rex Features
Getty Images
266 James Dimmock c/o Flexifoil
267 Kent Kochheiser, USA
Sandboard Magazine
268 Phil Shaw
Ross Parry
269 Vadim Vlassov
286 Designer's own
288 Betty Halvagi

ACKNOWLEDGMENTS

Special thanks go to the following people for their work during the production of this year's edition:

Kat Aalam
James Bradley
Sally Brown
Caroline Butler
Scott Christie
Ann Collins
Sam Fay
Simon Gold
Richard Gue
Mary Hill
Laura Hughes
Peter Laker
Helen Laughton
Joyce Lee
Anthony Liu
Andi Mercer
Shazia Mirza
David Roberts
Alistair Richards
Malcolm Smith
Amanda Sprague
Jamie Thackwell
Ryan Tunstall
Kate White
Sophie Whiting

The team also wishes to thank the following individuals and organizations:

A C Nielsen
ACI (Airports Council International)
Ernest Adams
Dr Leslie Aiello
American Birding Association
American Museum of Natural History, New York
Amnesty International
Dr Martyn Amos
Jorgen Vaaben Andersen
Anritsu
Argentinian Embassy
Arran Frood
Aviation Security International
Ron Baalke
Dr Peter Barham
BBC's *Life of Mammals*
Guenter Bechly
Roy B. Behrens
Clive Bevan
Richard Boatfield
Dr Richard Bourgerie
BP
Dr John Brackenbury, University of Cambridge, UK
Sean Breazeal
Dr Elliott Brent, Lindley Library
Britannica *Book of the Year*
British Antarctic Survey
British Museum
British National Space Centre
Professor John Brown
Oliver Brown
BT
Dr Robert Angus Buchanan
Caida
Caltech
Cambridge University
Dr Robert Carney
CERN
Dr Franklin Chang-Diaz
Dr Hubert Chanson
Professor Phil Charles
Christie's
CIA Factbook
Admiral Roy Clare
Isabelle Clark
Richard Clark
CNN.com
Competitive Media Reporting/TNS Media Intelligence
ConocoPhillips
Dr Mike Coughlan
Dr Paul Craddock
CRM Team
Crufts
Professor AM Cruise
Professor Mike Cruise
Margaret Cudlipp
Peter D'Amato
Daily Mail
Dr Pam Dalton
Professor Kris Davidson
Dr Ashley Davies
Department of Conservation, New Zealand
Dr David Dilcher
Discovery News
Martin Dodge
eBay
The Economist
Economist Intelligence Unit
EETimes
Chris Ecroyd, Forest Research, New Zealand
Dr Farouk El-Baz
Dr Cynan Ellis-Evans
Elysium
Dr John Emsley
ESA
Euromonitor
Everesthistory.com
Everestnews.com
Exeter University
FAI – Fédération Aéronautique Internationale
FIA – Fédération Internationale de l'Automobile
Dr Xiaohui Fan
Anton Fatti
Sarah Finney
Peter & Angela Folkard
Brian Ford
Forbes
Fortune
Mike Foster, Jane's
FTSE Group
Tim Furniss
Lorenzo Gallai
Martin Gedny
Genealogische Handbuch des Adels
Geological Society of London
Dr Richard Ghail
Andy Gillard, *Scootering* magazine
Tim Goodyear (IATA press office)
Stephanie Gordon
Professor John Guest
Dr Jim Gunson
David Hancock, Screen Digest
Mary Hanson
Harvard-Smithsonian Center for Astrophysics
D & L Hegarty
Hello! Magazine
Ron Hildebrant
Dr Paul Hillyard
History of Advertising Trust Archive, UK
Hoover's
Dr David Horne
Graham Hudson
IATA – International Air Transport Association
Imperial College London
Independent
Institute of Nanotechnology
Intel
International Boundaries Research Unit, UK
International Energy Agency
International Union for the Conservation of Nature
Intersec Security Exhibition, UK
IUCN Red List
Professor Steve Jones
Emily Kao
Abigail Keeny
Dr Nichol Keith
Sophie Kemp, Mycological Herbarium, Royal Botanical Gardens, Kew, UK
Keo Films
Professor Joseph Kirschvink
Sir John Kreb
Lancaster University
Dr Rolf Landua
Dr Roger Launius
Alain Leger
Daniel Lemin, Google
Lockheed Martin
M & J Long
Los Alamos National Laboratories
Dr Robert Loss
Louisiana State University
Neil Lucas, Knoll Gardens
Simone Mangaroo
Professor Giles Marion
Brian Marsden
Jenny Marshall

Dr Jim Marshall
MastroNet Inc.
Dave McAleer
Dr Alan McNaught
Met Office
Mi2g
Lucy Millington
Mirror
Dr Edgar Mitchell
Monell Chemical Senses Center
Moody's
Bill Moore, EV World
Dr Sir Patrick Moore
Professor Jon Morse
Munich Re
Martin Munt
NASA
National Academy of Sciences
National Amateur Gardening Show, UK
National Birds of Prey Centre, UK
National Geographic
National Maritime Museum
National Physical Laboratory
National Science Foundation
Natural History Museum
Nature Magazine
Dr Ted Nield
NetNames
Newsweek
Night Vision & Electronic Sensors Directorate (NVESD)
NOAA
Barry Norman, WKVL Amusement Research Library
Andrew Nottage
Nua.com
OANDA
Oracle
Oxford University
Peak Beam Systems Inc., USA
Hilary Pearce
William Pirowski
PPARC
Sean Price
Prison Activist Resource Center
Productschap voor Gedistilleerde Dranken
Qinetiq
Dr. Paul A. Racey
John Reed, WSSRC
Professor Sir Martin Rees
W, B & J Rees
Regional Planetary Image Facility, University College London
Reuters
Ian Ridpath
Scott Robb
Eileen Rodriguez, Google
Dr Mervyn Rose
Royal Astronomical Society
Royal Horticultural Society, UK
Royal Institution
Royal Philips Electronics
Royal Ontario Museum
Royal Society of Chemistry
Rutherford Appleton Laboratory
Ryan Sampson
John Satterfield, Boeing
Science Museum, London
Scottish Daily Record
Search Engine Watch
Istvan Sebestyen
Dr Paul Selden
Prof Dick Selley
SETI Institute
Dr Seth Shostak
Dr Martin Siegert
Siemens
Sotheby's
Lara Speicher
Standard & Poors
State Bank of India, New York
Danny Sullivan
Greg Swift
Charlie Taylor
Telegeography
Time Magazine
Tim Tindall
Tinsley
UK National Giant Vegetable Championship
Professor Martin Uman
UK Planetary Forum
UN Fact Book
United Nations
United Nations High Commission for Refugees
University of Aberdeen
University of Bath
University of Birmingham
University of Boston
University of Colorado
University of Dundee
University of Florida
University of Greenwich
University of Hertfordshire
University of Oklahoma
University of Southampton
University of Toronto
US State Department
Juhani Virola
Dr David Wark
Professor Kevin Warwick
Richard Winter
Dr Rick Winterbottom
Dr Richard Wiseman
Greg Wood
World Bank
World Federation of Exchanges
World Meteorological Organisation
World Roads Federation
WTO (World Tourism Organization)
Dr David Wynn-Williams
Professor Joshua Wurman
Paul Zajac, Wards Communications

BE A RECORD BREAKER

IF YOU THINK YOU'VE GOT WHAT IT TAKES TO BE A WORLD RECORD HOLDER WE WANT TO HEAR FROM YOU!

COULD YOU BE A RECORD BREAKER?

DECIDE WHICH RECORD YOU WANT TO BREAK

Guinness World Records features many people who have accomplished extraordinary feats. If you think you have what it takes to join this exclusive record-breaking club then read on. There are thousands of records to choose from. You could gather a large group of people to break a mass participation record, or perhaps you have an unusual collection that we would be interested in. You might even suggest something new, as we are always on the lookout for innovative and exciting categories.

What we are looking for in a new category is a challenge that is inspiring, interesting, requires skill and is likely to attract subsequent challenges from people all around the world.

MAKE AN APPLICATION

You need to contact us BEFORE you make your attempt. Every Guinness World Record is governed by a unique set of rules that MUST be followed. You need to apply for these rules before you can make an attempt. If you have a new record idea, you need to find out if we have accepted your proposal before you attempt the record. If we like your idea, we will draw up rules specifically for your attempt in order to set a standard for all subsequent challenges.

The easiest and fastest way to make an application is via our website. Click on the link that says 'Make a Record Attempt', this will take you to an online application form. You'll be asked to choose a password which we will send you with a membership number to allow you access to our new tracking feature. Through this you can monitor the progress of your claim and ask any questions that you have about your record attempt.

If you don't have Internet access, you can contact us by post. Ensure that you have provided adequate contact details. Please be advised that proposals received this way take much longer to process than those received via the website.

Our website:
www.guinnessworldrecords.com

Write to us:
GUINNESS WORLD RECORDS
338 EUSTON ROAD
LONDON NW1 3BD
UK

Call us: *+44 (0) 870 241 6632*
Fax us: *+44 (0) 207 891 4501*

WAIT UNTIL YOU HEAR FROM US

Once your application has been processed, your proposal will be passed on to one of our specialist researchers who will look into your claim. If the application is successful, we will write to you with the corresponding rules and regulations which must be strictly adhered to for the attempt to be considered. We'll also send you some general guidelines that explain the evidence you need to provide to have your record attempt verified. If we reject your proposal we will explain why and, if appropriate, suggest an alternative.

ORGANIZING THE RECORD ATTEMPT

We can provide you with advice and guidance regarding record-related queries. As long as there is no violation of the guidelines, your record attempt can be organized in any way you choose. Guinness World Record adjudicators are able to attend events but will charge a fee to do so. Please remember that all record attempts are undertaken at the sole risk of the competitor and Guinness World Records cannot be held responsible for any liability arising out of any attempt.

HAVE YOUR ATTEMPT VERIFIED

Once you've completed your attempt, you must send one package containing all the verification documents that have been requested by us (ie videos, photographs, witness statements, and, where required, other more specialized items that will depend on your specific record attempt).

All evidence must be sent to our mailing address clearly marked with your membership number and claim identification number, which will have been provided in prior correspondence. If your claim passes all inspections, including a final scrutiny from the Keeper of the Records, you will be declared a Guinness World Record holder!

RECOGNITION OF YOUR ATTEMPT

All Guinness World Record holders receive a complimentary certificate to commemorate their achievement, recognizing that they have become members of the exclusive Guinness World Records hall of fame. We can't guarantee that any specific record will appear in our book, as the record selection changes annually. But as long as you hold on to your current world record, there is always the chance that your record could appear in a future edition.

Good luck!